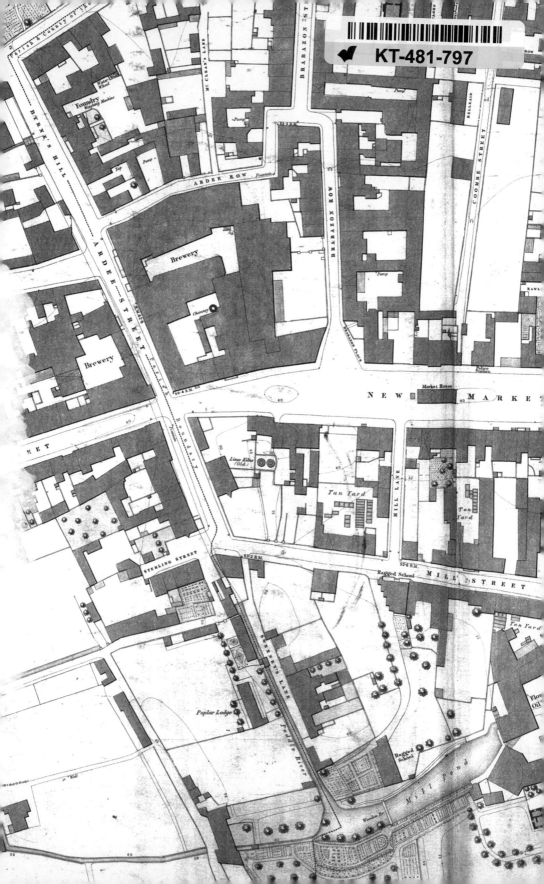

Raising Dublin, Raising Ireland: A Friar's Campaigns

Father John Spratt, O.Carm. (1796-1871)

By

Fergus A. D'Arcy

Carmelite Publications

Published by the Irish Province of Carmelites, 2018.
Design and Typesetting by Dave Twohig, O.Carm.
Printed and bound by Print Tender, Ltd.
Printing facilitated by a bequest.

ISBN: 978-1-5272-2177-2

*For Patricia*

# CONTENTS

# ACKNOWLEDGEMENTS

Fr Martin Kilmurray, when Prior Provincial of the Carmelite Order in Ireland and Zimbabwe, was the source and inspiration of this biography. To him as originator of the concept and as an unfailing supporter in its development, first thanks are due. His Carmelite confreres in many places are also owed a considerable debt of gratitude. In particular, in Dublin, Br Patrick Mullins and Fr Dave Twohig at Gort Muire, Fr Desmond Kelly and Fr Brian McKay in Whitefriar Street; in Rome, Fr Giovanni Grosso, currently Prior Provincial of the Italian Province, Fr Míceál Ó'Néill, Prior of Collegio Internazionale San Alberto, Fr Ton Van Der Gulik, and Fr John Keating Councillor General for Europe, all greatly helped to open doors, especially to the Archives of Propaganda Fide, to the Vatican Archives and to the Carmelites' own international archive in San Alberto. In Spain, the Carmelites, Fr Tomás Cámara Lopez in Salamanca and Fr Rafael Leiva in Seville assisted generously with guidance and historic material. Thanks are expressed to Mgr L M Cuña Ramos for permission to conduct research in the Propaganda Fide Historical Archives, and for the assistance of Mgr Ciarán O'Carroll, Rector of the Irish College, Rome.

To Ms Ruth Long, Librarian, and Ms Laura Magnier, Archivist, at the Carmelite Provincial Library and Archives in Dublin, thanks are expressed for their unceasing help, over years, in negotiating the extensive collection of material on John Spratt and his Carmelite contemporaries. Similarly, the help of the Carmelite legal advisor, Mr Denis Barror, is appreciated.

Debts were also incurred to many other librarians and archivists; notably to Ms Noelle Dowling at Dublin Diocesan Archives and her associate, Mr Peter Sobolewski; to Fr Gerald Powell, Chancellor of the Diocese of Dromore and Ms Agatha Larkin at Dromore Diocesan Archives, as also to the staff of the diocesan archives at Cashel, Galway and Kildare and Leighlin. In addition, thanks are offered to Fr Francis Puddister, Chancellor of the Diocese of St John's Newfoundland. As often before, one is grateful to the staff of the National Archives of Ireland, especially to Mr Gregory O'Connor, Mr Brian Donnelly and their former colleague, Ms Caitriona Crowe. The staff of the Jesuit Archives in Dublin and London, Damien Burke and Rebecca Somerset, greatly assisted; so also did Dr Brian Kirby, archivist at the Capuchin Archives in Dublin, particularly with the correspondence of Fr Theobald Mathew, and Ms Marianne Cosgrave, archivist at the Sisters of Mercy Congregational Archives, Dublin. Likewise, thanks are offered to Frs Patrick Conlan and Ignatius Fennessy of the Franciscan Library, Killiney, to Fr David Kelly, archivist at the Augustinian Archives, Ballyboden, Dublin, and Fr Christopher Clarke, formerly Prior of the Discalced Carmelites at St Teresa's Church and Monastery, Clarendon Street, Dublin. The support of the staff of the National Library of Ireland, the National Library of Scotland, the British Library, London, the National Library of New Zealand, the Royal Irish Academy, Trinity College Dublin, the Archives Department of University College Dublin, and of the Church of Ireland Representative Body Library, especially Dr Raymond Refaussé was greatly appreciated. No less so was the assistance of Mr George Moriarty and Mr John McCormick of the Irish Quaker Historical Library, Dublin, as also of Mr Eugene Roche of the Special Collections Library of UCD and his Library colleagues, Ms Jenny Collery, Ms Cathy Caplan and Ms Jane Nolan. The help of Ms Teresa Whitington of the Central Catholic Library, Dublin, is also heartily acknowledged, as is the help of my old friend, Fr Thomas Morrissey, SJ.

The staff of the public library system of Ireland were unfailingly helpful, in particular those of Dublin City Library & Archives, Mr Mario Corrigan, Mr James Durney and colleagues in Kildare Library Collections and Research Services, Ms Caitlin Browne in Roscommon Library and Ms Charlotte Crowe in Tipperary Family History Research.

Thanks are greatly due likewise to Mr George McCullough of Glasnevin Cemetery, to his late colleague, Mr Eamonn MacThomáis, to the latter's successor Mr Conor Dodd and to Dr Peter Harbison of the Glasnevin Cemetery Trust. The advice of Mr John McEvoy, Project Manager of the Sophia Housing Association at Brickfield Lane, Dublin, the successor body to John Spratt's famous Night Refuge, was invaluable.

To Dr Vera Orschel very special thanks are offered for her great help with nineteenth-century Italian correspondence and translation; a similar tribute is owed to a dear friend, Patricia Roche for her help with early nineteenth-century Spanish correspondence and to Mr Seamus O'Sullivan for his help, along with that of Br Pat Mullins, with some, at times, almost indecipherable Latin letters. I am very grateful to former colleagues at UCD, in particular Professor Cormac Ó Gráda for advice on a number of economic history issues, Dr Eileen Kane for her assistance with the identification of portraits of John Spratt, Mr Martin Cunningham for advice on nineteenth century Spanish history, and to Professors Roger Stalley and Christine Casey of Trinity College Dublin.

Ms Bernadette Faulkner came to the rescue at various critical stages with help in typing my own almost illegible handwriting. My daughter Ann was of very great assistance indeed, from the beginning, in early-stage proofing of the entire typescript in its several versions. Caitriona, Caroline, Andrew, Seamus, Leo and Lucy all offered moral support during many a demanding day. To Fr Dave Twohig, O. Carm. of Gort Muire is due a huge debt of gratitude for his friendship and his heroic work in making this book appear as it does, through arduous days of typesetting, image sourcing, cover designing and proofing. Finally, my largest and best thanks go to my dear wife, Patricia, who worked as hard, bore as patiently and endured as much on this project as John Spratt did in the many projects of his own life.

# ABBREVIATIONS

*(Titles of Newspapers in italics)*

BIMI:            Board of Irish Manufacture and Industry

CDA:             Catholic Defence Association
CISA:            Collegio Internationalize San Alberto, Rome
CSORP:           Chief Secretary's Office Registered Papers
*CT:*            *Catholic Telegraph*
CYMS:            Catholic Young Men's Society


*DDE:*           *Dublin Daily Express*
*DEM:*           *Dublin Evening Mail*
*DEP:*           *Dublin Evening Post*
*DEPC:*          *Dublin Evening Packet and Correspondent*
*DMR:*           *Dublin Morning Register*
*DWH:*           *Dublin Weekly Herald*
*DWN:*           *Dublin Weekly Nation*
*DWR:*           *Dublin Weekly Register*

*EF:*            *Evening Freeman*

*FJ:*            *Freeman's Journal*

| | |
|---|---|
| GRC: | General Relief Committee |
| HP: | Haliday Pamphlets, Royal Irish Academy |
| HT: | Haliday Tracts, Royal Irish Academy |
| HTS: | Hibernian Temperance Society |
| ICM: | Irish Church Missions |
| ISCA: | Irish Sunday Closing Association |
| *IT:* | *Irish Times* |
| ITAA: | Irish Total Abstinence Association |
| ITU: | Irish Temperance Union |
| *LR:* | *Limerick Reporter* |
| LNRA: | Loyal National Repeal Association |
| NAI: | National Archives of Ireland |
| NBPIMI: | National Board for the Promotion of Irish Manufacture and Industry |
| PBIMI: | Parent Board of Irish Manufacture and Industry |
| OCMC: | O'Connell Monument Committee |
| RIA: | Royal Irish Academy |
| SPIMI: | Society for the Promotion of Irish Manufacture and Industry |
| UPNBIMI: | United Parent and National Board of Irish Manufacture and Industry |
| *WFJ:* | *Weekly Freeman's Journal* |
| YMCA: | Young Men's Christian Association |

# INTRODUCTION

It is almost a century and a half since the death of John Spratt, Carmelite, and now a century and a quarter since the publication of the only book on his life until the present. Since then a substantial body of new material has become available from his own and his contemporaries' private papers, from newspapers and many other primary and secondary sources not available when A E Farrington wrote his biography in 1893. From all of these there emerges a fuller picture of a Dubliner, who, honoured by one of the largest funerals the city has ever seen, has long since been forgotten by its citizens if not by his fellow-Carmelites. The city and the country which he loved so well and whose historic artefacts he discovered, collected and treasured, was, in his own life, plagued by poverty, drunkenness and homelessness: his own special mission was to launch campaigns against all three, and much more besides. It makes the reconsideration of that life and the retelling of those crusades all the more timely in these years, in light of the problems of substance abuse, violence and homelessness that have come back to plague this city and this country today.

John Spratt has been overlooked in the modern histories of nineteenth century Dublin and Ireland, and this is all the more remarkable in that he was by far the most overtly political priest over the course of forty years of public life and discourse. From Catholic Emancipation, through the Repeal, the Young Ireland and Confederate movements and the convulsions of 1848, through the porous politics of the 1850s and on to the Fenian, Amnesty and Home Rule movements, this Carmelite friar was to be found at the centre of political activity , and always so in the spirit of reconciliation and moderation.

13

Although a foremost member of the church militant, in so far as advancing the Catholic claims to religious equality went, at the same time he was uniquely ecumenical in his age; if he was a man of his time in his fear of proselytism, he was ahead of his time in reaching out to those of a different dogma: he enjoyed a cordial and actively co-operating engagement with his Church of Ireland and Dissenter brethren, from Quakers to Unitarians. If it is true that *'the nineteenth century may be truly described as the century of philanthropy'*,[1] then John Spratt was truly a man of the age. If it is also true, as Virginia Crossman has suggested, that *'Irish charity workers of different faiths rarely worked together to address particular social problems'*,[2] Friar John proved an outstanding exception: by any measure his was a life remarkable in philanthropy. As the unfolding chapters will show, it was not simply a case that the number of this friar's charitable ventures grew, but also that the nature of his philanthropy evolved: his earliest undertakings were in the older tradition of what has been categorised as single, charity-specific benevolence, as witness his work for orphans, cholera relief and for the Sick and Indigent Roomkeepers (Chapter Five); and while such endeavours continued, they did so alongside later and wider ventures which grew into the newer, reformist expression of philanthropy that involved a total societal reform more widely conceived:[3] such was the nature of his commitment to temperance and teetotalism (Chapters Eight and Twenty Two); such too his commitment to the industrial regeneration of Ireland (Chapter Thirteen) and his campaign for the abolition of Donnybrook Fair (Chapters Eight and Seventeen)

One of the predominant concerns of the charitable in the nineteenth century was to distinguish between the 'deserving' and the 'undeserving poor': as Luddy has observed, *'one of the major problems facing philanthropists was to provide relief to the "deserving poor"'*: and, as Crossman noted, *'the*

---

1.  L. Geary & O. Walsh, *Philanthropy in nineteenth-century Ireland*, Dublin 2015, p. 13.
2.  V. Crossman, 'Middle class attitudes to poverty and welfare in post-Famine Ireland', in F. Lane, ed., *Politics, Society and the Middle Class in Ireland*, Basingstoke 2010, p. 131.
3.  See A. Boylan, 'Women in groups: an analysis of women's benevolent organisations in New York and Boston, 1797-1840', in *Journal of American History*, 71, 1984, pp. 497-523, cited in M. Luddy, *Women and Philanthropy in nineteenth-century Ireland*, Cambridge 1995, pp. 4-5.

*concept of the deserving and undeserving poor became deeply rooted in Irish culture'.*[4]
In this regard Friar John proved a man of his time: it was evident in
his early philanthropic work as seen in his commitment to the Sick and
Indigent Roomkeepers' Society, as a body aiming to help those who
through no fault of their own had fallen on hard times and were too
respectable to beg; it was as evident in his later humanitarian work in his
Night Refuge where he was concerned that no 'bad' characters gained
admission to contaminate the respectable and hard-working homeless
(Chapter Nineteen).

At the same time, against the growing individualism and *laissez-
faire* of the age, a hallmark of that philanthropy was *'to foster a sense of
community'.*[5] This was central to the friar's outlook and work: it was to
the fore in his support for the hapless depositors of the insolvent Cuffe
Street Savings Bank (Chapter Thirteen), as it was in his commitment to
the support of tontine societies as well as devotional confraternities:
likewise such commitment to community lay in his organising the
movement against early burial hours (Chapter Fourteen) as much as it
did in his organising the music bands and the summer excursions of his
Irish Total Abstinence Association (Chapters Eight and Twenty Two).
Insofar as the philanthropy of the time involved a cultural dimension,
as McEvansoneya has argued,[6] John Spratt could be found to express
this dimension in his giving also: it would be seen in his taking his
young charges of St Peter's Orphanage to see the annual exhibitions
of the Royal Hibernian Academy as later in his support for the Sunday
opening of the Botanic Gardens to the common people of Ireland.
(Chapters Fourteen and Twenty One).

When it came to the relief of poverty, he was no supporter of the
new poor law and its workhouses. Like most Catholic clergy who had
any interest in the matter, he thought it unacceptable that children of
the destitute be confined to and reared in workhouses and saw the

---

4. M. Luddy, 'Philanthropy in Nineteenth-Century Ireland', in A Bourke, ed., *The
   Field Day Anthology of Irish writing*, vol. 5, *Irish Women's Writing and Traditions*, Cork
   2002, p. 692; V. Crossman, *Poverty and the Poor Law in Ireland, 1850-1914*, Liverpool
   2013, p. 3; see also V. Crossman & P. Gray, eds., *Poverty and Welfare in Ireland, 1838-
   1948*, Dublin 2011, p. 11.
5. Geary & Walsh, op.cit., p. 17.
6. P. McEvansoneya, 'Cultural philanthropy in mid-nineteenth-century Ireland' in
   L. Geary & O. Walsh, *Philanthropy in nineteenth-century Ireland*, Dublin 2015, pp.
   210-224.

whole system as a British state imposition to be challenged.[7] As with his confreres, he would prefer a comprehensive system of welfare provided by religious institutions, as evident in the sheer range of his own charitable undertakings for the poor, from schools to orphanages, asylums for the homeless, the deaf and the blind. He had passed away before the state poor law system began to refocus from *'deterrence to assistance for the needy'*.[8] Not, however, that the Catholic Church was entirely at odds with the secular values of the Victorian age: that Church, like other agents and agencies, promoted the values of industry, self-reliance, sexual morality and sobriety, and some seriousness as against the carefree fecklessness of an earlier age. In espousing and promoting such values over the course of a long public career the Carmelite friar proved as much a moderniser as any in his time.

John Spratt, however, was not opposed to state intervention as such: even as his political and religious liberalism brought him into campaigning comradeship with leading Unitarian and Quaker Dissenters, he did not share their *laissez-faire* or economic liberalism: where emergency situations required it, he believed in state intervention. His economics, what he called *'the economy of mercy'*, came from an older, traditional Catholic moral economy and yet spoke beyond his age to ours. It was in this context, at the outset of the Great Famine, that he called for the state to intervene to prevent the diversion of grain going to brewing and distilling instead of to meeting the hunger of the masses (Chapter Eleven).

Co-existing with his commitment to a generous Christianity and philanthropy was his abiding commitment to political liberalism. This he learned in his unswerving support of and close engagement with Daniel O'Connell and his various political movements from the 1820s to the 1840s. With O'Connell dead and the ranks of Repeal nationalism sundered, a different political climate was ushered in, following the

---

7. See, *inter alios*, A. Clark, 'Orphans and the Poor Law: Rage against the machine', in V. Crossman and P. Gray, op.cit., pp. 97, 101, 103; also V. Crossman, *Poverty and the Poor Law in Ireland, 1850-1914*, pp. 24, 227.

8. V. Crossman, 'The humanization of the Irish poor laws: reassessing developments in social welfare in post-Famine Ireland', in A. Gestritch, S. King & L. Raphael, eds., *Being Poor in Modern Europe: historical perspectives, 1800-1940*, Oxford 2006, p. 229; V. Crossman, *Politics, pauperism and power in late nineteenth-century Ireland*, Manchester 2006, p. 3.

tumult of 1848. His was perhaps the foremost, if unheeded, voice calling for reconciliation. Thereafter, as noted by Hoppen, Comerford, and others,[9] came a period of fluid political alignments and of fluctuating allegiances: against the contesting forces of Orange unionism and ultra-Toryism on the one hand and militant Irish nationalism on the other, Spratt was significant in attempting to forge a distinctive Liberal middle ground, in his case as much in local ward politics as in the politics of national organisations (Chapter Twenty One). In this he would be found publicly promoting the political agendas and ambitions of MPs such as the Liberal Quaker Jonathan Pim as much as the Liberal Catholic MPs, John Reynolds and Sir Dominic Corrigan. Such middle ground soon collapsed from under their feet as the 1860s moved into the 1870s, leaving John Spratt's politics and theirs appearing anachronistic; for all that, his intense preoccupation with the registration of Liberal voters and the securing of his own and his fellow-Carmelites' right to vote made a genuine contribution to the development of popular political awareness and engagement. Friar John's commitment to religious, philanthropic and political liberalism did not endear him to his Catholic diocesan superiors, notably Cardinal Paul Cullen; yet, that co-operation across confessional chasms proved vital for the vigour of the interdenominational charities to which he devoted himself and to the viability of the liberal non-sectarian politics that he promoted.

Despite a life of such extensive and abiding philanthropic and political commitments, he was, however, first and foremost a priest and a pastor to his people. Long before the devotional revolution reportedly came to dominate the religious landscape of Ireland, this friar was to the fore in producing and disseminating devotional literature: among his many publications in this area, his *Sincere Christian's Manual of Devotion*, and his *Carmelite Manual* constituted major home-produced provisions for the needs of an increasingly devout Catholic readership: he became the friar who produced the most significant and extensive body of published work of any Irish Carmelite in the nineteenth

---

9. See K. T. Hoppen, *Ireland since 1800: conflict and conformity*, London 1989; K. T. Hoppen, *Elections, Politics and Society in Ireland, 1832-1885*, Oxford 1984; V. Comerford, 'Ireland, 1850-1870: post-famine and mid-Victorian', in W. E. Vaughan, ed., *A new history of Ireland*, vol. 5, *Ireland under the Union, 1801-1870*, Oxford 1989, pp. 372-95; R. Swift & C. Kinealy, eds., *Politics and Power in Victorian Ireland*, Dublin 2006, p. 13.

century. A reformer, building on the reconstructive work in discipline and observance of Archbishops Troy and Murray, his reforming zeal within his own Order made for uneasy relations within the friary and the Irish province. This notwithstanding, over the course of fifty years, he became the leading figure of his Order in Ireland, as Prior of Whitefriar Street and Prior Provincial. When to all of this is added his church and school building, together with his confraternities and other charitable commitments, the whole range of his achievements made for a substantial if unquantifiable contribution to the creation of the nineteenth century Irish Catholic community.

If John Spratt is casually recalled by the few today, it is most likely due to his remarkable and enduring campaign for temperance and total abstinence. This, however, as the following chapters will present, was but one of the host of causes and campaigns, organisations, institutions and movements which he founded, led or significantly supported, to the number of at least forty-two. For all that he was one of the best-known public figures in mid-nineteenth century Ireland, and the best-known Carmelite, Friar John nonetheless was something of an enigma. He left no diaries or journals that confided his personal hopes or apprehensions or his views of clerical confreres and lay associates. No letters to family or to friends have survived him. Letters about him or references to him by colleagues reveal a man who was at times ambitious, at times vain, not easy to live with in community and not always indulgent to younger friars. At the same time he was compassionate, generous and kind to a fault to those in need. He proved relentless in pursuit of the public good and never gave up in the face of adversity. Consequently, notwithstanding his flaws and failings, warts and all, one may hope to be forgiven for suggesting that John Spratt deserves to be the better remembered.

*Fergus A D'Arcy*

# CHAPTER ONE

## *From Cork Street to Cordoba*

For a figure of such significant public prominence as Fr John Spratt, Carmelite, surprisingly little is written about his family background or circumstances. Since his death in 1871 he has had four biographers who, apart from references to the piety and influence of John Spratt's mother, have little or, in most cases, nothing to say of his father or siblings. Furthermore, they differ in assigning his year of birth.[1] All that extant documentation will yield is that John Spratt was baptised on 5th January 1796.[2] Presumably, therefore, he was born in late 1795 or in the first week of January 1796.

John's parents were both Dubliners. His father, James, was born in or about the year 1758 and his mother, Esther Mary (Elizabeth) Bollard

---

1. See *Appendix 1: The Spratt Family Genealogy, problems of dates and names* for a full discussion of the issues of dating associated with John Spratt and his family. The first four biographies in date order are W. J. Battersby, *Authentic life and acts of the Very Rev Dr Spratt, S.T.M., Provincial, O.C.C.*, Dublin 1871; A. E. Farrington, *Rev Dr Spratt, O.C.C.: his life and times*, Dublin 1893; P. O'Dwyer, *John Francis Spratt, O.Carm., 1796-1871: a Dissertation submitted to the Faculty of Church History of the Pontifical Gregorian University*, Rome 1968; *Father John Spratt: beloved of Dublin's Poor: a centenary souvenir, 1871-1971*, Dublin 1971; *The Irish Carmelites (of the Ancient Observance)*, Dublin 1988; D. Murphy, 'John Francis Spratt, 1796-1871' in J. McGuire & J. Quinn, eds., *Dictionary of Irish Biography, from the earliest times to the year 2009*, 8 vols., Cambridge 2009, vol. iii, p. 1099. There are other biographical accounts in A. Webb, *A Compendium of Irish Biography*, Dublin 1878, p. 487; J. S. Crone, *A Concise Dictionary of Irish Biography*, Dublin 1928, pp. 236-37.
2. According to testimonials of the year 1819 signed by the parish priest, Patrick Duignan and his curate, Fr Brady. See Carmelite Provincial Archives, Gort Muire (henceforth cited as GMA), *Scrapbook A*, pp. 1-2; and O'Dwyer, *Dissertation*, p. 28.

three years later.[3] Apart from the record of her devout Catholicism, as stated by Farrington, almost nothing is known of her background, parents or siblings, if any; she may have had a brother, Richard.[4] Nor is there, as yet, any proven record of the date of their marriage.[5]

As for the children of James and Esther, the standard authorities are vague: Farrington simply refers to the existence of siblings without names or details, while O'Dwyer mentions a brother James who became an Augustinian priest and a sister, Catherine, who became a Carmelite nun. In fact the family was a quite a large one. It would appear that there were seven children, four boys and three girls, in the following order: James, the likely first-born, was baptised in September 1790; then came Michael, baptised on 16th September 1792. Next came the future Carmelite friar, John, who was baptised on 5th January 1796. One hazards that the next family child was Mary Ann who may have been born circa 1798.[6] The next extant record is for Catherine, the future nun, who was baptised on 11th September 1800. There then followed a second James, date of baptism not known but on his death in June 1879 he was stated to have been 76 years of age, suggesting a date of birth in 1803. That he was a different James from the first-mentioned earlier is clear from the fact that on his death he was described as '*a younger brother of Fr John*'.[7] This leads to the surmise that James the first-born must have died an infant or child. Of this second James more is known than of most of his brothers and sisters. He entered the Augustinian Order in Dublin, and as will emerge later, he had a varied career there, living for extended, alternating periods, in Italy and Ireland. Following upon James the younger, came the final child, Esther (Elizabeth), baptised in April 1806.[8] Michael therefore must have been the eldest surviving child of his parents and his godfather was one Richard Bollard, Esther's brother, presumably.

---

3. For the sources on James and Esther, see *Appendix 1: The Spratt Family, problems of dates and names*.
4. Ibid.
5. Ibid.
6. No baptism record is extant for her.
7. *The Nation*, 14th June 1879. All the other children's dates of baptism are to be found in the DDA, Parish Registers of St Catherine's.
8. Curiously, her names have bequeathed the same problem as those of her mother: see *Appendix 1*.

*The Family Business*

This large family lived at No. 104 Cork Street on the edge of the Liberties. The father James was a parchment and glue manufacturer in a district where the skinning and tanning trades were heavily concentrated. He was first listed in Dublin trade directories in this capacity, from the year 1818. James's business was almost certainly an extensive one, consisting of tan yards, drying lofts, mills, bark house and machinery, as well as the family dwelling. How long he may have been in this business before 1818 is not clear, but possibly for many decades: it emerges that he also rented a small holding of some fifteen acres, with cottage and stables, at Porterstown, in Castleknock.[9] It may be surmised that he grazed cattle there prior to their slaughter for skins. As for the Cork Street business, at the time of his death in 1828, it was mentioned that he was a large employer and it also appeared that he had had under-tenants. However, as the 1820s advanced, economic difficulties mounted for the trades associated with hides and tanning as much as they did for handloom weavers in the Liberties. Had he been in the business long before 1800 his trade would have prospered; however, not long after he first paid for a trade entry in *Wilson's Dublin Directory*, that situation would change, as shall be seen later.

If Michael were indeed the eldest surviving son, he would in due course effectively become the head of the Spratt family, being John's elder by four years. He settled for a life in trade, probably working with their father, James, but, in or around 1823, he went into business in his own right, as a tanner, at No. 105 Cork Street, next door to the family home and business. As will emerge later, Michael's was in some respect a tragic life, but not before he had married Anna, born in 1798, and had become a father to at least five children: these were Michael junior, baptised on 22nd December 1825, James, baptised on 27th December 1827, Andrew, baptised on 9th May 1828 and two others who followed but whose dates are not yet known, Eleanor and John.

As for the other family members not yet touched upon in any detail, these were Mary Ann and Esther Eliza. Mary Ann must have been born some years before Esther as she married in 1818. One hazards that she may have been born around 1798, between John (1796) and

---

9. Registry of Deeds, *Transcription Book*, Year 1830, vol. 857, No. 184, *Michael Spratt and William Forestal*, 26th March 1830.

Catherine (1800) since James followed these, in 1803. It is noteworthy that when she married Joseph Vickers in 1818 she was marrying into one of the oldest established trading families in the district of St Catherine's Parish. The Vickers (also spelled Vicars) were tallow chandlers of Francis Street. Mary Ann and Joseph had six children, some of whom will feature much later in this volume in the wake of the death of their uncle, Fr John.[10] As for the youngest of the Spratt family, Esther Eliza, born as stated, in 1806, she, like her mother, presented a problem of two Christian names. Almost nothing is known of her beyond her death at Monkstown in 1840.[11]

## From Child to Man

By all accounts the Spratt household of Cork Street was a devoutly Catholic one. Regrettably, few details have survived regarding John's early years. A few edifying accounts of his precocious piety and generosity to the poor of his district feature in the pages of Farrington's devoted memoir. He went to school, locally, it seems, in nearby Dolphin's Barn, at the top of Cork Street. He made his confirmation before Archbishop Troy, in St Catherine's Parish Church, in April 1806.[12] As he entered his teenage years he was taught Latin and Greek by the then Carmelite Provincial, Patrick O'Farrell. This link apparently came through his mother's association with the Carmelites. She attended the original church of the Carmelites in Ash Street – within ten minutes' walk of Cork Street – and was a member of the Confraternity of the Scapular there. It was here that John went on to serve Mass and so came into direct contact with the Order in which he would spend the rest of his life.[13] Given his early attachment to the life of the soul and his youthful commitment to helping the less fortunate, it was hardly any surprise to James and Esther Spratt when this son of theirs applied to Fr O'Farrell for admission to the Order.

It may well be asked why John chose to join a religious order, and indeed, why the Carmelites. It may be that parental influence was initially critical in this regard. The Spratts would have been modestly

---

10. For these family details, see *Appendix 1*.
11. Ibid.
12. Farrington, pp. 11-15. Battersby, p. 5, mentions that his initial schooling was provided by Fr Roche, parish priest of Bray, Co Wicklow.
13. O'Dwyer, *Irish Carmelites*, pp. 179-180; O'Dwyer, *Dissertation*, p. 29.

prosperous, were clearly devout and may well have been socially as well as spiritually ambitious for their children, within the social and professional constraints upon Irish Catholics in that age. It is significant that two of their three surviving boys and one of their three girls became regular religious and that the parents were prepared to forego the potential support of two of their male offspring and were prepared to devote resources to supporting their religious vocations. Furthermore, the conventual religious life may well have offered a more prestigious and attractive vocation than that of a hard-pressed diocesan curate who lacked the relative freedom of movement; in addition, membership of a religious community was to prove no barrier to clerical ambition or upward progression to the highest echelons of the Catholic hierarchy, in Ireland or internationally.[14] As to John's personal decision, there should be little surprise that it was the Carmelites he chose: his own and his family's closest contacts with clergy and the religious life had clearly been overwhelmingly with the Carmelites of Ash Street and then of French Street. John was just out of his teens when, on 20th August 1816, Fr O'Farrell decided to accept him, and another, Robert O'Neill, for the Order and sent them to Spain for their Carmelite formation. The destination was the community and College of St Albert, Cordoba.[15]

14. As witness the lives and careers of several Irish prelates of the age, such as the Dominican, Archbishop John Thomas Troy who confirmed him, the Augustinian James Doyle, Bishop of Kildare and Leighlin, or of John Spratt's Discalced Carmelite friend, Bishop Whelan of Bombay or of his Franciscan friend, Bishop Fleming of Newfoundland.
15. GMA, *Scrapbook A*, p. 4, Patrick O'Farrell, letter of reference, 20th Aug 1816.

**Fig 1.**     *Sketch of a young John Spratt, in Gort Muire Archives,* Scrapbook A.
            *The artist is unknown.*

# CHAPTER TWO

## *Committing to Carmel*

The Ireland which John Spratt left in 1816 was a troubled country; the Spain to which he went was more troubled still. The Church in Ireland may have been weak and wary as it slowly emerged from the shadows of the Penal Laws; the Church in Spain and its religious orders were warier still, having suffered grievous blows over the previous eight years: they would suffer yet more grievously in the twenty years after John's arrival there. As Charles Esdaile has described it:

> Between 1808 and 1814 Spain experienced the most devastating struggle in her entire history. French, Spanish and Anglo-Portuguese armies marched and counter-marched across the face of the Peninsula. A savage guerrilla war and burgeoning social unrest reduced large parts of the country to anarchy. Revolution in Latin America shattered Spain's tottering finances. Famine and epidemic swept the country.[1]

Cordoba, like Seville and other cities and towns, following the uprising of 1808, saw the rise of a revolutionary junta and, soon after, an invasion of a French army of 20,000 under General Pierre Dupont. On 7th June 1808 he sacked Cordoba, plundering its wealthy churches. As for the historic Carmelite community of Cordoba, the historian Ismail Carretero has chronicled how, under Joseph Bonaparte, in 1809, their convent was converted into a military barracks and their magnificent library and altar-pieces became fuel for the campfires of the French

---

1.  C. J. Esdaile, *Spain in the Liberal Age: From Constitution to Civil War, 1808-1939*, London 2000, p. 21.

soldiery.[2] Spanish guerrillas, more generally, responded in kind with massacres of isolated French military units. The ferocity of violence on both sides set the stage for the bloody Peninsular War. Dupont's army moved out from Cordoba to take Seville before suffering a major but rare defeat in the battle of Bailen. Upon Napoleon's reoccupation of Madrid that December, retribution followed: feudalism and the Spanish Inquisition were abolished and Napoleon proceeded to suppress two thirds of Spain's convents and monasteries.[3]

### Restoration

In the aftermath of Napoleon's final defeat and the restoration of the Spanish monarchy under Ferdinand VII, a series of decrees restored the Inquisition, the Jesuits and the religious orders,[4] but not such Church property as had been sold off before 1814. An uneasy peace now held until a new revolution in 1820 resulted in the secularisation of most of the regular clergy, in the halving of church tithes and once again in the suppression of the Jesuits. Such was the shattered country to which John Spratt and his fellow Carmelite postulant, Robert O'Neill, travelled in the summer of 1816. They arrived at Cadiz after an eventful voyage and made their way to Cordoba. The convent they found was now one of modest size and of limited resources.

John's future friend and soon to be his Master of Novices, Fr Alonso Jurado y Ruiz, writing in 1823, observed that he had done much to restore the monastery. By the time of his writing, Fr Alonso remarked that the monastery was not rich and not poor but that the first two years of its restoration, just as John was settling in, had been *'painful and there was much hunger'*. By the time John and Robert O'Neill would leave, matters had become tolerable – *'last year (1822) was so-so and this one seems to be good'*.[5] A report of 1823 described it as a house of some twenty religious while various notes from its Priors to the Vicar Provincial of Andalucía as late as 1834 reflected a situation of great

2. I. M. Carretero, *Exclaustracion y Restauracion Del Carmen en España, 1771-1910*, Roma 1996, p. 7; B. V. Boyan, *Historia del Carmelo Español*, vol. iii, *Provincias de Castilla y Andalucía*, 1563-1835, Roma 1994, p. 572.
3. Carretero, p. 26; R. Carr, *Spain 1808-1975*, Oxford 1983, p. 7.
4. Esdaile, p. 43.
5. Alonso Jurado y Ruiz to John Spratt, 11th July 1823, as cited by A. Gil, 'Documenta', in *Zelo*, vol. 10, No. 2, Summer 1958, pp. 90-97.

**Fig 2.**    *The Carmelite Church in Cordoba, photographed in the 19th century.*

penury. Their venerable theological college – El Colegio de San Roque
de Cordoba – founded in the early seventeenth century had just three
lecturers in theology and some twenty students in 1808. These were the
circumstances and context that greeted John Spratt and Robert O'Neill
on finally arriving in Cordoba in the autumn of 1816.

### Cordoba

Why it was that the Carmelite Friary of Cordoba became their
destination is not explicable, on the basis of extant sources, since their
Prior Provincial, O'Farrell, had recommended them for the Province of
Castile, not for that of Andalucía and Murcia.[6] It seems odd, however,
given that in its most recent past, the Irish Province had had its closest
links with their Carmelite brothers in Seville: it was in La Casa Grande
de Sevilla that Spratt's contemporary and future Provincial, Fr Thomas
Coleman, was professed in 1808 and where four other Irish novices
were professed during the very years when Spratt and O'Neill were

---

6.  O'Dwyer, *Irish Carmelites*, p. 180, citing GMA, *Scrapbook A*, p. 4, Fr Patrick
    O'Farrell, 20th Aug 1816.

located in Cordoba.[7]   Disturbed though Spain was in the first three
decades of the nineteenth century, in the actual year 1816 when Fr
O'Farrell decided to send the two young men there, the country was not
so troubled as to prevent them travelling to Castile and thereby forcing
them to settle for Cordoba.   One may hazard that O'Farrell did so on
the recommendation of unnamed others, or that Cordoba was chosen
in the absence of sufficient space in Seville for even more Irish novices.

Long fallen from its medieval grandeur under the Moors, Cordoba,
once the most populous city in Europe, had declined to a provincial
backwater of some twenty thousand people.   A somewhat hostile
contemporary English visitor described its citizens in unflattering terms
in 1831 as

> probably the most bigoted of any town in Spain...the very air
> of the city, its dark and narrow streets, and the general gloom
> which prevails are almost sufficient to indicate the character of
> people...in no place, probably, are there more outward and visible
> signs of religion than at Cordoba, not even excepting Seville...[8]

This notwithstanding, and though little enough is known about their
daily lives in the city, such limited evidence as survives suggests that
John Spratt and Robert O'Neill had settled in well and were not
unhappy.   John's progress in the Spanish language was subject to
differing accounts.  According to Farrington, during their novitiate year
under Fr Alonso, Spratt and O'Neill *'made great progress'*: a letter from Fr
Francis Egan in Madrid, spoke highly of them and that their knowledge
of the Spanish language was *'very extensive'*.[9]   Nevertheless, the same
letter of 13th June 1817 to Fr Finny in Dublin, while indeed stating
that *'the Prior of Cordoba is highly pleased with his Irish novices, as is the entire
community'*, added that the Prior *'complained that their progress in the Spanish*

---

7.  Ibid, Appendix IV, p. 397, citing CISA Archives, Archivo General II – Baetica 7, *Libro de Profesiones*.
8.  Sir Arthur de Capell Brooke, Bt., *Sketches in Spain and Morocco*, 2 vols, London 1831, vol. 1, pp. 260-261.
9.  Farrington, pp. 44-45.  Francis Egan may have been the same who was born in Roscommon in 1749, and was professed in Seville in January 1768; see O'Dwyer, *Irish Carmelites*, pp. 149-150, 244.

*language was rather slow'.*[10] Slow it may have been but in the end adequate enough that John was well able to correspond with his Spanish novice master in the early years after his return to Ireland.

## Carmelite studies

As for their religious training, the scheme of study which they had to undertake has been recorded in broad outline by Farrington.[11] The initial course of training under Fr Alonso as novice master was described as *'severe'*. With that year successfully negotiated, John was professed on 31st December 1817, as a member of the Irish Province. Although he took a vow of poverty, he did not make a full renunciation: presumably this was because the Irish Province was then only emerging from the shadows of the Penal Laws and that in this situation the common life and the vow of poverty had not yet been fully re-established as a normal part of Irish Carmelite life.[12] This was understandably a practical consideration for Carmelites and other regular clergy until they came to live in a less uncertain, hostile and penal climate. Nevertheless, when it came to John's case, this issue of living the common life and pooling all resources in common would single him out as unique among his Carmelite confreres in declining to do so.[13]

Immediately after his First Profession he was sent to study theology and philosophy outside the friary, at the historic Carmelite College of San Alberto in Cordoba. Founded in 1602 and named after St Albert of Sicily (c.1250-1307), this College became renowned as a place of learning for the Carmelites of Andalucía and Murcia. Here he followed a standard text, the *Cursus Philosophicus*, presumably that of Rodrigo de Arriaga (1592-1667), Jesuit scholar and Dean of Arts at the University of Prague. This work was first published at Antwerp in 1632: a formidable volume, it acquired wide popularity in religious institutions beyond the Jesuits and was reprinted several times up to Arriaga's own

---

10. GMA, Spratt Papers, Box 56, *Ledger 1*, Francis Egan to Thomas Finny, 13th June 1817; also see O'Dwyer, pp. 180, 245. Finny always spelled his name as appears here, whereas the GMA, *Catalogus Fratrum* spells his name as Finney.
11. Farrington, pp. 43-44.
12. O'Dwyer, p. 180.
13. For further discussion of this, see Chapters Ten and Twenty-Three.

death and beyond that.[14]  In addition to the work of Arriaga, he was introduced, predictably, to the philosophy of St Thomas Aquinas.

When it came to theological studies, he and his fellow students were able to rely significantly on the works of two renowned English Carmelites.  Their source for dogmatic theology was the work of John Bacon of Norfolk (c.1290-1347), also known as Baconthorpe, who was Provincial of England over the years 1327-1333.  A prolific scholar with over 120 volumes ascribed to him, he came to be recognised as the authority on Carmelite theology.  His commentary on the *Sentences* of Peter Lombard became a standard work in European universities for three centuries after his death in 1347.  In 1466 the General Chapter of the Carmelite Order recommended his writings as an authoritative source for their theology students, a recommendation endorsed by its General Chapter of 1593.[15]  '*The most important scholastic the Order produced*' and the '*first of the Order's Marian Scholars*', his works were issued in four volumes in 1764 and they were extensively used in the Carmelite colleges of Spain and Italy in the eighteenth and nineteenth centuries.[16]

The other English Carmelite of enduring stature whose work was studied by John Spratt and his fellow students was Thomas Netter of Saffron Walden (1372-1430), Provincial, diplomat and '*Prince of Controversialists*'.[17]  The esteemed Carmelite historian, Joachim Smet, described him as '*the only great theologian of the fifteenth century*'.[18]  He was, successively, confessor to Henry V and then tutor to Henry VI.[19]  He was best known, perhaps, for his polemics against John Wycliffe and the Lollards.  In addition to these sources, John Spratt studied canon law as expounded by the seventeenth century Spanish Carmelite, Juan Bautista de Lezana (1589-1659), and towards the end of these studies

---

14.  A. Alexander, *Infinitesimal: how a Dangerous Mathematical Theory shaped the Modern World*, London 2015, pp. 139-41, 144.  Farrington does not mention Arriaga as the author.

15.  J. Smet, O. Carm., *The Mirror of Carmel : a brief history of the Carmelite Order*, Darien, Illinois 2011, p. 150.

16.  Smet, pp. 389-390.  See also W. H. Kent, 'Catholic Theology in England', *The Dublin Review*, vol. 109, July-Oct 1891, p. 99.

17.  Farrington, p. 76.  Farrington had a special interest in the life and thought of Thomas Netter: see O'Dwyer, p. 297.

18.  Smet, p. 15.

19.  J. Bergström-Allen & R. Copsey, *Thomas Netter of Walden: Carmelite, Diplomat and Theologian*, Faversham 2009, pp. 23, 35-6, 61, 89, 108.

he encountered the mystical theology of St Teresa of Avila and St John of the Cross. By the time these labours were successfully concluded he had been professed in December 1817 – as noted earlier – and in May 1818 he received the tonsure and took Minor Orders and Subdiaconate. He became Deacon in March 1819 and finally, on 26th February 1820, he was ordained priest by Petrus Antonius de Trevilla, Bishop of Cordoba.[20] There was now the possibility of a further year of theology at the College of San Alberto in Seville but the troubled state of Spain prevented this and determined instead that he continue in Cordoba until March 1821. As a result, John was to be there at the start of another great social and political upheaval.

## Revolution 1820-1823

The restoration of absolutism in 1814 was not acquiesced in by all sides: a succession of conspiracies and insurrections came to a head in revolution. On the 1st January 1820, in the small town of Cabeza de San Juan, sixty kilometres north of Cadiz, a disaffected army officer – one of many – Lieutenant Colonel Rafael del Riego led a revolt in favour of the restoration of the liberal Constitution of 1812. His example spread rapidly. On 7th March 1820 his forces entered Cordoba, on the very day that King Ferdinand in Madrid agreed to restore that Constitution.[21] This second liberal revolution saw Ferdinand under virtual house arrest during what came to be called the Constitutional Triennium, up to 1823. These years became ones of convulsion. The new Cortes, opening on 9th July, decreed the re-expulsion of the Jesuits and the secularisation of most of the religious orders. On 25th October, Ferdinand, under duress, reinforced such drastic measures by decree: the Benedictines and Augustinians were suppressed altogether, new orders were forbidden, and all religious communities of fewer than twenty-four persons were abolished. As a consequence, more than half of all religious in Spain were disbanded and secularised.[22] By the autumn of 1821 the new liberal, bourgeois revolution was itself in trouble, the Treasury near bankrupt and the country convulsed by bitter

---

20. GMA, Spratt Papers, Box 56, Ledger 1, *Scrapbook A*, pp. 5-8 hold the certificates for the different stages in his path to ordination.
21. Esdaile, p. 49.
22. E. A. Peers, *Spain, the Church and the Orders*, London 1945, pp. 62-63; Esdaile, pp. 48-52.

divisions. The radical Cortes of February 1823 continued to pursue an extreme agenda which included the suppression of more monasteries that had survived the earlier purges. By that stage a virtual civil war was in train, with churches and monasteries being torched and monks and priests being hunted, murdered or executed.[23] John Spratt was by then safely out of the country but his confreres in Cordoba did not escape having to go into hiding. Fr Alonso gave him a dramatic account of these events.[24] The outcome was counter-revolution and an invasion of 60,000 troops of the restored French monarchy: the liberal government fled in turn from Madrid to Seville and then to Cadiz which finally fell to the counter-revolutionary forces on 1st October 1823.

*A Farewell to Spain*

It was against this background that Fr John continued his studies at Cordoba rather than pursuing them in Seville. Nevertheless, with his final year of theology completed in March 1821, he and Robert O'Neill prepared for their return to Ireland. Before a final farewell to Spain and despite the troubled state of the country, they travelled in April 1821 to visit Seville, Granada and Malaga.[25] Returning to Cordoba to pick up their belongings, they also gathered a sheaf of letters of praise and commendation, notably from their novice master, Fr Alonso, and from Fr Antonio Castro, Provincial of Andalucía. In May 1821 they departed from Cadiz and sailed home to Ireland by way of Liverpool. Arriving back in Dublin he went straight to the little Carmelite Friary at 12 French Street from where a very different life began.

---

23. Esdaile, p. 60.
24. A. Gil, 'Documenta', pp. 90-97.
25. GMA, *Scrapbook A*, passport to Sevilla, 2nd April 1821; also O'Dwyer, pp. 180, 244.

# CHAPTER THREE

## *Survival and Revival*

Battered and bruised after two centuries of harassment and repression, the Catholic Church in Ireland to which John returned as a priest in 1821 was a challenged and wary organisation. Its clergy and laity had been subjected to an extensive series of penal enactments from the Tudors to the Hanoverians. Haphazard in application, these were intensified in range and incidence after the Williamite victory in 1691. They included an Act of 1697 banishing Catholic bishops and regular clergy from Ireland as of 1st May 1698. Legislation against Catholic laity included provisions forbidding them from sending children abroad for education and prohibiting Catholics from teaching school.[1]

Although this entire code constituted a formidable array of repressive legislation, it was fluctuating and haphazard in its enforcement. James Kelly has cautioned that it is possible to exaggerate its impact but in general it left *'a legacy of institutional poverty and attitudinal deference'* which ensured that the Church *'still bore the scars of repression a century later'*.[2] Nevertheless, enforcement and the threats of enforcement waxed

---

1. All the penal legislation is listed by title, chronologically, in T. W. Moody, F. X. Martin & F. J. Byrne, eds., *A New History of Ireland*, Vol. III, *A Chronology of Irish History to 1796*, 1st ed. Oxford 2011 ed., pp. 256-258. For another list of all such legislation, see J. Bergin, et al., *New Perspectives on the Penal Laws*, Dublin 2011, pp. 275-280.
2. Kelly, 'The impact of the penal laws', in J. J. Kelly & D. Keogh, eds., *History of the Catholic Diocese of Dublin*, Dublin 2000, pp. 144-145. See also D. Keogh, 'The Catholic Church in Ireland in the age of the North Atlantic Revolution, 1775-1815', in B. Bradshaw & D. Keogh, eds., *Christianity in Ireland: Revisiting the Story*, Dublin 2002, pp. 155-163; T. P. Power & K. Whelan, eds., *Endurance and Emergence: Catholics in Ireland in the Eighteenth Century*, Dublin 1990.

and waned according to the fluctuating fear of external threats to the security and stability of the Protestant crown, state and society. Certain it was that, after 1760, a subsidence of anti-Catholic sentiment was apparent in a significant section of Irish Protestant opinion.[3] With the Hanoverian Protestant establishment secure after 1760, the most significant penal legislation was removed between 1778 and 1793.[4] For all this, certain significant disabilities and vexations still remained: among them were the prohibition on becoming a member of parliament, the ban on priests officiating at funerals or on their wearing vestments in public or using ecclesiastical titles or ranks. A persuasive presentation of this state of affairs over 1780 to 1829 is well expressed in James Kelly's description of *'a complex and variegated picture of toleration as well as disruptive repression'*.[5] All of this made for a cautious Catholic clergy and laity – wary at best, if not completely cowed at worst – but gradually growing in confidence and reconstruction until the rise of Daniel O'Connell and his Catholic Association quickened the pace of protest against remaining disabilities from 1823. Disabilities apart, the Catholic Church faced daunting challenges in the century after 1770 from what Larkin has described as *'a chronic shortage of clergy and an inadequate supply of places of worship'*, consequent upon the explosion of population: over 1770-1840 the Catholic population rose by 150 per cent, but the number of priests by only 50 per cent.[6]

---

3. Kelly, p. 169.
4. Most significant were Luke Gardiner's Acts of 1778 and 1782: that of 1778 permitted Catholics to take leases for 999 years and to inherit on the same terms as Protestants; that of May 1782 allowed Catholics to acquire land except within parliamentary boroughs; that of July 1782 permitted Catholics 'to teach school' and to act as guardians. Then came Langrishe's Act of 1792 allowing Catholics to practise as lawyers, followed by Hobart's Act of 1793 extending the parliamentary franchise to Catholics and enabling them to occupy most civil and military offices. Finally, in this series, came an act of June 1795 permitting the creation of Catholic seminaries. Effective toleration had already seen the opening in 1793 of St Patrick's College, Carlow, providing higher education for Catholics. Trinity College then followed in 1794 by permitting Catholics to take degrees.
5. Kelly, p. 174.
6. For the challenges and response of the Church in Dublin in particular see *Appendix 2: The Catholic Church in Dublin in an age of repression and reconstruction*. For Larkin's comment, see E. Larkin, 'Before the devotional revolution', in J. H. Murphy, ed., *Evangelicals and Catholics in Nineteenth-Century Ireland*, Dublin 2005, pp. 15-17.

**Fig 3.** *This drawing of the Portlester Chapel of St Audoen's Church, Dublin, in ruins, with no roof, illustrates the state of disrepair of the Catholic churches in Dublin at the time. Originally published in the* Dublin Penny Journal, *Volume 1, Number 26, December 22nd, 1832.*

## The Regulars

If the situation for Irish Catholics was very difficult but gradually ameliorating over the period 1770 to 1850, the same cannot be said for the situation of the male religious orders. Their numbers in Ireland declined from 800 in 1750, through 400 in 1800 to 180 in 1840, a 77.5% decline in ninety years. From having constituted over 30% of Catholic clergy in 1770, they fell to 7.5% by 1840. In the Dublin archdiocese the number of friars fell from 79 in 1800 to 63 in 1825. This phenomenon of decline was described by Larkin as *'a rout'*. As Fenning points out, restrictions imposed by Rome on the numbers and types of novices they could admit in Ireland was a significant factor.[7] However, Larkin argues that the more serious consideration was the negative effect on their community life – and therefore on vocations – caused by their entering into or being drafted into parish work during decades of extreme population pressure.[8] Recovery would eventually set in after

7. H. Fenning, *The Undoing of the Friars in Ireland,* Louvain 1972, pp. 278-285.
8. E. Larkin, *The Pastoral Role of the Roman Catholic Church in Pre-Famine Ireland, 1750-1850,* Dublin 2006, pp. 22-23, n. 12, p. 30; see also *Appendix 2.*

1860 so that by 1900, their numbers had risen to 260. It was only after they had been almost fully replaced in parochial work by diocesan priests that this recovery became manifest, and so, for much of John Spratt's life as a friar, their situation was a difficult one.[9]

Furthermore, relations between bishops and secular priests on the one hand and the regular clergy of the religious orders on the other hand in Ireland, as elsewhere, were not always harmonious.[10] From time to time there could be tensions over jurisdiction and more commonly over financial competition for alms, fees and bequests. Nevertheless, the Orders in Dublin played a very significant role in the pastoral ministry. The impressive church and school building programme which commenced under Troy and Murray owed a huge amount to the efforts and achievements of the Religious Orders, male and female. Of the twelve leading new Dublin city churches erected between 1780 and 1841, some five were those of the regular clergy.[11] Indeed, the very first churches to be built in the new dawn of the post penal era were those of the Dominicans in Dominick Street in 1780 (rebuilt 1835), and of the Discalced Carmelites who began their Church of St Teresa in Clarendon Street in 1793. Despite the banning and exiling of the male Religious Orders from Ireland as of May 1698, it is probable that at no time in the course of the penal era was the island devoid of monks and friars. A Privy Council return of April 1698 counted only 27 Catholic clergy in Dublin, of whom only one was of the regular clergy.[12] Until quite some time after this, however, they cannot be said to have advertised their presence. In this regard, the Carmelites, of course, were no exception.

### Carmelites in Ireland: Survival and Revival

The story of the Carmelites in Ireland has been well-chronicled by Peter O'Dwyer and needs no detailed repetition here. As with all other

---

9. Larkin, *Pastoral Role*, p. 47, esp. note 78.
10. Larkin, 'Before the devotional revolution', pp. 30-31.
11. They were the churches of the Dominicans, Dominick St, 1780, and rebuilt in 1835, the Discalced Carmelites in Clarendon Street in 1793, the Calced Carmelites of the Ancient Observance, Whitefriar Street in 1825, the Jesuits' Saint Francis Xavier Church in Gardiner Street in 1829, and the Franciscans' Church of St Francis of Assisi (Adam and Eve's), Merchant's Quay in 1834.
12. Kelly, p. 147, n. 11.

clergy, regular and diocesan, they suffered seriously in their numbers from the mid-sixteenth to the mid-eighteenth centuries. However, the distinguished Carmelite historian, Joachim Smet, has cautioned that

> Although there cannot have been many Carmelites in post-Reformation Ireland, there is no reason to believe that their number is limited to the few whose names have come down to us.[13]

Nevertheless, even in the darkest days of the penal era, the Carmelites through their continental colleges, especially in Spain, had re-established themselves in Ireland. By 1731 with 38 members, they were sufficient in numbers to embolden them to request that Ireland be reconstituted as a separate province, which was duly authorised by Pope Clement XII on 10th October 1737. By 1761 their numbers had risen to 50 in fourteen locations, at which point their future seemed promising.

It was therefore ironic that, having survived the worst of the penal times, their continued progress or even existence was threatened by an edict from Rome. Allowing for some exaggeration, indiscipline had become a problem; these men had grown accustomed to fending for themselves and while some of them may have yearned for the closed conventual life in common, others were too used to their own independence. As a consequence, the Roman authorities, in 1751, decreed that postulants were no longer to be professed in Ireland but instead had to subject themselves to a canonical novitiate on the continent. The problem of indiscipline was not unique to the eighteenth century Irish Carmelites – it affected many of the Orders of the regular clergy, and accordingly, this decree from Propaganda Fide applied to them all. Unfortunately the decree was a case of the cure being worse than the malady. As Hugh Fenning has observed, this disastrous decree almost *'constituted a death sentence for the Mendicants'.*[14] It hit the Carmelites especially hard: unlike the others, they had no native novitiate on the continent: the cost of getting their novices to Europe and of getting other Carmelite houses there to accept them, constituted a serious impediment. In the year of this decree, 1751,

13. Smet, pp. 355-359.
14. Fenning, *The Undoing of the Friars*, p. 44.

there were some 64 Carmelites in the Irish Province: by 1767 this had fallen to 34. Rome relented in a practical way: in 1774 they agreed to the creation of novitiates in Ireland but they limited the Carmelites to a maximum intake of 14 every three years and these to be not less than 25 years of age. This was hardly the remedy the Order needed. By 1801 their Irish Province was down to 28 priests in 10 friaries. Despite the fact that the Catholic Church in Ireland in general, and in Dublin in particular, experienced a powerful revival and a spectacular expansion over the years 1800 to 1850 and beyond, the Carmelite province saw little enough of this expansion. Its leading house in Ireland and its only one in Dublin, had as late as 1820 a complement of 6 priests, and the whole province only 21. The following thirty years saw no evidence of the modest growth that was to follow later: by 1840 their Dublin house numbered only 8 members, and still had that number in 1850, while the whole Province in 1840 had only 26 of whom 7 were living in solitude, without benefit of any community. For all that, and despite continuing challenges to common life and discipline, change was abroad and much would be achieved by the small band of brothers who lived or tried to live according to the *Rule* of St Albert.

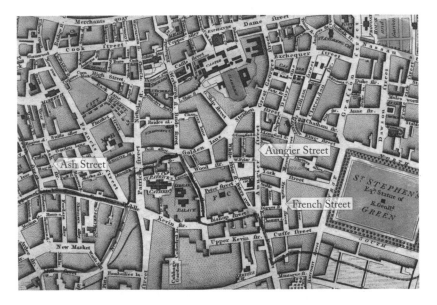

**Fig 4.**     *Map of Dublin 1798.*

*The Ash Street Carmelite Community*

By 1731 the Calced Carmelites had established a foothold in Ash Street, having previously perhaps been located in New Row.[15] It is interesting to note that their presence in Ash Street involved a move from one premises to another, possibly in 1739.[16] It appears that this second Ash Street chapel and friary may have been built from scratch: a report of the year 1749 observes that it *'was built as it now appears'*, and continued:

> the altar-piece is a painting of the crucifixion, on each side of which are those of Elias and Eliseus in Carmelite Habits, the former of whom that Order boasts as their founder. A handsome branch hangs before the altar, near which is a pulpit and four galleries. Adjacent to the Chapel is a convenient House, sufficient for the reception of six Carmelites.[17]

The move of the Carmelites into Ash Street indicates both the growing effective toleration of that time and the growing number of Catholics in the area. It was located in the Liberty of Thomas Court and Donore, part of the Liberties of the Earl of Meath – an estate hostile to the presence of Catholics in the later seventeenth and earlier eighteenth centuries.[18] As David Dickson has observed, respecting the year 1731,

> there was still, it seems, no chapel or resident priest on the Meath estate, although the Chapel opened by the Carmelites in Ash Street off the Coombe in the late 1720s (formerly a Quaker

15. For the earlier history of the Carmelites in 18th century Dublin, see *Appendix 3: The Carmelites of New Row and Ash Street, Dublin, in the 18th century.*

16. Registry of Deeds, *Book 94*, p. 341, No. 66611, Memorial of Deed of Lease, dated 16th May 1739. The move may have come in 1739 as, in May of that year, Matthew Lyons, then Provincial, and Owen Swiney, then Prior, signed a 31-year lease with the Meath Street property owner, Samuel Onge, for a plot of land containing two houses and yards. It fronted on to Ash Street on the west side, with a passage on its south leading to Meath Street.

17. N. Donnelly, ed., *Roman Catholics: State and Condition of Roman Catholic Chapels in Dublin both Secular and Regular A.D. 1749*, Dublin 1904, pp. 17-18.

18. Registry of Deeds, Dublin, Land Index Books, *Book 87*, p. 5; also N. Burke, 'A hidden church'? The structure of Catholic Dublin in the mid-eighteenth century', *Archivium Hibernicum*, vol. 31, 1974, p. 89.

meeting house) showed they were not far away.[19]

If the move represented a growing toleration and a growing Catholic presence, it also surely represented on the part of the Carmelites a growing confidence for their future. In their second move within Ash Street they had secured a site *'with an extensive street frontage, on which their church was adjoined by a tree-lined courtyard'*.[20] Located in the parish of St Nicholas Without, the Ash Street Carmelites served a growing community of Catholics, probably even then constituting a majority of the population in the area. Already by 1731 there were sixteen Catholic schools, eight diocesan and seven regular clergy to be found there.[21] By 1761 it is estimated that there were then 9,000 Catholics to 2,000 Protestants in this parish.[22] Here the Carmelites served in a bustling, noisy environment not without its plethora of public nuisances: unregulated slaughter houses and dairies, together with nearby tanneries, glue factories, breweries and distilleries. Their own premises backed on to a lime-burning yard and had itself previously been a coal yard.[23] The street was but a stone's throw from the old Newgate prison on Cutpurse Row, Francis Street, from where the processions of condemned criminals in trundling carts were taken to be hanged on the 'fatal tree' in Stephen's Green – on average once a month by the 1780s.[24] It was an environment hardly conducive to a contemplative life. Inevitably, Ash Street itself was not without its share of crime. Indeed, the Carmelites themselves could be victims, as happened in September 1771:

---

19.  D. Dickson, op.cit., p. 146. The author, however, is mistaken in observing that the Ash Street premises was formerly a Quaker meeting house: the Quaker meeting house in question was that of New Row, as they never had one in Ash Street.
20.  N. Burke, p. 89.
21.  P. Fagan, 'The Dublin Catholic Mob, 1700-1750', *Eighteenth-Century Ireland*, vol. 4, 1989, p. 140.
22.  P. Fagan, *Catholics in a Protestant Country: the papist constituency in Eighteenth-Century Dublin*, p. 35. Chapter 2, 'The population of Dublin in the eighteenth century' is an updating of his earlier article on the subject, *Eighteenth-Century Ireland*, vol. 6, 1991, pp. 121-156.
23.  Registry of Deeds, *Book 94*, p. 341, No. 66611, A Memorial dated 16th May 1739, between Samuel Onge of Meath Street, Merchant, and Matthew Lyons and Owen Swiney of Ash Street.
24.  B. Henry, *Dublin Hanged: crime, law enforcement and punishment in late eighteenth-century Dublin*, Dublin 1994, p. 16.

> About eight o'clock at night as the clergymen belonging to the
> Chapel in Ash Street were going into their houses in said street,
> they were attacked by three villains who robbed them of their
> watches and every other valuable thing they had about them,
> with which they got clear off.

It was little consolation to them that a few days later the Sheriff

> apprehended and lodged in Newgate a man charged with robbery
> of the two Romish clergymen in Ash Street... it is said he is an
> old offender, and has oftentimes been in gaol.[25]

For all that, the Ash Street Carmelites managed to serve here for three
quarters of a century before moving on.

Over the course of their seven decades there, the numbers of
these friars seems to have remained stable at around six or seven.
This was their estimated number in November 1751 as recounted by
William Burke.[26] Fifteen years later, the Ash Street community was
still numbered at seven friars, according to a report by the Spaniard,
Calahorra, in 1766.[27] Such was still the reckoning which Archbishop
John Carpenter made in 1780. He wrote of the existence in the city
of six chapels of the religious in which there served six, seven or eight
regular clergy. They were busy, fragmented lives they lived, it seems, for
he added that they neither lived in common nor dined in common.[28]

### *The Devotional Revival*
This small band of Carmelites was part of a significant Catholic cultural
revival of the later eighteenth century. The period saw the flourishing
of popular devotional practices and publications and the establishment

---

25. J. Brady, 'Catholics and Catholicism in the Eighteenth-Century press', *Archivium Hibernicum*, XVII, 1953, pp. 144-145, citing reports in the *Hibernian Journal* and *Pue's Occurrences*, Sept 1771.

26. W. P. Burke, *The Irish Priests in the Penal Times, 1660-1760*, 1968 reprint of 1st ed., Waterford 1914, p. 307.

27. F. Calahorra, *Breve Compendio del Origen y Antiquedad de la Santa Religion del Carmen*, Madrid 1766, pp. 111-112, cited in O'Dwyer, p. 131.

28. M. J. Curran, 'Archbishop Carpenter's Epistolae (1770-1780)' in *Reportorium Novum*, vol. 1, No. 2, 1956, p. 395: "qui nec commune vitam ducunt, nec communi mensa utuntur: v.e.... Franciscani, Dominici, Augusti, Carmelitae Discalci üdem Calceati et Capucini": the quotation is taken from Carpenter's *Relatio Status* of 1780.

of day, evening and Sunday schools, especially for the poor. While it has been stated that *'Ireland [then] had no native authors of devotional texts'* it is interesting to note that the sermons of the English Carmelite, Francis Blyth, were *'commonly found'* in Dublin's bookshops in the 1770s, notably Blyth's *Sermons for every Sunday throughout the year.*[29] This is but one example of a substantial volume of Catholic imprints that became available in eighteenth and early nineteenth century Dublin, as recently revealed, notably in the work of Hugh Fenning and Cormac Begadon.[30]

Similarly, there was a notable growth of popular devotional practices, promoted in particular by the city's religious orders through confraternities and sodalities. However, when it came to public displays of Catholic piety, the expression of such devotion through processions was both sporadic and discouraged during the eighteenth century. From Archbishop Lincoln in the 1760s to Archbishop Troy in the 1790s the Dublin diocesan authorities were not keen on such public displays at a time when their Church was still vulnerable and just about tolerated. At the start of the 1760s, Lincoln was caustic in his comments, describing some public processions consisting of *'three or four lubberly fellows with scapulars about their shoulders'.*[31] Then, in 1790, when the Calced Carmelite Provincial, Thomas O'Mahony, asked Troy's permission to conduct a monthly procession in honour of 'Our Lady of the Brown Scapular', he was refused, even though a similar request had already been allowed to their Discalced confreres. Troy was conscious of simmering

29. C. Begadon, 'The Renewal of Catholic Religious culture in eighteenth-century Dublin' in J. Bergin et al., eds., *New Perspectives on the Penal Laws*, Dublin 2011, pp. 227-248, esp. p. 235.

30. H. Fenning, 'Dublin imprints of Catholic interest: 1701-1739', *Collectanea Hibernica*, 39-40 (1997-1998), 106-154: 'Dublin imprints of Catholic interest: 1740-1759', *Collectanea Hibernica*, 41 (1999), 65-116; 'Dublin imprints of Catholic interest: 1760-69', *Collectanea Hibernica*, 42 (2000), 85-119; 'Dublin imprints of Catholic interest: 1770-1782', *Collectanea Hibernica*, 43 (2001), 161-208: 'Dublin imprints of Catholic interest:1783-1789', *Collectanea Hibernica*, 44-45 (2002-2003), 79-126; 'Dublin imprints of Catholic interest: 1790-1795', *Collectanea Hibernica*, 46-47 (2004-2005), 72-141; 'Dublin imprints of Catholic interest: 1796-1799'. *Collectanea Hibernica*, 48 (2006), 72-141; 'Dublin imprints of Catholic interest: 1800-09', *Archivium Hibernicum*, 61 (2008), 246-324; C. Begadon, 'Catholic Devotional Literature in Dublin, 1800-1830', and 'Catholic Religious Publishing, 1800-1891' in J. H. Murphy, ed., *The Irish Book in English, 1800-1891*, Oxford 2011, pp. 331-341 and 371-378, respectively.

31. P. J. Corish, *The Catholic Community in the Seventeenth and Eighteenth Centuries*, Dublin 1981, p. 85.

interdenominational tensions in the city and felt that another such procession might be unwise; furthermore, to have granted the request to the Calced Carmelites, would have only led to a different kind of procession – a procession to his door of Capuchins, Dominicans and Franciscans seeking similar concessions.[32] However, within the confines of their conventual chapels, the Regulars established their specific Third Orders for lay members and their particular devotional practices. Already, in the earlier part of the eighteenth century, even in their makeshift buildings, it was noted that the Dublin Carmelites in Wormwood Gate had *'a representation of Our Lady giving the scapular to Dr Simon Stock'*.[33] At the other end of that century, the Carmelites maintained their devotion to the Scapular of Our Blessed Lady of Mount Carmel. It was to this devotion that John Spratt's mother, Esther, made her way regularly from Cork Street to Ash Street.

From an early stage, too, these Carmelites were providing schooling in the locality. In their 1731 *Report*, the curates and churchwardens of St Nicholas Without remarked *'there are sixteen Popish Schoolmasters some of whom are Priests or Friars, in the said parish'*. Half a century later, when the Church of Ireland clergy were required to make a return of Catholic Schools in their Dublin Parishes, the Rev John Gast of St Nicholas Without gave a detailed report as follows:

> There is another popish School belonging to the Regulars of Ash Street where 20 boys are clothed and instructed. Its only support is a Charity Sermon and some subscriptions. The expense from 1st January 1786 to 1st January 1787 for clothes, linen, woollen, shoes, stockings, hats, books, paper was £73-19-1, master's salary £12.0.0, no rent paid for the schoolroom, being part of the chapel; besides the master has about £40 pay boys.[34]

This Report suggests the socially mixed nature of the local population at that time since the pupils were a combination of charity scholars and fee paying ones.

32. Begadon, 'The Renewal of Catholic Religious culture in eighteenth-century Dublin', p. 241.
33. J. Meagher, 'Glimpses of eighteenth-century priests', *Reportorium Novum*, vol. 2, No. 1, 1958, p. 130.
34. J. Brady, 'Catholic Schools in Dublin, 1787-1778', *Reportorium Novum*, vol. 1, No. 1, 1955, p. 195.

**Fig 5.**    *The former Carmelite Church and Temperance Hall at French Street.*

*French Street, 1806-1825*
In 1904 Nicholas Donnelly, the historian of Dublin Catholic parishes, wrote:

> The chapel here described [Ash St] served them until 1780, when they moved to the more retired and genteel neighbourhood of French Street, now Upper Mercer Street, where a nice little chapel was erected for them in Cuffe Lane, with a dwelling house attached in French Street.[35]

To judge from the tone of his somewhat inaccurate account, it is as if the Carmelites were seeking more respectable surroundings when they moved from Ash Street. At the start of the nineteenth century, French Street certainly was a safer and more respectable neighbourhood, with its medical doctors and solicitors, compared with Ash Street's labourers, artisans and traders. Nevertheless, whatever about their selection

---

35. N. Donnelly, *State and Condition of Roman Catholic Chapels*, note N, p. 37. He misdates the move to 1780 instead of 1806.

of French Street, their leaving of Ash Street had been a matter of necessity, not choice: the Ash Street lease expired and the landlord was not willing or able to renew it to the Carmelites. The move to their new location took place in 1806. In May of that year their new chapel, made possible by the generosity of the citizens of Dublin, was completed and dedicated on 6th June.[36] That it had been planned for some time is evident from what is called *The Ash Street Account Book* and, when it took place, it involved two separate premises: their friary or convent in French Street and their chapel, close by, in Cuffe Lane, and to which there became attached a school.

It is not fully clear when exactly this particular school was opened by the Carmelites. O'Dwyer records that they had opened a new school, St Patrick's, in French Street and the context in which he states this suggests that it was from their commencement in the area in 1806.[37] It is clearly the case that, from at least early in 1808, a St Patrick's school for forty orphan boys and sons of impoverished local tradesmen was being conducted and was supported by an annual charity sermon preached in French Street Chapel.[38] The French Street Chapel and School were both named St Patrick's. Despite the savings they had made in Ash Street towards this move, it cost them a lot more than the available finances. In consequence, they had to undertake serious fundraising. Typical of this was a concert of sacred music, followed by a sermon which they organised, appropriately enough, for St Patrick's Day of 1811. The sermon took the form of a panegyric on St Patrick, delivered by Rev. J F Cavanagh. The collection, as they advertised for the occasion, was towards *'liquidating the very heavy debts incurred by the building'.*[39]

Sometime before the death of Prior Richard Cosgrave, responsibility for these debts and for the new community fell on the shoulders of Fr Thomas Finny as Prior.[40] On 14th May 1813 he took over the

---

36. *SNL*, 23rd May 1806.
37. O'Dwyer, pp. 163-164, 174, n. 213.
38. *Hibernian Journal or Chronicle of Liberty*, 8th Feb 1808; *SNL*, 24th Jan 1809.
39. *FJ*, 16th March 1811.
40. Richard Cosgrave, the last Prior of Ash Street and the first Prior of French Street, died in March 1816: see *Appendix 3*.

management, leading a community of six friars.[41] Thomas Finny strove
hard to make the new church and community decently appointed and
to meet its debts. This task took some time but in July 1816 he was able
to record in satisfaction:

> I have this day cleared off the original Builder's bill for the whole
> of which was £1,842-2-6. During my term of three years I have
> expended for the Chapel and the house to this day:

| For the two additions to the Chapel: | £300 |
| | £374-1-3 |
| Expenses of house: | £296-10-6 |
| | £970-11-9.[42] |

Thomas Finny remained the most active of his community in fund-
raising, certainly so down to 1818. Soon after that, significant change
occurred in his career and in the composition of the French Street
Community. As a result of the Chapter of May 1819, he became
Provincial, a position he held until 1823, while Thomas Coleman
succeeded him as Prior in French Street.[43] He and John Spratt were
destined to have a close working relationship until Colman's death at
the age of 58 in 1838. Indeed, circumstances would quickly throw
them together into the same boat that faced very troubled waters in the
Dublin Carmelite community from the early 1820s.

41. These were Richard Cosgrave, William Kinsella, Thomas Coleman, John Cormick,
    Simon A. McCarthy and Edward Ryan: see C. Giblin, 'Papers of Richard Joachim
    Hayes, O.F.M., 1810-1824', *Collectanea Hibernica*, 21-22, 1979-80, pp. 120-134.
    This is a list of Dublin Catholic clerical signatories protesting against the proposal
    for a veto by the British Government on the appointment of Catholic Bishops
    in Ireland. See also GMA, *Ash Street Account Book*, p. 69 and O'Dwyer, p. 243,
    n.13.
42. GMA, *Ash Street Account Book*, p. 86. O'Dwyer, p. 179.
43. Thomas Coleman had been professed in La Casa Grande de Sevilla in 1808. He
    was aged 34 when he became Prior of French Street. A Dubliner, and indeed
    a fellow-parishioner of John Spratt, he was born in Meath Street and baptised in St
    Catherine of Alexandria: see AO, Rome II, *Baetica*, ff. 73 v, 290r, cited in O'Dwyer,
    243, n.4. For the changes in the office holders in 1819, see O'Dwyer, *Irish
    Carmelites*, pp. 185, 187, citing H. Young, *The Catholic Directory for the year 1821*, p.
    14; P. Cunningham, 'The Catholic Directory for 1821', *Reportorium Novum*, vol. 2,
    No. 2, 1960, pp. 324-63.

# CHAPTER FOUR

## *Priest and Prior in the 1820s*

When John arrived at French Street in the summer of 1821 he walked into a hornet's nest. Whatever may have been the personal relations obtaining in this community before John arrived, they had become strained, to put it mildly, from at least 1822. The next Irish Chapter was held in 1823 and Thomas Coleman now became Provincial. For whatever reason, Finny refused to recognise Coleman's elevation to that office as his successor. Finny was, without doubt, a dynamic and reforming friar. He was the first Irish Carmelite in post-Reformation Ireland to produce a specific *Ordo of the Divine Office* for his Order's Irish Province.[1] His energy was evident also from the manner in which he had built up and funded the physical structure of his French Street community. That he was an advocate of reform appears from the letter he addressed to his Prior General, Antonius Faro, in 1822. It will be recalled that Dublin's Archbishop Carpenter had noted of that city's communities of regular clergy, in the 1780's, that they neither lived in common nor dined in common even though living under the one roof. To judge by Finny's letter, little had changed in this respect as regards the Calced Carmelites.[2] They were hardly alone in this: the Franciscans' historian, Patrick Conlan, records how *'the concept of regular observance was new to the Irish Franciscans'* of the eighteenth and earlier nineteenth centuries, and that much needed to be done to encourage the adoption

---

1. T. Finny, *Ordo Divini Officii Pro Anno MDCCCXX…*, 14 pp., John Coyne, Dublin 1820. Copy in the Library and Archives, Gort Muire. I am grateful to the librarian, Ruth Long, for drawing my attention to this volume.
2. O'Dwyer, pp. 185-190.

of community meditation and the communal recitation of the Divine Office.[3] Among other problems, Finny's letter mentioned the habit of friars dining with lay friends and living at times outside the walls, their failure to share equally the funds from alms, the neglect of conducting the Divine Office and daily meditation together, the abuse of seeking or taking out loans of money, the failure to make wills leaving property to a named member or members of the Order, and the failure to record such wills and to archive them properly.[4]

Finny quickly became alienated from Thomas Coleman and from the Prior General, Faro. He defied all urgings and threats in his refusal to recognise the newly elected Coleman as Provincial. What precisely lay at the heart of this alienation is not clear. Certain it is that Coleman had begun collecting funds to create a new church and community house – the future Church of Our Lady of Mount Carmel, Whitefriar Street. It may be that, having put so much effort, time and money into the French Street community, Finny may have resented deeply the prospect of its being abandoned in favour of some new venture. As early as 1823, Coleman and Spratt had engaged a Mr Wall to draw up plans for a new foundation[5] and in late February of 1824 Coleman had complained to the Order in Rome that French Street was too small and that they needed larger premises, especially if novices were to be received. Nor

---

3.  P. Conlan, *Franciscan Ireland*, Mullingar 1988, pp. 56-57. See also P. Conlan, 'Reforming and seeking an identity', in E. Bhreathnach, J. MacMahon & J. McCafferty, eds., *The Irish Franciscans, 1534-1990*, Dublin 2009, pp. 102-131.
4.  O'Dwyer, *Irish Carmelites*, pp. 185-190. This letter, in its original draft form, may have been composed in Rome by the former Prior General Timothaeus Maria Ascensi. This Carmelite had been delegated to assist with arrangements for the Irish Provincial Chapter and his letter was despatched for consideration by Finny and the Irish Province through the young Carmelite, Richard John Colgan, then based in Rome. Destined to be Provincial of Ireland over the years 1843 to 1846, Colgan may well have been of some influence in the Roman Curia of the Order – as O'Dwyer suggests – but he had only completed his novitiate there in May 1819 and had been ordained not less than a year after that. He was helping the Prior of Dublin, Thomas Coleman, to prepare business for the Irish Provincial Chapter of 1823. However, Finny, an independent spirit, would never have sent the letter to the then Prior General, Faro, if he had not believed in its propositions.
5.  Wall was almost certainly a member or descendant of the important family of Dublin master craftsmen and builders who in the eighteenth century built a significant house in Leinster Street and who executed the plasterwork on the Provost's House, Trinity College Dublin. I am grateful to Dr Christine Casey of Trinity College Dublin for this information.

was that all – he referred to the difficulties with Fr Finny and to the fact that the French Street property, being in Finny's name, could have been bequeathed by Finny to anyone he chose.[6] This, however, was hardly the case: the property had been willed to the Carmelites, admittedly in Finny's name, by the prosperous Dublin merchant, James Corballis of New Street, but *'without power to the said Thomas Finney [sic] and to any other of the said clergy to alienate the said premises during the time they should be respectively entitled thereto subject to the payment of the yearly rent'.*[7] Not only did the Procurator General, Bonvicini, give permission for a new Church building, he instructed Coleman to expel Finny from the Order for disobedience and to inform Archbishop Murray to that effect.[8] Coleman and Spratt, a month later, wrote to Murray of their plans for a new foundation in Dublin to replace that of French Street.[9] Finny's defiance led Coleman to suspend him and there now developed a prolonged and acrimonious controversy. Ultimately, this led Finny and the Order to a final parting of the ways. In the end, he signed a legal document with the French Street landlords to terminate the lease, thereby freeing the Carmelites from any liabilities for the property there.[10] By 1828, Thomas Finny had become a diocesan priest serving in the relatively remote parish of Valleymount, Co. Wicklow.

At what precise point the young Fr Spratt became caught up in this conflict which so bitterly divided the French Street community is not quite certain. Is it possible that it was he, fresh from Spain, who planted in Coleman's mind the ambition for a new church? One matter is clear: within this divided fraternity, there was a close triumvirate of Thomas Coleman and William Kinsella, holding between them the office of Provincial from 1823 to 1841, and John Spratt. At the Chapter of

---

6. O'Dwyer, *Irish Carmelites*, p. 195.
7. Registry of Deeds, Land Index Book, *Book 93*, vol. 713, 397/488132, Corballis and another to Finney [sic], 21st March 1817, registered 9th Apr 1817. The Corballis family who had been neighbours of the Carmelites in the New Street area in the eighteenth century, moved to the Roebuck area of Clonskeagh in the nineteenth century. They were strong financial supporters of various Catholic causes, not least those undertaken by John Spratt.
8. O'Dwyer, p. 196.
9. DDA, *Murray Papers*, 30-8/81-86, Coleman & Spratt to Murray, 20th March 1824.
10. Registry of Deeds, *Transcription Book 94*, vol. 836, 427/561962, Finny to Kelly, Registered 8th July 1828.

**Fig 6.**   *Photograph of a young Fr John Spratt.*

1823, Fr John was elected Prior of Whitefriar Street.[11]  Then in May 1826 when Kinsella became Provincial by Apostolic letter, he appointed Spratt as Vicar Prior of French Street immediately, which office he held until May 1829.[12]  At the same time as this appointment, Kinsella made Spratt First Definitor, in effect the second most important post in the Irish Province.  It was a rapid and impressive progress for so young a friar and ought to have augured well for his standing in the Province for the future.  However, as Prior, he soon became caught up in the bitter struggle between ex-Provincial Finny and the then Provincial, Coleman.  Finny, fairly or unfairly, had been suspended and, by the start of 1823, was *persona non grata* in a section of his own community. If he is to be believed, Finny recounted how, in February 1824, Spratt ordered the house servants not to light the fire or carry out cleaning for Finny and ordered their confrere, Laurence Callanan, to break and enter Finny's rooms.  Callanan wrote to Finny to say that Coleman, Kinsella and Spratt promised to send him to any convent he wished provided (in Finny's account) Callanan '*said he was drunk when he broke*

11.  GMA, Box 56, Coleman to Spratt, 20th Apr 1823; *DEP*, 26th Apr 1823.
12.  GMA, Box 56, Kinsella to Spratt, 8th May 1826.

*my door'*: subsequently beside himself with anxiety for having done this, the distraught Callanan was reported as crying out *'you villain, Spratt, you done me'* [sic].[13] In his exasperation at developments, Finny could be intemperate in his observations. He certain did not spare his Prior, Spratt, in his vituperation. Even before the Christmas of 1822, hardly a year after Spratt's return and six months before he held any significant official position in the community, Finny castigated his Carmelite adversaries by reference to their origins, describing Coleman as a mere weaver, Kinsella a turner, and Spratt a glue-boiler and sheep-skinner, while Frs Coote, Colgan and Neil, were respectively a tailor, land-bailiff and huxter of cabbages.[14]

John's appointments as Prior, then Vicar Prior over 1823 to 1829, constituted a very early promotion and recognition for the young Dubliner. In this position he was not only head of a religious community: in effect, if completely unofficially, he was the head of a 'parish' of that population living between the lower Coombe and Clarendon Street area to the west, down to Dame Street in the east. By the time Spratt became Prior of French Street he was already becoming known in the roles of preacher and pastor. He would now become responsible for the St Patrick's Free Schools and he quickly became caught up in the ceaseless round of fund-raising sermons that would become so significant a feature of his pastoral and public life. The first such sermon, so far identified, was delivered on Sunday 24th November 1822, in aid of the St John the Baptist Orphan Society which had been founded in 1812.[15] Given what was to be Spratt's deep and lifelong commitment to the cause of orphans, it was perhaps an appropriate starting-point. As a relative newcomer it may have been also appropriate that he was to deliver the evening charity sermon at St John Street Chapel, following on from the day sermon on that Sunday, delivered by the Rev. Charles Stennett, parish priest of Donabate. Their efforts would benefit the Society's forty orphans.

*A Brother in Charity*
One of the collectors on the occasion of this early public role by Fr

13. DDA, *Murray Papers*, 30/9/25 & 30/9/26, Finny to Murray, 23rd March 1825, Callanan to Finny, 10th Aug 1825.
14. CISA, *Prov.Hib.Literae, 1715-1810*, II Hib. 3, Finny to Fato, 17th Dec 1822.
15. This particular Orphan Society appears to have ceased operating after the 1830s.

John was his older brother, Michael.  The latter had already established himself as generous with his time on charitable enterprises.[16]  Thereafter he soon became caught up in his brother John's public endeavours. When John first preached for the St John the Baptist Orphan Society, Michael was its vice-president.[17]  By January 1825 he had become its secretary and would come to associate with its leading supporters who included Daniel O'Connell, Andrew Ennis, the Hibernian Bank Director and leading O'Connell supporter, and the young James Haughton who was to feature so prominently in John's later life.[18]  Michael was still the Society's secretary as late as 1835.[19]  Apart from his political commitments – to be described later – a third area for his charitable efforts was on behalf of the Carmelites' St Patrick's General Free School in Cuffe Lane.  In November 1824 he was among the donors, following a charity sermon, for the school, in French Street Chapel. Michael continued his support of the school to the end of the 1820s and beyond, by which time he appears to have moved house, along with their mother, from Cork Street to Rehoboth Place, Dolphin's Barn, off the South Circular Road.[20]  It is clear from all of this that Michael Spratt worked closely with and for his brother John as the latter developed his charitable ministry from the 1820s.

---

16.  Even before John's return from Spain, Michael had been actively committed to     .
     charitable work, first in his own parish of St Catherine's where, in April 1821,
     he was organising donations for its Catholic Free Schools.  That same summer he
     featured among the great and the good of Catholic Ireland in organising an
     address of welcome to King George IV on the occasion of his visit to Ireland.
     Here Michael was a signatory in the company of aristocrats such as Gormanston,
     Killeen and Trimleston as well as of Archbishop Troy.  For these, see *FJ*, 30th Apr
     1821, 9th July 1821 respectively.
17.  *FJ*, 23rd Nov 1822.
18.  *FJ*, 18th Jan 1825.  For James Haughton see, in particular, Chapter Eight.
19.  *FJ*, 29th Jan 1835.  When he is mentioned in January 1837 as a collector of
     donations he is not described as the Society's Secretary.  Interestingly, in January
     1826, he is described as the President of the Society: *FJ*, 14th Jan 1826.
20.  Over the period 1826 to 1830 his address is given variously as Cork Street and
     Rehoboth  [also spelt Rahoboth and Rehoboath, it was not listed in Dublin
     directories before the year 1823].  *FJ*, 24th Jan, 27th Sept 1828, 30th Jan, 7th Feb
     1829, 20th May & 5th Oct 1830.  The Whitefriar Street Building Accounts have
     an entry of 1826 showing a donation from Michael with the Rehoboth address: it
     may have been his own personal house as distinct from the family home in Cork
     Street.

*Great Expectations*

John's mission as prior and pastor began at a time of profound expectation on the part of Catholics in Ireland. That expectation owed not a little to the mood of millenarianism that caught the popular imagination in the early 1820s, as it developed around the prophecies of Pastorini. Pastorini, nom-de-plume of the eighteenth century English Benedictine monk and bishop, Charles Walmesley (1722–1797), was the author of *The general history of the Christian Church from her birth to her final triumphant state in Heaven*. First published in England in 1771, it appeared in various Irish editions in Dublin and Cork over the period 1771 to 1825.[21] In these editions, and pamphlet versions of them, the author was taken to have prophesied the downfall of Protestantism and the triumph of Catholicism in Ireland for the year 1824 or 1825.[22] Coinciding exactly in time with these expectations of deliverance there came the heightened sense of expectation generated by the miracle worker and German Catholic priest, Alexander Emmerich, Prince Hohenloe. Identified with the gift of distant healing, Hohenloe's miraculous powers were so widely accepted that the intellectual Bishop James Doyle of Kildare and Leighlin and the cautious, conservative Daniel Murray, Archbishop of Dublin, publicly acknowledged two of Hohenloe's miracles – one of distant healing of a deaf-mute girl, Maria Lalor, in Co. Laois in June 1823, the other of a Carmelite nun, Mary Stuart of St Joseph's Convent, Ranelagh, Dublin, in August that year. She had been paralysed, mute and bedridden over four years.[23] The Hohenloe miracles and the bishops' endorsement of them gave a sharp and sudden lift to the politically excluded Irish Catholic community,

---

21. C. Walmesley, *The general history of the Christian church: from her birth to her final triumphant state in Heaven, chiefly deduced from the Apocalypse of St John the Apostle. By Signor Pastorini*, Dublin 1771.

22. I. Whelan, *The Bible War in Ireland: the 'Second Reformation' and the Polarization of Protestant-Catholic Relations, 1800-1840*, Dublin 2005, p. 143; T. McGrath, *Religious Renewal and Reform in the Pastoral Ministry of Bishop James Doyle of Kildare and Leighlin, 1786-1834*, Dublin 1999, p. 193.

23. L. M. Geary, 'Prince Hohenloe, Signor Pastorini and Miraculous Healing in Early Nineteenth-Century Ireland', in G. Jones & E. Malcolm, eds., *Medicine, Disease and the State in Ireland, 1650-1940*, Cork 1999, pp. 40-58; C. Connolly, 'Prince Hohenloe's Miracles: Supernaturalism and the Irish Public Sphere' in D. Duff & C. Jones, *Scotland, Ireland and the Romantic Aesthetic*, Lewisburg 2007, pp. 236-257; T. McGrath, *Politics, interdenominational relations and education in the public ministry of Bishop James Doyle of Kildare and Leighlin, 1786-1834*, Dublin 1999, pp. 107-108.

even as Pastorini's prophesies appeared to present deliverance and triumph as imminent. There is no extant direct commentary from John Spratt on the Hohenloe phenomenon: nevertheless, there is evidence that he was influenced by it, as shall shortly appear.[24]

## The Second Reformation

To whatever extent John Spratt became caught up in the excitement around the miracles of Prince Hohenloe he certainly was quickly immersed in the great contest between a recovering Catholicism and Protestant evangelical revivalism precisely at this time. Leading members of the Church of Ireland gentry became converted to a newly zealous and serious life in which the Bible became paramount. Contrasting with early eighteenth century movements of quietist piety, this movement aimed for a new moral world through a Second Reformation, targeting the wholesale conversion of Catholics. Taking the lead in this was the new Church of Ireland Archbishop of Dublin, William Magee. His first visitation charge to his diocese, delivered in St Patrick's Cathedral, Dublin, on Thursday 24th October 1822, proclaimed the Church of Ireland to be the sole legitimate religious body in Ireland. To his listeners he remarked:

> We, reverend brethren, are placed in a station in which we are hemmed in by two opposite descriptions of professing Christians: the one, possessing a Church without what we can properly call a Religion; and the other possessing a religion, without what we can properly call a Church: the one so blindly enslaved to a supposed infallible authority, as not to seek in the Word of God a reason for the faith they profess; the other, so confident in the infallibility of their individual judgement as to the reasons of their faith that they deem it their duty to resist all authority in matters of religion.[25]

With this assertion, directed against the Presbyterian and Roman Catholic churches alike, he went on to proclaim for the Church of Ireland a new missionary role to convert both persuasions and others

---

24. See below, p. 73.
25. W. Magee, *A charge delivered at his primary visitation in St Patrick's Cathedral, Dublin, on Thursday 27th of October, 1822*, Dublin 1822, pp. 21-22.

**Fig 7.** *Bust of William Magee, Church of Ireland Archbishop of Dublin, which can be found in Trinity College Library.*

on the island to Anglicanism. Thereby he created a storm.[26] His manifesto provoked confrontation with the Catholic bishops whose leading figures did not mince their words in response. Magee's and the evangelicals' crusade to convert the Catholic Irish to Protestantism resulted in serious rivalries, acrimonious public debates and, as a result, a new sectarianism.[27] Within a few months, the foundation of the *Dublin Evening Mail*, in February 1824, brought confrontation and vituperation to new depths: thrice weekly, with the widest circulation of any newspaper in Dublin, it poured out its stream of vitriol against Catholics.[28] This was against the background of the growing activities of the evangelical agencies, the Bible Society, the Hibernian Missionary Society and the Irish Society, from the early 1820s. All of this lent added urgency to the Catholic impetus to provide education for its flock, to develop a Catholic literature, and to challenge Protestant conversionist zeal head on. The young Fr

---

26. I. Whelan, 'The Bible Gentry: Evangelical Religion, Aristocracy and the New Moral Order in the Early Nineteenth Century', in C. Gribben & A. R. Holmes, eds., *Protestant Millenialism, Evangelicalism and Irish Society, 1790-2005*, London 2006, pp. 52-82; S. J. Brown, 'The New Reformation Movement in the Church of Ireland, 1801-1829', in S. J. Brown & D. W. Miller, eds., *Piety and Power in Ireland, 1760-1960: essays in honour of Emmett Larkin*, Indiana 2000, p. 181; J. Holmes, 'Irish evangelicals and the British evangelical community, 1820's-1870's', in J. H. Murphy, ed., *Evangelicals and Catholics in nineteenth century Ireland*, Dublin 2005, p. 219.

27. J. Leichty, 'The popular reformation comes to Ireland: the case of John Walker and the foundation of the Church of God, 1804', in R. V. Comerford, M. Cullen, J. R. Hill & C. Lennon, eds., *Religion, Conflict and Co-existence in Ireland*, Dublin 1990, pp. 159-187; D. Bowen, *The Protestant Crusade in Ireland, 1800-1870*, Dublin 1978.

28. F. O'Ferrall, *Catholic Emancipation: Daniel O'Connell and the birth of Irish Democracy, 1820-1830*, Dublin 1985, p. 47.

Spratt quickly found himself engaged in all of this. In addition to the Dublin Carmelites' commitment to their French Street day, evening and Sunday schools, Spratt now set up a new school in Longford Street in 1824.[29] For this he paid an initial annual rent of £15, together with teacher salary of £23, and he began this project with a modest outlay for twenty-four benches, a large table and various classroom sundries including books for the children and one hundred quill pens.

At this stage he was by now sufficiently well-known to his ecclesiastical peers and prominent lay Catholic colleagues, that he was invited to take part in a meeting that ultimately led to the foundation of the Catholic Book Society. In the early 1820s, in response to the evangelical mission, a paramount feature of which was the dissemination of Bibles and related pamphlet material, a number of Catholic laymen and clergymen were concerned to set up a means of countering this evangelical crusade by dissemination of cheap Catholic literature. W. J. Battersby among the laymen, and William Yore among the Dublin diocesan clergy publicly promoted the idea of establishing a society to this end.[30] They secured Bishop Doyle's enthusiastic support. There followed the convening of a meeting in November 1824 where the young Spratt joined Yore, Fr Patrick Dowling and Battersby in adopting the structure, rules and mission that led, after a delay of three years, to the foundation of *The Catholic Book Society for the diffusion of useful knowledge throughout Ireland*.[31] His associate, Fr Matthew Flanagan, was to be the Society's first secretary while Archbishop Murray acted as its first treasurer. It says something for its perceived importance in

---

29. Citing Farrington's biography of Spratt, O'Dwyer dates this foundation as being in the year 1822. However, the *Whitefriar Street Building Accounts* record the 'Roman Catholic Free School founded in St Peter's Parish anno 1824 by Revd John Spratt of French Street, Dublin'. O'Dwyer, *Irish Carmelites*, p. 197, citing Farrington, p. 116. Strangely, O'Dwyer's earlier Ph.D.dissertation, *John Francis Spratt, O.Carm., 1796-1871*, Pontifical Gregorian University, Rome, 1968, p. 54, proposes that Farrington is wrong in stating 1822 as the foundation year, since Spratt was then not long home from Spain, and suggests the year 1824 instead.

30. T. Wall, 'Catholic periodicals of the past, 2: the Catholic Book Society and the Irish Catholic Magazine', *Irish Ecclesiastical Record*, vol. 101, Jan-June 1964, pp. 289-303: it appears that it was Battersby who took the initiative to promote the idea, in a series of letters in 1824: see Wall, pp. 289-290.

31. Wall, p. 290; T. McGrath, *The pastoral ministry of Bishop James Doyle*, pp. 143-145. The reason for the three-year delay is not evident but it may have been because they were awaiting the endorsement of their bishops.

counteracting the endeavours of the evangelicals, that the majority of the Catholic prelates were enthusiastic in their support. Within three years the Society claimed to have produced a run of almost a million books and pamphlets and within its first ten years, it claimed to have printed five million.[32] Spratt became a member of the committee from its foundation and he remained active in the Catholic Book Society for many years to come: in addition, he was a founding member of the Catholic Society for Ireland, established in 1835 to secure the free distribution of Catholic literature, notably the imprints of the Catholic Book Society and in the mid-1830s he was simultaneously one of the new body's 37 vice-presidents, one of its 24 management committee members and one of its 3 trustees.[33]

At the same time, he became active in the reception of Protestants into the Catholic Church. In March 1827 he received seven converts from the Protestant faith in the French Street Chapel, a month later a further four former members of the Established Church, and then in July came the reception of a female member of the Society of Friends. By that date, it was claimed that over the previous six months Spratt had received *'upwards of sixty'* Church of Ireland converts to Catholicism.[34] One of the more famous or notorious cases involved the former Augustinian friar of New Ross, the troubled monk, Michael Murphy. Entering Maynooth in 1819 or 1820, he was ordained by Archbishop Murray in March 1824 and entered the Augustinians in New Ross.[35] There he had fallen out with his confreres, claiming that he had been persecuted by them. He converted to the Established Church in 1827 and in a setting of huge crowds and great expectations, he was received by the clergy of Christ Church Cathedral at their 10.30 service on Sunday 26th March: his aged father, three brothers and two sisters joined him to take Communion there on the occasion.[36] He had been converted by Rev. Caesar Otway, a Protestant next-door neighbour of the Whitefriar Street Carmelites and a noted evangelical, living at 55

32. T. Wall, loc.cit., p. 292; McGrath, *Pastoral ministry*, p. 147; Begadon, 'Catholic religious publishing, 1800-1891', p. 373.
33. *Catholic Directory*, 1836, p. 53.
34. *The Public Ledger and Daily Advertiser*, 21st March 1827; *DWR*, 21st Apr 1827; *SNL*, 6th July 1827.
35. *DEP*, 10th May 1827.
36. *SNL*, 27th March; *DMR*, 3rd Apr; *DWR*, 7th Apr; *DMR*, 13th June 1827.

Aungier St, where Murphy stayed during these days of high drama.[37] A year later, on 17th May 1828, he formally recanted. On Sunday 15th June with even greater solemnity, in a ceremony where Spratt was directly involved, he was received back into the Catholic Church in John's Lane. His signed recantation was read out by Dr William Yore and a suitable sermon was preached by Fr Patrick Dowling.[38] Leading figures of the Dublin Catholic clergy took part in the formal ceremony – priests whom Fr Spratt was meeting for perhaps the first time and with whom he would work closely together for decades to come. It was Fr Spratt who led Michael Murphy into the sanctuary, to read out his public recantation.[39] This decade of new sectarian rivalry featured notoriously-charged public platform debates between Protestant and Catholic clerical militants, yet Spratt was not to be found amongst them, neither in polemical pamphleteering nor on public debating platforms. No evidence to-date suggests that he himself participated in public debates of this kind in the 1820s.

Nevertheless, he could hardly avoid becoming caught up in the political and religious developments unfolding at the time. The years 1823 and 1824 constituted a climax of expectation and event. In February 1823, in the County Dublin by-election, a pro-Catholic emancipation candidate, Henry White, defeated the Protestant establishment candidate, Sir Compton Domville. On 12th May 1823 Daniel O'Connell presided at a meeting in Dempsey's Tavern, in Dublin's Sackville Street that founded the Catholic Association.[40] While its first year gave little hint of a commanding future, the adoption, in February 1824, of the penny-a-month Catholic rent, and the wholesale recruitment of the Catholic priesthood in supporting its collection, transformed the Association *'into a colossus of democratic power unprecedented*

---

37.  *DEM*, 26th, 30th March 1827.

38.  *DMR*, 14th June; *DWR* 14th, 21th, June 1828.

39.  GMA, *Scrapbook D*, Box 73, item 10, cited in O'Dwyer, p. 246, n. 113, undated and untitled newspaper cutting.

40.  *DEP*, 13th May 1823. This meeting was consequent upon an 'Aggregate Meeting of the Catholics of Ireland', chaired by Lord Killeen, in Townsend Street Chapel on 10th May 1823. J. A. Reynolds, *The Catholic Emancipation Crisis in Ireland, 1823-1829*, New Haven 1954, p. 14, misdates the foundation meeting of the Catholic Association to 26th April 1823, citing the *Dublin Evening Post* of that date. See also, P. M. Geoghegan, *King Dan, The Rise of Daniel O'Connell, 1775-1829*, Dublin 2008, p. 196.

**Fig 8.**     *Monument of Dr Daniel Murray, Catholic Archbishop of Dublin, in St Mary's Pro-Cathedral, Dublin.*

*in the annals of political organisations in Britain or Ireland'.*[41] Despite his implied claim, much later in life, to have been with O'Connell in the Catholic Association from the start, John Spratt and four of his confreres actually joined the Association on 3rd November 1824, eighteen months after its foundation.[42] In the meantime, the impressive Daniel Murray, in May 1823 had succeeded the aged John Troy as Catholic Archbishop of Dublin. Such developments fostered a new confidence in Ireland's Catholic leadership, clerical and lay. With this came a new sense of impatience, frustration and urgency for deliverance.

It is sometimes observed that the most galling of disabilities are those that remain after the worst is over.[43] Many overt prohibitions

41. Reynolds, p. 13.
42. *DEP*, 4th Nov 1824. An enrolment card showing Spratt's membership for the year 1826 is extant in the Carmelite Archives, GMA, Box 78, *Scrapbook 'G'*, p. 67: the card is dated 16th January 1826. For John's implied claim, see Chapter Twenty-one. The four confreres were named as Coleman. Kinsella, McCarthy and Fitzpatrick.
43. On this point, see, for example, T. Bartlett, 'The penal laws against Irish Catholics: were they too good for them?', in O. P. Rafferty, ed., *Irish Catholic Identities*, Manchester 2013, pp. 154-170.

and oppressive restrictions had been removed or allowed to atrophy over the period 1740 to 1820. Despite this, some major and minor ones remained in place as reminders to Catholics of their secondary status. Notable among these were the ban on Catholics becoming members of Parliament and their exclusion from the great majority of public offices.[44] In addition, in law there were prohibitions on the reading of Catholic (and Dissenter) rites at funerals in Church of Ireland parish churchyards and graveyards. Since in Dublin City, and elsewhere, the Catholics had no cemeteries of their own, this might have been a problem: but, until the 1820s, a blind eye had been turned on the recitation of Catholic prayers at their funeral services. With the changing climate arising from the rise of Protestant evangelicalism and Catholic revival in general, and with the arrival of William Magee as an evangelical Protestant Archbishop of Dublin in 1822 in particular, the issue became a significant one in practice. Archbishops Magee and Murray soon became embroiled in a serious dispute precipitated by a row over funeral rites at the burial of a young Catholic man, Arthur D'Arcy, in 1823. This led to further politicisation of the Catholic bishops and clergy.[45] With the dispute at its height, Murray summoned a meeting of all the clergy of his diocese, regular as well as parochial, in April 1824, to put the Catholic side of the issue, namely, that it had been 'the invariable practice' at Catholic burials in Church of Ireland parish graveyards that one of the Catholic clergy recited, at the grave, a form of prayer for the soul of the departed and that the other clergy and laity present joined in responses to this, everyone all the while standing with heads uncovered. This gathering insisted that nothing different or untoward had transpired at Arthur D'Arcy's funeral. Among those present at this diocesan meeting was John Spratt. Although he is not recorded as speaking, the fact that he appended his signature to the resulting joint statement from this meeting suggests that it was an initiating event for the young Carmelite Prior, a key moment in his own politicisation. It was a few months later that he joined the Catholic

---

44. Reynolds, p. 65. Reynolds cites 257 positions in the administration of justice in Ireland from which they were barred in law. Of 1,314 lower offices not barred, they held only 39 in 1828 and 653 civic offices of rank or honour were denied to them. Of 3,033 minor such offices from which they were not barred, they held only 134.

45. For the ensuing burials dispute, see *Appendix 4: The Burials Question in the 1820s and after*.

Association and thereby began a lifelong devotion to O'Connell and his various causes in the quest for political equality and religious liberty.

Although James Reynolds' observation that Fr L'Estrange was the only Carmelite to become involved in Daniel O'Connell's Catholic Association is not quite accurate, since John Spratt was a member from November 1824, it is true to say that Spratt does not appear to have been a very active member. Farrington claims that Spratt was

> ever at the side of the great Liberator in his work of obtaining Catholic Emancipation…In the cause of Catholic Freedom he laboured night and day, whenever and wherever his services were wanted. O'Connell praised his services very much, and made a speech on the young Carmelite when he joined him.[46]

This may well be, but the description is not borne out by extant sources.[47] Spratt was far from unique in this: most Catholic clergy while active in the country in supporting O'Connell, especially in facilitating collection of the Catholic Rent, did not very often appear at the meetings of the Association in Dublin.[48] Nevertheless, in the wake of the Catholic Emancipation campaign, John would become a politically active priest in many matters of public concern and debate and also in voting in parliamentary elections for forty years from the 1820s.[49] In the middle of the 1820s, however, even as he joined the Catholic Association, it may be suggested that he had other demanding engagements and preoccupations, personal, conventual and philanthropic.

---

46  Farrington, p. 129.

47.  His name is not mentioned once in the entire corpus of Catholic Association manuscript records in the Dublin Diocesan Archives, nor in any of the letters in the several volumes of the published O'Connell correspondence, nor in his own varied collection of newspaper cuttings. Furthermore, ten years later, in August 1836, when Spratt was admitted to the National or General Association, O'Connell's speech welcoming him, never mentioned anything of Spratt's having worked for the Catholic Association, whereas, in that same speech, O'Connell praised the work of the Discalced Carmelite, Fr L'Estrange, then three years deceased, for his work for that body: see *DMR*, 8th Aug 1836.

48.  Reynolds, p. 31. Reynolds does not name the Carmelite but there is no doubt, from various other sources, that it was Fr L'Estrange of Clarendon Street. Reynolds says of this 'lone Carmelite', that he 'remained for six years virtually the only priest who participated regularly in the Dublin meetings'.

49.  For his voting activities, see Chapters Seven, Nine and Twenty-one.

**Fig 9.**    *Fr John Spratt's Catholic Association membership card.*

*Economic Anxieties*

While the 1820s saw rising hopes and expectations for the Catholic cause, they also saw growing difficulties for the Irish and the Dublin economies. There had been severe difficulties through crop failures and fever epidemics in 1817 and 1822. Then, in 1826, there came a financial and economic crisis, combined with another serious fever epidemic. The economic collapse, especially in the textile industries, had a devastating effect and particularly so on the weavers of Dublin's Liberties, but it was *'felt brutally by all types of worker in the affected neighbourhoods'.*[50] For the city manufacturing interest, technological change and industrial competition from Great Britain caused severe hardship across a range of trades from textiles to tanning. This was exacerbated by the removal of the final protective tariffs between Great Britain and Ireland as of 1824 and by the deflationary effects of the amalgamation of the British and Irish currencies in 1826.

---

50.  D. O'Toole, 'The employment crisis of 1826', in D. Dickson, ed., *The Gorgeous Mask: Dublin 1700-1850*, Dublin 1987, pp. 157-171; T. O'Neill, 'A Bad Year for the Liberties', in E. Gillespie, ed., *The Liberties of Dublin*, Dublin 1972, pp. 76-83.

As a result, unilaterally-imposed wage reductions became common, combined with the increasing use of apprentices as a form of cheap labour. In addition, in certain trades, notably in textile and leather, the introduction of machinery and of new methods of production, undermined the economic and psychological position of the artisans. From 1823, in many cases they responded with strikes and acts of intimidation and violence, against masters and fellow-workers alike. By the spring of 1824 the situation in Dublin had become grave in this regard in the range of workshops and dwelling houses stretching from Cork Street, through the Coombe, to Golden Lane and Bridge Street, in the heart of which dwelt the Carmelites of French and Whitefriar Streets. In the middle of this unrest came two notorious incidents in the Cork Street area, where the Spratts had their family home and business. In the second of these a master-clothier, James Butterworth, was seriously assaulted.[51] In the ensuing arrest and trials of six men, Daniel O'Connell was the defence counsel and John Spratt and his brother Michael testified as character witnesses for one of the accused. Four of the accused were sentenced to death but the Spratts' testimonials may have helped to this extent: the death sentences were commuted to transportation for life.[52] They were taken away and lodged on the hulk while awaiting the outcome of an abortive appeal. One of the convicted was killed in an attempt to escape from the hulk.[53] This case brought the young Fr Spratt into immediate contact with the harsher aspects of Dublin life in the 1820s. From his own family's experience around this time, however, he will have appreciated the dire effects of economic dislocation and decline.

*Family Fortunes and Misfortunes*
Among the trades that suffered severely in this economic downturn was that of tanning and its related branches of skin curing, parchment and glue-making. Undoubtedly, the success of these in Dublin during the late eighteenth and earlier nineteenth centuries enabled the Spratt family

51. *FJ*, 2nd Feb, 13th May 1825. Butterworth was listed as a clothier of 33 Chamber Street in *Wilson's Directory for 1825*, p. 52, and for 1827, p. 50, but no longer listed from 1830 onward.
52. *FJ*, 30th Aug 1825.
53. National Archives, Kew, H.O. *Series 100*, 216, f. 200: Magistrates of the Head Office of Police to Henry Goulburn, 27th Jan 1826.

to fund the expense of sending John and his younger brother, James, into training for the priesthood, the one in Spain, the other in Italy. Doubtless, his own prosperity, garnered in this trade, enabled James senior to take a lease of a cottage and fifteen acres in Carpenterstown, Castleknock, close by the Phoenix Park, in 1814.[54] Nevertheless, the trade was among the first to show signs of deterioration in conditions: in 1818 the journeymen tanners were forced to accept a wage reduction.[55] By the mid-1820s John's father and fellow-employers were facing the pressure of technical change. In February 1825 James Spratt was among 53 employer tanners who called on the Corporation of Glovers and Skinners, otherwise known as the Guild of the Blessed Virgin Mary, to convene a meeting of its members to consider the best means of relieving these employers from *'the great losses we sustain by the flawing and gashing of sheep, lambs' and other skins'*. The Guild Master, David Scott, responded positively by calling that meeting but it is not at all clear as to the outcome.[56] One of James Spratt's neighbours, the tanner Christopher Weldon, had gone bankrupt at this time and his extensive business at 103 Cork Street was auctioned off in September 1826.[57] By this stage James Spratt was probably no longer all that active in the family business and it is likely that, by then, his eldest son Michael would have taken over. On 4th December 1828 James died at the age of seventy. It says something of his standing in business and the community that his passing was noticed in several newspapers, including the front page of the *Freeman's Journal*.[58] The reports noted that his death *'is now deeply regretted not only by his relatives and friends but by the numbers to whom he had given support by employing them in his establishment'*. For all that prominence, however, it is strange that there is no record of his funeral nor of the place of his burial. Although the Catholic Association was by that date well on the way to finding its own solution to the problem of Catholic burials in Protestant churchyards, by seeking

54. Registry of Deeds, *Transcription Book*, Year 1830, vol. 857, No. 184, A memorial of an indented deed of assignment between Michael Spratt and William Forestal, registered 26th March 1830.

55. Parliamentary Papers, *Third Report of the Commissioners for inquiring into the Condition of the Poorer Classes in Ireland*, HC 1836, (43), xxx, Appendix C, Part II: evidence of two operative tanners.

56. *FJ*, 22nd Feb 1825. The records of this guild are not extant.

57. *FJ*, 16th Sept 1826.

58. *FJ*, Sat 6 Dec 1828; *SNL*, *The Pilot*, 8th Dec 1828.

to procure their own cemeteries, the first fruits of that search, the cemetery at Goldenbridge, was not realised until 15th October 1829, with Glasnevin's Prospect Cemetery being opened by them some time later, on 22nd February 1832.

By the time of James' death, his son John had already secured one of his own major achievements in the construction of the new Carmelite Church in Whitefriar Street. It may be that James senior was laid to rest there and that it was Fr John who conducted the funeral service but there is no extant detail on either point. As for James junior, it is not likely that he could have attended his father's funeral as he had been admitted to the Augustinian Order by 1827 and would then have been in Rome completing his novitiate year, followed by further years of study. He was professed there in 1828 and then began his philosophy studies at Fermo in 1829.[59] Michael, now head of the household in Cork Street, remained there for a year or so with his widowed mother, Esther. He continued the business as a tanner and enjoyed the distinction of being one of the first Catholics to be admitted to the freedom of the Corporation of Tanners. This was on Tuesday 4th August 1829, just four months after the enactment of the Catholic Relief Act.[60]

*A New Foundation*

The outstanding major achievement for John, as priest and prior in the 1820s, was the foundation of the Church of Our Lady of Mount Carmel in Whitefriar Street. The genesis of the idea is obscure but almost certainly lay in the belief of Provincial Coleman, Prior Kinsella and John himself, in or about the year 1822, that current pressures and possible future growth required a move from French Street. Spratt and Coleman wrote to their Archbishop in March 1824 to say that their hope for a novitiate in Dublin could only be realised by a new foundation.[61] They now began that quest by employing the services of the builder, Wall, in order to draft preliminary plans and the site was identified – a narrow stretch of land, between Whitefriar Lane and York Row, now

---

59. Information provided by Fr David Kelly, OSA, Archivist of the Augustinians, Dublin, 5th Aug 2013.
60. *FJ*, 8th Aug 1829.
61. DDA, *Murray Papers*, 30/8/81-82, Coleman and Spratt to Murray, 24th March 1824, and Murray's reply, 26th March 1824.

**Fig 10.**   *Exterior view of the original church at Whitefriar Street.*

**Fig 11.**   *Interior view of the original church at Whitefriar Street.*

Whitefriar Place.[62] It was singularly fortunate that this plot became available because it was, in fact, part of the site of the historic original foundation which the Carmelites had established in Dublin circa 1280.[63] The land in question was owned by Patrick Campbell, Master of St Patrick's Hospital. On 5th October 1825, John Spratt and William Kinsella secured this site by lease of one thousand years, on payment of a sum of £800 sterling,[64] with an option to purchase outright at the end of seven years, on payment of £1,000. For this, Spratt and Kinsella secured for the Carmelites a site measuring 38 feet in breadth, fronting on to Whitefriar Street, 36 feet in breadth backing on to Aungier Street, with its north side measuring 264 feet and its south 252 feet. The site came with a dwelling house, No 57, fronting on to Aungier Street and which until recently had been in the possession of a Miss Jane Westby.[65] The annual rent payable was £80.

On securing this plot, John engaged the services of a leading, Dublin-based architect, George Papworth. Having trained in London, Papworth was in mid-career at this time. He had already executed or secured commissions for the cast-iron bridges of Oak Park, Carlow and King's Bridge, Dublin, and, later on, would be responsible for the reconstruction of 51 St Stephen's Green for the Museum of Irish Industry.[66] If the selection of architect was by reputation and word of mouth, Spratt may have chosen Papworth due to the fact that the latter was just then completing his own work on the vestibule and organ gallery of St Mary's Pro-Cathedral, Marlborough Street.[67] In this new commission he was constrained and considerably challenged since what Fr Spratt had acquired was *a narrow strip of ground*. Yet, a

62. J. Collins, *Life in Old Dublin*, Dublin 1913, p. 135.

63. S. A. Ossory Fitzpatrick, *Dublin: A Historical and Topographical Account of the City*, Cork 1977 ed., p. 285.

64. Registry of Deeds, Dublin, *Transcript Book*, year 1825, vol. 183, No. 807: Campbell to John Spratt and Another, registered 7th October 1825.

65. Mrs Westby and her two daughters were prominent in Dublin social life up to about the year 1820. They were generous donors to various charities, both in life and in death. The daughter Jane died circa 1825 and the house contents were sold then. See *FJ*, 16th March 1818, 19th May 1819, 29th Apr 1825, 8th Oct 1825, 13th, 21st June 1837, 14th May, 6th June 1840.

66. R. Loeber, H. Campbell, L. Hurley, J. Montague & E. Rowley, eds., *Art and Architecture of Ireland*, 5 vols, Dublin 2014, Vol IV, *Architecture*, 1600-2000, p. 532.

67. C. Casey, *Dublin, The City within the Grand and the Royal Canals*, New Haven and London 2005, pp. 129-130.

visitor to Dublin, Starrat, writing in 1832, described the *'new extensive Roman Catholic Church, one side of which extends nearly along the entire South side of York Row. It is a plain building and will require a considerable sum to render it complete, according to the original design'*.[68]  In those times of denominational tensions and rivalries it was a newcomer among its confessional neighbours.   Next door and north of it, in Whitefriar Street, was the large chapel accommodating 1,200 worshippers which was built for the Wesleyan Methodists in 1756, but now occupied by the Primitive Methodist Connexion.   There also was the Methodist Female Orphan School, founded in 1804.[69]  Before too long the Methodists would abandon their chapel, leaving it to accommodate the expansion of the Carmelite presence in the area.[70]  Around the corner in Aungier Street was the largest and most fashionable Anglican Church in Dublin, that of St Peter's, and just across the road was the York Street Chapel of the Independents or Congregationalists, built in 1808.  Two corners away, in Bishop's Street, was the Church of the Moravians, or the 'United Brethren', who came to Dublin in 1746.  Both the Moravians and the Methodists had houses for widows close by the Carmelites in Whitefriar Street.[71]

One may hazard a guess that John and his confreres regretted that the new Church was so narrow in width.  W J Battersby in his *Catholic Penny Magazine* of 1834 and in his first *Catholic Directory* of 1836 mentioned this, remarking that *'it is regretted that want of room prevented it from being more than thirty two feet in breadth'*.[72]  It was scarcely a remark that they would have made unless Spratt had mentioned it himself.  Nevertheless, although small in extent, the church was to have vaults, a practical step when the burials issue had still not been resolved by the provision of cemeteries for Catholics in Dublin, and a possible fashionable attraction for prosperous potential donors.  Surviving documentation shows that

68.   M. Starrat, *History of Ancient and Modern Dublin; or, Visitors' Guide to the Metropolis of Ireland*, Dublin 1832, pp. 179-180.

69.   *The Dublin Almanac and General Register of Ireland*, 1842, p. 310.

70.   See Chapter Fourteen.

71.   J. J. McGregor, *The New Picture of Dublin*, Dublin 1828, pp. 258, 332-333; Starrat, p. 180.

72.   *The Catholic Penny Magazine*, vol.1, no. 7, 29th March 1834; 'W. J. B', *A Complete Catholic Registry, Directory and Almanack for 1836*, Dublin 1836, p. 82.  See also T. Wall, 'Catholic Periodicals of the Past: 1: The Catholic Penny Magazine, 1834-35', in *Irish Ecclesiastical Record*, vol. 101, Jan-June 1964, pp. 234-244.

Spratt made provision for an initial three vaults during the construction stage: one came to be occupied by a supporter, Mrs Berry;[73] the second by a Miss Doherty, of whom more anon, and the third by John's own mother who was interred there after her funeral rites in 1836.[74]

The front entrance, reached by a flight of steps, was on the west end, facing on to Whitefriar Street, while the high altar and sanctuary were to the east, backing on to Aungier Street. Papworth rendered the exterior in roman cement and provided a simple, lofty hall, with *'an elegant Regency exterior'* of sixteen round-headed windows, looking on to York Row. Glazed in plain, leaded glass, these were set five feet apart, crowned with recessed panels which carried the inscription *Gloriosae Matri et decori Carmeli dedicata*.[75] From within, these windows lit up a series of statues set in niches along the north wall, while a Greek ionic canopy was constructed over the high altar. Pride of place in this new church, must surely have been given to the statue of Our Lady of Dublin.

## Our Lady of Dublin

In the course of his life, John Spratt displayed a keen interest in the history and antiquities of his native city. He became a considerable collector of books and was akin to that later Carmelite Dubliner, Dillon Cosgrave, in thoroughly knowing his Dublin and in frequenting its book and antique shops. Sometime between 1822 and 1824 that curiosity led him to the discovery and recovery of an ancient statue in wood, of the Virgin Mary, known as Our Lady of Dublin. The eighteenth century clergyman and antiquarian, Mervyn Archdall, claimed to have seen this statue on the altar of the Catholic chapel-of-ease in St Mary's Lane where it seems it was displayed in 1749.[76] According to Roger Stalley, it is like some work of the German sculptor, Michael Erhart, and that

---

73. Probably the late wife of his supporter, the seed merchant William Berry of nearby Kevin Street, and possibly related to the young Carmelite of Moate, Patrick Berry.

74. GMA, *Whitefriar Street Church Building Account Book*, May 1829: "Crowe, for two vaults....£3-0-0; to John Crowe for Mrs Berry's vault....£1-10-0". For Miss Doherty, see Chapter Five.

75. *The Catholic Penny Magazine*, vol. 1, No. 7, 29th March 1834.

76. M. Archdall, *Monasticon Hibernicum*, Dublin 1786, p. 147. Spratt's annotated copy is in Gort Muire Archives.

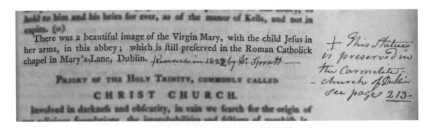

**Fig 12.**    *Spratt's annotation in Archdall's* Monasticon Hibernicum *states the statue was 'Removed in 1822/3 by Dr Spratt. This statue is preserved in the Carmelite Church of Dublin. See page 213.'*

**Fig 13.**    *The statue of Our Lady of Dublin in Whitefriar Street Church.*

it dated from circa 1500 to 1520.[77] Legend has it that it originated in the pre-Reformation Cistercian Abbey of St Mary, Dublin, and that here it bore a silver crown, allegedly used in the coronation of the Yorkist Pretender, Lambert Simnel, in Christ Church Cathedral on 24th May 1487. The antiquarian, George Petrie, who was sceptical of this connection, claimed that this *'double-arched crown'* was a feature unique to the coinage of Henry VII (1485-1509). In 1833, writing in *The Dublin Penny Journal*, he claimed that the statue was *'originally the distinguished ornament of St Mary's Abbey'*. With the suppression of the Cistercian Abbey of St Mary, in 1539, legend has it that the statue was spirited away, hollowed out from the back to be used as a drinking trough for pigs in a nearby yard. Spratt himself claimed that in 1588 the image was *'publicly burned by the common hangman'*.[78] Credible or not as these accounts may be, the statue somehow made its eighteenth-century appearance in the chapel of St Michan, which was a Mass-house erected by Dr Cornelius Nary over 1702-4, on the corner of Bull Lane and Mary's Lane.[79] It was Dr Nary who recovered the statue and set it up in this Mass-house.[80] Here it remained until a new chapel, commenced in 1811 under Fr Christopher Wall, was completed in 1817. The old Mass-house then became a school and, as Myles Ronan observed, *'for some unaccountable reason the statue was not removed from Mary's Lane Chapel to the new church'*. As he records, it somehow made its way to an antique shop and it was from here that Fr Spratt purchased it around 1822-1823.[81] Something similar is suggested in a marginal note in Spratt's own copy of Archdall's *Monasticon*.

### The Prior and the Pen
It is hardly without some relevance that, at this very time, John Spratt's devotion to Our Lady was expressed in his first-ever publication, *A Novena, or nine days' devotion to the ever glorious and blessed Virgin Mary of*

---

77. R. Stalley, *The Cistercian Monasteries of Ireland*, London & New Haven 1987, p. 223. I am grateful to Professor Stalley for this and for his observations on the provenance and style of the statue.
78. A margin note to this effect, signed 'J. Spratt', is entered on p. 577 of Spratt's copy of Archdall's work.
79. M. Ronan, *An Apostle of Catholic Dublin: Father Henry Young*, Dublin 1944, p. 27.
80. M. Ronan, *The Parish of St Michan*, Dublin 1948, unpaginated but 32 pp.; P. Fagan, *Dublin's Turbulent Priest: Cornelius Nary, 1658-1738*, Dublin 1991, pp. 199-201.
81. Ibid.; see also Battersby, *Catholic Directory*, 1836, p. 70.

*Mount Carmel*.[82]   In introducing this book of prayers for the use of the members of the Sodality of the Holy Scapular, Spratt implied that this novena constituted the revival of a practice which *'antecedent to the Reformation, was well-known to the Catholics of England and Ireland'* and which was still practised *'with great solemnity in all the Carmelite Churches on the Continent'*.  It may also have been the very first devotional publication for the laity produced by the Irish Carmelites since the Reformation. How widely it circulated is not known but he certainly dispatched 100 copies to Fr Michael Hughes of the Kildare Priory of the Carmelites. The latter managed to sell 50 of them and then wondered what he was to do with the remainder, *'as I see no great sign of disposing of them'*.[83] Spratt produced a second edition of it about four years later, printed by John Coyne of Cooke Street.  Slightly longer than its original, with some new prayers, it also had these interleaved with a distinct formula of meditation for each of the nine days.  Even as this appeared in print, his next publication, also aimed at members of the Scapular Sodality, was imminent.  This was his *Sincere Christian's Manual of Devotion* which he announced for publication in September 1828.[84]  These and his later writings may not have been particularly brilliant or original, but they did represent significant contributions to a home-produced devotional literature that had been conspicuously deficient in its supply until then. While Begadon does not mention Spratt's writings, the friar had the distinction of being among what Begadon states as *'only a few Irish*

---

82.  J. Spratt, *A novena, or nine days' devotion to the ever glorious and blessed Virgin Mary of Mount Carmel, compiled from* [sic] *the use of those pious individuals who wear the holy scapular*, 30 pp. Dublin, Richard Coyne, Capel Street, 1824.  There are two extant copies in the Royal Irish Academy's Haliday Pamphlet Collection.  The first is the dated edition of 1824; the second, published by John Coyne of Cooke Street, is an undated edition, 35 pp.: but it is housed in the series of pamphlets for the year 1828, as arranged by Haliday, and it mentions Whitefriar Street as the place where it may be obtained.  It should be noted that O'Dwyer, *Dissertation*, p. 82, stated that Spratt's first-ever publication was *A Sermon on the Love of God and Our Neighbour*, which he dates to 1825, citing Farrington, p. 184: however, the only extant copy of this, published by Courtney of Dublin, dates from 1830.

83.  GMA, Box 56, *Scrapbook A*, Hughes to Spratt, month not given, year 1824.

84.  J. Spratt, *The Sincere Christian's Manual of Devotion or Selection of Prayers Arranged Principally for the Use of the Members of the Sodality of the Holy Scapular*, 1st ed [?], Dublin 1828.  There is at least one subsequent edition of this, Dublin 1837, published by John Coyne, a copy of which is extant in the Gort Muire Archives and Library.

*devotional authors who were published in this period'.*[85] To that extent Spratt
made his contribution to *'the increase in the internal cohesion of the Catholic
community in Dublin'.*[86]

Spratt's serendipity in discovering the statue, circa 1823, and which
he had restored by 1824, he may have considered miraculous: this was,
according to himself, *'at the same time in which so many miracles were performed
on account of the prayers of Prince Hohenloe, as it may be believed'.*[87] Maybe then,
perhaps later, John had ordered an inscription in leather, as follows:

> Imago Beatissimae Virginis translata fuit ad Capellam Ejusdem
> nominis Mari[a]e postmodum cura Rev[eren]di Johannis Sprat
> [sic], Prior Carlimitarum [sic]. Restaurata fuit anno 1824 in
> eodem tempore in quo patrata sunt miracula quam plurima
> propter orationes Principis Hohenloe ut pie creditur. Imago
> h[a]ec est eadem qu[a]e inventa fuit in monasterio celeberrimo
> Div[a]e Mari[a]e. Dublin +.

> The image of the Most Blessed Virgin was afterwards brought
> in the care of the Reverend John Sprat [sic], the Prior of the
> Carlimites [sic], to the chapel of the name of the same Mary.
> It was restored in the year 1824, at the same time in which so
> many miracles were performed on account of the prayers of
> Prince Hohenloe, as is piously believed. This image is the same
> that was found in the most celebrated monastery of Holy Mary.
> Dublin +.[88]

This artefact, today in the Carmelite Archives in Gort Muire,[89] may have
been suspended around the neck of the statue, perhaps as an identifying
label, either before the move from French Street to Whitefriar Street in
the later 1820s or perhaps during reconstruction work on the church in
Whitefriar Street in the 1840s. The inscription may have been dictated
by Spratt to a workman: it was hardly incised directly by himself on to
the leather as it misspells his name and that of the word 'Carmelites'.
As for the statue itself, originally painted in several colours, at some

---

85. C. Begadon, 'Catholic Devotional Literature in Dublin, 1800-1830', p. 336, and
  'Catholic Religious Publishing, 1800-1891', p. 372.
86. Ibid, p. 333.
87. GMA, Box 73.
88. Idem. I am grateful to Dr Patrick Mullins, O. Carm., for this transcription and
  translation.
89. An image of this artefact can be seen on page 346.

point it was whitewashed, perhaps before Spratt acquired it, but, during a later attempt at restoration, in 1914, by removing the whitewash, the original colours were erased as well.[90]

### 'This Beautiful and Extremely Graceful Edifice'

The statue was truly an iconic symbol with which to grace the new church building. The foundation stone of this was laid on 25th October 1825 by Archbishop Daniel Murray. John and his Carmelite confreres celebrated the occasion in style. Paying sixteen shillings and eight pence for the cutting and delivery of that foundation stone, they laid out £2-6-10 for wine and cakes which were enjoyed immediately after the stone was put in place, and a hefty £7-7-10 for meat, wine and spirits for dinner that evening. Little was spared to make for a memorable day: even a military band was employed to entertain the guests on the occasion.[91]

However, in the course of its construction there was some grief. A year into the operation, the elegant south wall was defaced by individuals whom Prior John described as *'some sacreligious* [sic] *miscreants'*. He put up a reward of £10 for information leading to the apprehension of the culprits, but to what avail is not clear.[92] Nevertheless, another joyous day was celebrated on 11th November 1827 when the Archbishop returned to consecrate the new building. It was a historic moment for the Irish Carmelites as they reclaimed the site that had been theirs for over two hundred years from the late thirteenth century. The church was now usable, but still required completion. Within a year Prior John had installed an organ and was seeking the services of an organist.[93] Who that first organist may have been does not appear, but, by the mid-1830s one J Duggan had been installed and a layman, John Prenter, had been employed as the clerk of the church, a position he held well until 1851 at least.[94]

90. A. Corbett, D. Pochin Mould & C. Dixon, *Whitefriars Street Church*, Carmelite Publications, 88 pp., Dublin 1964, p. 41.
91. GMA, B 12 S 5, *An Account of Money Received for the purpose of purchasing a House and Concerns and Building thereon a Church for the Friars of the Carmelite Order in Dublin, 1825-1855.*
92. *DEP*, 21st Dec 1826.
93. *FJ*, 17th Nov 1828.
94. Battersby, *Catholic Directory*, 1837, p. 15; *FJ*, 25th March 1851.

When the church came into use, it is by no means clear whether the community followed immediately into the premises on Aungier Street. It is possible that they resided in the dilapidated house of Miss Westby from the outset of the initial completion of the church: so much might be gathered from a comment by Richard Colgan in a report to Prior General Cataldi in January 1840, when he complained that *'the convent is an old house in a somewhat ruinous state and too small to hold more than five religious'.*[95] Spratt paid for having repairs carried out on the roof of this dwelling in 1828, but, for all that, it is probable that they remained on in French Street for some time after this, perhaps until the major building works which commenced in the 1840s; it may be, therefore, that the church clerk, Prenter, occupied the former Westby dwelling. It appears certain that the friars had not got a new, dedicated convent or friary until 1841.[96] However, on 9th July of 1840, the foundation stone of the Carmelite Convent in Aungier Street was laid by Archbishop Murray, using the same silver trowel as had done service for the foundation stone of the church itself back in October 1825.[97]

The building of the new church at Whitefriar Street was a major undertaking that does not appear to have fazed John Spratt. He and his confreres financed it by a combination of loans and donations, large and small. From the outset, the most significant loan came from Patrick

---

95. O'Dwyer, *Irish Carmelites*, p. 203.
96. This appears to be borne out by the evidence of the Dublin street directories. That of Pettigrew and Oulton for the year 1841 records eight Carmelites, including John Spratt, as residing at No. 7 French Street, while that of 1842 records seven Carmelites residing there. At the same time, there are no names of Carmelites listed as living in Aungier Street or Whitefriar Street. Interestingly, in the *Directory* for 1843 there are no Carmelites listed as resident in French Street, and, No. 7 is then occupied by Richard Maher & Son, Carpenters & Builders. See *The Dublin Almanac and General Register for 1841*, p. 654, and 1842, p. 652. The Carmelites resident in French Street in 1841 were Richard Corrigan, William Withers, John Spratt, Michael Tobin, Andrew Day, Edward O'Rourke, William Kinsella and Joseph Dowling; in 1842 they were the same names, minus Joseph Dowling. This matter is not picked up in works of architectural history dealing with the Whitefriar Street-Aungier Street foundation: A. Grehan, *Aungier Street: revitalising an historic neighbourhood (Dublin City Council)*, Dublin 2013, pp. 20-21; C. Dixon, 'An Appreciation of the Present Buildings at Whitefriars Street', in A. Corbet, D. Pochin Mould & C. Dixon, pp. 55-57; Casey, p. 471. Dixon states that the building of an extension commenced in 1842, while Casey, op.cit., states that the extension was undertaken in 1844.
97. *The Catholic Luminary and Ecclesiastical Repertory*, No. 4, 1st Aug 1840, p. 93.

Campbell who had leased them the site in the first instance. In October
1825 he lent the Carmelites £1,000 at eight per cent annual interest. In
that same month, the friars of French Street themselves put up over
£200 while at the same time a Ms McDonnell lent them an initial £298.
Six months later, and now married as Mrs Rowan, she lent them a further
£80. A good friend of the Carmelites, Mrs Segrave of Harcourt Street,
gave them £100 in December 1825, and other borrowings, presumably
short-term, included some £50 from the St Peter's Orphan Society, in
July 1826, and £50 from Spratt's publisher, Coyne, in that same year.
The actual day of the consecration enabled Spratt to raise £200 and his
own family were not found wanting, in a more modest way. His brother,
Michael gave over £5 in April 1826, while their father, James, gave over
£2 that February, on top of a previous £2 in 1824, and some £5 came
in 1829, following his death. Indeed, many years later, Fr John stated
that his father 'gave large sums of money to the Order'.[98] Even the children
attending John's Free School brought in a modest sum in 1824 and he
himself was raising funds by way of raffles. One sign of desperation
to raise finance may have been manifest when in June 1826 he spent
£5 on a lottery ticket, 'to try our fortune', but with what outcome is not
evident.[99] It must have galled him as it did many Catholic and other
non-Anglican Christians, to have had to pay out over £2 on parish cess
and over £2 on minister's money at the same time. However, by May of
1829 his auditors, Provincial Coleman and the latter's secretary, Richard
Colgan, approved the accounts which showed an expenditure of over
£4,555.[100] Colgan may have co-authorised the accounts but, long after
the event, he was not very complimentary: in a report of 1840 which
he sent to Prior General Cataldi, Colgan recounted how Prior John had
been anxious to 'make a name for himself' by building this church, but that,
when he ceased to be Prior, in 1829, he left a church with walls and
roof, but without a finished ceiling. Furthermore, Colgan complained
that John had also left it with debts, the repayments of which had still
not been completed when Colgan wrote to Rome. He added that at
the front of the building Fr Spratt had placed an inscription 'to show

---

98. In October 1861, in testimony before the municipal revision court in Dublin, see
    Chapter Twenty-one, p. 13, citing *FJ, SNL,* 29th Oct 1861: just how large was
    never stated.
99. GMA, *Whitefriar Street Building Account Book.*
100. Ibid.

*future generations that he had built the church'*.[101]  Colgan's letter of 1840 invites caution: he told Prior General Cataldi that John had spent all the money collected by the Provincial and his confreres, *'the Lord knows how'*.  O'Dwyer rightly challenged this assertion, pointing out that the very detailed accounts of the monies collected for and spent on the new church were recorded carefully by Spratt and are still extant.  As to leaving the Church unfinished, especially with regard to the ceiling, Battersby in 1834 offered a decidedly contrary opinion:

> The interior presents a beautiful architectural view….The ceiling is coved and divided into rectangular compartments. The interior, just completed, will be particularly neat.[102]

In the early summer of 1829, when John had ceased to be Prior, he could look back on a very considerable achievement.  With that accomplishment there came recognition, in the form of the conferral of the title, Magister de Justicia, granted by the Pope, Pius VIII, on 28th August and conveyed by the Vicar General, Aloysius Scalabrini, in a letter of 12th September 1829.[103]  It was a recognition that came as a result of John's requesting it, which he had done that June in a letter to Scalabrini.[104]  His award came in the year when Catholic Emancipation was finally achieved through the Catholic Relief Act of 13th April. That achievement was secured at some price: the accompanying Irish Parliamentary Elections Act removed the franchise from the forty shilling freehold electors whose voting solidarity had led to Daniel O'Connell's original electoral triumph and the consequent achievement of Emancipation.

**Fig 14.**  *Aloysius Scalabrini, O.Carm.*

101. O'Dwyer, *Irish Carmelites*, p. 203.
102. *The Catholic Penny Magazine*, vol. 1, No. 7, 29th March 1834.
103. GMA, Box 56, Ledger 1, *Scrapbook A*.
104.  Ibid., Scalabrini to Spratt, 1st Aug 1829, mentions John's letter of 6th June 1829, requesting the title.

*Emancipation and Repression?*

The achievement came with another price as well, to be paid for by the male, regular clergy in Ireland and the United Kingdom at large. When the government's Catholic Relief proposals were published as a Bill, they contained clauses that threatened the eventual destruction of the male religious orders. Whereas the Relief Acts of 1791 and 1793 appeared to them to have legalised the existence of the regular clergy in Ireland, restrictions were now to be placed on the Orders, aimed, in theory, at their final extinction.[105]

Before it passed into law, the Augustinian Provincial, Daniel O'Connor, called a meeting of the regular clergy of Cork which decided to try to rally the clergy and laity at large to oppose the development. They appointed O'Connor and the Dominican, J.P. Leahy, to travel to Dublin to recruit the leaders of the regular clergy there. By this means, John Spratt, as Prior of the Dublin Carmelites, became involved in the attempt to have the punitive clauses in the draft Catholic Relief Bill removed. He attended the meeting of all the Dublin regular clergy, held in the Augustinian friary on Thursday 19th March. He joined with Leahy and O'Connor in drafting a remonstrating document, and the next day travelled with them to Carlow to secure the support of James Doyle, the Augustinian and Bishop of Kildare and Leighlin. Doyle fully endorsed their efforts and agreed a remonstrating memorial with them. Back in Dublin, two days later, the Provincial, William Kinsella, chaired a meeting of the Carmelites to discuss the situation.

Fr John's brother, Michael, was also to the fore to protest against the proposed legislative attack on the Orders. He and some fellow-parishioners of St Catherine's called on their parish priest, Dr Duignan – the same who had given John his references for Spain – to convene a meeting for this purpose. Michael proposed the first resolution at this gathering:

> That we consider that portion of the Relief Bill which has for its object the suppression of the Regular Clergy and Monastic Institutions of the Catholic Church in the United Kingdom, an unnecessary penal interference

---

105. R. Walsh, 'A List of the Regulars Registered in Ireland, pursuant to the Catholic Relief Act of 1829', *Archivium Hibernicum*, III, 1914, pp. 34-48.

and called for the Bill's amendment in this regard. He joined a committee to prepare a petition to the House of Lords.[106]

Thereafter, a delegation of Leahy, O'Connor and Edmund Ignatius Rice went to London to see Peel, Wellington and other parliamentarians, but their efforts were in vain. When the Bill finally became the Catholic Relief Act on 13th April 1829, it included clauses which, in theory, aimed at the control and eventual destruction of the regular clergy. Four clauses obliged regulars then living in the Kingdom to register their presence there, forbade other regulars to enter, banned the admission of new members, and threatened the banishment of any person who joined an Order.[107] These clauses could only have caused dismay to Spratt, his confreres and the other religious of the country, but O'Connell was confident in assuring them that these penal provisions would not be implemented.[108] So it proved: nevertheless, their existence on the statute book, together with other legal disabilities in the matter of wills and charitable bequests, remained a source of anxiety for the religious orders for a long time after. Furthermore, the regular clergy now had to register their existence with the state, with a penalty of £50 per month for every month of failing to do so.[109]

As for John Spratt, he was now no longer Prior and would not hold that office again for the remainder of his life in Whitefriar Street: other challenges beckoned.

---

106. *FJ*, 1st Apr 1829.
107. For these clauses of 10 Geo. IV, c.7, namely XXVIII, XXIX, XXXIII & XXXIV, see *Appendix 5: The Penal Clauses of the Catholic Relief Act, 1829*.
108. McGrath, *The Public Ministry of Bishop James Doyle*, p. 72.
109. Ibid, p. 35.

# CHAPTER FIVE

## *The Common Cause of Charity, 1824-1848*

Friar John was thirty-three when he completed his second and final term as Prior, in the summer of 1829. The relinquishing of this office may have come as a relief to him after the labours and responsibilities of the previous six years. One may speculate to the contrary, however, and suggest that he now experienced a certain anti-climax or frustration. His concern for recognition was evident in his request for the title *Magister de Justicia*. His successor as Prior was William Kinsella, and John, it seems, was critical of him for not insisting upon the rigorous standards the latter thought appropriate for his confreres in Dublin. He wrote in complaint to Scalabrini, the Prior General, in 1829. On not receiving a satisfactory response, he wrote again in the earlier half of 1830 and even suggested that he himself should come to Rome.[1] Scalabrini responded that he could not act upon a single complaint and exhorted him to be more prudent and charitable towards his superior. Scalabrini added that in any letters that he himself might send to the Dublin friary, he would conceal Spratt's name. As for the latter's proposal to come to Rome, that would be impractical since Scalabrini intended going south to Naples or Sicily to see out the rest of his term of office as Prior General. However, he invited Spratt to visit him in either of those places.[2] He wondered, in passing, and doubtless in response to whatever Spratt had written to him, why some unnamed individual – possibly Kinsella – could *'rage against your title in religious status'*. Finally, and almost contradicting his limp invitation to Spratt to

---

1. GMA, *Scrapbook A*, pp. 23, 27 and cited by O'Dwyer, *Dissertation*, p. 35.
2. GMA, *Scalabrini to Spratt*, 1st July 1830.

visit him in Naples or Sicily, he urged that John's place was best at home '*because your presence in your convent in Dublin seems very useful to me, with your prudence and dexterity, if anything bad can happen, you will be easily able to impede it*'. John remained on in Dublin – for the moment – but his discontent at the regime of his superiors, Coleman and Kinsella, may not yet have abated: two years later, in February 1832, in the course of thanking Spratt for the gift of a book, Scalabrini mentioned just having received a letter from Fr John, and he responded as follows:

> Then, regarding what you write in the letter that arrived here with the last post, I tell you that this being the year when a General Chapter will have to be held, and it being also the habit to grant Provincials the fourth year, beyond the three years of their Provincialate, for that reason I was sent the patent by your Provincial Coleman for continuing another year in his Provincialate, as I have done with the other Provincials who came to terminate their cares this year.[3]

It is hard to resist the surmise that Spratt wanted an election, with, perhaps, himself as prime candidate for Provincial: a year later, Propaganda Fide received a report from Dublin that all was not well with the Carmelites in Ireland and that the Order needed a good Provincial. This came at a time when Kinsella had just entered on that office, in succession to Coleman. This report was anonymous but, O'Dwyer speculates, with justice, if it may not have come from the pen of Spratt. Almost certainly it did, given Scalabrini's letter of 20th February 1832 and given also that the Prior General had earlier assured Spratt that his name would not be mentioned in correspondence with Dublin.[4]

*Resuming the writing*

In the meantime, Fr John returned to his writing. In 1830 he produced a new tract, *A Sermon on the Love of God*,[5] based on the passage in the Gospel of St Mark, xii. 30:

---

3. GMA, Scalabrini to Spratt, 20th Feb 1832.
4. GMA, Scalabrini to Spratt, 1st July 1830.
5. *A Sermon on the Love of God*, 18 pp., T & S Courtney, 1st ed. Dublin 1830, later ed., Dublin 1837. It was announced for publication in 1828 but the earliest extant copy is dated 1830, in Royal Irish Academy Haliday Tracts.

> And thou shalt love the Lord thy God with thy whole heart and
> with thy whole soul and with thy whole mind and with thy whole
> strength. This is the first commandment.

It is very much a sermon from the heart wherein he describes the
command to love God as containing *'the science of salvation'*. It is shot
through with the consciousness of sin and neglect: *'nothing is forgotten in
the world but the God that made it'*, and that *'our affection is denied to nothing else
but to that God who alone is truly worthy of our love'*. He goes on to ask *'how
many Christians, many probably in this assembly, who during a long life have never
performed a single act of charity or lived twenty four hours to their God?'* With
its recurring references to the threat of *'eternal misery and damnation'* on
the one hand, and the prospect of *'a blissful eternity'* on the other, it is
very much in the evangelical spirit of its time. He followed it up, soon
after, with *The Parents' Guide*. To date, no copy of this work has come to
hand. However, he sent a copy to Bishop Doyle in Kildare. The latter
expressed pleasure at receiving it and thought well enough of it to be
prepared to promote its circulation. However, he also felt the need to
offer some minor criticisms of interpretation and to mention that there
were some scriptural quotations used by the author that he himself
would not have employed in their particular contexts. He concluded by
expressing regret that Spratt had incurred so much expense by sending
the work through the Post Office instead of by less expensive means.[6]
Other writings would come from his pen in this, and in every other
decade of his life, making him one of the few Irish priests of the age
making a significant native contribution to the apostolate of the pen.

*The Resurrection Men*
The monastic peace that enabled John to write could rather readily be
shattered in so urban a setting as the Aungier Street-Whitefriar Street
area was fast becoming. Crime and violence were never far from the
friary precincts and, indeed, on occasion occurred within that sacred
space. On the night of Tuesday 15th April 1831 or in the early hours of
the morning following, the south gate of the Whitefriar Street Church
was broken open. The intruders made their way to a vault from which
they stole the body of *'the late lamented Miss Doherty'*. She was no more

---

6. GMA, *Scrapbook A*, p. 133, James Doyle to Spratt, 16th March 1831.

**Fig 15.** *A 19th century image depicting Resurrection Men.*

than thirteen years of age. Appalled by this *'most inhuman outrage'*, John organised a group of close supporters to raise money towards a substantial reward and contributed to this fund personally, as did his brother, Michael.[7] A sum of 120 guineas was raised as a reward for information leading to the prosecution and conviction of *'the perpetrators of so revolting a crime'.*[8] It is interesting to note that even though John was no longer in any position of formal authority in the Dublin friary, it was he who took the initiative: when the reward advertisement first appeared in print, it was under his name and no other.[9] The reward notice must have been effective: within days three 'resurrection men' were being sought by the Dublin police: Michael Farrell, Christopher Carney and James McClean. Farrell was the first to be arrested, in the last days of March. He appeared before the magistrates on Thursday 7th April. It transpired that the clerk of the church, John Prenter, who lived in a house on the premises, had locked up at ten o'clock on the night of Tuesday 15th April. When he arrived to open at six o'clock the next morning, he discovered that the doors had been forced, and

7. Others included old friends and new, who proved ever ready to contribute to his many and varied causes down the years: Andrew Ennis of Harcourt Street, Peter Slevin of French Street, Surgeon Mitchell, Fr Matthew Flanagan, Dr Keogh of Aungier Street and William Berry of Kevin Street for whose wife John had constructed another vault in the building of this church.
8. *FJ*, 21st March, 13th Apr 1831.
9. It is also notable that it was one of the few occasions that John ever appeared in the public prints without some of the letters or honorific titles that he used to append to his name: he signed the advertisement simply, for once, 'John Spratt'.

found that the vault and its coffins, one made of lead, had been broken open and emptied of its remains. When Farrell had effected his entry, he and his two accomplices, at three in the morning, took the body to the Anatomy School in nearby Peter Street. The porter on duty there told them, after some time, that the School could not accept the remains given from whence they had come, *'as it was feared there would be a great rout about it'*.[10] With this avenue of disposal closed off, all was not lost: an hour later, they contacted Dr MacCartney, of the Trinity College Anatomy School, and he paid £2 in advance for Miss Doherty's body.[11] The three resurrection men then took her body to the Trinity Anatomy School, leaving it with the School's porter, Nagle, and the College porter, Dongan. These two later recounted that when the three body-snatchers came back later for full payment, Dr MacCartney, having thought twice about it, left word that no money was to be paid over. When the three called on him later that day and MacCartney refused still to pay them, they threatened never again to provide him with bodies – or 'subjects', as they styled them – and one of them, McClean, insisted on taking the body away again. MacCartney refused to release it fearing that they would then try to export it, as he later testified.[12] Later that day, the distraught father of the dead woman came to Trinity College to identify and recover the body. On arrival, he found that her long hair had been shaved off, her upper and lower teeth extracted, and a gold crucifix from around her neck had been stolen.[13]

Farrell's trial, on 7th April, sheds much light on the grim world of these body-snatchers, but it also explains the exact nature and method of burials in the new Church of Mount Carmel, Whitefriar Street. John Prenter, as church clerk, explained in detail how Miss Doherty was buried in the actual aisle of the church:

> On the 14th of March, her grave was sunk in the earth; [it] had walls of brick work round about it; over her coffin were placed flags, over these flags, clay, and then the flags of the Chapel.[14]

---

10. *DEPC*, 9th Apr 1831.
11. *DEPC*, 31st March 1831.
12. *DMR*, 28th, 30th March 1831, *DEPC*, 31st March 1831.
13. *DMR*, 26th March 1831.
14. *DEPC*, 9th Apr 1831.

It transpired that Miss Doherty's remains had been placed in three containers, an original wooden coffin, then a leaden one, and finally an outer wooden one, and her father had himself placed her within, before all was sealed. In the event, Farrell was convicted and sentenced to one year imprisonment in Richmond Bridewell.[15] McClean and Carney were arrested shortly afterwards and, upon trial and conviction, they were sentenced to a surprisingly lenient three months' jail.[16] It was significant of the problem that at this very time, in 1831, when Prospect Cemetery in Glasnevin was actually under construction, its perimeter was fitted with watch-towers for vigilance against the 'resurrection men'.[17] The trade in corpses was shortly afterwards brought to an end by the Anatomy Act of 1832, in the turbulent passage of which through the Houses of Parliament, Daniel O'Connell played an important role in support. From having had to rely on the corpses of murderers or of those stolen from graves, the anatomy profession could henceforth rely upon a less toxic supply of cadavers and the deceased and their loved ones could thereafter rest in peace.

### King Cholera

There was little rest or peace, however, for Fr John Spratt. Death and its daily violations were never far from his view or from that of the little band of Carmelites in Whitefriar Street. As if the country and the city had not been plagued enough by endemic fever and periodic outbreaks of typhus, as in 1817-19, then in June-December 1822, and again in 1826-27,[18] at the beginning of the 1830s came the visitation of Asiatic cholera. Originating in India in 1826, it spread to Russia, reaching St Petersburg in 1829. It passed on into Germany in 1830 and entered Great Britain through Sunderland in November-December 1831.[19] By the end of February or start of March 1832 it had reached Belfast

---

15. Ibid.
16. *FJ*, 20th Apr 1831.
17. For the history of 'the resurrection men', see J. Fleetwood, *The Irish Body Snatchers: a history of body snatching in Ireland*, Dublin 1988. This work makes no mention of the Doherty case but does mention the Glasnevin watch-towers, p. 44.
18. T. P. O'Neill, *The State, Poverty and Distress in Ireland, 1815-1845*, National University of Ireland PhD Dissertation, 1971, pp. 54-63.
19. A. Briggs, 'Cholera and society', in *Past & Present*, 19, 1961, pp. 76-96; N. Longmate, *King Cholera: the biography of a disease*, London 1966, pp. 11-31; J. Robins, *The Miasma: Epidemic and Panic in nineteenth-century Ireland*, Dublin 1995, pp. 63-64.

**Fig 16.** *The Cork Street Fever Hospital and House of Recovery. Opened in 1804, the hospital was inundated over the next three decades with the fever epidemic of 1817/1819, the typhus epidemic of 1826 and the cholera epidemic of 1832.*

and by the end of March it had arrived in Dublin.[20]  By mid-April it had reached Cork and Kerry, by mid-May Limerick and Galway, and by August it stretched from Waterford and Wexford to Derry.[21]  With its widespread poverty and congestion, Dublin was probably the worst hit.  By 2nd May some 430 had died in the capital; by July 1,524 had fallen to the disease and by the end of the year it had claimed 4,478 of Dublin's citizens.[22]  The overall death-toll in Ireland was in excess of 25,000 souls.  This constituted 38% of all those who contracted the disease.[23]  Unlike the more prevalent typhus, this Asiatic cholera was socially indiscriminate and killed its victims usually within twenty-four hours of contracting it.  Eighty per cent of its victims died in Ireland's cities and towns and its rapid spread induced widespread panic.  This was so much the case that some who had the means to escape the city did so, including, it is alleged, Daniel O'Connell and his family who departed for London on 24th April 1832.[24]

---

20.  Robins, pp. 68-69; H. Fenning, 'The cholera epidemic in Ireland, 1832-33', *Archivium Hibernicum*, vol. 57, 2003, pp. 77-125.
21.  Longmate, p. 135.
22.  O'Neill, pp. 68-70.
23.  P. A. Grace, 'In time of cholera', *Irish Journal of Medical Science*, vol. 183, No. 1, March 2014, p. 133; Robins, p. 108.
24.  H. Reeve, *The Greville Memoirs*, 8 vols, London 1898, ii., p. 316; O'Neill, p. 177.

The situation was hardly helped by the pastoral letter of Archbishop Murray in which he berated his flock:

> You have disregarded the warnings of the word of God...Your sins have ascended to the throne of the Lord and demanded justice; before that withering justice shall be let loose against you, fall down in human compunction before him.[25]

While the Archbishop's words were hardly reassuring, his motives were understandable: he was at pains to discourage wakes and to encourage the speedy burial of the dead as a means of curtailing the contagion among the living. His pastoral had been prompted, in part, by a request from the General Board of Health, now being called The Cholera Board, for his support in the suppression of wakes and in the discouraging of intemperance. In their separate ways, the ecclesiastical and the health authorities of the age saw intemperance as a link to cholera. For all of his and their urgings, the epidemic intensified its hold on the city and country throughout April. In response to this, the Cholera Board established temporary hospitals in Dublin, notably the Townsend Street Cholera Hospital and the Grangegorman Cholera Hospital. Under the direction of Mary Aikenhead, the relatively recently-founded Sisters of Charity bore the main burden of the care of the cholera victims at Grangegorman while the Sisters of Mercy, under Catherine McAuley, shouldered the responsibility for the care of those victims who were brought to the Townsend Street facility.[26] They remained there in a critical capacity until December, with the last publicly reported cholera fatalities for Dublin City being recorded on 14th December 1832.[27]

John Spratt became greatly caught up in this cholera relief work. Farrington relates that Fr John and Fr Edward O'Rourke became actively involved in helping out during this crisis. He mentioned that they carried straw on their own backs to make beds for the poor and that

---

25. W. Meagher, *Notices of the life and character of His Grace Most Rev Dr Daniel Murray, late Archbishop of Dublin*, Dublin 1853, pp. 154-156, cited in Robins, p. 71.
26. M. C. Sullivan, *Catherine McAuley and the Tradition of Mercy*, Dublin 1995, pp. 64, 112, 174; M. C. Sullivan, *The Path of Mercy: the life of Catherine McAuley*, Dublin 2012, p. 116; O'Neill, pp. 275-276.
27. Sullivan, *The Path of Mercy*, p. 120.

they carried the dead to the carts to have them conveyed for burial.[28] Fr John's most enduring contribution and commitment in the cholera epidemic was his role in the work of the Cholera Orphan Society. This body was established on the first day of August 1832 at the Old Chapel, French Street, by a group of laymen of the locality and, by the end of October 1832, it was placed under the patronage of the Carmelite Provincial, Thomas Coleman, and his Whitefriar Street confreres.[29] From the outset it was made clear that it would receive orphans of any religious denomination and that it would guarantee not to subvert their religious beliefs. From the outset, also, Fr John was to the fore in raising money for the cause and in supporting it energetically.

*Father to Orphans*
One of the most prominent and enduring features of John Spratt's life mission was his concern for and his commitment to the city's orphans. Long before the 1832 cholera epidemic caught him up into this commitment, he had already established his credentials as a crusader for orphans. This became evident in his earlier work on behalf of the St Peter's Orphan Society. This institution was founded under Carmelite patronage on 28th July 1817 by a workman named Halligan and was run on a day-to-day basis by an elected committee of laymen. In time, the patronage and spiritual guardianship of St Peter's became a joint one between the Calced Carmelites of French Street and the Discalced of Clarendon Street: in August of 1822 the Society's President, Thomas Ryan, thanked Fr Finny of French Street and Fr Hanlon of Clarendon Street *'for their zealous co-operation in support of this charity'*.[30] Its organising committee met at No. 6 Cuffe Lane while the charity sermons in its support were frequently preached in the French Street Chapel. The foundation date is significant as it occurred during the middle of the epidemic and economic distress of 1816-1819, and just before the

---

28. Farrington, p. 139. See also O'Dwyer, *Dissertation*, p. 117.
29. *DMR*, 22nd, 24th, 30th Oct 1832, 29th July 1833. O'Dwyer, *Dissertation*, p. 116, states that it was founded at No. 12, Aungier Street.
30. *FJ*, 28th Dec 1821, 8th Aug 1822.

virulent typhus epidemic of 1817-1819 spread rapidly in Dublin.[31] This crisis, among other things, left in its wake, orphaned children. It was in response to this that Halligan and his fellow workers had established St Peter's to address the plight of the orphaned. By December 1821, they had rescued 34 victims, clothed, fed and set them on the road to education.[32] By 1825 they were caring for some 58 orphans and by that stage Fr John had become involved. In the year 1825 he arranged that the Sunday collections at French Street Chapel would go exclusively to St Peter's, and was active in securing donations for it.[33] The committee of St Peter's, possibly at Fr John's urging, planned to open a school for older orphans. Early in March 1825 they advertised for a husband and wife to act as teachers and foster parents to the orphans.[34] By May 1825 they had secured premises for the school and fitted it out, at 22 Charlemont Street, where some 22 of their orphans were being taught by trained teachers.

By mid-1825 the Society had nine guardians, headed by Fr Spratt and consisting of six clergy and three lay men. It had become responsible for some 58 children over the previous eight years. He himself proved deeply committed to the support of St Peter's: from the Sunday masses of 29th May 1825 he donated the entire collection to the Society.[35] Two years later the Committee praised him for the *'unremitting attention and uniform zeal he has always evinced for the interests of this important charity'*.[36] In June 1828 he chaired the annual business meeting of the Society in Whitefriar Street Church, was responsible for securing many donations, and chaired its proceedings again in 1829.[37] It may have been through his good offices that O'Connell was persuaded to support and preside at their charity dinner in November of that year, after his re-election as MP for Clare that July. The Committee certainly thanked Spratt for

---

31. By the end of September 1817 there had been almost 800 admissions to the city's four hospitals. When the epidemic peaked in the city, in October 1818, there had been over 3,000 admissions. The poverty, sickness and distress led the Lord Mayor, in November 1816, to convene a Mansion House Relief Committee: within a month this had raised some £10,000; see O'Neill, pp. 54, 156, 239.

32. *FJ*, 28th Dec 1821; *SNL*, 27th July 1822.

33. *DMR*, 22nd Jun 1825.

34. *SNL*, 9th March 1825.

35. *DMR*, 22nd June 1825.

36. *DMR*, 27th July 1827.

37. *DMR*, 7th July 1828, 9th July 1829.

his exertions in this regard.[38] By this time the School attached to the orphanage had moved from Charlemont Street to the much closer Peter's Row.[39] They incurred expenditure in fitting out these premises and the charity dinner of November 1830, chaired by Tom Steele, raised funds to defray this cost.[40] By that stage, John Spratt was the only Whitefriar Street Carmelite whose name was associated, publicly, with this Orphan Society. So it would remain until his death in 1871. The Society remained active during all the intervening years. He continued to co-chair its business meetings and to act as the conduit for its donations, as for example in July 1841 when he passed on some £73 from Dr Cahill's charity sermon.[41] By the following year the St Peter's Orphanage Schoolhouse was listed as being located at 51 Aungier Street.[42] By 1845 he was described as the Society's *'superintending guardian'*.[43] In the midst of his long commitments to famine relief and to the temperance cause in the mid-1840s, he could still be found chairing St Peter's business meetings, as in January 1847.[44] Interestingly, although from the outset in 1817, it professed to be non-denominational, by the later 1850s, while John was still very much in charge, it was now being styled *'St Peter's Catholic Orphan House at 51 Aungier Street'*.[45] John remained eloquent in his public appeals on behalf of St Peter's, none more eloquent perhaps than his Christmas Eve Appeals of 1861 and 1862.[46] By the early 1860s it had undertaken the care of some 400 orphans and by January 1871 it was still caring for some 45. The Society survived Spratt's sudden death four months later, but not without serious troubles between the lay management and the Carmelite friars, by the end of the 1870s.[47]

---

38. *DMR*, 24th Nov 1827.
39. *DMR*, 26th Oct 1829; it was located at No. 9 Peter's Row.
40. *DMR*, 29th Nov 1830.
41. *FJ*, 4th Aug 1841.
42. *FJ*, 16th Feb 1842.
43. *FJ*, 19th June 1845.
44. *FJ*, 22nd Jan 1847.
45. *FJ*, 17th July 1858. Perhaps this was a sign of the growing confessionalism of the 1850s; see Chapters Fourteen, Eighteen & Nineteen for John Spratt and the issue of proselytism in the 1850s.
46. *FJ*, 24th Dec 1861, 24th Dec 1862.
47. See Chapter Twenty-three.

*The Cholera Orphan Society*

As an orphan society, St Peter's inevitably felt the consequences of the cholera epidemic in Dublin and Spratt, his confreres and co-workers, found themselves more challenged than ever, as a result. Yet the Carmelites of Dublin soon saw themselves take on additional responsibility with the emergence of a kindred body, the County and City of Dublin Cholera Orphan Society. This body was founded by a group of concerned city layman on 1st August 1832.[48] Known originally as the Visitation Orphan Society, they sought out the Carmelites for support and were soon meeting in what had come to be known as The Old Chapel, French Street. Their initial meetings were chaired by John Spratt's young confrere, Andrew Day.[49] By the end of October 1832, the Visitation Orphan Society had come under the formal patronage of the Provincial *'Dr Coleman and the Reverend gentleman of Whitefriar Street'*. By that time they had secured offices at No. 3 York Street and from there they operated until their disappearance sometime in the later 1840s.[50] From the outset the society was at pains to stress and to guarantee its non-sectarian, non-proselytising credentials. At an early meeting, in October 1832, Fr Day insisted on this: *'the society has no respect to sect...we have nothing to do with differences of religion'*.[51] A few weeks later, a resolution was adopted stating that

> the creed or religious opinions held by the deceased, shall in no way prejudice the reception of their Orphan Children into this Institution and that we view with just abhorrence the offer of an Asylum to the destitute for the purpose of subverting their religious opinions, being contrary to the principles of Christian charity, the broad base upon which this Society is founded.[52]

The title of the Society evolved until, by the beginning of December, it became the 'County and City of Dublin Cholera Orphan Society'.

---

48.  *DMR*, 29th July 1833.
49.  *DMR*, 22nd, 24th Oct 1832.
50.  The last mention of the Society in the national press was in 1847 when it was mentioned as receiving a sum of £20 from the will of Richard Corballis, of Rosemount, Co. Dublin: see *DWR*, 11th Dec 1847.
51.  *DMR*, 24th Oct 1832.
52.  *FJ*, 9th Nov 1832.

There was a certain logic in this evolution of title. For one thing, those children they rescued were settled into homes stretching from Sandyford to Glencullen, Stepaside to Scalp. Indeed, for some time, they published the names of the children and the names and addresses of the foster parents with whom they were placed.[53] For another, as their fundraising efforts began to exhaust the generosity of Dublin's city dwellers, they extended their fundraising activities systematically beyond the city and into the county, from Clontarf and Raheny to Finglas and St Margaret's on the north, and from Donnybrook to Rathfarnham on the south.[54] A crisis of fundraising led the leaders to some desperate measures. One Sunday, in the summer of 1834, they resorted to the dramatic expedient of parading the unfortunate 'Cholera Orphans' through the main streets of Dublin in a long procession of misery: this wended its serpentine way from York Street to St Stephen's Green, Baggot Street, Merrion Square, Nassau Street, College Green, Sackville Street, Rutland (now Parnell) Square, Capel Street, South Great George's Street and back to York Street and Coburg Gardens, and, at the same time, there was held an 'Orphan Dinner' in the Gardens.[55] Later that year, with funds faltering and a claimed 350 orphans looking for help, they sought and secured an interview with Chief Secretary at Dublin Castle, Edward Littleton. No government subvention or promise of aid was forthcoming, but Littleton himself donated £10 while his superior the Lord Lieutenant, Wellesley, provided £50 and secured a further £50 from a friend in London.[56] Suddenly, from being £11 in debt they happily found the Society with a surplus of £130 and the city-wide parade of orphans and the dinner in the Coburg Gardens had raised a further £27.

John Spratt's role in the Society was not central or dominant, but neither was it negligible. Like Coleman, Kinsella and the other members of the French Street-Whitefriar Street community, he was an important conduit for donations throughout the 1830s and he was appointed as Vice-President, along with Fr Coleman, in January 1835.[57] Furthermore, he was instrumental in securing the *pro bono* services of

53.  *DMR*, 12th, 16th, 28th Nov, 4th, 11th Dec 1832.
54.  *DMR*, 9th May, 22nd June, 30th Aug, 17th Sept 1833, 11th Aug 1834.
55.  *DMR*, 4th July 1834.
56.  *DMR*, 11th Nov 1834.
57.  *FJ*, 22nd Jan 1835.

a medical doctor, James McKeon, from September 1833. Dr McKeon paid tribute to Spratt and the Carmelites in a letter of 26th September of that year:

> The very laudable and praiseworthy conduct of the Clergy of your Convent, since the Cholera made its appearance in the city, which left so many poor children without parents or protection, can only be equalled by your and their now, anxious endeavours to protect those children from disease,

and, in consideration of that, he accepted Spratt's invitation to become the medical officer for the Society, *gratis*.[58]

While most of the friars of the Dublin Carmelite community brought in donations for the society, including the young friars, Michael Tobin, William Withers and Richard Colgan, back from Rome since 1826, Spratt was not found wanting as a conduit for funds; apart from many modest donations, he secured one gift of £8 in March 1832, £20 in April 1835, £10 in July 1835, and a legacy of £21-17-6 in February 1834.[59] In that same period of the early 1830s he managed to find time to preach and collect for two other bodies, the Josephian Society and its Female Orphan House on Paradise Row, founded in 1770, and the St John the Baptist Orphan Society founded in 1812. One of his sermons for the Josephian raised a creditable £89 in March 1832 and this was but one of several sermons he preached for that body over 1831 to 1834.[60] His brother, Michael, acted as secretary to the St John the Baptist Orphan Society over many years, certainly from 1822 into the mid-1830s, and John was active in support of this orphan charity likewise.[61]

Over the years 1789 to 1832, with endemic poverty and recurrent epidemics, the numbers of Dublin's orphans tripled every fifteen years. On the eve of the cholera epidemic the city had 800 orphans being looked after by some 24 orphan societies.[62] The cholera epidemic then overwhelmed the city. Francis White, the Secretary of the Dublin

---

58. James McKeon, M.D. to Spratt, 26th Sept 1833, cited in *FJ*, 27th Sept 1833.
59. *DMR*, 12th NW 1832, 25th Feb 1834; *FJ*, 8th June 1839.
60. *FJ*, 17th Dec 1831, 13th March 1832, 14th Dec 1833, 22nd Dec 1837.
61. *FJ*, 21st Nov 1822, 8th Jan 1834.
62. O'Neill, *Dissertation*, pp. 276 ff.

Board of Health, estimated that the epidemic had left 1,000 orphans destitute.[63] Furthermore, he was to remark:

> It is with great regret I have heard that the humane exertions of the Managers of the Cholera Orphan Society, in St Peter's Parish, have not been attended with that success their praiseworthy undertaking so highly merited.[64]

All White was saying was that charity was not enough and that Dublin and Dubliners were no longer willing or else no longer able to give as they had done in the past. He recalled that in the midst of the hardship of 1831-32, the City's Mansion House Committee could raise only £2,000 whereas a call for distress funds in 1814 raised £10,000 and a second such call, during the crisis of 1816-17 raised £19,000. For all its limitations, however, and in the absence of radical government intervention and assistance, charity was all that there was.

Spratt's role in this particular society, when coupled with his crucial work for St Peter's Orphan Society, established for him, by the early 1830s, a reputation as a champion of the poor and as one who could work in a spirit of fraternity with Christians of other allegiances. It was this, doubtless, that led to the invitation to take on a new role in the *'common cause of charity'*.

### From Orphans to Indigents

In November 1833 John was invited to become joint secretary to Dublin's oldest surviving charity, The Charitable Society for the Relief of Sick and Indigent Roomkeepers of all Religious Persuasions in the City of Dublin.[65] One of the six major charities for the poor of Dublin, it was founded on 15th March 1790 by Samuel Rosborough, a linen cloth agent of St Michan's Parish, and nine other tradesmen

---

63. F. White, *Report and Observations on the State of the Poor of Dublin*, Dublin 1833, pp. 21-22.
64. Ibid.
65. NAI, 1028/2/2, *The Sick and Indigent Roomkeepers Society, Minutes of Monthly General Meetings and Trustees' Reports*, 1st Nov 1833. See also *A Statement of the Charitable Society for the relief of Sick and Indigent Roomkeepers of all religious persuasions in the City of Dublin for the year 1833*, Dublin 1834, p. 59.

**Fig 17.**   *Samuel Rosborough (1757–1832)*

neighbours.[66] It might have been well-nigh indistinguishable from the other one hundred and more charitable institutions found in Dublin at that time, had it not been for two outstanding features which it shared with few others. Firstly, it had been from its foundation, an expressly undenominational, non-sectarian, non-political body.[67] Secondly, those they aimed to help were

> poor roomkeepers who never begged abroad and who by unforeseen misfortune, sickness, death of friends, or other dispensations of Providence, have been reduced to indigence, and that such persons must be of good character, for sobriety and general good conduct.[68]

---

66.  D. Lindsay, *Dublin's Oldest Charity: the Sick and Indigent Roomkeepers Society, 1790-1990*, Dublin 1990, pp. 1-3; D. Lindsay, 'The Sick and Indigent Roomkeepers Society', in D. Dickson, ed., *The Gorgeous Mask: Dublin, 1700-1850*, Dublin 1987, p. 133; in both works p. 20, p. 148 respectively.

67.  When its ten founding fathers met in Mountrath Street, on 25th March 1790, they determined that *"as a charitable feeling for the relief of our fellow creatures must be pleasing to Almighty God, we have resolved unanimously to form a society to be called The Charitable Society for the Relief of Sick and Indigent Roomkeepers of all Religious Persuasions in the City of Dublin"*; see Lindsay, *Dublin's Oldest Charity*, p. 3.

68.  Ibid, pp. 3-4.

It was in keeping with the spirit of inclusiveness that the Society, in 1833, had created the two honorary secretaryships, one Protestant, one Catholic.  In each case, the recipients of the honour possessed established credentials in the field of charitable works and in manifesting a record of cordial relations that bridged religious divisions. The Protestant invited was the Rev Thomas Shore, a man who had done much to bring to notice the appalling poverty which obtained in the parish of St Michan's, where he was curate.[69]  Shore's evidence before the parliamentary inquiry of 1836 into poverty in Ireland was noteworthy in its presentation and analysis of poverty in the capital city.[70]  Furthermore, he had been a most active member of the Society for quite some time before this: in October 1828 he had been elected a trustee of the original Barrack Street Division and often chaired meetings of the general committee of the Society.[71]

As for John Spratt, his introduction to the Roomkeepers Society may have come through the agency of his French Street friend and charity associate, Peter Slevin, owner of a circulating library.  Slevin was not only secretary of the St Peter's Orphan Society for many years, he was also President of the St Stephen's Green Division of the Roomkeepers Society in the early 1830s.[72]  Slevin had first become a regular subscribing member of the Society in 1828 and was first elected a Divisional Officer for the Stephen's Green Division in 1829 for the year 1830.[73]  In July of that year he was elected President of the Stephen's Green Division, a position he held until 1832.  Thereafter he remained active in the Society and he and Rev Thomas Shore worked closely together on its committees.  It is reasonable to suggest that he may have been the

---

69.  J. Prunty, *Dublin Slums, 1800-1925: a study in urban geography*, Dublin 1998, pp. 212-13, 284.  See also Rev Thomas Shore, *Case of the Rev Thomas R Shore and the Protestant Orphan Society, with a statement of the circumstances under which he was removed from the Society*, Dublin 1851.

70.  Parl. Papers, *Appendix to First Report from the Commissioners inquiring into the State of the Poorer Classes in Ireland*, Appendix C, Part II, pp. 2-3.

71.  NAI, 1028/2/1 & 2, *The Sick and Indigent Roomkeepers Society, Minutes of Monthly General Meetings and Trustees' Reports*.

72.  For his role in the Roomkeepers, see Lindsay, p. 167.  He was a prominent O'Connellite loyalist right down to the end of the 1840s, remaining steadfast in his support of the O'Connells after the split with the Young Irelanders and the Confederation.

73.  NAI 1028/1, *Annual Report for the year 1828*, p. 34.

one who introduced John Spratt to the Society. However, another of Spratt's friends and supporters, the Kevin Street seed merchant, William Berry, had earlier been one of the Society's trustees in the Stephen's Green Division also: in his case, from October 1828.[74] It was doubtless through Berry and Slevin that the Carmelites of Dublin came into close relationship with the Roomkeepers Society. From 1828, the Friars had joined with the other Catholic churches in Dublin in granting a church collection once a year to the Society. Furthermore, in May of 1832, the Roomkeepers passed a resolution of thanks to

> Rev Mr Coleman, Provincial of the Carmelite Friary, Aungier Street, for the very kind manner in which he granted to the deputation who waited on him from Stephen's Green Division of this Charity, the use of the School House, French Street, for payment of the Sick and Indigent of that Division.[75]

John Spratt himself first contributed financially to the Roomkeepers with a personal donation in November 1830, and by the spring of 1831 he must have become a member, since he seconded a resolution at its annual general meeting in February of that year.[76] Nevertheless, it was some testimony to John Spratt's standing that he was soon invited to become joint honorary secretary with Thomas Shore. The Roomkeepers already had a full-time paid secretary, yet the honorary nature of Shore's and Spratt's position did not mean that theirs were merely prestige appointments, made solely in order to ease the attraction of funds. Both men worked hard and long together on behalf of the Society. From the outset, in accepting the invitation, they won the approbation of the Society's members for

> their prompt acquiescence in the wishes of the Trustees in accepting this office: thus showing the citizens of Dublin that, although differing in religion, men can be found to unite in the common cause of charity.[77]

---

74. Ibid, *Minutes of Monthly General Meeting*, 3rd Oct 1828.
75. Ibid, *Minutes of Monthly Meeting*, 4th May 1832.
76. Ibid, *Minutes of Monthly Meeting*, 5th Nov 1830, 4th Feb 1831.
77. *Annual Report of the Charitable Society for relief of Sick and Indigent Roomkeepers in the City of Dublin, for the year 1833*, Dublin 1834, p. 15.

Spratt's presence gave a new profile to the role of Catholics in inter-denominational charity work. There were about twenty small Catholic charities functioning at parish level before and during the 1830s but their visibility was not high. The St Peter's Orphan Society and the Cholera Orphan Society were exceptions, both in their visibility and in their being Catholic-inspired but anti-sectarian. These apart, the only other significant non-denominational Dublin charities were the Mendicity Institute, established during the economic and epidemic crises from 1817 and the Dublin General Dispensary, founded in 1782.[78]

Spratt, though apparently never a member of the Mendicity Association, was certainly well-disposed to it and had some dealings with it. When, for example, its long-serving honorary secretary, Thomas Abbott, had died, Fr John was to the fore in calling on Lord Mayor Hodges to give expression to the sense of loss felt by the Friends and Supporters of the Mendicity Association, among whom Spratt counted himself.[79] Furthermore, when the imminent arrival in Dublin of the new poor law and its workhouse system appeared to threaten the survival of the Mendicity Association, he was again to the fore in a public meeting called to support the Association. Indeed, he was one of the main speakers and proposed the second resolution to the effect that

> it is in the manifest interest of the public to prevent their streets from being inundated with misery, beggary and disease, which must eventually follow the closing of the Mendicity Institute.[80]

The Mendicity Association survived the introduction of the workhouse system but the fear that it might not was a considerable one at that time.[81] The Roomkeepers Society was also fearful of this same threat, so much that in 1837 they convened a special general meeting to consider the implications for their funds that the imposition of a

---

78. A. Woods, *Dublin Outsiders: a history of the Mendicity Institution, 1818-1998*, Dublin 1998, pp. 11-12; the initial meeting was held on 23rd May 1817 and it was launched at its first public meeting on 22nd Jan 1818; see also D. Dickson, *Dublin: The Making of a Capital City*, Dublin 2014, pp. 299, 611, n. 67.
79. *SNL*, 17th June 1837.
80. *SNL*, 20th April 1839.
81. Woods, pp. 105-116.

new 'poor law vote' might have. For the Roomkeepers to have held such a conference threatened their historic principle of avoidance of all political discussion, yet the national debate on the proposed new poor law system was indeed a profoundly and inescapably political one. However, their integrity remained intact in the wake of that conference: they had wisely anticipated and subsequently had found that the new system did not pre-empt their mission. Reporting for the year 1841, the Roomkeepers noted that

> Notwithstanding that the two poor-houses have been opened for the last two years and that the past year has not been distinguished by any particular calamity, the immense number of 25,640 individuals have actually received relief out of the Society's funds.[82]

If anything, the new Poor Law actually enabled the Roomkeepers to focus more clearly on their original vision, namely, to act as a

> resource for those who would not allow their private wants to meet the public eye, but would sooner die in their privacy than seek relief in a workhouse.[83]

Yet, the threat was not groundless: over 1837 and 1838 donations fell by a substantial £670 and the society had to strengthen its appeals to the public.[84] From his own entry into Roomkeepers, Fr John's ability at attracting financial support was evident. In its annual report for 1833 he is minuted as moving a vote of thanks to the Lord Lieutenant for his support to the Society. In that year, with an income of in excess of £2,600 they had expended some £2,597 in helping a remarkable 10,415 families or 36,902 persons.[85] He himself was able to bring in over £20 through the bequest of one John Quinn.

The ordinary business meetings of the Society were held monthly and John Spratt for almost forty years was dutiful in his attendance at

---

82. *Annual Report of the year 1841*, pp. 11-12.
83. Lindsay, *Dublin's Oldest Charity*, p. 21.
84. Ibid, p. 22.
85. *Annual Report of the Charitable Society for the relief of the Sick and Indigent Roomkeepers in the City of Dublin*, 1833, p. 4.

them. Indeed, frequently he acted as chairman of these. In the first half of 1835 he was especially active in his practical support. With Peter Slevin and one William Casey he visited the Superiors of the religious orders in Dublin to promote charity sermons for the Society's funds. It may well be, also, that it was due to his connections and efforts that Archbishop Daniel Murray preached the Charity Sermon for the Roomkeepers on All Saints Day, 1st November 1835, a sermon which, indeed, was subsequently published.[86] Under his chairmanship and at his initiative, in June 1836, when funds were running perilously low, another public appeal was decided upon.[87] Again, through his good offices, when there were difficulties securing a speaker for their 1836 charity sermon, they succeeded in getting Bishop Kinsella of Ossory to help out and, whether it was owing to the latter's abilities or not, the receipts for the year at £2,718 plus were the highest since Spratt had become joint Secretary.[88]

The city experienced even greater hardship during the year 1837 and it was decided to send a fund-raising deputation to London to solicit the support of the great. Spratt drafted two addresses for presentation, to the new Queen, Victoria, and to the Duchess of Kent, in the hope of eliciting bounty: these were duly signed by Lord Mayor Thomas Hodges, as chair. Whatever the result of this deputation to the mighty, receipts for 1837 constituted a record of £2,700.[89] As noted earlier, the passing into law of the new Poor Law Act, in 1838, and its implementation from 1st January 1839, appears to have had a dampening effect on the inflow of donations: the receipts for 1838 were lower by £200. The Society now wondered whether they could continue to offer assistance as extensively as before and, under Spratt's guidance, they began to consider if they could originate some scheme *'for the granting of small loans to the industrious poor'*: essentially to help them out of, rather than 'in' their poverty. This was to anticipate a larger such initiative that Spratt would take up with the Dublin working class as a whole in the 1840s and 1850s along with his friend and fellow-priest, Matthew Flanagan.[90]

---

86.  *Minutes of Monthly Meetings*, Dublin 1791-1835, vol. II, pp. 4-6, cited in O'Dwyer, *Dissertation*, p. 104.
87.  Ibid, 1836, p. 4, cited in O'Dwyer, *Dissertation*, p. 114.
88.  O'Dwyer, *Dissertation*, p. 105, citing *Minutes of Monthly Meetings*, p. 14.
89.  Ibid., p. 105.
90.  See Chapter Thirteen.

However, it was also to repeat a strategy which the Roomkeepers had attempted in its earliest years and again in the 1820s.[91]

His initiative in this raises the question, to what extent John Spratt ever theorised about the causes and possible remedies for the poverty of the city and of the age. Certainly, there are no published writings of his on economic issues or prescriptions, such as one finds in the case of his radical contemporary, Fr Thaddeus O'Malley of Dublin's Pro-Cathedral.[92] Equally, there do not appear to be any musings of his on these matters, in his surviving private papers. In this respect he did not differ from the overwhelming majority of his clerical contemporaries in Dublin, Ireland or the world at large: his perspective and his perceived solutions were moral rather than economic or political. Consequently, rather than dissecting or opposing the new Poor Law, in the way that Fr O'Malley did, he adopted a practical view in appearing to accept it, although later on deploring its excesses. Speaking in 1839 he observed that the great distress of the age had created a constituency of the utterly destitute whose desperate situation claimed prior attention over the quiet and respectable poor roomkeepers who were the original object of the Society's mission: the new Poor Law would remove the former from the scene and into the workhouses, leaving the latter to continue to be cared for by the Roomkeepers Society. It was a practical view until the Great Famine – in Dublin as in the country as a whole – completely overwhelmed the new workhouse system. That is another story.[93]

As the Society moved from the 1830s into the 1840s it soon felt the pressure of the rising influence of the temperance movement, especially under Fr Mathew's leadership. Hitherto, officers and collectors of the Society's four divisions – Barrack, Workhouse, Rotunda and St Stephen's Green – had conducted their business in public houses: the premises were free and the officials paid for their own drink.[94] However, at a monthly meeting in 1841, Fr Spratt seconded a motion

91. Lindsay, *Dublin's Oldest Charity*, p. 14.
92. F. A. D'Arcy, 'Federalist, social radical and anti-sectarian: Thaddeus O'Malley (1797-1877)', in G. Moran, ed., *Radical Irish Priests, 1660-1970*, Dublin 1998, pp. 91-110.
93. See Chapter Eleven.
94. M. J. Tutty, 'Dublin's Oldest Charity', *Dublin Historical Record*, XVI, 3, March 1961, pp. 73-74.

'that it was expedient for the further advancement of the interests. of this Charity, that some measure be adopted for holding the divisional meetings in the office of the Society so as to obviate the objectionable custom of holding them in other localities'.[95] As a consequence, in 1841 the Society established its headquarters at 85 Dame Street and in 1855 moved to their longest-standing location at No. 2 Palace Street, at the entrance to Dublin Castle.[96]

Through the various challenges of securing prominent speakers for charity sermons and the difficulties of sustaining income during the 1840s, Spratt remained the key figure in obtaining both. Typical of this success in the latter was his securing £20 from

**Fig 18.**    *The former headquarters of the Sick and Indigent Roomkeepers Society, on Palace Street.*

Lady Cloncurry in 1843 and £50 from the will of Fr John Ryan of St Paul's, Arran Quay, in 1846, and he was one of the trustees in the will of Mrs Catherine Lyons which annually brought to the Society a munificent £147 plus, from 1845.[97] On 5th November 1848 he himself was one of the preachers at the Society's Catholic Charity sermon in the Pro-Cathedral. The other speaker on the occasion was none other than the celebrated English Passionist preacher, Fr Ignatius, formerly the Honourable George Spencer.[98] For Fr Spratt, it constituted a high point indeed in his life in the city and in his role in the Roomkeepers Society: a role that would distinguish him as a champion in the common cause of charity for another quarter of a century.

---

95.  *Minutes of Monthly Meetings, 1841*, p. 43-4.
96.  Lindsay, *Dublin's Oldest Charity*, pp. 25-26.
97.  *Annual Report*, 1843, p. 30, 1846, p. 25 and 1845, p. 31 respectively.
98.  *DEP*, 21st Nov 1848.

# CHAPTER SIX

## *Education Odyssey, 1820–1848*

The cause of public charity was but one of the major commitments of John Spratt's life and of that of his confreres. Another was their lifelong dedication to the education of the poor. From the outset, Friar John's philosophy of education was simultaneously to Christianise and civilise the poor – to cultivate morality at the same time as literacy. In this regard his approach was not different from that of his contemporary education pioneers, Edmund Ignatius Rice and his Christian Brothers. However, John differed from them in one fundamental: his way was Christian but non-denominational, or even inter-denominational whereas theirs was distinctly denominational.[1] It was essentially a position that he would hold to the end of his days even as it eventually put him out of line with a later, more militant Church under Cardinal Cullen.

In the 1820s and 1830s John and his fellow-friars received significant support for their local educational endeavours. In late January 1831 the annual dinner for their St Patrick's General Free Schools Charity was held in Mahony's of Patrick Street. Daniel O'Connell was announced to attend and preside but, due to the demands of a law case, was unable to do so. In his stead came the redoubtable Protestant, 'Honest Tom' Steele, as remarkable an international champion of liberty as that age was to produce. He was one of O'Connell's most loyal and senior lieutenants. Chairing this meeting, Steele proposed the first toast to *'Daniel O'Connell and the Repeal of the Union'*. There then followed a toast

---

1. For Rice, see D. Keogh, 'Evangelising the Faithful: Edmund Rice and the reformation of nineteenth-century Irish Catholicism', in Lennon, *Confraternities and Sodalities*, pp. 57-75.

**Fig 19.**   *'Honest Tom' Steele (1788-1848).*

*'To The St Patrick's Institution'* and a third toast followed *'To the Reverend Spratt'*. Fr John was present, returned thanks and delivered a speech which was often interrupted by loud applause as he proposed the toast to Tom Steele.[2]

Later that year there was another public dinner in support of the Carmelite Free Schools, one that was significant for several reasons relevant to Carmelite and to national history alike.   For Carmelite history, and for the life of John Spratt, its significance lay in the fact that there was now no mention of St Patrick's Free Schools as such: indeed, the earlier dinner, in January 1831, seems to have been the final occasion when that title of St Patrick's would appear on the public record.   As shall emerge later, it would seem that St Patrick's Free Schools ceased to exist by that name in the course of 1831, apparently subsumed in a different educational entity, St Andrew's, under John Spratt's management.

In terms of national history, this later dinner, held on Wednesday 9th November 1831, for an assembly of 120 patrons, was notable. It was presided over jointly by Daniel O'Connell, the Carmelite Provincial

---

2.   *FJ*, 27th Jan 1831.

Thomas Coleman, and the Dublin Prior, William Kinsella. It proved to be a great success financially and, it would seem, socially: Friars Coleman and Kinsella were promptly called upon to render a few songs. Fr Kinsella declined, but Fr Coleman brought the house down with his rendition of some unnamed, humorous lyric which he delivered *'in excellent style'*.[3] More to the point, the occasion was highly significant politically. It took place during a critical transition period in O'Connellite politics, in the wake of the securing of Catholic Emancipation. Over the course of 1830-31, O'Connell became immersed in the great British and Irish struggle for parliamentary and electoral reform in particular and for political reform more generally. At the same time, he was also seriously considering the launch of a new campaign to secure the Repeal of the Act of Union. He chose this meeting of support for the Carmelites to announce his intention to establish a 'National Political Union' as a means to galvanise his countrymen for political reform. Pointing out how Ireland had suffered economically under the British Parliament, he deplored Ireland's economic decline. Indicating his growing alignment with Britain's radical democrats, he proposed a toast *'To The Reformers of England and the Cause of Reform'*. Following upon this, he then gave evidence of his close bond with the Carmelites. Rising to propose a toast *'To The Carmelite Free Schools and the Head of the Order, my excellent friend, Dr Coleman'*, he went on to recall how, eleven years before, in 1820, he had presided at the institution of the charity dinner for their schools where, now, some 400 to 500 boys and girls were receiving the benefits of a moral and literary education. He remarked upon the irony of history whereby, after three or four centuries of persecution, the Carmelites were now getting back to the point where *'their predecessors were obliged to terminate their activity in the works of charity and religion'*. After a pause, during which Fr Coleman rose to thank and to toast O'Connell, the latter launched into a long speech. Trenchantly, he referred to the injustice done to the religious orders by the punitive clauses of the Catholic Emancipation Act: they *'were singled out as the only persons unfit to share in the contemplated benefits of the Relief Bill, a gratuitous insult offered by a contemptible prejudice'*.[4] He went on to call for parliamentary and municipal reform, the secret ballot, and, above all, *'to see Irishmen governed*

3. *DMR*, 10th Nov 1831; *FJ*, 11th Nov 1831.
4. *FJ*, 11th Nov 1831.

*by Irishmen'.* Parliamentary and electoral reform was achieved two years later, and O'Connell's energy in politicising the Irish people certainly bore fruit in the case of John Spratt and his Dublin confreres: they, having secured the right to vote, through the Great Reform Act of 1832, endeavoured to exercise it thereafter, as shall emerge later.

### The Carmelite Schools from 1820

Interestingly, John does not appear to have been present at this historic dinner in support of the Carmelite Schools, no more than he had been present at their foundation since the latter happened at a time when the young friar was still in Spain. The foundation of these schools in 1820, unnoticed in the local or the national press of the time, was recorded by Fr Henry Young in his *Catholic Directory for the Year 1821*, when that illustrious Jesuit wrote:

> In St Andrew's Parish is the Calced or Grand Carmelite Convent, French-Street...St Patrick's General Free Schools, opened in October 1820, in Cuffe Lane, at the rear of French-street Chapel under the direction of the Revd Gentlemen of the Convent, Guardians; in which an unlimited number of poor children of that quarter of the city are educated and carefully instructed in the principles of morality, in a day, evening and Sunday School.[5]

This foundation date of 1820 was corroborated by O'Connell in his speech at the November 1831 charity dinner. It is noteworthy, especially in an age of growing sectarian animosity in Dublin, that these St Patrick's General Free Schools were, *'from their infancy'*, conducted *'without parochial or religious distinction'.*[6] The first-ever public appeal in their support, made in January 1821, revealed that they aspired to cater for some 400 boys, taught on Lancasterian principles and attending from 10 a.m. until 3 p.m. daily. Remarkably, a further 400, it was asserted, were taught from 6 to 9 p.m. in the evening, and, in addition, some 400 girls were taught on Sundays, by *'a schoolmistress perfectly qualified to undertake their charge'.*[7]

---

5. P. Cunningham, 'The Catholic Directory for 1821', *Reportorium Novum*, vol. 2, No. 2, 1960, p. 334.
6. *DMR*, 13th Jan 1821. It is not clear in what manner this foundation differed from the French Street-Cuffe Lane School of circa 1806-08, as mentioned in Chapter Three; one hazards that the earlier venture may have faltered at some point.
7. Ibid.

Conditions in these premises must have been fairly grim as, in 1824, they were described as being *'in a dilapidated state, so that up to one third of the 300 to 400 could not be accommodated that winter'*.[8] By the end of that decade the Carmelites feared that they would have to close the schools unless additional funding were forthcoming.[9] Although not present at the foundation, John was, throughout the 1820s, active in support of St Patrick's. As early as October 1823 he preached the evening charity sermon.[10] He did so again in 1825, 1826, 1827, and in his new Whitefriar Street Church in September 1828. He was the sole member of the Dublin Carmelite community to have done so in that decade. It says much about his energy and commitment to note how widespread was the advertising of the Schools' charity functions in the local and national press during those years. On the occasion in 1828, his brother, Michael, and Daniel O'Connell acted as donation collectors.[11]

## *A Carmelite School for Girls*

Whereas down to 1823, the girls of St Patrick's were taught only on Sundays, the Carmelites were hoping, through their 1823 appeal, to provide daily schooling for the girls *'of the numerous poor of the neighbourhood'*.[12] It may not be clear when exactly it was that the Carmelites realised this hope. It is noteworthy that late in 1823 they issued the following invitation:

> St Patrick's general free School for Female Children to be established in the neighbourhood of French Street. His Grace the Most Revd Doctor Murray, Patron. The friends of this new institution respectfully Solicit the honor of Your company at their first Dinner on Monday the 29th of December 1823, At
> ............
>
> Dr Tuomy in the Chair
> Tickets 10s Deposit 5s
> Dinner on the table at 5.30 precisely.[13]

---

8. *DEP*, 2nd Oct 1824.
9. *DMR*, 6th Feb 1829.
10. *DEP*, 2nd Oct 1823.
11. *DMR*, 2nd Oct 1825, 10th Oct 1826, 7th Oct 1827, 24 Sept 1828.
12. *DEP*, 2nd Oct 1823.
13. GMA. I am grateful to Laura Magnier, GMA Archivist, for this reference. See L. Magnier, 'Recent find in the Archives', *Carmelite Contact*, Issue 32, 2015, p. 10.

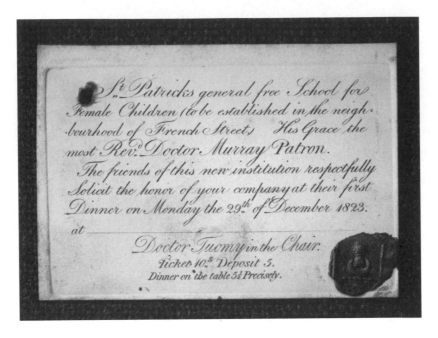

**Fig 20.**  *An invitation to Dinner.*

Consequently, it could well be that their hope began to be realised as early as the following year, 1824.

It is likely that this initiative was due to Fr John. It was around this time, it seems, that he had established his 'Roman Catholic Free School' in Whitefriar Street, in the Church of Ireland Parish of St Peter. The phrase and the reference were his own but there is conflicting evidence as to its origins.[14] John launched this enterprise on a wing and a prayer, financed by modest contributions from his friends, his confreres Coleman, Kinsella and McCarthy, and even from his father, James: in the accounts for 1829 there is listed a contribution of £5 from his father who had died in December 1828.

Just how many Carmelite premises or schools were involved at this point is unclear: in 1824 O'Connell's Catholic Association had launched a nationwide investigation into the nature and extent of Catholic schooling in Ireland and into the sources of funding for this. Circulars were sent out to various clergy. John Spratt's letter of response was

---

14.  GMA, *Accounts of Whitefriar Street Church and Schools*, p. 91. For the conflict of evidence, see *Appendix 6: The Carmelite and other Schools of the Whitefriar Street neighbourhood in the 1820s: some problems of evidence.*

read out at a meeting of the Association in April 1824. Here he stated that

> There were two schools belonging to French Street Chapel. In one of the schools 300 boys received religious instruction, and, in the other, 100 girls. They received no assistance from the Kildare Place Society.[15]

The various modest donations and the penny contributions from such pupils as could afford them, were not sufficient to make ends meet. By 1827 his schools had placed him in debt to the then sum of £100.[16] Some relief came by way of a bequest of £14 per annum *To The Roman Catholic Schools of the Parish*. This gift, from a person named Carey, possibly Archdeacon Oliver Carey of Elphin, came through the good offices of the Church of Ireland Archdeacon of Dublin, John Torrens. Torrens seems to have been well-disposed to Spratt and the Carmelites: he was Rector of St Peter's Parish and a neighbour of theirs, with an address at 38 Aungier Street. It may well be believed that he was embarrassed and dismayed when, a year before this, he had become embroiled in the unseemly row about the Burials Question as it erupted over the funeral of Arthur D'Arcy. In late 1824 he paid a courtesy visit to St Patrick's School, a month after the Carmelites reported that it was in *'a dilapidated state'*, and gave a practical donation of bricks and slates.[17] After his death, in June 1851, the administration of Carey's bequest would be conducted through Archdeacon Torrens' son, the Rev J H Torrens. This bequest was acknowledged in Spratt's school accounts in that year.

Debt-ridden as John's school project was, he struggled on until he was partly rescued by an unexpected development. A little more than two weeks after O'Connell had aided the Carmelites in raising money through their charity dinner, the government appointed a new permanent body, the Commissioners of National Education, on 26th November 1831. The previous September, Edward Stanley, Chief Secretary at Dublin Castle, had secured a parliamentary grant of £30,000 to fund a national system of undenominational primary

---

15. *Waterford Mail*, 21st Apr 1824, citing an undated report in the *Dublin Evening Express*.
16. GMA, *Accounts*, pp. 96-97.
17. *FJ*, 2nd Nov 1824; *DEP*, 2nd Oct 1824 for the report on 'dilapidation'.

education for Ireland. Although a significant minority of the Catholic bishops would later oppose the system, it proved a godsend for a great body of the poorer Irish Catholics and Protestants. It was certainly a godsend for John Spratt as he struggled with his school foundation. It helped him morally that his own Archbishop, Daniel Murray, was a keen supporter of the scheme and became one of the most actively committed of its Commissioners. It helped financially in that Fr John could now apply for funding towards the running costs of the school.

At the end of the year 1831, Fr John Spratt and the Church of Ireland's Reverend John H. Robertson of Queen Street, jointly signed an application for funding support, to the newly appointed Commissioners of National Education. It was submitted as an application *'of the 1st class'* – that is, an application jointly made by clergy of two separate denominations. Their application was submitted for a St Andrew's School, founded for females in 1824, and now with 150 pupils on its rolls. It may well have been the school for girls that the Carmelites had publicly expressed their hopes for, at the charity dinner of October 1823.[18]

### The National Education System to the rescue

Fr John Spratt's and the Rev J H Robertson's application was successful: on 13th April 1832 their St Andrew's School was formally taken into connexion by the Board of National Education and was assigned the Roll No 754.[19] The Reverend Robertson died in or about the year 1834 and, at some stage soon after that, St Andrew's appears to have bifurcated. By the end of March 1835 the Commissioners were reporting two of their recognised schools in the parish: the original female one, now with 235 girls with a single named teacher, and a New Model School of 394 pupils and three teachers which was subsequently

18. Parl. Papers, H. C. 1831-32 (445), *A Return of the number of applications to the Board of Education for new schools under their system, or for assistance in behalf of schools already established*, p. 10; and NAI, *ED* 2/150/12, Roll 754. This St Andrew's is not to be confused with a school of the same name in Townsend Street, in the Parish of St Mark's.

19. NAI, *ED* 2/148/80. Interestingly, St Patricks' Free Schools seem to have 'disappeared' or to have been subsumed into this entity, since there is no mention of St Patrick's in any of the education files of the Commissioners, nor in the Parliamentary papers or the national press after the two single mentions of January and October 1831 in the Dublin newspapers.

relocated to become the famous Marlborough Street Model School.[20]
A different parliamentary return of the same year, 1835, reported two
separate schools under the name 'St Andrew's', in St Peter's Parish.
Firstly, there was recorded a St Andrew's with 324 scholars under the
management of a Committee of *'The Misses Healy and Spratt'*, with the
latter named as Manager, and to whom was remitted the cost of £15
per annum for teacher salary, together with a grant of £2-5s-3½ᵈ for
school supplies.[21] Secondly, there was reported a St Andrew's under the
management of the Rev. John H. Robertson.[22] By the year 1837, while
these schools of St Peter's Parish were again being recorded separately,
that managed by Fr John was actually listed as *'St Andrew's – Spratt's'*.[23]

From the earliest years of his joining the National System Fr
John employed one Bridget Whelan – certainly from 1834.[24] Paid
£15 per year, she served until November 1840 when she moved to St
Catherine's in Meath Street.[25] She and her Carmelite manager worked
in difficult conditions. An inspector noted in 1836 that, because of
the poor condition of the school, the numbers attending had declined.
Three years later he complained that *'the apartment in which the school is
held is in a most wretched, ruinous and dirty state'* and there were threats of
salary discontinuance if matters were not mended.[26] The threat was not
carried out but it may have been enough for Bridget Whelan to make
her move, as the number of enrolments went into a decline from 156
in March 1836 down to 84 in March 1838 and to 81 by March 1839. Fr
John somehow managed to replace her with one Phebe [sic] Herbert in
March 1838 and then secured Mary Elizabeth Kearns in Phebe's place
in March 1839. It is not evident that the physical environment had
improved but school enrolments rose. It would be happy, perhaps, to
think that the enhanced enrolments reflected an improvement in the

20. Parl. Papers, H. C. 1835 (300), *Second Report of the Commissioners of National Education in Ireland for the year ending 31 March 1835*, p. 34.
21. Parl. Papers, H. C. 1835 (390), *Return of books, schools and of Roman Catholic, Protestant and children of other denominations, under the superintendence of the Commissioners of National Education*, p. 5.
22. Ibid, p. 55.
23. Parl. Papers, H.C 1837 (483), *Report of the Select Committee on the Plan of Education for Ireland*, p. 590.
24. NAI, *ED*, 4/1, *Salary Payments*, 1834-1836.
25. NAI, *ED*, 2/15/17.
26. Ibid.

teaching: certainly Miss Kearns stayed with St Andrew's and John Spratt until at least April 1843, and perhaps until September 1846 when one Mary Lennon was appointed around the period of a change of name and location.[27]

Although originally, and by designation, a girl's school, by the end of March 1838 it was reported as having enrolled some 13 boys in addition to its 80 girls. This girls' school, with Spratt as manager, was still recorded as such in January 1839 and would retain this formal designation for eight years to follow, even though the number of boys enrolled grew steadily. As 1839 proceeded, its numbers rose steadily from 44 boys and 72 girls, until by October 1842 the enrolments stood at 114 boys and 149 girls.[28]

*From St Andrew's to St Peter's*

In the course of the earlier 1840s Spratt's St Andrew's experienced growing numbers of pupils and an increasing number of boys among them. By the end of 1844, still with a sole government-salaried teacher, his school had 206 pupils, with 88 boys and 118 girls.[29] By now, hopelessly overcrowded, on 21st October 1845 the Education Board's superintendent reported the removal of the teachers, children and equipment *'to a more eligible situation'* in Whitefriar Street and with a request for permission to change its name from St Andrew's to St Peter's. This request was granted in October 1846. The National Education Commissioners' *Thirteenth Report, for the year 1846*, noted that *'St Andrew's (Spratt's)'* was also known as *'St Andrew's No. 2 Female'* and that it had now become St Peter's, with its relocation in Whitefriar Street.[30] A month before this approval, Spratt secured a new senior teacher, Mary Lennon, who worked for him for six years until July 1852. In the same month as the sanction for name change, he also secured an assistant teacher, Julia Whitty, at £8 per annum.[31] In May 1849 he

27. NAI, *ED* 2/15/177, *St Andrew's Female, Now St Peter's Whitefriar Street.*
28. Parl. Papers, H. C 1839 (429) *Education* (Ireland) pp. 66-67; H.C. 1840 (246), *Sixth Report of the Commissioners*, p. 49; H.C. 1842 (353), *Seventh Report of the Commissioners... for the year 1840*, p. 64; NAI, *ED* 2/15/17.
29. Parl. Papers, H. C. 1844 (569), *Tenth Report of the Commissioners*, p. 77; H.C. 1845 (650), *Appendix to the Eleventh Report of the Commissioners..*, p. 61.
30. Parl. Papers, H. C. 1847 (32), *Thirteenth Report...*, p. 91.
31. NAI, *ED* 2/15/177 and 2/15/17; Parl. Papers, H.C. 1847 (32), *Thirteenth Report...*, p. 91

obtained a new head teacher in the very youthful, nineteen-year-old Elizabeth Taylor who had qualified in February 1848. By the mid-1850s she would head up a team of five teachers in this school, on a salary of £16 a year and for at least another decade she would be paid various additional gratuities for training up new teachers and mentors.[32] In the course of 1847 John Spratt's education project finally resolved itself into two distinct schools for boys and girls. His girls' school retained its original 1831 roll number, 754, and a newly-designated boys' school, commencing on 15th March 1847, became school number 5008, under his management also. By the end of the 1840s these two schools had now enrolled a remarkable 611 girls and 631 boys.[33] For his new boys' school he employed a thirty-five-year-old Patrick Lyons who had trained in Marlborough Street and had previously taught in Carlow and Wicklow. Spratt employed Lyons on trust that the Commissioners would recognise him and agree to pay his salary, which they did as of 3rd June 1847.[34] Unlike the adversely critical reports visited upon the girls' school in the 1830s, this one, built by private subscription – in the middle of the Great Famine – was described by Inspector McDermott, in April 1847, as being *'in good order...built of brick and slates...sufficiently ventilated and warmed'*. Of its original 250 boys, some 50 were taught free while the remainder paid a penny a week.[35] Finally, on 27th August 1850 John could report that he had signed a lease to take over the Old Methodist Meeting House in Whitefriar Street – in a dilapidated state – and immediately commenced a collection in order to fit it out as a new school for the female children of the neighbourhood.[36] By the end of the 1840s, at last, John Spratt in his educational endeavours, could begin to look forward to better days, having, for over 25 years, soldiered on doggedly through tough times endured.

32. NAI, *ED* 1/29/90 and 2/150/12.
33. Parl. Papers, H. C. 1849 (1066), *The Fifteenth Report...for the year 1848*, p. 91.
34. NAI, *ED* 1/29/23, Application St Peter's Male, Whitefriar Street, 4th March 1847; and *ED* 2/16/30.
35. NAI, *ED* 1/29/23.
36. GMA, *Accounts of Whitefriar Street Church and Schools*, pp. 139 ff.

**Fig 21.** *The Old Methodist Meeting House in Whitefriar Street.*

# CHAPTER SEVEN

---

## *Travels, Titles, Troubles, 1830–1839*

The years as prior, church-builder, educator and fundraiser from 1823 doubtless took their toll. On 1st February 1834 John Spratt sought permission from Prior General Calamata to travel to Rome. His first request, based on grounds of ill-health, received a brief but friendly and positive reply.[1] For reasons unclear, he felt it necessary to ask a second time, now saying that it was partly because of health difficulties and partly because *'he had some business to transact with the Holy See'*.[2] Precisely what this 'business' was is not clear. However, from Calamata's second reply, on 11th June 1834, it would appear that there was concern about abuses in the Order in Ireland which, Calamata observed, *'were scandalous even to the seculars'*.[3] He added he was hopeful that the Provincial's *'prudence and zeal'* would *'uproot'* them, and he agreed, in principle, that Spratt be allowed to travel, subject to the Provincial's consent. This consent must have been forthcoming as, on 15th June 1834, Calamata gave formal approval.[4]

Spratt was armed with letters of introduction from Archbishop Murray, from Michael Hughes, the Prior of Kildare, and from W J Whelan, Vicar Provincial of the Discalced Carmelites. Later on, in February 1836, this Discalced friend and future Bishop of Bombay, supplied an additional one.[5] He left Dublin shortly after chairing a

---

1. GMA, Calamata to Spratt, 15th March 1834.
2. O'Dwyer, *Dissertation*, p. 35.
3. GMA, Calamata to Spratt, 11th June 1834.
4. GMA, Calamata to Spratt, 15th June 1834.
5. GMA, *Scrapbook A*, 6th Feb 1836, William J Whelan (1798-1876).

meeting of the Cholera Orphan Society at the end of October 1835[6] and travelled via Liverpool and London to Brussels where he visited the national cathedral of Saints Michael and Gudula. From there he travelled to Waterloo and thence on to Cologne and Milan where he viewed the cathedral of St Charles with its great stained glass choir window. He arrived in Rome on 15th December 1835.[7] Here he was welcomed by his Prior General and he stayed in the principal Carmelite house in the city. Another of his contacts there was Cardinal Thomas Weld.[8] The Cardinal was held in high regard by the Holy See, being one of its principal advisors on English affairs.[9] Weld, who famously carried kindness to a fault, provided Spratt with transport during his stay in Rome. He may well have been one of that distinguished congregation who heard Spratt preach at the Chiesa dei Santi Nomi di Gesù e Maria, the principal Jesuit church on the Via del Corso, on 28th February 1836.[10] What subject he chose for his sermon on the occasion is not

**Fig 22.** *The facade and pulpit of Chiesa dei Santi Nomi di Gesù e Maria, Rome.*

6. *FJ*, 27th Oct 1835.
7. Battersby, *Catholic Directory for the year 1837*, p. 267.
8. The eldest of fourteen children of the English Catholic landowner of Lulworth Castle, Dorset, who, in 1794, had freely given land in Stonyhurst, Lancashire, for the Jesuit foundation there: see F. J. Turner, 'Thomas Weld (1750-1810), landowner and benefactor', in *Oxford Dictionary of National Biography*, Oxford 2004-15.
9. R. Mitchell, 'Thomas Weld, (1773-1837), Cardinal', in *Oxford Dictionary of National Biography*, Oxford 2004-15.
10. Battersby, 1837, p. 268.

recorded but he clearly made a favourable impression where it mattered. Calamata honoured him with the position Titular Provincial of England and France for three years.[11] This was, perhaps, a consolation prize for not having been made Irish Provincial when, four years before, he had urged the Prior General to make a good appointment to that office. This honour excited envy or resentment in at least one of his clerical contemporaries: Fr John Nicholson complained to Dublin Diocesan Archdeacon John Hamilton against Spratt *'undeservingly'* getting the honour when he himself had been refused. Writing from London, this disgruntled Discalced Carmelite, and future Bishop of Corfu, did not mince his words:

> Mr. Spratt was made Provincial of England a few months ago by his General or by the Pope, upon his showing some necessity for personal Protection or comfort. That was not strictly according to rule, as there are none of his Order in England, but the Appointment carries with it what confers that protection. There is an example, and for a second time, in the very same person... But God's will be done.[12]

As a further mark of esteem, Pope Gregory XVI provided him the gift of the body of St Valentine for the Church of Mount Carmel in Whitefriar Street. John left Rome after 8th April 1836 and visited the historic Carmelite foundation of Loreto. Here, according to tradition, the house of the Holy Family was preserved after its translation from the Holy Land. On leaving Italy he visited Amiens, Rouen and Paris before travelling to London and arriving in Dublin in May.[13] For the rest of his life, he rarely ventured out of Dublin except on missions connected with the temperance movement.

*From Rome to Dublin – the remains of St Valentine*
The most enduring result of John Spratt's visit was undoubtedly the procuring of the remains of St Valentine, and later the securing of the indulgences related to his devotion. Much uncertainty attaches to

11.  GMA, Calamata to Spratt, 7th Apr 1836.
12.  DDA, *Hamilton Papers*, 35/6/54, Nicholson to Hamilton, 28th June 1836; the underlining is in the original. For details of Nicholson's life see P. MacSuibhne, *Paul Cullen and his contemporaries*, vol. 2, Naas 1962, pp. 380-382.
13.  *The Pilot*, 23rd May 1836.

**Fig 23.** *The relics of St Valentine at Whitefriar Street Church.*

the person or persons of St Valentine as there is debate as to who he was or how many St Valentines there may have been.[14]  The generally accepted traditional account is that he was a priest martyred in Rome on the Flaminian Way on 14th February 269, in the reign of Emperor Claudius II and that he was buried in the Cemetery of Hippolytus, off the Tiburtine Way.  The cult that developed around St Valentine in the later Middle Ages associated him with romantic or courtly love.

Upon his remains being exhumed, Spratt ensured that their translation and installation in the church in Whitefriar Street was attended with great ceremonial.  At mid-morning on Thursday 10th November 1836 an assembly of some forty robed priests, with Archbishop Murray at their head, received at the great gate of the Church, the remains of St Valentine encased in a special casket.  To the chanting of the Litany of the Saints, they processed down the aisle where friars Coleman, Kinsella, Colgan and Spratt received the relic and placed it on an elevation at the High Altar.  Thereupon, Spratt ascended to the pulpit, announced the indulgences pertaining, and preached the inaugural sermon of the rite.  Then, with Andrew Day as high priest, Michael

---

14.  One traditional account has him as Bishop of Terni, north-east of Rome, where a basilica is named in his honour, after he was martyred for his activities in converting people to Christianity.

Tobin as deacon and William Withers as sub-deacon, the Archbishop celebrated the Pontifical High Mass, all the while supported by the choir of St Andrew's, Westland Row.[15]

Given the temper of the time, it is not surprising that this inaugural event, and its later commemorations, attracted the ridicule of the ultra-protestant press: the latter did not hold back in pouring its scorn on John Spratt, the Carmelites and the veneration of St Valentine. Coming up to his February feast day, in 1837, the *Dublin Evening Packet and Correspondent* commented:

> It may be interesting to our readers to know that St Valentine the Martyr, besides this body which is now in Dublin, has a head in the Church of St Sebastian; another body at Boulogne; another head at the Abbey of Jumieges; half body at Milan; another body, almost entire, at Melun; and detached arms at Macerata, at the Abbey of St Denis de Mons, at the Escurial [sic] and in other places...The Church of Rome has an ingenious way of defending her absurd veneration for these quadruple-bodied, and quintuple-headed martyrs.[16]

A year later, the *Dublin Evening Mail*, on the occasion of the saint's day, launched a bitter editorial attack on '*the odious superstition*' around it.[17] Such ridicule hardly deterred the friars. Having inaugurated the proceedings in November 1836 – rather than on 14th February – a first commemoration festival was held a year later in October 1837, to remember the translation of the remains.[18] A year later again, the friars – possibly John Spratt himself – issued a publication entitled *Devotions in honour of St Valentine*.[19] Four years after the publication of the *Devotions*, that commemoration was still observed, on 8th November 1842.[20] How far the religious devotions to St Valentine may

15. *Kennedy's British and Irish Catholic Magazine*, No. 3, Dec 1836, cited in *DEPC*, 4th Feb 1837.
16. Idem.
17. *DEM*, 9th Feb 1838.
18. Battersby, *Catholic Directory for the year 1838*, p. 431.
19. *Devotions in honour of St Valentinus, Martyr, whose sacred body is deposited in the Carmelite Church, Whitefriar Street*, 8 pp., Dublin 1838. The only currently-known extant copy is in the Haliday Collection, Royal Irish Academy, Dublin. The work is without a named author and has no preface or introduction.
20. Battersby, *Catholic Directory for the year 1844*, p. 365.

have developed thereafter in Whitefriar Street Church is not clear. As late as December 1846 one journal inquired, in mocking tones, *'whatever has happened to the bones of St Valentine about which there was such a fuss a few years ago?'.*[21] As a religious occasion, presumably it continued to be marked there in a quiet, restrained way, but certain it was that it ceased to engage the interest of the press, hostile or otherwise. For the rest of the century their reporting on St Valentine's Day was cursory and generally confined to noticing the growing volume of mail handled by the Post Office in succeeding years.

## A Favour to a Friend

Fr Spratt was not long back in Ireland, having secured the favours of the Pope, when he himself was sought out to secure a significant public favour for another. The request came from the Franciscan friar, Michael Anthony Fleming, Bishop of St John's, Newfoundland. One of the most important figures in the political and religious development of Newfoundland in the nineteenth century, Fleming was a Carrick-on-Suir man who joined the Franciscan Order in 1808, at the age of sixteen. Ordained in 1815, he went as a curate to serve on the Newfoundland mission in 1823. In 1830, in succession to his uncle, Thomas Callan, he was appointed bishop.[22] Through his energy, persistence and persuasiveness over the next twenty years he transformed the fortunes of the Catholic Church there by successfully recruiting priests, nuns and religious brothers from Ireland, building schools and churches, and crowning his achievements by commencing the construction of the massive St John's Cathedral.[23]

In pursuit of these aims he visited Ireland, England and Rome on several occasions to lobby, to recruit and to raise funds. Despite the arduous journey entailed, he returned on recruiting missions to Ireland nine times in nineteen years, for the first time in 1828 and for the last

---

21. *DEPC,* 3rd Dec 1846.

22. J. B. Darcy, *Fire upon the Earth: the life and times of Bishop Michael Anthony Fleming, O.S.F.,* St John's Newfoundland 2003; R. J. Lahey, 'Fleming, Michael Anthony, 1792-1850' in *Dictionary of Canadian Biography,* vol. 2, 1836-1850, Toronto 2003-2005.

23. Darcy, p. 160.

in 1847.[24] Apart from direct visits to seminaries, convents and friaries in the quest for volunteers, he contacted leading clergy in Ireland. This was the context in which Bishop Fleming first approached John Spratt. It says much for Spratt's public standing that he became the first clergyman to whom Fleming wrote, with requests for the correspondence to be printed. Until 1844 and Fleming's correspondence with Fr Andrew O'Connell, Spratt

**Fig 24.** *Bishop Michael A. Fleming.*

appears to have been the only one who actually secured such publication for his supplicant.[25] It was as early as September and October 1834 that Fleming addressed Spratt on 'Newfoundland' and 'Religion in Newfoundland'.[26] How long Spratt and Fleming were acquainted is not certain but at the end of Fleming's third visit home, in 1833, Spratt had presented him with a gift of books, and the latter now referred to *'the ardent friendship you have testified to me'* and to *'the deep interest you have been pleased to take in the mission of Newfoundland'*.[27] In appreciation, Fleming now gave Spratt an account of his own experiences on that mission from his arrival in 1823 until his consecration as bishop on 28th Oct 1829. He told how he had prevailed on the Presentation Sisters in Galway to send out five nuns who established a school catering for 850 pupils, the whole cost of this enterprise being paid for by Fleming out of his own pocket. Consequently, he hoped the Irish people might

---

24. The years of his visits appear to have been 1828, 1830, 1839, 1836, 1837, 1840, 1842, 1843 and 1847.

25. Apart from Fleming's *Letters on the state of religion in Newfoundland, addressed to the Very Rev. Dr A O'Connell, PP*, Dublin 1844, Spratt's editions of Fleming's letters are the only ones that were published in the Irish newspaper press.

26. M. A. Fleming, 'Religion in Newfoundland' and 'Newfoundland' : two letters to the Very Reverend John Spratt, Dublin, 24th Sept, 8th Oct 1834, in *Most Important Letters of the Right Rev Dr Fleming, Catholic Bishop of Newfoundland to the Very Rev John Spratt of Aungier Street on the state of religion in that country*, 16 pp., Dublin 1835.

27. Ibid, pp. 1-2.

send money for the mission or to remember this cause in their wills.[28]
He concluded his second letter, on 8th October, 1834, having given an
account of the nuns' and of his own journeys through the island, with
expressions of affectionate regard to Daniel O'Connell and to Spratt's
Carmelite confreres of Whitefriar Street.

They maintained that correspondence over the next three years.
The most substantial body of this correspondence for which Fleming
privately urged Spratt to secure publication, appeared in print as a series
of five letters over the period August and September 1836.[29]  It was
in the first of these, dated London 28th July 1836, that he thanked
Spratt for a further gift of some 400 volumes: whether or not this was
a personal gift from Spratt's own resources or one made through the
auspices of the Catholic Book Society is not clear; however, it may be
significant that, during his October 1836 visit to Ireland, he was invited
to address the Catholic Society of Ireland – the distribution arm of
the Catholic Book Society.[30]  They organised a lavish public dinner for
him, chaired by the County Dublin M.P., Christopher Fitzsimon, a son-
in-law of Daniel O'Connell.  Fitzsimon was President of the Catholic
Society and, on this prominent public occasion, he had Fleming seated
to one side along with Spratt.  Some forty priests attended, along with
other worthies who included the *Morning Register*'s editor and proprietor,
Michael Staunton.

Fleming used this occasion to provide a detailed description of the
denominational and political difficulties that historically had beset the
Catholic Church in Newfoundland.  He recounted how, from the start
of his mission there, the number of churches had grown from six to
forty and the number of priests had increased from five to nineteen.
His last great ambition, and the object of his current visit to the United
Kingdom, was *'to secure a grant of waste land on which to erect a church, a
schoolhouse, a convent and a residence for the clergy'*.[31]  The church he now had
in mind was actually a cathedral.  He had come to England to lobby
the Colonial Secretary, Charles Grant, Lord Glenelg, on this matter.
Furthermore, he had recruited Spratt to do likewise.  Indeed, Spratt had
already done so, for on 15th August 1836 he had written to Sir George

28.  Ibid, pp 7-8.
29.  *DMR*, I, II, 20th Aug; *DWR*, 3rd, 17th Sept 1836.
30.  Darcy, p. 118.
31.  *DMR*, 20th Oct 1836.

**Fig 25.** *The Basilica Cathedral of St John the Baptist.*

Gray, Under-Secretary for the Colonies, to this end. Gray submitted this letter to his Superior, Glenelg,[32] and while it might be too much to assert that Spratt could claim a major share of the credit, nevertheless, Fleming's great quest was successful. He secured his site and on 20th May 1841 the foundation stone was laid for the great Cathedral of St John the Baptist, before a gathering of 20,000 people.[33] He lived to see the edifice take shape but died five years before its completion in 1855.

Between Fleming's first correspondence with Spratt in 1833 and these five letters of 1836, contact had been maintained and it is clear from the first of the five that Spratt had written to him from Dublin and from Rome.[34] Fleming's letters to Spratt revealed a considerable talent for clear, direct and engaging communication as he described the challenges of his mission and his journeying around the coast of Newfoundland. It was ironic, therefore, that when Spratt asked him, in the course of this Dublin visit, if he could oblige by preaching on behalf of the Sick and Indigent Roomkeepers Society, Fleming declined on the grounds that he was no orator, but he was not unappreciative of what Spratt had done for him:

> I thank you again and again for the trouble, the interest you take in my regard – I know well that you will not slacken in your exertions to advance the cause of religion in that interesting, although long-neglected colony.[35]

32. GMA, Gray to Spratt, 17th Aug 1836, in answer to Spratt's letter of 15th Aug.
33. Battersby, *Catholic Directory for the year 1842*, p. 408.
34. Most of the correspondence to Fleming up to the year 1842 was lost in the great fire which destroyed much of St John's in June of that year. See Darcy, pp. 239-241.
35. GMA, Fleming to Spratt, 18th Aug 1836.

Some months later, Fleming showed that appreciation in a most practical way. On 27th November 1836, John's mother, Esther Elizabeth, died at the family home in Cork Street: on Wednesday 30th November it was Bishop Fleming who presided at the funeral ceremony, receiving the remains *'with due solemnity at the great gate'* before they were *'deposited in a vault of the Church of Mount Carmel'*.[36]

### The Apostolate of the Pen

Apart from ensuring that Bishop Fleming's letters went into print, and despite the preoccupations of his Roman sojourn, Fr John still found time to resume his own writing. In 1835, he published *The Novena, or Nine Days' Devotion to the Seraphic Mother, Saint Teresa of Jesus*. This twenty-two page compendium he dedicated to his Archbishop, Daniel Murray, who had proven so supportive in preaching for the Sick and Indigent Roomkeepers Society and in accommodating Spratt with a testimonial for his Roman journey. Spratt was following a Carmelite tradition of commencing this devotion every year on 7th October, culminating with the feast day of the saint on the 15th. The prayers revolve around nine promises or resolutions towards moral reform, paralleling the nine privileges St Teresa reported on receiving through Christ in the course of her life.[37] In keeping with that Carmelite tradition, the novena prayers reference not only St Teresa but the Patriarch, St Elias. Equally, they stress that element of the fear of perdition that was to the fore in the age. There is now no direct means of knowing how popular this Novena may have become in the lives of those who attended the Church of Mount Carmel, but, doubtless, it contributed significantly to the liturgical tapestry of the Carmelite year in Whitefriar Street. The constant enrolments to membership of that Church's confraternity through the 1830s into the 1840s seem to point to a vibrant devotional life there at that time.[38]

Around the same time as this Novena publication, John produced a more substantial volume of devotional literature. This was *An Eulogium*

---

36.  *DEP*, 3rd Dec 1836.

37.  J. Spratt, *The Novena, or Nine Days' Devotion to the Seraphic Mother, Saint Teresa of Jesus*, 22 pp., J. Coyne, Dublin, n.d., c. 1835.

38.  GMA, *Ash Street Confraternity Book*: although this volume commences with Ash Street in the eighteenth century, it continues well into the nineteenth century following the moves to French Street and Whitefriar Street.

*on the Ever Blessed Virgin Mary of Mount Carmel.*[39] This seventy-two page work was published by the Catholic Book Society in 1835, and was adopted by the Catholic Society of Ireland, a body founded to promote the distribution of Catholic literature in general and the publications of the Catholic Book Society in particular.[40] Fr John dedicated this work to the Prior General, Aloysius Calamata, who led the Calced Carmelites from 1832 to 1838. It is possible that this work is a second edition of an original that he first published, perhaps circa 1832: this is not certain, but in February 1832 he received a letter of acknowledgement and thanks from Aloysius Scalabrini, Calamata's immediate predecessor. In that letter, Scalabrini mentioned receiving the gift of a volume from John via the hands of John's brother, James, who was then in Rome. Scalabrini did not mention the title of the work, but observed:

> By that Augustinian brother who is well-deserving of you, I have been favoured with the book written by Your Reverence....I have enjoyed your work and have admired your solicitude and zeal for promoting the devotion to our Mother Mary of Mount Carmel.[41]

The only other work of Spratt's on the subject of the Blessed Virgin, before 1832, had been his *Novena or Nine Days' Devotion* of 1824: it is unlikely that he would have presented this eight-year old pamphlet as a gift to his Prior General so long after its publication.

The *Eulogium*, florid in style but steeped in Old Testament allusions, stressed the concept of Our Lady as 'Mother of Carmelites' and the writer rejoiced that the *'sons of Carmel are called to be the privileged children'*. Indeed, with its emphasis on Carmelite history and references to St Simon Stock, the work has the appearance of an address to Carmelites or the devotees of the scapular.[42] The work expressly addresses itself to *'the illustrious order of Mount Carmel'* but the phrase may be meant to embrace Third Order or Confraternity members as much as the friars,

39. J. Spratt, *An Eulogium on the Ever Blessed Virgin Mary of Mount Carmel, chiefly from the Spanish*, 72 pp., Dublin 1835. In February 1846 Battersby published a new edition of this, entitled *A Panegyric on the Ever-Glorious and Blessed Virgin Mary, chiefly from the Spanish. By the Very Revd Dr Spratt*: see *FJ*, 17th Feb 1846.
40. Wall, loc.cit., p. 295.
41. GMA, Scalabrini to Spratt, 20th Feb 1832.
42. Spratt, *Eulogium*, p. 22.

especially since later it refers to an *'illustrious confraternity'* that in the course of history included *'kings and princes, joyful at wearing the scapular'*.[43] The work provides a long historical excursus on the obscure story of the Carmelites over the sixth to the tenth centuries before moving on to the story of the recovery of the Holy Land and later the revelations to St Simon. Written in a highly emotive style, it is fundamentally a celebration of the privilege of being Carmelite. The work coincided in time with another Carmelite publication entitled *The Subscribing members of the venerable confraternity of Our Blessed Lady of Mount Carmel, held in the Carmelite Convent, Whitefriar Street, Dublin.*[44] The publication of the two may have been linked.

Fr John's other publication in these years came in 1837. This was *The Sincere Christian's Manual of Devotion*, the publisher again being John Coyne. It was a substantial work of close on four hundred pages, consisting of prayers arranged mainly for use by members of the Sodality or Confraternity of the Holy Scapular.[45] The actual copy of this volume in the Carmelite Library of Gort Muire is in itself of considerable historical interest. Inside, a bookplate carries the Spratt family coat of arms, with the motto *Nunquam Non Paratus*. On the title page, in handwriting, is the inscription *'written for his young friend, Master J. Daniel O'Connell Spratt, by Daniel O'Connell M.P. for the County of Cork, 11th February 1845 Merrion Square, Dublin'*. Dedicated just over two years before O'Connell's death, the inscription on the volume gave witness to the close relationship between the Catholic faith and O'Connellite nationalism on the one hand and the close bond of friendship between John Spratt and Daniel O'Connell, on the other.

The work commences with a short seven-page exposition by Spratt on the nature of prayer and then, somewhat incongruously perhaps, a page on the sacrament of matrimony with a surprising attention to strictures concerning clandestine marriages.[46] Following a series of morning and night prayers, Spratt then provides a discourse on the nature and meaning of the Mass, together with guidance for serving a

43.  Ibid, pp. 10, 18.
44.  R.I.A. Haliday Tracts. 469/3.
45.  J. Spratt, *The Sincere Christian's Manual of Devotion, or selection of prayers arranged principally for the use of members of the Sodality of the Holy Scapular*, p. 29, Dublin 1837.
46.  Ibid, pp. 7-14.

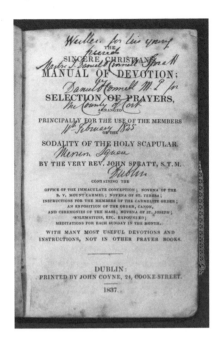

**Fig 26.** *Spratt's* Manual of Devotion, *with inscription by Daniel O'Connell.*

priest at Mass *'according to the ancient rite of the Holy Carmelite Order'.*[47] He
proceeds to provide devotions for Confessions and Holy Communion,
followed by an explanation of the major feast days of the Church's
year, with their attendant ceremonies.[48] He provides the text of three
novenas, to the Immaculate Virgin, to St Teresa and to St Joseph, as
well as the text of four litanies, of the Saints, of Divine Providence, of
the Blessed Sacrament, and of the Blessed Virgin. Finally, apart from
his description of the indulgences associated with the Carmelite Order
and with the veneration of St Valentine, he includes meditations for all
Sundays and prayers for the diverse circumstances of life. The work
constituted a *vade mecum* for the devout Christian, and certainly was one
of the most ambitious and comprehensive devotional compendiums
of its time.[49] The decade of these writings, however, was one which

---

47. Ibid, pp. 15-35, 39-47, 75-79.
48. Ibid, pp. 80-167.
49. For all that, the publishing history of this volume, after 1837, is not clear. How
many subsequent editions or reprints there may have been is not evident in the
standard catalogues such as those as the National Library of Ireland, the British
Library or the Library of Congress.

saw John committed even more widely than his literary, educational, charitable and pastoral endeavours indicated.

*A Priest in Politics*

Immediately in the wake of Catholic Emancipation, Archbishop Murray, with his fellow bishops, issued a pastoral on 9th February 1830, disavowing political activism or involvements for the future on the part of the clergy.[50] As though this counsel had been ignored, Murray spelled it out more explicitly in January 1834:

> We recommend to them [the clergy] most earnestly to avoid in future any allusion at their Altars to political subjects and carefully to refrain from connecting themselves with Political Clubs, acting as Chairmen or Secretaries at political meetings or moving or seconding resolutions on such occasions.[51]

It would appear that Fr. John, normally deferential in his dealings with archbishops, chose to ignore these admonitions. Whatever about his support or lack of support for O'Connell in the Catholic Association from the mid-1820s, from the moment of his taking part in the mission to prevent the anti-monastic provisions of the Catholic Relief Bill, he became a committed O'Connellite and nationalist, as did his brother Michael. When the reform of the electoral franchise was enacted in 1832, John Spratt was keen to exercise his vote and did so while he could, throughout the 1830s.

It was in the Dublin City election of December 1832 that he first cast his vote, not surprisingly for Daniel O'Connell and his running-mate, Edward Ruthven.[52] He had the satisfaction of seeing them successful. Interestingly, he was the sole Carmelite from the Whitefriar Street Community recorded as voting. He was exercising the £10 leaseholder qualification which may well explain why most of the rest of that

---

50. *DEP*, 11th Feb 1830 for the text. See also J. H. Broderick, SJ, *The Holy See and the Irish Movement for the Repeal of the Union with England, 1829-1847*, Rome 1951, pp. 45-47.

51. *DEP*, 18th Oct 1834: it was issued under Murray's name, on behalf of the entire hierarchy, on 28th January but did not appear in the press until 18th October 1834.

52. T. M. Ray, *A List of the Constituency of Dublin as registered prior to the City of Dublin Election in January 1835*, pp. 160, Dublin 1835, p. 141.

**Fig 27.** *Daniel O'Connell.*

friary did not vote – because they were not leaseholders. However, it does not explain why William Kinsella, then his senior in both years and office, did not vote, since Kinsella was a co-signatory of the lease with Spratt which they had signed with Patrick Campbell when they first leased the Whitefriar Street site from him. It would appear to be the case that, under the registration rules, joint leaseholders were enfranchised.[53] Whatever the reason, almost three years later again, in the election of January 1835 he was, once more, the only member of the friary either registered or recorded as voting – once again, for O'Connell and Ruthven.[54] He saw them triumphantly elected, only to see them unseated, on petition, in 1836. However, John Spratt turned out faithfully again in the summer of 1837, contributing his vote to the return of O'Connell and Robert Hutton.[55]

Fr John next presented himself for registration as a voter in November 1839 – on this occasion with an unhappier outcome. The registration officer refused to register him on the basis that John Spratt, although technically a leaseholder, did not personally possess a beneficial interest in the property but was, essentially, a kind of trustee.[56] A complex exchange ensued, with the registration officer putting it to him whether he had the power to sell his interest in Whitefriar Street.

53. This is a complex area and two of the contemporary expert commentators on the question were silent on the issue: see RIA, HP 1816, Anon, *The Irish Franchise and Registration Question*, London 1841, and RIA, HP 1643/7, E. Molyneux, *A practical Treatise of the law of elections in Ireland as altered by the Reform Act*, Dublin 1835; however, D. O'Connell, *Seven Letters on the Reform Bill and the law of elections in Ireland*, Dublin 1835, indicates that joint leaseholders with the relevant property qualification, were eligible to vote as a result of the 1832 Reform Act.
54. Ray, p. 141.
55. *SNL*, Tues 5th Nov 1839 contains a report of how Spratt voted two years before, in 1837.
56. Ibid.

Spratt replied that, in law, he could sell it but that in conscience he could not. On the latter basis the official ruled that Spratt in fact had not got a beneficial interest and so denied him the vote. It would appear that Fr John was not able to vote again, in parliamentary elections, until the *Representation of the People (Ireland) Act* of 1868 made it possible for him and indeed for the entire Carmelite community of Whitefriar Street to exercise the vote, through the 'lodger franchise', in the general election that November.[57]

The exercise of electoral interest and influence, however, was not confined exclusively to those who possessed the vote. Hoppen has shown just how strongly persuasive non-electors could be on the voting conduct of electors[58] and Spratt's political interest was not confined to the ballot box. This was evident from the outset of the 1830s. On 7th January 1830, at a meeting of collectors for the O'Connell Fund, he was prominent among those who subscribed and wrote a letter of support, as acknowledged by the Fund Secretary, Edward Dwyer.[59] Later that year, in September, controversy erupted around O'Connell's associate, 'Honest Jack' Lawless over allegations that he had accepted £2,000 from his opponent to stand down as a candidate for the Meath County constituency. A group of prominent O'Connellites called a public meeting in defence of Lawless. Here too, John Spratt and his brother Michael, were to the fore as signatories, in the company of leading figures like the Thunder brothers, Andrew and Michael, and other wealthy or influential O'Connellites such as Richard Corballis, Lawrence Finn, Patrick Lavelle, James Devereux, Michael Staunton and Richard Barrett.[60] It is noteworthy that Spratt was the only clergyman among the fifty-one signatories of the requisition.

Six years later, O'Connell, on 16th July 1836, established a new political body, the General Association of Ireland. Its objects were to maintain support in Ireland for the Whig-Liberal administration of Lord Melbourne, in order to achieve reform of the tithes and

---

57. NLI, *City of Dublin Election, 18th Nov 1868, List of Electors*, p. 71.

58. K. T. Hoppen, *Elections, Politics and Society in Ireland, 1832-1885*, Oxford 1984, pp. 71-73.

59. *FJ*, 8th Jan 1830. He signed himself as 'The Very Rev. John Spratt, M.S.O.B.V.M.' and was fifth in the list of those whose names were read out.

60. *DEP*, 4th Sept 1830; *DEP & C*, 7th Sept 1830. On this occasion Spratt signed himself John Spratt, O.M.C.

municipal systems and to promote the registration of sympathetic voters.[61] Michael Spratt was in the very first list of subscribers to this organisation.[62] Days later, John Spratt was proposed for and admitted to its membership: O'Connell expressed his delight and pleasure at having amongst them a Carmelite Friar

> so distinguished for his piety and zeal as the Rev. Mr. Spratt... he could not forget that one of the honestest and most zealous friends of civil and religious liberty that the old Catholic Association could boast of was a gentleman of the Order to which Mr. Spratt belonged, his esteemed and much-lamented friend, the Rev. Mr. L'Estrange.[63]

A year later Fr John was involved in a meeting of the Liberal voters of St Peter's Parish, convened for the purpose of ensuring the election of O'Connell and Robert Hutton as MPs for the City of Dublin. A particular concern of this gathering was to secure the maximum registration of Liberal electors and John actually seconded a resolution to exhort every Liberal voter to ensure that their full range of municipal taxes had been paid so that their registration might not be refused. It was ironic, therefore, that two years later he himself would be denied the vote, as earlier mentioned. This, however, did not deter him from continuing his commitment to and taking an active part in support of O'Connell and his political agenda throughout the ensuing 1840s.[64]

*Friary Matters*
Notwithstanding all his charitable and political preoccupations, John did not escape the impact of familial concerns – whether it was the family of Carmel or the family of Cork Street. As to the Carmelite family of Whitefriar Street, on the surface little appeared to disrupt the routine of regular life in the course of the 1830s. The community remained small in its members and stable in its personnel. At the start of the 1830s they counted just seven friars: Coleman, Kinsella, Spratt,

61. G. Lyne, *The General Association of Ireland, 1836-1837*, MA thesis, UCD, NUI, 1968.
62. *DMR*, 12th Aug 1836.
63. *DEP*, 9th Aug 1836. L'Estrange was actually a member of the Order of Discalced Carmelites.
64. See Chapter Nine.

Day, Colgan, Tobin and Withers. The arrival of Edward O'Rourke brought their number to eight in the course of the year 1835[65] and not until the later 1840s did the numbers increase to 10 friars. In the context of such size, the Carmelites' hope for a novitiate in Dublin, as expressed in the early 1820s, had little prospect of realisation even though the cost of sending their young men to novitiate in Spain or Italy constituted a considerable burden.

As to the leadership of the Order in Dublin, Fr. Coleman's three-year term as Provincial would normally have ended in 1832, but, as noted earlier, his Prior General extended it for a further year. In 1833, then, he was succeeded by the Whitefriar Street Prior, William Kinsella. When Fr Kinsella's term concluded in 1836, Friar John might well have entertained thoughts of preferment, but this was not to be: the role of prior fell to Andrew Day, even as Coleman became Provincial.[66] Thomas Coleman died at the relatively young age of 52 on 16th November 1837,[67] and was succeeded by Kinsella until 1840. On 5th March of 1840 the 39 year-old Dubliner, William Withers, was appointed Vicar Provincial with Richard Colgan succeeding Andrew Day as Dublin Prior. Withers bore his burden until the Chapter of 1843 almost unanimously elected Colgan as Provincial and Edward O'Rourke became Prior.[68] Clearly, over these thirteen years, there was no office for Fr Spratt.

## The Quest for Titles

If John could not gain office in Dublin he did not let matters rest and pressed for some kind of titled recognition. This came in April 1836 when Calamata made him Titular Provincial of England and France for three years.[69] Two years later, in one of his final acts before he stood down as Prior General, Calamata appointed Spratt as Commissary

65.  Battersby, *The Catholic Directory for the year 1836*, p. 82.
66.  O'Dwyer, *Irish Carmelites*, p. 203; Battersby, *Catholic Directory of the year 1838*, p. 288.
67.  *SNL*, 30th Nov 1837.
68.  Battersby, *Catholic Directory for the year 1845*, p. 226.
69.  O'Dwyer, *Irish Carmelites*, p. 207, citing GMA, *Scrapbook A*, p. 34: however, O'Dwyer, p. 212, note 197, cites a letter Spratt wrote to Joseph Palma, former Procurator General and later Prior General of the Order, to seek the title of Ex-Provincial: here Spratt claimed that it was in 1834 that he had been given the title Provincial of England and France and that two years later in 1836, he was given the title Commissary General of the Kingdom of England.

**Fig 28.**   *Aloysius Calamata, O.Carm.*        **Fig 29.**   *Pope Gregory XVI.*

General for England for a period of six years, from 27th April 1838: apparently he was concerned that the Prior General should have a personal representative for that country.[70] Although he would be busy enough in Dublin without this added responsibility, John's notebooks show he had developed an interest in the history of the Carmelite Order in late medieval England.[71] Nonetheless, no evidence has been encountered that Spratt ever did any practical work for the possible restoration of the Calced Carmelite Order in England. Apart from passing through the country on his journeys to and from Spain over 1816-1822 and Rome over 1835-1836, he never again set foot in England, with but three exceptions when, twice in 1846 and once in 1858, he made brief trips to Birmingham, Liverpool and London in the cause of temperance.[72] Nevertheless, he was not averse to using these titles in various situations and, of course, they gave him a certain status in the Irish Carmelite hierarchy.

These titular grants of 1836 and 1838 apparently did not suffice and Friar John appears to have been a discontented member of his community. So it might be deemed from a letter by Provincial William Withers to the Prior General in August 1842. Withers seems to have been a straightforward blunt man who did not mince his words. He gave an account of the state of the Province and of the ages and

---

70. GMA, Calamata to Spratt, 27th April 1838.
71. See GMA, Box 73, *Carmelite Convents in the reign of Henry VIII*.
72. See Chapter Eight, p. 39, Chapter Fifteen, p. 21.

conditions of its friars. Of Spratt, at this time, he wrote that he was one *'who has done more harm to the convent than can ever be undone'* but added *'now behaves better'*.[73] When the new Prior General, Joseph Palma, was elected to lead the Order in 1841, Spratt wrote to wish him well, and six months later he wrote requesting the title of Ex-Provincial.[74] If no positive response was forthcoming, success eventually attended his efforts: on 23rd January 1846, the Pope, following an audience with the Secretary for the Congregation of Bishops and Regulars, granted Spratt the title of Ex-Provincial and ordered the Irish Provincial Council to implement this.[75] Fr John lost little time in having it announced in the press, where a notice to this effect appeared on 21st March whereas it was not officially announced to his Carmelite community until the meeting of its Definitory on the 29th of April.[76] For Fr John it came not a moment too soon, as Pope Gregory died on 1st June 1846.

As for the Order in Ireland, from the early 1820s until 1840 its leadership rotated between Thomas Coleman and William Kinsella. In the early 1830s, when Spratt complained to Rome of the lack of rigour and of good governance, it may have appeared petulant and even self-serving. Nevertheless, from independent sources it would appear that there was some foundation to his misgivings. Richard Colgan, who was no friend of Spratt, complained to Cataldi in 1840 of the Provincial's and the Prior's management of the Dublin friary: its visitation was perfunctory, fast and abstinence were not adhered to, there was no meditation and no readings at meals, and even drunkenness was not being censured.[77] However, following upon the intervention of the Prior General, reform of observance did come about, almost immediately in the wake of this.

*A Family Disaster*
If the Carmelite family of Whitefriar Street at times caused Fr John some grief, so too did the Spratt family in Cork Street, largely through the misfortunes of Michael. Like so many Dublin trades from 1826,

73. GMA, Withers to Palma, 20th Aug 1842: O'Dwyer, *Irish Carmelites*, p. 211.
74. GMA, Spratt to Palma, 4th March 1843.
75. GMA, *Scrapbook A*, p. 36: outcome of papal audience, 23rd Jan 1846, announced at a meeting of the Definitory, Aungier Street, 29th April 1846.
76. *FJ*, 21st March 1846.
77. O'Dwyer, *Irish Carmelites*, p. 204.

his tanning trade encountered serious difficulties over the decade and a half which followed. As a Catholic, Michael had been one of the first six to gain admission to the Dublin Guild of Tanners, in August 1829.[78] It was small consolation: four years later, he was one of 23 tanners who called for a meeting of the trade in order to lay their grievances before the Commissioners of Corporate Inquiry.[79] Held at the public leather crane in High Street, it was in protest over serious grievances: these included the fact, as Michael pointed out in his speech, that contrary to the original charter of the Guild of Tanners, whereby those representing the Guild should *'be of the art or business of tanning'*, there were guild members who had nothing whatever to do with the trade.[80] For all their grievances and protests there was little or no redress or remedy. In 1835, Michael was declared bankrupt and on 21st October the family home was advertised for auction[81] together with a plot of land on nearby Brickfield Lane where, ironically, over a quarter of a century later, Fr John would found one of his most enduring charitable monuments.[82] Michael may have been in serious difficulties by 1830 for, in March that year, he sold the family interest in the fifteen acres of land his father had acquired in Carpenterstown in 1814.[83] It was on 15th June 1835 that he was declared bankrupt. That October he managed to pay off his creditors and was discharged from bankruptcy. His entire property was auctioned on 7th November 1835 and in stepped the brewer and family friend, Andrew Thunder, who purchased the lot and then gave it back to Michael.[84] However, he was soon in further difficulties and in February 1837, for a sum of £100 he mortgaged the property to the Caledonian Insurance Company.[85] Unable to keep up his payments, he was soon deeply in debt again and ended up in Kilmainham jail for his indebtedness. He was committed to prison

---

78. *FJ*, 8th Aug 1829.
79. *FJ*, 12th Oct 1833.
80. *Dublin Observer*, 19th Oct 1833.
81. *SNL*, 21st Oct 1835.
82. See Chapter Twenty.
83. Registry of Deeds, *Transcript Book*, Year 1830, vol. 857, No. 184, Michael Spratt to William Forestal, 26th March 1830.
84. Registry of Deeds, *Transcript Book*, Year 1839, vol. 1, No. 178, Bury to Clarke, registered 12th June 1839, and see also *SNL*, 21st Oct 1835.
85. Registry of Deeds, *Transcript Book*, Year 1837, vol. 2, No. 287, Michael Spratt to Low & others, registered 4th Feb 1837.

on 11th April 1838 following a Queen's Bench writ for a debt of £46 on behalf of a creditor, James Bury. Now owing £440, his property was taken over by a Thomas Street tanner, Patrick Clarke, in return for entirely paying off Caledonian, in December 1838.[86]

Through all these years of personal disaster, especially from 1835 through 1838 and beyond, Michael continued to be politically active: from collecting money for O'Connell's General Association in August 1836, to contributing funds to defray O'Connell's and Hutton's election expenses in July 1837 and to chairing a meeting of the Central Registration Board in August 1838, he remained in the public eye.[87] In the course of 1839, however, he did not feature at all in the Dublin or national press – although he would do so again in almost every year of the 1840s. At the end of the 1830s it is not clear how he survived: he managed somehow for, in 1838, he moved into the crumbling grandeur of Crumlin House as tenant and lived there for the next two years.[88] No. 104 Cork Street was now listed no more and No. 105 came to be occupied by Patrick Clarke, the tanner.[89] Michael was to emerge with several new careers and several new addresses in the course of the 1840s, as shall appear later.

As for Fr John, there is no hint or evidence as to how, or even if, he was involved in finding solutions to the disasters which led to the loss of the family home. However, for both of them and the rest of the family, the 1830s would end and the 1840s begin in further distress when their younger sister, Eliza, died – from cause unstated – in later October 1840, at the early age of thirty-four.[90] Yet, for all this adversity, the new decade would offer new challenges and career directions for the three brothers John, Michael and James.

86. Registry of Deeds, *Transcript Book*, Year 1839, vol. 1, No. 177, Low and others to Michael Spratt, registered 12th Jan 1839.
87. *FJ*, 12th Aug 1836, 14th July 1837, 8th Aug 1838 respectively.
88. Pettigrew & Oulton, *The Dublin Almanac and General Register of Ireland, 1839*, pp. 499, 660; *Wilson's Dublin Directory*, 1840, p. 790. For the history of Crumlin House, see F. Watchorn, *Crumlin and the way it was*, Dublin 1985.
89. *Wilson's Dublin Directory*, 1840, p. 512.
90. *DMR*, 2nd Nov 1840. The notice does not give the date of death. Her age was given as 27 in *DEPC*, 29th Oct 1840.

# CHAPTER EIGHT

## The Search for Sobriety, 1830-1849

On 17th March 1840 John Spratt was to find himself in a position of unprecedented public eminence. As the *Dublin Morning Register* recorded:

> It was with no ordinary pleasure we contemplated the scene which the city presented on yesterday so different from what Patrick's Day in Dublin used to be. From an early hour in the day large groups began to assemble. At about eleven the principal streets were almost impassable...the crowd was particularly dense in the neighbourhood of the Rotunda...[where a] procession commenced about twelve and on leaving the Rotunda Gardens presented a very imposing appearance. Each member carried a wand with a ribbon attached to the top, the two bands of the 97th and 88th added not a little to the animation of the scene.[1]

Leading the procession was John Spratt in his capacity as Patron of the Irish Total Abstinence Association and seated with him in the leading carriage was the Methodist Minister, Rev Mr McClure, chairman of the Irish Temperance Union.[2] Some two thousand members of the Irish Total Abstinence Association followed the Carmelite friar's lead. They, in turn, were followed by five other temperance and teetotal societies whose own leaders were becoming prominent in a campaign for temperance or even for total abstinence from alcohol:

---

1. *DMR*, 18th March 1840.
2  *DWH*, 21st March 1840.

the Mariners' Total Abstinence Society, led by Captain Jackson and with its two hundred parading members carrying a Union Jack; the National Total Abstinence Society led by Rev Dr Doyle and carrying banners which proclaimed *'no religious distinctions, no political discussions'*; St Paul's Temperance Society led by Dr William Yore, Catholic Parish Priest of the Arran Quay district – and accompanied by the regimental band of the Connaught Rangers; next came the St Nicholas of Myra Temperance Society, led by Parish Priest Matthew Flanagan and then the Metropolitan Total Abstinence Society led by the Rev Andrew O'Connell of Westland Row, accompanied by Daniel O'Connell's disciple, Thomas Reynolds, City Marshal; then came the Dublin Total Abstinence Society, led by the Unitarian, Charles Corkran, and which boasted 800 members, and finally the National Temperance Society whose 250 members were based in Stanford Street.

The procession presented an imposing spectacle and its extent was conveyed by the *Register* as follows:

> It would give some idea of the members who were present when we state that, at the time the banner of the first section was at Carlyle Bridge, after having passed up Cavendish Row, round by Mountjoy Square and Sackville Street, that a considerable number were still in the Rotunda Gardens waiting to join the train…

Having reached Dublin Castle the Lord Lieutenant, Viscount Ebrington, came out to witness it and when the first band struck up 'God save the Queen' the crowds cheered heartily and his Excellency acknowledged them with repeated bows. It was a remarkable occasion not only in its extent, but by the fact that it was strikingly an inter-denominational event. In some cases the individual societies were of a single allegiance as with St Nicholas of Myra, for the Catholics, or the Congregationalist Dr William Urwick's National Total Abstinence Society, for the Protestants; in other cases, the specific society could be multi-denominational, as in Spratt's Irish Total Abstinence Association and Dr J P Doyle's National Total Abstinence Society. For John Spratt the occasion marked the beginning of several glorious years when the cause of sobriety and moral reform seemed set to triumph, followed by

**Fig 30.** *Portrait of Fr Theobald Mathew by James Butler Brennan.*

a further quarter of a century when a heroic dedication was needed to sustain the cause.

*Temperance-Teetotal Beginnings*

The origins and history of the Irish temperance movement have been very well chronicled over the past thirty years, as has the role of its most famous advocate, the Capuchin Friar, Fr Theobald Mathew. It is unnecessary, therefore, to rehearse in detail either that history or biography here.[3] However, John Spratt's hugely significant role in the movement has not had any comprehensive treatment in print. That role shows him, with whatever faults or failings, as a man of independence, courage, charisma and great persistence. That commitment for over

3. For the Irish Temperance Movement, see among others: G. Bretherton, *The Irish Temperance Movement 1829-1847*, Columbia University PH.D dissertation, 1978; D. Ferriter, *A Nation of Extremes: The Pioneers in Twentieth-century Ireland*, Dublin 1999; E. Malcolm, *'Ireland sober, Ireland free': drink and temperance in nineteenth-century Ireland*, Dublin 1986. For Fr Mathew and temperance, see among others: H. F. Kearney, 'Father Mathew: Apostle of Modernisation' in A. Cosgrave & D. McCartney, eds., *Studies in Irish History*, Dublin 1979, pp. 164-175; C. Kerrigan, *Fr Mathew and the Irish Temperance Movement, 1838-1849*, Cork 1992; J. F. Quinn, *Fr Mathew's Crusade: temperance in nineteenth-century Ireland and America*, Boston 2002; P. A. Townend, *Father Mathew, temperance and Irish identity*, Dublin 2002.

forty years and, quite literally, until his actual dying day, in some sense
entitles him to the title 'Apostle of Temperance' as much as it belongs
to Fr Mathew: with the difference that John's apostolate, in the end,
would cover so much else besides abstention from alcohol.

From the outset, his commitment to the cause of sobriety marks
him out as unique among Catholic priests of the age and movement.
Although leading Dublin Catholic priests like William Yore, Matthew
Flanagan and Andrew O'Connell may have become pre-eminent in
the city in that cause, they were not believers in it *ab initio*. Yore and
O'Connell came to the cause early in 1840 when the movement had been
growing in dynamism and extent, and had begun to capture support of
the populace at large. Both were doubtful that such a movement could
succeed and actually joined and led it in their own areas under pressure
from their parishioners. Both feared they would lose control of their
flocks if they did not reluctantly take up the leadership roles thrust
upon them.[4]

In complete contrast, Fr John Spratt believed profoundly in the
cause and far from being a newcomer in that famous spring of 1840,
he was by then a veteran.[5] John Spratt had gone public and beyond his
own flock in the cause from as early as 1830. In that year he founded
his temperance society in Cuffe Lane, off French Street. That society
may have been small and invisible to the Dublin press, but it continued
in existence throughout the 1830s and may have been the nucleus for

---

4.  Bretherton, p. 244. William Yore admitted as much in a speech to his St Paul's
    Total Abstinence Society on Tuesday 19th June 1841: he recollected that when
    many deputations waited upon him to induce him to go at the head of a teetotal
    society, he initially refused, thinking he knew human nature too well to think such
    a society would succeed: see *DWH*, 3rd July 1841.
5.  P. MacSuibhne, *Paul Cullen and his contemporaries*, Naas 1962, vol. 2, p. 49 is the
    only modern historian or biographer to note that Spratt was long in the field
    before Fr Mathew arrived, but he errs in referring to James Haughton as John
    Haughton. Spratt was not the first Catholic priest to preach temperance in
    Dublin: Fr Michael Blake of Sts Michael and John Parish and later Bishop of
    Dromore had been preaching temperance in the 1820s. So too had the celebrated
    Fr Henry Young, Fr Blake's curate in that parish at the time. However, they
    preached the cause within their own church and parish and without organising
    a body or a movement: see Ronan, *An Apostle of Catholic Dublin*, pp. 91-92, 163.
    Spratt was not the only Carmelite to advocate temperance in print in the 1840s,
    as his confrere, Matthew Scally of Knocktopher, did likewise: see M. Scally, *The
    Teetotaller's Catechism*, Dublin 1846.

the Irish Total Abstinence Association in 1840. In 1830 it had the distinction of being one of only three little societies founded in the city, the others being The Operatives' Temperance Society in the Liberties, and the St Peter's District Temperance Association of Hatch Street. The first temperance society founded in Dublin in 1829 by the Unitarian clergyman, James Henry, and the Anglican medics, Dr John Cheyne and Dr Joshua Henry, was composed of Anglicans, Congregationalists, Unitarians and Quakers.[6] Ambitious for the spread of the movement, they held a public meeting in Dublin on 7th April 1830 and changed the Dublin Temperance Society into the Hibernian Temperance Society.[7] They recruited a significant number of prominent citizens, including the banker John David Latouche, the former head of the Dublin Police, Major Henry Sirr, the Trinity College Fellow, Dr Franc Sadlier, the Congregationalist minister, Rev William Urwick, and the aristocratic philanthropist and future supporter of Spratt, Valentine Lawless, Lord Cloncurry. At what point John Spratt joined the Hibernian Temperance Society is not precisely certain but he was a member within the first twelve months of its existence. When the HTS issued its *Appeal…to all Persons interested in the real welfare of Ireland*, in February 1831, he had already joined it and, indeed, was a member of its committee – the only Catholic priest in Dublin to be so involved.[8] How long he remained active in the HTS is uncertain, but certainly for at least three to four years: he was still a committee member in January 1834.[9] After that he may have drifted away from it because of its conservative Protestant character, as Malcolm intimates.[10] However, Spratt never had any problem working with Protestants as such. This was already clear from his active co-operation with them in education and in the Sick and Indigent Roomkeepers Society, and it may well be that it was simply his commitment to the latter from 1833 as well as his education and cholera relief work that directed him into other channels and away from the HTS. Nonetheless, it remains true that the temperance and teetotal

6.   *The Address of the Dublin Temperance Society to their fellow citizens*, Dublin, (R. D. Webb) 1830.
7.   *Sketch of the Rise and Progress of Temperance Societies: Hibernian Temperance Society, Paper A*, Dublin 1830, p. 3.
8.   *The Pilot*, 28th Feb 1831.
9.   *The Dublin Temperance Gazette*, vol. 2, No. XIX, Jan 1834, p. 3, in RIA, *HT* 464/12.
10.  Malcolm, pp. 84-85.

movement from 1829 to 1838 was almost predominantly Protestant –
and notably Dissenter Protestant at that – with the isolated exception
of Spratt himself, whose Cuffe Lane temperance society appears to
have continued its existence throughout the decade. Some of these
Dissenters could be decidedly anti-Catholic, as was the case with Arthur
E Gayer who came to prominence in the movement, especially through
his sole editorship of the *Irish Temperance and Literary Gazette* over 1836
to November 1838. While he gave publicity to even the smallest of the
Dublin Protestant Temperance Societies, Bretherton has commented
that Gayer took no notice of the Cuffe Lane Society and speculates '*was
it because its president was a Catholic Priest?*' [11]

If Spratt's four-year active involvement with the HTS may have been
relatively short in contrast to his almost forty years of commitment to
the Sick and Indigent Roomkeepers, one important consequence of it
was almost certainly the beginning of his friendship with the celebrated
James Haughton: they became companion-campaigners for forty years,
in a litany of great public causes, both moral and political, and especially
so in the cause of teetotalism.[12] From the outset of the Dublin, then
Hibernian Temperance Society, Haughton provided it with financial
support and sometime between 1836 and 1838 he became a total
abstainer or 'teetotaller'.

*From Temperance to Teetotalism*
Teetotalism was a radical version of the temperance movement that first
emerged in Paisley in 1832 and manifested in Dublin in 1835 when the
City Sheriff, R G White, founded Dublin's first total abstinence society.
In February 1839, Haughton along with the Quaker families of Allen,

---

11.  Bretherton, pp. 91, 169. An alternative version of the editorship of this journal is
     given by Richard Harrison who claims the founding owner, the Quaker Richard
     Allen, was editor. See R. Harrison, *Richard Davis Webb, Dublin Quaker Printer 1805-
     1872*, Cork 1993, p. 20.

12.  In the 1820s Haughton, a Carlow-born Quaker turned Unitarian, came to Dublin
     as a corn merchant in 1817, having learned his business first in Cork City.
     Through his relentless letter-writing to the national press, as well as his activities
     in a plethora of organisations, he became one of the most prominent public
     figures of the age, especially through his two greatest public commitments, the
     causes of anti-slavery and of sobriety: see S. Haughton, *Memoir of James Haughton*,
     Dublin 1877; J. Rowlands, 'James Haughton and Young Ireland', *Carloviana*,
     Christmas 1971, pp. 9-12.

**Fig 31.** *James Haughton.*

Bewley, Pim and Webb, had established the Irish Temperance Union to try to unify and support the various individual teetotal societies that were now springing up.[13] The ITU challenged the more moderate HTS for the leadership of the movement and by the early 1840s had prevailed.[14] As for Friar John, the origins of his original commitment to temperance and his later conversion to teetotalism are not evident in the existing secondary sources. As to his initial commitment, it is possible that he was influenced by the important if qualified support that Bishop Doyle of Kildare and Leighlin gave to it in 1829. When Ireland's first temperance society of the 1820s was founded at New Ross in 1829, its creator, the Rev George Carr, had written to Doyle to solicit support. Although Doyle was sceptical of the prospects of temperance through the bottom-up efforts of such a local society, in the absence of government action in terms of the taxation and licensing of drink, he nonetheless, gave the support of his name. The timing of this, by way of a letter to Carr on 19th December 1829 which the latter then published in the *Dublin Evening Post* of 2nd January 1830,[15] could possibly have inspired Spratt to found his Cuffe Lane Society

---

13. Malcolm, p. 92.
14. Bretherton, p. 244.
15. *DEP*, 2nd, 16th Jan 1830.

shortly after. Furthermore, Doyle, as well as Spratt, became a member of the HTS. However, when it was that John personally adopted a temperance position is unknown: it could well have been that he learned his temperance in the family home.[16]

As to when he might have become teetotal, Quinn suggests that Spratt, Haughton, Webb and others had *'discarded their moderationist policies for teetotalism in the mid-1830s'.*[17] Whatever about the latter three, there is a problem in Quinn's observation as far as he includes John Spratt. As shall appear in another context shortly, by his own admission in February 1841, Spratt became teetotal in November 1840 when he took the pledge from Fr Mathew.[18] By late 1838, Spratt's lone Cuffe Lane Temperance Society began to be joined by the first stirrings of Catholic clerical anti-drink initiatives. The parish priest of St Michan's, Dr J P Doyle, founded the National Total Abstinence Association, based in Denmark Street, Dublin, in August 1838 and, within eighteen months, it claimed 1,000 members.[19] It was largely responsible for the first St Patrick's Day teetotal procession in Dublin in March 1839.[20] On 3rd November 1839 in Arran Quay parish, was founded the St Paul's Total Abstinence Society, based around St Peter's church, Phibsborough: patronised by the local parish priest, Dr William Yore, who was by then diocesan Vicar General, it claimed 6,000 members by early 1840.[21] Even before the Capuchin friar, Fr Mathew, came to Dublin that year to promote the cause, there were at least eight largely Catholic-led teetotal societies in the city.[22]

As with the Protestant-inspired societies, the Catholic ones were often initially founded by laymen and then 'patronised' or led by clergymen, either at the behest of their lay founders, or at their own initiative in order to control them. Regardless of which it was, by the autumn of 1839 it was clear that teetotalism was finally expanding beyond its largely Protestant origins. Fr Spratt, doubtless witnessing

16. Farrington, pp. 15-16. Although this work was not published until 1893, Farrington had been a member of the Order when John was Vicar Provincial in the later 1860s and they were confreres in the Aungier Street Friary.
17. Quinn, p. 52.
18. *DWH*, 13th Feb 1841.
19. *DWH*, 5th Sept 1840.
20. Malcolm, p. 95.
21. *DWH*, 21st March 1840.
22. Battersby, *Catholic Directory*, 1841, p. 290.

this development from his friary, was clearly gratified that almost a decade after his own initiative, the movement was at last finding a place in the minds and hearts of the Catholic common people. This much is evident in his unconcealed joy at the foundation of what soon would be his Irish Total Abstinence Association.

## The Irish Total Abstinence Association

It was on the 11th August 1839 that a group of working men led by one Michael Groome began meeting together as the Irish Total Abstinence Association. They first convened in the rooms of a George Birkett of Stafford Street, then in those of John Battersby of Cross Lane, and, finally, in the Old Chapel, French Street. The chapel was then *'fitted out in the neatest manner'* as a temperance hall,[23] and so it would remain for well over thirty years. They were supported early on by the Dublin draper, Richard Allen, of the Society of Friends and by his fellow-Quaker, Thomas Mason.

That the founding members of the fledgling ITAA met in the Old Chapel indicates that the Carmelite friars, or at least Friar John, had provided them with this facility. John was first publicly associated with the ITAA when he appeared at their meeting on 29th December 1839. Here he was gratified at *'the great change that had taken place since the period that he had been president of a temperance society'*; he *'anticipated the most glorious results from the present moment'*, expressed his determination to give the association his support and patronage, and *'heartily rejoiced to see that here there existed no distinction either of religion or politics among them'*.[24] Two months later, the *Dublin Evening Post*, formerly hostile but now supporting the movement, since the teetotal conversion of its owner and editor, F W Conway,[25] reported on *'one of the most densely-crowded meetings we ever witnessed'*: some two thousand people pressed themselves into a meeting of the ITAA in the Old Chapel. Fr Spratt presided, and by his side stood O'Connell's disciple and future Marshal of Dublin City, Thomas Reynolds.[26] This self-confessed and long-time heavy drinker had been converted to teetotalism, and, as with Conway, this conversion was symptomatic of the dramatic and interdenominational

---

23. *DWH*, 5th Sept 1840.
24. *DWH*, 4th Jan 1840.
25. Bretherton, p. 81.
26. *DEP*, 5th March 1840.

revival the cause was experiencing from 1839.[27] By early March Spratt was actively heading the ITAA, as its patron, and clearly was not only directing it, but bringing it to a leading position in the growing teetotal movement in Dublin. This became abundantly clear when he led his ITAA to head the St Patrick's Day teetotal parade in Dublin on 17th March 1840, as described earlier. For the next thirty years Spratt would become almost synonymous with the ITAA and, whatever were the fortunes and misfortunes of the Irish teetotal movement, in its rise and decline over the next ten years under Fr Mathew, John Spratt reported the ITAA alive and active when other associations fell by the wayside. Not only that, but he came soon enough in time to head up or take over several other well-known Dublin teetotal bodies, as shall emerge later. He would, along with James Haughton, became the dominant figure in Dublin teetotalism and might well be remembered today as the dominant figure in teetotalism's history in Ireland at large, had it not been for the conversion of Fr Mathew and his meteoric rise to national leadership of the cause from 1839-40. Before considering the complex relationship between Fr Mathew and Fr Spratt in the course of the 1840s, it might be appropriate to mention some aspects of John's contribution before their crossing of paths in 1840.

## John Spratt's Moral Vision

Over the next thirty years, John's commitment to preaching and promoting sobriety was unswerving. In the immediate ten years it seemed to become all-consuming, so great was his activity in the cause, whether in the ITAA or more broadly. However, it was not so much for him that sobriety was an end in itself: rather it was part of a wider moral vision that he imagined for his countrymen. *The salvation of Ireland depends on the movement'*, he was to say, in early November 1840 at a densely-packed ITAA meeting, attended by the Vincentian, Father Henry Young, the Quaker, Richard Webb, the Unitarian, Charles Corkran, and the Catholics, W J Battersby and Thomas Reynolds.[28] It was a profoundly Christian moral vision and, at the same time, a practical one of creating a society that would not only be sober, but literate, industrious, patriotic and prosperous. Literacy figured in it

---

27. *DMH*, 3rd Oct 1840 for Reynolds' conversion; Malcolm, p. 13 for Conway's.
28. *DWH*, 7th Nov 1840.

to the extent that he was anxious to promote the dissemination of knowledge and public piety through the written word. This was already long evident in his educational work and in his involvement in the Catholic Book Society: now he aimed to apply it to the ITAA, as it began meeting in the Old Chapel, French Street. With the money the members were now saving, having foresworn alcohol, he urged them to join or establish tontine and benefit-societies and to stock libraries and reading rooms: he rejoiced that the ITAA had opened such facilities in the Old Chapel and had provided the new hall with improving literature and teetotal publications.[29]

Industry and prosperity featured in this vision in that he became a supporter of the workers' co-operative and Irish manufacture movement as it emerged in 1840 and would become prominently and very proactively involved in its renewal circa 1850, as will be seen in due course.[30] Patriotism featured in this vision also in so far as he came to support O'Connell's Repeal Movement and came to see both Repeal of the Act of Union and the adoption of teetotalism as being two sides of the same coin.[31] In a sense he was hereby emerging as an advocate of and contributor to the modernisation of Irish society, aiming to produce an educated, literate, sober and industrious people. Apart from drunkenness in general, one very flagrant affront to this moral vision for Fr John was the notorious annual extravaganza known as Donnybrook Fair.

## *This Sink of Pestilence and Carnival of Crime*
The annual fair at Donnybrook every August had been in existence since the grant of a charter in 1204. In the course of the eighteenth century it had become notorious for its scenes of public disorder, drunkenness and worse. As the nineteenth century wore on, it became slightly more subdued in its excesses but still remained for respectable society as a moral blemish on the face of Dublin.[32] As the temperance and teetotal movements gained ground in the course of the 1830s, Donnybrook Fair became increasingly seen as a source of drunkenness, debauchery

29. *DWH*, 12th Sept 1840.
30. See Chapter Thirteen.
31. See Chapter Nine.
32. F. A. D'Arcy, 'The decline and fall of Donnybrook Fair: moral reform and social control in nineteenth-century Dublin', *Saothar*, 13, 1988, pp. 7-21.

**Fig 32.** *'A Scene at Donnybrook Fair' by Samuel Watson, 1842.*

and the undoing of the city's young families, especially servants. No more than Spratt was the first to raise the flag of teetotalism in Dublin, neither was he the first to commence a campaign for the suppression of the Fair. That honour fell to the city's evangelicals, sabbatarians and Protestant teetotallers who publicly deplored this annual carnival of vice and called, in vain, for its abolition. Not the least of its abominations was that, because by charter it was conducted over 14 days, this included two Sundays each August, a deep affront to the sabbatarians. But the chief offence was that it was more about drink – and plenty of it – than it was about anything else. Their first major attack on the holding of the Fair, in 1837, led the Lord Mayor, William Hodges, to secure a military force to clear the site on Saturday 26th August. Having done this, he then faced a series of legal actions from outraged booth-owners for breach of their chartered rights. His plea to government for financial assistance towards his legal costs fell on deaf ears and so ended the first assault on the humours of Donnybrook. But soon after, a moral campaign, led in particular by the Irish Temperance Union and its organ, the *Irish Temperance and Literary Gazette*, took up the campaign against the Fair in 1839.[33] The ITU appointed a deputation that July to press the Lord Mayor to secure the removal of *'this grave of morality and virtue'*.[34]

---

33. Harrison, *Webb*, p. 21.
34. *DWH*, 13th July 1839.

If, then, Fr John was not the first out of the blocks on this issue, he was quick to follow the temperance evangelicals in taking it up; and because of his growing public prominence and perceived authority, his adherence to the cause was signally important. He was to become the most formidable and to remain the most persistent campaigner for abolition of the Fair. Once Fr John took up the cause, early in 1840, he spared no effort to galvanise the troops. He prepared a major temperance festival of his ITAA for Sunday 21st June and organised for it to be held *'on the ever-noted fields of Donnybrook'*. He again secured the services of the band of the Connaught Rangers to entertain the 500 to 700 teetotal guests who sat down to a festival tea-party. With him on the occasion were his by now usual loyal supporters, Battersby and Reynolds, and present also was the indefatigable Dublin temperance lecturer, John Mackey. After two hours, with the tents and coffee tables cleared away, Fr John rose and spoke of

> this glorious day when so many of the different ranks came together in the sacred cause of total abstinence...on the very spot which has been for ages the scene of so much drunkenness, riot and debauchery.

Temperance was not enough, he declared; teetotalism was essential, and referred in this to *'Fr Mathew, to whom they were all so indebted'* and who had found this too to be the case.[35]

This was, on John's part, a particular crusade only then beginning, but it proved to be one that would take much longer to bring to a successful conclusion than he could have imagined. He followed it up two months later, as the Donnybrook fortnight drew near, with a spirited attack by way of a circular address issued to his ITAA members, launched from his Aungier Street friary on 22nd August 1840. He did not pull his punches:

> One of the most common temptations at this particular period is that of visiting Donnybrook Fair. For many years back this has been considered one continued scene of drunkenness and debauchery; it has been the theatre of every scandal, the abode

---

35. *FJ*, 25th June 1840.

of every vice and the cause of endless misery to thousands…this sink of pestilence and carnival of crime.[36]

His denunciations were joined the very next day at Sunday Masses by pulpit broadsides against visiting the Fair, from Frs Yore at St Paul's, Doyle at St Michan's and O'Connell at Sts Michael and John.[37] How far these warnings were heeded is a moot point: when the Halls came to Ireland in 1840 and stopped by the Fair, they reported:

> We heard nothing and noticed nothing that could offend the most scrupulous: there was no quarrelling approaching to a brawl; we did not encounter a single intoxicated person of either sex and enquiry at police offices the next day revealed 'no charges preferred'.[38]

From this it might appear that clerical admonitions were having some effect. John Spratt was certainly not discouraged, and when the next August came around he published an *Open Letter to the Citizens of Dublin and its vicinity*. In this he called on all teetotallers to use their influence with their friends and acquaintances to avoid patronising the Fair which, to him, was still *'that continued scene of drunkenness and debauchery'*, *'that theatre of every scandal, and abode of every vice'*.[39] He implored people to prohibit their apprentices, servants and children from going there. Four years later, on 2nd June 1845, John organised the largest teetotal meeting that Donnybrook Fair had ever experienced. On this occasion, apart from his stalwart teetotal supporters, Haughton, Battersby and Reynolds, he was even joined by his brother Michael and by his brother James, now back from Italy. Furthermore, on this occasion, he did not need the Connaught Rangers to supply the festive music as his ITAA now had its own brass band and its junior society, the St Joseph's Juvenile Association, also based in French Street, had its band too.[40] Several thousand reportedly took the pledge from him on that

---

36.  *DWH*, 29th Aug 1840: *Donnybrook Fair: Address to the members of the Irish Total Abstinence Society by the Very Rev Dr Spratt.*

37.  *DWH*, 29th Aug 1840.

38.  S. C. & A. M. Hall, *Ireland, its scenery and character*, 3 vols., London, 1841, i. 332-345.

39.  *DWH*, 14th Aug 1841, *Donnybrook Fair: to the citizens of Dublin and Vicinity.*

40.  Battersby, *Catholic Directory*, Year 1845, p. 501.

occasion. Over two months later, on 25th August 1845, he challenged the organisers of Donnybrook Fair by staging yet another monster meeting of teetotallers and postulant teetotallers in a field nearby. Reporting on *'one of the most extraordinary meetings ever perhaps witnessed at or near Donnybrook, in an immense meadow within a quarter of a mile from the Green'*, W J Battersby described Fr John addressing the huge crowd, congratulating them on *'the miraculous change which had taken place in the morals of the people, particularly on the occasion of frequenting the great Fair'*. He concluded:

> Witnessing the egress and ingress of perhaps fifty thousand persons to and from the 'Brook, not even one individual was seen in the slightest degree inebriated, and that within a circumference of two miles.[41]

This may have been a high point in John's mass demonstration approach to tackling the Fair. He does not appear to have repeated it during the remainder of the 1840s. The Fair would survive despite these heroic efforts and John would have to adopt new tactics in the battle against its debauchery in the course of the 1850s and 1860s.[42]

*The Growth of the ITAA*
Over the years 1840 to 1845, his ITAA grew in strength and was joined by a youth branch, St Joseph's, in 1841. By 1842 each would have its own teetotal brass band, and that of the ITAA would outlive John himself, surviving into the 1890s. By March 1840 his ITAA was shaping up to be *'one of the most influential'* teetotal societies in the city and quickly grew from some 500 members at that time. He was proud of its interdenominationalism, announcing with some satisfaction, in September 1840, that the new Association had elected two joint-presidents, Browne, a Protestant and Harte, a Catholic.[43] Two months later he had further cause for rejoicing when, in some elation, he announced:

---

41. Ibid, p. 503.
42. See Chapter Seventeen.
43. *DWH*, 19th Sept 1840.

The society here, of which I am patron, has received the full approbation of the Archbishop of Dublin and they are to have a place reserved for them next Sunday, in the Metropolitan Church, to hear Fr Mathew's sermon. Dr Miley has spoken in the highest terms of our society. You are all to have a place reserved for you, next Sunday, for my society I consider the most respectable in Dublin, even the Archbishop bears testimony to that. I am sure Protestants as well as Catholics, will go to hear Fr Mathew.[44]

In the grip of his elation at this token of esteem, he may have overstated the Archbishop's approval: one of the notable features of the teetotal movement throughout its history in those times was that Daniel Murray as Archbishop, declined to warmly endorse it, being among seven prelates who had reservations while ten were warmly supportive and ten definitely hostile to Fr Mathew's movement.[45]

However, Murray did engage Fr Mathew to preach at the Marlboro Street Church, not in the cause of temperance, but rather to raise funds to complete the church building there.[46] For all that, the invitation to Spratt and his ITAA was a recognition of sorts and encouraged him to ever greater commitment to the cause. His efforts emanating from the French Street Hall met with growing success. On 21st November 1841 the St Joseph's Juvenile Total Abstinence Society, for those under 17 years of age who took the pledge, was founded at 12 Whitefriar Street: four days later he accepted an invitation to become its patron.[47] For all his animus against Donnybrook Fair and its excesses, it is clear that Spratt was no killjoy when it came to festivals and festivities. Apart from being proud of the ITAA's and the St Joseph's temperance brass bands, he was greatly to the fore in organising and supporting teetotal banquets indoors and teetotal parties and parades outside. In December 1840, through his ITAA, he hosted a Grand Christmas Teetotal Festival at the Rotunda, with Daniel O'Connell as guest of honour, attended

44. *DWH*, 21st Nov 1840.
45. Townend, pp. 64, 168-171.
46. Capuchin Archives, *Mathew Correspondence*, No. 2215, Murray to Mathew, 11th July 1840. This sermon, in November, was Mathew's third one in that church in 1840. The two earlier ones, in March and September, were in aid of the Female Orphan Society and the Widows' Asylum, respectively: see *DMR*, 25th March, 28th Sept 1840.
47. *DWH*, 4th Dec 1841.

by some 1,500 guests. O'Connell praised Spratt as only Dan could and Fr John, in reply, congratulated his members for having put down *'the demon of intemperance'.*[48] While the political significance of this gathering will be considered later,[49] it is worth noting, in passing, how, once again, Fr John stressed publicly his great commitment to interfaith harmony:

> In assembling here, my friends, on this and similar occasions, no party feelings or religious dissension shall or can...endure among us: we have assembled - in peace and Christian charity – the priest and the minister – the Protestant and the Catholic – the Presbyterian and Methodist – the Quaker and Unitarian – all united together in the bonds of friendship and brotherly love, to better the condition of our fellow creatures. My friends, this we shall continue to do in our respective spheres for the remainder of our lives.[50]

Apart from his concern to promote harmony between the denominations, he was also anxious that his ITAA occasions would be cheery rather than gloomy gatherings and he either initiated or responded positively to the note of festivity in the ITAA's endeavours; indeed, he was criticised by some of his stuffier followers for allowing dances at his tea-party festivals.

By mid-1845 his ITAA claimed a membership of some 10,000;[51] by the year 1846 it was claiming 30,000[52] and by 1847 it claimed 40,000, while its youth section, St Joseph's, claimed 1,000. Over the years 1843 to 1846, Fr John was said to have administered the pledge to some 160,000 people. By 1848 he stated that his ITAA now had 52,000 members, and by 1850 he claimed it numbered 60,000.[53] Such figures smack of exaggeration but even if they were only one half or even one third of that, these would still be remarkable figures for a single society. Initially, the huge growth over the years 1841-1845 clearly owed much to Spratt's own effort but also to the charismatic mission of Fr Mathew,

---

48.  *FJ*, 31st Dec 1840.
49.  See Chapter Nine.
50.  Ibid.
51.  Ibid, p. 233
52.  Ibid, pp. 186, 262.
53.  Ibid, 1848, p. 284; 1850, p. 346.

and it owed not a little also to the expectations of deliverance generated by the rise of the Repeal Movement under O'Connell, over the years 1840 to 1843.

### Capuchin and Carmelite

The role of Fr Theobald Mathew in transforming teetotalism into a mass movement of astonishing extent has been well-documented.[54] Inevitably his evangelism, his triumphs and tragedies, brought him into close contact with Dublin's leading teetotallers, Spratt, Haughton and others, for the rest of the 1840s. For John Spratt, Mathew's forays into the Dublin region would be a source of support but, simultaneously, a challenge: their relationship would turn out to be a complicated and at times an uneasy one, as together and separately, they pressed the cause of teetotalism.

It is significant of the standing of John Spratt that the first overtures came from Fr Mathew. At the start of February 1840 it was mentioned in the temperance press that he had written to Spratt to announce his intention of visiting Dublin in the cause.[55] The Capuchin made his first foray into the capital over eight days from 19th March, and on his final day, he arrived up to the Whitefriar Street Church at the very moment when Spratt was administering the teetotal pledge there.[56] It was certainly a fraternal gesture and presumably it encouraged the Carmelite to intensify his own efforts in promoting the cause. For his own part, Fr John continued to organise impressive public gatherings. However, on 7th July 1840 the Lord Lieutenant issued a proclamation cautioning temperance societies against processions which displayed party emblems or which were accompanied by music bands *'playing party tunes'*.[57] Spratt had no problem with this and would continue to organise parades and processions that complied with the spirit of the Lord Lieutenant's caution but it would lead to some tension between Mathew and Spratt as shall be seen. In the meantime, however, Spratt clearly grew in his admiration of Mathew's achievements and gave evidence of this growing support for the Capuchin. In August 1840 he went out to Sandyford in Co. Dublin to hear Mathew preach to many

---

54. See note 3, ante.
55. *DWH*, 1st Feb 1840.
56. *FJ*, 6th April 1840.
57. *DEP*, 9th July 1840.

**Fig 33.**   *Temperance Association Card of Thomas Kent signed by Fr Theobald Mathew, OFM Cap., 12th April 1838.*

thousands there.[58]   He certainly became involved during Mathew's fourth visit to the city over the days from Sunday 15th to Wednesday 18th November.   This visit began with Mathew's sermon that Sunday in aid of the Metropolitan Church.   This was the occasion to which Spratt and his ITAA were invited – to his great elation.   There followed *'the three glorious days'* when Mathew administered the pledge to an estimated 33,000 people.   The visit was a truly significant one for both men.   In the case of Mathew it represented something of a breakthrough in that he was now attracting and 'converting' the middle and upper echelons of society to the cause.   One of his most notable converts on that Monday 16th November was none other than John Spratt himself.   Fr Mathew announced *'I am happy to tell you that Rev Dr Spratt is going to take the pledge; he has practised it for twelve months and, knowing its sweets, he is now going to seal it by taking the pledge'.*[59]   To mark the event Mathew presented

58.   *Dublin Monitor*, 1st Sept 1840.
59.   *DEP*, 17th Nov 1840.

Spratt with a splendid silver medal and then made him a vice-president of the Dublin branch of his Cork Total Abstinence Association, based in the Capuchin Friary, in Church Street.[60]

The two friars had in common that they were both unusual in their ecumenism, and in their actual record of working with Protestants of diverse denominations, especially in this great cause. Spratt around this time told the following story:

> A man one time came to me and said, sir, I am a Protestant, but I think I will turn Catholic. I told him to go home and say his prayers, and beg of God to direct him, and then to come to me after considering the matter.[61]

The two friars also shared a strikingly 'liberal' view on the nature of the pledge: each saw it as a non-binding promise rather than a perpetual vow. On one occasion at this time John assured his hearers that *'the pledge is only to be kept as long as the party wished'* and he cited Fr Mathew as making clear that one could relinquish it by informing the society or person who had administered it in the first place.[62] This was in strong contrast to the hard-line position of clergy such as Dean Miley who had written a tract entitled *Will Teetotalism Last? An Exhortation to the People on the Heinous Guilt and Disastrous Consequences of the Violation of the Temperance Pledge.*[63]

By that stage Spratt's ITAA was going from strength to strength, had created three separate savings clubs – for Christmas, for sickness and for mortality expenses, and Spratt as its effective leader displayed an energy for the cause greater than ever.[64] By early February 1841 he was already making preparations for their next great procession – that scheduled for St Patrick's Day.

On 8th February he issued a formal address to ITAA members urging that for this procession they *'observe the greatest caution and*

60. *Dublin Weekly Register*, 21st Nov 1840.
61. *DWH*, 21st Nov 1840.
62. *DWH*, 8th May 1841.
63. RIA, HP 1783/11: J. Miley, D.D., *Will Teetotalism Last? An Exhortation to the People on the Heinous Guilt And Disastrous Consequences of the Violation of the Pledge*, 22 pp., Dublin 1840.
64. Ibid.

*circumspection: no party tunes shall be played, no political emblems exhibited...
you will honour God and St Patrick and you will respect the great and good Fr
Mathew'*. However, in patriotic mode, all concerned were to wear a
scarf of Irish manufacture and a determination was expressed to try to
unite all the city's other teetotal societies to form a central organising
committee.[65] The cautions concerning public display coincided with
and were doubtless prompted by the concern of his teetotal clerical
associate, Dr Andrew O'Connell of Sts Michael and John, who had
written to the Lord Lieutenant on 4th February regarding temperance
processions on St Patrick's Day. Dublin Castle replied to O'Connell on
8th February, assuring him that while the Lord Lieutenant was anxious
to promote the success of the cause of abstinence, he urged the need
for another abstinence – that from party displays, emblems and music
– from any St Patrick's Day procession.[66] Dr O'Connell communicated
this immediately to John Spratt who then stressed the message at his
ITAA meeting two days later.

However, Dr O'Connell's concern did not deter the Carmelite friar.
Spratt and his clerical colleagues proceeded with the St Patrick's Day
Parade through Dublin, from the Phoenix Park to the Coombe, to the
sound of church bells pealing, then across to Capel Street, Mountjoy
Square, Sackville Street and ending in St Stephen's Green: all the while
the ITAA contingent were led by *'marshals on horseback'*:

> The Very Rev Dr Spratt, President, Mr J Reilly, Vice-President,
> went in the first chariot, drawn by six horses, with postilions and
> outriders, in white livery, with a profusion of gold lace. The
> members of the committee and band filled several carriages.
> The Society, which contains upwards of 16,000 members, had
> a very fine appearance, the men, dressed in white scarves and
> bands, with pink flowers and knots, marched two deep.[67]

Whether or not John's persistence in parading troubled Fr Mathew or
led to some dilution of their alliance at this precise time, as it would
later on, is not clear. However, in April 1841 Spratt organised an

---

65. *DWH*, 13th Feb 1841.
66. *DEP*, 11th Feb 1841, N. H. MacDonald, Dublin Castle, to Rev A. Connell, PP,
8th Feb 1841.
67. *FJ*, 18th March 1841.

Easter temperance festival in the Rotunda, at which Daniel O'Connell attended. It was a significant meeting in indicating the extent to which the Dublin temperance movement was becoming allied with and almost fused with O'Connell's movement for Repeal of the Act of Union.[68] Spratt's growing closeness to O'Connell's Repeal Movement was not something Mathew would welcome: he certainly deplored James Haughton's commitment to Repeal but, equally, he deplored what he regarded as Haughton's malign influence on Spratt. In an undated letter to a fellow-Capuchin, Mathew remarked, *'there is no man more kind-hearted than Dr Spratt but he is led away by artful men'.*[69]

Over the course of the years 1842-43 O'Connell's movement for Repeal of the Act of Union strengthened its hold over the temperance movement, and fund-raising for his movement diverted financial support from Mathew's cause.[70] By 1843 Mathew's temperance movement appeared to be losing some of its momentum and he himself was entering a period of serious financial difficulty: indeed, as early as the end of 1841 he had incurred debts in excess of £5,000.[71] By the end of 1842 moves were made to set up a testimonial for him, in which Spratt played a leading part over the next two years.[72] Haughton, who was particularly dismayed, was highly critical of Mathew's financial mismanagement and led the committee in asking for details from the Capuchin: indeed, he organised a new, more active committee himself, in October 1844. Unsurprisingly, in turn, Mathew was dismayed by Haughton's and his associates' interventions. At the beginning of November he pleaded with Spratt:

> Do not, I entreat, commit me to their keeping. You and my other sincere friends can act independently of the Testimonial Committee. You can say it is my wish to have donations forwarded to myself and I will acknowledge them.[73]

---

68. This development is addressed in greater detail in Chapter Nine.
69. Capuchin Archives, *Mathew Correspondence*, No. 1716, Mathew to Patrick Duff, no date given.
70. Malcolm, p. 131; Kerrigan, pp. 116-126; Townend, p. 224.
71. Malcolm, p. 139.
72. *Dublin Monitor*, 9th Nov, 7th Dec 1842, 6th Dec 1844.
73. *Mathew Correspondence*, No. 934, Mathew to Spratt, 1st Nov 1844.

A few days later, he added:

> To you, very revd dear Mr Spratt, besides the large sums of
> money you have remitted, I am indebted for my deliverance from
> Mr Haughton…I would not have noticed the resolutions of
> this self-appointed guardian if you had not charitably called my
> attention to them. It was a monstrous assumption of despotic
> authority on the part of Mr Haughton.[74]

Some weeks after this, he angrily confided in Charles Gavan Duffy, in a
revealing complaint that included John Spratt within its censure:

> I wish Mr Haughton would consult me for the good of the
> Society and not injure it by causing a schism. 'Divide et impera'
> is the cry of our enemies. He wishes to place at the head of
> the Teetotallers of Dublin, Rev Dr Spratt, who is weak enough
> to arrogate to himself the title of Founder of the Irish Total
> Abstinence Society.

At the same time, Mathew was prepared to acknowledge some
obligation to the Carmelite in respect of Haughton and the reconstituted
testimonial committee:

> I would have been bound up, hand and foot, if I had not
> extricated myself from his grasp, and I am grateful to the help
> of the Rev Dr Spratt for help [sic] in that struggle.[75]

Thereafter, in 1845 and beyond, with his financial difficulties continuing,
Fr Mathew's temperance evangelism suffered, even as Spratt's appeared
to intensify. The Capuchin's temperance meetings grew relatively fewer
and their coverage in the national and Dublin press diminished even
as the latter seemed to devote more space and attention to the teetotal
work of the Carmelite friar.[76] Nevertheless, even for Spratt, the glorious
years of the St Patrick's Day temperance parades of 1840-1842 were no
longer to be repeated exactly.

---

74. *Mathew Correspondence*, No. 935, Mathew to Spratt, n.d.
75. Bretherton, pp. 264-5, citing Mathew to Gavan Duffy, Nov-Dec 1844.
76. Kerrigan, p. 76.

*The passing of the parades*

By most accounts, the St Patrick's Day temperance parades which John Spratt organised for 1840 and 1841 were impressive and successful. That for 1842 had, it seems, less success and walking fatigue may have begun to set in. The next year, Fr John did not hold or organise a parade for St Patrick's Day, but switched the event instead to Easter and so it would remain until his final Easter temperance parade in 1845. What lay behind this change of date? For one thing, over the course of the previous six months, the political atmosphere had become more tense and the government more anxious about stability and public order, as O'Connell's campaign for Repeal of the Act of Union intensified. For another thing, his growing sequence of mass meetings for Repeal proved a major contributing factor to the political tension, and, on 9th March, by which date, ordinarily, John Spratt would have been preparing for his St Patrick's Day annual temperance outing, O'Connell held one of his most imposing monster meetings at Trim, Co Meath. In due course, this was to be followed by an equally impressive meeting at Tara Hill, on 15th August, and would culminate in the government's proclamation on 7th October prohibiting the great gathering at Clontarf due for the

**Fig 34.**   *Daniel O'Connell speaks at the monster meeting in Trim.*

next day. O'Connell cancelled that meeting and was summoned, with his son, John, to appear in court to face charges of conspiracy.

Against this background Fr Mathew had himself suppressed his own annual temperance parades. Fr John, by contrast, merely switched the event from St Patrick's Day to Easter Monday, 16th April 1843. Writing from the Carmelite friary, Aungier Street, on 5th April, in his capacity as President of the ITAA, he explained that, following upon a deputation of the various city temperance societies, he decided to proceed with a *'public, peaceful and joyous manifestation'* on Easter Monday. He therefore called on Dublin employers to facilitate their workers in participating and remarked that *'without being a strict holiday, it is usually kept as such by even the most necessitous'*. He made it clear that no party tunes would be played and no party emblems displayed.[77] These assurances notwithstanding, his decision caused concern to Fr Mathew who asked Spratt *'if the great risk of holding an Easter procession was worth the benefit'* and reminded the Carmelite that *'upon your head rests the responsibility'*.[78]

John's first Easter Monday parade went ahead on 17th April and even as it proceeded past the offices of the *Evening Mail*, the editor commented:

> Father Spratt has triumphed over the prudence of the Government and the good sense of Fr Mathew. Whilst we write, the streets are crowded to the most inconvenient excess with processions of teetotallers, headed by bands of music and distinguished into officers, and rank and file, by badges and decorations...One distinguishing characteristic was observable throughout the procession – almost every society had a banner of a Harp without a Crown, indicative of the accordance of the brethren, in the cry for Repeal, and symbolically pointing to the separation of the countries.
> SEPARATION![79]

---

77. John Spratt to 'Fellow Citizens: The Grand Teetotal Procession', 5th April 1843, in *FJ*, 6th Apr 1843.

78. *Mathew Correspondence*, No. 1038, Mathew to Spratt, n.d.; Townend, p.128, places this letter circa 1840, but it clearly belongs to one of the years 1843 to 1845 as these were the only years when Spratt held temperance parades at Easter; the newspaper context, especially that provided by the *Dublin Evening Mail*, suggests that the year in question is 1843.

79. *DEM*, 17th Apr 1843.

A triumph for Spratt it was, as a record 16 societies took part, watched by an estimated 20 to 25,000 people.[80] Consequently, he was not at all put off from repeating the Easter Monday procession the following year. In preparation for this, he convened a meeting of 5,000 Dublin teetotal society members to prepare: all his principal associates were there: Haughton, Martin Brennan, Thomas Reynolds, the Quakers Webb and Allen, and so too, his brother Michael, who seconded a resolution condemning the manufacture of *'ardent spirits'*.[81] On the day itself, Monday 8th April, the event, held in *'glorious weather'*, was a great success. Present with Spratt in his splendid carriage were T M Ray, secretary of the Loyal National Repeal Association, and Thomas Reynolds, the City Marshal. It is hard to avoid the conclusion that the strength of the 1844 Easter Monday teetotal procession owed a great deal to the political tensions of the time: the State Trials of O'Connell, Ray, Reynolds and others had commenced on 15th January; guilty verdicts were returned by the jury on 10th February and the sentences would be handed down in May. It is, perhaps, in this context, that the *Freeman's Journal* comment on the procession is to be understood: *'It is unavailing to deny the fact, there was a formidable demonstration of popular power in the movement of yesterday'*. It went on to express the sense of unity between the temperance and the nationalist movements:

> The illusions of centuries have disappeared before the mingled enthusiasm of religion and of country...[the marchers] have formed a conspiracy of sober men, pledged to good order and obedience to the law – bound together by a community of wrong and consolidated into a fine league of practical morality.[82]

The point was unmistakeable when the procession stopped for some minutes outside O'Connell's home in Merrion Square, whereupon a band struck up *See the Conquering Hero Comes*, and it did not go unremarked that *'In the Rev Mr Spratt's carriage we noticed Mr Ray and the City Marshal'* – two of the O'Connellites convicted with him for conspiracy and, like him, then awaiting sentence.

---

80. *FJ, DEP*, 18th Apr 1843.
81. *DEP*, 6th Apr 1844.
82. *FJ*, 9th Apr 1844.

The following year saw the last of Spratt's Easter Monday temperance parades, but in addition, it saw him adopt an alternative strategy when he initiated a new development for St Patrick's Day. He had decided to commence open-air meetings, first at Newmarket in the Coombe, just around the corner from the home of his birth. In an open letter, *To the Tradesmen of the Liberty*, he urged the workmen of his old neighbourhood to meet him *'in large numbers'* in order to take the pledge and to *'enlist under the banner of the good Fr Mathew'*. This event, held on 17th March 1844, was a notable success with many thousands turning up and with some 1,000 taking the pledge. It seems, however, that after 1845 the days of John Spratt's temperance parades were over, but his evangelism for the cause was certainly not, as he directed new energy into great open-air meetings, without parades or processions; and these, in fact, gave rise to further and serious disharmony with Fr Mathew.

*Friar against Friar – altar against altar*
On Sunday 21st June 1846 John Spratt held a well-advertised pledge-giving mission in Finglas village. Serious offence was taken at this by Fr Mathew who, also on the same day, was conducting a pledge-giving rally at Sandyford village.[83] The unfortunate Friar John was accused by Friar Theobald of causing division in the temperance ranks and, more darkly, of entertaining *'other objects besides the promotion of teetotalism'*.[84] Worse was to follow when, that autumn, Spratt visited Belfast and Drogheda on a temperance mission and did so without securing the prior permission of the local Catholic diocesan clergy. Fr Mathew was displeased, to put it mildly.[85]

The Belfast mission constituted one of Spratt's singular triumphs in the cause and its circumstances invite the conclusion that there may have been an element of resentment or jealousy, on Mathew's part, at Spratt's popularity. As it happened, the Carmelite was invited to Belfast by *'the magistrates, bankers, merchants and manufacturers, with the Total Abstinence Association of Belfast'*. This invitation concluded: *'signed by one*

---

83.   *FJ*, 25th June 1846.
84.   *Mathew Correspondence*, No. 1090, Mathew to Patrick Duff, 27th June 1846.
85.   *Mathew Correspondence*, No. 1091, Mathew to Duff, 1st Oct 1846, No. 1093, Mathew to Duff, 24th Nov 1846. See also Fr Augustine, *Footprints of Fr Mathew, OFM, Cap: apostle of temperance*, Dublin 1947, p. 408; Kerrigan, p. 166.

*hundred and twenty gentlemen of the town of Belfast, of different denominations'.*[86]
In the event, Spratt could rejoice in a successful visit when, on Sunday
13th and Monday 14th September, he administered the pledge to
an estimated 5,000 people. This was the first time that Belfast had
experienced an open-air, pledge-giving service, one which *The Northern
Whig* described as *'a demonstration of a novel and gratifying description'.*[87]
Spratt was accompanied on this visit by W J Battersby and they were
both impressed by the *'order and decorum'* which prevailed that Sunday, in
the assembly of some 6,000 to 7,000 people *'of all religious persuasions'.*
As if to emphasise this, Spratt's speech on the occasion was followed
by those of the Rev E J McAlester of Hollywood and by the Methodist
minister, the Rev Mr McClure. On the following day, John spoke on the
Falls Road where a number of mill owners had closed their works to
allow their workers to attend. In his exhortations to all concerned, John
urged the establishment in Belfast of a temperance hall, a temperance
reading room and a mechanics' institute. In an editorial the following
day, praising his work, the *Northern Whig* commented:

> Yet, strange as it may appear, scarcely a clergyman of town or
> country presented himself, either day, to aid in promoting this
> great moral movement…not one Catholic priest was found to
> countenance this brother in his high moral work.[88]

This comment, unsurprisingly, elicited a tetchy response from one
Catholic curate of the city, Fr Patrick Dorrian, future Bishop of Down
and Connor.[89] Taking issue with the implied censure, he indirectly
criticised Spratt for *'thrusting his sickle into another's corn…gathering another's
vintage, be the crop ripe, or be it yet green'.*[90] The comments came at a time
when relations between Spratt and Fr Mathew were at their worst,
following John's foray into Finglas on the day when Mathew was in
Sandyford.

In a letter of 1st October 1846 Mathew confessed that he had

---

86.  *FJ*, 19th Aug 1846.
87.  *Northern Whig*, 15th Sept 1846.
88.  Ibid, 15th Sept 1846.
89.  A. Macauley, *Patrick Dorrian, Bishop of Down and Connor, 1865-85*, Dublin 1987,
     pp. 56-59.
90.  Ibid, 19th Sept 1846.

cherished Spratt *'as a sincere friend'* until Spratt had held his *'opposition meeting'* in Finglas. Since then, and since John's temperance mission to Dundalk without the permission of the parish priest, Dr Coyne, Mathew *'disclaimed all connexion with the Very Rev Dr Spratt'* and deemed the latter's Dundalk visit as *'dangerous to the faith of the people by raising altar against altar'*.[91] He added:

> If instead of 5,000, had he administered the total abstinence pledge to the whole population of Belfast, it would be as dust in the balance, weighed against the injury he has inflicted on the holy religion of which he is a Priest. He has taught the Catholic people…that 'they can do without their Pastors'. The Very Rev Dr Spratt was well aware of the strictness with which I adhered to the rule of not holding a temperance meeting in any parish unless expressly invited by the Parish Priest…it is to be deplored that the Rev Dr Spratt has adopted his present line of conduct.[92]

In light of the Carmelite friar's repeated acts of kindness and financial support, this attack and subsequent ones smacked of 'eaten bread soon forgotten' especially given the litany of Mathew's previous expressions of gratitude.[93] Now in its place came bitterness:

> Dr Spratt, blinded by vanity, would soon lead us into a pit from which we could not extract ourselves. He is a good man, but excessively weak.[94]

---

91. *Northern Whig*, 13th Oct 1846, citing *The Pilot* and *Freeman's Journal*.
92. Ibid, 13th Oct 1846, citing letter of Fr Mathew to James Nagle of Kingstown, Co Dublin, 1st Oct 1846. Nagle had supplied Mathew with articles from *The Pilot* and the *Freeman's Journal*, praising Spratt's temperance work.
93. In the worst days of his indebtedness he wrote: 'Your untiring solicitude on my behalf is above all thanks…I am indeed truly grateful…when I look back upon the awful precipice upon whose brink I stood and from which you snatched me and placed me in safety…'; again, he was to write: 'You have extricated me from a gulf…I can only say I am grateful and shall ever cherish the remembrance of your truly fraternal protection and affection'. These sentiments dated from circa 1844 and two years later, he added: 'I feel so overwhelmed by the weight of your kindness…you have proved yourself the kindest and most sincere friend.': see Capuchin Archives, *Mathew Correspondence*, Nos. 576, 935, 1037-8, Mathew to Spratt, n.d.
94. Ibid.

Elsewhere he wrote, with his characteristic animus against the Unitarian teetotaller, *'Mr Haughton makes a cat's paw of Dr Spratt'*.[95] His comments on Spratt, arising from the latter's northern visits, were both extreme and unwarranted and suggest a person no longer in control of his own utterances and emotions. On 9th October 1846 John Spratt responded vigorously and wrong-footed Mathew in a most telling way. The Carmelite put it to Mathew:

> Did you not, when charged from various quarters…with making the pledge an act of religion, declare that 'it was nothing more than a simple promise, wholly foreign from the jurisdiction of the Church'? Either it is an act essentially religious or it is not. If it be essentially religious, and requiring ecclesiastical jurisdiction, I am justified in asking you from what Bishop did you derive or ask authority to administer the pledge? If you have no authority but your own, has not *every Priest* who is a teetotaller, *equal authority with yourself?*[96]

Spratt reminded Mathew of his own frequent admissions that it was the Society of Friends and Protestant Dissenters who had converted him to teetotalism and that Mathew's own Total Abstinence Association was not a sectarian or political body, but rather one embracing all creeds and political persuasions. The Carmelite denied having conducted *'an opposition meeting at Finglas'*: for one thing, it was held at six o'clock in the evening while Mathew's Sandyford meeting was held before that, at noon; for another, the places were seven miles apart; and, finally, the Finglas meeting had been *'advertised and placarded long before I heard of your intended visit to Sandyford'*. Spratt wondered:

> Has jealousy done its evil work here? Is there no cause in Ireland to be free from jealousy? Nor any work, however sacred, secure from individuals squabbling about superiority?[97]

---

95.  Ibid, Nos. 1095, Mathew to Duff (1846), and 1092, Mathew to Duff, n.d.

96.  *Cork Examiner*, 16th Oct 1846.

97.  Idem.

He continued:

> I recollect hearing from yourself, when in Dublin, (and I now
> quote your own words in print) that the first who came forward
> to cheer you on in your great work were members of the Society
> of Friends, and Protestants of different denominations.

Spratt, therefore, asked Mathew:

> What would you think of the man who would charge you of
> setting up 'altar against altar' when you were thus acting to
> promote a good work amongst all classes of Christians?

Since, by Mathew's own insistence,

> the pledge is only a moral act, then I violated no law and interfered
> with no ecclesiastical jurisdiction by going to Belfast or Dundalk.

Spratt could name parishes to which Mathew had gone without
parochial permission and asked which bishop or pastor Mathew
consulted when he went on his temperance missions to England, and
Spratt himself provided the answer – none – since Mathew had gone
there on the invitation of the British Association for the Promotion
of Temperance, not by invitation of the Catholic Church. Only once
in this long and passionate riposte did he allow a note of bitterness or
sarcasm to protrude, as Spratt defended his visit to Belfast, to which he
had been invited by members of all classes:

> I went there and returned at my own expense – I would not
> accept one shilling from the people. I had nothing to do with
> medals or cards, so I cannot understand how anyone could be
> jealous with [sic] me.[98]

The editor of the *Northern Whig* supported Spratt and took up the
theme of jealousy on Mathew's part:

---

98. *Northern Whig*, 13th Oct 1846, citing Spratt to Mathew, 9th Oct 1846.

We have read Fr Mathew's letter with surprise. He writes in an apparent pique and jealousy as if he were more anxious to preserve his own fame unrivalled than caring about the progress of the great cause...For nine years he has declined to visit us; and now he is angry when another does.[99]

Unsurprisingly, although Spratt may have been upset by Mathew's attack, he was in no way deterred. He paid a second visit to Belfast a month later. He preached teetotalism at the village of Whitehouse on Sunday 12th October and then went on to the Falls Road in further evangelism over the next two days. Over the course of this second visit, some 3,000 were said to have taken the pledge. On this venture, James Haughton went with him. Against the background of the serious rift with Fr Mathew, Spratt's speech in Whitehouse was pointed:

I stand before you, friends, not in the capacity of a Minister of Religion – the temperance platform is free from party and sect...[but] as an advocate of that cause in which Catholic and Protestant are united together.[100]

As if to underscore this point, the Methodist minister, Rev McClure, spoke at this Sunday event also. On the Falls Road, next day, some mill owners again closed their works to allow their workers to attend and take the pledge and, reportedly, some 2,000 did so.[101] On the final day, Tuesday, some 500 young people of the Falls Road received the pledge at Spratt's hands. Later that evening, he and Haughton addressed a united assembly of the three main Belfast teetotal societies and Spratt was presented with a formal address and with an invitation to make a third visit to the city. All things considered, Mathew's description of Spratt's Belfast missions as *ill-advised and unhappy* was hardly fair or accurate. Furthermore, Spratt's reputation as a temperance champion had spread beyond Ireland. In August 1846 he travelled to Birmingham to preach teetotalism to the Irish emigrants there and in late November 1846 he accepted an invitation to promote the cause in Liverpool, opening a new temperance hall on the occasion, in Bond Street. He

99.  Ibid.
100.  *Northern Whig*, 13th Oct 1846.
101.  *Vindicator*, 14th Oct 1846.

spent two days on Merseyside, to some effect, before returning to Dublin on 1st December 1846, with an invitation, as with Belfast, to return to Liverpool for another visit.[102]

Mathew was not well pleased:

> On my repeated refusal to attend the opening of the new Temperance Hall in Liverpool, Very Rev Dr Spratt was invited and accepted the invitation. The ceremony was announced for yesterday. Nothing could have induced me to take so unnecessary and fruitless a voyage.[103]

He would have been even more jaundiced if he had read the report in the *Liverpool Mercury* concerning

> The Rev Dr Spratt who has acquired of late such popularity in the sister kingdom by the vast numbers of persons he has been the means of converting to the principles of teetotalism. He was received in the Clarence Temperance Hall with three cheers from the audience of 500, and administered the pledge there.[104]

Yet, for all that, in his letter on this matter, Mathew indicated a qualified regret:

> Though I regret having given pain to Dr Spratt, I do not regret having written a disapproval of his proceedings at Belfast. Had I been silent, all the bishops of Ireland would have become opposed to the Temperance Movement.

He had a point, even if exaggerated: a majority of the bishops who were opposed to the movement, were from northern dioceses, including Bishop Denvir of Down and Connor who was opposed to Fr Mathew visiting on any temperance mission for fear of generating sectarian troubles.[105] Yet, Mathew was beginning to relent even as Spratt's teetotal evangelism intensified.

102. *The Pilot*, 7th Aug; *DWN*, 8th Aug; *FJ*, 1st Dec 1846.
103. *Mathew Correspondence*, Mathew to Duff, 24th Nov 1846.
104. *Liverpool Mercury*, 27th Nov 1846.
105. Kerrigan, pp. 159-160; Townend, p. 171

*Reconciliation*

This was only a beginning of a thaw and the full melting of the ice was to take somewhat longer – in fact, not until the summer of 1848. Most of the steps in that process are missing, but, in some manner or other, the path to reconciliation was paved by the Dublin diocesan archdeacon, John Hamilton. Hamilton had written to Mathew on some private or pastoral matter, in late March or early April of 1848. In a reply of 4th April, Mathew mentioned that he would be in Dublin during Easter Week (Sunday 23rd April) and expressed himself as *'exceedingly anxious to see you as I have many subjects to speak to you on'.*[106] As it happened, just at this time, Spratt had been in direct contact with Hamilton, having preached a charity sermon for him on Sunday 2nd April. Hamilton was duly grateful, as acknowledged by Spratt on the 7th.[107] Some weeks later, the Capuchin called on the Carmelite. The latter reported the result to Hamilton on 30th June 1848:

> The good Father called on me yesterday, he was in good spirits, we are friendly once more. I am sure I may thank you for bringing about this reconciliation which affords me so much pleasure and for which I truly feel grateful to you.
>
> > I remain, Very Revd dear Sir,
> > Yours faithfully,
> > John Spratt.[108]

This reconciliation, long overdue, yet was timely: Mathew had suffered a stroke that April and this may have indicated that it was time to repair relations. As a result of this blow and other developments in his life, as Townend observes, Fr Mathew *'never returned to sustained labour on behalf of the Temperance Movement'.*[109]

*Adhering in Adversity*

As for Fr Spratt, like Mathew, he too had many other commitments. Nevertheless, although the days of the great parades and processions

---

106.  *DDA*, 37/1/274, Mathew to Hamilton, 4th Apr 1848.
107.  Ibid, 37/1/279, Spratt to Hamilton, 7th Apr 1848.
108.  Ibid, 37/1/278, Spratt to Hamilton, 30th June 1848.
109.  Townend, p. 258.

**Fig 35.**   *The front (face) shows the Good Shepherd. The outer-rim inscription reads*
*'I have found the sheep that was lost Luke Chap. 15 v. 6'.*
*The obverse: Cruciform text of pledge reads: 'I have voluntarily promised in*
*the presence of the Revd. Dr. Spratt to abstain from all spiritous liquors and*
*intoxicating drinks except used medicinally and then by order of a medical*
*man and the discountenance of all the vices and practices of intemperance and*
*also to attend to my religious duties'.*
*The outer-rim inscription reads 'The Dublin Total Abstinence Pledge The Very*
*Revd. Dr. Spratt Patron 1840'. The maker of the medal was J. Taylor.*

were over, he continued assiduously to promote the cause for the rest
of the 1840s – and well beyond – with an exhausting schedule of
engagements. Over the three years to the time of the Belfast missions
and the serious rift with Mathew, it was claimed that the Carmelite friar
had administered the pledge to some 160,000 persons in Dublin. By that
stage, apart from leading his ITAA with its claimed 40,000 members,
he was now also heading the Metropolitan Teetotal Association with its
24,000, on behalf of its titular leader, Fr Andrew O'Connell: so claimed
his friend, Battersby.[110]

By the end of that year, while now claiming a membership of 52,000
for his ITAA, John had now become President of the National Total
Abstinence Society of Denmark Street, in addition to his presidencies
of the ITAA and the Metropolitan.[111] It was as if, while other clergymen
were relinquishing their leadership roles, he was expanding his. Apart

110.   Battersby, *Catholic Directory for the year 1847*, p. 307.
111.   Battersby, *Catholic Directory for the year 1849*, p. 347.

from his many Dublin City temperance commitments in 1849, he again went to the north, this time to preach temperance in Newry.[112] Here he received, for once, a warm Catholic episcopal welcome in advance from an old friend, Bishop Blake of Dromore. The latter apologised for not being free to attend the sermon by *'the distinguished preacher, Dr Spratt, who so efficiently fills the place of the immortal Mr Mathew'.*[113]

By the end of 1849, with Mathew now in America, Spratt had taken over as the apostle of temperance. Apart from the weekly Sunday evening events in French Street and Denmark Street, he daily administered the pledge in Whitefriar Street Church.[114] In addition to all of this, as the decade drew to a close, he turned again to the pen to promote the cause. It was in 1849 that he produced *An Appeal to the People on the Horrid Crime of Drunkenness.* Printed by John Fowles and published by Battersby, this 64-page exhortation to sobriety enjoyed many editions and reprinting in the years ahead. Indeed it was taken up by the Irish Temperance League, founded in Belfast in 1858 and which body's Dublin branch printed 5,000 copies of John's *Appeal* in the 1860s.[115] The work is unremarkable, but written in an accessible manner, expounding the message of eternal salvation and temporal, social redemption that constituted the core of Spratt's unremitting temperance evangelism.

How can one judge if the search for sobriety and moral reform 'failed'? It has been noted that between the years 1838 and 1842 the consumption of both legally and illegally produced spirits fell significantly, and in the case of legal whiskey, by more than half. Taking the history of excise duty and other factors into account, Malcolm concluded that the impact of the teetotal movement during that period offers a credible explanation for this fall.[116] However, from 1843 to 1846 legal consumption recovered significantly. Townend, similarly, has pointed out the falling consumption of spirits per head of population

112. Battersby, *Catholic Directory for the year 1850*, pp. 150-156.
113. *Newry Examiner* and *Louth Advertiser*, 7th Nov 1849.
114. Battersby, *Catholic Directory for the year 1849*, p. 205; *1850*, p. 150.
115. Marsh's Library contains a 32 page edition which is catalogued as being published circa 1848: however the RIA's edition is 1849 with 64 pp and an edition was printed in London as late as 1870, held by the University of London Library. For the Irish Temperance League's promotion of Spratt's *Appeal*, see Chapter Twenty-three and Malcolm, p. 177.
116. Malcolm, pp. 144-145; see also Townend, pp. 248-251.

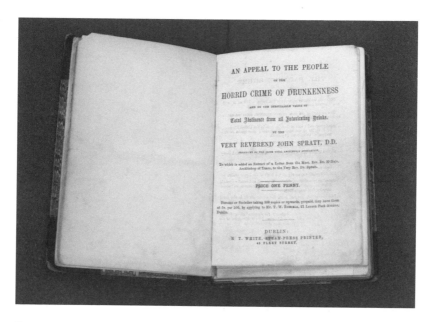

**Fig 36.**   *An Appeal to the People on the Horrid Crime of Drunkenness.*

over 1838 to 1842, and then, with the exception of the year 1847 – the severest in the Famine – its steady rise, to a doubling over 1843 to 1852.[117] It is safe to assume, despite heroic efforts by the guerrilla army of teetotal warriors, that there was a significant extent of backsliding and pledge-breaking and that teetotalism, as a mass movement, faltered. Indeed, that faltering had a very personal reference, close to home, in Fr John's case, as shall be seen elsewhere.[118] All this notwithstanding, the friar never abandoned the search for sobriety and moral reform by direct appeal to the person. Nevertheless, as he and the movement entered the 1850s and 1860s, a new strategy of moral reform by appeal to the legislature, was to be adopted in addition, as shall be seen later. In the meantime, even as Mathew and others became somewhat side-tracked from the movement by other calls and claims, John Spratt too was compelled, simultaneously, to face other challenges and commitments in the national politics of the 1840s and in the national calamity of the Famine.

117.   Townend, pp. 248-251.
118.   See Chapter Sixteen

# CHAPTER NINE

## The Politics of Repeal, 1840-1847

On 15th April 1840 Daniel O'Connell presided over the foundation meeting of the 'National Association' which, on 13th July of the same year, was renamed the Loyal National Repeal Association. It was a decisive moment in O'Connell's career and one not without impact on the Carmelite friar, John Spratt. John had witnessed the collapse of the family business and the loss of the family home in the course of the previous five years, and during the following ten he would witness the descent of his brother, Michael, into misfortune and into Michael's many changes of address as he sought a livelihood and tried to keep ahead of his various landlords. It was a time of disaster for many trades and businesses in Dublin, as elsewhere in Ireland. Any recourse which offered a prospect of recovery was eagerly sought or seized upon by the small traders, masters and workers of the city at the time. Many of these distressed folk looked back to the prosperous years that coincided with the independent Irish parliament of the final two decades of the eighteenth century, and fondly believed that a restoration of the independent legislature could secure the recovery in their economic fortunes.

Consequently, when O'Connell, after several years of alliance with the Whigs in the 1830s, decided that the time had come for a campaign to restore the Irish parliament by way of repeal of the Act of Union, he found a ready response from the Irish masses in general and from the Dublin masters, artisans and labourers in particular. He found ready support also from the rank and file of the Catholic clergy, and not a little even from some of its bishops. A letter of 12th March

1839, from Cardinal Giacomo Fransoni, the long-serving Prefect of Propaganda Fide, urging Irish bishops, and by extension, their priests, to keep out of politics,[1] certainly fell on deaf ears as far as Fr John Spratt was concerned.

From an early stage Spratt showed his support for the movement for Repeal. He joined the LNRA from the start, according to himself,[2] and soon engaged directly with O'Connell in a public meeting that was, ostensibly, a 'Grand Christmas Teetotal Festival'. On this occasion O'Connell made public

**Fig 37.**   *Cardinal Giacomo Fransoni.*

avowal of his adoption of teetotalism. Four months before this he had foresworn *'all species of intoxicating or fermented liquors'* and he now stood before this assembly wearing the badge of the Kilkenny Total Abstinence Society.[3] Whatever about his sincerity in this – that lifelong commitment did not long endure – it certainly suited his purposes in advancing the infant Repeal movement, to hitch it to the then far more advanced popular movement of temperance. John Spratt's 'Grand Christmas Teetotal Festival' provided one significant public occasion to commence that hitching process. His movement for Repeal rode to dominance on the back of the temperance crusade. Before too long, much to Fr Mathew's dismay, O'Connell's movement overshadowed and dominated the movement for temperance. Spratt and his temperance associate, James Haughton, both became caught up in this development and the Carmelite saw no difficulty in this alliance. By the early 1840s, O'Connell's leading lieutenants, Thomas Reynolds and T M Ray, had become close associates of Spratt. Reynolds became a teetotaller

---

1.  J. F. Broderick, *The Holy See and the Irish Movement for the Repeal of the Union with England: 1829-1847*, Rome 1951, p. 102.

2.  In January 1848, in sending in his annual membership remittance, he claimed that he had been a member since its foundation. See *FJ*, 4th Jan 1848.

3.  *FJ*, 31st Dec 1840.

**Fig 38.**  *The Rotunda in the 19th century.*

– publicly announced as such by Fr John – and he and Ray were prominent beside Spratt in his temperance processions.  Within four months of that Christmas Teetotal Festival at the Rotunda, Spratt and O'Connell would reconvene there.  This time the occasion was Spratt's Easter Temperance Festival but it was dominated by O'Connell and his promotion of the Repeal cause.  They entered the venue together, to acclamation.  O'Connell immediately took the chair, proceeded to lavish praise on the teetotallers and went on to propose *'the prosperity of Ireland'*.  Working up his audience he urged that

> if they would all join with him in making a long pull, a strong pull and all pull together they would soon rescue their country from the mire of degradation in which she was at present plunged, and place her on that pinnacle of national independence to which she was entitled.[4]

His speech was received *'with immense cheering'* and he went on to urge support for Irish manufactures.  In the detailed account supplied by

---

4.  *FJ*, 15th April 1841. This newspaper reported 'a numerous attendance', the *Dublin Evening Post* recorded one 'not so numerous'.

the *Freeman's Journal*, O'Connell had the floor exclusively to himself and there was no suggestion that Fr John intervened at any stage. It would appear that Fr John's Easter Teetotal Festival had been turned into a great concourse for the promotion of the Repeal. This appeared to cause John no difficulty and he and James Haughton became ardent Repealers. It was a development that was not lost on the establishment press. Commenting on Spratt's Easter Temperance Festival, the *Dublin Evening Mail* observed bitterly, but not inaccurately, that *'the Temperance Movement has openly and avowedly become an Association for the Repeal of the Union'*.

Then in June he actually presided as chairman at a meeting of St Peter's Parish Liberal Club, which O'Connell attended. Held next door to the Carmelite Friary, at 58 Aungier Street, this general meeting of the Liberal electors of the parish was convened to ensure the election of two Liberal members of Parliament for the City of Dublin.[5] Although parliamentary electoral success was not sustained on this occasion when the Liberal candidates, O'Connell and Robert Hutton, failed to be returned again as MPs for the City in the general election of July 1841, there was some consolation in a Liberal victory in the municipal elections to the now reformed Corporation of Dublin. The Liberals captured 49 of the 60 seats on 25th October 1841. On the first of November their triumph was complete when O'Connell was elected Lord Mayor, the first Catholic to occupy the position in modern Irish history.

Although Spratt may have been unpopular with his confreres in the Dublin Carmelite community at this time, it did not seem to deter all six other friars from appending their names below Fr Spratt's in supporting a meeting of the parishioners of Sts Michael and John, convened to organise the 'O'Connell Tribute' – that financial contribution widely-levied and widely-supported which enabled O'Connell to devote his energies exclusively to political life.[6] This was in early November 1841 and later that month Fr John's brother, Michael, now Secretary of the County Dublin Liberal Registration Club, was busy organising a general

5. *FJ*, 25th June 1841.
6. *FJ*, 8th Nov 1841. Fr Andrew O'Connell, parish priest of Sts Michael and John – no relation of Daniel's – was the convenor. The friars were: William Withers, William Kinsella, Richard Colgan, Michael Tobin, Andrew Day and Edward O'Rourke.

meeting of this body to consider how best to secure the maximum registration of Liberal electors at the ensuing Quarter Sessions.[7]  By October of the following year, 1842, younger brother James, now back from Italy, joined his two older brothers in the cause.  Together with his Augustinian confreres, James was among the signatories calling a meeting of St Catherine's Parish to make arrangements for the collection of their 'O'Connell Tribute' at the end of that month.[8]

## Clontarf and after

A culmination of the campaign for Repeal came on 7th October 1843 with the Government banning, and O'Connell cancelling, a great meeting scheduled for Clontarf the next day.  Conspiracy charges were brought against the O'Connells, father and son, John: their immediate aides and supportive newspaper editors soon followed.  The Spratts, like so many others, remained steadfast in their commitment to O'Connell and his cause.  For Michael that autumn was an especially difficult time, but this did not prevent him from continuing his active political commitments.[9] That August he was collecting funds for the Repeal Association and was equally occupied in charity work for the Franciscan Orphan Society, thanking his brother John and the Carmelites of Whitefriar Street for allowing the use of their Church for a fund-raising evening sermon.[10] Months later, in November 1843, at a meeting of the 'Friends of the Liberator', he was accepted as one of the collectors of St Mary's Parish, Donnybrook, in raising money for O'Connell, to honour the latter's forty-three years in public service.[11]

His brother John was equally active in the cause.  When a group of parishioners of Sts Michael and John called a meeting to arrange for the collection of 'The O'Connell Compensation Fund', the

7.  *FJ*, 24th Nov 1841.
8.  *FJ*, 18th Oct 1842. Two months later James was involved with other St Catherine's residents in protesting against the Poor Law Commissioners' handling of a case of alleged mistreatment of a female workhouse inmate, Martha McKeon.
9.  Over 1840-1842 he had operated as an auctioneer, presumably unsuccessfully, and now described as a 'Commission agent and accountant', living in Fairview Avenue, he was cited in the Insolvent Debtor's Court, initially on 9th September 1843. He was to have had the case against him heard on 8th November 1843. The outcome of this has not been located.
10. *The Nation*, 19th Aug 1843; *FJ*, 30th Oct 1843.
11. *DEP*, 14th Nov 1843.

**Fig 39.** *John Spratt's Volunteers of 1782 Revived membership card, dated 10th November 1844, in GMA Archives,* Scrapbook A.

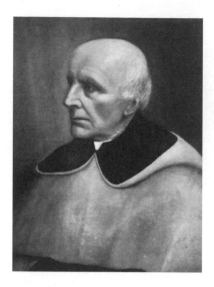

**Fig 40.**    *Fr Thomas Bennett, O. Carm.*

Carmelite's name immediately followed those of the diocesan clergy of that parish in supporting that call. Interestingly, his name was followed in turn by those of six Franciscan friars, and several city councillors and then by all remaining seven of his Whitefriar Street fellow-Carmelites, including even the normally apolitical Fr Thomas Bennett, future Provincial and President of All Hallows College. Exactly one week later, brother James was counted among the parishioners of St Catherine's, along with four other Augustinians of John's Lane friary, in calling a meeting for identical purpose.[12] This rallying to the cause of O'Connell by Carmelites, Franciscans and Augustinians had its own significance just about this time.[13]

The trial, conviction and jailing of O'Connell and associates for conspiracy did nothing to detach the clergy, no more than the mass of the people, from support for O'Connell and the cause of Repeal. Their subsequent release in September only served to deepen the excitement around the cause. It was against this background that, on 15th October 1844, Cardinal Fransoni issued another letter to the Irish Catholic Primate, urging clergy to abstain from engagement in politics and secular matters and to promote peace and obedience to the temporal authorities.[14] What was true of the clergy in general, in these matters, was true of Spratt in particular. Within days of the jailing of O'Connell and his eight fellows, Fr John and his Carmelite confreres were signatories to a requisition to get the inhabitants of Castle Municipal Ward to prepare an address of support to the Liberator and to express their determination to continue to press for Repeal. As in

---

12. *Dublin Monitor*, 10th Nov 1843.
13. See Chapter Ten.
14. Ibid, pp. 184-186.

the past, John's was the first of the Carmelite names appended to the requisition, immediately after those of the diocesan clergy led by Fr Andrew O'Connell. When this meeting was held, it was Spratt who proposed the first resolution.[15] A month later, he was among a group of fifty supporters who visited O'Connell and his fellow 'martyrs' before their release from the Richmond Bridewell.[16] A week later again, when Spratt himself was honoured at a grand dinner in Dalkey, attended by some 120 guests, including his brother James, his temperance friends Haughton, Martin Brennan and the Reynolds, Thomas and John, it was inevitable that the speeches praising Fr Spratt and temperance were accompanied by others lauding O'Connell and Repeal.[17] At that stage, the agitation for Repeal had passed its peak and the following year saw the beginnings of disunity and disaster: disunity within the ranks of the Repeal Association and disaster in the country as the first reports of the failure of the potato crop began to appear in the press that September.

The jailing of O'Connell and his leading Repeal associates had a dampening effect on that cause. Dissension within the Repeal Association then became a major problem with the rise of the Young Ireland movement and disputes over the Government's Irish Colleges' Bill. Matters came to a head in a very public row in the Association on 26th May 1845. The row was made deeper by frustration over the virtual stagnation of the Repeal cause over the period 1844 to 1846, and by despair with the onset of the Great Famine. Fifteen months later, on 28 July 1846, the Association split over the theoretical issue of the use of physical force to obtain political ends. The Young Irelanders seceded from the Repeal Association. This disunity caused dismay and attempts by Daniel O'Connell to effect a reconciliation foundered on the rocks of mutual intransigence: the split now deepened when the dissidents from the Repeal Association established the Irish Confederation, at a meeting in the Rotunda on 13th January 1847.[18] By that stage, beset by political stagnation and economic disaster in

---

15. *FJ*, 5th, 8th June 1844.
16. *FJ*, 23rd July 1844.
17. *FJ*, 1st Aug 1844.
18. See, *inter alia*, G. Owens 'Popular mobilisation and the rising of 1848: the clubs of the Irish Confederation', in L. M. Geary, ed., *Rebellion and remembrance in modern Ireland*, Dublin 2001, pp. 51-63; and R. Davis, *The Young Ireland Movement*, Dublin 1987.

the country, and by declining personal health, O'Connell made his final appearance in the House of Commons on 8th February 1847. Even as O'Connell faded, attempts were made to reunite the Repeal Association and the Confederation but these attempts foundered again on 4th May 1847. Eleven days later, O'Connell was dead.

## The ever-faithful friar

This dismal chain of events, from May 1845 to May 1847, naturally concerned Fr John as a devotee of Daniel O'Connell. The Carmelite doubtless witnessed the growing tensions during these two years with apprehension, but his loyalty to O'Connell was not in doubt. On 12th January 1846, in sending in his Repeal Association membership renewal, together with that of his confrere, William Withers, he informed O'Connell that he did so

> as a pledge of my conviction of the necessity of an independent parliament to do justice to Ireland...hoping that all classes of Irishmen will continue to co-operate heartily, and labour strenuously with you in your legal and constitutional struggle to effect the Repeal of the Legislative Union between Great Britain and Ireland.

His reference to your *'legal and constitutional struggle'* was doubtless an admonishing allusion to the Young Ireland dissidents. Certainly, O'Connell was duly appreciative and moved a vote of thanks *'by heartfelt acclamation, to Dr Spratt'*.[19] Alas, the friar's hopes for co-operation were to be dashed when the split in the Association came, decisively, on 28th July 1846. There would be no doubt where Fr John's allegiance would lie: on Sunday 16th August 1846 he attended an open-air meeting of the residents of St Patrick's Ward, off Camden Street, for the purpose of *'expressing confidence in the wisdom and prudence of O'Connell'* and to give their *'unqualified adhesion to the moral force principle'*. Alderman Butler, as chairman, expressed the appreciation of the meeting at Fr Spratt's presence, *'showing that the clergy were with them in these peaceable moral force struggles for working for the regeneration of Old Ireland'*. Spratt, seconding a motion of confidence in O'Connell, observed:

---

19.  *DWN*, 17th Jan 1846.

I am an ardent Repealer from conviction…I did not expect that I would have to come forward and express my determination, which is well-known, to stand by O'Connell when he is retarded in his efforts to make Ireland a nation…and he that supports O'Connell, stands by his country.[20]

Within nine months O'Connell was no more. Although he passed away in Genoa on 15th May, his funeral in Dublin did not take place until 5th August 1847. By that stage, the divisions in the Repeal movement appeared beyond repair.

Fearing the worst, the Carmelite called for an end to the dissension, all the more urgent as it might spill over to mar O'Connell's eventual funeral journey. On 10th June 1847, the friar issued a plea by public letter, 'The Liberator's Funeral – To the Citizens of Dublin'. He implored that

No political difference shall be alluded to on this occasion and that nothing but forbearance and brotherly love will be manifested on all sides…Whatever may be the political differences of any portion of the people, at such a moment, nothing but deep regret and Christian sympathy should be manifested by all classes…All political differences should be avoided and the recollection of all past dissensions be buried in oblivion…thus will the foundation be laid of a lasting peace amongst Irishmen.[21]

His friend, Battersby, who had been actively but unsuccessfully involved in an attempt at reconciling O'Connell and his opponents the previous November, fully endorsed Spratt's plea for peace and harmony. Calling on all concerned *'to stand up for nationality'*, he echoed Spratt's words when he implored *'all interested for our common cause and common country to make a sacrifice of their mere personal feelings for the sake of the people'*.[22] Friar John's fears that there might be disorder and disruption at O'Connell's funeral led him to call a special meeting of dockers and canal workers – two groups at one time notorious for their labour violence. Assembling

20.  *FJ*, 19th Aug 1846.
21.  *FJ*, 11th June 1847.
22.  *FJ*, 5th July 1847.

at his Cuffe Street Temperance Hall, in the middle of July, he exhorted them to be temperate, peaceful and harmonious during the funeral and, indeed, during the imminent general election. He then administered the teetotal pledge to a large number of them.[23] As it transpired, the friar's fears for the funeral on 5th August proved groundless. As the *Dublin Evening Post* observed:

> Whether we regard the number of persons, the solemn order with which the ceremonial was concluded, the air of religious zeal which pervaded the moving masses and the melancholy occasion upon which they assembled, we must pronounce the procession of O'Connell's funeral, this day, as the most imposing spectacle ever beheld in Ireland.[24]

In the wake of the funeral, Spratt remained politically active and committed to the Repeal cause. Towards the end of September 1847 he delivered a forthright speech at a banquet for John Reynolds who had just won election as one of the two MPs for Dublin City. At this gathering of some eight hundred guests, Spratt was very much the pre-eminent one, being the first-named of the platform party. When he spoke it was as though the Church authorities in Rome or Ireland had never cautioned against priestly involvement in politics. He declared:

> It is the duty of the clergy to stand by the people of Ireland, for the people of Ireland in the worst of times have stood by them... While the clergy of Ireland were anxious to promote the cause of religion, they have ever been indefatigable in the discharge of what they consider a sacred duty – they have always been zealous and energetic in aiding and assisting to obtain liberty for Ireland by encouraging and upholding the people in their constitutional struggle for that liberty. My own object, for some time past, has been to use all my exertions to promote the cause of charity, temperance and peace amongst all classes of my countrymen. But, I feel bound to take this, and every opportunity like it, to declare that, in my humble judgement, nothing less than a Repeal of the Legislative Union will ever confer permanent prosperity

23.   *FJ*, 17th July 1847.
24.   *DEP*, 5th Aug 1847.

on this country. It is the duty of the clergy to stand by the people of Ireland, for the people of Ireland, in the worst of times, have stood by them.[25]

In short, he called for a united clergy and people in order to obtain the political and religious freedom of Ireland. However, some three years before these developments diverted and diminished the energies hitherto devoted to Repeal, Fr Spratt had simultaneously become immersed in a new, quite different commitment which went a long way to sunder the unity of the clergy, whatever about the laity.

**Fig 41.** *The crypt of Daniel O'Connell, Glasnevin Cemetery.*

---

25. *The Pilot*, 29th Sept 1847.

# CHAPTER TEN

## *The Battle of Bequests, 1844–1845*

It has been noted how Carmelites, Augustinians and Franciscans displayed a deep devotion to both Daniel O'Connell and to the cause of a native parliament. That devotion clearly originated in his achievement of Catholic Emancipation. For the male religious orders, however, that triumph had been tempered by the penal clauses of the Emancipation Act as directed against these regular clergy. The situation in regard to property-holding by Catholic religious institutions was fraught with insecurity, and for the monastic orders the issue of property bequests was one that was worrying in its uncertainty. That uncertainty, born of the outlawing of the orders in the penal age, was compounded by the punitive clauses against their very existence as set forth in the Catholic Emancipation Act. It was then exacerbated by a piece of legislation that reached the statute book as the Charitable Donations and Bequests (Ireland) Act of 1844.[1]

It proved ironic that this Act was intended as a reform measure by the Robert Peel administration, to offer a greater say to Catholics in the matter of the disposition of certain charitable donations. In the year 1800 the Act of Geo. III c. 75 had established a Board of Bequests, comprising some fifty members whose purpose was to hinder the concealment and to prevent the misappropriation or the misapplication of bequests and donations contrary to the intentions of the donor. This Board was exclusively Protestant in its membership but could claim a statutory remit in respect of all charitable donations that may have been suspected of concealment or misapplication. This situation,

---

1. 7 & 8 Vict. c. 97.

especially for the Catholic regular clergy, was compounded by the 1829 Emancipation Act which nominally outlawed the religious orders and which, therefore, also appeared to render unlawful any donations or bequests to them or to any member or members of them.

It is this uncertainty for the male religious orders, officially illegal as they were, that may go some way to explain Spratt's peculiar position within his own religious community when it came to matters of money,

**Fig 42.** *Sir Robert Peel.*

property and the making of wills. In the Carmelite Provincial Chapter of 1843 the friars had adopted a decree that each would make a will to leave everything to members of the Order. Spratt was the sole dissenter, and declined to take the oath to this effect. As the Carmelite historian, O'Dwyer, explains, Spratt pleaded that he was holding so much money in trust for different charitable purposes, it was inappropriate for him to take the oath. Under pressure from his confreres, however, he promised to leave everything to the Order.[2] As it transpired, the wills made by the rest of the Carmelite community, following upon the 1843 Provincial Chapter, turned out to be invalid under the law, and, after the 1849 Chapter, they all had to make out new wills and to commit in writing that all their temporal goods would go to the Order through the person of the Provincial.[3] Spratt, presumably, was still the sole exception. As the one Calced Carmelite who had been prominently involved in the last-ditch endeavour to contest the penal clauses of the 1829 Catholic Relief Act, he may have been more conscious than most of the legal uncertainties in the matter of wills, donations and bequests. This notwithstanding, it is difficult to avoid the judgement that his refusal to take the oath, along with the rest of his confreres in 1843, is suggestive of special pleading.

---

2. O'Dwyer, *Irish Carmelites*, p. 213.

3. O'Dwyer, p. 218.

As to the genesis of the 1844 Act: in early 1840 an appeal by the Catholic hierarchy to the Chief Secretary, Viscount Morpeth, to consider the inequity of the Board of Bequests in its composition, secured no immediate result.  However, in February 1844 the Prime Minister, Robert Peel, in keeping with his emerging policy of trying to conciliate Ireland, announced to his cabinet his intention to bring in a measure to address the issue of wills and donations.[4]  However, in March 1844, Daniel O'Connell tried to seek redress by introducing his own bill on the subject.[5]  It proposed to endow Catholic bishops and parish priests with the same legal powers in respect of receiving and transmitting Catholic Church property as those enjoyed by the Established Church. Unfortunately, O'Connell's conviction and jailing on the one hand, and the hostility of an anti-Catholic parliament on the other, ensured the premature death of O'Connell's bill.  Peel's administration then introduced its own bill, coming before the House of Lords in June, and this measure became the Charitable Donations and Bequests (Ireland) Act, which received the Royal Assent on 9th August 1844. This Act proved to be highly controversial and within a few months it deeply divided the Irish Catholic hierarchy, clergy and Catholic political establishment as led by O'Connell.  Before considering this upheaval, a summary of its provisions may be appropriate.

*The Act of 1844*

The Act replaced the old Bequests Board by a new one of thirteen members.  It provided that there were to be three ex-officio judges and, of the remaining ten members, five, and not more than five, were to be Catholics.  All ten would be appointed by the Government.  Its purpose was to ensure that donations and bequests were executed in conformity with the intentions of the donors.  Only in cases of doubt or of suspected concealment or misapplication were the Board's Commissioners required to intervene.  There were four sections of the Act that became problematic or the subject of controversy.  Section 15 provided, *inter alia*, that '*nothing contained in the Act was to be construed as rendering lawful any donation, devise or bequest to or in favour of any religious*

4.  W. J. Walsh, *O'Connell, Archbishop Murray and the Board of Charitable Bequests*, Dublin 1916, p. 7; K. B. Nowlan, *The Politics of Repeal: A Study in the Relations between Great Britain and Ireland, 1841-50*, London 1965, p. 66.
5.  Walsh, p. 16; Nowlan, p. 67.

*order prohibited by the Act of 1829, known as the Catholic Emancipation Act or any donation, devise or bequest to or in favour of any member or members thereof'.* Section 16 provided that no donation or bequest for pious or charitable uses in Ireland should be valid unless the deed had been executed three calendar months before the death of the testator and duly registered in the Registry of Deeds. Section 22 laid down that nothing contained in this Act would render void or unlawful any donation or bequest which but for this Act would be lawful. Finally, Section 6 provided for situations where the custom and practice of a Protestant Church or the Catholic Church became an issue – in which circumstance a Committee of Protestant members could consider and advise the Board in respect of Protestant cases and a Committee of Catholic members would advise in the circumstance of Catholic cases.

Within weeks of obtaining the Royal Assent, the Act became the subject of a wave of attacks by O'Connell and those newspapers that supported him, notably, *The Pilot* and *The Freeman's Journal*. His assaults on the Act were expressed in two formal legal opinions published on 24th August and 5th December 1844. His attacks were also conveyed in a series of some ten public addresses delivered in Dublin, over the period from 3rd December 1844 up to 10th February 1845.[6] In his assaults upon the Act he and his press allies whipped up a frenzy of fear and opposition and he made it clear that no Catholic worth the name could consider having anything to do with it.

## The Plundering of the Friars?

Although the new Commissioners of Bequests would not be named publicly until 18th December, and although they would not hold their first meeting until 9th January 1845, within three days of the Royal Assent of 9th August 1844 the press attacks commenced in *The Pilot*.[7] These attacks were extreme and went beyond the facts of the case in declaring that the Act interfered with the power of testators or donors to choose their own trustees, which it did not, and in stating that the Act obliged testators or donors to have their charitable intentions submitted

---

6. Eight of the meetings were formal protest meetings of the inhabitants of various Dublin parishes; the other two were addresses delivered at meetings of the Repeal Association. See W. J. Walsh, *O'Connell, Archbishop Murray and the Board of Charitable Bequests*, Dublin 1916, pp. 55-88.
7. *The Pilot*, 12th Aug 1844.

to the Commissioners, which again was not the case.[8] Twelve days later, having been consulted by Bishop Cantwell of Meath for advice as to the implications of the Act, O'Connell delivered his first professional opinion. He held that the Act gave the Board dangerous powers and since the Board, by statute, comprised a Protestant majority, it would be Protestant power that would prevail in its decisions: in general, therefore, no Catholic charity could feel safe in the hands of such a tribunal.[9]

This first opinion was sufficient to galvanise three of the Catholic bishops, Cantwell of Meath, McGettigan of Raphoe and McHale of Tuam, to draft and circulate a 'Protest of the Hierarchy and Clergy of Ireland' against the Act. This first appeared in the press on 21st September and gathered growing numbers of signatures until its final list, of one archbishop, fourteen bishops and over 700 clergy of dioceses and religious orders, was published on 26th November.[10] However, while no Catholic bishop was happy with the Act, not all were totally against:

three of them, Armagh's Crotty, Dublin's Murray and Down & Connor's Denvir, were prepared to accept it and work it for all its faults.

McHale, however, was at one with O'Connell in assailing the Act. In a letter to Fransoni, on 25th November, he informed the Cardinal that, among other things, the Act annulled all bequests made to religious orders.[11] Factually incorrect, McHale's claim was probably based on respect for O'Connell's legal authority in these matters. As William

**Fig 43.** *Statue of Archbishop McHale of Tuam, in the grounds of the Cathedral of the Assumption.*

8.  *Walsh*, p. 34.
9.  *The Pilot*, 24th Aug 1844.
10. *DEP*, 21st Sept 1844; *FJ*, 26th Nov 1844.
11. B. O'Reilly, *The life of the Most Rev Dr McHale, Archbishop of Tuam*, 2 vols., New York 1890, i. 554; H. Andrews, *The Lion of the West: a biography of John McHale*, Dublin 2001, p. 104.

Walsh pointed out, the Act did not annul or make void bequests to religious orders but simply left unrepealed the annulling implications of the Catholic Relief Act of 1829. Back then, O'Connell had assured the Franciscan, Dr O'Meara, that these powers were theoretical and practically inoperable since only the Attorney General could prosecute a friar or monk under the 1829 Act.[12] Now, however, he appeared to have changed his mind, and publicly expressed regret that he had acquiesced in the outlawing of the regular clergy. He reiterated this regret quite explicitly at a public protest meeting at St Michan's on 3rd December:

> The Emancipation Bill prohibited any more the existence of regular clergy in Ireland, and I admit that it was a base thing of us to consent to connect our emancipation with that clause...I regret and deplore it...we should not have consented to introduce such a clause. It was a sacrifice we should not have made.[13]

Over November and December 1844 he intensified the campaign, stressing the disastrous nature of the Act upon the property of the religious orders. He now argued that the Charitable Bequests Commission, once up and running, would be obliged, under Section 12, to *'recover'* and *'apply the other purposes'* donations to religious orders: in effect, the Catholic Commissioners would find themselves involved in the plundering of the friars. This became the principal theme of his campaign. At his public protest meeting in St Michan's, on 3rd December, he advised his audience that any Catholic commissioner would find himself duty bound, under the Act, to recover such 'misapplied' donations and could therefore find himself *'robbing the friars of all their property'*. Unsurprisingly, the religious orders were appalled at the implied threat and, as an alarmed Archbishop Murray confessed to the Lord Lieutenant, Heytesbury, *'the religious orders...are...open-mouthed against the bishops for the decision to which they have come'*.[14] As Bishop Blake of Dromore put it, in a letter to Dr Paul Cullen in Rome, *'the Charity Bequests Bill has been a Pandora's Box in Ireland'*.[15]

12. *The Pilot*, 6th Dec 1844.
13. *The Pilot*, 6th Dec 1844.
14. Heytesbury to Graham, 21st Nov 1844, *Graham Papers*, cited in Kerr, p. 186.
15. Dromore Diocesan Archives, *Blake Papers*, Blake to Cullen, no date given.

Doubtless it was concerns such as these, together with their steadfast commitment to O'Connell, that led John Spratt, his brother James, and all the Carmelite confreres of Whitefriar Street to add their names to the *'Protest of the Hierarchy and Clergy of Ireland'* as circulated by McHale.[16] What precise role, thereafter, John played behind the scenes is not immediately evident in the extant sources but, it is a fair hazard from what follows, he was not an idle bystander. In the final week of November the heads of the religious orders sought from O'Connell his legal opinion on the implications of the Act for the orders and their property. On 30th November he gave the opinion. He pointed out that under the Emancipation Act, any donation to any male religious community was, by implication, *'void in point of law'*. As to donations to individual members of an order, under the same 1829 Act *'the question is one of some doubt'* but he felt that it was legal. However, he insisted that under this new Bequests Act

at present, not only no community of religious but no single regular can take or enjoy any species of property, either in land, houses or money, for the support of the Order or of any portion of the Order.

He proceeded to assert that any Catholic Commissioner would thereby be placed *'in direct antagonism with all the regular clergy'*, as

it makes it the duty of every Catholic Commissioner to sue for the recovery and application to other purposes of all charitable property, withheld or misapplied. Now, the property of the regulars is, in point of law, misapplied and every Catholic Commissioner is, in discharge of his duty, under this new act, bound to take away from the regulars, their property and apply it to other purposes.[17]

16. The list initially appeared in the press on 21st September; they added their names in the first supplement to the list, as published on 24th September. See *DEP*, 21st, 24th Sept 1844.
17. *FJ*, 5th Dec 1844: 'The Regular Clergy – The Bequests Act – Opinion of Mr O'Connell', dated 30th Nov 1844.

**Fig 44.**    *Lord Lieutenant Heytesbury.*

*Breaking Ranks*

This stark opinion, first published in the press on 5th December, caused alarm among the religious orders and came only three days after the press first revealed that Murray, Crolly and Kennedy of Killaloe had been announced as the three Catholic bishops nominated to the Bequests Board.[18]    Kennedy soon after buckled under pressure and resigned the appointment and was later replaced by Bishop Cornelius Denvir of Down and Connor.[19]    It is certain that the heads of the orders lost no time in conveying that alarm to Murray: on Monday 2nd December *'he hastened to the Vice-Regal lodge to consult with Lord Lieutenant Heytesbury and Chief Secretary Elliot'.*[20]    He was assured by them that the Government, in this Act, had no intention of pursuing the predatory aims which O'Connell had ascribed to the framers of the legislation and they insisted that, in relation to the property of the religious orders, O'Connell was mistaken.    They undertook to secure confirmation of this by consulting the law officers of the Crown and if, as a result, they were advised that they themselves were mistaken, they undertook to introduce amending legislation.[21]

18.    *Dublin Monitor*, 2nd Dec1844; *Dublin Gazette*, 17th Dec 1844: by the time the official announcement was published in the Irish administration's *Gazette*, Denvir had been substituted for Kennedy.

19.    *FJ*, 11th Dec 1844; *Roscommon Journal*, 4th Jan 1845.

20.    *FJ*, 6th Dec 1844 publishes Murray's letter of 6th December to Spratt in which Murray mentions that he went to consult them 'yesterday'.

21.    Kerr, p. 185.

In reporting these assurances immediately the same day, it is notable that Murray chose John Spratt as the prime recipient of this news and not Spratt's religious superiors, the Provincial, Colgan, nor the Prior, O'Rourke, nor, for that matter, any of the heads of the other orders concerned. Murray then put this in writing to Spratt on the next day, 3rd December.[22] On the evening of that same day it chanced to be the annual fund-raising dinner for the St Brigid's Orphan Society, at which Spratt was the officiating clergyman and where, by his side, sat Daniel O'Connell as chairman of the proceedings. While most of the speeches were concerned with Repeal of the Union – and not on the plight of orphans – O'Connell chose also to speak at length on the Bequests Act. In proposing a toast to Archbishop Murray, he warned that he *'did not wish Catholic clergymen to go to the Castle at all because they could not come back as good as when they went there'*. Regarding Dr Murray, he had the greatest confidence *'in his spotless integrity and the only fear he entertained was that he (Dr Murray) might think others as honest as himself but in that he feared he (Dr Murray) might be mistaken'*. He went on to reiterate that under this Act the regular clergy would be doubly worse off and that the legislation *'furnished machinery to rob them of all they possessed'*. He then proposed a toast to John Spratt. The latter spoke briefly but sufficiently to convey where he stood. He made no mention of Dr Murray's letter to him of that very day but instead observed, with some feeling that

> his Order, after the 4th of January when the bill alluded to would come into operation, would be worse than the fellow returned from transportation, for he could enjoy a property left to him by a friend, while the persons belonging to his Order could not do so because they had taken religious vows.[23]

His remarks appeared to have been much commented upon in the days that followed so that he felt obliged to comment further a week later, as shall be presently noted. His scepticism of Dr Murray's assurances was sharply endorsed the very next day, 4th December, when a meeting of the provincials of the orders, held in Clarendon Street Church, passed

---

22. *FJ*, 6th Dec; *DEPC*, 7th Dec 1844. Printed on these dates, Murray's letter was dated 3rd Dec 1844.
23. *FJ*, 4th Dec 1844.

two resolutions: the first condemned the Bequests Act as *'a penal enactment against us'*, the second called on *'our reverend and beloved Archbishop'* to bear in mind *'the apprehension and terror with which we are filled'*, and implored him *'to discountenance the penal law and prevent, if possible, its being ever carried into execution'*.[24] They brought these resolutions by deputation to Murray on 7th December, were received with his customary courtesy, and his verbal response – the substance and tenor of which was not reported – was considered by them at a reconvened meeting on Monday 9th December.[25] The alarm and scepticism of the orders' superiors would have been reinforced by O'Connell on the eve of their deputation. At a protest meeting of three Dublin parishes at the market-place in Spitalfields, on Friday 6th December, O'Connell read out Murray's letter to Spratt and then proceeded to pour scorn on the Lord Lieutenant and Chief Secretary for being party to an act that they did not know the meaning of and at having to refer the Act to their law officers. Again he insisted that the Act would lead to robbery of the friars' property.[26]

Spratt fully shared O'Connell's antagonism to the Act and now felt the need to expand on his remarks of 3rd December at the St Brigid's Orphan Society dinner. Eight days later, in a letter to the press, he commented that his earlier observations related to the Act *'in its present objectionable state'* and *'burthened as it is with a clause highly prejudicial to the regular clergy of Ireland'*. He pointed out that, with due respect to Dr Murray, the Archbishop's letter *'did not alter my opinion of the Bill as it is'*. Consequently, Spratt now urged that a petition be got up to have the Act amended as far as it affected the regular clergy and hoped that his Grace would support this. Expressing again his respect for the Archbishop, Spratt then added:

> We have every reason to place the most unlimited confidence in his Lordship's wisdom and long-tried prudence; and rest perfectly satisfied, *that in his official capacity of commissioner*, he would - should necessity require it – throw the shield of his protection over us in case of impending danger.[27]

24. *WFJ*, 14th Dec 1844.
25. *DEP*, 10th Dec 1844; *WFJ*, 14th Dec 1844.
26. *FJ*, 7th Dec 1844.
27. *The Pilot*, 11th Dec 1844; *FJ*, 11th Dec 1844. See also Kerr, p. 188.

In referring, conditionally, to Murray as one of the Bequest Board Commissioners Spratt was simply publicising what by then was common knowledge: mention of the Archbishop as a potential commissioner had been in the public prints since at least 19th November and was stated as though it were a fact from at least 2nd December.[28]  Spratt's reference came only two days after Archbishop McHale had issued a pastoral letter expressing outrage and disbelief at rumours that any Catholic bishop might dare to accept such a position.[29]  The official press announcement that three Catholic prelates had accepted the appointment was not published until 17th December, but rumours or the 'news', as mentioned by McHale and then by John Spratt, were sufficient to impel the regular clergy once again to send a deputation to Murray.  They sought to dissuade him from accepting a place as commissioner.  Murray conceded that *'certain alterations or modifications'* to the Act should be sought.  Nevertheless, he insisted that he could not regard the Act as *'dangerous or objectionable to the Roman Catholic religion'*, therefore, he did not *'see himself called upon to comply with their wishes'*.[30]  This response and his own subsequent pastoral letter on the subject did nothing to dampen down clerical and lay agitation.[31]  Protest meetings in city and country continued and indeed intensified, and in leading these protests, O'Connell's position on the Act seemed to become more radical: at the Dominican Church in Denmark Street, on 19th December, he took the extreme position that all charitable bequests would have to go before the Commissioners, even as he admitted to *'a feeling of defeat'* and that the Dublin Castle 'hacks' had triumphed insofar as three Catholic bishops had agreed to take office.  He concluded that *'this law cannot but have a most disastrous operation on the fortunes of the regular clergy'*.[32]

On the very next day, 20th December, the press carried the opinion of the Crown's law officers on the Act.  They disagreed directly with

28.  *DEPC*, 19th Nov 1844; *Dublin Monitor*, 2nd Dec 1844.
29.  *FJ*, 9th Dec 1844.
30.  *Dublin Monitor*, 18th Dec 1844.  The Monitor does not report a date for this encounter and none of the other newspapers report on it.
31.  *DEP*, 24th Dec 1844.  Extracts were published in the *Freeman's Journal* on 23rd December 1844, based on text supplied by the publisher, Coyne, but the first full version was that which appeared in the *DEP* on 24th December.
32.  *FJ*, 20th Dec 1844.

O'Connell on the two key issues raised by him in his opinion of 30th November. They held that in the Catholic Relief Act of 1829 there was no express provision making bequests to religious orders unlawful: they were unlawful as being against the policy of the Act. They found that the 1829 Act did not render unlawful, bequests to individual friars, that any bequest to a friar for his own use was legal, and that the 1844 Bequests Act had not changed this. They advised, in addition, that under the Bequests Act there was no obligation to compel the commissioners to take away the property of the religious orders.[33]

On several occasions over the next two months O'Connell promised a reply to this opinion, but none was forthcoming. In the interim, the new Commissioners held their first meeting on 9th January. At the same time, Spratt's suggestion for a petition had not been forgotten. On Tuesday 14th January, after the annual meeting of the diocesan clergy of Dublin, a separate conference of these, together with some Augustinians including James Spratt, took up John's suggestion for a petition. Initially over ninety signatories called for the repeal of the penal clauses of the Emancipation Act, the total discarding of the Bequests Act and its replacement by O'Connell's Bill of March 1844.[34] By the end of the first week in February the petition had grown to a final list of over 140 from a total of 173 parish priests, curates and regular clergy of the Dublin Diocese. It now included John Spratt and his six Carmelite confreres. This petition was presented to the House of Commons by John O'Connell on 14th March 1845.[35] A separate, more mildly expressed petition was also got up in the diocese, at the same time, with Archbishop Murray heading the list. This *'Petition of the undersigned Archbishop and Secular Clergy of Dublin'* called for the removal of the legal disabilities of the regular clergy under the Acts of 1829 and 1844.[36] The laity also took up the call for the repeal of the 1844 Act and Michael Spratt was among the signatories of parishioners

33. *FJ*, 20th Dec 1844. The Opinion of the Law Officers was actually dated 13th December but was not published in the national press until 20th December.

34. *FJ*, 6th Dec,1844; *DEPC*, 7th Dec 1844. Spratt immediately conveyed the letter, verbatim, to the press and it was published in various Dublin newspapers on 6th and 7th December.

35. *FJ*, 6th Feb, 17th March 1845. The six confreres were: Andrew Day, William Withers, Michael Tobin, Richard Colgan, Edward O'Rourke and William Kinsella.

36. *DEP*, 21st Jan 1845.

of St Mary's, Donnybrook, calling a meeting for this purpose, for
Donnybrook Green on 10th February 1845.[37] Similar meetings of laity
and clergy took place in these days throughout the country and Spratt's
Carmelite colleagues outside of Dublin were not absent from the lists.
At Knocktopher on 6th January, Friars Eugene Cullen, Matthew Scally
and at least four others had become involved in a great meeting in
and around their Carmelite Chapel, where an estimated forty thousand
gathered to petition for the cause. Cullen did not mince his words on
the occasion:

> I raise my voice and complain of those reprobates who have
> taken the liberty – without the nation's consent to make the
> Royal Mandate of Queen Victoria – whom God may preserve –
> their authority for regulating the affairs of the Catholic Church
> of Ireland.[38]

Indeed, the Carmelites Cullen and Scally would prove persistent in
continuing to fight for the repeal of the disabilities against the religious
orders, long after the rest of Ireland, clerical and lay, had let the dust
settle on their undisturbed disabilities. In January 1845 they headed up
a protest meeting and organised another petition among the people of
Knocktopher calling for the repeal of the 'obnoxious' 1844 Bequests
Act.[39] Three years later Scally issued a rallying call to the heads of the
religious orders in Ireland, urging a new campaign for the removal of
their legal disabilities.[40] It appears to have fallen on deaf ears, like the
various petitions against the Bequests Act in 1845.

For all that, the Bequests Commission commenced its work in
January 1845 and in all of its sessions until the century ended, and
beyond that, according to Walsh, it never had to hear or decide
upon a single case involving any adverse finding against any of the

---

37. *FJ*, 8th Feb 1845.
38. *DEP*, 9th Jan 1845.
39. *Kilkenny Journal*, 4th Jan 1845.
40. *Dublin Weekly Register*, 5th Feb 1848, Matthew Scally, OCC., 'Emancipation
    of the Regular Orders – To the Superiors of the Regular Orders of Ireland',
    Kildare 26th January 1848. The history of the male religious orders in respect of
    their legal disabilities, and indeed the history of the penal clauses of the 1829 Act
    in the century after its enactment, remain to be written.

religious orders in the matter of their properties, bequests or charitable donations.[41] Despite the hostile legislation against the religious orders remaining on the Statute Book, they survived and even prospered as the century wore on, conducting and constructing more friaries and monasteries, colleges and charities, than any friar or monk could have imagined in the agitating days of the passing of the Bequests Act.

*The Historical Bequest*
It is clear that, in a narrow legal sense, O'Connell, McHale and Spratt and their fellow-opponents of the Act were mistaken in regard to its negative implications. Furthermore, on a distinctly positive note, the Act, for the first time since the Reformation, recognised Ireland's Catholic bishops and archbishops by their titles, conferring on them a titular equality with their Protestant counterparts. In a wider political sense, however, the instincts of the Act's opponents were sound, since the whole point of Robert Peel's religious reform programme for Ireland was to detach the Catholic bishops and clergy from their support of O'Connell and thereby to kill off his movement for Repeal of the Act of Union by way of more modest reforms.[42] To a limited extent, this intention succeeded, since a minority of the bishops, led by Murray, broke ranks with the majority. To this extent, as MacDonagh observed, the whole affair constituted a significant defeat for O'Connell.[43] However, the great body of the Catholic religious leaders, diocesan and regular, remained united behind O'Connell, against the Act. Among them, John Spratt never wavered in that allegiance. Nevertheless, their agitation collapsed.

It was not until the year 1961 that the Charitable Donations and Bequests Act of 1844 was repealed by the Charities Act. As for the penal clauses of the Emancipation Act of 1829, they were not done away with until 1983 when that Act in its entirety was removed by the Statute Law Revision Act:[44] in the long duration of that intervening

41.  Walsh, p. 11.
42.  See Kerr, *Peel, Priests and Politics*, p. 151 and K. B. Nowlan, *The Politics of Repeal*, London 1965, pp. 59-63, 65-69.
43.  See also O. MacDonagh, *The Emancipist, Daniel O'Connell, 1830-47*, London 1989, pp. 259-60.
44.  I am grateful to Mr Seamus Haughey, Research Librarian of the Oireachtas, for this information.

century and a half, the property and the lives of Ireland's monks and friars remained undisturbed by predatory threats. Fr John could have had more trust in the *bona fides* of the new Bequests Commission: Archbishop Murray's confidence in it did not prove ill-founded. In June 1866, for example, a lady named Jane Etchingham, of York Row, made her will and provided that £200 be bequeathed to Fr Spratt to be used for whatever charitable purpose he deemed best. The friar, however, predeceased her, she dying in March 1872 without revoking or altering her will. The Commissioners of Charitable Donations and Bequests directed that the sum concerned be now paid to Fr John Carr, as Spratt's successor, to be expended on charity to the poor in whatever manner Fr Carr deemed fit.[45] However, back in 1844-45, the fever and heat of the agitation against the Act did much to distort perceptions, not least those of Fr John Spratt: for him the sudden collapse of that agitation was soon to be followed by graver threats and preoccupations more dire.

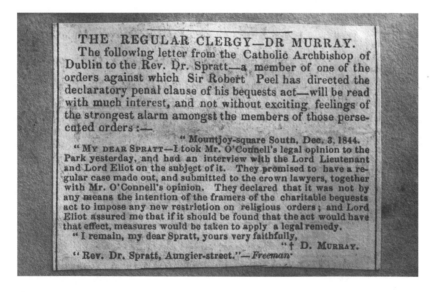

**Fig 45.**    *A clipping from the* Freeman's Journal, *6th Dec, in GMA, Scrapbook A, showing Archbishop Murray's letter of 3rd December 1844.*

---

45.    *FJ*, 7th Nov 1872.

# CHAPTER ELEVEN

## *The Carmelite and the Great Calamity, 1845-1850*

The first reports of the failure of the potato harvest were published in the national press from 9th September 1845. By the second week of November, the Prime Minister, Robert Peel, had ordered the purchase of Indian corn for Ireland from the USA and had appointed a relief committee to supplement the provision of workhouse relief under the Poor Relief Act of 1838. By the spring of 1846 a programme of public works had been organised. It was not until the latter part of 1846, however, that the onset of severe winter weather compounded the widespread distress, in the wake of the disastrous second failure of the potato crop that summer. On 13th November the Quakers established their Central Relief Committee and it was a fortnight before this that John Spratt began his public contribution to the debate on the relief of famine. On 1st November 1846 he published a letter entitled *The Distress of the People.*[1] Here he called for an end to the use of grain for brewing and distilling and urged the closure of the breweries and distilleries in order to save the grain for the feeding of the poor. The letter spoke more for his heart than his head, even if it was an understandable product of his temperance crusade which then was at its height. By that stage the famine had already had devastating effects on the country and soon was to manifest itself in the capital.

This became clear from the inexorably rising number of admissions to the North and South Dublin Union Workhouses. Whilst Dublin City never experienced the range and depth of the sufferings and mortality of significant areas of rural Ireland, the city, nevertheless, experienced

---

1. *The Pilot, FJ,* 2nd Nov 1846.

a growing influx of desperate people, from further afield, who came
in search of relief, or on their way to the emigrant ships.[2]  By early
November 1846 the North Dublin Union Workhouse had exceeded its
official capacity of 2,000 inmates and, within a year, had to double its
accommodation provision to 4,000: its numbers did not then reduce to
pre-famine levels until 1860.[3]  Similarly, the number of inmates relieved
in the South Dublin Union Workhouse tripled between 1840 and 1850:
from around 3,000 in 1841 the numbers rose to almost 6,000 in 1846
and rose relentlessly thereafter to close on 9,500 by 1851.[4]

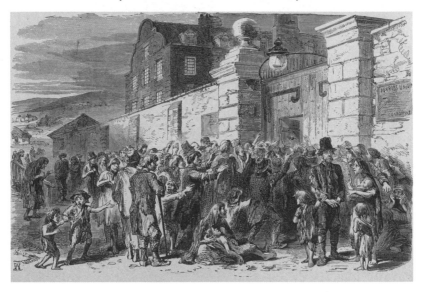

**Fig 46.**    *Scene at the gate of the workhouse, c. 1846.*

When, on 21st December 1846, the Lord Mayor was called upon
to convene a meeting to *'address the alarming and unparalleled distress of
the poor of this city'*, the requisition was an interdenominational one,
headed by the Church of Ireland and Catholic Archbishops of Dublin.

2.  O. Callaghan, *The Impact of the Great Famine on a city : a Study of Dublin, 1845-1850*,
    University College Dublin, B.A. dissertation, 1971, pp. 24 ff.; C. Ó Gráda, *Black '47
    and Beyond: The Great Irish Famine History, Economy and Memory*, Princeton 1999, esp.
    pp. 157-93, 'Famine in Dublin City'.
3.  C. Ó Gráda & T. W. Guinnane, 'Mortality in the North Dublin Union during the
    Great Famine', in C. Ó Gráda, ed., *Ireland's Great Famine*, Dublin 2006, p. 94.
4.  H. Burke, *The People and the Poor Law in Nineteenth Century Ireland*, Dublin 1987, p. 43.

In the list of 56 signatories of the requisition, John Spratt's was the only Carmelite, indeed the only signature by any regular priest.[5] That call to action resulted, on 23rd December, in what was designated a 'metropolitan' relief meeting. It was notable, amongst other aspects, for its multi-confessional composition. Among the prominent personalities attending were the O'Connells, Daniel and John, together with John Spratt, the only identified friar or monk present. When it came to the matter of establishing a Central Relief Committee, a considerable division appeared in the ranks of those present. Was this to be a committee for providing relief to the distressed in Ireland as a whole, or was it exclusively for the relief of the distressed of Dublin? When the formal resolutions had been adopted it became clear that what they had established was 'the Metropolitan Relief Committee for the Poor of the City of Dublin'.[6]

It was also notable that Spratt does not appear to have spoken at the proceedings and, for once in his life, he did not appear to have ended up on a committee. The new body met on 26th, 28th and 30th December, chaired by Daniel O'Connell, and then continued to meet for a further six months, usually under the chairmanship of Fr Andrew O'Connell. Its members included Spratt's friends and associates, Battersby and Haughton. This committee was active in raising and allocating funds and in calling on the government to save the starving people.[7] A few days after its launch, a separate group of prominent individuals, including the Marquis of Kildare and Lord Cloncurry, met on 29th December, to establish 'The General Central Relief Committee for Ireland'. This body raised an initial £1,438-5-0 in a limited number of substantially generous personal contributions.[8] Interestingly, despite the membership of his friend and benefactor Cloncurry, Spratt does not appear to have been involved in this organisation. For the first two years of the Great Famine, the Carmelite friar appears to have been exclusively active and engaged at local level. The historian, Fitzpatrick, suggests that there developed a serious difference of opinion between Cloncurry and Spratt over the General Relief Committee: that this body soon split and that Spratt headed up a separate Catholic Relief

---

5.  *The Pilot*, 28th Dec 1846; *FJ*, 21st Dec 1846.
6.  *DEPC*, 24th Dec 1846.
7.  *DEPC*, 31st Dec 1846; *DEP*, 29th Dec 1846.
8.  *SNL*, 30th Dec 1846.

Committee or Fund and that Cloncurry did not want to be associated publicly with a confessional charity. Fitzpatrick went on to say that privately, Cloncurry contributed £150 to Spratt's organisation while officially remaining committed to the General Central Relief Committee as established on 29th December 1846.[9] The present author has found no basis for this and surmises that the actual division was between the Metropolitan Relief Committee as founded on 23rd December, to aid relief in Dublin, as just described, and the more aristocratic General Central Relief Committee, established with a national remit. There was no element of sectarian or denominational exclusiveness associated with either body: each featured leading members of the Protestant and Catholic confessions. There had been difficulties at the start, but, as the editor of the *Evening Packet* observed, *'the difficulties did not, we are happy to say, arise from sectarianism, nor from politics'*, but related solely to remit, whether metropolitan or national.[10]

It is certainly curious that the friar did not speak at or become involved in the organisation of the Metropolitan Relief Committee, since ever before and ever afterwards he tended to end up a committee man or officer of an array of national bodies. However, in this instance, it may be that local demands had first call on his time and energies. There was, for example, his ongoing weekly commitment to the Sick and Indigent Roomkeepers Society of which he was joint honorary secretary. The history of the organisation during the Famine years amply illustrates the effect of the crisis on the respectable Dublin poor and the demands the crisis made on its own committee members.

*The Sick and Indigent Roomkeepers and the Famine*
In the course of 1846 the Sick and Indigent Roomkeepers Society experienced an unprecedented demand on its resources. It offered help to over 30,000 cases of want, an increase of 6,455 more than the year before. It was enabled to do so by virtue of an income of £2479, some £578 over what had been donated in the previous twelve months. That income in 1846 represented also an increase of almost £450 over the average receipts of the previous five years. Despite these impressive

---

9.  W. J. Fitzpatrick, *The Life, Times and Contemporaries of Lord Cloncurry*, Dublin 1855, p. 507.
10.  *DEPC*, 24th Dec 1846.

statistics, the Society rued the fact it was not able to answer every call for aid, because of insufficient funds. Such was the situation that it actually sent Spratt and the Church of Ireland Dean of Ossory as a deputation to the recently instituted Metropolitan Relief Committee in search of additional funds, but to what effect is not clear.[11]

In the course of the next year, the 'Black '47', they had relieved even more needy persons, at 33,577, but had to do so on a reduced income of £2,397, only £82 below the income for 1846.[12] While the figures for the numbers assisted superficially appeared impressive, Fr Andrew O'Connell pointed out that the figures amounted to a mere 2.5 pence per day per person relieved. However, it was the difference between staying alive with the hope of being able to work, or else staggering into the poorhouse. In the course of 1848, with both economic stagnation and famine fatigue setting in, even the Sick and Indigent Roomkeepers Society was now seriously experiencing the repercussions. Want of means meant that, despite a number of hugely generous bequests, the Society could relieve only some 26,500 persons and many applications for relief had to be declined.[13]

The following year, 1849, was again a disastrous one in terms of the impact of the Famine, but Spratt, in his annual report, was relieved to inform the members that the income had improved greatly over that for 1848. This and his fellow-committee members' attendance weekly over many years, and especially during the Famine, constituted a considerable commitment. To some extent the burden of the honorary secretaryship for him must have been lightened by the assistance of a paid general secretary. From 1844 this post was held by Myles Casey. Unfortunately, when Casey died suddenly in 1861, it was discovered that he had been embezzling some of its funds, amounting to a sizeable sum in excess of £2,000. Since it was for long undiscovered, the theft must have been proceeding over many years: it says much for the trusting

---

11. *The Pilot*, 27th Jan 1847.
12. *FJ*, 20th Jan 1848.
13. *FJ*, 19th Jan 1849. The Society was bequeathed two impressive donations of £1,000 each from the wills of a Ms Shee of Gardiner Street and a Mr Peter Ward of Lennox Street, together with a further bequest of £600 from the estate of James Martin of Fitzwilliam Square and £200 from that of Henry Willis of Henry Street. Such, however, were the laws' delays, that only £500 of this total of £2,800 had been made available to the Society in the course of 1848.

nature of Spratt and his committee fellows, if not for the level of his and their scrutiny, that the embezzlement went undetected over what presumably was an extended period.[14]

## The Poor of St Peter's

In the initial years of the Famine, Spratt's work was principally confined to local endeavour. Apart from his work for the Sick and Indigent Roomkeepers, he soon became involved in the local (Church of Ireland) parish of St Peter's. Even in this most prosperous of parishes, where the Whitefriar Street Carmelites were based, the pressure of an intensified poverty and distress began to manifest from late 1846. In face of this, on 30th December 1846, a group of twenty-nine male parishioners called upon the parish churchwardens to convene a meeting to consider *'the alarming and destitute state of the poor of the parish'* and to adopt measures for their *'immediate relief'*. Led by Archdeacon John Torrens, rector of St Peter's, and his four Church of Ireland curates, the names of John Spratt and two of his Carmelite confreres, Andrew Day and Michael Tobin, followed immediately, together with those of eleven local medical doctors.[15] Thereafter, throughout the famine years, the inter-faith co-operation between Anglican and Catholic clergy in St

Peter's was noteworthy and this may well have owed a great deal to the friendly relations between Fr Spratt and Archdeacon Torrens. Evidence of those good relations has already been noted in connection with John's schools in the 1820s. It was borne out again, early in the 1840s when, at a meeting of the St Peter's Parish Vestry, John stood up and asked Torrens that the Carmelites be exempted from the payment of

**Fig 47.**   *Archdeacon John Torrens.*

14. D. Lindsay, *Dublin's Oldest Charity,* pp. 39-40.
15. *SNL,* 30th Dec 1846. There may have been a third Carmelite: between the names of Day and Tobin there was the name of Richard Corrigan and this may have been a misprint for Richard Colgan. It appears as Corrigan in the *DEP* and *FJ,* for this date also.

the hugely-resented 'minister's money'. Torrens immediately granted this exemption. The friar was so effusive in his gratitude that he immediately offered to use his influence to prevent any *'Catholic party'* from offering opposition at any future such vestry meetings. When this was adverted to, *'as a boon made by one gentleman to another'*, at a similar St Peter's Vestry meeting in 1842, uproar ensued, which lasted over an hour, between opponents and supporters of minister's money. However, Spratt's relations with Torrens remained cordial, as they worked together down the years on the Roomkeepers Committee.[16] Now, five years later, the call of the twenty-nine Protestant and Catholic parishioners led to the foundation, on 1st January 1847, of the St Peter's Parochial General Relief Committee. A series of daily meetings over the following fortnight saw the establishment of a Provision and Finance Committee which divided the parish into districts and appointed two visitors per district to establish the extent of the distress, to collect subscriptions and to administer relief. Each pair of visitors was to comprise a member of each faith in order to inspire confidence that religious harmony prevailed and to avoid any suggestion of denominational bias in the distribution of aid. A soup depot and coal depot were quickly provided and all members took turns in organising the giving of relief. The actual operation of serving bread and soup commenced on 12th January 1847.

Inevitably, John Spratt himself was to be found at the centre of this parochial charity, becoming joint honorary secretary of the St Peter's Relief Committee along with one B B Smyth.[17] In these early days they had collected £120 and this had to cater to the needs of some 2,000 destitutes – a far greater number of the needy than these limited resources could satisfy. Such was their anxiety in this situation that the

---

16. FJ, 31st March 1842. 'Minister's Money' was an urban equivalent of tithes, levied in certain Irish towns and cities. It was a source of considerable resentment on the part of non-Anglicans; some of these had their goods seized and sold in order to pay, if they had been in default. The Dublin Quaker printer, and associate of Spratt, Richard Webb, had furniture valued at £6-19s seized for a debt of £1-12s of minister's money, levied on the instructions of the absentee Church of Ireland minister of St Mark's Parish. See R. S. Harrison, *Richard Davis Webb, Dublin Quaker Printer 1805-1872*, Cork 1993, p. 36.

17. *FJ*, 13th Jan 1847. Among those actively involved was the local Catholic curate, Fr M. Farrington, an uncle of Spratt's future biographer and confrere, Andrew Elias Farrington.

St Peter's Committee applied to the Metropolitan Relief Committee for supplementary aid, only to be rebuffed, as the St Peter's deputation had provided insufficient evidence of *'adequate exertions in the raising of funds for the relief of the poor in so extensive and wealthy a parish'.*[18]

For all that, it was to its credit that the St Peter's Parish Relief Committee made no distinction, not only between Protestant and Catholic, but also as between residents and migrants. There is no doubt that a significant body of those desperately seeking food in the parish over the years 1846 to 1849 were destitutes from beyond the parish and even from beyond the county. As Callaghan pointed out, over the years 1846-51 as many as 400,000 migrants may have passed through Dublin, and, as Dickson indicated, by 1850, 65% of all admissions to the North Dublin Union workhouse were non-Dubliners, while 80% of the beggars passing through the Mendicity Institute in 1849 were from beyond Dublin City. He observes that the population surge in Dublin over the 1841 and 1851 censuses was *'the direct result of the Famine'* and that many of the additional 36,631 Dubliners in 1851 were *'crisis migrants'.*[19] The extensive St Peter's Parish, on the western edge of the city, would have been a natural arriving point for distressed migrants of the west and south, coming through Wicklow and Kildare in search of support or on the way to emigrant ships. It is notable that the mortality rate in St Peter's and the neighbouring St Luke's parishes almost doubled between 1844-5 and 1846-7.[20] By the end of March 1847 the St Peter's Relief Committee was in dire straits. Their funds had become exhausted as they tried to feed some three thousand seven hundred parishioners and migrants every Tuesday, Thursday and Saturday.[21] During this period the various parish relief committees in the city were trying to feed and clothe some 36,000 men, women and children.[22]

For Fr John, the work for St Peter's Relief Committee became a daily commitment well into the middle of 1847, as shall be expanded upon shortly. However, he did not neglect wider concerns in the matter of famine relief. At the end of January 1847 he organised a well-attended

18.  *FJ*, 26th Jan 1847.
19.  Dickson, pp. 308, 317.
20.  Ó Gráda, *Black '47*, p. 170.
21.  *FJ*, 1st April 1847.
22.  *FJ*, 13th, 20th, 23rd, 25th Jan 1847. See D'Arcy, *Dublin Artisan Activity*, pp. 119, 123.

meeting of Dublin citizens in the Music Hall, Abbey Street, to direct attention, yet again, to the use of grain for alcohol production, when people were dying throughout the country for want of food. Convening this meeting he was assisted by his brother, Michael, who acted as its secretary. He was supported also by his Dissenter allies, Haughton and Allen. Spratt also secured the services, as chairman, of the Lord Mayor, Michael Staunton, who was just then commencing his term of office. Spratt was himself responsible for the passing of a resolution calling on government to ban the use of corn for distillation, in order *'to meet the unparalleled pressure on the starving millions'*. He insisted that the famine was not due, exclusively, to the failure of the potato crop, as there was sufficient alternative food in the country but that it was either exported or *'destroyed'* for drink. Despite being mutual supporters in many public causes, Spratt on the one side and Haughton and Allen on the other, found themselves at odds on this. As ardent Free Traders, these two Dissenter friends of the friar expressed themselves against any government interference with private enterprise.[23] Nevertheless, Spratt's resolution resulted in the adoption of a petition calling for drastic government intervention in the economy. The fact that the petition fell on deaf ears did not deter the Carmelite from continuing to explore all recourses for relief. In February he engaged his Irish Total Abstinence Association in the cause. On Sunday 7th February, at their French Street Temperance Hall, he proposed that they use their common bank fund to purchase flour in bulk *'at the lowest wholesale market price'* and sell it to their members at cost, *'during each week of this unprecedented period of distress'*. He thought that by this means *'thousands in Dublin will benefit'* and he hoped this example could be followed by other temperance societies in Ireland.[24] At the same time, although apparently not a committee member, he was actively involved in meetings of the Metropolitan Relief Committee that spring.[25]

## Soyer's Soup Kitchen
By now he and his co-workers were desperately awaiting government intervention in the calamitous situation. It came eventually in the form

---

23. *FJ*, 27th Jan; *DEPC*, 28th Jan 1847.
24. *FJ*, 12th Feb 1847.
25. *FJ*, 22nd March 1847.

**Fig 48.**   *Alexis Soyer.*

of the Destitute Poor (Ireland) Act of 26th February 1847, known as the 'Soup Kitchen Act'.[26] This authorised the appointment of commissioners to supervise the administration of relief outside of the workhouse system. This was followed, on 5th April 1847, with the opening by the celebrated French chef, Alexis Soyer, of his Model Kitchen, on the esplanade of the Royal Barracks. Friar John was among the distinguished guests invited to join the Lord Lieutenant, Bessborough, at the inaugural demonstration of Soyer's famine soup kitchen.[27] Chef to the Reform Club in London, Soyer had acquired much publicity by developing soup recipes for a trifling three farthings a quart and distributing this, daily, to several hundred of London's poor. Medical practitioners in England and Ireland alike were unimpressed, claiming that Soyer's soup offered little or no sustenance and, as far as the starving poor of Ireland were concerned, it *'runs through them, affording no nourishment'.*[28] Dr McKeon of the South Dublin Union had, with his fellow-parishioner, Spratt, witnessed the making of Soyer's soup and described it as

> a splendid humbug. It was completely sour. It was not nutritious and…was unfit for the consumption of human beings…The sending over of this French Cook was a scheme on the part of the Government to direct the attention of the people away from their do nothing policy.[29]

26.  10 Vict., c. 7.
27.  *DEP*, 6th April 1847. See also C. Woodham-Smith, *The Great Hunger*, London 1962, pp. 178-9.
28.  Woodham-Smith, pp. 178-9, citing a Mr Bishop, Commissariat Officer in West Cork.
29.  *Tipperary Free Press*, 3rd April 1847.

In spite of such comments, Soyer insisted that a meal of the soup and one biscuit was sufficient to sustain a healthy male adult. His forty foot long wooden kitchen, with its 300-gallon soup-boiler, soon had starving Dubliners queuing in droves and being admitted in batches of one hundred at a time. The chairman of the Dublin-based government relief commission, Major-General Sir John Burgoyne, was not impressed and thought the whole operation amounted to feeding the destitute like wild animals.[30] One estimate had it that Soyer's model soup kitchen would need to serve 5,000 bowls a day: it turned out to require 8,750 servings daily. For all its crudeness and contested nutritional value, Soyer's model kitchen was purchased by the government and given to the Relief Committee of the South Dublin Union, despite Dr McKeon's misgivings.[31] His scepticism was shared by other medics. Surgeon McCarthy, another fellow-parishioner of Spratt, wrote on 27th April to the press as official spokesman for St Peter's Relief Committee, to alert the public to the inadequate nature and amount of bread and soup being doled out to the destitute poor by the South Dublin Union under the 'Soup Kitchen' Act.[32] Such judgments by the medics, McKeon and

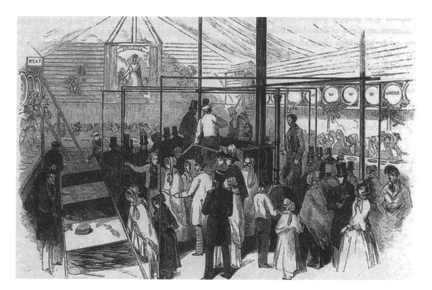

**Fig 49.**    *Alexis Soyer's soup kitchen on the esplanade of the Royal Barracks.*

30. Woodham-Smith, pp. 13, 173, 179.
31. Ibid, p. 179.
32. *SNL*, 29th April 1847.

McCarthy, have been sustained in the most recent specific scholarly treatment of Soyer and his soup kitchen by Strang and Toomre.[33]

Fr Spratt was likewise appalled.  He felt compelled to share his dismay at the treatment of these destitute people by a government agency that was now replacing the efforts of St Peter's and other Dublin relief committees as well as the Metropolitan Relief Committee itself.  With the arrival of the South Dublin Union Soup Kitchens, the Metropolitan Relief Committee was now being wound down by Fr O'Connell.  In a brief, blunt letter to Dr John Gray, owner of the *Freeman's Journal*, Fr John testified to the literal truth of what Surgeon McCarthy had revealed.  Being on relief duty at St Peter's Food Depot on 27th April, the Carmelite was *'eye-witness to the most melancholy and heart-rending exhibition'*.  Words failed him to describe the *'mock-relief administered to our poor fellow-creatures'*, and he went on to reproduce the examples the surgeon had supplied to *Saunders' Newsletter*.[34]  Together with the Church of Ireland counterpart, Rev Stack, he soon found himself involved in the administration of the new system, by issuing ration vouchers to the destitute, to take to the Union soup kitchens.[35]  By mid-May he was becoming desperate at the extent of this local  In a letter of 18th May he wrote of *'the urgent and unceasing appeals of hundreds who surround the chapel-house in Aungier Street, on every day, looking for food'*.[36]  He added that, whatever about keeping down the pressure of local taxation, the ratepayers of Dublin might find it *'in their interest to pay a few shillings more in the year in favour of 'famishing objects, than be visited with the awful concomitants of starvation – fever and pestilence which I fear are entering the city'*.  He was not misinformed: the North Dublin Union suffered a fever outbreak just then, and its guardians were commenting that large numbers were crowding the streets in fever.  The Union had to open a fever hospital in Drumcondra, over the months from May 1847 to July 1848.[37]  The famine fever reached its heights in Dublin, as elsewhere, over the period July to December 1847.  Indeed, while the use of the

33.  J. Strang & J. Toomre, 'Alexis Soyer and the Irish Famine', in A, Gribben, ed., *The Great Famine and the Irish Diaspora in America*, Amherst 1999, pp. 66-84.

34.  *FJ*, 30th April 1847; *DEPC*, 1st May 1847.

35.  *FJ*, 8th May 1847.

36.  *FJ*, 21st May 1847.

37.  NAI, *Minutes of the North Dublin Union*, 5th May 1847, 26th July 1848.  See also Prunty, *Dublin Slums*, p. 229.

soup kitchens helped to reduce starvation deaths, by the summer of 1847 deaths from disease rose.[38]

Spratt went on to attack the *'absurd rule'* that, in order to obtain food, the heads of families had to present themselves in person at the depots. He himself had to spend hours examining duplicates of pawnbrokers' dockets of pledged clothes where the owners – being heads of families – were at home, naked: otherwise their wives and children were left without a particle of food. Even then, the outdoor food relief offered by the South Dublin Union was *'such a stinted and insufficient ration'* that his associate, Thomas Arkins, poor law guardian for the North Dublin Union, launched a public attack on the South Dublin Union: so poor were the rations of the latter body that *'an influx of paupers'* descended on the North Dublin Union, instead, for relief.[39]

### *Outdoor Relief and the South Dublin Union*

Soon the February 1847 legislation for temporary relief by way of the 'Soup Kitchen Act' would be replaced: in June 1847 the Poor Relief (Ireland) Act empowered poor law union boards to grant relief outside the workhouse, but excluding persons who held more than a quarter acre of land.[40] It came at a time when the workhouses were overwhelmed by the numbers admitted and seeking admission. A month later, additional legislation created an independent Poor Relief Commission for Ireland, which, as Prunty has observed, *'made an important dent in the iron structure of the poor law'*.[41] The operation of the new legislation was viewed by Fr John as harsh. On 3rd July 1847, in a letter to Lord Mayor Staunton, he criticised the inspectorate under the new relief system as operated by the guardians of the South Dublin Union. The finance committee of this body had introduced a vetting system of double inspection, whereby the visiting inspectors were themselves inspected. He asserted that as a result of the increased bureaucracy involved in the double-checking of relief claimants, some hundreds were being deprived of

---

38. T. O'Neill, 'The organisation and administration of relief, 1845-52' in R. D. Edwards & T. D. Williams, eds., *The Great Famine: Studies in Irish History, 1845-52*, 1997 ed., pp. 243-244.
39. *FJ*, 21st May 1847; Thomas Arkins to editor, 20th May 1847.
40. 10 Vict. c. 31. The quarter-acre clause was known as the Gregory Clause, after its proposer, Dublin City MP, William Gregory.
41. 10 & 11 Vict. c. 90. See Prunty, p. 231.

relief previously given, with days, even weeks, elapsing before some of the applicants secured any relief at all.[42] He deplored the situation where

> many of these unfortunate creatures – to my own knowledge, have been left in such a starving state that it is heart-rending to look on them as fathers and mothers, accompanied by their innocent children, without an article of covering fit for human beings, or a morsel of food to satisfy their hunger, crowd about the food depot in Cheaters Lane and the Chapel-house in Aungier Street, crying for a bit of bread and receiving nothing but refusals.

At times, having signed as many as eight recommendations for some of these unfortunates, he still found that they were delayed by red tape up to ten days before getting help.[43] He even urged the Lord Mayor to rescind the bye-laws that forbade public begging: he hoped thereby that when the compassion of the prosperous failed, then the sight of pestilential paupers, begging in the streets, might foster the fear of fever among the better off, to almsgiving effect.

Over the ensuing weeks, the famine-induced fever spread throughout the city, and St Peter's was not spared. While additional fever hospital sheds were being planned, Fr Spratt and confrere, Andrew Day, attended a thinly-supported parish vestry meeting to consider stop-gap measures of medical aid. A proposal by Rev Stack to provide for two doctors to attend fever cases, paid for from privately-raised funds, fell foul of the medics present and the meeting had to disband with no action being agreed or adopted.[44]

*The Friar and the General Relief Committee of 1849*
The crop failures and starvation of 1846-7 were replicated when the potato failure over July-September 1848 led during 1848-9 to a repetition of the miseries of 1846-7.[45] This was then compounded by the arrival of cholera from November 1848, reaching Dublin City in

42.  *The Pilot*, 5th July 1847.
43.  *FJ*, 5th July 1847.
44.  *FJ*, 15th Sept 1847.
45.  Woodham-Smith, p. 363.

January 1849. Whilst it appears that in Dublin City during the course of the famine years, 1845-1849, only some 68 died of actual starvation, some 40,000 contracted fever and 5,513 died from it, while 3,723 died from cholera in the same years, 3,482 of them in 1849.[46]

It was against this background that Fr Spratt's labours for famine relief now expanded: from the confines of the work for the poor in St Peter's Parish on the one hand, and his commitment to the mission of the Sick and Indigent Roomkeepers Society on the other, in 1849 he took on a role that became a national one. He did this not only at a time of cruelly renewed and acute distress, but in a situation where leading relief agencies had by then folded their tents and departed the desolation. The Quakers, who had begun their relief operation in November 1846, collecting an astounding £200,000 during the disaster, had ceased their Dublin Soup Kitchen on 20th July 1847 and their relief fund distribution terminated on 1st May 1848.[47] The British Association, formed in London on 1st January 1847 to organise the supply of food, fuel and clothing, collected over £470,000 and spent almost £400,000 in Ireland (and the remainder in distressed Scotland). This it distributed through local Irish relief committees and through the Commissariat of the British Army in Ireland. The funds of the British Relief Association had run dry, by 1st July 1848, and its relief role in Ireland ceased. Then, even as the failure of the 1848 potato crop became evident, the British Army Commissariat itself ceased its role and left Irish relief to Irish devices. As Woodham-Smith observed: *'Ireland was left to face a winter of total failure, bankruptcy and starvation'.*[48] Dublin itself experienced greater distress in the course of 1849 than in any earlier famine year and it experienced higher mortality than even in the Black '47.[49]

In face of this unfolding near catastrophe, Fr John, on 12th April 1849, addressed a public appeal to Cloncurry. He was prompted by

---

46. Callaghan, pp. 45-49; Ó Gráda, *Black '47 and Beyond*, New Jersey 1991, p. 165; *Census of Ireland for the year 1851, Part V, Table of Deaths*, vol. i, Dublin 1856, p. 202.
47. Callaghan, pp. 103-4. Their Quaker Relief Committee funds, however, were not completely closed until the middle of the 1860s; T. O'Neill, 'The charities and famine in mid-nineteenth century Ireland', in J. Hill & C. Lennon, eds., *Luxury and Austerity*, Dublin 1999, p. 146.
48. Woodham-Smith, pp. 367-368.
49. Callaghan, pp. 34-35.

the sight of *'thousands of our people every day leaving Ireland'* and by reports of thousands more *'still dying on the public roads from actual starvation'*. He was baffled that no effort any longer was being made *'to arrest such general, continuous and all-withering destruction'*. He therefore called on Cloncurry to convene a public meeting to try to halt these evils.[50] Cloncurry was at that time away in England but was not unsympathetic to some initiative. Support for Spratt's call now came from the Catholic philanthropist and successful ship-owner, Richard

**Fig 50.**    *Statue of Sir John Gray on O'Connell Street, Dublin.*

Devereux of Wexford. The latter urged the need for a public meeting in Dublin to institute some kind of relief committee. He immediately donated £100 to Spratt to expedite such an initiative. The friar then won the support of John Gray of the *Freeman's Journal* who praised the Carmelite's initiative in convening a meeting at the Royal Exchange. Gray observed ruefully that *'the parliamentary representatives of the people have abandoned them'* and he urged the need for a committee such as Spratt envisaged,

> to act with vigour and earnestness and to make the case of the dead and of the dying their hourly study and nightly labour till that case, in all its horrors, is made patent to the whole human family.[51]

The resulting foundation meeting of what would become Spratt's General Relief Committee was held on 3rd May 1849. It secured the immediate support of old friends and associates, Haughton and

---

50.  *FJ*, 12th April 1849.
51.  *FJ*, 3rd May 1849, editorial.

Battersby, Dr John Miley and Tom Reynolds, as well as that of his confreres, Richard Colgan of Whitefriar Street and Matthew Scally of Knocktopher. An important new associate was the justice of the peace, John D Browne of Mount Browne, Co Mayo. This initial meeting was a considerable success in that it secured the interdenominational support of Archbishops Whately and Murray, as well as that of the MP, John Reynolds, the barrister and future MP, Isaac Butt, together with the banker, David Latouche, and leading Dublin City clergymen.[52] In calling them together, Spratt hoped modestly that he was not being presumptuous. His friend, Battersby, delivered an impassioned speech, deploring the disastrous relationship with England whereby

> after what is called a connexion of 700 years and a union of 49…their land was a desert and all that remained of themselves, skeletons in human form: they were in the fourth year of famine, desolation and death.

One of the first actions of this gathering, which collected funds on the spot, was to agree to send £140 immediately to Archbishop McHale for the relief of distress in Mayo, in a resolution proposed by Dr Miley and seconded by the Carmelite, Matthew Scally. A few days later, Gray, in his *Freeman's Journal*, praised Spratt for his initiative and he himself suggested that the committee issue a circular to all public servants asking them to donate the equivalent of one day's pay to the relief fund and that the Committee appeal also to people in England and Scotland for support.[53] The latter suggestion was taken up at the next meeting where Battersby was appointed secretary and Spratt became, simultaneously, honorary secretary and joint treasurer. This meeting set up a sub-committee to consider a deputation to England. In addition, the Protestant and Catholic clergy of Ireland were requested to bestir their congregations to assist with distress funds for the West and South of Ireland.[54] Spratt's General Relief Committee acted with urgency and impressive commitment. Over the period May to September 1849 it met almost daily to keep up the pressure of fund-raising and its work

---

52. *FJ*, 4th May 1849.
53. *FJ*, 8th May 1849.
54. *FJ*, 8th May 1849.

of fund distribution. At meeting upon meeting, Fr John read out, in full detail, the desperate letters from rural clergymen asking for help and describing the sufferings of their people. Long lists of subscribers were published and parish congregations in Dublin City were to the fore in collecting and forwarding funds to the General Relief Committee. One example of this local action was when parishioners of St Anne's, Dawson Street, met in the Shelbourne Hotel to arrange the division of their parish into districts and to appoint collectors for these.[55] Spratt's clerical connections and the friendships he forged through his temperance crusade stood him in good stead in this new work of charity. Thus, at the start of early July 1849, his friend, Fr William Yore, was able to contribute an impressive £112 from his parishioners of St Paul's, Arran Quay, and at that month's end, an additional £28. Similarly through Fr Staunton of St Lawrence O'Toole's – for whose new church in a poor district Fr John had preached the opening sermon – came £33 at the end of May. In that same month the parishioners of Fr John's birth-parish contributed some £87 to his Committee.[56] By the middle of May 1849, £300 had been raised by these local Dublin parish committees, out of the then collected total of £547, all of which had been sent to Protestant and Catholic clergymen for joint distribution.[57]

As for the call to public servants and others to subscribe, at the end of its first month of operation, the General Relief Committee reported a donation of £11-3s-3d from the Superintendents, Inspectors and Sergeants of the 'C' Division of the Dublin Metropolitan Police, and a gift of £5.5s from twenty-nine Dublin postmen.[58] In June the officers and men of the Royal Irish Constabulary in King's County donated £28, being the proceeds of a day's pay.[59] The staff of various Dublin commercial houses also tendered support: the young men of McBirney's retail store on Aston's Quay gifted a day's pay in late May 1849, while the directors and staff of Glasnevin Cemetery provided £20 in August.[60] Furthermore, individual friendships proved valuable, as when Fr Walsh of Rolestown contributed £20. One of the most remarkable of

---

55. *FJ*, 21st May 1849.
56. *FJ*, 12th, 29th May, 2nd June, 9th, 28th July 1849.
57. *FJ*, 14th, 15th and 16th May 1849.
58. *FJ*, 23rd, 25th May 1849.
59. *FJ*, 23rd June 1849.
60. *FJ*, 22nd May, 16th Aug 1849.

individual donors to Spratt's GRC was the mysterious Andreas George Moller, of Hardwicke Street, a man of unknown occupation.[61] He was the most generous of all repeat donors who contributed to the GRC. Although not a Catholic, Moller confessedly admired Spratt's charitable efforts and it is possible that they may have known each other through the Sick and Indigent Roomkeepers Society.[62] Within two weeks of the foundation of the General Relief Committee, he made his first donation of £12, but not before he had satisfied himself as to the *bona fides* of the GRC. He came to its meeting on Friday 18th May, asked to see and was shown the registers of donations and disbursements. Satisfied, he made the first of his many donations and, subsequently, some of his grants were made almost on a daily basis. During a particularly lean time for the GRC, in the course of July 1849, he contributed £60 on the 7th, £30 on the 10th, and sums of £25, £20, £100, £10 and £150 on each of the days from the 17th to the 21st.[63] In all, he gifted some £700 to the GRC, at times giving the impression that it consisted of sums he had collected from others. However, a leading article in the *Freeman's Journal,* in September 1849, probably written by the GRC Committee member, Dr John Gray, singled Moller out for special mention and intimated that this large sum came from Moller's own pocket.[64] Moller was soon drafted as a member of the Committee and went on to chair a number of its meetings.[65]

Moller was but one of a number of Spratt's supporters who coalesced into a dedicated and energetic corps who met almost daily, from 7th May to 17th September, and weekly thereafter until mid-October 1849. Prominent among the other leading members were Rev Robert King who was Church of Ireland rector of Kilmore, John Denis Brown who was a Co. Mayo landowner and magistrate, Dr John Miley, O'Connell's private chaplain in the Liberator's last days, the diocesan curate and

---

61. *FJ*, 24th April 1866 for his death notice. The various Dublin trade and street directories provide his address but not his occupation. Although residing in Hardwicke Street he was the lessor of a house and small yard at 21 City Quay, according to Griffith's Valuation in 1854. He was born in 1792 and died in 1866.
62. Moller may have been a member: he was certainly a supporter and contributor in the 1850s, for which see *Daily Express*, 23rd Jan 1855 where he is the seconder of a resolution at the annual general meeting of the Society.
63. *FJ*, 9th, 11th, 17th, 18th, 19th, 20th, 21st July 1849.
64. *FJ*, 5th Sept 1849.
65. *FJ*, 18th, 26th May 1849.

social radical Fr Thaddeus O'Malley, the City Marshal and teetotaller, Thomas Reynolds, and Spratt's old friend, James Haughton.[66]

Apart from organising local collections in Dublin parishes where they received almost £7,000 over the period May to September, the GRC issued a number of public addresses. Their *Address to the American People*, thanking them for past support to Ireland and requesting further immediate aid was written by Robert King and published in late May 1849.[67] In the same month John Miley prepared an *Address to the People of England*, while Spratt published two addresses and Haughton wrote three, all of them aiming at maintaining the inflow of funds. At the same time, Spratt sent out some 500 circulars to clergy, throughout the country, to garner detailed information on the state of the people in their localities.[68]

*The Appeal to England*

From an early stage in its proceedings, the GRC was determined on sending a deputation to England to raise both funds and public awareness that Ireland needed employment and wages as well as alms.[69] There was in Dublin, at this same time, a separate relief organisation called The Central Relief Committee. It confined its efforts specifically to the West of Ireland while Spratt's GRC collected funds for and distributed relief to all affected

**Fig 51.**   *John Bright, MP.*

66. For O'Malley, see F. A. D'Arcy, 'Thaddeus O'Malley, 1797-1877: federalist, social radical and anti-sectarian', in G. Moran, ed., *Radical Irish Priests, 1660-1990*, Dublin 1998, pp. 91-110; F. A. D'Arcy, 'Religion, radicalism and rebellion in nineteenth-century Ireland: the case of Thaddeus O'Malley', in J. Devlin & R. Fanning, eds., *Religion and Rebellion*, Dublin 1997, pp. 97-105.
67. *FJ*, 18th May 1849.
68. *FJ*, 22nd May 1849.
69. *FJ*, 1st June 1849.

areas across the country. Early in June 1849, Spratt and King went to see David Latouche, secretary to this Central Relief Committee, to explore the possibility of their constituting a joint deputation to England. That invitation was declined by the Central Relief Committee and Spratt subsequently proposed that Rev King and Dr Miley constitute the GRC delegation to London.[70] On arrival there, they were met by the Quaker radical MP and Free Trader, John Bright. His efforts, and theirs, to secure support fell far below expectations. As Dr Miley reported: they were

> met with coolness by some from whom they naturally expected sympathy, if not earnest and active support – met with indifference by others and with a chilling hopelessness by all who considered the condition of the country…opinion had already decided that all efforts were in vain.

It may well be that the delegation was encountering donor fatigue; but equally, given the Irish attempt at revolution in the previous year, it may have been facing plain political hostility from an uncomprehending or unforgiving British public. Whatever the reason, the consequence was unpalatable.[71]

By the first week in July, the GRC had completely exhausted its funds and had to leave unanswered some twenty-five letters of supplication. Becoming desperate, the Committee wondered if they should contact their London deputation to see if they had raised any funds that they could quickly transfer. In the meantime, at Thaddeus O'Malley's suggestion, they decided to appeal to areas of the country that had not been tapped before, including Belfast, Newry, Limerick and Kilkenny. It was at this point of desperation that Moller came to the rescue with the most generous of his multiple donations. When the deputation reported in the second week of July, it had held its first public meeting in London, but, despite the support of the illustrious MP, Richard Cobden, together with his colleague, John Bright, they had managed to raise only £250 and remarked that *the public is already tired of giving*. Some of the GRC members in Dublin, notably Haughton, Reynolds

---

70. *FJ*, 5th, 7th June 1849.
71. *FJ*, 27th June 1849.

and John Dennan expressed themselves as profoundly disappointed. Spratt was silent in face of this discouraging news.[72] The deputation, now joined by John O'Connell MP and Dr Gray, managed to secure an interview with Prime Minister Russell, but to little or no effect in terms of practical support.[73] In a letter to Spratt, from London, on 27th July, Miley deplored the failure to raise significant sums and now laid the blame squarely on the shoulders of Lord John Russell, as the latter had happened to mention that, in his opinion, *'the famine was over'*. Worse still, the Queen had decided to visit Ireland over 3rd to 12th August and, in preparation, Dublin's Lord Mayor proposed to spend some £7,000 on illuminations. As Miley ruefully recorded, this was something Londoners now threw in the deputation's face: he himself commented to Spratt that *'it is like illuminating a graveyard, like fireworks in Glasnevin'*.[74] In some despondency, Miley sent over £36, saying that it could likely prove to be the last remittance from London, as Russell's remarks about the end of the famine diminished any chance of further donations.[75] Russell's remarks proved premature: at the GRC meeting on 2nd August, a letter from Fr Wallace, parish priest of Ballygar, Co. Galway, reported the death from starvation, of a parishioner, Patrick Kelly, on Friday 27th July 1849.[76]

The GRC members were angered at the money being spent on preparations for the Queen's visit. Haughton proposed that instead of paying for illuminations, that all citizens pay a tribute to Her Majesty by way of a great grant to charity.[77] It seems that the authorities in Glasnevin Cemetery had taken this hint when they devoted their £20 to the GRC in mid-August. The best hopes, therefore, continued to come from local donations. By the beginning of August the GRC had raised over £5,000, most of it from Dublin's citizens. Despite this generosity, distress reports kept coming to the GRC from rural clergy and, consequently, Spratt felt the need to re-ignite the spirit of giving among his fellow citizens. On 3rd September 1849 he convened

---

72. *FJ*, 14th July 1849.
73. *DEP*, 1st July 1849.
74. *FJ*, 31st July 1849.
75. As it happened, in the end Miley was to transfer a final remittance of £127 from London at the end of August. See *DEP*, 1st Sept 1849.
76. *FJ*, 2nd Aug 1849.
77. *FJ*, 1st Aug 1849.

a public meeting that attracted a very large audience. At this, he had the GRC give an account of its stewardship. He described the GRC administration as being *'one of union, energy and fraternity...in the economy of mercy'*, and, as providing more substantial relief, at less cost and less time, *'than perhaps ever was given before in Ireland'*.[78] He reported how he had read out at their meetings some 2,000 letters from parochial clergy describing the extent of the distress. He reckoned that the GRC was responsible for saving 100,000 souls from death by starvation.

This public meeting of the GRC constituted something of a turning point. Here Haughton indicated that the country was now in the midst of an abundant harvest and suggested that the committee might cease its labours for the present, but Spratt countered that they continue to meet on a weekly basis.[79] There was considerable reluctance to watch the GRC disappear altogether. While Haughton and Reynolds thought the time had come to cease its labours, some thought otherwise. At its meeting on 12th October, Andreas Moller thought it *'unwise to break up the society altogether'*. O'Malley supported Moller's view, but characteristically, went further and called for some kind of 'national association' to press the government for reforms. In the end, however, they simply agreed to adjourn for one month.[80] When they reconvened on 16th November, a number of small donations had been received. Spratt moved, successfully, that the remaining funds be granted to the Sisters of Charity in Kinsale for the support of the poor they visited there.

Following upon this November meeting, the GRC passed into history but not without the widespread expression of gratitude to John Spratt and his colleagues for all they had accomplished. To a considerable extent Spratt's work on the GRC – even more than his teetotal crusade – gave him a national standing. He was now one of the best-known and well-regarded figures in the country, in both clerical and political circles. The passing of the GRC, however, left no vacuum in a busy life: even as it faded out of sight, he was already caught up in other momentous national and local developments.

---

78. *FJ*, 25th Aug 1849.
79. *FJ*, 4th Sept; *DEP*, 8th Sept 1849.
80. *FJ*, 13th Oct 1849.

# CHAPTER TWELVE

## A Time of Tumult, 1844–1850

Spratt remained loyal to O'Connell's memory and to the Loyal National Repeal Association, at least until its dissolution in the summer of 1848. In November 1847, he headed the list of seven Dublin Calced Carmelites in supporting a local collection towards an O'Connell monument.[1] Two months later he renewed – for what would be the last time – his annual subscription as a member of the Repeal Association. On the occasion of this renewal, in a letter to John O'Connell, he repeated his insistence on Repeal and Total Abstinence as being the only remedies for the evils of Ireland.[2] At the same time, notwithstanding that loyal membership, he manifested his own commitment to political reconciliation and the re-uniting of the sundered elements of the Irish nationalist community, in the months and years ahead. Spratt's faith in the Repeal Association was not shared by Lord Cloncurry. The latter considered himself a Repealer even before the word or the Association had been invented, but he remarked in June 1847:

> I would not join the Repeal Association, nor would I join the Young Irelanders, nor any other body where mutual vituperation and mutual denunciations are so largely indulged in.[3]

Instead, from that time he joined and frequently chaired the meetings of a new body, the Irish Council, which had emerged six months

---

1. *The Pilot*, 10th Nov 1847.
2. *FJ*, 4th Jan 1848.
3. *FJ*, 22nd June 1847.

before. Consisting originally of aristocrats and substantial landowners, it sought to develop an overarching alliance with disparate elements, in its quest for social and economic reforms for Ireland. Repealers such as John O'Connell supported it, and Young Irelanders and Confederates including Gavan Duffy, Smith O'Brien, Meagher, Mitchel and Doheny became members. Spratt, too, attended meetings of this Irish Council but, as Nowlan fairly commented, *'it proved powerless to achieve any lasting results'*. In effect, it proved to be little more than a talking shop.[4]

Disagreements on fundamentals invariably divided the Irish Council but they also divided the members of the Irish Confederation itself, as Ireland descended into a hopeless pit of disease, death and despair. Frustration with the Confederates' lack of an agreed radical programme led John Mitchel and Thomas Devin Reilly to resign from its council. Mitchel went on to found *The United Irishman* newspaper in February 1848, as a vehicle for his radical views and he was to experience growing popularity in the artisan Confederate Clubs of Dublin.[5] Together with Devin Reilly and James Fintan Lalor he aimed to pursue a radical agrarian agenda and to prevent the exportation of food. While this last point was one which John Spratt had advocated before, in 1846, this did not place him as any friend of these radical nationalists. He was far from sharing the views of John Mitchel or of Fr John Kenyon, the radical nationalist friend of Mitchel, or the views of that other clerical Confederate, the socially radical priest Thaddeus O'Malley – notwithstanding that O'Malley would be one of Spratt's closest supporters and associates in his General Relief Committee. Unlike the peaceful and conciliatory Carmelite, Kenyon and O'Malley were clerical firebrands. As for Mitchel, his denunciations of Britain over the famine and the exportation of food drove him into a revolutionary position. The incendiary tone of his writings in the *United Irishman*, in the words of James Quinn, *'caused a sensation'*.[6] The example of the February Revolution in France, which overthrew the monarchy of King Louis Philippe, led Mitchel to proclaim his own republicanism and to call for social revolution. His arrest, trial and conviction of treason, by a packed jury, in May 1848, were inevitable. However, his sentence

4. Nowlan, pp. 152-153.

5. Nowlan, p. 172; D'Arcy, *Dublin Artisans*, pp. 67-68.

6. J. Quinn, 'John Mitchel' in *Dictionary of Irish Biography*, vol. 6, p. 524.

**Fig 52.**    *Young Irelanders (clockwise from top left): Michael Doheny, William Smith O'Brien, John Blake Dillon, Thomas Devin Reilly, Thomas Francis Meagher and Charles Gavan Duffy.*

of fourteen years' transportation and his exile to Bermuda evoked widespread sympathy among all shades of nationalists, and contributed to the Rising of 1848. John Spratt, despite his far distance from the politics of Mitchel, was among the first to come to Mitchel's aid by engaging in what John Spratt did best – fund-raising.

It was a signal testimony to Fr John's standing and to the respect and trust in which he was held that the very first mention in the national press of a support fund for Mitchel's family, should have involved the Carmelite friar. *The Pilot* newspaper, an unlikely source of support for rebellious Young Irelanders, carried a leader on 31st May 1848, four days after his sentencing to transportation, asserting that *'the duty of supporting the family of Mr Mitchel has devolved upon Ireland'*. It went on to reveal that, on 29th May, Cloncurry had written to Spratt, to enclose £100 to assist Mitchel's wife and family.[7] Either Cloncurry had 'appointed' Spratt as a conduit for such aid or else Spratt had privately indicated to Cloncurry, in advance, his willingness to assume such a role. It was soon announced that a national committee of eight had been formed to raise funds for Mitchel's wife and children. The list of public figures was headed by John Spratt, followed by Richard O'Gorman senior and included the Young Irelanders, Thomas Frances Meagher, John Blake Dillon and Richard O'Gorman junior. Spratt quickly became a leading recipient of Mitchel family donations. These included an early one from his old friend, Matthew Flanagan, parish priest in St Francis Street. Flanagan, like so many after him who were not of Young Ireland radical nationalist views, was moved to act not only out of sympathy for the Mitchel family but just as much by outrage at the trial by a packed jury.[8] Among the other contributors Spratt acknowledged at this time were two of his Carmelite confreres in Moate, John O'Flynn and John O'Connor.[9] The Moate Carmelites pointed out that their donations included

> Voluntary contributors of poor but honest people who, though they do not subscribe to all Mr Mitchel's opinions, yet, like ourselves, have a holy hatred of injustice and jury packing.

---

7. *The Pilot*, 31st May 1848.
8. *The Pilot*, 5th June 1848; see also *FJ*, 3rd, 10th, 24th June.
9. *DWR*, 8th July 1848.

By the end of the first week in June, Spratt had transmitted over £100, including his own contribution, to the treasurer, O'Gorman senior. In so doing, Fr John wrote:

> Because of the important duties I have to discharge in the great movement of temperance, I have not taken a conspicuous part in matters of a more political character, yet I could consider that I had lost the feelings of an Irishman and the spirit of a patriot, if I did not come forward at this eventful crisis, to sympathise with the amiable and afflicted lady of that sincere and disinterested patriot, John Mitchel.[10]

Despite his admitted preoccupation with the temperance cause, he could not avoid becoming immersed in the wake of the political upheavals of that tumultuous year. The perceived indifference of the Whig-Liberal administration of Lord John Russell, the worsening Famine crisis, and the failure of Repeal politics to achieve success or to provide solutions drove some previously moderate men to extremes. Thus, William Smith O'Brien, and his colleague Thomas Francis Meagher, felt driven to call for a physical force response – in speeches at the Irish Confederation on 15th March 1848. April then found them in Paris, leading a Confederate delegation to congratulate the revolutionary government in France for the overthrow of the monarchy and the institution of the Second Republic. That resolution turned sour in the 'June Days' when the labour left was massacred in the Paris streets by General Cavaignac. This outbreak of violence and bloodshed, Spratt, in a public letter, *To the People of Ireland*, on 4th July 1848, attributed to the excesses of drink. He urged the working people of Ireland not to follow suit but forever to foreswear drink in the interests of moral and political sobriety.[11]

Meanwhile, on 15th May, O'Brien was tried on a charge of sedition, but the jury failed to agree, two days after the arrest of Mitchel. Their Confederate colleague, Charles Gavan Duffy, was arrested on 8th July, and Fintan Lalor on the 27th. Two days after this, O'Brien led the confrontation at the police barracks in Ballingarry, Co. Tipperary, where the Irish attempt at revolution in 1848 began. He, Meagher,

---

10.   *The Pilot*, 7th June 1848.
11.   *FJ*, 4th July 1848.

**Fig 53.** *John Mitchel.*

Terence Bellew McManus and Patrick O'Donohoe, after arrest, were tried and convicted of treason over the weeks from 28th September to 23rd October 1848. All four were sentenced to be hanged, drawn and quartered.

### The Campaign for Clemency

Almost immediately after O'Brien's death sentence, on 7th October, Spratt became involved in a campaign for clemency. On Friday 13th October, on the initiative of the Quaker, Richard Webb, and of Gavan Duffy's friend, Charlton Stuart Ralph, a meeting was held at Webb's house to consider how best to pursue a campaign for clemency for O'Brien.[12] It was Webb's friend, Haughton, who revealed that it was an initiative by Webb and Ralph. According to Haughton, they, he and a few friends had met to consider drafting a petition to the Lord Lieutenant, Clarendon, and decided to call a larger meeting of potential supporters for the following day, Saturday 14th October. It is not unlikely that Spratt was a participant in the first meeting. One suggests this, not least because Haughton and Webb were known as committed opponents in principle of capital punishment and, uniquely amongst

---

12. *DEPC*, 17th Oct 1848.

**Fig 54.**  *John Reynolds, MP.*

Irish Catholic clergy of the age, so too was Spratt. In early February 1848 he attended a public meeting called to petition parliament for the abolition of capital punishment. He seconded a resolution proposed by the local MP, John Reynolds, that *'death punishments are directly opposed to the principles of morality and to the spirit and the letter of the Christian religion and ought therefore to be immediately and forever abolished in every Christian country'*. He felt that Reynolds spoke so well on the matter that he himself needed to add little or nothing, except to express *'the detestation, the abhorrence in which they held the barbarous custom of putting their fellow creatures to death'*.[13] On that same day, he wrote publicly on the issue in a letter entitled *Punishment of Death*. While conceding that theologians, in certain extreme cases, might allow that the power of execution may be vested in the supreme authority, as far as he was concerned the exercise of the death penalty did no good; far from it, it demoralised those who attended public executions and did not stop the perpetration of crimes. He urged that this extreme punishment be changed for one more likely to produce a salutary effect on society.[14] Now, in October 1848, the issue of principle had become an urgent one of practice. As a result of the Webb and Ralph initiative, a well-attended meeting of leading citizens was held to consider the Smith O'Brien sentence. It included Spratt, the only Catholic clergyman reported as present.[15] This meeting adopted Haughton's draft petition, agreed on the urgency of securing as many signatures as possible, and appointed a deputation of seven to seek an interview with the Lord Lieutenant. Spratt and Haughton were nominated to the deputation and, such was the felt urgency of the matter, they sought and secured,

---

13.  *FJ*, 4th, 5th February 1848.
14.  *FJ*, 5th Feb 1848, letter dated 4th February.
15.  *FJ*, 13th Oct 1848.

that same day, an interview with Clarendon. This was with a view to learning if the warrant for O'Brien's execution had already been issued and to establishing if Clarendon would agree to receive the petition once the signatures had been secured. To their relief, Clarendon assured them on both counts – no warrant had yet been issued, and he would '*be happy*' to receive a signed petition.

They lost no time in proceeding to obtain signatures, and experienced rapid success in doing so. Spratt's committee sat all day, Saturday 14th October, to receive a constant stream of laity and clergy who came to support their cause. By mid-afternoon they had secured a remarkable 17,000 signatures including those of leading clergymen of all denominations, together with MPs, JPs, lawyers and medics. They sat again that Sunday, 15th October, as all classes of citizens came to add their names. On the very next day, the committee, with Spratt at its head, joined forces with members of Dublin Corporation to constitute the formal deputation to the Lord Lieutenant. They came armed with 24,200 signatures. Although the deputation felt that Clarendon was well-disposed to the petition for clemency, he could not then commit to a definitive reply as the legal proceedings at Clonmel, of Smith O'Brien's co-accused, were still ongoing. In fact, the three fellow-prisoners, Meagher, McManus and O'Donohoe were sentenced on 23rd October, but it was not until 5th June 1849 that the campaign for clemency was partly successful when all four were spared the death penalty and were sentenced, instead, to transportation for life. In the course of the year leading up to the commutation, however, the arrests and prosecutions of other confederates and radical nationalists interposed. Charles Gavan Duffy, editor of *The Nation*, and, separately, John Martin, editor of the *Irish Felon*, had been apprehended on 8th July, Kevin Izod O'Doherty of *The Irish Tribune* on the 9th,[16] James Fintan Lalor on the 27th and ten staff members of Duffy's *The Nation* on the 28th.

John Martin had been rightly convinced that in his case he was tried before a packed jury, in the sense that, as in Mitchel's case, every Catholic juror was ordered to stand down; likewise, in the trial of O'Doherty, the sole Catholic juror was set aside. It was widely feared that a similar experience would befall other accused in due course. As

16.  *DWN*, 15th July 1848.

it happened, it took three trials and three juries to convict O'Doherty on 30th October 1848. For some time before that, it was feared that Gavan Duffy would become the victim of trial before a packed jury. The Catholic Duffy feared as much, as he made clear in a letter to Robert Shaw, High Sheriff of Dublin, on 22nd November. Typical of this widespread concern was the comment of the *Limerick and Clare Examiner* at the time:

> The Catholics of Ireland have too long submitted to the crying evil – the degrading and unjust system of excluding them from juries when political offences are the subject of enquiry,

and it noted with approval *'a copy of a memorial to the Lord Lieutenant on the subject, emanating from Dr Spratt and other influential Clergymen'*; but, in commenting on this initiative, the editor *'had no sanguine hope of success'*.[17]

This initiative for a petition against the exclusion of Catholics from juries, in political cases, came from a committee for which Spratt and N H Delamere were joint secretaries. Very quickly again, therefore, in November 1848, Spratt found himself caught up in the frenzy of signature procurement. The essential hope of this new committee was that

> The scene they witnessed at the trial of John Martin and others would not be repeated and that in the forthcoming trial of their good friend, Charles Gavan Duffy, there would be no exclusion, but that it would be conducted fairly and properly.[18]

In similar spirit, on 5th December, Lord French of Castle ffrench, Co. Galway, in a letter to Spratt and Delamere, offered the support of his protest at

> the violation of constitutional rights and at the insult to the Catholic religion implicit in the exclusion of Catholics from the juries during the state trials...we shall offer no insult to the religion of others, and, why then, should we suffer insult

17. *Limerick and Clare Examiner*, 25th Nov 1848.
18. *The Pilot*, 1st Dec 1848.

to be offered to our own? We do not advocate, but abhor, the principles of sectarianism. All we require is fair play. On that we will insist, and vindicate our religion from infamy and insult.[19]

French's backing was soon followed by that of other notabilities, including Cloncurry, Henry Grattan and Sharman Crawford, all writing to Spratt in support.[20] Over the immediately following days the tempo of indignation and response quickened: as the editor of the *Freeman's Journal* observed:

> From all parts of the country, from men of every rank and class, indignant remonstrances are being poured forth against the systematic 'packing' of political partisans into the jury-box, and the systematic exclusion of 'the country' from all participation in the administration of the law in political cases.[21]

Spratt must have been both truly grateful and somewhat overwhelmed. On 9th October, the *Freeman's Journal* again commented:

> The complete and singular success of this movement has left the committee at a loss how to deal with it. They have received upwards of thirty thousand signatures, notwithstanding the shortness of the time since the protest was circulated, including all ranks in the land and embracing an unparalleled number of Catholic clergy of all degrees…The country was thought to have fallen into apathy, but this insulting and destructive system has awakened it thoroughly.[22]

Three days later the Carmelite found himself on a delegation to the Viceregal Lodge, this time leading the team of five that included his old friends and fellow-soldiers, Haughton and Battersby, the others being Delamere and J N Ralph. Their outstanding success in securing

---

19.  *FJ*, 11th Dec1848.
20.  *FJ*, 7th Dec 1848, publishing letters of 4th, 5th and 6th December, respectively, from Sharman Crawford, Grattan and Cloncurry.
21.  *FJ*, 8th Dec 1848.
22.  *FJ*, 9th Dec 1848.

**Fig 55.**   *Lord Lieutenant Clarendon.*

the final 41,000 names should have impressed, but they were destined to disappointment in the absence of any encouraging response.[23]     Clarendon took refuge in stating that the government could not interfere with county sheriffs in the matter of jury selection.  He denied outright that there had been any policy of excluding Catholics from serving in juries in the recent state trials and cited his Attorney-General in support.    He remarked that the law required that not only should jurors be fairly and impartially chosen, but that the jurors themselves should be fair and impartial.  He added that their petition failed to acknowledge that even more Protestant than Catholic jurors had been set aside.  He concluded his reply to the deputation by making it clear to them that he had no intention of interfering with the exercise of discretion in jury selection.  That was the end of it.

It was, therefore, ironic that when Duffy finally came for trial, after various postponements, the jury was discharged, on 22nd February 1849, having failed to reach an agreed verdict.  In the wake of this, another committee was established to petition for an end to his prosecution and to seek his liberation.  Signed by some 17,000 individuals, it was given to a deputation of 27 Irish MPs who presented it at a meeting with Clarendon at the Irish Office, in London, on Monday 2nd April 1849.  They left that meeting, *'not much gratified by their reception'*, when Clarendon told them with remarkable impropriety that he held Duffy to be guilty and that to grant their petition *'could be an extremely bad precedent and one he could not sanction'*.[24]  When Duffy's retrial commenced in April, a majority

23.   C. Kinealy, *Repeal and revolution: 1848 in Ireland*, Manchester 2009, p. 216.
24.   *DEM*, 4th April 1849.

of the jury pronounced him not guilty, but with a minority believing that there was some element of guilt, the jury was discharged and Duffy was granted bail, after serving ten months in custody.[25] This news was tempered by the consideration that Mitchel had been transported, that Martin and Doheny were awaiting transportation, while Smith O'Brien, Meagher, McManus and O'Donohoe still lay under sentence of death.

It was against this background that, on 16th May 1849, a meeting was held, with Spratt as chairman, to form a petition committee to seek clemency for these prisoners. All that day this new committee worked in Radley's Hotel, to produce multiple copies of yet another memorial to the Lord Lieutenant and to gather signatures. As on former occasions, the new committee enjoyed immediate support. Within that first day, they had secured 5,000 names; by Saturday 19th May some 7,000, including Spratt's famine committee co-worker, Rev Robert King, as also Cloncurry, Haughton and Charles Bianconi. By close of business, on Monday 21st May, they had garnered 15,000 signatures, including John's brother and fellow-priest, James. The *Freeman's Journal* was buoyant and strongly felt that:

> No motive can now exist save one of vengeance, to demand the expatriation of these gentlemen. State policy no longer requires a harsh course of action. The stillness of death has come over the country, and the ministers who caused that death to brood over the land, no longer pretend to fear that any result, dangerous to their sway, can now follow the liberation of the state prisoners.[26]

The collection of signatures accelerated and among them those of Fr Theobald Mathew – on his way to America – and of Spratt's Carmelite confrere, Thomas Bennett, as professor in All Hallows College: oddly, no other Carmelite friar's name was to be found among the legions that signed up:[27] nor, for that matter, apparently no signature from Fr John's other brother, the very politically-conscious Michael, but that is another story, for later surmise. Eventually, on 2nd June, it was indicated that Clarendon would receive a deputation two days later. There was a

---

25.  *FJ*, 16th April 1849.
26.  *FJ*, 21st May 1849.
27.  *FJ*, 25th May 1849.

sixteen-man delegation, comprising Spratt and Haughton, for the committee, together with, among others, Duffy's defence counsel, Isaac Butt, and Sir Colman O'Loghlen, and Dublin's Lord Mayor, Sir Timothy O'Brien. The latter read the text of the memorial and then Clarendon responded with a terse comment, at once non-committal but ominous: *'justice should be administered without any severity beyond that which the interests of society demand'.*[28] He then withdrew, leaving the delegation without any indication as to hope or success. Yet, significantly, on the very next day after the meeting with the Lord Lieutenant, the death sentences on O'Brien, Meagher, McManus and O'Donohoe were commuted – to transportation for life. A few weeks later, on 9th July 1849, Smith O'Brien, Meagher, McManus and O'Donohoe were on their way to Van Diemen's Land.

## The Quest for Conciliation

Tempered at least by the fact that these four lives had been spared, nonetheless the sentence of transportation for life must have come as a bitter blow to Fr Spratt and his colleagues who had worked so hard for clemency. For 'Old Ireland' or O'Connellite Repealers, such as John Spratt, these were bleak years indeed. John had renewed his Repeal Association membership in January 1848 and he hoped for political reconciliation of 'Old' and Young Ireland. Six months after this, in the first week of June 1848, attempts were made by John O'Connell on the one side, and by William Smith O'Brien, on the other, to achieve reunion. By 4th June it was agreed that the Repeal Association and the Confederation would both be dissolved, to be replaced by a new organisation, the Irish League. The attempt failed, not least because Charles Gavan Duffy, with supreme unwisdom, claimed the development as a victory for the Confederates.[29] This caused O'Connell, on 12th June 1848, to delay the final wind-down of the Repeal Association for two weeks, though, to his own discomfiture, sentiment within the Association was pressing impatiently for the union to come about. By late June 1848 the Repeal Association had ceased to exist. O'Connell, however, declined to join the new body and decided instead to concentrate on his parliamentary career at Westminster.

---

28.  *FJ*, 6th June 1849.
29.  Nowlan, pp. 206-207.

The new Irish League held its first meeting on 11th July 1848 but it never really gained momentum. With the Repeal Association now effectively moribund, and with many of the leading Young Irelanders and Confederates either now transported or on the run, both moral force and physical force alike seemed impotent. Repeal as a goal was dead. To the old faithful this was not immediately evident. O'Connell tried to revive the Association in October 1849 but he could attract few supporters. It was a feeble and a fruitless attempt and the initiative, it appears, now lay elsewhere.

In November 1849, largely through the efforts of Gavan Duffy, a national conference was called, to consider how, if possible, to revive the country's fortunes. The outcome, on 20th November, was the establishment of The Irish Alliance *'for the protection of the lives and interests of the Irish people and the attainment of their national rights'.*[30] A prominent role in this foundation conference was played by Spratt's friend and co-worker in so many causes, W J Battersby. Interestingly, Fr John himself was not involved. Instead, even though he was no longer a member of the dead-and-alive-again Repeal Association, nevertheless he soon re-engaged himself in efforts to foster the reunion of nationalist elements. His old friend, Bishop Michael Blake of Dromore, had observed with interest the foundation of the Alliance and the resurrection of the Repeal Association. In a letter to a Dublin City Councillor, Martin Burke, who had bemoaned the long silence of the Repeal Association and who had joined the Alliance, Blake praised John O'Connell, without naming him, but added that *'it appears the National Alliance is the more popular'*, yet Blake now called for a union of the two bodies.[31]

At the same time, about ten days after the foundation of the Irish Alliance, Fr Spratt also took an initiative. He drew up the text of a requisition calling for delegations from the Alliance and from the Repeal Association to confer on how best to achieve reunion. He gave

---

30. *The Advocate, or Irish Industrial Journal,* 21st Nov 1849; Kinealy, *Repeal and revolution,* pp. 226-7.

31. *FJ,* 3rd Dec 1948, Blake to Burke, 30th November, responding to a letter from Burke, 29th November 1849. This was not Blake's first foray into the quest for reunion: two years before that he had written to Daniel O'Connell, asking the latter 'to devise some proper mode for reconciling all Repealers to each other in Conciliation Hall...Repeal cannot be accomplished without a union of hearts': see Dromore Diocesan Archives, Blake to O'Connell, 20th November 1846.

this requisition to John Gray of the *Freeman's Journal*, to make available to the public for support and signatures.[32]  When Bishop Blake also continued to pursue his hope for reunion, Gavan Duffy responded in a tentatively positive way: ironically, ignoring his own role in causing the failure of the June 1848 initiative, due to his own triumphalism back then, he now urged *'restraint from vituperation'*, stated that he had always supported calls for reunion, and believed that such reunion was still possible.[33]

In the meantime, Spratt's initiative was taken up both by the Repeal Association and by the Council of the Irish Alliance.  At the Association's meeting on 10th December, John O'Connell referred to the negotiations and lavished praised on Spratt:

> This negotiation has been opened by an individual who, if anyone could work it to a successful issue, would by the influence of his character, do so.  It has been opened by my Reverend friend, Dr Spratt (cheers).

O'Connell added that he could not refuse *'so good, so venerated and so truly respected a man'.*[34]  As for the Irish Alliance, on 12th December, through their secretary, Maurice Leyne, they sent forward to Spratt a 'peace' proposal.  Doubtless elated at this positive response, the Carmelite friar wrote to John O'Connell on that same day, enclosing the Alliance document, and remarked:

> I can entertain the hope that you will accede to the peace proposition so fairly put, in order to obtain the much-desired junction.[35]

O'Connell lost no time in responding but his reply must have dashed Spratt's hopes.  He referred, in a gratuitously ungracious and maladroit way, to *'the very unusual letter of my misguided and unfortunate young relative, Mr. Maurice Leyne'.*  This was, without doubt, a reference to Leyne's having left the Repeal Association for the Confederates and to his having been

---

32.  *FJ*, 6th Dec 1849.
33.  *DWN*, 8th Dec 1849, Duffy to Blake, 7th December 1849.
34.  *DWN*, 15th Dec 1849.
35.  Ibid.

arrested, along with Thomas Francis Meagher, near Thurles on the night of 13th August 1848, during the suspension of Habeas Corpus.[36]

O'Connell then went on to ask the Alliance's former Young Irelanders *'why will they not accept my father's rules as repeated by him with full explicitness in 1846?'*, and he then declared *'We must consider the negotiations completely at an end'.*[37] One has no record of Fr Spratt's reaction and can but surmise that he must have been crushed by John O'Connell's response. It was small consolation to the Carmelite that the dying Repeal Association expressed its appreciation for his efforts. Meeting on 17th December, O'Connell reported the end of the negotiations that never really began and he went on:

> Whatever may be said of the negotiation itself, this much at least is certain, that the motives of the very Rev Dr Spratt were most admirable and excellent and that his conduct throughout was entirely in accordance with those motives.[38]

It is interesting to note that Fr John appears not to have re-joined the Repeal Association upon its resurrection by O'Connell, nor did he join the Alliance. This is evident from the fact that, when these negotiations were being prepared and the Alliance had appointed its delegation, it asked Fr Spratt if he would chair the imminent reunion conference: since *'he was belonging to neither body, we thought that he would best mediate between us'.*[39] If Spratt was now disillusioned with the Repeal Association it would appear that he was not the only one. Two of its former stalwarts, the Dublin City MP, John Reynolds, and its Lord Mayor, Sir Timothy O'Brien, were denounced in the Repeal Association with the jibe that having made their careers in Conciliation Hall, they now deserted it.[40] They were far from alone in that forsaking: two of John Spratt's closest friends, Battersby and Martin Brennan, both joined

36. *Tipperary Free Press*, 16th Aug 1848. Habeas Corpus suspension came into effect from 28th July 1848 until 1st March 1849.
37. *DWN*, 15th Dec 1849, J. O'Connell to Spratt, 13th December 1849.
38. *DWR*, 22nd Dec 1849.
39. *FJ*, 20th Dec 1849.
40. *DWR*, 22nd Dec 1849.

the Irish Alliance and served on its Council.[41] The Alliance, however, no more than its predecessor, the Irish League, ever experienced significant growth: instead, it languished. In August 1850 it merged with the pro-labour, radical organisation of Chartist antecedents, the Irish Democratic Association. These two bodies became the Irish Democratic Alliance.[42] It was an unhappy union: a correspondent to Duffy's journal, *The Nation*, put it succinctly, in February 1852: '*The Irish Democratic Association and the Irish Alliance, twin brothers, came into the world at strife and strangled each other in infancy*'.[43]

*Troubles abroad – troubles at home*
The failure of the non-negotiations of December 1849 terminated a truly dismal year for Spratt as for so many Irishmen. These national political disappointments apart, it was as if, wherever he turned, horrors and disasters befell, internationally and locally. Paradoxically, while fostering sympathy and promoting support for the personal plight of the

imprisoned or exiled nationalists and republicans of Ireland, the Carmelite was, simultaneously, witness to the plight and the flight of Pope Pius IX at the hands of nationalists and republicans in Italy.

In late November 1848 the pontiff had fled to the kingdom of Naples after the assassination of his prime minister, Pellegrino Rossi. Then, on 9th February 1849, the Pope's temporal power collapsed – temporarily – as

**Fig 56.**    *Pope Pius IX.*

---

41.   *DWN*, 5th Jan 1850. Brennan took up a position on its Land Committee – at a time when the land question in the form of tenant-right was just about to replace Repeal as the emergent dominant goal on the Irish political landscape. At the same time, Battersby took up a position on its 'City Committee' whose remit was to drum up membership in Dublin.

42.   *DWN*, 5th Jan 1850. For the Irish Democratic Association, see D'Arcy, *Dublin Artisan Activity*, pp. 68-69.

43.   *The Nation*, 14th Feb 1852, citing P. McEntee to editor, 19th January 1852.

Italian nationalists rose up and proclaimed a Republic in Rome. It was not until after a French Army occupied the city and overthrew the Roman Republic that the Pope was reinstated. In the course of these unfolding events, Spratt, as with most Irish Catholic clergy and laity, became caught up in the wave of sympathy. Typical of the reaction was a meeting convened by Fr Andrew O'Connell for the faithful of his parish of Saints Michael and John in December 1848. Spratt was to the fore at this meeting and proposed the first resolution urging that Ireland and its Catholics owed the Pope their sympathy and support, not least in consideration of the way in which the Pontiff had helped during the Famine.[44] Rome and the Pope had been extremely generous during Ireland's disaster. He had donated 1,000 Roman dollars to the Irish bishops for famine relief, and had called on Rome's clergy and laity to help. They responded in kind, including the staff and students of the Irish College who went without meals to save money for donations. Pius IX went further still by issuing an appeal to the entire Catholic world for aid when he published the encyclical, *Praedecessores Nostros*, in March 1847.[45]

## A very local calamity

While such international upheavals affecting the Papacy caused the Carmelite, his confreres and fellow-Catholics great anxiety, as they would again a decade later,[46] they were not the only ones. As if the political, economic and financial woes of country and city were not bad enough, there occurred in the very neighbourhood of the Carmelites, a more local misadventure. This was the collapse, on 10th May 1848, of the St Peter's Parish Savings Bank. More usually referred to as the Cuffe Street Savings Bank, from its location, the bank was established in 1818. Its early patrons and trustees came from the ranks of the wealthier Protestant clergy and laity of the parish, including Archdeacon John Torrens, rector of St Peter's, and his Church of Ireland curates. The bank's more substantial depositors came from all parts of the city and from distant parts of Ireland, from Antrim to Cork. However, its smaller depositors and savers were neighbourhood folk of lesser

---

44. *The Pilot*, 15th Dec 1848.
45. D. A. Kerr, *The Catholic Church and the Famine*, Dublin 1996, pp. 33-35.
46. In 1859 and again over 1866-1871.

means, mainly Protestant working class, including mechanics, domestic servants, widows and unemployed or retired artisans.

Over its first ten years the bank built up its clientele among all social classes and, by 1828, it counted close on £190,000 in deposits. Twenty years later, in the course of 1848, rumours were circulating concerning serious mismanagement of its funds – not for the first time. The problem originated almost two decades before this but was concealed by the trustees. It transpired that one of its officers, the cashier and book-keeper had been embezzling funds. It was little wonder that the Church of Ireland trustees tried to conceal the fact: it turned out that the culprit was none other than William Bruce Dunne, sexton of St Patrick's Parish – the same who had prevented the Catholic funeral rites at the burial of Arthur D'Arcy in St Kevin's Cemetery in September 1823.[47] Described as *'a very correct man'*, Dunne had in fact misappropriated over £16,500 – or £30,000 according to evidence before a House of Commons Select Committee of Inquiry in 1850[48] – before being discovered. He quit, or was 'resigned' from the bank in January 1831, and subsequently absconded. A superficial investigation was conducted for the National Debt Commissioners in London but no action was recommended by their officer, John Tidd Pratt. The continuing failure to take action and continued mismanagement by later trustees and managers led to a rising level of indebtedness, from £8,000 in 1833 through £19,000 in 1844 to close on £33,000 in 1847.

In this climate of undeclared crisis, rumours re-erupted and, in November 1845, a run on the bank developed which lasted until the spring of 1846.[49] By 20th November 1845 over £60,000 had been withdrawn by more suspicious savers. In all, this particular run saw £223,000 being paid out. The National Debt Commissioners now recommended that the bank be closed down but the trustees refused for fear that they would be personally liable for the consequences. A contagion now spread to the much larger Dublin Savings Bank. Its secretary, testifying ten years later to yet another parliamentary committee of inquiry, described the refusal by the Cuffe Street Bank to act responsibly as *'one*

47. See Chapter 4 and also *Appendix 4: The Burials Dispute in the 1820s and after.*
48. *Report from the Select Committee on Savings Banks*, HC 1850 (649), p. xiv. See also C. Ó Gráda, *The early history of Irish savings banks*, UCD School of Economics Working Paper, WP 08/04, Feb 2008, unpaginated.
49. Ibid., pp. xiv, xvi.

*of the most reckless and audacious
acts of spoliation and robbery on the
part of the trustees, managers and
officers'.*[50] Although the blight
was contained for a short while,
the growing uneasiness could
not be stayed. At the start of
1848 another run commenced.
On 22nd April the Cuffe Street
Savings Bank trustees asked
the government for aid. It was
refused. This time there was
no way out. On 10th May 1848
the bank closed its doors, its
clients clamoured in vain for
admission, and mounted police
had to restrain the depositors.
As Ó Gráda recounted, in the
week which followed, some
depositors sold their pass
books at a discount.[51] The
bank closed, never to reopen,

**Fig 57.**    *The headquarters of the
Bricklayers' and Stonecutters'
Guild, originally built as St
Peter's Parish Savings Bank.*

with liabilities close on £65,000 and assets of less than £100.

The majority of the local depositors were Protestant working people,
widows or the retired. Some of them, desperate to gain admission but
unable to do so, approached Fr Spratt for assistance. He offered the
use of his Cuffe Street Temperance Hall for emergency meetings and
from these sprang a committee that now laboured long and hard to seek
redress for the casualties. There were varying estimates of the numbers
of unfortunate depositors and the total sum of their losses. In a House
of Commons debate on the matter, in March 1849, the Dublin City MP,
John Reynolds, spoke of 1,664 unfortunates deprived of £50,000. He
himself had witnessed the most distressing scenes in Dublin at the time

50.  *Report from the Select Committee on Savings Banks,* HC 1857-58 (441), p. 238: evidence
     of Robert Deaker, honorary secretary of the Dublin Savings Bank.
51.  C. Ó Gráda. 'Savings banks, famine and financial contagion: Ireland in the 1840's
     and 1850's', *Irish Economic and Social History,* vol. 36, No. 1, 2009, p. 28.

and claimed to have known of consequential suicides.[52] The solicitor for the distraught depositors, William Keating Clay, put the number of the aggrieved at 1,554 and the amount at £47,000.[53]

As for Fr John, he was already heavily committed to other major undertakings, charitable, educational, political, on top of his temperance crusade and his daily priestly duties. Now, over 1848-1849, he became drawn into the accelerating maelstrom of the Cuffe Street crisis. Having lent his Temperance Hall, he attended the first emergency meeting of depositors on 19th May 1848. That meeting was told that some 1,670 depositors were being denied access to £49,350 of their own deposits. A committee of twelve to seek redress was set up. It included the local Church of Ireland curates, the Rev J McSorley and the Rev E Groves. Almost inevitably, Fr Spratt was elected to this body, as was his friend Haughton.[54] The latter proposed and the Carmelite seconded a resolution which held the government responsible for compensating the victims. Fr John knew hundreds of these savers and, while most were local working class and lower middle class Protestants, a sizeable minority would have been Catholics of similar circumstances,[55] and, conceivably, they counted among his own parishioners. Many of these hapless depositors were facing ruin. Some thirty of them came to Fr John to seek his help to actually gain admission to the workhouse, as they were starving. What happened to these is not known but a decision was taken to petition the Lord Lieutenant for redress. Spratt now found himself participating in yet another deputation to the Viceregal Lodge. His colleagues on this delegation were led by the Rt Hon Frederick Shaw, a leading Dublin Conservative and former MP for the City and for Dublin University. They included the two sitting Dublin City MPs, John Reynolds and Edward Grogan, together with the depositors' solicitor, William Keating Clay and fellow Committee member, Carew Smith.[56] The trip to the Phoenix Park was to little immediate effect: the Lord

52. Hansard, *Parliamentary Debates*, 3rd series, vol. 104, 29th March 1849, cols. 20-54.
53. *Savings Banks Ireland: Minutes of Evidence taken before the Select Committee on Savings Banks (Ireland). Appointed in the last session.* HC 1849 (21) p. 92.
54. *FJ*, 11th Jan 1849 provides a detailed account of the history of the bank and its crisis.
55. Ó Gráda has conducted a study of the likely denominational ratios, based on an analysis of their names. See Ó Gráda, *Early History*, Appendix 1.3, 'The names of the Cuffe Street Depositors'.
56. *DEPC*, 20th Jan 1849.

Lieutenant sympathised but was not in a position to offer a definitive or even a hopeful response. However, in no small way, due to the efforts of John Reynolds in parliament, over the course of the years 1848 to 1850, some three House of Commons Committees of Inquiry issued four bodies of evidence relating to the financial calamity.[57] Reynolds had his work cut out for him. The first investigation, in August 1848, issued a very brief and largely useless report as, in the Commission's own words, *'owing to the late period of the session, they have found themselves unable to bring it to a satisfactory conclusion'*; but, at least they recommended a further inquiry.[58] In March 1849 Reynolds pressed hard in the Commons to secure this second investigation. Unhelpfully, the Chancellor of the Exchequer, Sir Charles Wood, demurred, claiming it would be pointless. Reynolds' fellow Dublin MP, Edward Grogan, however, attacked Wood and the government for not having closed the bank, since the Commissioners of the National Debt and the various government administrators from 1831 to 1847 knew that the Cuffe Street Bank was insolvent but had ignored the problem.[59] Eventually, the Commons carried a motion for a new inquiry, by a slender majority of seven. Unfortunately for Reynolds, Spratt and the Cuffe Street Committee, this second parliamentary investigation, in 1849, issued a whitewashing one-page report: it exonerated the National Debt Commissioners for failing to intervene in a timely or an effective fashion and absolved the Government from all liability. However, a third investigation, in 1850, produced hard-hitting findings, recommended criminal proceedings against the officers of the Bank, and urged the Chancellor to look favourably upon the plight of the depositors.[60] Government relented and, within that year, parliament approved a compensation package of

57. In order of publication they were:
   *Report from the Select Committee on Savings Banks (Ireland)*, HC 1847-8 (693);
   *Savings Banks (Ireland): Minutes of Evidence taken before the Select Committee on Savings Banks (Ireland), Appointed in the last session.* HC 1849 (21);
   *First Report from the Select Committee on Savings Banks*, HC 1849 (437);
   *Report from the Select Committee on Savings Banks*, HC 1850 (649).
   There was, at the end of the 1850s, a further investigation: *Report from the Select Committee on Savings Banks*, HC 1857-58 (441).
58. *Report from the Select Committee on Savings Banks (Ireland)*, HC 1847-8 (693), p. 3.
59. Hansard, *Parl. Debates*, 3rd Series, vol. 104, Thursday 29th March 1849, cols. 20-54.
60. *Report from the Select Committee on Savings Bank, HC 1850 (649)*, p. xvii.

£30,000.[61] This must have been some comfort to the Carmelite friar for his efforts to help his neighbours, Protestant and Catholic: it was little enough consolation to desperate depositors as a dismal episode brought an end to a decade of disaster for Dublin and for Ireland.

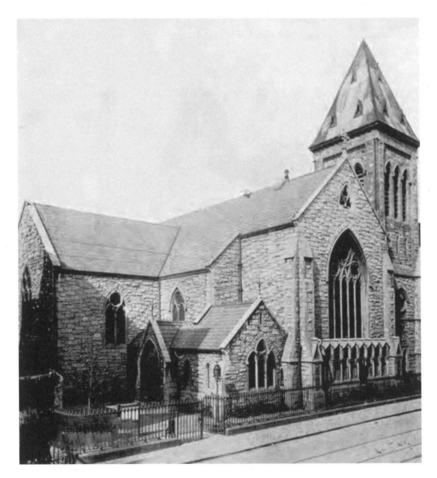

**Fig 58.** *St Peter's, Church of Ireland, Aungier Street, as it was rebuilt in 1867. In Spratt's time, it was the largest Church of Ireland parish church in Dublin. The church closed in 1950, and was demolished in 1983.*

---

61. *Return showing how the sum of £30,000 voted by the House of Commons for the relief of depositors in the late Savings Bank, Cuffe Street, Dublin, has been disposed of.* .... HC 1851 (295). Claimants of sums of less than £5 constituted the largest group, at 507, and this is the group where local people predominated: it was in contrast to the 294 claimants of sums in excess of £50 who mainly came from further afield.

# CHAPTER THIRTEEN

## *Regenerating Ireland, 1850-1853*

The desolate state of Ireland after the Famine led one group of men to meet to take some small steps towards helping the recovery of their country. On foot of a privately-circulated invitation some thirty of them gathered on 14th May 1850, in the Ormond Quay offices of solicitor James Moran. Like the rest of their contemporaries, they had witnessed the mass exodus of Irish with little education and no skills, equipped for life with nothing but the brute ability to dig the earth. Their meeting resulted in the birth of a new movement for the revival of Irish manufacture.[1] They aimed to promote where possible the exclusive purchase of Irish goods and sought to develop the industrial training of the young. Those present included the representatives of twelve different trades and, apart from these artisans and employers, there were, initially, at least two medical doctors, John Ryan of Francis Street and William Bevan of Leeson Street, and a solitary clergyman, Fr Fay of Meath Street. Fr Spratt was not present at this foundation meeting, but his friend and fellow temperance campaigner, the schoolmaster, Martin A Brennan, attended, as did two other of Spratt's lay acquaintances, Surgeon Mitchell and Martin Burke, the owner of the

---

1. This movement does not feature in modern standard surveys of nineteenth century Irish history: see, for example, D. G. Boyce, *Nineteenth Century Ireland*, Dublin 2005; A. Jackson, *Ireland, 1798-1998*, Oxford 1999; K. T. Hoppen, *Ireland since 1800: Conflict and Conformity*, London 1989; W. E. Vaughan, ed., *A New History of Ireland*, vol. 5, *Ireland under the Union, 1801-1870*, Oxford 1989; nor in specialist studies, see, for example D. Dickson, *Dublin: the making of a capital city*, London 2014; J. Brady & A. Simms, eds., *Dublin: through space and time*, Dublin 2001; J. Prunty, *Dublin Slums, 1800-1925*, Dublin 1998.

Shelbourne Hotel.[2]  The idea of handicraft revival was doubtless one
that arose in many minds at the same time, and diverse uncoordinated
initiatives had been evident in various parts of the country over the
previous decades.  However, in terms of establishing a co-ordinated
national organisation and movement, Martin Burke claimed that he and
Patrick Sheridan, carpet-manufacturer of Parliament Street, were the
ones who had taken the initiative.[3]  Burke's claim was contested: the
founding meeting was almost certainly convened by another significant,
but sinister, individual who attended on that occasion, one Thomas
Mooney, bankrupt baker and erstwhile banker of Francis Street,
of whom more anon.  Another foundation member, Bartholomew
O'Connor, provided a summary history of the movement in October
1852 – at a time when he was no longer well-disposed to Mooney – and
stated that the first meeting had been convened by the latter.[4]  The
founding members called their group The Board of (Irish) Manufacture
and Industry.[5]  They quickly found a permanent meeting place at Mason's
Rooms, 22 Essex Bridge, and their first meeting there was chaired by
Martin Burke.  However, from the outset, the driving force proved to
be Thomas Mooney, together with the Capel Street hatter, Christopher
Coyne, and the Harcourt Street physician, Dr George T Hayden.[6]  It
was Mooney who secured the premises and, at the very first meeting of
the Board of Irish Manufacture and Industry, on 21st May 1850, he was
temporarily appointed secretary.  The founders constituted themselves

2.  For accounts of this foundation meeting, see *FJ*, 18th May 1850, 8th Oct 1852.
3.  Burke made this claim at a public meeting organised by Spratt in October 1850;
    however, Patrick Sheridan was not at the foundation meeting of 14th May: see *FJ*,
    29th Oct 1850, 8th Oct 1852.
4.  *FJ*, 8th Oct 1852.  Burke's claim was supported by the Capel Street hatter,
    Christopher Coyne.  In a letter to the editor of the *Freeman's Journal* on 1st
    November 1850, Coyne remarked to Burke that the movement 'had originated
    with you and your friends…before Mr. Mooney had been aware of it'.  But no one
    disputed that it was Mooney who had issued the covering circular.
5.  Hereafter referred to as BIMI.  To avoid a proliferation of abbreviations, this
    abbreviation is retained although, at one stage, it changed its name to 'Parent Board
    of IMI'.
6.  George Hayden (1798-1857) was father to Thomas (1823-1881), professor of
    anatomy in the Catholic University and a protégé of Spratt; George's
    granddaughter, Mary Hayden, was first professor of modern Irish history in
    University College Dublin: see J. Padbury, 'Mary Hayden, 1862-1942, Feminist', in
    *Studies*, vol. 98, 2009, pp. 145-158.

as a Provisional Committee, with the aim of holding elections for a twenty-one member Council, and adopting a constitution when their membership would have exceeded 200.[7] Their early endeavours were devoted to recruiting members in order to bolster the funds needed for their two main objectives: to establish *'schools of industry'* to educate young people in the basic skills that would make them employable, and to propagate the message of supporting Irish-made products that would create that employment. These 'industrial schools' became a major thrust in the work of the BIMI.

The idea for schools of industry and training workshops for the labouring poor was hardly new and was very much in the air at the end of the 1840s. In London, the Christian Socialists, led by the theologian, F D Maurice, and his associate, J M Ludlow, had established the Society for the Promotion of Working Men's Associations and were deeply engaged in promoting workers' producer co-operatives over the period 1848-1855. In France, the Socialist Louis Blanc in his book *The Organisation of Work* (1840) had pioneered the idea of 'social workshops' and sought to realise it through the National Workshops set up following the February 1848 Revolution in Paris.[8] Spratt's clerical associate, Fr Thaddeus O'Malley, was to take up some of these ideas in the pages of his short-lived newspaper, *The Christian Social Economist* over November-December 1851.

However, Dublin artisans and masters, under the leadership of Fr Matthew Flanagan[9] had already tried to establish a movement of worker's co-operatives back in 1840-43, but the BIMI was the first body to try to establish a national movement. Sometime between May and July 1850 it secured a large warehouse in Prince's Street, behind Henry Street in Dublin, in order to create *'a central industrial school for girls'*, and appointed a Mrs Whitters to teach shirt-making and muslin embroidery.[10] At the same meeting where this was announced, Spratt's friend, W J Battersby, was in attendance and handed in a membership subscription from the

7. *FJ*, 13th Sept 1850.
8. A. S. Lindemann, *A History of European Socialism*, New Haven 1983, pp. 77-85.
9. Born Smithfield, Dublin, curate of St Catherine's Parish, then parish priest of St Nicholas Without, in Francis Street, for 30 years from 1826; secretary to the Catholic Book Society; built the Church of St Nicholas of Myra; died in April 1856.
10. *FJ*, 2nd Aug 1850.

**Fig 59.**   *Valentine Brown Lawless, 2nd Baron Cloncurry.*

Carmelite friar.  In announcing Spratt's membership, *'to loud cheers'*, Battersby paid an explicit tribute to the friar's faith in the initiative, claiming that Spratt had been part of every previous movement for the revival of Irish manufacture[11] and that *'his greatest virtue, perhaps, [was] that he never despaired'*.  Battersby claimed for his friend that *'it was but two years ago that he proposed a comprehensive plan for carrying on a movement for Irish manufacture, the principle of which is affirmed by this Board'*.  He then read out the text of a public letter on the subject which Spratt had written in 1848, but *'which was not then responded to by the public only because the country was about plunging into revolution'*.  The BIMI meeting was greatly enthused at Spratt's becoming a member.  One week later, he attended his first public meeting of the Board, on Tuesday 15th August 1850. He brought with him a contribution of £12 from Cloncurry.[12]

Three weeks later, on 8th September 1850, at a meeting in the former Wesleyan Methodist Meeting House, in Whitefriar Lane, the audience

---

11.   A claim of literal but hardly substantial truth: the only other significant revival 'movement' in Dublin was over 1840-1843 and there is no evidence to-date that Spratt was ever deeply involved in this, although he lent his signature to a requisition calling a foundation meeting of that movement, as he did again in February 1845 when another manufacture revival movement was attempted: see *FJ*, 10th Nov 1840, 3rd Feb 1845.

12.   *DWN*, 17th Aug 1850.

was informed that Fr Spratt had taken over the Meeting House with a view to establishing a school of industry.[13] However, it is not certain if this was his primary intention from the outset or if he had planned to use the new premises as an extension to his existing, traditional national school until he saw what was developing under Mooney and his BIMI associates with their industrial school in Prince's Street. Certainly, at the weekly meeting on 10th September, Battersby announced that Spratt had taken the premises for an industrial school to train up to 2,000 girls.

*Reviving Irish Manufacture and Industry – the BIMI*
When Spratt first joined the Board of Irish Manufacture and Industry, a promising future for it appeared to beckon. By mid-September 1850 the BIMI counted 250 members and, consequently, its provisional committee were preparing for elections to constitute the organisation on a regular and permanent basis. Its school in Prince's Street was training 100 girls; a new branch school was announced for the Canal Harbour area of St James' Parish; Kilkenny had set up its own Board of Trade along similar lines, with BIMI assistance and advice. The Board's propaganda at last appeared to be creating a demand for Irish-made clothes. John Spratt himself was able to place a large order of black and grey serge for despatch to *'certain religious orders'* in British Guiana as requested by Bishop Hynes.[14] Over the next few months the BIMI appeared to make good progress: the training schools of Prince's Street and Canal Harbour were reported to be flourishing and the Board seemed to enjoy growing success in persuading various poor law union workhouses, from Inishowen to Kinsale, from Balrothery to Galway, to adopt Irish made goods.[15] Spratt led a BIMI delegation out to Maretimo in Blackrock, Co. Dublin, to thank Cloncurry for his support. His lordship replied that he always employed Irish artisans and labourers, even when in Rome where he had commissioned a memorial for a departed friend.[16] In the same period, the BIMI

---

13. See Chapter Fourteen for a full account of this development.
14. *DWN*, 24th Aug 1850.
15. *FJ*, 24th Oct 1850.
16. Cloncurry had commissioned the celebrated Irish sculptor, John Hogan, to produce a memorial to Amelia, daughter of John Philpot Curran, for the Chapel of St Isidore in Rome. Amelia Curran had died there early in 1847. See V & R Di Martino, *Irish Rome: Roma Irlandese*, Rome 2015, p. 24.

had set up subcommittees to report on the condition and potential of various Irish industries.[17]   By November 1850, industrial schools founded or encouraged by the BIMI, seemed to spring up, overnight, like mushrooms. It had trained and sent out teachers to such schools in the North and South Dublin Union workhouses, to St Vincent de Paul's in Phibsborough, St Laurence O'Toole's in Seville Place, to Baltinglass and to Tipperary. They had even sent a teacher, Mrs Anne Murphy, to Spratt's Industrial School in Whitefriar Street. By year's end, the BIMI claimed to have created or helped to create 20 industrial schools.[18]   By the end of November 1850 the BIMI Council, which now included Spratt, had issued an impressive *Address to the People of Ireland*, setting out a comprehensive vision for creating a broad-based manufacturing industry for the country. However, despite external appearance, all was not well within the ranks of the BIMI.

### The Ominous Mr. Mooney

With its adherents now exceeding 250 in number, the election of 26 Council members and officers was conducted without a hitch, that September. Among the successful candidates were the temperance trio of Spratt, Brennan and Battersby. Dr William Bevan became treasurer, and Thomas Mooney with 100 votes, was elected permanent paid secretary. While claiming that he had not canvassed for a single vote, Mooney sounded a warning note when he remarked, on accepting the office, that he would '*do the work, provided that the management of the movement were left in his hands, under the direction of the Council'*.[19]

However, at that very time, September 1850, he himself mentioned that damaging letters about him had been circulating, in Drogheda, seeking to drive him from '*any share in the management of this movement'*. What the nature of these '*damaging letters'* may have been was not then disclosed, but Mooney was a man with a colourful past, destined to an even more colourful future. He was patriotic, charismatic, a confidence man and a bully. Bankrupt as a baker, from Francis Street, he was also at that time a fraudulent banker and insurance agent who had set up the singularly ill-named Provident Bank in Dublin in the 1830s. By the

---

17.  Fr Thaddeus O'Malley, for example, headed a committee to report on the slate industry.

18.  *FJ*, 7th Nov 1850; *DWN*, 28th Dec 1850.

19.  *DEM*, 20th Sept 1850.

**Fig 60.**   *Drawing of Thomas Mooney, originally printed in* The Irish World, *26th May 1888.*

end of that decade he had briefly been in jail as a result of his banking adventures. Such, however, was his charm and ability to persuade, that he was able to emerge as secretary to an earlier movement for the revival of Irish manufacturers, under the presidency of Fr Matthew Flanagan, in the early 1840s.[20] Amid complaints about mounting expenses incurred in securing publicity for Fr Flanagan's movement, Mooney resigned as secretary, amid uproar, in April 1841, and left Dublin for America, or, as one Dublin newspaper expressed it,

> Thomas Mooney of Bubble Provident Bank and Scheming Loan Fund notoriety deemed it prudent to make America his home... to continue his career of scheming trickery.[21]

In the United States he involved himself in the Irish-American dimension of the Repeal movement – not without further personal controversy and allegations of wrong-doing – and there wrote a monumental history of Ireland that was later highly regarded among some extreme

---

20. D'Arcy, *Dublin Artisan Opinion*, pp. 72-81. John Spratt supported the foundation of this movement in November 1840, but does not appear to have been active in it thereafter: see *FJ*, 10th Nov 1840.

21. *The Dublin Monitor*, 5th Aug 1842.

Nationalists.[22] In 1850 he returned to Dublin with the intention of setting up an emigration scheme for Irish people contemplating departing for America. Instead, having spoken with some old acquaintance from Fr Flanagan's early 1840s movement – most likely Martin Brennan – he became caught up with the idea of a relaunch of the campaign for the revival of Irish manufacture and industry.

Mooney was a man of considerable talents, great energy and persuasive power who attracted unswerving loyalty from many, but not from all of his associates. That loyalty was secured from some men of much higher educational attainments and social standing. To some extent he may have had a messianic complex: he certainly was given on occasion to using metaphors that cast himself in a Christ-like role. As before, in the early 1840s campaign, his dynamism soon led him to unbridled expenditure in promoting the BIMI dream. In the autumn of 1850 he was the chief among the BIMI Council who pressed to secure a central premises for the organisation, as a training school for its teachers, a meeting place for its members and an exhibition space for Irish manufactured goods. Mooney's impatient ambition in this led to the first of a series of resignations and secessions. When Mooney persisted in pressing the BIMI executive council to commit to the rental expenditure involved, two founding members, Spratt's friend Martin Burke of the Shelbourne Hotel, and Matthew Moran, resigned.[23] The Council endorsed Mooney's aim to take the premises in Mason's Rooms, 2 Essex Bridge, Parliament Street, for BIMI's headquarters. It was, however, not a unanimous decision. Spratt's friends, Battersby and the law student C S Ralph, objected strongly to the potential financial liabilities so that a subcommittee was set up to look further into the matter. The report of this subcommittee is not extant, but the seeds of dissension had now been sown. By late November the rumblings of discontent were unstilled and Spratt moved a resolution for a committee of twelve *'to consider the differences existing among some members of the Society'*. It is not clear what happened to Spratt's proposal, as there is no account

22. T. A. Mooney, *History of Ireland, from its first settlement to the present time*, 1st ed. 1845, 2nd ed. Boston 1846. It was published in Ireland as *The People's History of Ireland*, 2 vols., Dublin 1869-70. O'Donovan Rossa reviewed the work very favourably: see *The Irishman*, 21st June 1879. Mooney also wrote *Nine years in America, in a series of letters to his cousin, Patrick Mooney, a farmer in Ireland*, Dublin 1850.
23. *FJ*, 7th Nov 1850.

**Fig 61.** *A view from Capel Street overlooking Essex Bridge, by James Malton.*

given in any of the national newspapers from November 1850 to late January 1851. It may be noted, however, that apart from other traits, Mooney generally insisted that no newspaper men attend the meetings and that he communicated reports of BIMI proceedings directly from his own pen to the press.[24] Further trouble soon ensued.

*Mooney, mayhem and Spratt's secession*

At its weekly meeting, on 31st December 1850, Mooney delivered an extremely unwise and provocative speech. Were it not for the fact that he was a committed teetotaller it might be well supposed that he did so under the influence of intoxicating drink. The account of the speech was conveyed by himself to the newspaper press. In the course of his remarks he commented:

> Theology and letters alone will not fit a people to support themselves...Neither the Queen's Colleges nor the Pope's Colleges were calculated to supply the knowledge which the people want...

---

24. Thus, a report of a controversial meeting of the BIMI, on 31st December 1850, was described as "communicated by the Secretary". See *FJ*, 3rd Jan 1851.

Uproar ensued. The chairman on the occasion, John Dennan, who had been Spratt's co-worker on famine relief the year before, warned Mooney that he was *'treading on dangerous ground'*, but Mooney persisted and asked, *'Of what use is your dogmatic theology to those wretches who have to pickpocket?'* He then proceeded to attack the clergy, Catholic and Protestant, for generally failing to rally round in support of the movement, with, as he pointed out, the notable exceptions of Fr Spratt, Fr Fay of Meath Street and Archdeacon Hamilton.

Far from being pleased to be numbered among these exceptions, Spratt was outraged and publicised his outrage in a letter to the press on 4th January 1851. He began immediately by suggesting the need for a board and council of Irish Manufacture to be formed *'on sound principles'* so as to afford *'perfect confidence and satisfaction'*. He launched a blistering attack on Mooney, as

> not only the paid secretary but reporter, dictator and chief
> manager of all the affairs of the Society. Therefore, nothing
> appears in the public journals but what is favourable to himself
> and to his adherents.[25]

If Mooney wanted to know *'why the present Board of Trade is not supported'*,

> the reason is simply this: the great majority of the people have
> no confidence in some of its managers – the reporters from the
> public press are not allowed to attend its meetings; hence the
> most arbitrary and despotic acts take place there, contrary to the
> rules and regulations of any well-regulated society.

Spratt went on to describe an atmosphere of menace where anyone who disagreed with Mooney would find themselves, next time, confronted by Mooney's doorkeepers to prevent them entering a meeting. Spratt was not entirely exaggerating: some time later, Mooney found himself in court for assault, having seized a difficult attender by the neck and hurled him down the stairs.[26]

---

25. *FJ*, 4th Jan 1851, 'The Irish Manufacture Movement', John Spratt, 3rd Jan 1851.
26. *FJ*, 14th Feb, 22nd Apr 1852. The victim of Mooney's assault was one James W. Pollard.

However, at the heart of the conflict between them was the hard core of belief. Mooney wanted industrial schools to provide an exclusively secular, industrial training, with no reference to religion. Spratt wanted industrial schools that provided a non-denominational Christian education that would be simultaneously literary, moral and vocational. The Carmelite ended by urging a public meeting to establish a board and council of manufacture which would command public confidence and not affront the religious or political principles of anyone. He therefore concluded that he *'must cease to act with the present Board'* and, in a highly significant dig at Mooney, he insisted that

> I will not be accountable for any monies received, debts incurred or the management of female schools gotten up by Mr. Mooney and his friends.[27]

Four days later Mooney and Bartholomew O'Connor of the BIMI Council replied to Spratt, denying that Mooney ever dictated to the Board, that the press were excluded from meetings and denying that Mooney had given any offence to the clergy.[28] Spratt, in rejoinder, stood over all he had already alleged against Mooney and added that, contrary to their rules, the financial accounts were not being presented regularly or properly. Furthermore, in direct contravention of the instructions of the Board, Mooney had written offensive letters to Martin Burke and others who had resigned when the Board had ordered him *'to entreat them to return'*, and that he had suppressed letters unfavourable to himself. As for Mooney's 'neutral' approach to education in the industrial schools, the Carmelite insisted that it was not right for the girls to be kept in school from nine to five with *'no religious, moral or literary education'*, but then, what else could be expected of Mr. Mooney *'who treats religious instruction so lightly as to designate it "the parrot recitation of theology"'*.

## A Deepening Division

A serious split was now in the making and it was one which would divide Spratt's closest associates who hitherto had worked together for years in diverse other causes. At the next BIMI meeting, on 8th

---

27. *FJ*, 4th Jan 1851.
28. *FJ*, 8th Jan 1851.

January, Battersby rose to condemn Mooney for declining to retract his attack on the clergy and for failing to answer Spratt's charges. Against this, Martin Brennan, stating that *'he had ever been upon the most intimate terms with his venerated friend, his bosom friend, Dr Spratt'*, nonetheless could find nothing offensive in the speech of Mooney which he himself had heard.[29] Mooney himself then spoke and denied that he had intended to offend the clergy: he merely meant to point out that

> if you wanted to make the masses of the Irish people religious, moral, virtuous, honest and upright you must educate them in the arts and methods of industry. Without you doing this, your moral, or rather, your theological education by itself will fail: look at the state in which our people leave the country – with no practical skills and fifty in every one hundred illiterate. Ninety percent can do nothing but dig.[30]

He went on to insist that the accounts had been properly audited. At this point in the meeting, the silkweaver, O'Neill, and Spratt's associate, John Dennan, resigned, as did Fr Fay.

A week after this stormy gathering, Martin Burke convened a meeting of the Board, along with Spratt, Dennan and some 56 others, in the Shelbourne Hotel, on 20th January 1851. They passed a series of resolutions calling for a general meeting of the BIMI in order to remodel its structure and governance. They sought to elect a new council that would be socially and religiously representative: to have two honorary secretaries, one Catholic and one Protestant, a paid secretary and a Council of 21 to comprise 7 manufacturers, 7 workers and 7 independent of either. The press would be requested to attend and report all meetings and three auditors would examine all the accounts. Significantly, the meeting also proposed that all future industrial schools would be united with approved national schools of the various parishes and those responsible for conducting them were to be approved by the pastors and parents of the children so as *'to secure them, with industrial pursuits, the blessings of a literary and moral education'*. These resolutions were signed at this Shelbourne Hotel meeting by all 56 present and a

---

29. *FJ*, 10th Jan 1851.
30. Ibid.

further 111 signed them later. Among the signatories, along with Spratt, was his Carmelite confrere, Andrew Day. Not among them was Martin Brennan who remained firmly in Mooney's camp to the bitter end – and bitter the end would prove, but not before further fragmentation.

## The Split

The 150 dissidents, led by Spratt, met again on 13th February, in the Shelbourne, and called themselves the National Board for the Promotion of Irish Manufacture and Industry (NBPIMI). Spratt then made the decisive move in formalising the split and secession when he successfully proposed that

> A Provisional Committee be appointed to form a Board for the Promotion of Native Manufacture on such a basis as will give satisfaction and secure the confidence of the Public.

A provisional Committee of 21 was thereupon appointed and the first funds collected for the new organisation. The Carmelite then moved that Martin Burke be appointed treasurer, and in turn, Spratt and carpet manufacturer, Walter Bell, were appointed joint honorary secretaries. The final act of his secessionist meeting was that the new body adopted Spratt's proposed title, the National Board for the Promotion of Irish Manufacture and Industry.[31] Hitherto in his public life, Spratt usually had been a conciliator and unifier rather than a rebel and a splitter. It says much, therefore, of the depth of his misgivings about Thomas Mooney, in terms alike of the latter's personal character and of his ideology, that the Carmelite initiated so decisive a breakaway. The editor of the *Freeman's Journal*, Dr John Gray, supported Spratt in this, while deploring the circumstances which had precipitated the split.[32]

On 17th February the NBPIMI held it first public meeting at the Royal Exchange. The initial attendance may not have been great – the names of 25 people were recorded. With Burke as chairman, Frs Spratt and Gilligan proposed the resolution that all industrial schools be united with approved national schools, while Battersby and Dennan proposed that once the NBPIMI membership had reached 300, a

---

31.  *FJ*, 14th Feb 1851; *DWN*, 15th Feb 1851. Hereafter cited as NBPIMI.
32.  *FJ*, 14th Feb 1851.

**Fig 62.**   *The Royal Exchange, Dublin in 1810 (Modern day City Hall).*

general meeting would be convened to elect the officers and 21-man representative council.[33]   It was characteristic of Spratt in relation to public meetings that his speeches and interventions were kept brief, if he spoke at all; on this occasion, however, he spoke at length.   He regretted the failure of their efforts to unite with those who had *'legitimately engaged in this momentous movement'*, went on to deplore the godless situation of the factory children in England, and hoped that *'in a short-time he would have one of the most extensive industrial schools in Ireland'*, sufficient to accommodate 2000 children.   He revealed that Cloncurry had written to him to deplore the disunity and told Spratt that a BIMI deputation, including Mooney, Martin Brennan and Christopher Coyne had called on him to see if some solution to the division might be found. The deputation agreed to accept the thrust of the Shelbourne Hotel resolutions and to meet Spratt pretty well all the way.   The letter written by Cloncurry to Spratt was actually brought by hand to the Carmelite in his friary, in a delegation led by Martin Brennan, on Saturday 18th January.   They told Spratt that they accepted his reform propositions. Spratt then recounted that, when he received this delegation at the friary, he was the only one present on the secessionist side and so he asked that they put in writing their confirmation of acceptance of his

33.   *FJ*, 18th Feb 1851.

Shelbourne Hotel reform proposals. They apparently agreed to this and Mooney promised to deliver the written acceptance in person on the next day, Sunday 19th January: but, *'whatever the cause, he (Spratt) had not since received it'*. However, while willing to try for reunion, and having waited long and in vain that Sunday night for Mooney's delivery of the written acceptance, Spratt pressed ahead with the foundation meeting of the NBPIMI at the Royal Exchange on the next evening.

All of this emerged at a meeting of the original BIMI on 18th February. Here the Dame Street shoemaker, Manly Thacker, asserted that Spratt had brought religious differences into the movement by insisting on both a Protestant and a Catholic honorary secretary. The fact was true, the motive was not; ever-conscious of religious differences in Dublin, Spratt aimed to be inclusive in order to avoid religious contention: hence he had introduced joint Protestant and Catholic office holders into his Irish Total Abstinence Association and subscribed to an identical arrangement in the Sick and Indigent Roomkeepers Society. Thacker was right that one of the critical issues at the heart of the manufacture movement was that Spratt wanted an interdenominational approach whereas Mooney, and other leading figures of the BIMI, such as Thacker and Dr George Hayden, wanted a secular approach to industrial education. However, this was far from being the only source of conflict. Spratt made this abundantly clear in a letter to the press on 23rd February:

> I am surprised at their saying that it narrows down to this because our declaration of 20 January 1851 listed a whole range of reforms we sought.

He went further:

> I deny the assertion that I object to Mr. Mooney' school on merely religious grounds…I object to a system which keeps young girls at manual labour from morning to night without affording them an opportunity to read, write, keep accounts, and of obtaining a knowledge of those moral and practical duties of life which are indispensable to the security and welfare of society.[34]

---

34. *FJ*, 25th Feb 1851.

Nevertheless, the first meeting of the old BIMI after the secession revealed a large degree of support for Mooney, without whose energy and commitment its progress to that date could not have been realised. For his part, Mooney, now disregarding the secession, spoke enthusiastically of future developments including the building up of industrial schools within the workhouse system: this, later on, would become another source of rancour and division between the rival manufacture movements.

Before the end of February 1851 Spratt's breakaway NBPIMI had become a fully-functioning, separate organisation. At its meeting on 17th February, when it was announced that the substantial Kilmainham wool manufacturers, Thomas and Obadiah Willans, had joined, Spratt was in buoyant form, telling the assembly that the Prioress of Cashel Convent had asked him to find a training teacher for the industrial development of their schools. He himself had already managed to procure work orders for them as well as for the children of Whitefriar Street Industrial School. Martin Burke, meanwhile, announced the good news that, although only a week old, the NBPIMI now had over 420 members.[35]  A week later, they claimed their membership had risen to 527, but, in the interests of prudence, they decided to defer the appointment of a paid secretary until the membership would have reached 1,000. Despite, or perhaps because of this growth, the key members of the old BIMI professed to be anxious for reconciliation. However, complicated manoeuvrings to secure an end to the secession failed for many reasons, one of which being that Dr Hayden and some others of the old Board wanted to stand fully behind Mooney: consequently, Spratt and the NBPIMI proceeded to promote their own manufacture revival campaign.

At this stage, in March 1851, Spratt's Whitefriar Street Industrial School was fully in operation, with 120 girls attending daily and Messrs Wallace of Glasgow supplying them with raw materials and work orders.[36] Burke reported that a sub-committee was searching for large premises to serve as an exhibition hall. At the same time, in consolidation of the split, a new council of 21 was duly elected and new rules adopted. Among the 7 independent, non-employer, non-worker members, were Spratt and his close associates Burke, Battersby and C S Ralph. Spratt

---

35.  Ibid.
36.  *FJ*, 22nd March 1851. See also Chapter Fourteen.

and Ralph became the honorary secretaries and the growing volume of correspondence led to the appointment of the barrister, James Burke, as paid secretary.[37] Spratt's influence drew in more clergymen to membership, including his confrere, Andrew Day, three Discalced Carmelites of Clarendon Street, his Church of Ireland associate the Rev J J McSorley of St Peter's and, of particular note, Fr Matthew Flanagan, founder and president of the original manufacture revival movement of 1840-1843. Fr Flanagan deplored the division in the movement but hoped *'your original associates will have the good sense to join you again'*, and requested Spratt's aid in introducing an industrial branch into his own schools in Francis Street.[38]

The NBPIMI's concerns soon extended beyond the creation of industrial schools to the issue of public contracts and, in particular, to the large contracts for clothing the police of Dublin and of Ireland. In the hope of securing such contracts for Irish firms, Spratt soon found himself leading the NBPIMI in yet another deputation to the Lord Lieutenant.[39] The annual requirement was for 70,000 yards of cloth and the Lord Lieutenant promised the deputation that he would request the Board of Ordnance to look into the matter even as he was shown and admired a splendid sample of embroidered cloth from Spratt's industrial school.[40] However, like so many other of Spratt's delegations to the Viceroy's lodge, this one too appears to have been fruitless: it was reported on October 1851 that the DMP clothing contract had gone to an English firm.[41] Despite such disappointments, Spratt and the NBPIMI continued to work hard for the general revival cause. By mid-May his industrial school had over 190 girls in training and he had already sent newly trained teachers to emerging industrial schools in Cork and Tipperary.[42] At the same time, Martin Burke was still pressing to acquire permanent premises for the movement and declared himself willing to invest up to £2,000 to realise this.[43]

---

37.  *FJ*, 23rd May 1851.
38.  *DWN*, 12th April 1851. For Fr Day's admission see *FJ*, 5th June 1851: he was the only Carmelite of Whitefriar Street to join Spratt in the NBPIMI.
39.  *FJ*, 20th April, 15th May 1851; *EF*, 29th May 1851.
40.  *EF*, 29th May 1851.
41.  *FJ*, 29th Oct 1851.
42.  *FJ*, 23rd May 1851.
43.  *FJ*, 3rd July 1851.

*A Reunion once again?*

Down the road from the Royal Exchange, the rival BIMI in Essex Bridge claimed to be flourishing, and, in order to copper-fasten its status as the true original body of the revival movement, it had changed its name to the *Parent* Board of Irish Manufacturer and Industry, or PBIMI. However, despite claims to the contrary, all was not well in Essex Bridge. At a meeting of Spratt's NBPIMI, Ralph reported on growing dissensions in the parent body: *'it was a matter of notoriety that affairs were not so peaceably conducted elsewhere'*, he remarked. A document signed by a majority of its remaining members was circulating among the citizens calling for the correction of abuses in the BIMI and threatening a new secession. Ralph indicated that now

> from the very bosom of that gentleman's (Mooney's) supporters, opponents had now arisen and have placed their opposition now, as was ours formerly, on its true and proper basis as a money and financial question, for the protest, however delicately put, expressly declares that Mr Mooney is no longer 'to have any interference with the cash'.[44]

The reported rumours were well founded and soon a second split occurred, largely over Mooney's handling of money and publicity. By the end of July 1851, the manufacture revival movement, little over a year old, was now split three ways: the rump of the original BIMI, now called the PBIMI, Spratt's NBPIMI, and the second reform breakaway initially also calling itself the PBIMI.

The two secessionist bodies soon came together to form the United Board when, on Monday 4th August 1851, the Lord Mayor, Benjamin Lee Guinness, held reunion talks between them. These developments were viewed with a jaundiced eye by

**Fig 63.**   *Benjamin Lee Guinness.*

---

44. *FJ*, 11th July 1851.

the original (P)BIMI. Brennan rebuked the Lord Mayor for having conducted an arbitration with their two rival bodies, without consulting them. Mooney, who wrote in protest to the Lord Mayor, added:

> When Dr Spratt, in a pout, created the first secession, the Countess of Clarendon rewarded the exploit by ordering an embroidered petticoat from the worthy priest. When Mr Bagot, in a pout, created a second secession, there were agents from Dublin Castle and from England to reward him with money and fine letters. Split after split may take place, but he (Mr Mooney) would remain united to the great principle he preached, and, while twelve Irishmen can be found to gather round him and listen, he would remain in Ireland, preaching her regeneration.[45]

Although he did not comment, in return, Mooney's messianic tone and apostolic imagery would not have been lost on Spratt and his comrades. Undeterred, the second secessionist PBIMI proceeded with their endorsement of the merger with Spratt's NBPIMI and, on 12th August 1851, the United Board held its first public meeting with the manufacturer, Thomas Willans, as chairman. When Spratt entered the venue he was received *'with deafening and repeated peals of cheering'*. He rose to propose that *'the union of the Parent and National Boards do now take place and that henceforth they shall be designated as the United Parent and National Board of Irish Manufacture and Industry'*. He expressed his heartfelt wish that this union long continue.[46] The newly merged body then issued an *Address to the People of Ireland*, stating that some 50 to 60 industrial schools had been formed throughout the country and that a Model School had been established in Dublin to train industrial school teachers. Pointedly, they stressed the freedom of the press to attend and report their proceedings and some 35 leading figures signed off on this *Address*, including Spratt and Battersby of the former NBPIMI and Thacker, Alderman Andrews and the others of the former PBIMI. A special committee on industrial schools was set up of which Spratt became a member.

---

45. *DWN*, 9th Aug 1851. At the end of this speech, the newspaper account added 'Report supplied by the Secretary'.
46. *FJ*, 16th Aug 1851.

*From the United Board to SPIMI*

The United Board was not long united before Fr Spratt found himself ensnared in a bizarre situation of his own making. One of the first tasks of the new United Board was to advertise for a salaried secretary.[47] In the course of seeking a candidate, it appears that the Carmelite, in a chance conversation with Matthew Moran, observed that the old BIMI should now give up its opposition to the new United Board as it could never secure public support as a separate body. He went on to say, with remarkable un-wisdom, that regarding the position of secretary, Thomas Mooney could put in an application as a candidate and Spratt added that he was *'quite sure the members of the United Board would give it all the consideration it deserved'* – a loaded phrase if ever there was one. This conversation was reported to Mooney. He promptly took out an advertisement in the *General Advertiser* newspaper and publicised the account, rendering it so that it appeared Spratt had purposely sought out Moran to request that Mooney be a candidate; and that not only would he, Fr Spratt, vote for Mooney, but that most of his fellow-members would do likewise. Spratt, of course, denied outright that he had promised Mooney a vote and Spratt's account of this episode was greeted with loud applause. Apart altogether from their profound ideological and political differences, given the attacks Mooney had launched on Spratt, it seems scarcely credible that Mooney's version of events is believable over the friar's. Yet, accepting Spratt's version, it was either naïve in the extreme or Machiavellian in the extreme that Spratt should have in any way mentioned any potential candidacy by Mooney. If Machiavellian, perhaps Spratt wished to secure a revenge humiliation of Mooney who clearly stood no chance whatever of being appointed; if naïve, perhaps even he, like so many others, was once again beguiled by Mooney's charm. This, however, is unlikely: in the course of his self-exculpatory speech at the United Board, on 16th September, Spratt apparently expressed critical comments about Mooney, referring to *'Mooney's advertisement'* and remarking, understandably, that the BIMI Council *'was Mr Mooney'*. In response, his old friend, Martin Brennan, took issue:

---

47. *FJ*, 30th Aug, 13th, 15th, 18th Sept 1851.

He could not refrain from alluding to the extraordinary speech
attributed by the papers to the Very Rev Dr Spratt. Yielding to
the Reverend Gentleman all deference upon spiritual matters,
he (Brennan) must, however, enter his solemn protest against
any man in Ireland attempting to say that 'the Council was Mr
Mooney'. No, they were a Society and a Council and not Mr
Mooney.[48]

Curiously, despite Brennan's public reprimand of Fr Spratt, they
somehow continued to sustain their friendship. This was evident two
months later when Brennan, in December 1851, publicly thanked
the Carmelite friar for assisting with the Christmas examinations at
Brennan's Bolton Street 'Collegiate Seminary'.[49] Clearly, neither man
was the bearer of grudges. Brennan's, however, was not the only
attack on Spratt at this point. Simeon Fraser, ironmonger of Mary's
Abbey, a founding member of the BIMI in May 1850,[50] also attacked
the friar for designating the reports of their Board as "Mr. Mooney's
advertisement". Fraser deplored Spratt's failure to use his influence
to have had their BIMI invited to Lord Mayor Guinness' arbitration
conference:

the reverend gentleman called upon them to give up their
meetings and to dissolve. He only hoped the gentlemen who
seceded would work as well for the country as they had done.
They had trained teachers for 42 industrial schools in as many
parts of Ireland and not a single fault had been attributed to
them. That was their answer to the slanderers.[51]

The new organisation bore an altogether unwieldly name and in early
October it was agreed to simplify it as the United Board of Irish
Manufacture and Industry.[52] As some members felt that even this was
not sufficient to distinguish it from Mooney's BIMI, a month later it was
unanimously agreed to change its name again, this time to the Society

48.  *DWN*, 4th Oct 1851.
49.  *FJ*, 29th Dec 1851.
50.  *DEPC*, 18th May 1850.
51.  *The Irish Trades' Advocate*, 27th Sept 1851.
52.  *The Irish Trades' Advocate*, 4th Oct 1851.

for the Promotion of Irish Manufacture and Industry, henceforth abbreviated to SPIMI.[53] By this stage the membership numbers and the funds were sufficient to enable them to acquire a headquarters, at No. 33 Anglesea Street, for a yearly rent of £150. Spratt, initially, remained active in this reunited body, chairing some of its meetings, sitting on its council and channelling financial contributions.[54]

The new premises were to serve partly as a training centre for teachers destined for the industrial schools, partly as an exhibition centre for Irish manufacturers and also as a meeting place for the new body.[55] A Mrs Wood was appointed as matron for the teacher-training centre.[56] The SPIMI continued to enrol new members and to secure funding into the spring of 1852, and could report that its training school was proceeding successfully and its exhibition rooms were now open to the public. They claimed to have 100 children in employment and had sent two of their best pupils for advanced training in Belfast.[57]

## The Last Stand of the BIMI

Despite suffering its second secession, in July 1851, the original BIMI appeared to go from strength to strength in the year which followed. Credit for much of its continued vitality must go to the Harcourt Street physician, George Hayden and his wife, who gave it substantial financial assistance, including a transfusion of £100 immediately after the July 1851 haemorrhage. This was soon followed by further donations of £30 from himself and £50 from Mrs Hayden. Similarly, the indefatigable Christopher Coyne continued to bring an evangelical zeal to its endeavours and travelled widely, north and south, to spread the word of supporting Irish goods. In the immediate wake of the second secession, they began styling themselves The *Parent* Board of Irish Manufacture and Industry and they were determined, despite *'some irregularities that had recently occurred'*, to press ahead positively. They claimed to continually receive requests for teachers and, despite the breach with Frs Spratt, Fay and Gilligan, they continued to have

---

53. *FJ*, 2nd Oct, 6th Nov 1851.
54. *DEM*, 15th Oct; *Irish Trades' Advocate*, 18th Oct; *FJ*, 23rd Oct; *Dublin Mercantile Advertiser*, 5th Dec; *DWN*, 6th Dec 1851.
55. *DWN*, 29th Nov 1851.
56. *DWN*, 6th Dec 1851.
57. *DEP*, 19th Feb 1852; *FJ*, 15th July 1852.

contact with clergy throughout the country. In addition to this, they were planning to open a central depot to display Irish manufactures and Mooney let the ground floor of their premises to a subcontracting retailer, Geoghegan and Company, who undertook to sell only Irish-made goods and who opened to *'a vast crowd of delighted citizens'* in late October 1851.[58] In addition, they now began to press the concept of industrial training and gainful employment for workhouse inmates, and commenced with two handlooms in the South Dublin Union, thanks to the efforts of their Council member, Dr John Ryan. Soon they claimed to have erected ten looms in that institution.[59] By December 1851 the BIMI were promoting the idea of converting workhouses into self-sustaining establishments. They issued a bold invitation to the poor law guardians of Ireland, the nobility, MPs, mayors and newspaper editors to attend a great public meeting in January 1852 to promote this and the related idea of providing industrial training in all public institutions from schools to workhouses to prisons.[60] The BIMI had a genius for publicity – largely Mooney's genius, one suspects – and that meeting, held in the Rotunda on 26th January, attracted a great rake of the respectable, including Lords Aldborough and Cloncurry, the MPs Grattan, Grogan and Reynolds, and the Lord Mayor as chairman. Mooney opened the proceedings, boasted that they now had 120 industrial schools in operation and presented for view various exhibits that had already been produced in workhouses. Mooney and BIMI colleagues were determined to enlist the boards of guardians throughout Ireland in the movement. For some it was an attractive notion since it offered the prospects of employment for the idle poor and of lower poor law charges for the ratepayers.[61]

Not everyone agreed: the Spratt-supported SPIMI condemned the conversion of workhouses into industrial establishments as being utterly detrimental to free labour outside.[62] Leading elements of organised labour in Dublin agreed with Spratt's body: in June 1851, the Regular Carpenters of Dublin issued an address to Spratt's NBPIMI,

58.  *FJ*, 25th July; *WFJ*, *DWN*, 20th Sept; *FJ*, 28th Oct 1851.
59.  *FJ*, 28th Oct 1851.
60.  *DEP*, 18th Dec 1851.
61.  *FJ*, 5th Nov 1851, letter of J. B. Kennedy of Great Denmark Street, cited at BIMI meeting of 3rd Nov 1851.
62.  *DEP*, 19th Feb; *FJ*, 8th Sept 1852.

fully supporting the latter organisation,

> knowing you to be opponents of the pernicious system so
> fraught with mischief to the regular mechanic and ruin to his
> family – the establishment of trades in the workhouse.[63]

A week later, Spratt was present at an NBPIMI meeting where his
friend Ralph, as Secretary, urged their Council to prepare a report
on the subject: Ralph declared he was not opposed to workhouses
being self-supporting but it was unfair to place struggling tradesmen
in competition with workmen in poorhouses.[64] Mooney responded to
the criticism that his BIMI was interfering with the rights of labour by
retorting that no one seemed to object to the cheap labour competition
of England's manufacturers.[65]   However, despite Mooney's gift for
publicity, the distinguished academician and historian, Dr R R Madden,
in a letter of 25th July 1851, regarding the BIMI, commented:

> It has always appeared to me that the nature of Mr. Mooney's
> understanding of his position as Secretary of the Board was such
> as must inevitably prove, at some time or another, a complete
> obstacle to the working of the institution, and must, in the long
> run, wholly neutralise all his powers of utility and the energies
> which he devoted to the cause.[66]

Madden had actually visited Mooney and advised him to resign for the
good of the movement *'on which such great hope for the wretched people of this
country rested'*.  Madden's plea was in vain: he abandoned the BIMI and
joined the rival body of the second secessionists.  For the immovable
Mooney this was doubtless just another passing irritant.  However, over
the next twelve months his extravagant use of BIMI funds, notably for
paid publicity, deepened the anxieties of even his most ardent adherents:
none more so than Dr Hayden.  As late as December 1851, even more
clearly taken in by Mooney as ever Dr Spratt had been, and looking
forward to the great Rotunda meeting which Mooney was organising,

63.   *FJ*, 13th June 1851.
64.   *FJ*, 20th June 1851.
65.   *FJ*, 24th Dec 1851.
66.   *FJ*, 4th Aug 1851.

Hayden could laud *'the able, hardworking secretary who would not allow their machinery to stand still'.*[67] However, six months later, Hayden discovered that Mooney had incurred worrying financial liabilities to the newspaper press and, in self-preservation, Hayden *'severed himself from the body'.*[68] As the most loyal and substantial supporter of Mooney and the BIMI, Hayden's sudden withdrawal must finally have rattled Mooney: in a BIMI meeting at the end of July

**Fig 64.** *Dr R R Madden.*

1852 Mooney gave indications of doubt and self-doubt, but Martin Brennan and Bartholomew O'Connor urged that *'he must not falter now'.*[69] On Monday 2nd August, Mooney appeared and spoke at the usual weekly meeting of the BIMI but suddenly, according to an account by Bartholomew O'Connor, he resigned abruptly and took, or was given, some money to quit the country. O'Connor told how, on 5th August, Mooney left Dublin for Liverpool where, allegedly, he boarded a vessel – the appropriately named *John Bunyan* – en route for Australia.[70] It was to his and Spratt's old friend, Brennan, now signing himself O'Brennan, that Mooney wrote from Liverpool, on 7th August, as he was about to leave *'for the New World'.* He explained his departure as follows:

---

67. *FJ*, 24th Dec 1851.
68. *FJ*, 8th Oct 1852.
69. *FJ*, 28th July 1852.
70. *FJ*, 8th Oct 1852. This is according to O'Connor's account which, given all that had transpired, is impressive in its summation of the history of the movement and its secessions to October 1852. However, it is not certain, at this stage, if Mooney went to Australia or if, perhaps, he may have gone straight back to America where he was active in the 1850s and 1860s: it is likely that he did go, at first, to Australia, to judge from Martin Brennan's *Ancient Ireland*, Dublin 1855, p. xiii, where the list of subscribers acknowledges a subscription from a Thomas Mooney, Melbourne.

It is useless to talk of the causes that have led me to take this step. Among them are the troubles of the Board of Manufactures, which appeared to me beyond my power to surmount. The Dublin people can never be brought to forgive a man who has been commercially unfortunate. No matter how good my plans – no matter how useful my labours – there never would be forgiveness for me, and therefore, I separate myself from my plans, that men less objectionable may be suffered to carry them out.[71]

He admitted to Brennan that he owed the BIMI *'a few pounds'* which he would remit *'when I get a footing in the new world'*: he added that he himself left Ireland poorer than when he came home in 1850 and that he had sunk his own savings in the premises of the BIMI. When the dust of his departure had settled, it appeared that Mooney had left the BIMI in debt – largely in unpaid printers' invoices. At the same time, it seems he had incurred personal liabilities in some unnamed speculative venture involving the sale of Irish-made goods. Still, the depth of loyalty to Mooney, even following his departure, was noteworthy. Martin Brennan spoke warmly of his talents and lightly of his debts. Likewise, Simeon Fraser could only remark:

his leaving us so abruptly was to be deplored. We all regret that he did not unburden his need to one of us before he decided to depart suddenly.[72]

Over the previous thirteen months the BIMI had brought in some £1,400 in funding – £400 of this from Dr Hayden – and Mooney had left a personal debt to the Society of some £23 and overall business debts of between £130 and £150.[73]

Following Mooney's exile, Brennan acted as secretary and very soon there was renewed talk of reunion again. Intriguingly, in the fortnight before Mooney left, there had been obscure references to

71. *FJ*, 21st Aug 1852; *DWN*, 28th Aug 1852.
72. *FJ*, 27th Aug 1852.
73. *FJ*, 3rd Sept, 8th Oct 1852.

a proposed amalgamation of BIMI and SPIMI.[74] Now Christopher Coyne observed:

> When they had the aid of their late secretary there were many questions on which they could not agree. That was all removed now. It (reunion) was the objective of the other Board [SPIMI] and the country now called for amalgamation.[75]

Cloncurry, engaged to the end, wrote to Coyne a fortnight later to express the view that now that *'your late, most talented Secretary'* was gone, *'the most lamentable differences will now, I hope, terminate with his resignation'.*[76] One week later, perhaps as a reconciling overture on his part, Spratt wrote to the BIMI, enclosing a donation of £10 from *'an anonymous friend'*. As if to reciprocate, Coyne then paid a visit to Spratt's industrial school where, he reported, some 800 girls were receiving *'literary, religious and industrial education'.* Coyne was at his unctuous best and *'never felt greater delight than when visiting that beautiful school and he hoped that Dr Spratt would soon become a member of the Board. (hear, hear)'.*[77]

### From Disunity to Dissolution

Spratt and Coyne had given evidence of the possibility of reunion in the wake of Mooney's flight, and serious efforts were made to bring both sides together, over the period November 1852 to the spring of 1853. The most notable effort was made by the Co. Louth MP and Monaghan estate manager, Tristram Kennedy.[78] The possibility was not realised, however: leading figures in both camps had become too entrenched in their attitudes to overcome the mutual mistrust and

---

74.  *DEP,* 29th July; *FJ,* 28th July 1852 mention it only in passing and without any detail, and there seems to be no mention in any other paper, not excluding the *Express* which sometimes carried accounts that appeared in no other newspaper.

75.  *FJ,* 19th Aug 1852.

76.  *FJ,* 8th Sept 1852, Cloncurry to Coyne, 5th September 1852.

77.  *FJ,* 16th Sept 1852.

78.  *The Advocate,* 3rd Nov 1852. See also *Dublin Daily Express,* 4th June 1883, for an account of Kennedy's remarkable work in creating industrial schools in Carrickmacross and the Farney Estate of the Marquis of Bath. In addition, there is his own account in T. Kennedy and W. K. Sullivan, *On the industrial training institutions of Belgium and on the possibility of organising an analogous system in connection with the national schools of Ireland,* Dublin 1855.

antipathy. Ironically, the BIMI had cleared its debts by the end of 1852 whereas the SPIMI had gone into debt. This acted as an excuse for delaying reunion.[79] However, serious policy differences also prevented rapprochement. The BIMI still cherished a vision of converting workhouses and jails into factories while the SPIMI adhered to a view that this would compromise the rights of masters, artisans and apprentices.[80] In the end, each body went its own way but, ironically, to the same destination – dissolution.

Curiously, for a long time after the September overtures between Coyne and Spratt, the Carmelite was ceasing to be actively involved in routine SPIMI business. When it held a general meeting in July 1853, Spratt sent an apology for his absence.[81] By that point, the SPIMI was meeting only monthly and although it was still receiving new members and still training some 250 girls in its Anglesea Street School, it was, in fact, running out of steam. Spratt did attend the annual general meeting on 23rd August 1853 but it would prove to be his and its final annual gathering. When elections to the SPIMI Council were called, no candidates came forward, not even after a postponement to 10th September. Consequently, on that date, the SPIMI resolved, with only two dissenting voices, to dissolve itself. Deploring the fact that not one person came forward, the chairman, John Gallie, pronounced that they therefore had to let *their Society and their schools sink*.[82] As for their rival, the BIMI, it disappeared before this, without even a public announcement. It sank without trace, sometime in May 1853.[83]

It is profoundly ironic that, disunity and fatigue aside, the main identifiable cause of their demise should have been the Great National Industrial Exhibition of 1853 in Dublin, forever associated with the name of the engineer and entrepreneur, William Dargan. Back in 1852, the idea of such an exhibition as a hoped-for inspiration to the industrial regeneration of Ireland was floated and took hold so well as to be realised over the months to the opening on 12th May 1853. The BIMI and the SPIMI both welcomed the idea. Dr Hayden of the former, now

79. *FJ*, 21st Dec 1852.
80. *FJ*, 19th Feb, 7th Apr, 1853.
81. *FJ*, 27th July 1853.
82. *FJ*, 12th Sept 1853.
83. *FJ*, 17th May 1853, records what appears to have been its final reported public meeting.

**Fig 65.** *The Great National Industrial Exhibition, RDS, Dublin 1853.*

back in the fold after Mooney's flight, was particularly enthusiastic and actually proposed to Dargan that, at the end of the Exhibition, a great industrial conference might be held. Alas, as the Exhibition project grew into reality over the spring of 1853, both societies suspended their meetings and their propaganda as they perceived the public to be too preoccupied with Dargan's dream. The final resolution to be passed in the BIMI simply read:

> that as public interest is at present absorbed by the Great Exhibition, they deemed it right to adjourn the public meetings of the Board.[84]

It never met again. Dargan's dream sucked the life out of the two Dublin rival manufacture bodies and they quietly expired. Now Irish society became exercised over the most suitable manner in which to honour and to thank Dargan for organising the Great Industrial Exhibition. Opinions began to crystallise around the idea of a 'Dargan Institute'. What exactly this might be, was unclear. One suggestion, eminently interesting and appropriate, came from the editor of the *Dublin Weekly Nation*:

---

84. *FJ*, 17th May 1853.

A College of Irish Industry and Resources. An Irish Polytechnic. A School of Mines, of Mechanics, of Science and Art applied to Industry. That is the idea worthy of Dargan's name and services. He cares as little for a statue in the public streets as for the bauble title he refused.[85]

Instead of a School of Industry, what he eventually got was exactly what he did not want – a statue in a public place – on the lawn of a gallery devoted to Art, not Industry.

*Postscript*
The inglorious demise of the Irish manufacture movement, in the wake of the Dublin Exhibition, ought not, perhaps, to be the last word. For all their faults and failings, the competing manufacture revival movements did achieve something, as was acknowledged by the Cork MP, John Francis Maguire. His contemporary tribute was surely not misplaced:

> We believe the agitation of the Manufacturing Board [sic] was the most effective and the most durable, in its efforts, of all the agitations of that nature yet instituted. There is a perceptible revolution in public opinion with reference to the value of Irish manufacturers.[86]

Similarly, Tristram Kennedy, looking back from 1855, two years after the demise of the rival Dublin organisations, considered that they

> did a vast amount of good. They stimulated public opinion, irrespective of creed or political party, upon the subject of industry generally...the greatest benefit which arose was the organisation of industrial training schools throughout the country...[87]

---

85.  *DWN*, 6th Aug 1853. William Dargan (1799-1867) had declined Queen Victoria's offer of a baronetcy. See also F. Mulligan, *William Dargan: An Honourable Life, 1799-1867*, Dublin 2013, pp. 145-150.
86.  *DWN*, 3rd Sept 1853; J. F. Maguire, *The Industrial Movement in Ireland, as illustrated by the National Exhibition of 1852*, Cork 1853, p. 275.
87.  Kennedy & Sullivan, p. 43.

**Fig 66.**   *William Dargan.*

As for John Spratt's 'Great Schools of Industry', they survived the demise of the BIMI and SPIMI and continued to aid young girls to become employable, into the 1850's. For how long into that decade they may have remained as a distinct entity is not quite clear. In October 1861, during a serious dispute over the maltreatment of young girls in the South Dublin Union, Spratt called for the creation of a system of industrial training for the disadvantaged young, which suggests that his own industrial school had ceased as a distinct entity.[88] It may well be that his 'Great Schools of Industry' became fully absorbed into the fabric and the curricular life of his original national schools thereafter.[89] It is certainly the case, as shall be seen in what follows, that if the Carmelite friar began to distance himself from the politics and proceedings of the SPIMI in the course of 1853, he had not distanced himself from the formation of the young even as many other engagements vied for his energies.

---

88.  *DDE*, 1st Oct 1861; *DEPC*, 3rd Oct 1861.
89.  See Chapter Fourteen.

## CHAPTER FOURTEEN

### *Creating Community, 1850–1871*

Fr John's continuing commitment to old causes and his adoption of new ones from the 1850s were conducted in the context of his daily spiritual life in the Carmelite community of Whitefriar Street. This is an obvious enough point to make, except that, such was the extent of John's public engagements and interests, it is perhaps too easy to overlook that they were pursued against the background of daily prayer and conventual commitment. No spiritual diaries of his exist and no records now of everyday communal living. One can but surmise that his many taxing public commitments were made supportable by the sustaining ritual of the Carmelite way. The devotional life of his church in Whitefriar Street was a rich one as the 1850s progressed. Celebrating its 25th anniversary in the autumn of 1852, its conduct of diocesan jubilee occasions was marked by magnificent display. That October, the church ornately decorated with flowers, lights, richly coloured fabrics and banners, commenced the Forty Hours Adoration with a High Mass at its most solemn. It was celebrated by Fr Fernando of Ceylon, assisted by Fr Spratt, and the attending dignitaries included Dr O'Connor, Bishop of Pittsburgh, Dr Salvados, Bishop of South Australia, Dr Woodlock and the seminarians of All Hallows College,[1] as well as the Archbishop of Dublin, Dr Cullen, who had been transferred from Armagh only six months earlier. Three days of devotion concluded with another High Mass celebrated by Fr Day, with Spratt as master of ceremonies. Its solemn procession was led by young men in soutanes and surplices, followed by members of the

---

1. *CT*, 30th Oct 1852; *FJ*, 28th Oct 1852.

Church's Confraternity wearing the emblems of the Order, and the rear was brought up by the friars of the Whitefriar Street Community while the choir chanted the *Pange Lingua* and the litanies.[2] The pageantry was enhanced seven months later when, in April 1853, the friars took delivery of '*a magnificent embroidered canopy after the model of those used in Rome*'. It was made of rich white satin, by the Sisters of Mercy in Baggot Street, with the word 'Jehovah' wrought in gold lace, centred in a large, radiant star. Its side panels bore the arms of the Carmelite Order and the whole composition was fringed in gold lace and was borne aloft by means of six treble-gilt bronze poles. A '*costly work of sacred art*', its initial funding was made possible by the generosity of the members of the Whitefriar Street Church confraternity.[3]

Such magnificent occasions, while special, were not a rarity. A similar public occasion of equal splendour was conducted in Whitefriar Street Church only three months later,[4] and every year was marked by similar solemn processional events in the church and its environs. Thus, in October 1854, with Fr Bennett acting as master of ceremonies, Spratt celebrated the concluding High Mass for the Forty Hours Adoration, assisted by Fr McGee as deacon and Fr John Carr as subdeacon, supported by the choir, in a church densely crowded in sanctuaries, nave and galleries. Then followed a procession of the confraternity in their habits, with Spratt bearing the monstrance for Solemn Benediction.[5] These ceremonies were conducted in the district throughout this and the succeeding decades,[6] and brought dignity and colour to an area that was grim and became grimmer as the nineteenth century wore on.

### *A declining, dangerous district*

It was in consequence of this deterioration that the Carmelites' neighbour, the Methodists, felt the district was no longer respectable enough in the 1850s to remain there. Far back, in 1756, they had established an Almshouse for aged Methodist families in Whitefriar Street, alongside their preaching house.[7] However, their quest for

---

2.  *WFJ*, 30th Oct 1852.
3.  *FJ*, 14th Apr 1853, citing *The Tablet*, no date given.
4.  *FJ*, 27th Dec 1852.
5.  *FJ*, 16th Oct 1854.
6.  See for example, *FJ*, 8th Sept 1855; *CT*, 12th Dec 1857; *DWN*, 23rd July 1859.
7.  J. McGregor, p. 332. This author gives the year as 1756.

**Fig 67.**    *Former Methodist Centenary Church, Stephen's Green, now the Department of Justice.*

gentility led them to move their preaching house to their new chapel in Stephen's Green in 1843, although the old lease did not expire until 1849.  Likewise, although their Almshouse lease would not expire until 1863, they decided to move this facility to Grantham Street, off Upper Camden Street, in 1858, because the Whitefriar Street locality *'has rapidly declined'*.[8]  Daily life in the quadrangle of Whitefriar Street, Whitefriar Lane, York Row and Aungier Street was certainly not salubrious.  On one occasion in 1851, Fr John had to complain about the disgusting state of Whitefriar Lane with its broken paving and piled-up filth backing on to an entrance to his schools.[9]

The area was, at times, dangerous as well as dirty.  One summer evening, in 1852, a pedestrian, Stephen Rogers, was passing along Whitefriar Street when set upon by a mob of youths and suffered severe lacerations by a sharp weapon.  He was treated in nearby Mercer's Hospital before making his way home to Mount Street.  Hours

8.   *SNL*, 3rd March 1858.
9.   *FJ*, 8th Feb1851.

later, on news of the assault spreading, a large crowd gathered outside the Carmelite church on foot of rumours that the victim had been Fr Spratt and that he had been stabbed with a sword. It chanced by coincidence that a sword was being borne, innocently, by a man in the crowd and he, in turn, was set upon, was seriously injured and the crowd, mostly made up of youths, had to be dispersed by the police.[10] Nor were the precincts of the church free from mischief. In March 1851 its long-serving sacristan, John William Prenter, apprehended a woman in the pews after she had entered the vestry and departed with some vestments.[11] Much more seriously, on Sunday morning, 5th May 1850, Fr Colgan was celebrating the 9.30 Mass at the main altar of the crowded church when a young man charged forward and bludgeoned him on the back of the head and followed with a second blow to the back of his neck. Fr Colgan collapsed at the altar and when Fr O'Rourke, then saying Mass at a side chapel, ran to his rescue, he was felled by a severe blow to his forehead. At this point, some of the male worshippers came forward to attempt to seize the young man, until Fr Spratt, hearing the commotion, rushed from the vestry to restrain the assailant and saved him from the wrath of the congregation. He managed to restrain and confine the attacker until the police arrived. A covered car was sent to the chapel house door at the Aungier Street entrance, in a feint to draw the crowd away until the assailant was secretly bundled out to custody via the main Whitefriar Street entrance. The two local Church of Ireland curates of St Peter's, Rev Richard Ardill, the senior curate, and Rev J J MacSorley, came to assist the two stricken friars who were bathed in blood. Both friars were in a precarious state of injury, but survived. The assailant, Francis McMahon of Cabinteely, was a deaf mute, prone to seizures and to mental illness. It was a reflection of the religious sensitivities of the age, which would intensify in the course of the ensuing decade, that it was deemed appropriate by the press to report that the parents were Catholics who, for want of any alternative care, had sent him to the Protestant Claremont Institution. The supposition was soon made that in this place he had been imbued

---

10. *DEPC*, 15th July 1852.
11. *FJ*, 25th March 1851.

with rabid anti-Catholicism.[12] McMahon was arraigned before a grand jury which found him to be insane and incapable of standing trial.[13] He was subsequently committed to an asylum.

*Deathly debates in Dublin City*

Deaths and burials are never far from the daily concerns and duties of any pastor and, in this, John Spratt was no exception. However, at the start of the 1850s, in a more general social way, he became engaged in two public controversies around death and burial which brought out his deep concern for and connection with the common people of Dublin City. It will be recalled how in the early 1850s he was still greatly involved in the battle for the rights of the Cuffe Street Savings Bank depositors. At the very same time, commencing in October 1850, he found himself enmeshed in a concern of the local and citywide benefit and burial societies. In the age before the coming of the welfare state, such societies played a critical role in the lives of the common people. The numbers and the significance of such societies grew rapidly in the mid-nineteenth century, not least in the area where the Calced Carmelites lived. Indeed, the church premises were host to a large number of such local associations and they had at least two of their own in the Saint Simon Stock and the Grand Carmelite Tontine Societies. Just as British free trade in industry and commerce had come, from the 1850s, to dominate Irish trade and manufacture, it seemed too that an invasion of British tontine societies was imminent. So it appeared to the officers of the Dublin burial societies when they approached Fr Spratt for the use of his school for a large meeting. Its purpose was to expose and repel the advances of an English-based rival. Consequently, on 28th October 1850, a press notice was published urging that *'The Working Classes are requested to attend the aggregate meeting of the Benefit and Burial Societies to be held this day...in the Great School Rooms of the Very Rev Dr Spratt (late Old Meeting House, Whitefriar St)'.*[14] Spratt was requested to conduct the meeting and very quickly he would find himself leading a short sharp campaign to defend and preserve the home-grown benefit

12. *FJ*, 6th May 1850. Such was the theory espoused by the *Freeman's Journal.* For additional accounts of this incident, see *DEM* 6th, 8th May; *DEP*, 7th, 9th May; *DWR*, 11th; *DWN*, 11th May 1850.
13. *DWN*, 22nd June1850; *WFJ*, 22nd June 1850.
14. *FJ*, 28th Oct 1850.

and burial societies. This meeting's main resolution was

> ...to warn the working classes against a clique of adventurers from England [who] come to establish in Dublin a branch of the United Burial Societies of Toxteth Park, Liverpool.

One of the concerned citizens who joined Spratt on this occasion was Martin Burke of the Shelbourne Hotel. He and Spratt were already becoming staunch friends and close associates in the movement for the revival of Irish manufacture and industry.[15] Burke was highly complimentary of the Carmelite, describing him as *'the friend of the poor, the protector of the widow and orphan'*.[16]

A succession of speakers attacked the attempts of the Liverpool Society to seduce the members of these independent local bodies with the blandishments of supposedly superior benefits. The *Freeman's Journal* warmly supported the meeting, praising the Dublin societies for their growth over the previous twenty-five years, and lauded Spratt for the aid he had so readily given.[17] Spratt, indeed, was unusually outspoken: the meeting, he asserted, was of the greatest importance to the working classes of Dublin who *'constituted the support and comfort of the other classes of society'*. Commending them for their independence and self-reliance, he expressed shock that emigrant Irishmen in England should seek to subvert and destroy the local institutions:

> He felt surprised that any persons professing regard for Ireland and her people, and calling themselves Irishmen, though resident in England, should come over here and seek to induce the tradesmen of this impoverished city, to give up their own humane institutions and commit the care of even burying their dead, to a committee in England. This was really too much. They had too much Irish business managed in England already...and they knew how, at least, to bury their dead without assistance from England.

---

15. Martin Burke (1788-1863), as a juryman in Charles Gavan Duffy's trial in February 1849, famously refused to find him guilty: for this, and his career see *DWN*, 24th Jan; *SNL*, 19th Jan; *IT*, 17th Jan 1863. For his contribution to the campaign for the revival of Irish manufactures, see Chapter Thirteen.
16. *FJ*, 29th Oct 1850.
17. *FJ*, 30th Oct 1850.

**Fig 68.** *The Mortuary Chapel in Goldenbridge Cemetery, erected in 1829.*

It is not certain how successful this repulse proved to be: certainly, the Dublin societies continued to prosper and the Liverpool institution does not seem to have put down roots in the city.[18]

### A Grave Dispute

Two years after this episode, Spratt became involved in another 'burials battle' – this time against an unlikely enemy in the form of the Glasnevin Cemetery authorities. Once again, Fr John and the Dublin burial benefit societies came together in a public meeting in his Cuffe Street Temperance Hall. It was convened in response to a decision by the Glasnevin Cemetery Committee to curtail the hours during which interments would be permitted in Goldenbridge and Glasnevin. Since their opening in 1829 and 1832 respectively, interments had taken place from early morning to late afternoon and evening. They now proposed to have all burials completed before noon on any of the seven days a week.[19] In opening the first protest meeting in response, on 6th February 1852, Spratt, to loud cheers, observed that:

---

18. The Toxteth Park body is not listed among such institutions in *Thom's Directory* from 1850 onwards.

19. Glasnevin Cemetery Archives, *Proceedings of the Catholic Cemetery Committee,* vol. 5, June 1846 to Feb 1855, *General Minutes,* pp. 252-253, 4th Dec 1851.

The closing of the gates to Glasnevin and Goldenbridge Cemeteries, against the people of Dublin and its vicinity, after twelve o'clock, was indeed a grievance of no ordinary character... Unfair in principle and a serious infringement not alone upon the convenience but upon the liberties of the inhabitants of this city.[20]

The new restrictive hours cut across Church regulation and working class custom alike. As to the former, through the Synod of Thurles in 1850, the Church had already brought in its own new regulation whereby priests were now obliged to commence the final Sunday Mass not later than noon. As to the latter, Dublin workers' funerals were normally conducted in the afternoon. In these circumstances, Spratt insisted, many hundreds of working class Dubliners would be forced to miss Sunday Mass in order to attend a Sunday burial. Furthermore, under the proposed new cemetery regulations, in order to attend weekday funerals, working class mourners would have to lose a day's work and pay as a consequence. In the light of these issues, under Spratt's direction, the meeting formed the Anti-Early Burials Committee and it was Spratt that doubtless provided them with premises at 51 Aungier Street, the home of St Peter's Orphan Society of which he was the guardian.[21]

One old friend, Martin A Brennan of the Bolton Street Academy, and his recently-acquired friend, Martin Burke of the Shelbourne, joined him on this new body. Over the weeks and days leading up to this public meeting, they had already contacted the Cemetery authorities, had held several meetings with them, including one that comprised deputations from the Dublin trade unions and benefit societies.[22] Of the latter, there were then some eight hundred, ranging in numbers from 30 to 1,200 members, representing some 40,000 *'of the industrial classes'*. A written response to these deputations, from the Cemeteries Board secretary, M J O'Kelly, received on 6th February 1852, was deemed *'evasive'*, with its promise of *'a definitive response tomorrow'*. Burke, followed by Brennan, condemned this response, and it would be more than one day before a fuller reply was forthcoming.

20.  *FJ*, 7th Feb 1852.
21.  *FJ*, 7th, 13th Feb 1852.
22.  Glasnevin Cemetery Archives, *Proceedings,* vol. 5, pp. 263-265, 3rd Feb, 7th Feb 1852.

**Fig 69.** *A 19th century illustration of a funeral taking place in Glasnevin Cemetery.*

Spratt's Anti-Early Burials Committee thereupon issued a dramatic *"Address to the Citizens of Dublin…(the last sacred rites invaded)…"*. Although only recently-formed, this Committee had already worked hard against *'a most foul and infamous blow'* and asserted that *'it was our duty to combat these autocrats'*. It reported on a meeting with the members of the Cemeteries Board to whom it had presented a remonstrance, only to be told that the Board required more reasons to abandon their new regulation than those expressed in the remonstrance. The Cemeteries Board even went so far as to suggest that the Anti-Early Burials Committee should request Dublin City Corporation to erect 'dead-houses' where remains could be stored pending interment. Their only concession was to appoint a subcommittee of its own to report back on the question. Pending that report, it held the view that early interment would put a stop to drunkenness and indecorum at working class afternoon and evening funerals – an injudicious point to make to Fr Spratt, the teetotal crusader.

At a densely crowded subsequent meeting of the benefit society members and the citizens generally, held in the Mechanics' Institute on 23rd February 1852, Spratt again took the chair. He immediately launched a blistering attack on the Glasnevin Cemetery authorities:

Charges of the foulest and most unfounded character had been made against the working people of this city which it was their duty to repel…He emphatically contradicted their uncharitable and unwarranted accusations…[of] habits of intemperance and debauchery of the worst kind which they asserted were practised by persons attending funerals.[23]

He himself had attended many a funeral of burial and benefit society members, after the official cemetery chaplains had left the scene, and he '*never saw better or more excellent conduct*'. He described as a calumny, the assertion that the majority of burial benefit societies held their meetings in public houses – he knew that up to 30 such local societies held their meetings in St Peter's Orphanage premises and that, out of 800, only 10 or 12 held meetings in taverns: he then concluded by condemning this infringement of citizens' rights. His associate in many public causes, Surgeon James Mitchell, followed him by proposing a resolution attacking the Glasnevin decision as '*an unjustifiable aggression upon the rights of free citizens and a tyrannical infringement on the privileges of the industrial classes of the community*'. As a professional who had worked among them for twenty-six years, he knew the Dublin working class to be '*of regular and respectable conduct*' and noted '*their charity and humanity towards each other*'.

Considerable light was then shed on the background to this controversial regulation, by one Patrick Costello, a former member of the Cemeteries' Committee. He pointed out that the feeling in that Committee in favour of exclusively pre-noon burial was a relatively recent one which actually originated in Dublin City Council. Of the nine members who comprised the Cemeteries Committee who voted for this regulation, some six were City Councillors. According to Costello, as recently as 1846, when a bill for regulating the hours of interment in Dublin cemeteries came before parliament, the Cemeteries Committee objected. Four years later, under pressure from the 'sanitary' or public health movement, a second attempt was made to limit the hours of interment: the Cemeteries Committee instructed four of the members, the MPs John Reynolds, Sir Timothy O'Brien, James Fagan and Maurice O'Connell, to oppose this attempt. The two MPs for Dublin County were inclined to support the measure but Costello, being in London

---

23. *DEP*, 26th Feb; *FJ*, 24th Feb 1852.

at the time, prevailed on them to change their stance. However, over the two years from 1850, opinion within the City Council and within the Cemeteries Committee altered, resulting in the latter's adoption of the new bye-law. Costello thereupon resigned from the Cemeteries Committee in protest.[24] He added that their having spent £1,200 to £1,300 in securing the 1846 Act, he hoped the Cemeteries Committee would think again and rescind the regulation.

In seconding Mitchell's resolution, Martin Brennan commented, sarcastically, how remarkable it was *'that the answer of the Cemeteries Committee in which so much anxiety was exhibited for the promotion of temperance, was adopted, among others, by two distillers'.*[25] There were three members of that committee who had been Spratt's associates in the Repeal movement of the 1840s, the barrister Stephen Coppinger, Maurice O'Connell and his brother-in-law, Christopher Fitzsimon: they were opposed to the regulation and it was felt that if Daniel O'Connell, the effective founder of the Glasnevin and Goldenbridge Cemeteries, had been still living, the Cemeteries' authorities would not have adopted it.[26] The meeting ended with a decision to send yet another delegation to meet with the Glasnevin Board.

In the weeks which followed, both sides apparently competed to secure the support of the Dublin Catholic diocesan authorities, and it would appear that Spratt's Anti-Early Burials Committee had the edge in this. Although Archbishop Murray had just died, on 26th February, his most-senior clergy supported Spratt's Committee. On 15th March 1852, an address 'To the Catholic Cemeteries Board', drawn up on 5th March, had been signed by upwards of 60 diocesan clergy, including Archdeacon Hamilton, Vicar General William Meyler, as well as Bishop Daniel O'Connor of Saldes and, of course, the Carmelites of the Whitefriar Street Community. The address urged the cemetery authorities to reconsider their decision since it caused such inconvenience to the Catholic public at large and to working people in particular. Very reasonably, it suggested a compromise arrangement: that, for the six darker months of the year interments be conducted from 8 am to 3 pm,

---

24. Glasnevin Cemetery Archives, *Proceedings,* vol. 5, p. 254, Mon 19th Dec 1851, Extraordinary Special General Meeting of the Committee, resolution accepting Costello's resignation.
25. *FJ*, 24th Feb 1852.
26. *The Tablet*, 10th April 1852.

and for the six brighter months from 6 am to 6 pm.[27] Upon this address being presented personally by Spratt and his delegation, a debate took place within the Committee, at its meeting on 6th April 1852, where this compromise proposal was put as a resolution. However, an amendment to it was tabled by two members, Dolan and Ford, *'that we adhere to our original decision of 4th December last'*, as *'it has conduced in great measure to the peace and order, decency and propriety which should always attend on funerals'*. This amendment was carried by a large majority and Spratt's campaign ended suddenly in defeat.[28]

## *A Model of Model Schools*

Frustrating though the outcome of this campaign was, the friar at this time had other more uplifting ventures to foster. Not the least of these were his Whitefriar National Schools. Having helped his boys' and girls' national schools to survive and grow, he seized upon a new opportunity in education after the Methodists had abandoned their chapel in Whitefriar Lane. On 19th August 1850 he signed a lease for these premises.[29] A month later he gathered an audience there and informed them that he had taken the premises in order to establish *'a great industrial school for this and the surrounding parishes'*. The complex was extensive enough for education of up to two thousand young persons. Supporting him at this meeting, and in subsequent endeavours in fundraising for it, were his friends, Martin Burke, who chaired it, and Battersby who served as secretary. Another close associate of many years, Patrick Slevin, secretary of St Peter's Orphan Society, moved the key resolution that promised financial support for the new enterprise.

---

27. *FJ*, 15th March 1852. The Carmelite signatories were: John Spratt, Prior Provincial Michael Tobin, Andrew Day, Cornelius Crotty, Edward O'Rourke, John Carr, Thomas Bennett and William Withers. It was also signed by the radical priest and associate of Spratt, Thaddeus O'Malley.

28. Glasnevin Cemetery Archives, *Proceedings,* vol. 5, p. 270, 6th April 1852. Six voting members and the chairman, Alderman Moylan, supported the amendment and only two, Stephen Coppinger and the MP, Reynolds, could be found to oppose it. While the *Freeman's Journal* declined to comment on this decision until it could hear the response thereto from Spratt's Committee, that response was never forthcoming in the national press: *FJ*, 9th April 1852. *The Tablet* covered the story up until 10th April 1852 but had no reports or comments thereafter.

29. Registry of Deeds, *Transcript Book*, Year 1852, vol. 10, No. 112.

On top of his existing commitments, this represented a considerable undertaking on Spratt's part. He required to engage in extensive remodelling and refurbishment of the premises and, to this end, he needed to raise some £300. On 9th September 1850 he launched his first appeal in the public press.[30] There was rejoicing that the hall, once known as 'Gregg's Meeting House' or 'The Greggite No Popery Hall' where the Rev Tresham Gregg had used it *for rabid bigotry and proselytising*, would now serve *'the vast and densely populated district'*: the nearest alternative school for the poor was in Francis Street. Spratt was able to gather some 200 people at a public meeting to launch his appeal for funds.[31] A leading article in the *Freeman's Journal* commended his courage: noting that few would burden themselves with such a challenge, it commented that *'Fr Spratt's presidency is an earnest that everything shall be done as effectively and economically as close attention and supervision can render it'*, and reported happily that some £70 had been raised at this gathering.[32] A week later, Spratt was able to announce a single donation of £20, probably from Lord Cloncurry.[33] By the beginning of December he had raised and expended £200 on fitting out.[34] On the feast of St Stephen he announced 'an open day' as *'these splendid halls are now fully prepared for the reception of two thousand children'* and would open immediately after the Christmas holidays.[35] Classes were intended to be held day and evening and the premises were gas lit for this purpose. The extensive upper floor was set aside for the industrial training of young females and the lower rooms were dedicated for his female national school, while the former St Peter's male and female schools were now designated exclusively as the national school for boys.[36] In effect, as a result of this development, Fr John could claim to have opened five separate schools and he classified them as being, one each for 'adult boys' and 'adult

---

30. *FJ*, 11th Sept 1850, 'Great Schools of Education and Industry: to the charitable and humane', dated 9th September 1850.
31. *FJ*, 23rd Sept, Oct 1850. On the millenarian, evangelical cleric, Tresham Gregg, see J. Crawford, '"An overriding providence': the life and ministry of Tresham Dames Gregg (1800-1881)" in T. C. Barnard & W. G. Neely, eds., *The Clergy of the Church of Ireland, 1000-2000*, Dublin 2006, pp. 157-168.
32. *FJ*, 3rd Oct 1850.
33. *FJ*, 16th Oct 1850.
34. *FJ*, 7th Dec 1850, John Spratt to Editor, 5th December 1850.
35. *FJ*, 26th Dec 1850.
36. *FJ*, 28th Dec. 1850.

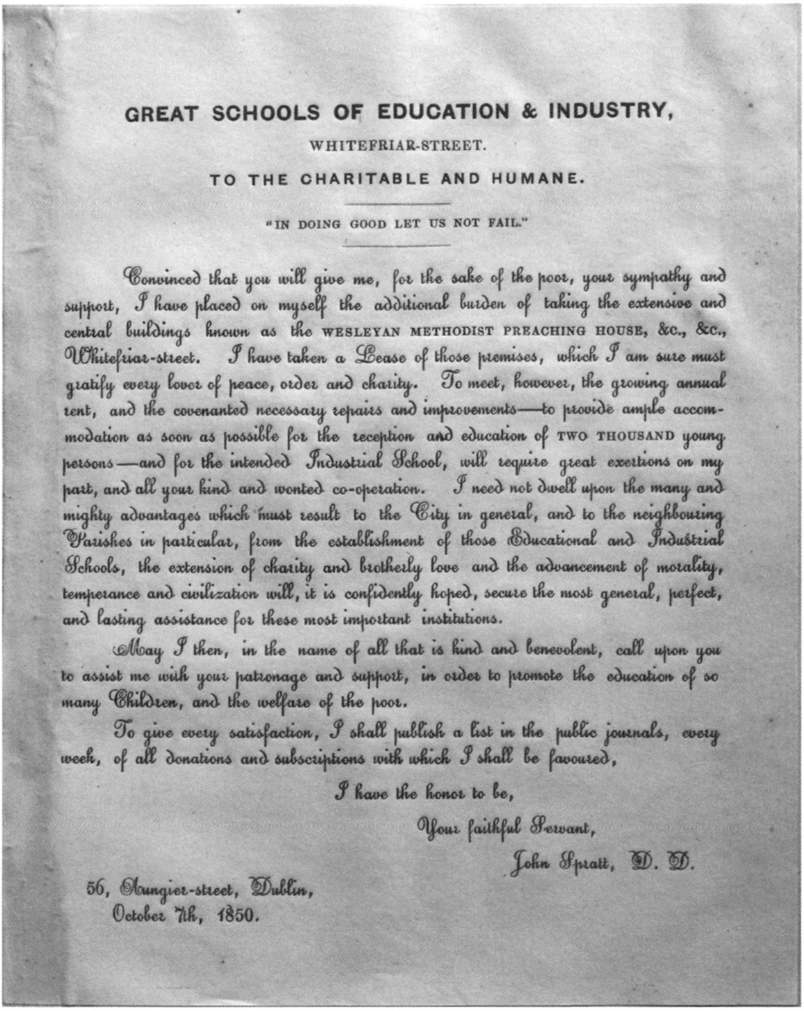

### GREAT SCHOOLS OF EDUCATION & INDUSTRY,

WHITEFRIAR-STREET.

### TO THE CHARITABLE AND HUMANE.

*"IN DOING GOOD LET US NOT FAIL."*

Convinced that you will give me, for the sake of the poor, your sympathy and support, I have placed on myself the additional burden of taking the extensive and central buildings known as the WESLEYAN METHODIST PREACHING HOUSE, &c., &c., Whitefriar-street. I have taken a Lease of those premises, which I am sure must gratify every lover of peace, order and charity. To meet, however, the growing annual rent, and the covenanted necessary repairs and improvements—to provide ample accommodation as soon as possible for the reception and education of TWO THOUSAND young persons—and for the intended Industrial School, will require great exertions on my part, and all your kind and wonted co-operation. I need not dwell upon the many and mighty advantages which must result to the City in general, and to the neighbouring Parishes in particular, from the establishment of those Educational and Industrial Schools, the extension of charity and brotherly love and the advancement of morality, temperance and civilization will, it is confidently hoped, secure the most general, perfect, and lasting assistance for these most important institutions.

May I then, in the name of all that is kind and benevolent, call upon you to assist me with your patronage and support, in order to promote the education of so many Children, and the welfare of the poor.

To give every satisfaction, I shall publish a list in the public journals, every week, of all donations and subscriptions with which I shall be favoured,

I have the honor to be,

Your faithful Servant,

John Spratt, D. D.

56, Aungier-street, Dublin,
October 7th, 1850.

**Fig 70.** *A letter written by Fr Spratt on behalf of the new industrial school.*

girls', one each for 'infant boys' and 'infant girls' and the industrial school: all five with separate teaching staff, providing for *'a full system of Literary, Industrial and Moral Education'*. By the middle of January 1851 he needed only a final £40 to finish the project completely.[37] Within six months, his industrial school was engaged in the production of finished lace cloth and Fr John had secured an order from no less a notable

---

37.  *FJ*, 14th Jan 1851. Boys and girls aged 9 years and over were designated as 'adult'. For this see *FJ*, 10th July 1851.

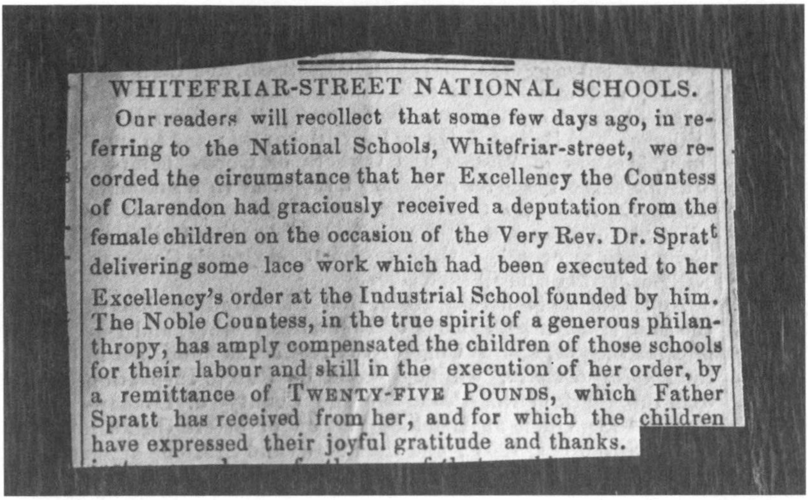

WHITEFRIAR-STREET NATIONAL SCHOOLS.

Our readers will recollect that some few days ago, in referring to the National Schools, Whitefriar-street, we recorded the circumstance that her Excellency the Countess of Clarendon had graciously received a deputation from the female children on the occasion of the Very Rev. Dr. Spratt delivering some lace work which had been executed to her Excellency's order at the Industrial School founded by him. The Noble Countess, in the true spirit of a generous philanthropy, has amply compensated the children of those schools for their labour and skill in the execution of her order, by a remittance of TWENTY-FIVE POUNDS, which Father Spratt has received from her, and for which the children have expressed their joyful gratitude and thanks.

**Fig 71.** *An untitled newspaper clipping from GMA, Scrapbook A, discussing the delivery of some lace work to Lady Clarendon, subsequent to her visit at the school.*

than the Countess of Clarendon, wife of the Lord Lieutenant.[38] In July 1851 he and his confreres enjoyed the distinction of a formal visit and tour of the schools by the Countess. She appeared to be greatly impressed by what she witnessed: the total complement was then 1,600 children of whom 600 were girls of the industrial school, aged from 10 to 15 years who were learning a variety of textile-related skills. It was a gala occasion in the life of the young industrial school and Spratt laid on musical entertainment, courtesy of his ITAA temperance band.[39] By the autumn of 1852 he claimed to have some 800 girls enrolled in the industrial school and, increasingly, he was being called upon to identify, from among them, young teachers, who could be assigned by request, to trade schools elsewhere in the country.[40] A year before this, in September 1851, Spratt and the industrial school had already won high praise from the *Dublin Weekly Nation* newspaper, when a leading article commented that

> One school in particular, in this city, deserves to be supported as a model of model schools. It is the school in Whitefriar

38.  *DEP*, 3rd June 1851.
39.  *FJ*, 11th July 1851.
40.  *FJ*, 16th Sept 1852.

Street, established by the Rev Dr Spratt...a temple of fanaticism, where Gregg ranted and Orange arms were piled in '48, has been converted by the reverend and benevolent gentleman into a temple of education and industrial arts...hundreds of children (are) acquiring education and habits of cleanliness and industry in the midst of a district where destitution and idleness and the negligent and filthy habits which attend them, heretofore prevailed...[41]

How many may have attended or were able to attend the industrial school on a daily basis, all year round, is a moot point. In December 1851, when Spratt stated that there were 1,821 children on the rolls of the five schools, he added that 1,000 were in daily attendance – a remarkable number, but of these, only 140 were daily attending the industrial school, out of a total of 800 on its rolls.[42] When the new Lord Lieutenant, Eglinton, paid a 'surprise visit' to the schools in March 1852, some 600 were present on the day but how many of these were attending the industrial school is not stated.[43] Nine months later, when Fr John made his annual appeal for funds for the schools, they counted 10 paid teachers and 800 pupils, with 200 of them *receiving monthly Communion, clean and tidy in attire*.[44] Nine months later again, during the Great Exhibition of 1853 in Dublin, it was noted that some 200 pupils of the industrial school had produced specimens of Limerick lace, duly inspected by Queen Victoria when Spratt was introduced to her during her fourth visit to the Exhibition that August.[45] One month later, as a special treat, he took all the pupils of his schools to visit the Exhibition themselves.[46] In a time before compulsory school attendance and in a setting where poverty and illness must have militated against attendance, even the lowest figure of 140 attending the industrial school, on a day when 1,000 were attending all five schools, was remarkable. It was all the more so when one considers the logistical challenge in the supply of raw materials and the disposal of the finished products. The context for the development of the industrial school at this time, as noted

41.  *DWN*, 13th Sept 1851.
42.  *DEP*, 9th Dec 1851.
43.  *DEP*, 30th March 1852.
44.  *CT*, 4th Dec 1852.
45.  *SNL*, 3rd Sept 1853.
46.  *DEP*, 13th Oct, 27th Oct 1853.

previously, was that created by the emergence of the movement for the revival of Irish manufactures, in which the friar played a pivotal part.[47]

At the personal level, there are few indications of Spratt's relations with the pupils. However, from the later 1850s it appears that many of the children of his national and his industrial schools were being sent to a friend, Fr W H Anderdon, for formal religious instruction in Newman's University Church, perhaps in preparation for the sacraments of Communion and Confirmation.[48] In January 1858, with Anderdon's help and that of the ladies of the St Vincent de Paul Society of Francis Street parish, Fr Spratt organised a splendid evening for 800 boys and girls of the Whitefriar Street schools. Regaled with tea and coffee, cakes and sweets, they were then treated to a magic lantern show arranged by Fr Anderdon while Fr Spratt engaged the uniformed band of his Irish Total Abstinence Association to provide the music. Beginning at 4 pm, the party went on until 9.30, assisted also by Carmelite confrere Fr Henry McGee and Bishop Whelan of Bombay.[49] A year later, through Anderdon's kindness, he was able to provide a similar special evening, with his ITAA band again supplying the music. In addition to the tea and cakes for 1,000 boys and girls, a Punch and Judy show was laid on in the gas lit and colourfully decorated hall. The children of his St Peter's Orphanage were included in the festivities.

*St Peter's Orphanage*

Along with the Whitefriar Street National Schools, the orphanage of St Peter's, at 51 Aungier Street, remained as a continuing responsibility for Fr John from earlier decades. Through the 1850s and 1860s it catered for around 50 orphans: the numbers fluctuated, from 53 in 1846, down to 40 in 1853, falling to 32 over 1856 and 1857, rising again to 40 in 1858 and peaking at 52 in 1872.[50] Originally a home for both girls and

---

47. See Chapter Thirteen.

48. *FJ*, 21st Jan 1859. Former Anglican priest and convert, a nephew of Cardinal Manning, William H. Anderdon (1816-1890) served as chaplain in Newman's Catholic University Church on Stephen's Green, Dublin, in the 1850s and 1860s. He gifted the porch of the church to Newman. He joined the Jesuits in their English Province in the 1870s. I am grateful to Rebecca Somerset, Jesuit Archives, London, for the English information on Dr Anderdon.

49. *EF*, 15th Jan 1858.

50. *SNL*, 9th May, 1846; *FJ*, 2nd April 1853; *DEP*, 29th March 1856, 25th April 1857; *SNL*, 13th April 1858; *DWN*, 13th April 1872.

boys, from March 1856 it ceased to present itself as accommodating girls.[51]   Furthermore, its title began to vary between the simple St Peter's Orphan Society and the more denominational St Peter's Catholic Orphan Society.  This may have been, perhaps, an indication of the growing confessional emphasis of the 1850s; or, perhaps, fewer Protestant orphans were placed there as time went on and as Protestant alternatives expanded.  Nevertheless, even as there was a fluctuating incidence of including or excluding the title 'Catholic' from the name, Spratt continued to assert that orphans were accepted *'without parochial or religious distinctions'.*[52]  The description 'Catholic' was not used by him until July 1856 and it was not until January 1859 that it came to feature permanently in the title of the orphanage society.[53]  By 1860, therefore, it was Catholic in name and probably so in fact, thereafter.

On a day to day basis the orphanage was conducted by a matron, Mrs Moore, from 1843 into the 1850s at least, and by a schoolmaster, Michael Connolly, later O'Connolly, from the 1850s to the 1870s.[54]  Fr John appears to have been kind to the orphans: despite busy days with diverse public engagements, he can be found taking them on various outings: to the Great Exhibition in October 1853, to a historical slide show or diorama in June 1859, and to view the paintings at the Royal Hibernian Academy in September of that year, in addition to the post-Christmas parties in the Whitefriar Street schools.[55]

Life at the Orphanage, however, was not without grief.  The Orphanage house, at 51 Aungier Street, was home to many societies for meeting rooms and in colder weather these rooms were heated with open fires.  After the evening dinner the children were allowed to run freely about the house.  In November 1854 one six-year-old orphan, William Brennan, was at play in one of these rooms when his clothes caught fire.  He died from his burns and the inquest in its verdict was critical at *'so young a child as the deceased having been allowed to run about unattended to'.*[56]

---

51.  *DEP,* 29th March 1856.
52.  For this point, see *FJ,* 2nd April 1859, 13th April 1858, 28th April 1859.
53.  For this situation in the 1850s, see *FJ,* 17th April, 24th May, 14th Aug 1852, 2nd April, 16th April 1853, 14th April 1855; *DEP,* 29th March 1856; *FJ,* 26th July 1856; *DEP,* 25th April 1857; *SNL,* 28th July 1857, 13th April, 16th July 1858; *EF,* 4th Aug 1858; *FJ,* 14th Sept 1858; *SNL,* 15th Jan 1859.
54.  *SNL,* 22nd Nov 1854; *EF,* 13th April 1858; *FJ,* 9th April 1875.
55.  *DEP,* 27th Oct 1853; *FJ,* 3rd June 1859, 12th Sept 1859.
56.  *SNL,* 22nd Nov 1854.

St Peter's depended exclusively on private charity. In that circumstance, John Spratt's ability as a networker and a fundraiser was critical to its survival. People he came to know in the various public campaigns in which he became involved were soon persuaded to help out or contribute. Typical among those he enlisted were Martin Burke, Lord Cloncurry, the corn merchant, James Haughton, the shipping merchant, Richard Devereux, and town councillors, John Bagnall and Alderman Andrews: many had been or were co-workers in his different causes, from clemency for State prisoners, through temperance, famine relief, and the movement for the revival of Irish manufactures.[57] The main annual charity sermons, where distinguished preachers were joined by equally distinguished 'collectors', normally were held in the Carmelite church in Whitefriar Street. Typical of such preachers were Dr Daniel Cahill, Dr Richard O'Brien of All Hallows and the CYMS, and indeed, Dr Anderdon, chaplain of the Catholic University.[58] Within the year of his own translation from Armagh to Dublin as Archbishop, Paul Cullen had become patron of the Orphanage.[59] Such sermons could bring in up to £80 or £90 a year and greatly helped St Peter's which was run on a very modest budget. Personal bequests were important to the viability

**Fig 72.**   *Dr Daniel Cahill.*          **Fig 73.**   *Dr Richard O'Brien.*

57.  *DEP*, 24th July 1851.
58.  *FJ*, 7th Aug 1852; *SNL*, 13th April 1858; *DEP*, 25th April 1857; *SNL*, 19th Aug 1859; *EF*, 10th Aug 1863.
59.  *FJ*, 2nd April, 16th July 1853; Cullen became Archbishop of Dublin on 3rd May 1852.

of the society but by their nature were a haphazard source.[60] In March 1860, the Orphanage enjoyed a particularly helpful windfall when it was bequeathed £100 from the will of the very rich James Murphy of Mount Merrion who left £150,000 upon his death in 1858.[61] The generosity of the local benefit and loan fund societies and of the local trade unions was also significant, especially around Christmas time.[62]

In the six months up to January 1859, and again in the months up to January 1860, thirty separate loan fund societies helped out: doubtless, Spratt's public campaigns for them, through his work for the Cuffe Street Savings Bank depositors, the defence against the inroads of British-based benefit societies and his role in support of the Dublin burial societies against the Glasnevin authorities will have stood him in good stead. These benefactors ranged from the Tontine Society of the Grand Carmelites through the Pawnbrokers' Assistants and on to that of the Dublin Warehouse Porters.[63] But it may well say something more about Spratt's charm and open spirit that even some who differed profoundly with him could overlook their differences and contribute to his orphanage. Thus, although he had serious differences with Thomas Mooney and Dr George Hayden of the Board of Irish Manufactures, they contributed to St Peter's.[64] Even more remarkably, when it came to bitter enmity between the Carmelite and the Licensed Vintners and Grocers Society, as shall be seen later, it did not prevent their leading officers, the local publicans, Carey and Brady, from acting as the auditors for the orphanage accounts.[65] Furthermore, although a publican, Daniel O'Hara of York Street was a supporter from at least 1837, and served as President of the Orphanage Society from the early 1860s at least, until well into the 1870s.[66] These diverse sources of aid enabled Spratt's orphanage generally to meet Mr Micawber's measure: in the later 1850s annual income was in the region of £240 to £320

60. For modest examples, see *FJ*, 22nd May 1850, 25th Jan 1853, 14th Sept 1858.
61. *SNL*, 21st March 1860.
62. *FJ*, 18th Jan 1851; *DEP*, 24th Jan 1851 for the Regular Carpenters of Elephant Lane; *EF*, 28th Jan 1863 for the Bricklayers' Society.
63. *SNL*, 13th Jan 1859; *EF*, 19th Jan 1860.
64. See below Chapter Thirteen.
65. See, for example, *SNL*, 19th Aug 1859.
66. *FJ*, 22nd Sept 1837; *DMR*, 26th May 1838; *The Pilot*, 23rd May 1838; *EF*, 19th Jan 1860; *Irish Times*, 10th April 1877.

and expenditure came in between £200 and £210.[67] Available accounts during the 1850s and 1860s show the Society facing growing inflation but also generally living within its means:

|  | Year | Income | Expenditure |
|---|---|---|---|
|  | 1857 | 249 | 201 |
|  | 1858 | 265 | 171 |
|  | 1859 | 327 | 211 |
| Half Year to Jan | 1862 | 227 | 229 |
|  | 1863 | 659 | 478 |
| Half Year to Aug | 1867 | 287 | 310 |
|  | 1869 | 486 | 493[68] |

Finally, apart from money, support in kind was extremely important for the Society: there was, for example, the generosity of a Mr Rispin of Clarendon Market, who supplied the orphanage with its Sunday dinner over many years, and that of the physician, Dr MacSwiney, who gave free medical attention to these orphans.[69] It is clear that the Carmelite friar commanded a sustained loyalty from his friends and supporters over five decades. When it came to St Peter's Orphan Society, none were more loyal than the Slevins, father and son: Peter, of French Street, later of Irishtown, and his son, Patrick Holmes Slevin of Charlemont Street and later of Ranelagh Road. Peter has already been encountered in connection with the Sick and Indigent Roomkeepers Society in the 1820s and 1830s. He was a devoted follower of O'Connell's, a member of his Precursor Society and his Repeal Association as late as 1850,[70] and was a leading light of the National Trades' Political Union. The owner of a circulating library, operating near the Carmelites on French Street and Whitefriar Street, he may have been one of the beneficiaries of O'Connell's success in opening up state and municipal offices to Catholics as, before his death in 1854, he had become a water-bailiff

67. *SNL*, 28th July 1857, 16th July 1858, 19th Aug 1859.
68. *EF*, 28th Jan 1862, 28th Jan 1863, 10th Aug 1863; *DEP*, 7th Aug 1867; *EF*, 13th Aug 1869.
69. *EF*, 4th Aug 1858.
70. *The Tablet*, 26th Jan 1850.

for the City of Dublin. Peter Slevin was Secretary of the St Peter's Orphan Society from at least 1825 until 1835, and remained one of its stalwarts into the 1850s.[71] His son, Patrick, who worked in the General Post Office, served as Secretary of the Orphan Society from 1838 at least until the end of the 1860s.[72] Patrick was present to assist the move from the School House at 9 Peter's Row, which the Society had occupied since at least 1832, to the spacious new premises at 51 Aungier Street, which occurred in late 1841; he was still present to assist in its final move to 44 York Street in 1865.[73] With Fr John, as one of the trustees, he did not long survive the Carmelite, as he died on 25 January 1872.[74]

---

71. *DMR*, 9th March 1825, 14th July 1835; *FJ*, 31 Aug 1848; *DWN*, 8th Dec 1849; *FJ*, 17th Oct 1854; *CT*, 21st Oct 1854; *SNL*, 2nd Nov 1854.

72. Sometime between September 1837 and November 1838 Patrick Holmes Slevin became honorary secretary in succession to one John Prendergast who held the post from 1835 after Peter Slevin's tenure. See *SNL*, 8th March 1825; *DMR*, 8th and 9th March 1825, 14th July 1835, 7th Sept 1837, 20th Nov, 1838; *CT*, 21st Oct 1854. At 51 Aungier Street, by November 1865 its address had changed to 44 York Street.

73. *DMR*, 12th June 1832, 17th Dec 1841; *EF*, 15th Nov 1865. Up to July 1864 the Orphan House was listed.

74. *FJ*, 26th Jan 1872.

# CHAPTER FIFTEEN

## *Charity, Co-operation and Conflict, 1850–1866*

If Fr John and Patrick Slevin had been mainstays of St Peter's Orphan Society for over forty years, the Carmelite was as deeply committed to that other charity, the Sick and Indigent Roomkeepers, over almost as long a period. He was prominent in their monthly business and annual general meetings through four decades. Year after year, Fr John was the one who read out the annual report – an exercise in his case that normally involved not just a technical report on finances and the numbers of unfortunates aided, but just as much an extended sermon on Christian charity by way of preface. Despite the growing confessional exclusiveness of those decades, and notwithstanding the increasing incidence of proselytism and sectarianism, the offices and members of this Society not only constituted a charity, but also a bulwark against these growing interdenominational animosities. On rare occasions the Society was accused of denominational selectivity in the distribution of its charity, and was swift to reject any such allegations. Thus, in 1860, a senior counsel, Henry H Joy, a member of the Association for the Relief of Distressed Protestants, asserted that the Roomkeepers Society was exclusive, and that *'while other societies are doing good, it is doing evil instead of good'.*[1] Joy was challenged by the Roomkeepers' secretary, Myles Casey, as to whether these remarks had been correctly reported, but Joy declined to comment beyond saying that his remarks applied to the Society in its *'former years'.* Further challenged by Casey on this, no further comment was forthcoming.[2] Three years later, Church of Ireland Archdeacon,

1. *SNL*, 29th March 1860.
2. *DEM*, 11th April 1860.

**Fig 74.**   *Dr Franc Sadlier.*          **Fig 75.**   *Dr Richard MacDonnell.*

John West, at a Roomkeepers' meeting, was concerned that the Society was perceived as sectarian: in response, and to alleviate his concerns, the Society published the testimony of twelve Protestant clergymen to the contrary, adding, *'which we trust will forever silence misrepresentation on this head'.*[3] Such misgivings are surprising considering not just the Society's constant insistence on its denominational impartiality, but also given the fact that Spratt himself was the only senior Catholic cleric holding office in the Society or even in constant attendance at it. His joint secretary was the Church of Ireland Dean of Ossory and the treasurer for very many years was the Provost of Trinity College, Dr Franc Sadlier, followed by his Provost successor, Dr Richard MacDonnell. Indeed, when the latter died in 1867, Spratt and his fellow committee members urged Dr Trench, the Archbishop of Dublin, to agree to the appointment as treasurer of his Provost successor, Humphrey Lloyd.[4] Church of Ireland diocesan clergy were in regular attendance at monthly committee meetings, individuals such as Thomas Shore of St Nicholas Within and William G Carroll of St Bride's, whereas, Spratt apart, Catholic clergy were only occasional attenders, such as fellow-priests, P J Gilligan and Andrew O'Connell.

---

3. *DDE*, 20th Jan 1863.
4. *DEP*, 21st Jan 1868.

*Repulsing Sectarianism*

Spratt himself, in his annual reports, repeatedly insisted on the non-sectarian message, declaring in 1850 that

> ...it knows no distinction in the receipt and distribution of its alms. Protestants and Catholics are united together in the bonds of Christian charity for the purpose of relieving their fellow creatures who are in distress and destitution.[5]

A decade later he stated that *'those who will be relieved will never be questioned as to class or creed'*, and, a year later again, he insisted that *'the entire absence of all religious distinctions in the distribution of its charity is amply borne testimony to by the most enlightened divines of all denominations'*.[6] It was not only a question of preaching ecumenism: he practised it too in the daily life of the Society. Thus, he and Rev Carroll of St Bride's went collecting funds for the Society, together door to door, on one occasion collecting £29 on a single side of one street in St Bride's Parish.[7]

Given the growing religious tensions of the time, and the mutual suspicions between Protestant and Catholic Church leaders in Dublin, it was a challenge for Spratt and his Protestant co-workers within the Society to keep that spirit of mutual respect and co-operation to the fore. It was less difficult in the 1830s and 1840s during the episcopate of Daniel Murray. Murray was a trustee of the Society and six months before his death, when he apologised for his inability to attend its annual general meeting, he wrote generously of this *'admirable society'*, praised the *'prudence and impartiality with which it administered the funds imparted to it'*, and enclosed his annual subscription.[8]

However, with the arrival of Archbishop Cullen matters might have been expected to deteriorate given that there was no love lost between the new Catholic archbishop and his Church of Ireland counterpart. However, Cullen maintained Murray's tradition of supporting the Society: he annually gave the use of his Cathedral for the charity sermon and, indeed, on 4th November 1860 he himself delivered it, raising

---

5.  *DWR*, 19th Jan 1850.
6.  *DEM*, 13th Feb 1861; *FJ*, 29th Jan 1862.
7.  *DDE*, 23rd Jan 1863.
8.  *FJ*, 23rd Jan 1852, Murray to Spratt 22nd January 1852.

over £84 on the occasion.[9] Such occasions as these were ones where Protestants and Catholics interacted: thus, at the Pro-Cathedral charity sermon in 1870, the meeting to thank Cullen, which took place in the vestry immediately after the sermon, was chaired by Sir William Wilde.[10]

Spratt was clearly comfortable enough with his Protestant fellow-members to be outspoken in the matter of the Church of Ireland's charity sermons for the Roomkeepers. In January 1864, at the annual general meeting, he remarked quite pointedly on the *'falling-off'* of the amounts raised *'of late years'* by the Church of Ireland's annual sermon. He recalled that, back in 1828, the charity sermon in St Andrew's, delivered by the Dean of St Patrick's, had raised £202,[11] whereas by the 1860s it was hardly one tenth of that. He now suggested that the Church of Ireland authorities might consider the Catholic practice of conducting simultaneous collections in all of the city churches on the day of the Roomkeepers' charity sermon. He successfully pressed for a Roomkeepers' deputation to meet the new Archbishop, Richard Chenevix Trench, with a view to securing an increase in the funds raised

and also to explore the possibility of the simultaneous collection. His Church of Ireland friend, the Rev William Carroll, supported this call.[12] The deputation was well received. Archbishop Trench could not promise a simultaneous collection without consulting his clergy, but did promise personal support. He was true to his promise and annually, thereafter, at least from 1864 to 1870, he himself delivered that sermon, usually in St Patrick's Cathedral, and became an annual

**Fig 76.** *Dr Richard Chenevix Trench.*

9. *EF*, 14th Nov 1860.
10. *DEP*, 8th Nov 1870.
11. *EF*, 9th Jan 1864.
12. For Rev William Carroll, see J. Crawford, *The Church of Ireland in Victorian Dublin*, Dublin 2005, pp. 22, 115. Carroll was the clergyman who baptised George Bernard Shaw and taught him Latin.

subscriber.[13]  Trench was at one with the ethos of the Society, telling
the deputation that *'such a charity as this had a peculiar claim because it enabled
us, without any sacrifice of principle, to unite together'*.  Two years later, in the
course of the Roomkeepers' charity sermon he remarked:

> In those days when so many things occurred to draw them apart
> – and must continue to draw them apart – from their Roman
> Catholic brethren, they should thank God that there were still
> some points of contact remaining, and, amongst these, was this
> Society in which they could work together, as disciples of the
> same God.[14]

The ability of the Society to transcend denominational divisions
continued to be manifest to the end of Spratt's days as honorary
secretary.  The city's Jewish congregation came in to support the
Roomkeepers in 1868 and, from that same year, Dublin's Unitarians
began to conduct a charity sermon for the Society.[15]

### Confessional Strife

Such developments were something of a triumph when one considers
the denominational disputes which came to litter the 1850s and 1860s –
disputes in which Spratt himself became embroiled.  As Miriam Moffitt
put it: *'The intensity of religious hostility in the mid nineteenth century between
Roman Catholicism and evangelical Protestantism cannot be overstated, as both
sides vehemently protested their own viewpoint'*.[16]  The litany of contention,
as a newly-robust Catholicism challenged an entrenched, evangelically-
revived Protestantism, included conflicts over denominational chaplains
to prisons and poor law union workhouses, and flashpoints of discord
over proselytism and alleged proselytism of vulnerable people, not
least of children in care institutions.  Such concern led the Catholic
authorities to press on with the foundation of Catholic equivalents,
be it in schools for the destitute poor, asylums for the deaf and blind,

---

13.  *SNL*, 13th May 1864; *EF* 29th Nov 1864; *DDE*, 1st Jan 1866; *DEM*, 28th March
     1868; *FJ*, 3rd April 1869.  That for 1864 he delivered in Christchurch and thereafter
     he preached the sermon in St Patrick's.
14.  DDE, 1st Jan 1866.
15.  *DEP*, 21st Jan, 14th Feb 1868, 3rd Dec 1870.
16.  Moffitt, p. 128.

or in refuges for 'fallen women'. Spratt became engaged in quite a number of these initiatives and embroiled in quite a number of the precipitating conflicts.[17] He himself, notably, became the target of Irish Church Missions ridicule.

By the late 1850s the Irish Church Missions was holding controversial discussions and classes, north and south of the city, and had established their own children's schools on Spratt's doorstep in the Coombe.[18] From their headquarters in Townsend Street, the Irish Church Missions from the end of the 1850s had the Carmelite friar as a target. Typical of this, in the summer of 1858, was an invitation to 'Roman Catholic friends' to

> come to the controversial class on the subject 'Is salvation by Fr Spratt's Brown or Fr Grimley's Red Scapular taught in Dr Cullen's bible...? Why no miracles brought by the Scapular now? How many can Fr Spratt claim or prove for his Scapulars? Can Fr Spratt tell what has become of the original scapular made in heaven and given to Simon Stock?'[19]

The protagonist was Rev Charles Fennell MacCarthy who kept up the attacks on Friar John into the next decade. On the same day, for example, in July 1860, when the evangelist, Alexander Dallas, Honorary Secretary to the ICM, presided in their Townsend Street premises, Rev MacCarthy held an evening discussion again on the subject, 'The Carmelites' Cloth of Grace', and wondered aloud, *'Will Fr Spratt prove that all Carmelites who duly use the brown scapular of Simon Stock shall not suffer eternal fire?'* and asked *'would a Scapularian be sure of salvation even in the*

---

17. He became, for example, vice-president, with Dr Yore as president, of St Mary's Asylum for Industrious Blind (Females) at Lower Dominick Street, when it opened in August 1858. See *DEP*, 24th Aug 1858. Spratt helped Yore to raise money for this institution, founded 'to rescue them [the Catholic blind] from their enemies', in Yore's own words.
18. See for example, *DDE*, 9th Jan 1858; see also, Moffitt, pp. 76-79; J. Prunty, 'Battle plans and battlegrounds: Protestant mission activity in the Dublin slums, 1840's – 1880's', in C. Gribben & A. R. Holmes, eds., *Protestant Millennialism, Evangelicalism, and Irish Society, 1790-2005*, Basingstoke 2006, pp. 119-143.
19. *DDE*, 27th July 1858.

*Adelaide Hospital?*'.[20]  Such discussion was inevitably one-sided as, since the Synod of Thurles, Catholic clergy were precluded from engaging polemically with Protestant divines in public debates.    However, MacCarthy's reference to Spratt, the scapular and the Adelaide Hospital would have resonated at that time with Dublin readers, Protestant and Catholic alike.

**Fig 77.**   *A sketch of the Adelaide Hospital.*

### The Friar and the Adelaide Hospital

On 20th July 1859 John Spratt issued a public letter entitled *Caution to the Catholic Poor of Dublin*.  Remarkable for its forthrightness, it announced:

> A hospital has been opened in Peter Street, called 'The Adelaide Hospital'.  It has been got up and is exclusively managed by that class of Protestants who seem to consider a hatred of Catholicity the greatest virtue and, acting on this illiberal feeling, though they admit Catholics as patients, yet no Catholic priest is allowed to enter the wards of that hospital or attend to any patient in it.

---

20.  *SNL*, 14th July 1860. The dating of the subject was strategically chosen since it was ten days before the feast of Our Lady of Mount Carmel when Fr John was due to preach on the subject.

In effect, argued Spratt, all dying patients, regardless of denomination, were ministered to by Protestant clergy. He asserted no wish to denigrate *'the liberal and noble-minded'* Protestants who did so much for charity in Dublin, and he felt that the latter *'would scorn a charity stained with the horrors of the forcible proselytism of the dying'*. Bluntly, he warned Catholics that if they entered that hospital *'the destruction is on their own head'* and concluded abruptly, *'let no Catholic enter the walls of the Adelaide Hospital in Peter Street'*.[21] His manifesto was soon noticed and endorsed by leading Irish journals, with the *Weekly Nation*, among others, commenting that *'we seldom have to chronicle anything so revoltingly intolerant'* as the situation revealed by his letter.[22] An alternative response was not slow in coming. On 30th July 1859 the Protestant *Warder and Dublin Weekly Mail* unleashed a blistering tirade on the Carmelite:

> Moved by the new ultramontane inspiration Fr Spratt has...come out as an opponent of the only exclusively Protestant Hospital the city possesses...As long as the Protestant public had no exclusive hospital, like the Roman Catholic edifices in Stephen's Green and Eccles Street, the policy of the Romanists was to screw all the money they could get out of Protestants for the support of those institutions on the pretext that they were erected 'out of the common love of all' and under a strict guarantee against proselytism...But the moment the Protestants, becoming aware of the dangerous character of these hospitals, erected one of their own, Dr Cullen and Fr Spratt came forth to denounce us for doing exactly what they themselves have done – namely – building a denominational hospital. Their anger is accounted for by the fact that, since the Adelaide Hospital opened, the Protestant subscriptions to St Vincent's and the Eccles Street Misericordiae have almost ceased.

*The Warder* insisted that *'the quiet and insidious proselytism'* of the nuns' hospitals had *'caused the erection of the Adelaide'*. It concluded that those entering the Adelaide were told the rule that no Catholic priests or sisters can enter: *'Fr Spratt has no business to complain'* and urged that all

---

21.   *FJ*, 21st July 1859.
22.   *DWN*, 30th July 1859.

Protestant donations be taken away from *'the Romish religious hospitals'*.[23]
The friar lost little time in answering back, publishing a reply in which
he charged the managers of the hospital with bigotry and intolerance
in refusing priests admission to visit their patient co-religionists. This
he sent to several newspapers and also had it printed as a handbill
distributed in the streets and posted on walls and church doors.

The recently launched *Irish Times*, whose owner-editor, Captain
Knox, worked with Spratt in certain public causes, in response published
readers' letters attacking the Carmelite and even dedicated an editorial
condemning his position on and activities against the hospital. On 15th
September the editor commented:

> It is with sincere regret we observe that our excellent fellow-
> citizen, the very Rev Fr Spratt, continues his ill-judged crusade
> against one of our most valuable local institutions. Why the
> Adelaide Hospital should be the object of such persevering and
> bitter hostility is really difficult to conceive.

It reminded readers that the Adelaide's rules were open and well-known
and that there were a number of other City hospitals which Catholics
could use.[24]

The controversies did not end here. On Sunday 9th October Dr
Cullen issued a pastoral at the beginning of which he targeted *'some recent
instances of bigotry and intolerance'* starting with the Adelaide Hospital:[25] He
quoted verbatim from its rules that

> no emissary or official of the Church of Rome shall ever be
> permitted to cross the threshold of the Adelaide Hospital for the
> purpose of administering any rite or imparting any instruction or
> so-called consolation to the patients.[26]

The Irish Church Missions now joined the fray when it invited Roman
Catholics to a discussion on the subject, *'is not the real trouble for Dr Cullen
and Fr Spratt that Roman Catholics are found content to die without the priests*

---

23.   *The Warder and Dublin Evening Mail*, 30th July 1859.
24.   *IT*, 15th Sept 1859.
25.   *Lloyd's Weekly Newspaper*, 16th Oct 1859, citing *Daily News*.
26.   *Cork Examiner*, 14th Oct 1859.

*and prayers of Rome?*'.[27]   Perhaps – or perhaps not – but the one real trouble for them was mentioned by Cullen in his pastoral; namely, the circumstance where a Catholic entered or was brought to the hospital who might be in little or no state to object.

### The French Patient

At the beginning of February 1859 one Henri Roebet, a French chef in the employment of the military at Portobello Barracks, fell seriously ill and ended up in the Adelaide Hospital.  Two dramatically opposed and irreconcilable accounts of the key circumstances soon arose.  John Spratt, on learning of the man's admission, *'in a dying state'*, requested a friend, Fr Nolan, to visit him.  Fr John, being very well-known in the district, presumably surmised he would be refused admission and therefore asked Fr Nolan of Donnybrook to make the approach. On the latter's being refused permission to visit, the friar called on the French Consul to secure leave for a priest to visit or else to have Roebet removed to St Vincent's Hospital instead.  At a first attempt to do so the French Vice-Consul, M E de Meric, was turned back, it not being 'visiting day'.  On returning a day later, according to John Spratt's account, de Meric was told that Roebet did not wish to see a priest.  On persisting in seeing his fellow-countryman, de Meric was led to see the patient, and again, according to the Carmelite's account,

**Fig 78.**   *St Vincent's Hospital at Stephen's Green.*

---

27.  *SNL*, 25th Oct 1859.

on asking Roebet if he wished to see a priest, he replied affirmatively. The Vice-Consul then left the hospital to consult his superior.[28] Three days later, Frs Spratt and Nolan called to the hospital to secure Roebet's release, for transfer to St Vincent's. They were refused admission and were told that the French Consul would have to call in person to secure the chef's release. On Wednesday 8th February, accompanied by Spratt and Nolan, the French Consul presented himself and secured Roebet's discharge and transfer to St Vincent's at Stephen's Green. As the *Freeman's Journal* commented:

> The Rev Fr Spratt has thus succeeded in vindicating the true principle of charity and the duties of religion whilst exposing to the reprobation of the civilised world a system of intolerance as hideous as any that could degrade humanity.[29]

However, from the pen of the clerk of the hospital, Rev D A Browne, came a forthright rebuttal of the *'violent attack up on the managers'* made by Fr Spratt *'who grossly misstates the facts of the case'*. According to this account, the Frenchman was first taken to St Vincent's Hospital. Here he was refused admission as *'his case was hopeless and they could do nothing for him'*. Consequently, he was then admitted to the Adelaide. Here, for three weeks he never asked for a priest and, according to the Portobello Barracks mess man, a friend named Rankley, he expressed himself happy with the attentions of the hospital chaplain, Rev Stone. Browne mentioned that a priest, *'at the request of some party outside'*, had called to see Roebet but was refused admission. Browne explained that the Vice-Consul also had indeed been refused admission – by error on the part of a minor functionary – in his first calling but was admitted the next day. Browne's account then flatly contradicted the statement in John Spratt's letter that the man asked to see a priest. According to Rankley, who visited him throughout, Roebet expressed no wish to leave the hospital and feared that the Consul might secure this against his wishes. Some days later, one Dr W H Tomlinson, on asking the same question, was told by Roebet that he wished to remain in the hospital.[30] However,

---

28. *The Irishman*, 11th Feb 1860.
29. *FJ*, 8th Feb 1860.
30. Tomlinson confirmed this in a letter of 10th February 1860: See *DEPC*, 11th Feb 1860.

after successive denials that he wanted a priest, he finally indicated that
if he deteriorated he might then wish to. The hospital committee
informed him that this was not possible and while happy to continue
to treat him, they recommended that *'while he yet had strength, to move to
another hospital'*. Browne's account continued:

> Shortly afterwards, the Vice-Consul and a priest were at the
> door of the hospital and the man was in a short time removed;
> but before he left he expressed to Mr. Rankley who called to
> see him and who was surprised to find him leaving, very strong
> indignation against those who had busied themselves in removing
> him from a place where he had received so much kindness. Such
> are the facts of the case.

Browne insisted that Roebet had been *'worried into consenting to leave the
hospital'* and did so *'with loud censures against the conduct of those who interfered
with him, and with declarations oft-repeated, that he left contrary to his wish'*.
Rev Browne concluded: *'I leave it to your readers to say on whose side was the
'revolting bigotry'.*[31] However, his was not the last word. On the very next
day, the Consul, Frederic de Burggraff directly challenged Browne's
assertion that Roebet had been removed against his will: *'I repeat that
your assertion is completely contrary to the fact. I could prove the same of many of
the various items of your letter'* and, he added, *'I will say, in all my life I never met
with such uncharitable regulations as those now in force in the Adelaide Hospital'*.[32]

By this stage the case had become notorious, being taken up by
the press all over Ireland and even reaching London where the *Evening
Standard* reported:

> The religious world of Dublin, Protestant and Catholic, has
> been in a state of ferment and excitement for the last four
> days by reason of the refusal of the managers of the Adelaide
> Hospital to permit a Catholic priest to have access to a native of
> France. The Rev Fr Spratt, fancying that the spiritual state of
> the sick Gaul was not in safe keeping, insisted on his removal
> to a more congenial atmosphere...Fr Spratt is, of course,

---

31.  *SNL*, 10th Feb 1860, D. A. Browne, clerk to editor.  Browne was sole honorary
     secretary of the hospital from 1862 to 1868 and joint honorary secretary until 1874.
32.  *SNL*, 13th Feb 1860, Frederic de Burggraff to Rev D. A. Browne.

glorified exceedingly for thus saving 'the faith and morals' of the Frenchman from the possibility of Protestant contamination.[33]

The friar was not content to leave matters to the French Consul. Asking the editor of *Saunders' Newsletter* for fair play, he wrote to challenge Browne, on 12th February, by reproducing a sworn statement of that day, made before the Lord Mayor by himself, by physician, Dr Daniel Dwyer of Camden Street, and two others, duly signed. They solemnly swore that on Sunday 12th February they were present in St Vincent's Hospital when Henri Roebet replied to a series of questions they put to him: he denied point blank that he told the Vice-Consul in the presence of a hospital official that he did not want to see a priest; he denied outright that he told Rankley that he did not want to leave: on the contrary, he now insisted that he was at all times anxious to see a priest but felt too weak to leave the hospital; he denied utterly that he told Rankley on the occasion of finally leaving the Adelaide that he was indignant at having to, or against those who came to transfer him; he now asserted that he was not pleased with the religious instruction given to him there by the Protestant chaplain and had never asked for the Bible that had been given to him.[34]

Whether it was the illness that laid him low or the strain upon him of the religious rivalry that arose from it, the unfortunate Henri Roebet passed away in St Vincent's in the early hours of Thursday 20th March 1860. By the Catholic or pro-Catholic city press he was lamented as *'the poor Frenchman who had been caught in the toils of the heartless proselytisers of the Adelaide Hospital'.*[35] For the Protestant journals, *The Warder, The Mail, The Packet* and *The Irish Times* came no mention of Roebet's demise. His passing did not mean the passing of the problem. Both sides to the controversy found cause to keep up the conflict of views in the immediately following months and years.

In June 1860, Cullen took up Spratt's crusade when, at a crowded general meeting of the Catholic Young Men's Society, he reeled off a litany of complaints against proselytisers, and reciting that list, he commented *'it is not charity to open the doors of the Adelaide Hospital to*

33.  *London Evening Standard*, 9th Feb 1860.
34.  *SNL*, 15th Feb 1860.
35.  *DEP*, 29th March 1860; *FNL*, 30th March 1860; *The Irishman*, 31st March 1860; *CT*, *WFJ*, 31st March 1860.

*poor Catholics, and then to prevent them from receiving the last rites of their holy religion*'.[36]  The opposition replied in kind, when the *Packet* two days later detailed '*the malignant and unscrupulous hostility which this institution has to encounter*'.  Spratt, in turn, remained relentless in his attentions to the Adelaide.  Early in 1861 he recounted the case of a Catholic, Fitzpatrick, '*detained against his will*' there.  Wanting to leave the hospital so that he could receive the ministrations of a Catholic priest, he urged his wife Bridget to intercede with Spratt for intervention.  In a partial repeat of the Roebet case, the friar and a medical friend were denied access and were informed, he told, that Fitzpatrick was a Protestant and did not wish to leave.  Mrs. Fitzpatrick managed to force her way through to her husband's bed and he, '*in the hearing of the attendants*', asked her to secure his transfer to Jervis Street Hospital.  Spratt once again published the correspondence between himself and the Adelaide and once again there was a direct and absolute contradiction of facts, one side claiming that the man's wife, Jane Fitzpatrick, said he was Protestant, the other side holding that he was Catholic, and that his wife insisted as such.  In the end he was transferred to Jervis Street, where he died four days later, with the rites of the Catholic Church.[37]  On 15th January, before his death, he made and signed a solemn written declaration that he had ever been a Catholic: '*I never was a Protestant, nor ever expressed a wish to be one*'.  He insisted that the chaplain, Rev Stone, in the Adelaide, had tried to convert him but he had refused to conform.[38]  The annual general meeting of the Adelaide, on 5th February 1861, heard an entirely different account, asserting that Fitzpatrick had converted to Protestantism a year before and had sent his children to a Protestant school, while his wife remained Catholic: so reported the *Dublin Evening Mail* and *Saunders' Newsletter*.[39]

Such conflicts served to sour not only Catholic-Protestant relations within the city, but even relations within the Adelaide itself.  As the Adelaide's historian, David Mitchell, has recounted, some leading members of its own medical staff found it difficult to accept '*the strict interpretation of the* Fundamental Principle *that non-Protestant patients should*

---

36.  *FJ*, 12th June 1860.
37.  *DEP*, 31st Jan 1861; *DEM*, 6th Feb 1861.  *The Mail*'s account insisted that he had become a Protestant a year before and asked to remain so.
38.  *DEP*, 31st Jan 1861.
39.  *DEM*, *SNL*, 6th Feb 1861.

*only be admitted if they agreed their clergy could not visit them'.*[40] Following further
such incidents and difficulties, its authorities decided in December
1863 to confine admissions to hospital or its dispensary exclusively to
Protestants. This decision was due to be ratified at the annual general
meeting of the following February but it was opposed and deplored
by the Honorary Secretary, Rev Dr Charles Stanford, and the honorary
treasurer, John Walsh. Despite pleas, Stanford resigned and the new
rule took effect from 2nd February 1864.[41] A further emergency general
meeting that April reversed the exclusion of Catholics from treatment
in the dispensary, but the prohibition on exclusion from the hospital
remained.[42] This notwithstanding, two years later Spratt recounted an
incident whereby a man, falling ill in the street, was admitted to the
Adelaide. Word was sent to the Carmelites in Whitefriar Street that
the man was dying and his sisters asked for Catholic clergy to attend to

him. Frs Crotty, Leybourne and
Spratt went to the hospital but
were denied access. They asked
for him to be removed to a nearby
house. According to Spratt this
was refused, until the man's sisters
demanded his discharge: blankets
having been brought from that
house, the man was carried out in
them and brought there and given
the last rites: Spratt commented,
*'how different is this from the parable
of the Good Samaritan'.*[43]

**Fig 79.**   *Fr Joseph Crotty, O.Carm.*

40.   D. Mitchell, *A 'Peculiar' Place: the Adelaide Hospital Dublin: its times, places and personalities, 1839 to 1989*, Dublin 1989, p. 59.
41.   Stanford's position is interesting since Bowen, in *The Protestant Crusade*, p. 242, described him as a lover of evangelical controversy and brought that propensity with him when he moved from being Rector of St Michan's to being Rector of St Thomas'. Moffitt lists him as one of Dublin's leading evangelicals involved in the Irish Church Missions. His curate at St Thomas's was the controversial Rev Charles Fennell MacCarthy, Dublin superintendent of the Irish Church Missions over 1852-77, for which see Moffitt, p. 76.
42.   Ibid, pp 59-61.
43.   *CT*, 2nd June 1866.

# CHAPTER SIXTEEN

## *Desolations, Consolations, 1850-1870*

The exclusiveness of the Adelaide authorities can be seen as a defensive reaction to the growing confidence and expansion of Catholicism in the period. It was clearly visible, in the 1850s and 1860s, in the case of their nearest Catholic institutional neighbours, the Carmelites of Whitefriar Street. Apart from the splendour of ceremonial in and around the Church of Mount Carmel as earlier described, the 1850s saw the physical enlargement of the church building and the numerical growth of the Carmelite community, their confraternities and their congregations. At the start of the decade, the community of friars had little changed in numbers from what it had constituted when John Spratt arrived back from Spain in 1821. In January 1850 they numbered eight priests.[1] Over the course of the next ten years that community doubled. In October 1856, the Provincial, Fr Thomas Bennett, informed the Order's Prior General in Rome that his Whitefriar Street community now numbered sixteen, and that there were three others anxious to join them.[2] Three months later he could now report some thirteen priests, two professed friars and four novices.[3] Throughout the 1860s, Battersby reported the numbers of the Carmelite friars in Whitefriar Street from twelve to thirteen, but by 1871 he recorded twenty-one.[4] These growing numbers would be far from idle as they

---

1. O'Dwyer, *Irish Carmelites*, pp. 219, 249, n. 228; Battersby's *Catholic Directory*, 1851, p. 336, which relates to 1850, states that there were nine Carmelites in Whitefriar Street.
2. O'Dwyer, *Irish Carmelites*, p. 227.
3. Ibid, p. 228.
4. W. J. Battersby, *Catholic Directory*, years 1851 to 1871.

were heavily committed not just to the Whitefriar Street congregations but to teaching in Bennett's thriving Dominick Street Academy and in Spratt's Whitefriar Street schools. Additional teaching demands would soon be made upon them when they opened Terenure College in 1860.

It was in these happy circumstances that Fr Bennett, in January 1857, sought permission to enlarge the church. That permission was secured and, although little noted by architectural historians, the extension, completed in 1859 by the renowned J J McCarthy, first Professor of Architecture in the Catholic University, was a significant one.[5] In securing some neighbouring properties by March 1857, they announced that they had acquired the space to extend.[6] They constructed along the entire length of the Church, a new aisle, using large open arches along the building's north side. This enabled them to realise a new chapel, dedicated to St Joseph, at the eastern end. The result was that they had added fifty per cent to the original area of accommodation. The work commenced in 1857 and, by good fortune, in the course of 1858 they also acquired the property of the Wesleyan Methodist Widows' Alms House. This enabled them to further extend the newly constructed aisle, right up to Whitefriar Street and to erect additional living quarters for the friary.[7] By September 1859 they seem to have expanded sufficiently so that Spratt was able to let two houses in Whitefriar Street for 31 years at £30 per annum, to a leasing landlord, Thomas McIntyre, who rented them out to some fourteen or fifteen tenants.[8]

The Carmelites had constructed or reconstructed a splendid room

5. C. Dixon, in A. Corbett, D. Pochin Mould and C. Dixon, *Whitefriars Street Church*, Dublin 1964, does not mention it, while C. Casey in *Dublin: the City Within the Grand and Royal Canals*, New Haven and London, 2005, pp. 471-2 gives it only a very brief mention. For J. J. McCarthy, see R. Loeber, H. Campbell, L. Hurley, J. Montague & E. Rowley, eds., *Architecture, 1600-2000*, vol. iv of A. Carpenter, ed., *Art and Architecture of Ireland*, Dublin 2014, p. 128; this volume does not mention the McCarthy extension of 1857-59 either.
6. *FJ*, 2nd March 1857.
7. *WFJ*, 20th May 1858.
8. *SNL*, 13th Sept 1859: so it emerged when McIntyre sought to be enrolled in the register of electors. Why Spratt should have had charge of the leasing is not clear – the Provincial Bennett was certainly preoccupied with Dominick Street Academy and his major role in All Hallows College, yet Spratt was neither Prior nor Provincial; it may have been because he had been the original leaseholder and had been a signatory to most of their various leases from the 1820s through the 1850s.

**Fig 80.** *A liturgical celebration in Whitefriar Street Church, c.1920s.*

for their Confraternity around this time also. At the end of this room stood two side-altars of carved oak, and its high altar featured a reliquary donated by Fr John. The sides of the room exhibited two carved angels on pedestals, and on two other pedestals stood figures of the Virgin and St Joseph. In addition, the room held two carved figures of the Virgin presenting the scapular to St Simon Stock. The writer of this account claimed that these were the only two statues left in Dublin at the time of the Reformation, that *they had occupied a place in the old Carmelite Church in Ash Street. They were thence taken to the Carmelite Church in Moate where they were for years over the high altar'*. At some unstated date they were restored to Whitefriar Street. The room boasted a framed autograph letter of Pope Pius IX, thanking the confraternities of Dublin for their support, and the walls of this room were covered in *'grand religious oil paintings'*, while the writer added that *'the decorations of the altar baffle description'*.[9]

It is not clear, however, following the general extension of the church at this time, that the Carmelites had been able to afford to decorate it to the standard that they desired. It appears that they postponed this final project and it would be over a decade later that they returned to this task. In June 1870 Spratt organised a meeting after Sunday Mass to raise funds to redecorate the whole building. He brought some of his most prestigious old friends and collaborators into the enterprise, including the Hon Judge Little, the MP and QC, Sergeant Sherlock, as well as Peter Paul M'Swiney and A M Sullivan.

In stressing how the Carmelites had had to postpone the final decoration of the church, Sherlock urged that *'the Rev Dr Spratt had claims on the people of Dublin unsurpassed by those of any other man, lay or clerical, in the city'*. Sullivan reminded the congregation that *'this church is peculiarly dear to the citizens of Dublin'* and, retracing history, also reminded them that under the law as it stood, the Carmelites were not supposed to exist in Ireland and that it was a reproach that the penal clauses of the 1829 Catholic Relief Act still remained on the statute book. M'Swiney took the opportunity, as a resident neighbour for the previous twenty-one years, to praise its priests for their unflagging service to the people. When all the speeches were done, a subscription list was opened, with £200 being donated immediately.[10]

---

9.  *WJF*, 19th July 1862.
10.  *EF*, 7th June 1870.

Employing the architect, Burke, and the interior decorator, John Entwistle, the friars set about their project and, by October 1870, the refurbishment of their church, *'made more beautiful by the magnificent decoration it has undergone'*, had been completed.[11] Such development doubtless brought great cheer to the Carmelite community and although, as in any family, there might be tensions and differences, nevertheless by the second half of the 1850s, Fr Bennett could testify that harmony and good feeling marked the life of the friary.[12]

## *Departures – fraternal*

This decade of progress was not without its setbacks for the friars in general and for Fr John in particular. The violent attacks on Fr O'Rourke and Fr Colgan, as noted earlier, were doubtless a considerable shock to the community. It may well be that Colgan never fully recovered. From his earliest days as a young Carmelite in Rome, as Provincial from 1843 until 1846, until his appointment as Assistant General, he enjoyed the highest repute and confidence of the authorities in Rome.[13] However, after taking up the office of Assistant General at Traspontina in late 1850, he was complained of as causing serious problems for the community friary there, including calumniating his confreres.[14] Upon his return to Dublin, during the provincialate of Thomas Bennett, his conduct caused the latter great anxiety and, by 1856, both Archbishop Cullen and Bennett wondered if he suffered from 'insanity'. For Bennett and his Whitefriar Street community, the problem was solved when Colgan left Ireland to become a parish priest *'somewhere in England'*.[15]

The other victim of that 1850 attack, Edward O'Rourke, did not too long survive it. A highly-regarded friar of great erudition and gentleness, he had become Prior in Whitefriar Street from 1849 but had been obliged to resign that position in the wake of the assault. Aged fifty-nine at the time of the attack, he died on 2nd February 1855 at the age of sixty-four. Upon resigning, his position as Prior was taken up by Andrew Day. Like John Spratt, Day had entered the Order in Spain, and on returning to Ireland five years later, in 1829, he was assigned to

---

11. *FJ*, 22nd Oct 1870.
12. O'Dwyer, *Irish Carmelites*, p. 227.
13. Ibid, pp. 185, 188, 195, 202-3, 208-11, 213, 218.
14. Ibid, p. 222.
15. Ibid, p. 227.

**Fig 81.**   *Lord Cloncurry's estate at Lyons, Co. Kildare.*

Dublin, just as Spratt's term as Prior of Whitefriar Street was coming to its close. Only twenty-five at that time, he became Spratt's closest friend in that community. Day, in turn, became Prior there in 1840, but he suffered much with ill-health. His own great wish was to pursue his Carmelite vocation as a priest to Irish emigrants in the United States of America, but this was not to be: he died aged forty-nine in December 1853. His requiem Mass was conducted by Fr John as chief celebrant, on that Christmas Eve. It was recorded at the time that, at that High Mass, Spratt was *'most evidently poignantly afflicted for the loss of Mr Day whom he regarded with intense affection'.*[16] It was a particularly impressive funeral in which some sixty carriages, plus a procession of mourners on foot, moved from Whitefriar Street through Stephen's Green and on to Townsend Street, past the house where Day had been born, before wending its way to Glasnevin where Spratt again officiated.[17]

The year 1853 was not a good one for Fr John with the loss of friends and supporters. In the month before Day's demise, Fr John, and Ireland, lost the esteemed philanthropist, Cloncurry.[18] The foremost of Spratt's charitable supporters over a wide range of causes from

16.   *FJ*, 27th Dec 1853.
17.   A submission made by regular clergy, as required by the terms of the Catholic Relief Act of 1829, has an entry for Day stating that he had been born in Taghmon, Co. Wexford. O'Dwyer follows this source in his *Irish Carmelites*, pp. 196, 246, n. 127, citing R. Walsh, OP, 'A List of Regulars Registered in Ireland (1829), in *Archivium Hibernicum*, III, 34-86. However, the *Freeman's Journal*, cited above, states that he had been born in Townsend Street, Dublin.
18.   Valentine Lawless, Lord Cloncurry (1773-1853), one-time United Irishman, later a supporter of Catholic Emancipation and of Repeal, and an enthusiast for agricultural improvement on his estate at Lyons, Co  Kildare.

the 1840s, he and Spratt had known each other from at least 1830.[19] Cloncurry admired Spratt's work for education, temperance, famine relief and political reconciliation.[20] An ardent opponent of proselytism and sectarianism, Cloncurry on one occasion asked Spratt to investigate suggestions of proselytism on the part of a clergyman in the Coombe Charitable Hospital, a body Cloncurry supported with donations.[21] He was a frequent contributor to Spratt's various enterprises, beginning with St Peter's Orphan Society in 1840.[22] Cloncurry's funeral, intended to have been a private one, proved far from that when Spratt was among the prominent personalities who turned up in carriages at Maretimo, Blackrock, Co. Dublin, and accompanied the funeral party from there to Cloncurry's estate at Lyons, Co. Kildare.[23]

*Losses – familial*

Far less publicly lamented and little noticed was the death, in February 1853, of Fr John's own brother, Michael. He passed away, *'after a long and painful illness'*, at No. 15 North Anne Street, Dublin, and therein lies a sorry tale. There were no details of any kind regarding his funeral, nor of his place of burial, but it is now known that he was buried in Glasnevin Cemetery, in what became a family plot.[24] Even when recording his death, the sole press report erred in stating his age as fifty-five: he was, in fact, sixty-one, having been baptised on 16th September 1792. Michael and Fr John had been side by side in various charitable and political engagements from the early 1820s to the middle of the 1840s. As earlier noted, Michael had suffered bankruptcy, brief

19. They were both involved in the campaign to secure financial support for O'Connell's lieutenant, 'Honest' Jack Lawless: see *FJ*, 3rd Feb 1830.
20. See, for example, *FJ*, 1st June 1848, 14th Apr 1849 and W. J. Fitzpatrick, *The life, times and contemporaries of Lord Cloncurry*, Dublin 1855, pp. 512, 527, 536, and O'Dwyer, *Irish Carmelites*, pp. 226, 250.
21. *DWN*, 14th April 1855. See also W. J. Fitzpatrick, *The Life, Times and Contemporaries of Lord Cloncurry*, p. 574, Cloncurry to Spratt, 1st March 1852. A search of *Thom's Directory* of the decade has not indicated the names of the Coombe Hospital chaplains so the identity of "Rev Mr S" remains unclear. It may have been the Rev Mr Stone, Adelaide Hospital chaplain involved in the affair of the French patient, Henri Roebet: see Chapter Fifteen.
22. *FJ*, 10th Nov 1840.
23. *FJ*, 2nd Nov 1853.
24. Thanks to the assistance of the Glasnevin Cemetery historian, Conor Dodd, and Director, George McCullough.

imprisonment for debt and the loss of the family home in the later 1830s. Misfortune remained his companion thereafter. He had tried his hand at auctioneering, but evidently without success as he was soon bankrupted again: in September 1843 he was summoned to appear before the Insolvent Debtors Court, as *'auctioneer, commission agent and accountant'*.[25] In the later 1840s, Michael secured employment as clerk to the North Dublin Union Workhouse, possibly through Fr John's good offices.[26] By now he was on a downward path in terms of at least five different residential locations until finally, in 1853, he was domiciled at Anne Street North.[27] Here he may have been a tenant of or have been accommodated by the noted Irish Chartist leader and wool merchant, Patrick O'Higgins, an irony since his younger brother, Fr John, was a strong opponent of the Chartists and their attempts to organise in Dublin.[28] He parted company with his North Dublin Union Workhouse employers and became Master of the Naas Union Workhouse, in the autumn of 1849. Described in the local Kildare press as *'brother to the Rev Dr Spratt'*, he produced *'testimonials of the highest possible character'*, and was duly appointed Master by a large majority vote of the Board.[29]

25. At one point during this phase of his career, he was claiming to auction the finest of fine art. His auction notices included references to 'specimens from the most admired masters of the Flemish and Italian Schools' and to the 'sale of a splendid collection of Pictures...of the most esteemed Ancient and Modern Artists...the Collection includes a splendid Picture by Carravassio [sic], St John Preaching in the Wilderness': see *FJ*, 19th Jan, 25th March, 18th April 1841; see also *DMR*, 18th April 1840, where he represents himself as auctioneer for properties in the Dolphin's Barn area of the city.

26. *FJ*, 1st July 1847: in this notice he appeared as secretary to the Finance Committee of the North Dublin Union, and in *FJ*, 15th Jan 1848, as secretary to the Union's Fever Hospital in Drumcondra, involved in inviting tenders for meat supplies.

27. He had lived in Cork Street until 1838. Over 1839 and 1840 he lived in the erstwhile comfort of a deteriorating Crumlin House. No home address has been found for him over 1841 to 1843 when he was listed as having his auctioneer's office at 19 Upper Ormond Quay. From 1844 to 1849 he lived at Triton Terrace, Sandymount, and over 1850 and 1851 he was listed at 41 Aungier Street. From there he moved in 1852 to 20 Richmond Place, Summerhill.

28. Pettigrew & Oulton's, and *Thom's Directories*, 1830s to 1850s. O'Higgins had an extensive property, richly furnished, and with wool warehouses in its back yards, located at the same 15 North Anne Street address where Michael stayed. O'Higgins died in October 1854 and the house was vacant for two years after this. For O'Higgins's death, and the auction of his goods, see *DWN*, 14th Oct 1854; *DDE*, 20th Jan 1855.

29. *Leinster Express*, 6th Oct 1849.

**Fig 82.** *Michael Spratt's Headstone, the inscription reads:*
*Erected by Michael Thomas Spratt in memory of his beloved Father, Michael*
*Spratt, Late of Cork St, Dublin, who died Feb 19th 1853, aged 59 years.*
*Also in memory of Susan, the beloved wife of the above named Michael*
*Thomas Spratt, who died in Childbirth Dec 29th 1861, aged 30 years.*
*Requiescant in pace.*

Unfortunately, the subsequent record did not bear out the promise of
the testimonials. In July 1850 the Naas Union Workhouse porter, Peter
Shaughnessy, accused Michael Spratt of being out late at night and
of arriving back to the Workhouse intoxicated. The Board accepted
Michael's version of events.[30] However, he was in trouble again a few
months later. He had been ordered to produce two solvent securities;
upon failing to do so within the two weeks allotted for this, he resigned
on 5th October 1850, ahead of dismissal. It seems that he never again
secured gainful employment. Less than a month before his death, the
unfortunate man was cited to appear at the Insolvent Debtors Court
for 15th January 1853.[31] He died, presumably in poverty, in North
Anne Street, on 15th February.[32] What happened to his widow, Anne,

30. Naas Board of Guardians, *Minute Book*, 20th July 1850. I am grateful to Mario
    Corrigan and James Durney of Kildare Library and Archives for locating this
    information.
31. *FJ*, 22nd Dec 1852; *General Advertiser for Dublin*, 8th Jan 1853.
32. The headstone, in Glasnevin Cemetery, erected at the request of his son, Michael
    Thomas Spratt, contains several inaccuracies, including the date of death as 19th
    February 1855. It was erected sometime after 1861, probably when Michael
    Thomas had already gone to New Zealand: see *Appendix 7: Michael Thomas Spratt
    (1825-1885)*.

and the family thereafter is not certain.[33]  In 1868 she went to live with her youngest son, John, at Eldon Terrace, Harold's Cross, and it was here that she died, on 27th October 1870, at the age of seventy-two.[34] She was buried beside her husband in Glasnevin Cemetery, within a stone's throw of the O'Connell Circle, where Michael's more fortunate and more famous brothers, Frs John and James, would eventually lie.

### Sister Mary John of the Cross

For John and James, the death of Michael was not their only loss in the 1850s.  Their sister, Catherine, at the age of fifty-six, had entered the Carmelite convent of Our Blessed Lady of the Assumption, in Firhouse, County Dublin, on 8th June 1856.  She was solemnly professed as Sister

Mary John of the Cross on 15th October 1857 but passed away only two years after entering, on 11th October 1858.[35]  Although she had been the member of an enclosed Order, her passing was widely noticed and marked with full and public obsequies.  Her *'amiability of disposition, piety and zeal, endeared her to everyone who had the happiness of knowing her'*.  John Spratt's friends, Bishop Whelan of Bombay and Bishop O'Connor of Saldes, presided, along with Dean Meyler of St Andrew's,

**Fig 83.**   *Headstone of Sister Mary John Spratt at Firhouse Carmelite Convent.*

33.  Immediately after his death she may have gone to live with her children at Wharton Terrace, Harold's Cross.  She herself is listed as living there in 1857 but, interestingly, in 1853 the eldest son, Michael Thomas, was living at that address.  Anne Spratt was at this same address until 1861, but not listed so thereafter.  However, her son, John Spratt, and his family lived in Harold's Cross, at No. 6 Parnell Place, from 1861 to 1866.  In 1867 he was listed at No. 14 Middle Parnell Place but, in the next year he moved to No. 5 Eldon Terrace, Harold's Cross, where Anne Spratt joined him.  For the life of their eldest son, Fr John's nephew, see *Appendix 7*.

34.  Registry of Births, Marriages and Deaths: Death Certificate of Anne Spratt, widow of Michael Spratt, tanner; registered 5th Nov 1870; also *FJ*, 29th Oct 1870.

35.  Archives of the Carmelite Monastery, Firhouse: information courtesy of Sr Breda, 19th Nov 2013.

Westland Row. Fr John himself was High Priest at the Requiem Mass. His brother, Fr James and most of John's Carmelite brothers of Whitefriar Street, attended the solemn occasion. The detail of the press coverage was in stark contrast to the sparse reporting of Michael's death five years before.[36]

Friar John lost other friends to death or departure in these years too. One of his most steadfast supporters, Fr Matthew Flanagan, passed away in April 1856. A curate of St Catherine's for eighteen years, before becoming parish priest of St Nicholas of Myra in Francis Street for another thirty, Spratt would have known him as the effective founder and secretary of the Catholic Book Club from 1824. He was as generous as he was rich and gave ready support to many of Spratt's charitable and educational ventures. It was indicative of the closeness of their friendship that Fr Flanagan made Friar John the executor of his will.[37] Another loss came with the departure from Dublin of the scholar, schoolmaster, teetotaller and nationalist, Martin A Brennan, who had soldiered side by side with Spratt in so many campaigns. At the very end of the 1850s Brennan gave up his Bolton Street Academy and moved back to the west of Ireland to found and edit *The Connaught Patriot*. Spratt organised and chaired a farewell dinner in his honour. His departure must have been a keen loss to the Carmelite, especially in his campaign for temperance.[38]

**Fig 84.** *Portrait of Fr Matthew Flanagan in St Nicholas of Myra Church.*

---

36.  *FJ, EF*, 14th Oct, 1858; *DEP, Newry Examiner, CT, WFJ*, 16th Oct 1858. The national press only carried a single, very brief notice of Michael's death, namely three lines in the *Freeman's Journal*, with no reference to his clerical relatives: see *FJ*, 21st Feb 1853.
37.  *FJ*, 28th April, 12th Aug 1856.
38.  *DWN*, 20th Aug, 24th Dec 1859.

*The Consolations of History*

Despite such losses, defeats and relentless commitments, the friar found time in the 1850s for the pursuit of some leisure and some vanity. During these hectic years he exhibited a considerable interest in history and historical artefacts. He became a member of the Irish Ecclesiological Society founded, in 1849, to promote the study of Christian antiquities and to encourage the practice of ecclesiastical architecture.[39] Fr John was a notable finder of antiquarian treasure and was not laggard in communicating the excitement of his discoveries. His rescuing and restoration of the Virgin of Dublin was but the best-known of his contributions in this regard. On another occasion he discovered, in the lumber room of Christ Church Cathedral, a small statue of St Laurence O'Toole, carved in Irish oak and allegedly bearing a likeness to the saint. Spratt maintained that it once *'occupied an honourable place'* in the Cathedral, and he found it together with what he thought was an old tabernacle belonging to the Cathedral. In November 1853 he offered the statue to Archbishop Cullen: it is not evident if Dr Cullen took up the offer or what happened to the statue subsequently.[40] In sequence, this was the third of three historic statues that he unearthed. Three years before this, he revealed that he had come into possession of an ancient Madonna and Child, a carved artefact, found at Donabate in north Dublin. So he informed the Royal Irish Academy, in June 1850, when he made a present of it to them. This was accompanied by a square-shaped antique bell uncovered from the site of an ancient ruin in Kildare when the foundations for a new chapel were being laid down.[41]

---

39. *Wexford Independent*, 26th May 1849; *DWN*, 17th Nov 1849; *FJ*, 7th Feb 1851. The co-founder and honorary secretary of the Society was J. J. McCarthy, the architect responsible for the major extension to Whitefriar Street Church over 1857-59.

40. DDA, *Cullen Papers*, 325/8/147, Spratt to Cullen, 10th November 1853. Inquiries of St Laurence O'Toole Church, Seville Place, and of the Pro-Cathedral indicated no present-day knowledge of the statue's whereabouts. The offer from Spratt came exactly two years after he had preached a panegyric on St Laurence O'Toole before Archbishop Cullen, in the church of the same name. See P. MacSuibhne, *Paul Cullen and his contemporaries*, Naas 1965, vol. 2, p. 106.

41. *The Advocate, or Irish Industrial Journal*, 26th June 1850; *DWR*, 29th June 1850, letter from Dr Todd, honorary secretary of the Royal Irish Academy.

**Fig 85.** *The Blessed Stone, currently located in St Audeon's.*

*Blessed Stone, Lucky Stone*

Apart from the Virgin of Dublin, his best-known discovery was that of 'The Blessed Stone', also known as The Ancient Sculptured Stone of St Owen's – or St Audeon's. Carved from hard granite, measuring 3 feet 5 inches long, 1 foot 10 inches wide and 5 inches deep, it bore two sculptured crosses, each enclosed within a circle. From ancient times it had stood in Owen's Lane, leading through St Audeon's Arch, from Cornmarket to Cook Street, at the base of the tower near to the western door of St Audeon's Church.[42] In 1826, when the church was undergoing repairs, the Blessed Stone was taken up and, according to one account, was supposedly deposited by workmen in a yard in Cook Street for a number of years, until they later alerted Fr John to the object and thereby it came into his possession.[43] An alternative account suggests that once removed, it was taken home by a tradesman in search of better luck in his business but, after twenty years, he belatedly thought the better of it and suddenly it reappeared at the entrance of the newly-erected Catholic Church in High Street. This account, by the

---

42. *The Irish Builder*, 1st July 1886, p. 190.
43. *FJ*, 17th Aug 1853.

antiquarian writer, W F Wakeman, records an interview he had with Fr Spratt shortly before the latter's death, in which the friar told how he had come across the Stone in its new location and sought permission to have it removed to the Whitefriar Street friary, pending restoration.[44] Having secured the Stone, Fr John sought the opinion of the Royal Irish Academy antiquarian, George Petrie. The latter deemed it a sepulchral monument of a type *which are now rarely to be met with in Ireland*', of a *very early Christian age*' and much older than the church beside which it used to stand.[45]  It was also known as 'The Lucky Stone' because sellers of small wares used to visit it daily to seek good luck in their business by kissing the Stone, from which practice, it was alleged, a portion of it had become smooth and polished.[46] This artefact had an interesting later history.  In 1855 Spratt's hopes were that the object might be cleaned up and mounted on a granite pedestal and erected in a prominent place in Glasnevin Cemetery; so reported *The Dublin Builder*, many years later, and added:

> probably adjacent to the new Mortuary Chapel which was then in contemplation to be erected after a design by the late Dr Petrie who, we may venture to suppose, designed the plan for Dr Spratt as the best means of preserving the Stone. And for that reason, Dr Spratt intended having the following suitable inscription, which he had written, inserted on the pedestal:

This Interesting Relic
of remote antiquity, which, according to tradition
marked, the grave of an early Irish
Saint, formerly stood near the ancient
Parish Church of St Audeon, Dublin, and
from time immemorial was called The Blessed
Stone. It was carefully preserved by the
Very Rev Dr Spratt of this city, and in
the year 1855, presented by him to the Catholic
Cemetery Board who have erected it on this
handsome and substantial pedestal.

---

44.   *WFJ*, 23rd July 1887, reprinted from *The Evening Telegraph*, No. XXVIII in a series on 'Old Dublin', by W. F. Wakeman.

45.   *The Dublin Builder*, 6th June 1859, George Petrie to John Spratt, 21st October 1853.

46.   *The Irish Builder*, 15th Aug 1886, p. 235.

**Fig 86.** *An image of the pedestal for the Blessed Stone, designed by Spratt, in* Scrapbook A.

Whether Spratt offered it to the Glasnevin authorities in 1855 and had his offer declined, or whether he simply procrastinated in making that offer is not certain. In either case, the intention was not realised. Instead, it appears that he had the Stone inserted into an outer wall of Whitefriar Street Church, in some kind of niche. There it remained, as Wakeman described it, *'as one of Dr Spratt's antiquarian treasures'*, and *'unquestionably the oldest form of Christian Cross known to this country'*.[47] The editor of *The Irish Builder*, recalling a discussion with the Carmelites of Whitefriar Street in 1884, was told that they recollected the Stone's being set into the wall near the door which entered their vestry from the Community House in Aungier Street. He added that:

> in a short time previous to our visit, when the church was undergoing exterior repairs, the walls of the vestry were plastered on the outside with a thick coat of cement, covering over the Stone also. It appears the plastering over the Stone was done accidentally as all were ignorant of what it was and why it should be placed there.[48]

---

47. *WFJ*, 23rd July 1887, reprinted from *The Evening Telegraph*, No. XXVIII in a series on 'Old Dublin'.
48. *The Irish Builder*, 1st July 1886, p. 190.

Confusingly, this account is not consistent with that given by the same journal just one month later when it records that in the October after John Spratt's death, in 1871, his executor and his solicitor came upon the draft inscription among his papers. With it were his instructions that the Stone should be removed from where he had had it erected outside the wall of Whitefriar Street Church. On 18th October 1871 the executor had the Stone removed to Glasnevin Cemetery and in 1886 it was still deposited in the Cemetery weigh-house.[49] In the same year, the *Irish Builder* reported that the old disused graveyard of St Audeon's was being cleaned up and converted by the Open Spaces Committee of Dublin Corporation into a *'pleasure ground'*. The journal's editor suggested that the Stone ought to be brought back and erected on this new recreational site. It was a suggestion, it felt, Dr Spratt would have heartily approved as a means of preserving what he had called *'an interesting relic of remote antiquity'*.[50] It did not happen thus, and seven years later, the medical doctor, E McDowell Cosgrave, bemoaned this failure and called for a movement to have the Stone erected there: the *Irish Builder* editor supported him in this and, in October 1893, commented:

> We have seen this stone in an out-office at Glasnevin Cemetery, and we hope that an effort will be at once made for its transfer to the vicinity of its original *locale*.[51]

What happened in the years since is not fully clear but, eventually, in the 1990s, it was restored to its original home at St Audeon's.[52]

Apart from his dealings with the Academy, Fr John was in communication with the Kilkenny Antiquarian Society in these years. In June 1855 he wrote to them about the 'Blessed Stone', enclosing a text on the subject which he had previously published in *Duffy's Fireside Magazine* in 1854, where his article also carried a woodcut image of the object.[53] He came back to the Kilkenny Antiquaries in 1856 when he donated *"one of those curious antique stone articles commonly called 'stone*

---

49. Ibid, 15th Aug 1886, p. 235.
50. *The Irish Builder*, 15th Aug 1886, pp. 235-6.
51. Ibid, 1st Oct 1893, p. 219.
52. It can now be viewed in St Audeon's Church at the Visitors' Centre.
53. *Duffy's Fireside Magazine*, vol. iv, 1854, p. 46.

**Fig 87.**    *An example of a 'bulla' or leaden seal of Pope Gregory IX, one of which was donated to the National Museum by Spratt.*

*chalices', but by others supposed to be crude lamps"*. This was found near the old church of Carrigacurra, Holywood, Co. Wicklow, and with it he donated a small, square, ancient Irish bronze bell, found in the ruins of the famous White Abbey Church in Kildare.[54] Finally, in 1858, he featured twice in the Society's publications: first, when he donated what he called "Wilson's Dublin Tradesman's token", found in an ancient well in Aungier Street; and then, more substantially, a 'bulla' or leaden seal of Pope Gregory IX, found by workmen opening a sewer *'within the precincts of the Cathedral Church of the Blessed Trinity, Dublin'*. The bulla, or seal, had been appended to a papal document dated between the years 1227 and 1238 and bore, on one side, the bearded heads of Saints Peter and Paul, and on the other, the name of the Pope.[55]

It seems that he did not donate every artefact that he acquired. Apart from the history of his possession of the "Blessed Stone", Wakeman records that when he met Spratt before May 1871, the friar showed

---

54. *Journal of the Kilkenny and South East of Ireland Antiquarian Society*, vol. 1, n. s., 1856-7, part ii, 1857, *Proceedings and Papers*, p. 358. These are now known as cresset-stones, for which see M. J. Moore, 'Irish Cresset-Stones', *Journal of the Royal Society of Antiquaries of Ireland*, vol. 114, 1984, pp. 98-116. I am grateful to Ms Isabella Mulhall of the National Museum of Ireland for identifying some of Spratt's artefact finds of the 1850s: it would seem that he donated some of these varied items to the Royal Irish Academy who subsequently gave them into the keeping of the National Museum.

55. Ibid, vol. 2, n. s., part 1, 1858, p. 62, and p. 201.

him parts of a bishop's mitre and a couple of ecclesiastical finger rings, found by labourers when they were excavating the floor or ground of Christ Church Cathedral. They believed that these items had belonged to an Archbishop of Dublin, Dúnán (Donatus) who held office from 1074 to 1084, or else Donngus (also Donatus) who occupied that office from 1095 to 1121.[56] Fr John's interest in such matters of the past was further borne out by his own heavily annotated copy of Archdall's *Monasticon hibernicum* into which he inserted relevant newspaper cuttings and personal notes. Indeed, his interest in history was evident in the copious newscuttings relating to the 1798 Rebellion, and relating also to the history of the Carmelite Order from medieval times. There is also one suggestion that he had had *'a zeal for the old language...surpassed only by that for religion and temperance'*, a suggestion that came from the pen of his old friend, Martin A O'Brennan, in his book, *Ancient Ireland.*[57]

*Projecting self – portraits and titles*
Spratt's antiquarian publications in the 1850s served not only to call attention to the past, but, it may be suggested, to himself. His critics sometimes characterised him as attention-seeking, and it is hard to avoid the surmise that, with all his sterling qualities, he was a vain man. It is notable that when Martin O'Brennan produced his first book, *Ancient Ireland*, in June 1855, he wrote a fulsome dedication to Fr John that is worth reproducing at length:

> I take leave to dedicate to you, whose friendship it has been my pride to enjoy for many years, this poor effort of my pen...I have selected the name of one, whose untiring exertions in the cause of charity and temperance have ranked him among the greatest benefactors of the human family. It is not titles or riches that confer elevation...It is moral worth conferred dignity; not dignity, worth. In you I behold this worth which, in my mind, constitutes the great and good man...

It is little wonder, therefore, that when it came to subscriptions for the

---

56. *WFJ*, 23rd July 1887, W. F. Wakeman, 'Old Dublin', 'The Blessed or Lucky Stone, now in Glasnevin Cemetery'.

57. M. A. O'Brennan, *Ancient Ireland*, Dublin 1855, 'Dedication'. Brennan had changed his name to O'Brennan in the course of the 1850s.

book, Fr John far surpassed all other subscribers by putting himself down for eight copies.

Of all the Irish Carmelites between 1800 and 1870, he is the only one whose image has come down to us in diverse and multiple forms. Flattering images are to be found in the pages of his scrapbooks and he was not averse to having his likeness reproduced more than once. In 1853 the lithographer, William Forster of Crow Street, embarked upon a series of *'eminent Catholic divines'* and had already commissioned and completed *'a portrait of the Very Rev Dr Spratt'*: even though Forster said it himself, it was *'an admirable and beautifully executed likeness of this amiable and respected clergyman'*. The *Freeman's Journal* was suitably impressed: *'we have rarely seen a better lithograph portrait'*.[58] There are at least four lithograph portraits, created at different times, in addition to portraits in oils and a bust. One of these portraits was completed in the later 1850s by Joseph Crowley, RHA, and was exhibited at the Royal Hibernian Academy in 1858, the year after Crowley's death.[59] A bust of the friar, by whom commissioned is unknown, had been completed and exhibited in the Academy in 1866 by the eminent sculptor, James Cahill, and for long lay unclaimed in the sculptor's studio, awaiting its purchaser.[60]

All of them, if flattering, had something to be flattering about, since their subject was handsome, engaging and famous.[61] If there may have

---

58.  *FJ*, 13th Dec 1853.
59.  I am grateful to Dr Eileen Kane for researching and sharing this information. There were two other portraits in oils but it is not certain if they were completed during Spratt's lifetime: one was commissioned for the Sick & Indigent Roomkeepers Society where it hung in its Castle Street premises for almost a century, and the other was displayed in his St Joseph's Night Refuge and is now in the keeping of the Sisters of Mercy in Baggot Street: this latter information was kindly supplied by Mr John McEvoy, Projects Officer, of Sophia Housing, Cork Street, Dublin.
60.  Cahill was the creator of the renowned statue of O'Connell in Ennis, as also of busts of Spratt's associates, Dr Thomas Hayden and Sir William Wilde, the latter being a noted patron of Cahill's work, for which see P. Murphy, 'James Cahill (1832-90)', in P. Murphy, ed., *Art and Architecture of Ireland*, vol. 3, *Sculpture, 1600-2000*, pp. 58-9.
61.  See R. M. Elmes, *Catalogue of Engraved Irish Portraits*, Dublin 1975, p. 188. See also National Library of Ireland, main catalogue. The first Forster lithograph is not dated in Elmes nor in the NLI catalogue, but it clearly dates from 1853, as the *Freeman's Journal* so reports it. Another, by T. H. Ellis of London, entitled *The Very Rev Dr Spratt, D.D., V.Provincial of the Carmelite Order*, is dated 1869: see Elmes, p. 188. The remaining two, *Yours faithfully and truly, John Spratt, D.D.*, by Forster, Crow Street Dublin, and *John Spratt, D.D., President of the Irish Total Abstinence Society, Dublin*, also by Forster, are undated. The lithographs are in the National Library of Ireland.

been in the Forster lithograph of 1853 a suggestion of its subject's self-satisfaction, it is perhaps understandable: within polite Dublin society Spratt was in demand. In July 1850, for example, he was one of the honoured guests at the Lord Mayor's banquet, at which he said the Grace,[62] and continued to be an invited guest at these banquets throughout the 1850s and 1860s.[63] In 1855 the new Lord Lieutenant, George Howard, 7th Earl of Carlisle, invited him to dinner at the Viceregal Lodge.[64] Spratt was not tardy in cultivating the great. In a personal capacity he would

**Fig 88.** *Lord Lieutenant George Howard.*

send congratulations to incoming Priors General of the Order, and sent a letter of condolence to the Marchioness Wellesley upon bereavement, to which he received a two-page response of appreciation.[65]

Within the Whitefriar Street community in particular and the international Order of Calced Carmelites in general he had, by the mid-1850s, acquired an unofficial status of some eminence and authority. Regardless of who may have been Prior or Prior Provincial, Spratt was their best-known personality. He was the one who transacted their property dealings and building expansion in that decade, as well as being the one who most recognisably fought their public battles for Catholicism. During the long time when Fr Thomas Bennett was Provincial, from 1852 to 1863, he accomplished a great deal for the Order. However he was also heavily engaged with his role as founder-

62. *FJ*, 10th July 1850.
63. See for example, *FJ*, 24th Jan 1854, 20th Feb 1857, 21st Feb 1860, 8th Feb 1861, 5th Feb 1862, 27th Jan 1865, 20th Feb 1867.
64. GMA, Box 78, Aide-de-Camp of Lord Lieutenant to Spratt, 5th July 1855.
65. GMA, Box 56, *Scrapbook A*, Marchioness of Wellesley to Spratt, 6th March 1852.

manager of his Dominick Street Academy, and equally in his role as Professor, Vice-President, from 1856, and then President, from 1861, of All Hallows College. In these circumstances, Fr Bennett was not the most assiduous correspondent with either the Order's General or with the authorities in the Holy See. Spratt increasingly filled that partial vacuum. As O'Dwyer points out, *from 1855 he was the member of the Province who had most dealings with the General*.[66]

Fr John, it proved, was no more averse to titles than to portraits. His proclivity in this regard from 1829 to the end of the 1840s has been noted earlier, and nothing changed in this regard in the 1850s. In July 1855 he received from the Prior General, Jerome Priori, *'the attestation of the esteem which I acknowledge towards you'*. He added:

> Your zeal, the great good which you do for the young, all these things suggest to me a means to show you the esteem in which I hold you and the only means is that of the Laurea…Finally, I rejoice at the beautiful manner you write so well our Italian language…I salute you with all my heart…[67]

Priori fulfilled his promise when, shortly after, he sent the award of the doctorate to Friar John.[68] Five years later, in 1859, Priori honoured Fr John again, this time with the award of the title, Provincial of England. This news was announced in the national press that October, and, given its wording, the announcement may well have been supplied by Spratt himself:

> We are rejoiced to learn that the religious solicitude of the most Rev Father General of the Calced Carmelite Order has reached even our shores. Anxious to promote the devotion of the faithful towards the ever-Immaculate Virgin Mary of Mount Carmel, he has appointed the Very Rev John Spratt, D.D., to the Office of Provincial of England, with all due privileges.[69]

---

66. O'Dwyer, *Irish Carmelites*, pp. 226-7.
67. DDA, *Cullen Papers*, 332/7/51, Priori to John Spratt, 13th July 1855. The letter, it seems, was sent via Fr James Spratt to John by way of Archbishop Cullen.
68. GMA, *Scrapbook A*, Priori to John Spratt, 4th Aug 1855.
69. *EF*, 5th Oct 1859, citing the *Weekly Register*, no date given.

It is curious that there is no reference to these honours in any of O'Dwyer's works on Spratt. For all that, it did not go unnoticed at the time. Spratt's Carmelite confrere of Knocktopher, Matthew Scally, who at times was in trouble with his Provincial for writing to the press without permission, could not restrain himself from offering public congratulations on Spratt's elevation to the *'high and most important office of Provincial of the Carmelites of England'*. He added that, by accepting it, *'Dr Spratt has undertaken a most serious responsibility'*, and, while the General had made *'a most judicious selection'*, Scally ended on a strangely interrogative note: *'how Dr Spratt can give effect to his position as Provincial of England demands a long consideration'*.[70] Fr Scally's long consideration came to fruit in a second letter, ten days later, when he raised the question *'Why appoint a Provincial of Carmel to a country in which the Order had not a single convent?'* He answered simply: *'Dr Spratt is destined to restore Carmel in all its glory to England'*.

Such a prospect was both very timely and exceedingly welcome to the Knocktopher Carmelite. His own friary and college there, established on 1st January 1852, had been under serious threat from Fr Bennett. The latter wanted the college closed down, even as he himself was about to found Terenure College in Dublin.[71] If Spratt succeeded in restoring the English Province from its long extinction, then, as Scally put it, *'Dr Spratt will have in Knocktopher a College in which he may educate his future apostles for the English mission of Carmel'*.[72] For John Spratt the award brought recognition from on high, at the end of an exhausting decade of devotion to multiple causes. However, after a very brief three-day visit to Spitalfields, London, to promote the temperance cause, in September 1858, he never again set foot in England and, as shall appear later, he did nothing to initiate or to support the restoration of the English Province of Carmel. Other demands would take precedence.

---

70.  *EF*, 15th Oct 1859, M. Scally, OCC., to Editor, no date given.
71.  D'Arcy, *Terenure College, 1860-2010: A History*, pp. 3, 17, 20; O'Dwyer, *Irish Carmelites*, pp. 228, 251.
72.  *EF*, 25th Oct 1859.

**Fig 89.** *Painting of Fr John Spratt currently at Whitefriar Street Church.*

**Fig 92.** *Bust of John Spratt by the eminent sculptor, James Cahill, currently situated in the Whitefriar Street Community Centre.*

**Fig 93.** *Two images of John Spratt from the Gort Muire Archives. The source is unknown.*

**Fig 94.** *Lithograph of Fr John Spratt, by Forster & Co., Crow Street, Dublin. Courtesy of the National Library of Ireland.*

**Fig 95.**  *Lithograph of Fr John Spratt, as President of the Irish Total Abstinence Society, also by Forster & Co. Courtesy of the National Library of Ireland.*

THE VERY REV. D. SPRATT, PRESIDENT OF THE
Irish Total abstinence Society.

**Fig 96.** *Lithograph of Dr John Spratt, as President of the Irish Total Abstinence Society. Courtesy of the National Library of Ireland.*

**Fig 97.** *An Irish Total Abstinence Association Pledge signed by Spratt. Image courtesy of the Irish Quaker Historical Library, Dublin. Text reads as follows:*

I voluntarily promised to abstain from all Spirituous Liquors & Intoxicating Drinks, except used medicinally & then by order of a Medical Man & to discountenance all the Causes & practices of Intemperance. I also promise to attend to my Religious Duties.

_____ has taken the Total Abstinence pledge this day of August 1845.

John Spratt, Patron.

**Fig 98.** *Wooden plaque on portrait of John Spratt in the Roomkeepers Society dates it to 1872. Courtesy of the Roomkeepers Society.*

**Fig 99.** *A leather tag identifying the statue of Our Lady of Dublin. For a translation of the text, see p. 73.*

**Fig 100.** John *Spratt kept many scrapbooks containing images, newspaper cuttings, notes and correspondence. This is* Scrapbook A *at the Gort Muire Archives.*

**Fig 101.** *The Shrine of Our Lady of Dublin in Whitefriar Street Church.*

**Fig 102.** *One of Spratt's prayer books with his name inscribed on brass clasp.*

**Fig 103.** *The breviaries of John Spratt in the Gort Muire Library.*

349

**Fig 104.** *The monument to John Spratt stands at the foot of the O'Connell monument in Glasnevin Cemetery. His vault is within the O'Connell circle. The base of the monument has four panels illustrating his life's work.*

**Fig 105.** *The front panel of the Spratt monument outlines his life and accomplishments. It reads:*

*Sacred*
*to the memory of*
*the Very Rev John Spratt D.D.*
*who departed this life on the Eve of Pentecost 1871*
*in the 75th year of his age and the 51st of his ministry.*
*He was for many years the Provincial of the Carmelite Order in Ireland.*
*It was by his exertions and under his superintendence that*
*the church of that Order was erected in Whitefriar St, AD 1826.*
*He was the vigilant guardian of St Peter's Orphanage from its foundation*
*and for upwards of forty years he was honorary secretary of the*
*Roomkeepers Society. He was one of the first to join Father Matthew*
*in the crusade against intemperance, and with Monsig. Yore continued*
*to be the champion of that Holy Warfare to the latest moments of his*
*earthly career. He was the zealous founder of St Joseph's Night Refuge,*
*Cork St, for the homeless poor, and the asylum for the Catholic female blind,*
*formerly at Portobello and now at Merrion, was one of his happiest inspirations.*
*To him the schools at Whitefriar St, male and female owe their origin and efficiency.*

**Fig 106.** *The second side illustrates The Temperance Pledge, his work with the Temperance Movement.*

**Fig 107.** *The third side shows St Joseph's Night Refuge, which he founded in 1861.*

**Fig 108.** *The fourth side shows the Carmelite Church, Whitefriar Street.*

**Fig 109.** *The oldest of the Carmelite Plots in Glasnevin Cemetery, dating from 1853.*

# CHAPTER SEVENTEEN

## *The Friar and the Fall of Donnybrook Fair, 1853-1868*

As has been seen earlier, the existence of Donnybrook Fair was increasingly an affront to the sensibility of post-Famine Ireland, even as its worst excesses seemed far in the past. This *'sink of pestilence and carnival of crime'* continued to exercise the indignation of Fr Spratt and his combative Catholic and Protestant contemporaries. Over the period 1840 to 1847 he had proven the most formidable and most persistent foe of the Fair. His largest demonstration against it had been in August 1845 and a further impressive protest followed in August 1847.[1] Thereafter came a pause in his campaign until the early 1850s when a new curate, Fr Patrick J Nowlan, came to the care of the combined Parish of Donnybrook-Irishtown. He would raise the banner of protest and soon would rouse Fr Spratt to join him in a renewed crusade against the infamy. A reforming priest of great zeal, he initiated a new attempt to end the Fair. Doggedly and successfully organising public opinion on the issue, he secured the support of Lord Mayor Joseph Boyce who summoned a public meeting to the Mansion House on Monday 14th May 1855. The aim was to create a committee to raise funds to buy out the rights of the Madden family to the revenues of the Fair. Those present constituted a social confluence of considerable clout, from the Marquis of Westmeath, through aldermen and town councillors to some of Dublin's leading social and moral crusaders of the age. Among them, inevitably, were Friar John and his teetotal ally, Haughton.

Opening the meeting, the Lord Mayor's very first observation was

---

1. See Chapter Eight.

that they aimed *'to do away with the annual nuisance of Donnybrook Fair, the burden of which every artisan must have felt'*.[2] He revealed that the present owners of the rights were willing to be bought out for £3,000, a small price to pay to end a place where *'numbers of citizens and labourers spent a large portion of their time in drinking and idleness'*. Significantly, he added

> There was scarcely a servant in any house in Dublin that had not a desire to pass a portion of the week at Donnybrook and by their connection with their fellow servants the evils resulting from the Fair were brought home to their very doors.

An edifying resolution, denouncing Donnybrook as having been for long *'the theatre of immorality, drunkenness and its concomitant evils'*, was proposed by the Marquis of Westmeath and seconded by John Spratt; a subscription list was then opened and an abolition committee appointed. This committee was notably interdenominational: it included the Church of Ireland Archdeacons of Dublin and Kildare, the Unitarian Haughton, the Congregationalist neighbour of Spratt's in York Street, Dr William Urwick[3] and their neighbouring Church of Ireland curate, Rev J J MacSorley, in addition to the Donnybrook Catholic curate, Fr Nowlan. Others included Cheyne Brady, Churchwarden of St Peter's Church of Ireland parish and William Dargan of Great Exhibition fame, in addition to the Marquis of Westmeath and the committee secretary, Stephen Radcliff Fetherston-Haugh,

**Fig 110.** *Dr William Urwick.*

2. *FJ*, 15th May 1855.

3. Interestingly, although Spratt and Urwick had worked cordially together in the temperance movement in Dublin from the early 1830s, as well as in the campaign against Donnybrook Fair in the 1850s, and would do so again into the late 1860s, there is not a single mention of Spratt in W. Urwick's monumental *The life and letters of William Urwick, D.D., of Dublin*, London 1870.

**Fig 111.** *Rev Dean Andrew O'Connell.*

city solicitor and Eccles Street neighbour of James Haughton.[4] Soon
after this, Spratt was happy to inform the Lord Mayor that Rev Dr
William Yore of St Paul's, Arran Quay, had joined the Committee and
provided his subscription *'to carry out the treaty with the proprietors of the
patent under which fairs are held at Donnybrook'.*[5] Additional support from
the clergy soon followed when the local parish priest and long-time
ally of Spratt, Rev Dean Andrew O'Connell, lent his name to the
committee. He commented:

> so convinced have I been of the evil consequences of this
> annually occurring intrusion upon the morality and quiet of this
> parish that, since my appointment to it, I have felt it my duty
> to strictly prohibit those under my spiritual jurisdiction from
> frequenting that scene of vice.[6]

The committee soon secured supplementary support from other
significant quarters. First came the all-important backing from the

4. *DEP*, 31st May 1855.
5. *SNL*, 7th June 1855, John Spratt to Lord Mayor, 6th June 1855.
6. *FJ*, 21st May 1855.

press: the *Freeman's Journal* commented editorially that there was neither commercial nor recreational need for the Fair, its importance as a market having declined and its recreational value having been superseded by cheap daily rail excursions to country and seaside.[7] Then the Commissioners of the Dublin Metropolitan Police, Colonel George Browne and John Lewis More O'Ferrall, wrote to say they wished to see the Fair abolished, having already themselves taken great pains to reduce its excesses. Generously, they enclosed £5 each.[8] Not to be outdone, the army chiefs joined in when garrison commander, Major General Falls, sent his contribution to the funds:

> from the conviction that the proposed abolition will prevent crime amongst the garrison and may materially save the non-commissioned officers and men from exposure to temptation and disgrace.[9]

More support followed in the person of Lord Downes, and then from employers on behalf of their workmen.[10] One of these, William Baxter of fashionable Grafton Street, retailer of military footwear, urged every employer in the city to induce workmen to subscribe to the fund. The men in his employment had *'in the most cheerful manner put down a subscription of one shilling each'*.[11]

With such a procession of dignity and worth, it was inevitable that the Association for Discountenancing Vice should join in. On 21st June it duly did so with a public resolution of support and a contribution of £10.[12] Within four months the requisite £3,000 had been raised and the proprietors of the revenues were accordingly bought out. By indenture dated 17th September, 1855, between the members of the Madden family on the one hand, and the trustees, led by Lord Mayor Boyce, on the other, the ancient rights to the tolls and customs, originally conferred by King John, were finally transferred for extinction.[13]

---

7. *FJ*, 17th May 1855.
8. *FJ*, 21st May 1855.
9. *FJ*, 29th May 1855.
10. *FJ*, 2nd, 9th, 14th June 1855.
11. *FJ*, 14th June 1855.
12. *FJ*, 22nd June 1855.
13. NAI, *Chief Crown Solicitor's Papers*, 1859/79. (Hereafter cited as NAI/CCS).

Congratulations now poured in from on high, and, not least, on the head of Fr John. No less a luminary than Fr Mathew, the apostle of temperance, wrote from the Imperial Hotel on 10th August 1855 to congratulate the people of Dublin *'on the total removal of that moral plague-spot, Donnybrook Fair'*. He went on to include praise of the Carmelite friar, whom, not many years before, he had censured:

> this most necessary event was, with the Divine assistance, effected by the united efforts of your worthy Mayor, Very Rev Dr Spratt, *my dearest friend*, the universally respected James Haughton Esq and many other benevolent personages.[14]

Praise more direct for Friar John came from further afield. Writing from Liverpool, one Moses Cullen observed:

> Sir,
> I am glad to find that the great national nuisance, Donnybrook Fair, has at last been abated…I have for the last twenty-five years witnessed the unceasing efforts of the good Dr Spratt regarding this fair. He had seen the misery it produced and he laboured zealously to combat – and thank God he has been successful and his efforts are now perfected.[15]

However, perhaps the praise he would most have welcomed was that which came, without naming him directly, from the Archbishop and Apostolic Delegate, Dr Paul Cullen. In a letter of 15th August to his clergy, he expressed *'sincere delight'* at the *'measures adopted to suppress the Fair'*:

> Everyone acquainted with the city is aware that that Fair, to say nothing of the loss of time and other temporal considerations, was the occasion of innumerable offences against God: that riotousness, drunkenness, debauchery and profligacy of every kind prevailed to an awful extent and seemed to walk in it in triumph.[16]

---

14. *CT*, 18th Aug 1855 (Italics mine).
15. *CT*, Moses Cullen to Editor, letter dated 15th Aug 1855.
16. *FJ*, 20th Aug 1855.

At the same time, the two commissioners of the Dublin Metropolitan
Police, having seen their £10 contribution bearing fruit, now issued a
notice stating that they

> will not permit any hackney car stand in any of the streets of
> Donnybrook or in any place adjacent thereto. No crowd or
> assemblage of persons will be allowed on the Green. All public
> houses will be visited by the police and restricted to legal hours.[17]

The Fair, it seemed, had at last been abolished.

*Resurrection*

Amid all these grave expressions of support and approval from on high,
only two small voices managed to squeak in slight notes of disbelief
or protest. One, signing himself 'An Artizan', wrote to the *Freeman's
Journal* on 23rd August 1855, to reject the idea that those who resorted
to Donnybrook Fair were bad characters and claimed that this was a
slur on himself and on the many thousands of artisans who were used
to going there and who were determined to uphold *'the only remnant of
amusement left to them'*.[18] Even before this letter, while the authorities were
rejoicing, one J.L.D. of Donnybrook wrote to express astonishment
that anyone could call the fair *'a moral plague-spot'*: this, in itself, was a
slur on the police, since neither crime nor outrage had been perpetrated
in the previous sixteen years. He took issue seriously with *'the reverend
and other gentlemen'* who subscribed largely for *'what they call the general
good without having consulted any of us on the matter'*, and whose actions
now threatened the welfare of local people who obtained a living from
the Fair. He ended by throwing down the gauntlet: he invited Dublin
friends to continue to pay their annual visit, *'as we have ample space on our
licensed premises to entertain and comfortably accommodate the public generally'*.[19]
This J.L.D. was one Joseph Dillon, none other than the nephew of John
Madden who had died in 1850 and whose heirs had sold off the rights
to the abolition committee. A public house-owner of Donnybrook
village, Dillon had been the effective organiser of the Fair since the

17.   *FJ*, 25th Aug 1855.
18.   *FJ*, 23rd Aug 1855.
19.   *FJ*, 15th Aug 1855.

**Fig 112.** *Donnybrook Fair 1859, by Erskine Nichol.*

death of his uncle in 1850, and naturally was not going to take his own economic extinction quietly.[20] With his daughter, Eliza, he took up the task of reviving Donnybrook Fair. Although the Madden family interest had been bought out, there was nothing to prevent the nephew Dillon from using his own licensed premises, which included a two and a half acre field facing on to the old fair ground, from organising the animal market and the public amusements of old. To the consternation of clergy and police, this he proceeded to do. On 25th August 1855 he boldly published in the newspapers a notice of his intention to continue the Fair by accommodating it on his property. When published, this notice appeared beside that of the police in which they had announced their intention to crack down on hackney cab drivers in the area *'in consequence of the abolition of Donnybrook Fair'*.

The *Catholic Telegraph* now took issue with the *Freeman's Journal* for having dared to publish the protest letter of 23rd August from 'An Artisan', and attacked its editor for encouraging Dubliners to ignore the death sentence on the Fair, and for defying Archbishop Cullen's letter of 15th August. It also printed an epistle from Fr Spratt to the citizens. Warning against *'any unlawful attempt to perpetuate that disgraceful scene'*, Spratt commented:

---

20. NAI, *Chief Secretary's Office Registered Papers, 1859/79* (hereafter cited as NAI/ ICSORP); also *Thom's Dublin Directory for the year 1855.*

permit me to congratulate you on this most happy event. Too long hath this scandalous exhibition continued, which was called a Fair, but which might more appropriately be designated the theatre of all that was foul and disgusting...the source and scene of crime and infamy and the cause of the ruin and disgrace of millions of our people...We have, therefore, reason to rejoice that Donnybrook Fair no longer exists.

He continued with a passionate exhortation:

In order, therefore, to give no pretext for the continuance, in the slightest degree, of this annual nuisance, let all those who lay any claim to respect for themselves, or for their country, come to the solemn determination of not going near Donnybrook during the ensuing week, but to seek healthy and innocent amusements in other places.[21]

Fears for the possible resurrection of the Fair were not ill-founded: in some dismay, early in the next year, J D Fitzgerald, a legal adviser to the Irish Office in London, confirmed to Col Thomas Larcom, Undersecretary at Dublin Castle, that from the legal aspect, the abolition committee's work had been all in vain, and that some special legislation would be needed.[22]   As a consequence, in the years immediately following the apparent abolition of 1855, Dillon and his daughter Eliza continued to hold the Fair, in defiance of church and state.  For the Fair of August 1858 they had a large poster printed, entitled *Amusement for the Millions*, and, when the Police Commissioners sought advice as to its legality, they were formally advised that only some special measure could stop the Dillons.  To add insult to injury, in anticipation of the Fair of August 1859, Eliza Dillon actually wrote to the Commissioners of Police that July:

I am about holding 'the annual fair at Donnybrook'.  And in order to preserve peace and regularity I humbly require the aid and protection of the Metropolitan Police.[23]

21.  *CT*, 25th Aug 1855.
22.  NLI, *Larcom Papers*, J. D. Fitzgerald to Thomas Larcom, 16th Feb 1856.
23.  NAI, *CSORP*, 1859/79: Case to advise proceedings to prevent a repetition of the holding of a Fair at Donnybrook.

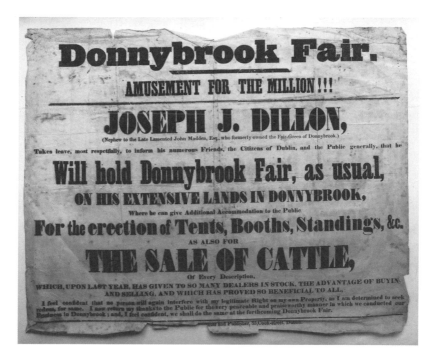

**Fig 113.** *A poster printed by Joseph Dillon advertising the Fair.*

To his chagrin, the Divisional Superintendent for the area, James McMahon, had to admit that since the Custom House records showed her licence to be for 'House and Premises', the law was not being violated by holding festivities and selling drink in the Dillon field. He had to add that, as a consequence of this loophole, every day of the Fair some 20,000 people visited the village and availed of the entertainments laid on by the Dillons in 1859; that this, in turn, required the presence of one hundred officers and men of the DMP and that *'scenes of the most demoralising nature have occurred within this enclosure'*.[24]

In response to the dilemma now posed, the legal officers of the Crown suggested that the Chief Secretary should fully support the Dublin police magistrates in refusing to renew the Dillons' licence. This proved to be the key weapon in the fight against the Dillons' efforts to preserve the Fair. On 8th November 1859, Eliza Dillon's application for a renewal of the licence came before the magistrates of College

---

24. Ibid, Superintendent James McMahon to Commissioners of the Dublin Metropolitan Police, 22nd Sept 1859.

Street Police Office. Superintendent McMahon was happy to report to the Police Commissioners that her application had been refused.[25] But, if this looked like the end of the road, it was not.

*Raising the Bar*

In the summer of 1860 Joseph Dillon published a placard announcing that Donnybrook Fair would be held this year *'as usual'*. He intended to apply for a spirit grocer's licence to replace that refused to his daughter in November 1859. Determined to thwart him, the Police Commissioners requested Dublin Castle to ask the Commissioners of Inland Revenue, in turn, to authorise their Dublin officials to refuse the issue of this licence.[26] With some misgivings Inland Revenue replied on 14th August 1860. They insisted that they had no legal authority to withhold the licence, but, given that the Dublin police request had the backing of the Lord Lieutenant of Ireland, they instructed their Dublin revenue officials *'not to grant licences without further order'*. Nervously, the London revenue authorities insisted that since they had no power to refuse Dillon *'they must therefore rely upon His Excellency's authority, in case their conduct in refusing the licence should be called in question'*.[27] The eventual result of these and further exchanges between Dublin police and Inland Revenue was that no spirituous liquors or beer (other than ginger beer) were sold in Dillon's field during the days of the Fair, and the police were able to report that the Fair passed over *'without any of the scenes of drunkenness and disorder which took place at former times'*. Still, if Dillon was partly frustrated, nevertheless the Fair was held; horses were offered for sale and bought in his field; *'four or five hundred persons of the very lowest class collected in this field each day'*; drink was served in the village public houses, and there was sufficient animation about the place for twenty eight arrests to be made for various transgressions.[28]

By the beginning of the new decade, then, the *'moral plague-spot'* was still not out. It was in these circumstances that relentless Friar John and Fr Nowlan redoubled their efforts to end the infamy. In February 1861 they wrote to the Chief Secretary of Ireland to insist that legislation was

25. NAI, *CSORP*, 1861/9340, McMahon to Commissioners, 8th Nov 1859.
26. Ibid, 1860/17819, Commissioners of Police to Undersecretary, 7th Aug 1860.
27. Ibid, William Corbett to Undersecretary, 14th Aug 1860.
28. Ibid, 1860/18577, William Campbell to Commissioners of Police, 5th Sept 1860.

absolutely necessary.[29] The government's response to their overtures, even though they were endorsed by Police Commissioner More O'Ferrall, was unhelpful. Frs Spratt and Nowlan claimed that government had promised legislation in the past and so they now requested that clauses abolishing the Fair be inserted in the Fairs and Markets Bill just then before Parliament. In response, the government claimed that this was a Bill dealing with places of business and not of amusement and that Donnybrook Fair did not fit into the former category and that, in any case, it was a police matter. Dublin Metropolitan Police Commissioner, More O'Ferrall, supported Spratt's representations and claimed that Donnybrook Fair was indeed a place of business, but to no avail.[30] The anxieties of clergy and police, therefore, remained unallayed and, a few months later, were to be intensified: on 1st July, 1861, with yet another fair in prospect, Crown Solicitor Matthew Anderson informed the Undersecretary that Eliza Dillon, whose spirit licence was successfully quashed, was about to apply for another licence for the same house and field, but was likely to use some other person's name *'in order to deceive the authorities'*. He suggested that the Commissioners of Excise refuse the licence *'if not to the person, then at least to the house and place in which such gross immorality was proved to have been practised in past years'*.[31] Next day, in reply, Corbett of the Inland Revenue in London informed Larcom, the Undersecretary, that they had ordered the refusal of *'any spirit licence for the house and premises at Donnybrook lately licensed as a public house in the name of Miss Dillon'*. Significantly, however, he added that the Revenue Commissioners pointed out that *'the course now adopted is not a legal one'*.[32] Despite this warning, the Lord Lieutenant went ahead and telegraphed Edward Steel, Acting Collector of Revenue in the Dublin Custom House, not to grant any spirit licence whatever in respect of these premises without further instruction. Four days later, when Eliza applied for a beer-dealer's licence, he also ordered that none be given to her before 31st August 1861.[33]

29. NAI, *Official Papers*, 1861/85, J. Spratt & P. J. Nowlan to E. Cardwell, 14th Feb 1861.
30. Ibid, *Official Papers*, 1861/45, Spratt & Nowlan to Cardwell, 14th Feb 1861 and J. More O'Ferrall to Larcom, 28th March 1861.
31. NAI, *CSORP*, 1861/4862, Matthew Anderson to Undersecretary, 1st July 1861.
32. Ibid, 1861/4863, William Corbett to Thomas Larcom, 2nd July 1861.
33. Ibid, 1861/17097/4997, Anderson to Larcom, 6th July 1861.

At this point both police records and the press were silent as to what actually happened at the Fair of 1861, but it seems likely that, having been refused licences, the Dillons proceeded to let other retailers of spirits and beer sell on their field. This conjecture is based on two points. Firstly, this is precisely what the Dillons did in the years after 1861 for which there is police information, as shall be seen presently; and secondly, even as the authorities themselves were acting illegally, according to Inland Revenue, moves were made to give the authorities the clout to act decisively in a legal manner: on 13th June 1862 the royal assent was given to a bill dealing with customs and excise duties.[34] Section 13 of this empowered the Revenue Commissioners to grant or to refuse an occasional licence for the sale of beer, wine, spirits or tobacco to existing licence holders at places outside their originally licensed premises. In the summer of 1862 Dillon placarded his field and gates with posters proclaiming that Donnybrook Fair would commence on 'Walking Sunday', 24th August, and that he had accommodation for tents, stands, cattle and horse trading, and for the erection of booths for the sale of drink by licensed traders. Divisional Superintendent McMahon acted immediately. He requested Inland Revenue to refuse all licences to sell drink in Dillon's field or in any field adjacent *'during the so-called Fair Week at Donnybrook'*. This request was swiftly and completely complied with. Nevertheless, despite all this, Commissioner More O'Ferrall had to admit to the Undersecretary that *'the fair has been more numerously attended this year than for some years past'*, and McMahon reported from the spot that, on Sunday 24th August 1862, Joseph Dillon had opened his field and conducted the Fair until Saturday 30th August. According to McMahon some 6,500 people visited Dillon's field to enjoy four swinging boats, two merry-go-rounds, thirteen roulette tables, twenty shooting galleries, five ginger beer stands, eleven fruit and cake stands, one tent with stuffed whale and shark, one circus, one machine for weighing men and five tents for the sale of spirits and beer. Adding to this defiance, Dillon's neighbour, publican John Lawlor, who also had a field, opened his premises for the sale of horses: and, apart from the drink on sale in Lawlor's place, three village street publicans and one just outside the village had kept music and dancing going in their pubs till eleven o'clock each night of the Fair. McMahon's officers

---

34.   25 Vict. c. 22, 3rd June 1862.

had to admit that no drink had been sold in Dillon's house or by the Dillons personally, and the Police Superintendent had to concede that *'Dillon will succeed in continuing and reviving the Fair unless his interest in the place is purchased or a legislative enactment for its abolition is passed'.*[35] Dillon had defied the authorities by getting licence holders from different parts of the city to sell their wares on his field, thereby flying in the face of the law. It proved to be a pyrrhic victory, however. He continued to hold or to organise the Fair in the succeeding years of 1863 to 1866, using different sets of publicans from widely separated parts of the city each year, but police reports recorded dwindling numbers in attendance and dwindling entertainments. Average daily attendance fell from 2,500 in the early 1860s to a mere few hundred in 1865 and 1866.

*The Vanquishing of Vice*
The symbolic climax of the conflict came in August, 1866. In that year Dillon and Donnybrook Fair vied locally with Dr Cullen and the Catholic Church for the support of the masses, resulting in a decided victory for the latter: the foundation stone for the new Church of the Sacred Heart, looking across to the old Fair Green, was laid in 1863 and the official opening for the completed edifice was set for the traditional Walking Sunday in August, 1866, the opening day of Donnybrook Fair. Thousands poured into the village on that August Sunday of 1866. The church opening ceremony was conducted by Paul Cullen and special lustre was conferred on the occasion by virtue of the fact that he had become a Cardinal a mere eight weeks before this, the first such in Irish history. The local parish priest, Dr O'Connell, had intended the church not just as a means of providing much needed extra space but as an expiatory monument for the vices and wickedness of Donnybrook Fair. On this point the press agreed with him, seeing it as *'a great landmark which will point out where vice and immorality were vanquished'.*[36] The event proved one of the most memorable and impressive of public occasions in the life of Dublin in the nineteenth century.

On that very same day, Dillon opened his field as usual in order to commence the annual festivities of Donnybrook Fair. This time he

---

35. Ibid, 1862/16948 & 17561, Superintendent McMahon to Commissioners of Police, 11th Aug & 1st Sept 1862.
36. *FJ*, 27th Aug 1866.

could only produce one licence holder willing to sell drink in the field. Divisional Superintendent, Daniel O'Donovan, reported that a good number of gamblers were amongst the crowds who came to attend the rival events, but, he added, their numbers were lessened *'by the appearance of some constables who interfered as far as possible to intimidate them'*. He admitted that this intimidation had good effect for *'their numbers grew less each day'* and that the attempt to revive the old Fair *'was a failure in toto this year'*. It was his opinion that *'the last attempt had been made'*. In this he was not quite correct: whereas, by his own admission, Joseph Dillon had finally given up the attempt,[37] two years later his daughter Eliza made one last effort: but after a few days the original *'120 persons of the lowest class'* who visited the field had fallen to a mere handful of *'horse dealers and ragged idlers who are often to be seen lolling about corners'*. In the triumphant words of Inspector Peter Fitzpatrick of the new Donnybrook Police Station, *'thus ended the great failure of the attempt to revive Donnybrook Fair'*. He had his own explanation for the failure:

> I attribute the fall of Donnybrook Fair to the absence of music in the public houses of Donnybrook and the neighbouring locality as there was not a sound of music to be heard in any public house in the whole subdivision: no doubt they all dreaded the refusal of their licences if they went against the police arrangements which were carried out effectively.[38]

Donnybrook Fair finally ended in 1868, thirteen years after its abolition had been prematurely announced. The police were not slow to take credit for its decline and fall. They had harried the hackney men, thwarted the publicans, silenced the music and intimidated the gamblers. Their Commissioners had publicly given written and financial support to this particular cause of moral reform and social control. They did this at a time when the DMP force was run with a ruthless regimen and when its average police constable was so badly paid that protest on their conditions appeared in print in the very month and year that the abolition committee thought it had won its victory, in August

37. NAI, *CSORP*, 1866/14573, Daniel O'Donovan to J. L. More O'Ferrall, 4th Sept 1866.
38. Idem.

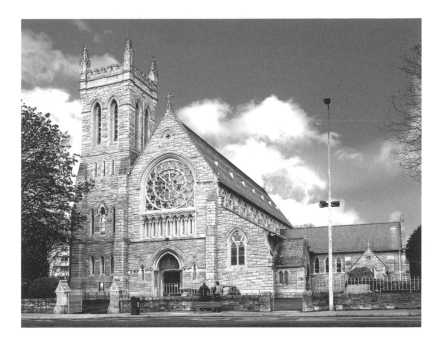

**Fig 114.** *Church of the Sacred Heart, Donnybrook.*

1855. The Police Commissioners believed they had wrought a social and moral revolution of which the Donnybrook saga was only one episode. Rough sports and popular pastimes, from bull-baiting and cock-fighting to street wrestling, and other 'excesses' were suppressed or fell into abeyance over the period 1830 to 1860 and while the police claimed credit, some of their number would concede that wider forces were at work, including those of education and religion.[39] In the case of the assault on Donnybrook Fair, it is quite clear that the command of these forces was in the hands of Cardinal Cullen, Fr P J Nowlan and Fr John Spratt. Of these three, the veteran was clearly the Carmelite friar, who was the earliest, the longest-serving and the most persistent officer of the Church militant, leading from the front, in that particular battle. It was the single most significant victory in his long war in the cause of temperance. As the *Freeman's Journal* commented:

---

39. For a fuller treatment of this, see F. A. D'Arcy, 'The decline and fall of Donnybrook Fair: Moral Reform and Social Control in Nineteenth Century Dublin', in *Saothar*, 13, 1988, pp. 7-21.

Yesterday was 'Walking Sunday' which used to be the preliminary
to the orgy of Donnybrook Fair. The recurrence of the day,
however, caused no unusual concourse of visitors to the locality,
thanks to the Rev D Spratt and the other advocates of progress
and morality.[40]

The battle and the victory did nothing to diminish the esteem in
which Spratt was held. In the same month of 1866 when the new Church
in Donnybrook, overlooking the old Fair Green, was consecrated, a
great reception was held in Holy Cross College, Clonliffe. It was the
first public honouring of Paul Cullen in his new role as Cardinal. Huge
crowds gathered outside the College even as the prelates and leading
pastors gathered inside to welcome him. The Carmelite friar was
present and one newspaper, the *Dublin Daily Express*, as often hostile as
favourable to him, commented:

> The Rev Dr Spratt was only second to the Cardinal himself so
> far as regards this demonstrative and, no doubt, well-deserved
> guerdon of public approbation.[41]

When the Cardinal, later that day, received an address of congratulation
from Spratt's Catholic Young Men's Society, he remarked, in reply:

> I hope that you will remain under the guidance of Dr Spratt and,
> for as long as you do, everything must go on well with you.[42]

---

40.  *FJ*, 23rd Aug 1869.
41.  *DDE*, 21st Aug 1866.
42.  *DEP*, 21st Aug 1866.

## CHAPTER EIGHTEEN

---

# *The Church Militant: from CDA to CYMS,*
# *1850-1867*

In the course of the 1850s the Catholic Church in Ireland exhibited a growing confidence and developed a new militancy. This owed not a little to the appointment of Paul Cullen as Archbishop of Armagh.[1] The defensiveness of an earlier age was replaced with a new boldness as the Church experienced an unprecedented growth in the numbers of its personnel – their numbers rising even as the population was declining.

At the same time, Protestantism's evangelical revival exhibited a fresh intensity through the work in Connaught and in Dublin City of the Irish Church Missions and its agents, Alexander Dallas and his colleagues.[2] The militant anti-Catholicism of Dallas and the Irish Church Missions virtually coincided in its arrival, with Cullen and his anti-Protestantism: these concurrent developments led to new tensions and animosities. Within their neighbourhood of Cuffe Street, Camden Street, Aungier Street and Whitefriar Street John Spratt and his Carmelite confreres cultivated and continued to experience cordial relations with their Church of Ireland counterparts in St Peter's Parish. Nevertheless, by the end of the 1850s it would seem that the bitter anti-Catholicism of Dallas and the Irish Church Missions on the one

---

1. He was informed of his appointment on 19th December 1849 and was consecrated Archbishop on 20th February 1850; he arrived in Ireland in April 1850: see C. O'Carroll, *Paul Cardinal Cullen, portrait of a Practical Nationalist*, Dublin 2008, p. 27.
2. M. Moffitt, *The Society for Irish Church Missions to the Roman Catholics, 1849-1950*, Manchester 2010, p. 76; D. Bowen, *The Protestant Crusade in Ireland, 1800-1870*, Dublin 1978, pp. 224ff; P. MacSuibhne, *Paul Cullen and his contemporaries*, Naas 1965, vol. III, p. 365.

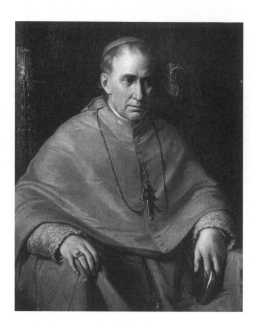

**Fig 115.** *Cardinal Paul Cullen.*

hand and the equally explicit anti-Protestantism of Cullen on the other, would deeply influence inter-faith relations in Dublin City as in Ireland as a whole. Fortunately, and unlike elsewhere in Ireland, this fresh sectarianism never spilled out into open violence in Dublin, but an undercurrent of mutual suspicion and antagonism was never far below the surface. More anxious Protestants in Ireland and Britain had understandable reasons for unease when the Pope restored the Catholic hierarchy on 29th September 1850. Nicholas Wiseman's pastoral marking that restoration, *From Out the Flaminian Gate*, with its statements of territorial jurisdiction, appeared provocative enough to lead even Victoria to exclaim *'Am I Queen of England or am I not?'*.[3] The British Government response was to introduce the Ecclesiastical Titles Bill against this perceived 'Papal aggression'. It proposed to outlaw the use of territorial titles by British or Irish Catholic bishops and to prohibit the publication of papal decrees in the jurisdiction. The progress of this legislation took place against a background of anti-

3.   E. R. Norman, *Anti-Catholicism in Victorian England*, London 1968, p. 56. See also O. P. Rafferty, *The Catholic Church and the Protestant State: nineteenth century realities*, Dublin 2008, Ch. 3, 'Nicholas Wiseman, ecclesiastical politics and Anglo-Irish relations in the mid-nineteenth century', pp. 69-90.

Catholic outrage and riots in England and against a growing movement of Catholic protest in Ireland. Although the legislation received the royal assent on 1st August 1851, Cullen was ultimately right that it could not be implemented: it proved a dead letter in the end, but it served to reflect Protestant outrage even as it cautioned Catholics that a new penal regime might follow. Indeed, from its first reading in February 1851, the bill generated a campaign of Catholic protest in Ireland, ultimately led by the bishops, and supplemented by the opposition of some twenty-four Irish MPs. These became the nucleus of the Independent Irish Party. The mass Catholic agitation came to a head on 11th May 1851 when protest meetings were held in every Catholic parish in Ireland.[4] The protests failed to prevent the enactment but they were accompanied by the emergence of a new body, the Catholic Defence Association of Great Britain and Ireland.

## *John Spratt and the Catholic Defence Association*

Forever associated with the name and person of Paul Cullen, the Catholic Defence Association was, in fact, founded by John Spratt and W J Battersby, supported by Dr Daniel William Cahill.[5] It is remarkable that leading authorities on the subject have ascribed the foundation to Archbishop Cullen and have overlooked the initiating role of Spratt and Battersby.[6] It was in Battersby's bookshop premises, at No. 10

---

4. O'Carroll, pp. 36, 39.

5. Daniel William Cahill (1796-1864), educated in Carlow College and then Maynooth, was Professor of Natural Philosophy in Carlow from 1825 until opening a school at Seapoint, Dublin. He became a well-known lecturer and apologist for Catholicism against the Established Church. Spratt prevailed on him on quite a number of occasions to deliver charity sermons for his different charities. He fell foul of Archbishop Cullen for his outspoken nationalist speeches; see O'Carroll, *Cullen*, p. 92 and T. Wall, 'Catholic Periodicals of the Past: 2: The Catholic Book Society and the Irish Catholic Magazine', *Irish Ecclesiastical Record*, vol. 101, Jan-June 1964, p. 303.

6. See P. MacSuibhne, *Paul Cullen and his contemporaries*, vol. IV, Naas 1974, p. 292; D. Bowen, *Paul Cardinal Cullen and the shaping of Modern Irish Catholicism*, Dublin 1983, p. 246; E. R. Norman, *Anti-Catholicism in Victorian England*, London 1968, p. 78; A. Macauley, 'Strong views in very strong forms': Paul Cullen, Archbishop of Armagh (1849-52)', in D. Keogh & A. McDonnell, eds., *Cardinal Paul Cullen and his World*, Dublin 2011, pp. 84-85; exceptionally, C. O'Carroll, *Paul Cardinal Cullen, portrait of a practical nationalist*, Dublin 2008, p. 40, avoids direct ascription to Cullen and notes that it was 'formally established at a meeting in the Dublin Rotunda on 19th August 1851'.

Essex Bridge, on 31st March 1851, that Spratt and Battersby convened a meeting of Catholic clergy, laity and Dublin City confraternity members to consider an association in defence of Catholic interests.[7] They persuaded Cahill to chair their first meeting. They were at pains to stress, from the outset, that they were not a political body and they had circulated the leading clergy, including Primate Cullen, in advance of the meeting and generally received approbation for their initiative. It is not clear that Spratt and his co-founders had secured approval from Archbishop Murray of Dublin: Murray may have been exceptional among the senior clergy in withholding support. However, the convening circular laid strong stress on the non-political nature of this essentially politico-religious initiative. Its object, after all, was to challenge, thwart or prevent the Ecclesiastical Titles legislation and its means would amount to the politics of public meetings, agitation, petitions and lobbying. In introducing the founding document, Cahill was at pains to develop the theme of the Catholics as a still-persecuted people in Ireland and Britain, about to be persecuted even more. This last was hardly a groundless assertion on his part since Prime Minister Russell had already threatened renewed penal legislation against Catholics if the Holy See did not withdraw its condemnation of the Queen's Colleges.[8] Interestingly, the founders of the embryonic Catholic Defence Association were clearly trying to keep their bishops onside by the tone and content of the only other resolution by which:

> We consider the association for Catholic purposes, unconnected with politics, admirably calculated to meet the present and future wants of the Catholic body.

They called on Catholics to support it. Spratt then brought this foundation meeting to a close, thanking Dr Cahill for his stirring contribution. At this early point in its emergence, Spratt and Battersby were the leading lights. It was under their names only that the next meeting was convened, and again, significantly, with the advertising notice stating *The Catholic Defence Association (unconnected with politics)*.[9]

---

7. *FJ*, Tuesday 1st April 1851; *DEP*, 3rd April 1851.
8. MacAuley, loc.cit., p. 84, citing *The Tablet*, 29th March 1851.
9. *FJ*, 7th April 1851.

At this second meeting, Spratt was received with great warmth when he declared how grateful he was that so many devoted Catholics had come together to support the new initiative. Thereafter, even as this venture gained momentum in the course of the spring and summer of 1851, Spratt's role would become submerged: this happened as the movement was taken up by others, at first by the politicians, notably his associate, the Dublin MP, John Reynolds, and the MP, William Keogh, and then by the bishops. Presumably, with so many other ongoing and emerging commitments on his plate, this may not have been entirely unwelcome to the friar, and he and Battersby may even have been gratified that their initiative would grow beyond them, in time, into a more considerable movement.

Even before this second meeting of theirs ended, he and Battersby were preparing for the first major public meeting and demonstration of Dublin's Catholic citizens and sympathisers, on 22nd April 1851, in Conciliation Hall. All of Spratt's oldest supporters and co-workers were present – Battersby, Brennan, Frs Gilligan, Young and O'Malley – but significantly also, the Dublin City MPs, Henry Grattan and John Reynolds who chaired the meeting. Reynolds led the attack not only on the Ecclesiastical Titles Bill but also on the Religious Houses Bill which sought to institute inspection of convents on the pretext of ensuring that no female was being forcibly confined therein – a legislative proposal which Reynolds denounced *'as not only an insult to the virtuous, chaste and religious women against whom it was directed, but a bill calculated to insult their fathers, brothers and relations'.*[10] The meeting adopted petitions against these bills. Two days later, the infant Catholic Defence Association met at Battersby's premises and announced that:

> arrangements were being made for the purpose of holding a public meeting of the citizens of Dublin at as early a date as possible to inaugurate the Association, which will be duly notified.[11]

The formal inauguration of this Catholic Defence Association, however, did not take place through Spratt and Battersby. Instead, they

10. *FJ*, 23rd April 1851.
11. *FJ*, 26th April 1851.

were overtaken by a wider movement, led by Reynolds and Keogh. Under the latter's inspiration another meeting – a so-called 'Aggregate Meeting of the Catholics of Ireland' – was announced for 29th April 1851 in Dublin's Rotunda. Up to that meeting, the Catholic bishops had not been in public attendance at such gatherings, but all of them supported this proposed convention: Paul Cullen could not attend but commended the proposed meeting and referred to *'some few of the important objects to be attended to by the Catholic Defence Association which you propose to establish…The institution of such an association appears to be most desirable'.*[12] It was as if he was unaware of or chose to overlook the initiative already taken by Spratt, Battersby and colleagues.

As a rallying occasion for aggrieved Catholics, this gathering was a success, attended by seven MPs, various notabilities of the Catholic gentry, and extensively by Catholic clergy including Spratt. Following the meeting, an organising committee convened at rooms in Sackville Street to prepare for a more formal launch. Spratt was active on this committee and, indeed, chaired an important meeting of it in early June 1851 when it sought the support of the English convert, now Cardinal, Nicholas Wiseman, for what it called an "Association for

**Fig 116.** *Cardinal Nicholas Wiseman.*

the Defence and Increase of Catholic Liberty".[13] Wiseman was cautiously non-committal, remarking that he hoped it would not be a political body – an appropriate prudence given that he had been in considerable part responsible, through his injudicious pastoral, *From Out the Flaminian Gate*, for bringing a cascade of anti-Catholic abuse down upon the heads of Catholics in Britain and Ireland.

It was not until 19th August 1851, with a further meeting in

12.   *FJ*, 30th April 1851, Cullen to Reynolds, 27th April 1851.
13.   *FJ*, 5th June 1851.

the Rotunda, that the Catholic Defence Association was at last formally launched in the presence of Archbishop Cullen as chairman, with twelve other prelates attending.[14]   The requisition calling this meeting was signed by 21 of 28 bishops, 14 noblemen, 26 MPs and numerous clergy including Spratt and all 7 of his friary confreres.[15]   Now led by Cullen, the CDA was an alliance between the bishops and leading members of the 'Irish Brigade' of MPs led by Reynolds, Keogh and Sadleir.

Pending the appointment of a permanent secretary these three MPs acted in a secretarial capacity on a temporary basis, with Keogh as the effective administrator.  As regards the permanent position, Spratt's close comrade, Battersby, came forward as a candidate and by any measure of experience, he ought to have been a very strong one.  He not only had been producing the annual *Catholic Directory* since 1836, but had served in a host of Irish Catholic organisations since 1823.  In the later stages of that career he had been secretary to the Famine Relief Committee in 1849, to the preliminary committee for the Catholic University in 1850 and as he put it himself, *'Secretary to the Catholic Defence Association which I suggested five years ago'*, and he added, significantly:

> the rules of which were long since submitted to the judgement of the bishops, individually and collectively and which, of course, at their will is left to be merged, if necessary, in the present organisation.[16]

Spratt earnestly supported Battersby, declaring *'few persons [were] better entitled to fill the vacant situation'*.  Despite this endorsement and the support of the other prominent clergymen, Yore, O'Connell and Cahill, Battersby was not successful.  The appointment of an English convert, Henry Wilberforce, was made by Cullen on 17th December 1851, despite the strong opposition of fellow-archbishop, McHale,

---

14.  *EF*, 19th Aug 1851.

15.  *WFJ*, 19th July 1851. Archbishop Murray was not among the signatories. The others missing were: Cornelius Denvir of Down and Connor, Francis Haly of Kildare and Loughlin, Edward Walsh of Ossory, John Ryan of Limerick, and Lawrence O'Donnell of Galway.

16.  *FJ*, 13th Oct 1851.

and the leading MPs of the Irish Brigade.[17] Cullen's action caused a controversy that split the Catholic Defence Association. It was not that Battersby himself was in the running, up to the eve of Cullen's announcement, rather the other contender against Wilberforce was a Galway man, George Burke. It emerges from a quite different context that, two months before he finally returned to Ireland as Archbishop, Paul Cullen had indicated little time for John Spratt and William Battersby, as shall be seen shortly in connection with the origins of the Catholic University.

Cullen's insistence on the appointment of Wilberforce caused a furore in the ranks and leadership. William Keogh publicly appealed against Cullen's decision, with Cullen publicly replying.[18] Within the ranks of the Catholic Defence Association there was a division between those such as Cullen who saw it as detached from Irish nationalism and essentially viewed it as a United Kingdom Catholic defence body, and laymen like the MP Keogh and clergy like Spratt and Cahill who identified their Catholicism with Irish patriotism. As Ciaran O'Carroll points out, the clash between these two schools of thought as regards Irish nationalism was to intensify following the transfer of Cullen to Dublin, as archbishop and also as apostolic delegate. This occurred on 3rd May, following the death of Daniel Murray on 26th February 1852.

Despite mutual suspicions and tensions, Cullen's Catholic Defence Association and the Tenant League co-operated in contesting the general election of July 1852. That election constituted a peak in Catholic clerical involvement in electoral politics and saw the return of some 42 Catholic MPs – many of them members of the Irish Brigade and Tenant League. Altogether the Brigade comprised some 48 out of 105 Irish MPs; these were committed to independent opposition to the government until religious freedom and land reform legislation would be enacted.

*The call of politics*

As for John Spratt, given his active political engagement over the previous two decades, it might have been expected that, in the 1850s, he

---

17. Macauley, loc.cit., p. 85, D. Bowen, *Paul Cullen and the Shaping of Modern Irish Catholicism*, Dublin 1983, p. 247.
18. O'Carroll, pp. 46-47.

would show continued interest. In this he did not disappoint. As already seen, he had been energetically engaged in trying to secure clemency and remission for the exiled Smith O'Brien. It was in the middle of 1850, when he was caught up in the emergence of the Catholic Defence Association, that his work for Smith O'Brien reached its end-point in the abortive deputation which he led to the Lord Lieutenant. On that occasion, on 17th May 1852, as one of the secretaries of the 'clemency committee', he was a member of the deputation which presented a petition seeking clemency for O'Brien and his exiled comrades: that petition was signed by 9 peers, 15 Catholic bishops, 19 baronets, 42 MPs, 66 Deputy Lieutenants of counties, 288 magistrates, 11 high sheriffs, over 500 clergy of several denominations and 10,000 lesser mortals. As far as the Lord Lieutenant was concerned, after being found guilty of high treason, they had already been spared by exile, had attempted to escape and had displayed no remorse: consequently, he declined to recommend the prayer of the petition. For all these efforts on his behalf, Smith O'Brien was not ungrateful. A year later, Spratt received from him a letter from Van Diemen's Land, dated 15th October 1852, thanking the Carmelite for these efforts, *'all the more since your sentiments differed upon many points from those of the party with which I was connected'* and he concluded in a dignified way in deploring the response of Lord Eglinton.

Such political disappointment to Spratt was not his only one at this time. His interest in electoral politics was to be manifest also in his continued efforts to secure recognition as a voter. In January 1851, he and his confreres applied for registration. Their application was challenged by the local Conservatives but they were admitted to the electoral register. The Conservatives announced they would appeal against the decision to admit the Carmelites but the outcome of that appeal is not evident.[19]

When it came to the general election of July 1852, famous for clerical involvement throughout the constituencies, Fr John was deeply engaged. His close associate in the Cuffe Street Savings Bank campaign, John Reynolds, was the sitting MP, seeking re-election. Such was Spratt's support that despite his teetotal antipathy to taverns, he found himself in Daniel O'Hara's College Tavern, York Street, on 1st

---

19. *FJ*, 15th Jan 1851.

July, at a Reynold's campaign meeting, with the MP as main speaker. Here the friar moved the second resolution, giving evidence of the heightened emotions around this particular election, fought in the red haze of sectarian agitation:

> That as a bigoted and unscrupulous faction are using every exertion to return men pledged to trample on…civil and religious liberty won after years of toil and struggle, we, the electors must be up and stirring to counteract their plans and return at least one member, willing and capable of vindicating our rights.[20]

Temperance gatherings and sermons apart, it was unusual of Spratt to speak at any great length in public meetings, but this occasion was an exception. He spoke earnestly and extensively to urge the duty of everyone to come out to support Reynolds who had done so much for the people of that area and of Dublin, Catholics and Protestants alike, notably in the recovery of some money for the Cuffe Street bank depositors. He told how Protestant electors had promised that in return they would favour Reynolds next time out. The friar hoped *'they would fulfil their promise, but he greatly feared that bigotry would prevail'*.[21] Right he was: Reynolds lost his seat in a menacing, bare-knuckle contest, claiming that some 700 to 800 dead and absentee voters had been personated. Certain it was that he won the majority of property-qualified voters and lost out to the freeman electors. It was a bad blow to the nationalist cause and to that of the Catholic Defence Association.

*The Friar and the Friends of Religious Freedom and Equality*
Despite Reynold's loss, the election saw the return of some 48 Irish MPs pledged to independent opposition in the quest for Catholic redress and land reform. However, the promise inherent in this significant cohort of Irish independent MPs was never realised. The acceptance of office in the Aberdeen coalition government by William Keogh and John Sadleir, becoming public knowledge on 17th December 1852, blighted

---

20. *FJ*, 2nd July 1852. The publican Donal O'Hara was one of the many laymen, not a few of them publicans, who actively helped Spratt in his charities. O'Hara was president of St Peter's Orphan Society for many years: see Chapter Twenty-Three.
21. *DEP*, 3rd July 1852.

that promise. By the summer of 1852, in any case, the Catholic Defence Association was waning and disappearing from public view: rumours of its demise had to be denied officially that October, but it remained moribund until, on 29th November 1853, Cullen announced its dissolution.[22]

During the unhappy final period from the defections of Keogh and Sadleir in January 1852 until that dissolution, Spratt remained active in the Association, as active as its own lethargy allowed. He

**Fig 117.** *John Sadleir, MP.*

was present at its large and protracted meeting on 29th January 1852, chaired by Cullen, to consider *'the system of proselytising now being carried out in several parts of the south and west of Ireland'*, and to take steps *'to defeat the machinations of the preachers and upholders of that odious system'*.[23] Furthermore, he remained a paid-up member of the Association, the only Calced Carmelite of his community or in Ireland to be so.[24] However, his active engagement in the fight for Catholic liberty in the face of the anti-Catholic hysteria in Britain and Ireland, from the autumn of 1852 to the winter of 1853 effectively, took place not in the Catholic Defence Association but rather in the ranks and leadership of the Friends of Religious Freedom and Equality. This body had been established by the Mayo MP, George Moore, in September 1852, to fight for religious equality and the disestablishment of the Church of Ireland.[25] Spratt was involved from the outset, attending its first major

---

22. O'Carroll, p. 88.

23. *EF*, 29th Jan 1852.

24. To judge by the list given in *DEP*, 10th Feb 1852.

25. George Henry Moore (1810-1870), Mayo landowner, had been a member of the Catholic Defence Association, was the pioneer and real leader of the idea for Irish Independent opposition, based on religious equality and tenant rights, and led the attack on Sadleir and Keogh after their defection.

public conference on 28th October,[26] as were old friends from repeal days, Martin Brennan and Thomas Arkins. He was not present at a critical meeting of this body in January 1853 when it condemned Sadleir and Keogh but renewed its commitment not to support government until it made religious equality a matter of cabinet policy. Although absent, commending reference was made to Spratt for his deputation to Viceroy Clarendon on the subject of the exclusion of Catholics from juries.[27]

### The Invasion of the Convents

The main thrust of Spratt's activity within the Friends of Religious Freedom and Equality centred on the issue of threatened legislation for the inspection of convents. Known euphemistically as the bill 'to facilitate the recovery of personal liberty in certain cases', it was generated by the fervour of anti-Catholic evangelicals against nunneries and their supposed forced detention of females therein. The campaign, led by the MPs Chambers, Whiteside and Newdegate, comprised a series of efforts in parliament in 1853 to secure an official investigation into convents. In May 1853 Chambers' motion to bring in a bill for the 'inspection of nunneries' was carried against the government by 138 to 115.[28] The Dublin City MP John Vance was among the 12 Irish MPs who supported Chambers, with 44 Irish MPs opposing.[29]

The campaign by Newdegate, Chambers and others in the House of Commons was sufficient to secure a Royal Commission of Inquiry into Maynooth College and more than sufficient to increase greatly the apprehensions of Catholics in Ireland and Britain. On the first day of June 1853, Spratt chaired a meeting of the Friends of Religious Freedom to consider how best to challenge and defeat this bill. This gathering resolved to call on Catholic parishes throughout the country to petition against the bill and a petitions sub-committee to pursue this agenda included Spratt and Martin Brennan as members.[30] It followed on a scathing pastoral on the subject from Archbishop Cullen issued on

26.  *FJ*, 29th October 1852, *DWN*, 30th October 1852.
27.  *FJ*, 13th Jan 1853.
28.  *SNL*, 11th May 1853.
29.  *DEPC*, 14th May 1853.
30.  *SNL*, 2nd June 1853; *FJ*, 4th June 1853.

14th May 1853.[31]  At a subsequent committee meeting, Spratt moved the opening of a subscription list to finance the movement while his committee colleague, the English Jesuit, Dr Henry Marshall, with the support of Spratt and Brennan, secured the adoption of a public *Address to the People of Ireland*.[32]  Their efforts were rewarded when an impressive list of the great and the good appended their signatures to the call for a public meeting of Ireland's Catholics to petition parliament against *'the bill for the inquisitional inspection of convents'*.[33]  The meeting duly took place on 13th June, in the Rotunda, *'against the audacious and insulting attempt of the bigoted fanatics to obtain legislative sanction for invading the convents'*, with Fr Spratt the only Carmelite listed as attending.[34]  This agitation and the flood of petitions against Chambers' inspection may have had some effect: almost a fortnight later, Russell and the government successfully opposed the second reading with a majority of 29 against.[35]  One Protestant Dublin journal commented ruefully that

> Clamour and misrepresentation have done their work in reference to the Bill for the Inspection of Nunneries, but the triumph of Ultramontanism on this occasion has been dearly bought.  The government have yielded to the pressure brought upon them… they must en masse pander to the bigotry of the Roman Catholic party…[36]

On a personal political level, the autumn of 1854 would see a reverse for the friar: Spratt's application for inclusion on the register of electors, and that of nine of his Whitefriar Street brothers, were objected to and they were denied the vote.  In this they were not alone: seven confreres of the Discalced Carmelites in Clarendon Street were also

---

31.  *SNL*, 21st May 1853; also Sunday 15th May 1853; MacSuibhne, vol. 1, p. 366, citing P. F. Moran, *Pastoral letters and other writings of Cardinal Cullen*, 3 vols, Dublin, 1852, 1, 244-7.

32.  *EF*, 6th June; *FJ*, 7th & 8th June 1853.

33.  *FJ*, 10th June 1853.  Apart from the long list of aristocrats, gentry, MPs, magistrates, and citizens in general, appeared the name of Michael Thomas Spratt, Fr John's nephew, soon to depart for New Zealand from a colourful past in Ireland to an equally colourful future in Otago.

34.  *FJ*, 14th June 1853.

35.  *SNL*, 23rd June 1853, House of Commons debate, 22nd June 1853.

36.  *DEPC*, 23rd June 1853.

struck out, as were six Augustinians of John's Lane.[37] Dublin remained
a city of divided, sectarian politics. It would not be until the general
election of 1868, following upon the Irish electoral reform act of that
July, that Fr John and his confreres living in Whitefriar Street would
enjoy the vote unchallenged.[38] The denial of his vote in 1854 may have
been academic. Even Cullen's curbs on clerical engagement in secular
politics, embodied in the national synod decrees of May 1854, ratified
by Rome in 1855,[39] did not prevent the friar's continued active political
engagement. In March 1855, along with other Dublin clergy, such as his
old associates, Frs Yore and Gilligan, Fr John was active in the Liberal
Registry Association set up in Dublin the previous September.[40] Two
years later he was actively organising a petition in favour of *'a uniform
oath for parliamentary representatives of all religious persuasions'*. He collected
some three thousand signatures within the precincts of Whitefriar
Street Church, which the Limerick MP, John O'Brien, presented to the
House of Commons in June 1857.[41] However, it would not be until
the mid-1860s before Fr John again greatly engaged in secular political
activity. Throughout the 1850s he had many other new ventures to
absorb his abundant energy and zeal.

*The Catholic University*
Not the least of these new ventures was his involvement in the quest
for a Catholic University. Once returned to Ireland as Archbishop
of Armagh, Cullen was determined to establish a Catholic University,
whereas Murray doubted it was practicable. However, at the start of
1850, the editor of the *Freeman's Journal* wondered impatiently why no

37.  *SNL*, 19th Sept 1854.
38.  *City of Dublin Elections, 18th November 1868: list of electors*, Dublin 1868, p. 71. There
     was one Carmelite exception: Fr Thomas Bennett, listed with an address at 41
     Lower Dominick Street, held the vote in 1859 and 1865 but did not cast it: see *City
     of Dublin Election, May 1859, List of Electors in the year 1859*, Dublin 1859, and S.
     Tudor Bradburne, *City of Dublin Election, July 15th 1865, List of Electors for the year
     1865*, Dublin 1865, p. 15. The Representation of the People (Ireland) Act, 1868
     (31 & 32 Vict. c. 49) reduced the rental qualification from £8 to £4 and introduced
     the lodger franchise.
39.  O'Carroll, p. 92; Norman, *The Catholic Church and Ireland in the Age of Rebellion*,
     London 1965, p. 28.
40.  *DEP*, 13th March 1855; *EF*, 14th March 1855.
41.  *FJ*, 17th June 1857.

effort had actually been made to found a national Catholic University. He argued that *'all that is required is a zealous committee of ways and means'*, and asked *'when will the formation of a zealous committee enable the erection of a fitting university?'*.[42] Exactly two weeks later, the English convert, Frederick Lucas, owner of *The Tablet*, urged the *'necessity of immediate action'*.[43] The response came a few days later where John Spratt commenced a public campaign on the issue. On 30th January he addressed a letter to the bishops of Ireland announcing that the Wexford philanthropist, Richard Devereux, had written to him to offer £200 as a first donation *'towards establishing a Catholic University in Ireland'*.[44] Acknowledging that Pope Pius IX had urged such a foundation and that Catholic clergy and laity had been talking about it for some time, Spratt was anxious that something be actually done about it, and had begun discussions with some prosperous laymen who agreed that a preliminary fund-raising committee should be formed.[45] At the same time he hastened to add *'that such a university should be entirely under your lordships control'*. Spratt won the praise of Archbishop McHale for undertaking this preliminary committee. McHale wrote to the friar on 5th April and commented:

> Your plan is admirable. Leaving the regulation of the University in its plans and details to the hierarchy, to whom all such institutions should be confided, you kindly and generously anticipated their wishes in coming forward to lighten their labours by collecting funds…[46]

It was both open praise and barely concealed admonition against trespassing on episcopal authority.[47] Four days later, at Battersby's book shop in Parliament Street, Spratt convened the first meeting of the committee to collect funds for the projected university. He drew upon the support of some of those who had helped him in the General

---

42. *FJ*, 12th Jan 1850.
43. *The Tablet*, 26th Jan 1850, 'A Catholic University Possible'. Lucas had moved his weekly newspaper from London to Dublin around this time.
44. *FJ*, *DEP*, 31st Jan 1850. Interestingly, the *Freeman's Journal* announced this as 'The First Contribution towards a National University'.
45. 'To the Most Rev and Right Rev, the Catholic Archbishop and Bishops of Ireland' … John Spratt, DD, 30th January 1850.
46. *FJ*, 7th Feb 1850.
47. *FJ*, 7th Feb 1850, McHale to Spratt, 5th February 1850.

**Fig 118.** *Frederick Lucas.*

Relief Committee the previous year and secured the adoption of a circular letter to the bishops, nobility and gentry of the three kingdoms. In this he referred to the Pope's prescripts of 9th October 1847 and 11th October 1848 urging the establishment of a Catholic University in Ireland along the lines of the Belgian one at Louvain. He described himself as the honorary secretary of this committee, with Battersby as actual secretary.[48] However, all was not plain sailing. He hoped that Archbishop Murray might agree to act as treasurer, but the latter, always unenthusiastic about the proposal, declined on the grounds that he had too many other commitments.[49] Furthermore, there had already appeared a hostile editorial in the pages of *The Tablet*. Having complained, in late January, of the lack of action on the matter, Lucas, on 9th February, now attacked Spratt for taking this initiative. He deplored it as premature and *'calculated to damage the cause'* and caustically referred to the pretensions of anonymous gentlemen constituting themselves as a 'Central Committee'. He wanted to know by whom they had been 'appointed' and insisted that it had not been by any public meeting *'and not by any episcopal authority'*.[50] Spratt countered that he had the authority to use the names of Archbishop McHale and of the new primate, Archbishop Cullen. Technically this was correct, but in fact he had not directly asked Cullen's permission. Instead, McHale had assured him that it would be in order for Spratt to name

---

48.   *FJ*, 12th Feb 1850; 21st Feb 1850. By its next meeting, on 20th February, Battersby was described as its secretary.
49.   Murray to Spratt, 16th February 1850, cited in *FJ*, 21st Feb 1850.
50.   *The Tablet*, 9th Feb 1850.

McHale and Cullen as treasurers.[51] It was not until March 1850 that Spratt actually got round to writing to Cullen directly and explained how McHale, offering his own name, had added *'As the Primate, Most Rev Dr Cullen is absent I will venture to give you his name also for the same purpose'*. Spratt explained that it was in these circumstances that he had already lodged some £260 to accounts in their name. He added, no doubt in reference to Lucas, that

> although it is the opinion of a few that *'the movement ought to be delayed still longer'*, many of us are convinced that the moderation and prudence with which the present movement has commenced have defeated an opposition which would have interfered with the realisation of the wishes of those who are most anxious to see the University established with as little delay as possible.[52]

If, understandably, he supposed that Cullen was with him in wanting as little delay as possible he was badly mistaken. Cullen, very soon after this, would write to McHale, from the Irish College, in less than flattering terms:

> I fear that the Committee now acting will do no good. Mr Battersby and Fr Spratt are not well-fitted to commence the work. Perhaps it may be discredited unless some of the first men in Ireland, lay and clerical, be induced to give their names to the Committee. It would be better to delay a few weeks in order to get a regular committee together.[53]

Could it be that Lucas had contacted Cullen at the time of the former's editorial against Spratt and his committee? It is interesting that, in commenting on this somewhat ungenerous letter of Cullen's, MacSuibhne wondered if Cullen had lived in Rome as a recluse, unfamiliar with Irish conditions or if, on the contrary, he may have been thoroughly well-informed. Almost certainly it was the latter, for Cullen had in Fr Peter Cooper, priest and canon of the Pro-Cathedral in

---

51. *DEP*, 21st Feb 1850.
52. DDA, *Cullen Papers*, 45/3/1/3, Spratt to Cullen, n.d. March 1850.
53. Cullen to McHale, 24th March 1850, cited in MacSuibhne, vol. 2, pp 44-49.

Dublin, a confidante who kept him fully-informed of Church politics in Dublin and Ireland. Cooper wrote frequently and regularly to Cullen in Rome, almost as his agent, right up to Cullen's return thence to Armagh in 1850 and his translation from Armagh to Dublin in 1852.[54] In due course Cullen would come to see Spratt in a more favourable light. The friar, presumably, was unaware of these comments at the time and had printed an elaborate two-page *Address of the Central Committee in Dublin, appointed to collect donations and subscriptions...*[55] He pursued the fund-raising goal with his customary zeal and success. Devereux's £200 came in, as did £40 from Castlebar Catholics, £30 from a priest in Ferns and a donation from John O'Connell.[56] He was advising potential donors to lodge gifts to the names of McHale, Cullen and Devereux in various Irish banks, and hoped there would soon be simultaneous collections in all the parishes of Ireland.[57] Yet, somehow, between the spring and autumn of 1850, Spratt, Battersby and their committee had been stood down or taken over. Cullen's wish to see *'some of the first men in Ireland'* in command had come to pass. When the Catholic University Committee met that October, in new premises on Wellington Quay, the meeting comprised Cullen, McHale, Slattery of Cashel, Cantwell of Meath, and the reluctant Murray of Dublin who had been induced by Cullen to come on board in the wake of the Synod of Thurles. This committee also included the esteemed layman, Charles Bianconi. Furthermore, by 17th October 1850, they had formed a new fund-raising subcommittee with Cullen's informant, Fr Peter Cooper, as one of three secretaries.[58] Neither Spratt nor Battersby were to be found on it. It may well have been these two and their original committee co-workers who were intended when Cullen's new University Committee thanked *'the zeal and services of the gentlemen who have recently exerted themselves for and generously contributed towards the establishment of a Catholic University'*:[59] if so, they were frozen out thereafter. Battersby may well have taken offence – not

54. Bowen, *Cullen*, pp 109-110, 114, 116 & 127.
55. DDA, *Cullen Papers*, Catholic University 45/3/1/2.
56. *DEP*, 21st Feb, 5th March 1850; *FJ*, 1st March 1850.
57. *DEP*, 12th March 1850.
58. DDA, *Cullen Papers*, 45/3/1/13/2, Catholic University of Ireland. The new subcommittee was functioning from at least 17th October 1850, if not before this.
59. *DEP*, 19th Oct 1850.

too long afterwards, having also been rejected for the secretaryship of the Catholic Defence Association, he would exclude all mention of Cullen's published pronouncements from his *Catholic Directory*.[60] If Spratt had taken offence he certainly did not express it: a year later, on the feast of St Lawrence O'Toole, on 14th November 1851, it appears that Spratt delivered the panegyric, before Cullen, after High Mass.[61] In addition, he attended Newman's famous public lectures on university education, delivered in Dublin in May-June 1852.[62]

**Fig 119.** *Portrait of Cardinal John Henry Newman by Sir John Everett Millais.*

Furthermore, when Newman faced enormous costs for the libel case brought against him by the Italian ex-priest G G Achilli, the Irish Catholic University Society convened a Dublin meeting to help his expenses, and it was Spratt who moved the resolution inviting Dr Cullen to chair the meeting. However, the resulting eighteen-member Newman Indemnity Fund Committee, including Cullen, Lucas, John O'Connell and Charles Gavan Duffy did not include the Carmelite friar,[63] though he and his Carmelite community contributed. Two years later, Spratt attended Newman's inaugural lecture as Rector of the Catholic University on 9th November 1854, following Newman's installation on 4th June of that year. Spratt remained an invited guest at the new University's public occasions in the later 1850s[64] and he had the gratification, after his own

---

60.  So maintains MacSuibhne, vol. 2, pp. 46-47.
61.  So MacSuibhne states, vol. 2, p. 106, but I can find no other references to it.
62.  *FJ*, 25th May 1852; *CT*, 5 June 1852.
63.  *FJ*, 14th Aug 1852; *DWN*, 21st Aug 1852. They gave a donation of £5. The Clarendon Street Discalced Carmelites also contributed £10.
64.  He attended the opening public lectures of its Cecilia Street Medical School in November 1858 and November 1859: see *DEP*, 4th Nov 1858, 3rd Nov 1859.

early efforts, of seeing the institution set up and survive, even if it can hardly be said to have flourished in its first decades: but the friar was never counted in its inner circles. By the time of its eventual launch, in May 1854, however, Spratt was busily preoccupied with a new launch of his own, that of the Catholic Young Men's Society.[65]

**Fig 120.** *Newman House, Stephen's Green, formerly the Catholic University of Ireland.*

*The CYMS*

On Sunday 9th April 1854 Fr John held a meeting in the Carmelite Friary with a view to establishing what he called the 'Young Men's Society' or the Guild of the Blessed Virgin Mary and St Joseph. He had drawn up draft rules, and had them submitted and approved by the Archbishop. These rules were thereupon adopted and plans were made for a formal public foundation meeting.[66] Essentially they sought to promote the spiritual welfare of the members '*by means of mutual improvement, brotherly love and devotedness to the holy Catholic and Apostolic Church*'. Each member committed to live soberly, in justice to his neighbour and in the practice of prayer, meditation and the frequenting of the sacraments. Central

65.  Hereafter referred to as CYMS.
66.  *The Weekly Telegraph*, 22nd April 1854.

also to the cultivation of a sense of community among the members was the commitment to provide for a library, a reading room and classrooms. It was truly a sign of the times when there was added the *'duty to protect the rising generation from the poisoned arrows of the proselytisers'*. Furthermore, whereas it began its existence with the simple title 'Young Men's Society', within two months it was calling itself the 'Catholic Young Men's Society'. Fr John felt *'there was an absolute want of such a society...aware of the awful prevalence of bigotry, irreligion and immorality'*.[67]

Dublin City was not the first in Ireland to see such an organisation for Catholics. That distinction went to Limerick where a parish curate of St Mary's, Fr Richard Baptist O'Brien, set up the Limerick Young Men's Society in May 1850. Cork City followed in November 1852 when Fr John J Murphy, P.P., instituted the Cork YMS.[68] While John Spratt owed his inspiration to the Limerick example of Fr O'Brien, as he acknowledged in June 1854,[69] and with whom he was on friendly terms, all three bodies had in common a determination to emulate the foundation and expansion of their Protestant counterpart, the Young Men's Christian Association. This was founded in London in June 1844 and in Dublin in 1845-6,[70] with broadly similar aims except for the defence of their own version of orthodoxy. For much of his own pastoral and educational ministry, from the early 1820s until the

---

67. *FJ*, 28th June, 13th July 1854, 31st Oct 1855.
68. *Limerick Reporter*, 4th July 1851. Within less than a year it boasted some 900 members: see *Limerick Reporter*, 18th Feb 1851; *DWN*, 22nd Feb 1851. M. J. Egan, *Life of Dan O'Brien, Founder of the Catholic Young Men's Society*, Dublin 1949, p. 30, states that it was founded on 19th May 1849, as also does the anonymously written *Catholic Young Men's Society Centenary Record, 1849-1949*, Dublin 1949, p. 21. Both sources were probably relying on J. J. Healy's *Notes by J. J. Healy on Revd Richard O'Brien, Founder of the Catholic Young Men's Society of Ireland*, which is now archived at NLI Ms 28870. This dating of 1849 was likely obtained from O'Brien's successor in Newcastle West, Dr Hallinan, later Bishop of Limerick. None of the Limerick newspapers carry any reports of Fr O'Brien's Young Men's Society before the year 1851 and provide no evidence of its existence before 1850.
69. *Cork Examiner*, 5th Nov 1852. Spratt stated that it was the Dominican friar, Dr Leahy, who founded the Cork Young Men's Society – see *EF*, 14th June 1854.
70. The original Dublin body was called the Dublin Young Men's Association. It was founded in November 1845 but had its first public meeting on 30 January 1846. The Young Men's Association of Ireland was soon after formed and had its public inauguration in June 1846. It was not until the 1850s that it came to be referred to as the YMCA. For the foundation bodies see *The Statesman and Christian Record*, 3rd Feb, 16th June 1846.

early 1850s, Friar John's endeavours had been directed towards the poor. Now, from the middle of the 1850s, he added a concern for the spiritual and cultural welfare of working and middle class males of his native city. This new direction may well have been his response to the growing impact of proselytism, to the palpable new presence of sectarian tension in general and to the presence of the Protestant YMCA in Dublin in particular.

**Fig 121.** *The Christian Union Buildings in Lower Abbey Street were erected on the site of the Metropolitan Hall, formerly the Music Hall.*

It was on 12th June 1854 that Spratt organised the formal launch of the Dublin CYMS in the Abbey Street Music Hall.[71] Old friends rallied round, including Patrick Slevin, Battersby and Brennan, while Fr Gilligan and Fr Flanagan of Francis Street were also supportive. It is interesting to note, in addition, that this was one of the few public occasions in his career that his Carmelite confreres were to the fore in participating. Frs Henry McGee and John Carr were in full support and each spoke at considerable length in celebrating this development.[72] Fr McGee, who ran the Carmelite Confraternity in Whitefriar Street, was received with

71.  *FJ*, 31st Oct 1855, First Annual of the Dublin C.Y.M.S.
72.  *EF*, 14th June 1854; *DWN*, 17th June 1854.

enthusiastic cheering. The meeting appointed officers, with Fr Spratt very much in charge as 'Guardian'. The Committee was provided with temporary meeting rooms at 54 Aungier Street. Their prime tasks were to recruit members and to build up a reading room and library. Within days they had signed up one hundred members and in January 1855, following a row in the Mechanics' Institute, when Catholic members walked out in protest over anti-Catholic remarks made by its professor of French, these protestors now joined the CYMS.[73] Very quickly the members had fitted out the reading room, providing it with newspapers and Catholic publications.[74] As one member, Matthew Fitzpatrick of nearby Peter Street, observed,

> as to newspapers, they had not the infidel *Sun*, nor the bigoted *Despatch*, but papers in which they had firm trust and reliance, such as *The Freeman* and *The Tablet*, which would not hurt their feelings as men nor outrage their faith as Catholics.[75]

Thanks to the latter's own generosity, the nucleus of a library was in place when he gifted some seventy volumes of books, while Fr John also gave generously of books.[76] By November 1856 they had acquired 1,500 volumes.[77] Fellow-clergy too provided encouraging financial aid, with £5 from John Henry Newman, then just a month installed as Rector of the Catholic University; another £5 from Fr Matthew Flanagan, and £1 each from Fr Michael Farrington, from the Augustinian Prior, William Walsh, and from Dr Yore.[78]

Their first year had been a successful one: they had secured over 240 new members in the three months up to October 1855 and the expansion required new premises. In their early months they had used the lecture hall of the Catholic University's Medical School in

---

73. DDA, *Cullen Papers*, 332/7/3, Spratt to Cullen, 11th January 1855.
74. *FJ*, 28th June 1854.
75. *FJ*, 26th Sept 1854.
76. *FJ*, 31st Oct 1855. Library donations not long after included over 100 volumes from Michael Murphy of Belfield, Roebuck, and a set of the *Encyclopaedia Britannica* from an engineer, John Dwyer of London: see *FJ*, 16th Nov 1855, 26th July 1855 respectively.
77. *FJ*, 11th Nov 1856.
78. *FJ*, 13th July, 29th Aug 1854. Newman had been installed as Rector on 4th June 1854.

Cecilia Street for their public lectures – the attendance on one occasion included the illustrious Orientalist, Peter le Page Renouf who held the Chair of Ancient History and Oriental Languages in the University.[79] On 29th May 1855 the CYMS moved to extensive premises in the Anglesea Buildings in Lower Abbey Street and, by October of that year, with a still-expanding membership, they took four additional rooms there. This enabled them to offer courses

**Fig 122.** *Portrait of Sir Peter Le Page Renouf, by Alberto de Rohden.*

in French, English and Irish, the latter provided by Martin Brennan: all of this in addition to their library and reading room facilities.[80] Gratified by their progress, they ascribed not a little of it to the fact that they were *'governed by the benign suavity and mild wisdom of Dr Spratt'*.[81]

*From Praise to Blame*

Their sense of significance would have been enhanced that August when Spratt led the young men on a courtesy visit to Dr Cullen. They came to welcome the Archbishop's return from Rome where he had been participating in the ceremonies to mark the proclamation of the doctrine of the Immaculate Conception. Complimenting him on his *'improved health and increased vigour'* and wishing him *'length of years'*, Cullen reciprocated, discussed the Society's progress with Spratt and its officers, and was warm in his thanks and praise.[82] However, it would not be too long before the 'increased vigour' manifested itself in a less auspicious manner. In the spring of 1856 a serious row broke

79.   *DEP*, 26th Apr 1855. K. J. Cathcart, *The Letters of Peter le Page Renouf, 1822-1897*, 4 vols, Dublin 2002-4; D. McCartney, *UCD: A National Idea*, Dublin 1999, pp. 5, 15.

80.   *Catholic Telegraph*, 26th Jan 1856.

81.   *DEP*, 25th Oct 1855.

82.   *EF*, 27th Aug 1855.

out involving the CYMS, Dr Cullen, Fr Spratt and several Dublin newspapers.[83] It arose remotely from Dr Cullen's ordinances against clerical involvement in politics, following the defections of Sadleir and Keogh from the ranks of the Independent Irish Party and the cause of the Tenant League. It arose more immediately from the disenchantment of Archdeacon Fitzgerald, parish priest of Rathkeale, Co. Limerick, with these ordinances. A passionate supporter of the League and champion of the rural poor, Fr Fitzgerald, after Mass on Sunday 2nd March 1856, delivered an impassioned homily against landlordism and the *'extermination'* of the poor. In the course of this speech he defended the unguarded comments of another Tenant League priest, Fr Tom O'Shee or O'Shea. In a letter to the Tenant League leaders, Fr O'Shea, deploring Cullen's *'ban'* on politics, called the Archbishop the *'Arch-Apostate'*. Archdeacon Fitzgerald excused O'Shea with the comment that

> if instead of calling Primate Cullen an apostate, he had said that Primate Cullen was an obstacle and the greatest of the obstacles in the way of tenant justice...that [if] Dr Cullen had used the same means to establish tenant justice as he did to establish the Catholic University...he (O'Shea) would have found some that I know of to agree with him...[84]

In less flagrant language, Archdeacon Fitzgerald himself launched a barely-concealed attack on Cullen:

> those who wheedle and coax you and dazzle your eyes by their perhaps honest zeal for your religion, at the same time that they obstinately refuse to join the ranks of your only true and faithful friends, the Independent Opposition, seek not your good but their own...They secure power and distinction for themselves...A Bishop's nephew may reasonably hope to be a collector or a stipendiary [while] the masses are left to the tender mercies of evicting landlords...[they are] victims of extermination...

---

83. The dispute was not covered in the pro-Catholic press, *The Freeman's Journal* and *Dublin Evening Post*, but it was given detailed treatment in the *Dublin Weekly Nation* and in the anti-Catholic *Dublin Evening Packet and Correspondent*.

84. *DWN*, 15th March 1856.

In an ill-disguised reference to the prelate, he continued: *'it is a great comfort to the evicted that we have Italian names for our prayers'*, and, referring to *'the political feelings and misdeeds of certain church dignitaries'*, he concluded to his parishioners

> what filial affection do you or I owe to the suffragens of Connaught or Leinster? ...everyone ought to respect bishops, so long as they respect themselves....[85]

It was not the Archdeacon's only excursion into episcopal criticism. In January 1856 there had been a Tenant League Council meeting in Dublin where Fr O'Shea's letter concerning the 'Arch-Apostate', Dr Cullen, had been read, with O'Shea claiming that he had been muzzled by his ecclesiastical superiors. A draft resolution then followed, criticising Cullen for trying to prevent Catholic participation in political meetings in Dublin. Dwyer Gray of the *Freeman's Journal* objected to the critical wording of the resolution and moved an amendment to have the wording deleted. Archdeacon Fitzgerald proposed that the wording remain and his proposal was carried.[86]

The *Tablet* and *The Nation* had reported on Fr O'Shea's letter and on Archdeacon Fitzgerald's sermon.[87] At a subsequent CYMS meeting, Fr Spratt's fellow 'guardian', Fr James Mulligan, curate of the Pro-Cathedral in Marlborough Street, read out the offending publications and, reportedly under instructions from Dr Cullen, ordered the removal of the two papers from the CYMS reading-room. Uproar ensued, with, apparently, many members protesting. However, the chairman, Matthew Fitzpatrick, overruled them by insisting that the spiritual guardians *'had absolute power in the matter'*. A week later *The Tablet* reported the cancellation of the paper's subscription by the CYMS.[88] *The Nation* expostulated:

> If a newspaper is to be censured for the speeches and writings it inserts and not for its own expressions, what a ridiculous position the Directors of the CYMS have placed themselves in,

85.  *DWN*, 15th March 1856.
86.  *Warder and Dublin Weekly Mail*, 2nd Feb 1856.
87.  *The Tablet*, 22nd March 1856.
88.  *The Tablet*, 29th March 1856.

and added:

> To speak plainly, we believe it (the expulsion) to have been made
> by the orders of His Grace, the Archbishop...we look upon it
> by far the most obnoxious act of this proceeding, that no one
> regards the Rev Mr. Mulligan as the real author of it.[89]

For some reason not quite evident to *The Nation*, the *Catholic Telegraph*
was included in the expulsion order. *The Nation* remarked:

> Why the *Telegraph* we cannot conceive...but the fact is that the
> resistance of the Society was so strong to the course first pursued
> by the Father Guardian that the *Telegraph* was immolated in order
> to secure the expulsion of the other two papers without causing
> the absolute dissolution of the Society.

In truth, however, the *Telegraph* had reproduced the same account of
the Archdeacon's role in the January Tenant League meeting in Dublin
and of the reading there of Fr O'Shea's 'Arch-Apostate' letter.[90]  The
Protestant *Dublin Evening Packet and Correspondent* made much of the
dispute and noted that while both *The Tablet* and the *Telegraph* backed
away from the conflict and were *'disposed to lick the hand that smites them'*,
the editor of *The Nation* dug his heels in.[91]  The latter described how
some 100 CYMS members signed a protest *'against the interdict of their
crafty bishop'* – not their words, rather those of the *Packet* – and the
*Nation* went on to condemn *'the Cullen system as "mean, dark and despotic".'*

Fr John was absent from most of that tumultuous meeting but
became embroiled in the aftershocks.  He waited the best part of a
week before writing to the *Nation's* editor, on 28th March, to dispute
the accuracy of that paper's report of the 22nd.  He insisted that the
expelled journals had been expressing *'gross slanders against the episcopacy'*.
The *Nation*, in response, regretted that he had now identified himself
with the expulsions, since he had taken no part in the proceedings,
having arrived after chairman Fitzpatrick had quelled the revolt.  The

---

89.  *DWN*, 22nd March 1856.
90.  *CT*, 2nd & 9th Feb 1856.
91.  *DEPC*, 1st April 1856.

*Nation* regretted out of hand *'Dr Spratt's monstrous charges of "slandering the episcopacy" and of adopting an "unCatholic tone,"'* and concluded:

> Let him reconcile with his own conscience and with the opinions
> of better and wiser men than, with all respect, anyone supposes
> him to be.[92]

### From protest to progress

The Dublin CYMS survived the upheaval of that spring, and when it held the annual general meeting that November it was as if there was a rallying to its side by the great and the good. Chaired by Dean Meyler, the crowded attendance included two MPs, two Catholic University professors and an array of senior diocesan ecclesiastics, with solicitors, barristers and doctors of divinity aplenty, not omitting Dr Spratt and his Knocktopher confrere, Fr Eugene Cullen. The continued growth in its membership was such that resolutions were adopted to institute a fund-raising campaign to build premises of their own from the ground up. It was a lofty ambition and one never realised, as likewise its hope to expand their educational provision so that the CYMS might become 'The College of the Working Classes', but all this gave clear evidence of a growing confidence for the future. Spratt was elated, euphoric even, when he announced that he had in his hand

> the most important document that had even been addressed to
> any public meeting. It came from one of the most illustrious,
> venerable and venerated prelates in the United Kingdom – it
> came from the Apostolic Delegate, the Most Rev Dr Cullen.

The letter from Cullen, dated 9th November, to 'My dear Dr Spratt' apologised for not being present, offered best wishes for success and enclosed a gift of £5. In fairness, it was an unusually long letter, expressing gratification at the achievements of the CYMS over the previous year, rejoicing that *'thanks to the Liberator, Ireland has entered a new era'* and that Catholics were now rapidly acquiring the position to which they were entitled. He particularly celebrated the creation of their own university and paid tribute to Newman, its Rector. He reserved his final

---

92. *DWN*, 5th April 1856.

and warmest praise for the CYMS members and Fr John:

> Having so many proofs of the good effected by your society all
> that remains for me to do is to beg of you to exhort the young
> men to persevere on the course in which they have entered...
> [and] to assure you, my dear Dr Spratt, of the great esteem with
> which I remain your obedient servant.[93]

**Fig 123.** *Patrick O'Brien, MP.*

To Dr Cullen's praise was added that of the MPs, Rickard Deasy and Patrick O'Brien,[94] bringing to a close an evening of which John Spratt might well have been proud. It would seem that it was with no sense of irony that Dr O'Connell and the City Coroner, Dr Kirwan, proposed, seconded and spoke to a resolution praising the press for its support of the CYMS.[95] No mention was made of earlier discord and the occasion ended with general satisfaction.

Over the following years the Carmelite remained an ever-active presence at CYMS meetings. In August 1857, for example, he moved the resolution to take over the entire Anglesea Street premises pending their securing a building of their own, as the increasing prosperity of the society now enabled them to commence their building fund.[96] They maintained close relations with professors from the Catholic University and secured distinguished speakers for their annual series of public lectures on science and history, including the Cork MP and Catholic historian, John F. Maguire, and the Irish scholar, Eugene

---

93.  *FJ*, 11th Nov 1851, Cullen to Spratt 9th November 1856.
94.  Rickard Deasy (1812-1883), MP for Cork from 1855, Solicitor-General in 1859 and Attorney-General in 1860. Patrick O'Brien (1823-1895), MP for King's County from 1852 until 1885.
95.  *DEP*, *FJ*, 11th Nov 1856.
96.  *FJ*, 19th Aug 1857.

O'Curry.[97] They also maintained close relations with their Archbishop. In February 1858 he attended their annual general meeting on an occasion that was graced with an impressive array of dignitaries, clerical and lay, and attended by several thousand. Cullen actually chaired the meeting and delivered a substantial address on science and art and on the historic role of the Catholic Church in fostering both. He went on to praise the English converts, Newman, Manning, Faber and others and to denounce proselytism and *'souperism'*. Commenting on the proselytisers, he went further:

> I tell you with whom we should be very much displeased – with the respectable Protestants of Dublin because they suffer themselves to be compromised by so low and degraded a class of persons. Strangers who read the placards about our city must think that all Protestants of Dublin were engaged in calumniating their Catholic neighbours; that is not the case; but the respectable Protestants of Dublin should raise their voices against these Souper Schools.[98]

He congratulated the CYMS members on their *'truly gratifying progress'*. For Fr John Spratt and his young men, this occasion was recognition of a high order. It was hardly undeserved. The CYMS membership had grown greatly: by November 1858 it had 900 members according to one source.[99] Some 250 were using the reading room on a daily basis, and their library now contained some 2,260 volumes, 700 of them donated in the previous twelve months. To their language and literature classes in English, Irish and French they had now added Italian and music. An oratory had been opened in the December 1857 and the first mass there was celebrated by Fr John, with Dr Cullen's approval.[100] To the prayer sessions before each formal reading night were added quarterly communion and an annual retreat in the Marlborough Street Church.

97. *FJ*, 16th Dec 1857. John Francis Maguire (1815-1872), MP for Dungarvan from 1852 and for Cork from 1865 to 1872. Eugene O'Curry (1794-1861) was appointed Professor of Irish History and Archaeology in the Catholic University in 1854.
98. *DEP*, 2nd Feb 1858.
99. Egan, p. 60.
100. *WFJ*, 6th Feb 1858.

Their public lectures continued to attract distinguished speakers and substantial attendances. In September 1858, for example, they hosted a lecture by Cardinal Wiseman which attracted an impressive audience that included four bishops and the presidents of Salamanca and Maynooth Colleges. Three months later, Dr Anderdon of the Catholic University, a new but warm friend of Spratt's in these years, drew over 3,000 to a CYMS lecture at the Rotunda.[101] Under Spratt's guidance the CYMS also founded "the Musical Guild of St Cecilia" to promote the performance of the works of great Catholic composers. In September 1859 they staged their first public performance of Haydn's Grand Mass, No. 16, with 100 vocalists.[102] That same month they decided to form a limited company in order to set about acquiring a site and building their own premises. They would seek to raise £5,000 in £1 shares. Apart from the problem of space, they felt some of their public venues were not ideal. As Dr Anderdon, for one, confessed:

> he felt a little uncomfortable when going to the lecture at the Rotunda, either the day before or the day after Lola Montez lectured there.[103]

The summit of the CYMS's public presence was reached at the very end of the decade. The issue was the expression of support for and sympathy with the Pope. While numerous meetings of support for the Papacy were held throughout Ireland at this time, that organised by Spratt and the CYMS was by no means the least. Spratt had sent an invitation to Dr Cullen on 13th November expressing the determination of the CYMS to hold such a meeting and to adopt an address. Cullen replied two days later, pleading inability to attend, due to illness but remarking that if the authority of the Holy See were overturned

> the ties of family would soon be broken...the practice of divorce would be facilitated...and polygamy as taught by the Mormons ...would overrun the earth with its accompanying evils.[104]

101.  *FJ*, 7th Dec 1858. Anderdon became a loyal and active supporter of several of Spratt's ventures and institutions. See Chapters Fourteen & Twenty.
102.  *EF*, 1st Sept 1859.
103.  *FJ*, 16th Sept 1859.
104.  *EF*, 16th Nov 1859.

He added that Socialism and Communism would then destroy the rights of property, and dismissed the notion that the Papal States were badly governed. Despite Dr Cullen's inability to attend, the meeting on 15th November was as impressive as any on the issue. The Rotunda was thronged, *'immense crowds'* gathered outside, and the platform party boasted some four MPs, and a great number of senior clergymen and lay notabilities. Spratt's confreres, Thomas Bennett and Henry McGee, joined him on the occasion. Following appropriately long and impassioned speeches, the CYMS President, Thomas Cosgrave, proposed the adoption of the address to the Pope. A month later, Fr John and his Whitefriar Street brethren organised a similar meeting of the Confraternities of Dublin in support of His Holiness.[105] A year later, almost, Fr John had the gratification of receiving two formal letters of gratitude from Pius IX, conveyed with evident warmth and pleasure through Dr Cullen.[106]

*Decline and Demise*

Dr Cullen's relationship with Dublin CYMS and its founder, John Spratt, developed as a cordial and supportive one over the next few years. The Archbishop supported the Society financially and morally and undoubtedly regarded it as a significant expression of the Catholic mission: it was, after all, established as a bulwark against the perceived proselytising of the YMCA. He attended its principal public lectures and acted as chairman of some of its more important gatherings, at least down to 1865.[107] As for John Spratt and the CYMS, from its foundation until 1856 when the row over the Archdeacon Fitzgerald and Fr O'Shea attacks on Cullen broke out, he had been sole 'Spiritual Guardian'. However from that time and, whether to assist him or to monitor him, a pro-Cathedral curate, Fr James Mulligan, had been appointed as 'Co-Spiritual Guardian'. When Fr Mulligan died prematurely, later that year, Fr John Pope, a canon of the Cathedral, was appointed in his place. Consequently, for the next decade he and Spratt appeared in harness at various CYMS events. Gradually, as the 1860s wore on, Spratt became

105.  *FJ*, 5th Jan 1859.
106.  *CT*, 13th Oct 1860, reproduces the Pope's thanks to Spratt and the Confraternities; *WFJ*, 24th Nov 1860, conveys Pius IX's thanks to Spratt and the CYMS.
107.  For his support and attendance see, for example, *FJ*, 12th June 1860; *FJ*, 20th Oct 1863; *FJ*, 7th June 1865.

less involved and Canon Pope more involved in the supervision of the Society. It was from the mid-1860s that the CYMS peaked and then declined. It had moved location twice – from Abbey Street to Ormond Quay in August 1860 and then from there to the disused Dominican Chapel in Denmark Street in October 1861.[108] As far as Fr John was concerned this first move was a retrograde step. He regarded the money spent on it as *'thrown away'*. Furthermore, it came at a time when there were problems in retaining the large number of members. It was clear that there had been discussions about decentralising the organisation by the creation of local clubs or 'guilds', but he had not been consulted. This the friar would not countenance and he pointed out that any such change would have required the agreement of the spiritual guardians, and ultimately of the Archbishop. He cautioned the CYMS committee to concentrate on immediate practical challenges instead of *'fanciful'* schemes of restructuring, *'if the present apathy would be overcome'*. In what amounted to a printed public rebuke, he claimed that the rudeness of some of the staff and bad management had *'stripped the society to a very serious number'*.[109] By late 1865, it emerged that the second move to Dominick Street also had been unwise. The cost of upkeep proved beyond them but, more importantly, the location was not central enough. As a consequence, the membership declined dramatically, even at a time when the CYMS was trying to widen its appeal and portfolio by developing a wide range of evening classes in association with the Catholic University. In October 1863, at a time when their library had expanded to 4,000 volumes, thanks in particular to Fr Spratt, came reports of *'fluctuating membership'* and this was put down to the economic depression at the time.[110] By autumn 1865 they were in financial difficulties, despite donations from laity and clergy including Cullen, Woodlock and Spratt, and they decided to reduce considerably the annual membership fee from 8 to 5 shillings, in

---

108.  *EF*, 18th Aug 1860; *FJ*, 25th Oct 1861. The Dominicans had constructed a new, larger St Saviour's Church and presbytery. By coincidence, and unrelated, Spratt's confrere, Thomas Bennett, had opened a 'Collegiate Seminary' or secondary school in Denmark Street in 1854: see D'Arcy, *Terenure College, 1860-2010: A History*, pp. 22, 128.

109.  GMA, *Box 73*, printed circular letter, Spratt to President, CYMS, 19th February 1861.

110.  *FJ*, 20th Oct 1863. For this economic depression see Chapter Twenty.

the hope of recovering recruitment. In August 1866 came the last documented public outing for the CYMS when Spratt and Canon Pope led it as a deputation to congratulate Dr Cullen on his elevation to Cardinal.[111]   Only two months later the CYMS held an emergency meeting '*with a view either to its continuance or its dissolution*' as '*the members of the Society had diminished to a painful extent*'.  They now numbered only 180, down from the many hundreds of their happier Abbey Street days, when they were '*the most flourishing Society in Dublin*'.[112]  By this stage the Carmelite friar appears to have opted out or drifted away from active involvement and, it was in some desperation that Canon Pope, in a public letter of mid-October 1866, suggested a radical appeal to Dublin laity and clergy for support, concluding, with more hope than faith, '*but perhaps the citizens of Dublin may yet throw us a plank to save us from sinking*'.[113] The plank was not thrown.

The CYMS officers quietly abandoned Denmark Street sometime between October 1866 and May 1867.  The one and only report of any Dublin CYMS activity to appear in print for another forty years came on 3 May 1867: when an advertisement announced a general meeting in the school rooms of Cecilia Street to make arrangements for elections. The rest was silence.[114]

---

111.   *FJ*, 21st Aug 1866.
112.   *FJ*, 11th Oct 1866.
113.   *FJ*, 16th Oct 1866.
114.   *EF*, 3rd May 1867.  No other report of any Dublin CYMS has been found in the
         newspaper press until 22nd February 1907 when the *Dublin Daily Express*
         mentioned a meeting in the Mansion House of a 'Dublin Roman Catholic Young
         Men's Society'.  The CYMS Centenary Record of 1949 mentioned a CYMS unit
         in Aughrim Street in 1896 and another in North Frederick Street in 1908: see
         Anon, *Catholic Young Men's Society of Ireland: Centenary Record, 1849-1949*, Dublin
         1949, p. 31.  It is ironic that the demise of the CYMS in Dublin came at a time
         when similar societies were founded and flourished in Dundalk, Newry, Sligo,
         Galway, Cork, Wexford, Waterford and Navan.

# CHAPTER NINETEEN

---

## Harbouring the Homeless:
## The Night Refuge, 1860-1961

> In the wretched religious distractions which divide and harass our country it is unusual to allude [thus] to a brother of a different sect but there are signs and tendencies abroad which seem to indicate that this system of mutual anathema is passing away...[1]

So commented the Church of Ireland rector, Rev W G Carroll, that shining light amid the gloom and poverty of St Bride's Parish. He was speaking of his Carmelite friend and charity co-worker, John Spratt, in May 1871. Sectarian jealously and mutual anathema may have been *'passing away'* in 1871: a decade before this, however, William Carroll and the friar, together and separately, felt the sharp edge of sectarian rancour and denominational rivalry. At the beginning of the 1860s, in both Protestant and Catholic camps, there was a morbid preoccupation with religious perversion; on both sides, protestations of abhorrence of proselytism. In April 1860, Henry Joy, Q.C., as a spokesman for the Protestant Orphan Society, expressed concern that orphans were *'exposed to the insidious arts of Romish proselytism'.*[2] On the other side, that January, the Ladies' Association of Charity of St Vincent de Paul spoke of *'perils to the faith of Catholic orphans'* and continued, *'we shall now enumerate some of the institutions, machinery and snares contrived for the destruction of our poor children's faith'.* They began by listing first the Protestant Orphan Society, to the latter's consternation, in a long list of Protestant orphan institutions.[3]

---

1. *EF*, 30th May 1871: sermon of the Rev W G Carroll, Rector of St Bride's Parish, on Pentecost Sunday, on the death of John Spratt, three days before.
2. *SNL*, 14th April 1860.
3. *CT*, 21st Jan 1860.

Such confessional concern was toxic enough to infect even the issue of the national census, due to be conducted in April 1861. When the project came before parliament for approval, from April 1860, there was an initial government position that the Census of Ireland would contain no inquiries as to the religion of its inhabitants. The editor of the *Dublin Evening Packet and Correspondent* was not best pleased:

> There are particular reasons for desiring a religious census of Ireland and the Government must not be allowed to cheat us of it, out of concession to Ultramontane prejudices. A number of causes have conspired to thin the Roman Catholic population and, just as steadily as they have left the country, Englishmen and Scotchmen have settled here, bringing with them their enlightened religious convictions.[4]

The *Packet* reverted to the subject several times later that year, describing Ireland as *'at present the most Ultramontane and priest-ridden country on the face of the globe'.*[5] While the *Warder and Dublin Weekly Mail* agreed, it added:

> Census or not, Ireland is fast becoming a Protestant country. Twenty years more, like the ten last, might be enough to turn the scale.[6]

Such confessional demographic challenges were largely ignored by the Catholic clergy but the sole exception, John Spratt, could no longer contain himself. On 11th December 1860, he addressed the challenge in a letter to the *Freeman's Journal* and referred to an evening paper *'gloating'* over the anticipated results of the next census:

> With an almost jubilant spirit, the editor has gone into the calculation of the hundreds of thousands destroyed by the famine or driven to expatriation, and the gratifying decrease of Popery in consequence; the continued and increased emigration to America and Australia and also to England, with the same happy result; the vaunted progress of the proselytism of the

---

4. *DEPC*, 26th April 1860.
5. *DEPC*, 15th Nov 1860.
6. *WDWM*, 1st Sept 1860.

Bible Societies, their agents and sympathisers...and the influence of some 40,000 English settlers...[the editor] exulting in the mighty vision he has conjured up, insists with fanatic emphasis that the coming Census will prove that the name 'Catholic' should no longer be applicable to Ireland.

When the commencement date of 8th April neared, the *Evening Packet* re-entered the fray: observing that anxiety was increasing concerning *'honest returns'*, it adverted to the *'strong desire to learn...the numerical proportions of Protestantism to Romanism in Ireland'*, as, *'for the purposes of struggling against Romanism, we are all Protestants together'*. It continued:

That the Romish Church will, to speak in electioneering phrase, poll to the last man, is absolutely certain...and from the silence which its dignitaries have hitherto maintained upon the subject, no priest having publicly written on it except our old opponent, Dr Spratt, whom nobody minds, we may rest assured that the ecclesiastical 'instructions' have preceded the civil and that the Altar has anticipated the Registrar-General's Office.[7]

The *Packet* was, however, ill-advised to characterise John Spratt as he *'whom nobody minds'*: somebody in authority must have minded him as, in April 1861, a Catholic, George W Abraham, was appointed as one of the two Assistant Commissioners.[8]

In the end, the Census returns hardly did much to overexcite the confessional contenders. As a percentage of the total population, over the period from the previous religious census in 1834 up to 1861, Catholics experienced a decline of 3.2%, falling from 80.9% to 77.7%; over the same period, the Church of Ireland and Presbyterian membership experienced a rise of 3.5% from 18.8% to 22.3% of the whole. While that trend would continue down to the year 1911 and

---

7. *DEPC*, 23rd March 1861.
8. George Whitley Abraham was joint Assistant Commissioner along with Sir William Wilde. Both were made full commissioners for the 1871 Census. Abraham translated a life of St Dominic by Lacordaire, donated to various Catholic Church charities and contributed widely to the national and international press. He died on Christmas Day, 1885, in Dublin. See *Census of Ireland for the Year 1861*, Dublin 1863; *Tipperary Vindicator*, 12th Jan 1864; *DDE*, 28th Dec 1885.

beyond, it proved a far cry from the scale reversal in twenty years that the *Warder* had anticipated back in April 1860.[9]  As the *Dublin Evening Post* pointed out, the membership of the Established Church of Ireland had also declined, from 852,064 to 678,661 and the Dissenters in similar extent:

> All, in fact, have suffered by the common calamity…and those who had so cruelly speculated upon the disappearance of the Catholic majority have now reason to rejoice that their uncharitable anticipations have proved altogether groundless.[10]

*The Portobello Hotel*
Such melancholy reflections did nothing to assuage the 'mutual anathema' that marked the beginning of this decade.  Proselytism continued to be problematic, but, paradoxically, productive – for its opponents.  The fear of religious apostasy or piracy proved a potent stimulus to all sides in the protection of their flocks, especially the disabled and the destitute.  As one sympathetic editor expressed it, many charitable institutions *'had been perverted to sectarian uses'*.[11]  It was in this atmosphere of confessional rivalry and mutual fear of proselytism that Fr John and his long-time clerical comrade, William Yore, were moved to open a temporary asylum for destitute blind females in a house in Lower Dominick Street.  It admitted its first blind woman on 18th August 1858, under the care of the Sisters of Charity.[12]  A parallel initiative led, on 31st January 1859, to the opening of an asylum for the destitute male blind in Glasnevin under the care of religious brothers. By October 1859 the male asylum cared for some seventy persons while the female asylum had a maximum capacity of forty.  By the summer of 1859, the pressure for places in this latter exceeded its capacity and the concerned Carmelite was already seeking for a solution.  That spring he had come upon the vacant and deteriorating Portobello Hotel.

---

9.  N. C. Fleming & A. O'Day, eds., *The Longman Handbook of Modern Irish History since 1800*, London 2005, p. 452, for the denominational percentages.

10.  *DEP*, 16th July 1851.

11.  *EF*, 24th Sept 1859.

12.  GMA, Box 73, *An Appeal on Behalf of the Catholic Blind Asylum, Dublin*, July 1858; also, *FJ*, 11th April 1861: the date was given then by George Gordon Place, secretary of St Mary's Asylum for the Industrious Blind, in his annual report.

One-time pride of the Grand Canal Company from its first opening in 1807, it had since become redundant by the coming of the railways.[13] Spratt conceived the idea of becoming its tenant, to create a new home for the destitute female blind and, as so often before, he engaged his network of lay supporters to fund the refurbishment and the yearly rent. Putting together a volunteer committee, they cleared the tons of rubbish from the basement, restored the building and converted it into St Mary's Catholic Asylum for the Female Blind.

**Fig 124.** *Monsignor William Yore.*

For Fr John, not the least gratifying element in the restoration project was the fact that a large space on the premises had been previously devoted to a spirits warehouse for a liquor store in Camden Street: this they now converted into the chapel of the Asylum. Yore and Spratt made arrangements with the Irish Sisters of Charity, led by Mrs Telford, to take over and manage the institution as they had done in Dominick Street. In August 1859 the blind residents of Dominick Street were transferred to the new facility in Portobello, which could accommodate up to 150 blind women.[14] By the start of 1862 it was sheltering some 100 souls and providing *'remunerative industry'*. They were trained in basket-making, stocking-weaving and in the making of fibre mats. Music, too, was taught in the Asylum and in 1862, during

---

13. For a brief history of this establishment, see M. Curtis, *Portobello*, Dublin 2012, pp. 113, 117-8. The author dates the take-over of the hotel for a blind asylum as 1858, whereas it was in fact 1859: see *FJ*, 3rd Feb 1862. It was in business as a hotel up to late November 1858; following financial difficulties, its contents were auctioned off on 18th January 1859: see *SNL*, 14th, 17th Jan 1859. The title to the hotel itself was to have been sold on 29th January 1859. Sometime between then and June 1859 it was acquired as the new location for St Mary's Female Asylum, replacing the Dominick Street facility: see *Tipperary Vindicator*, 14th June 1859.

14. *FJ*, 11th April 1861.

**Fig 125.** *Portobello College, formerly the Portobello Hotel.*

a courtesy visit, the Lord Lieutenant was received by Yore, Spratt and Mrs Telford and was entertained to an organ recital by a blind boy and girl. The residents were enabled to contribute to their own keep. Greater ambitions were conceived by the Sisters: they planned to increase the intake so that the Asylum could become a 'national' charity. The result was that this Asylum at Portobello became a staging post as the Sisters and their organising support committee secured a new, larger site at Harold's Cross and engaged the architect, Charles Geoghegan, to design a completely new facility.[15] As the time to move from Portobello to Harold's Cross approached, the Sisters entered negotiations with a businessman, Isaac Cole, who wished to take over the building and return it to its original use as a hotel. Spratt cannot have been too pleased with this as he had asked the diocesan vicar-general, Monsignor McCabe, to approach Mrs Telford with a view to securing the premises for some other venture, most likely for his contemplated Night Refuge for Homeless Women and Children.[16] Whatever his plan for the Portobello premises might have been, at this point, he had left it too late. McCabe was informed by Mrs Telford, on 9th April 1868, that much as she would wish to see the building *'devoted to the interests of religion'*, she had pledged her word to the entrepreneur that she would

---

15.  Ibid.; *EF*, 3rd Feb 1862.
16.  See p. 411.

give him first refusal.[17] The premises, in consequence, re-opened under Cole, as a hotel, which proved eminently convenient for British Army officers from the nearby Portobello Barracks.[18]

Spratt probably asked McCabe to approach Mrs Telford on this matter as his own relations with her had not always been cordial: he was not pleased with the way the Portobello Asylum was being filled with all-comers, to the exclusion of cases he considered to be particularly deserving. One such case revolved around a young inmate of the Molyneux Asylum for Blind Females, a Protestant charity, founded in Peter Street in Dublin in 1815. Originally intended to admit blind persons of all creeds, by the mid-1850s it claimed to have none but Protestant blind residents. However, it did employ two Catholic servants *'to the detriment of its true Protestant character and to the danger of the young inmates who must, more or less, associate with them – an impropriety persevered in to the present moment'*. So discovered a committee of investigation established in 1856-7 and which discovered malpractice and corruption in the Institute.[19] Whether, by the 1860s, it had begun to take in Catholics again, is not clear, but in 1866 Fr Spratt clearly tried to gain the admission of a former inmate, presumably Catholic, to the new St Mary's at Portobello. He may have tried first to secure admission for her by directly approaching Mrs Telford, to no effect. This is inferred from a letter of Mrs Telford to Archbishop Cullen on 9th April 1868: he had intervened on the girl's behalf but Mrs Telford held firm as she knew

---

17. DDA, *Cullen Papers*, 341/1/IV/1, Telford to McCabe, 9th April & McCabe to Spratt, 13th April 1868.

18. Curtis, p. 118. In the 20th century it became a nursing and retirement home: among those who spent their last years there was the painter Jack B Yeats and the owner of the Gate Theatre, Lord Longford.

19. It had failed to publish annual reports or accounts for over twenty-five years, had deprived the residents of proper diet and had paid its suppliers over the odds for goods and services. Although its numbers had remained stable over these many years, its income had 'greatly increased' but its expenditure to an even greater extent so that it was in debt by over £200 by 1857: see L. H. King Harman & H. Allnutt, *The Veil Partly Withdrawn, or further revelations in connection with the Molyneux Asylum for Blind Females, Peter Street, Dublin*, Dublin 1857, p. 20. See also Anonymous, *A Statement of the Efforts Made by the Committee Desirous for Reforms in the Molyneux Asylum for Blind Females*, Dublin 1857, pp. 4-8, 16.

from sad experience how dangerous the influence of such persons is over our dear Catholic blind children, having received two from that Asylum at the opening of our Institution and I am sorry to say, notwithstanding all that has been done to remove their protestant impressions, they still remain tainted, and it is with great difficulty they are prevented from injuring the souls of their companions.[20]

Spratt was written to by Mrs Telford on the same day or a day later, and while her letter is not extant, it is clear that it left Spratt in something of a fury: he wrote to Mrs Telford and did not mince his words:

My dear Mrs Telford,
I return your pound note which is a wretched compromise for what Religion and Charity should render imperative on "Sisters of Charity" to do for the poor blind girl. Mr Smith, the Souper Agent, in consequence of your refusal to give shelter to the unfortunate blind girl, is unwilling to part with his victim, and he possesses zeal in his wretched vocation, very little of which, I am sorry to say, exists in certain quarters on our side. The parent of the girl in question is a wretched pauper, and, as far as I can learn, in the fangs of Soupers, and the idea of sending her home is now out of the question.
I hope the perversion of our Blind Asylum at Portobello to a mere boarding house for inmates of Work Houses in the Provinces may rest lightly on your conscience in your dying moments, as I must say that the manner in which this case and some others that I knew of, have been dealt with entirely outrages my idea of what true charity consists in.
I am your obedient servant,
John Spratt.

However, by that stage he had too many other engagements to dwell for long on this disappointment. Indeed, back at the start of the Portobello project, at the commencement of this decade, his concern for the destitute engaged him in several other commitments to the poor, one of which would constitute perhaps his greatest challenge, his greatest achievement and his most lasting legacy.

20. DDA, *Cullen Papers*, 327/6/VI/12/1, Telford to Cullen, 20th April 1866.

*Sheltering the Destitute: The Night Refuge*

On 24th October 1860 Fr John addressed an open letter to the editors of the *Dublin Evening Post* and the *Freeman's Journal.* In a public life of over five decades littered with such letters to the press, this was one of his most dramatic and effective. Directed to the problem of "The Homeless Poor", in its urgency and poignancy it anticipated by over twenty-five years those two great classics of social protest, *The Bitter Cry of Outcast London* and *Maiden Tribute of Modern Babylon.*[21] As such, it merits some citation:

> Dear Sir,
>
> I have for a long period, with feelings of sorrow and commiseration, looked upon the pitiable condition of the homeless poor of this city – those utterly destitute creatures who are under the dire necessity of spending the night in the streets, crouching and shivering under an archway or the passages of houses – outcasts, as it were of humanity, forlorn and deserted by all. There are hundreds of these homeless creatures in Dublin... [who]...spend even the most bitter nights without any shelter, save that which a doorway or a dismal hall of some old house affords: but this is not the worst of it; destitute young women repeatedly call at the police stations, and ask permission to sit at the fire until morning; this request is on all occasions refused, and the poor creatures are turned out – for what? Because there was no charge against them. Can we wonder that many of these, unable to bear up against cold and hunger, succumb and lose their virtue. I have also been informed, that many poor creatures sleep in the hall of one of the daily morning papers every night; and trifling as is the shelter it affords, they could not have it only that the gate is open all night for workmen to pass in and out......I well know that the amount of misery in this city is so great that it cannot be expected that all could be grappled with; but still it appears to me that some of its most appalling results would be prevented by the institution of a Night Refuge for Homeless Women and Children...It may be considered unreasonable of me, where so many charities are supported, so many claims generously responded to, to expect that an additional burden

---

21. A. Mearns, *The Bitter Cry of Outcast London*, London 1883; W. T. Stead, 'The Maiden Tribute of Modern Babylon', in *Pall Mall Gazette*, 6th, 7th, 8th, 10th July 1885.

should be undertaken.  But can we ever do too much in the cause of Him who has shed the last drop of his sacred blood for our salvation in the name of suffering humanity...I make this appeal...for the means of establishing a night asylum, the details connected with which shall command my earnest and constant attention.

I have the honour to be, dear Sir, your obedient servant,

John Spratt, D.D.[22]

*Proselytism and Poverty*

The timing of this plea, just then, is the subject of two divergent accounts given some years after its publication.  The first, dating from 1865, relates how a French *'author of eminence'*, was visiting Dublin with a view to writing a book about Ireland.  Determined to see the city at its worst as well as its best, with two Irish companions he visited the only night refuge in Dublin at the time.  This was an unnamed facility, actually the Bow Street Night Asylum, being run by *'lay Scripture expounders'* and the author was appalled by the poverty and distress encountered.  This account suggests that the author reported the situation to the Catholic authorities in the city and thence it was resolved that they should set up a proper night shelter for the homeless and that John Spratt was approached to take up the challenge.[23]  This account, given in the *Dublin Weekly Nation* by its editor and owner, A M Sullivan, a close associate of Spratt's in many undertakings in these years, has some credibility.  The account does not identify the French author and *'true friend of Ireland'*.  However, the most likely 'French author of eminence' is Adolphe Perraud.  He visited Ireland in 1860 and produced a comprehensive and insightful account of the country, entitled *Etudes sur l'Irlande Contemporaine*, published in Paris in 1862, and in Dublin the year following.[24]  He provided detailed accounts of poverty and distress in the west of Ireland and in Dublin, wrote extensively on the poor

---

22. *DEP, FJ, EF,* 25th Oct 1860, *CT,* 3rd Nov 1860.
23. *DWN,* 23rd Dec 1865.
24. A. Perraud (1828-1906), priest, professor of history and later Cardinal.  An English translation published by James Duffy in Dublin in 1863 is entitled *Contemporary Ireland,* but another Dublin edition which appeared in 1864 is entitled *Ireland under English Rule.*

**Fig 126.** *A M Sullivan.*          **Fig 127.** *Cardinal Adolphe Perraud.*

law system and mentioned the existence of the Night Refuge and its foundation by John Spratt.

The second account, in August 1871, some three months after Spratt's death, appeared in the *Freeman's Journal*. It tells a more dramatic story. It relates how, on a cold January night, in 1861, in a biting east wind, Fr Spratt drove through sleeting rain and half-melted snow, to the offices of the *Freeman's Journal*, to deliver copy to the sub-editor. On the way up, on an exposed landing, he came upon a group of homeless women and children in a huddle against the elements. Having completed his business with the sub-editor, they descended the back stairway together and encountered two or three shivering humans lying inside cardboards boxes and six little girls huddled in the doorway, *'drenched to the skin and as cold as corpses'*. He then encountered and spoke with two young women who had lost their employment a fortnight since and had nowhere to stay, having exhausted their meagre funds. He returned to the *Freeman's* office, to discuss the situation with the editor. He learned that the greatest threat to such unfortunate women was other women, namely, their employers, since domestic servants such as these were liable to instant dismissal for trivial offences. This idea and very phrasing occurs in his powerful letter, *The Homeless Poor* of October 1860. At the time of these encounters around the offices of the *Freeman's Journal*, there were no casual wards in workhouses where the transient destitute could find lodging overnight: short of entering the workhouse, such women were homeless. The account continues that following these encounters, Spratt laid the results of the experience before Archbishop Cullen and received encouragement to pursue some solution.[25]  This account has a ring of authenticity in its immediacy and may have been given to its anonymous author by Spratt himself, or else may have been written by Sir John Gray as editor and friend of the friar. However, the dating cannot be correct as to January 1861 since Spratt's first public mention of the problem had been delivered in his letter of 24th October 1860.  Furthermore, over a year before this again, in September 1859, the Carmelite wrote to Archbishop Cullen, *'out of the blue'*, as it were, a revealing letter on this same subject: he urged the need for such an asylum, not least because the only one in the City was the Bow Street Night Asylum, *'the great recruiting Depot for the Souper Schools of the Church Mission Society'*.[26]  It is not evident what reply Dr Cullen may have offered and a year went by before Spratt took the critical initiative with his letter, *The Homeless Poor.*  It had an immediate impact. The *Evening Post* editor urged that Spratt's call for a night asylum *'has the strongest claims upon all who are blest with affluence and upon whom devolves the imperative duty of assisting in this good work'*.  At the same time, the *Evening Freeman* recommended the friar's *'admirable letter'* to the *'consideration of the affluent and benevolent'* and urged that *'all true philanthropists, regardless of sect or party, should lend a co-operating hand to this work of real humanity'*.[27]

*Finding a Home*

Thus encouraged, Spratt set about locating premises that might provide the structure for a refuge.  He had not far to look.  It was in Cork Street, where he had been born and where brother Michael's bankruptcy had lost them their own family hearth, that the friar found the makings of a home for the homeless.  Here, at Brickfield Lane, stood the now abandoned Stove Tenter House, itself a charitable initiative, by an earlier remarkable philanthropist, Thomas Pleasants.  Pleasants, immensely wealthy from inherited property and his wife's estate, was as generous as he was prosperous.  He left behind him an impressive record of charitable foundations which included the Cork Street Fever Hospital, Pleasants' Asylum, and the Stove Tenter House.  This last-

25.  *FJ*, 30th Aug 1871.
26.  DDA, *Cullen Papers*, 319/7/II/20, Spratt to Cullen, 25th September 1859.
27.  *DEP*, *EF*, 25th Oct 1860.

named, for which he donated £13,000 in 1815, was a very large, four-storey structure, built on the eastern side of an extensive lawn; it was effectively a drying house for the cloths of the weavers of the Coombe, in the Liberties. Here, by means of great coal-fired stoves that circulated heat throughout the building they could stretch out their cloths and dry them, suspended on tenter hooks, in winter.[28]  With the collapse of the Liberties textile trades, over 1820 to 1850, the Tenter House itself became redundant and fell into decay.  It lay idle until in the 1850s the poor law guardians of the South Dublin Union, overwhelmed by applications for admission to their overflowing poorhouse, took over the lease of the Tenter House from the Thomas Pleasants' Trust and converted it into an auxiliary workhouse.  The South Dublin Union re-installed the stoves to heat the edifice and refurbished the building. They built a covered walkway along its western front and overall made the place habitable, housing juvenile paupers.  By the end of the 1850s the Union no longer needed it and once again it was abandoned.  Such was the situation when, between October and December 1860, John Spratt came upon it, in the very streets where he had played as a child.

**Fig 128.**  *South view of the Stove Tenter House in 1818.*

---

28.  For Pleasants, see C. Doyle, 'Thomas Pleasants (1728-1818)', in *DIB*, vol. 8, pp. 151-2. For the Stove Tenter House, see J. McGregor, pp. 182-83.

*Finding the Funds*

Apparently without a penny to his name, he entered into a tenancy agreement with the Pleasants' Trustees, in December 1860, to lease the premises initially for ten years, at £100 a year rent.[29] It seems he trusted in Providence and in his own good name to source the funds he needed. By this move he secured a building with three floors and a basement, each floor over 200 feet long, situated on a green-field plot the size of Fitzwilliam Square. This land was, presumably, the famous Tenters' Fields where the weavers of the eighteenth century had stretched out their fabrics for bleaching. Now it was surrounded by a wall, with proper entrance and gate-lodge. As with Portobello, he formed a project committee and prepared a public appeal for funds. If not in any spectacular way, his appeal bore fruit. Soon sufficient people came forward with modest but welcome contributions: £7, for example, from his old friend, Fr Anderdon; £1 each from the Police Commissioner Lake, the City Marshall, Thomas Reynolds and the poor law guardian and honorary secretary to his Portobello project, George Godfrey Place.[30] Even his current arch-enemies, the Licensed Vintners' and Grocers' Society, rallied to the cause. First was their president, Carey who gifted £10 that December, and then the Society itself, through its secretary, Bernard Brady – who was Spratt's most searing critic in the trade – came forward with another £10.[31] In addition, Spratt himself had already asked a supporter, Thomas McEntyre, to put in a good word with a mutual acquaintance and former Repeal comrade, P J Murray, soon to be Inspector of Reformatories and Industrial Schools.[32] Murray undertook to guarantee the £100 annual rent for the ten years of the lease. Furthermore, he provided a separate donation of six guineas.[33] McEntyre, writing in the wake of this donor's death in 1873, indicated that Murray objected to having his acts of charity publicised during his lifetime, but McEntyre insisted that *'such acts should*

---

29. *FJ*, 8th Dec 1860.
30. *FJ*, 18th, 27th, 31st Dec 1860, 8th, 9th Jan 1861.
31. *FJ*, 13th Dec 1860, 7th Jan 1861.
32. *FJ*, 18th Feb 1873, Thomas McEntyre to editor, 17th February 1873, in an encomium on the death of Murray. The latter held this position from 1863: see *Thom's Directory*, 1863, p. 834.
33. *EF*, 10th Dec 1860, 29th Jan 1861.

*not be allowed to pass unrecorded*'.[34] Murray's generous undertaking was one of the most significant donations in enabling Spratt to realise the vision, not least as the Carmelite mentioned, early in 1862, that it cost £9 a week to sustain the project.[35]

Other donations, large and small, local and international, personal and commercial, all helped. Small sums came from afar, such as the gift of two guineas from a lady emigrant in Sydney, who promised a similar sum for every year thereafter, £1 from a lady in Melbourne, a similar sum from Dr Mullock in Newfoundland, or the £5 from Madame d'Abbadie in Paris.[36] Fr John was happy to acknowledge interdenominational support also, such as £1 from 'a Protestant lady', £2 from Rev Richard Dickson, rector of Wickham, Berkshire, to the munificent £50 initial gift from Benjamin Lee Guinness, coupled with a promise of an annual £5 subscription, all came Fr John's way in the course of January 1861, even before he had opened the Refuge.[37] Other prominent early donors included clergymen such as Yore and Woodlock, together with businessmen such as Bianconi and Devereux, and local politicians such as Atkinson and Reynolds.[38] Commercial houses also rallied and were acknowledged, even if some were dealers in alcohol, such as with Findlater & Co.[39] Other retail houses, such as Cannock & White and Arnott & Co of Henry Street, would become regular

---

34. *FJ*, 18th Feb 1873. Called to the Bar in 1848, Murray had been a founder of both the *Dublin Review* and the *Irish Quarterly Review*. Only fifty years old when he died, his passing was marked by contradictory characterisations. For the *Freeman's Journal* he had been *'a most amiable and kindly gentleman'* whose death *'will be regretted by a very large circle of friends and acquaintances'*. For the extremer nationalist organ, *The Irishman*, which speculated *'whether his end was accelerated by extreme labour in the discharge of his duties, or by the depressing influence of debt and drunkenness'*, he was a villain who ignored and suppressed chaplains' and physicians' reports on the mistreatment of Fenian prisoners and, as Director of Prisons, punished the temerity of Dr Robert McDonnell for exposing the inhumanity of the prison regime by forcing him to live permanently within the prison walls himself. For these opposing assessments see *FJ*, 10th Feb 1873, *The Irishman*, 22nd Feb 1873. He was one of the two Directors of the Government Prisons' Office from 1864 to at least 1867: see *Thom's Directory*, 1864, p. 836 and 1867, p. 863.
35. *EF*, 6th Feb 1862.
36. GMA, Box 73, newspaper cutting from *Catholic Telegraph* of letter dated 23rd November 1862; *EF*, 21st, 24th June 1862; *FJ*, 14th July 1863, respectively.
37. *WFJ*, 16th Feb 1861; *FJ*, 10th Jan 1861; *DDE*, 29th Jan 1861 respectively.
38. *FJ*, 27th Dec 1860; *EF*, 31st Dec 1860; *FJ*, 9th, 10th, 14th Jan 1861.
39. *FJ*, 9th Jan 1861.

donors of modest cash gifts. The project had been prompted as much by fear of Protestant proselytism as by the shock of female destitution, yet it was presented as strictly non-denominational. Although soon it would be called St Joseph's Night Refuge, and although from the start, it featured evening and morning prayer, it insisted that *'it knows no distinction of creed in its benevolence'* and *'was open to all creeds and none'*.[40]

*Opening the Doors*

By early February 1861 Fr John was ready to launch his project. He invited the press and the public to view his premises over Sunday and Monday, 10th and 11th of that month. Those who came to inspect found an impressive structure consisting of cast-iron pillars and joists, with the iron lathwork floors overlaid with timber. There is a remarkable description of the layout of the Refuge given in a letter of 24th July 1871 by one Marian St John Neville, who knew Fr Spratt, and this supplements contemporary newspaper accounts. Her letter describes the ground floor as containing the washing facilities and a dormitory *'for the lowest class of persons such as street dealers and hawkers, charwomen and others'*. Along this two hundred-foot dormitory, with its twelve windows, were wooden platforms, one foot from the floor, and on these were arranged *'the cocoa fibre mattresses supplied with warm though coarse and plain covering'*.[41] The second floor dormitory held one hundred iron bedsteads – *'the covering a little better than that below'*. This was designed for *'a more respectable class, such as servants out of place'*, the *'better class of aged poor'* who needed temporary support, and out of work governesses. On this floor also there was located a smaller dormitory *'containing five or six comfortable beds'*. Here Fr Spratt afforded shelter and privacy to *'many a sad and sore-tried creature who had been born in wealth and respectability but who had been reduced to destitution by unforeseen circumstances'*. The writer, St John Neville, recalled that *'Fr Spratt was very tenderly considerate to all such. I remember his telling me not to look earnestly at the women as he received them – that he would not like them to think he was making a show of them'*. Each dormitory had a waiting room *'for its respective classes'*, *'lit by gas and cheered by a warm fire in winter'*, and to each was also attached a small room in which the dormitory matron slept overnight, with access to a

40.  FJ, 30th Aug 1871.
41.  GMA, Box 57, Envelope and letter from Veronica Crowley, SMG, to Laura Magnier, Archivist, 24th April 2013, containing typescript copy of letter from Marian St John Neville to Miss Blake, 24th July 1871; also EF, 29th Jan 1861.

**Fig 129.** *St Joseph's Night Refuge for the Homeless Poor.*

bell-pull alarm in case of fire or other mishap. The general matron was paid, and the other matrons were simply given free lodging in return for their service. The top floor housed a chapel, a breakfast room and a schoolroom for the children of the destitute residents and of the poor of the locality. An elaborate system of piping heated the whole building from large stoves, located presumably in the basement. These also served to warm up or dry out the cold and wet arrivals, while a heated outhouse served to dry their clothes.[42]

Spratt was at pains to assure his public and supporters that this would be no place for professional beggars or ladies of ill-repute. His aim was to

> afford shelter to such well-conducted females as may be under the dire necessity of spending the night in the street, crouching under an archway or in the passages of old houses and thus be placed in circumstances of moral danger.[43]

All that was required for such unfortunates to secure shelter was to procure a note from some clergyman or *'other respectable person'* and to present themselves before eight o'clock at night, after which hour the Refuge was closed. Every evening for the remaining ten years of his

---

42. *EF*, 29th Jan 1861.
43. *FJ*, 12th Feb 1861.

life, Fr John made his way before eight, through the little wicket gate, where he stood *'and examined each applicant at the gate lodge endeavouring thereby to avoid the admission of bad characters'*.[44] On summer evenings the poor women worked or read on the benches along the covered walkway, until nine o'clock, at which point Fr Spratt led the night prayers for the residents. Every morning, whenever it might be available, they received a breakfast of bread and tea, before setting off to spend another day on the streets in search of employment or support.

### I was a stranger and you took me in

The question arises, who were these people, and in what numbers did they seek this Refuge? At all times, the vast majority of the adult females were out of work domestic servants, bringing home the truth of Spratt's observation that woman's worst enemy was woman, in the sense that such servants were liable to dismissal at the whim of their employer mistresses. After domestics, the next largest category tended to be those engaged in branches of the clothing trade, either as dress and shirt makers, weavers or milliners. Then came the street traders or hawkers, sellers of newspapers or petty wares. Next followed the varying numbers of shop assistants, child minders and governesses. Finally, at all times there were the children of these homeless women, constituting from ten to thirty per cent of the nightly population of the Refuge. Spratt published the numbers of all these unfortunates almost every week without fail, from March 1861 until his death in May 1871, and these numbers continued to be reported, if sometimes sporadically, down to the year 1910 and beyond.

Their lowest weekly numbers came in that first year when, in October 1861, they registered an intake of 161 adults and 19 children. Just a year on from opening, the Refuge admitted a record 1,142 souls in one week of March 1862: some 208 of these were children. Over that first year, the Refuge took in 29,124 destitute persons, averaging 560 a week. By any standards, the figures were daunting, and, given the seasonality of distress, the weekly figures were at times astonishing. In the month of March 1862, the Refuge averaged 1,095 a week.[45]

---

44. GMA, Box 57, Marian St John Neville to Blake, 24th July 1871.
45. The full returns for that first year are tabulated in *Appendix 8: The Night Refuge: Table No 1: Weekly returns of the numbers of women and children, 5th April 1861 to 27th March 1862.*

The numbers sheltered over the next ten years never dropped below 300 a week and were often in the 700s. In the last year of John Spratt's own life, from May 1870 to May 1871, the Refuge was as badly needed as ever: it provided 23,797 overnights in the forty weeks for which there were returns, averaging 595 a week.[46] This situation remained the case for long after his own passing: in the week ending 16th February 1880, the Refuge sheltered 902 unfortunates; in the week ending 29th March 1890 some 1,054 used the Refuge, and in the week ending 6th January 1900 it provided beds for 776 souls.

*Bread and Bequests*

John Spratt's Night Refuge received no state aid and was entirely dependent on charity of cash, food and clothing. The published reports of cash donations show a weekly stream of very modest sums, perhaps five or six donations a week, featuring shillings more than pounds, and, even when pounds, they were normally one or two rather than five, ten or twenty: Benjamin Lee Guinness' £50 was exceptional.

Bequests were a godsend, but of their nature, sporadic: and, of bequests received during his lifetime, they most commonly amounted to relatively modest sums of £5 to £10. The Dublin newspaper press recorded one such gift of £5, seven gifts of £10 and one of £15 made during the ten years Friar John was in charge of the Refuge.[47] In the two months before his death in May 1871 there was one bequest

**Fig 130.** *Benjamin Lee Guinness.*

---

46. See *Appendix 8: The Night Refuge: Table No 2: Weekly returns of the numbers of women and children, 6th May 1870 to 15th May 1871.*

47. These bequests from wills were as follows: £5 from Mrs Cecilia Moran, *FJ*, 13th Sept 1869; £10 each from Fr Flanagan of St Andrew's, *Penny Despatch*, 15th April 1865, Peter O'Neill of Shillelagh, Co. Wicklow, *EF*, 18th Sept 1867, Dr James Fitzpatrick, *FJ*, 2nd Nov 1867; J. Crofton, *DEP*, 24th Sept 1870; Mrs Dallaghan, *FJ*, 5th Sept 1871; Francis Connolly of Haddington Road, *FJ*, 14th Dec 1871; Thomas Hughes of South Gloucester Street, *FJ*, 12th Oct 1870; and £15 from P. K. Doyle, *FJ*, 13th July 1871.

of £50 and another of £100,[48] but it was only after this that a few large sums came to the Refuge: one for £200 was received in 1876 and one for £1,000 in 1884.[49]

There were also, from the outset, modest and generally haphazard gifts of goods. Insofar as any trend was discernible for such gifts in kind, they tended to cluster around Christmas and New Year when coal merchants and bakeries supplied fuel and food. The one notable exception in the regularity of his gifts was the heroic baker, James Moone of Francis Street. Week after week, from the foundation of the Night Refuge until Spratt's demise, and even for some years after that, he supplied from ten to fifteen 4lb loaves a week, without fail.[50]

Whether it was cash from wills and donations, or gifts of food, the total income of the Night Refuge, as publicised in the press, was pitiably small and simply could not have been sufficient to provide heat, linen and food to cater for even 100 nightly residents a week, let alone the total complement of some 300 to 1,200 who occupied its beds and its floors. It constitutes something of a mystery, or a miracle of food and fuel, as to how Fr John kept it going. The Carmelite archives in Dublin and Rome shed no light on this and one surmises that there must have been substantial private charity, unpublicised, from friends, friars or Fr John himself that enabled it continuously to receive the destitute without once in his lifetime ever closing its doors. He himself may have had a substantial income from Mass stipends which he may have directed to the Refuge, but the evidence is not to hand and the mystery of survival not only remains unresolved, but deepens.

### The End of a Tenancy
Fr Spratt's ten-year lease of the Tenter House and land at Brickfield Lane, Cork Street, was coming to a close as the 1860s ended. He

48. Mary Wade of Nelson Street, FJ, 6th May 1871 and Patrick Murray of Amiens Street, FJ, 1st Aug 1871 respectively: this last will was made before John's death but not executed till after it.
49. William Hogan of Great Britain Street left a will of £10,000, of which £200 went to the Night Refuge, FJ, 30th June 1876. James Viscount Netterville of Cruicerath, Co. Meath, bequeathed £1,000 to the Refuge: he died in April 1882 and the will was executed in 1884, FJ, 14th April 1884.
50. Almost every single week that the press recorded any information concerning the Night Refuge, James Moone's name featured as supplying loaves of bread. The final such record which this author could find was in FJ, 17th May 1873.

would, thereafter, have become a tenant at will, renting on a monthly or yearly basis, with no security of tenure. The landlords were the Thomas Pleasants' Trustees. They were, at this time, in charge of two other charities, Pleasants' Asylum[51] and the Cork Street Fever Hospital. As Spratt's lease was about to expire there was a possibility that the Trustees would put the Tenter House up for sale. The management of Pleasants' Asylum wanted to take it over for their own use, under the terms of Thomas Pleasants' will, a development that would have jeopardised Spratt's charity. He therefore got his legal advisers to move to try to purchase the interest in the lease. By the time the case came on for hearing, in *Barrett versus Attorney-General*, in June 1871, Spratt was dead. However, his case continued and it transpired at the first major hearing, that the Trustees required £1,100 for the interest in the lease. Surprisingly, Spratt's team indicated that Fr Spratt had been prepared immediately to offer that sum. From where he had or could find that sum, straight up, is not evident. The Master of the Rolls judged that the Cork Street Fever Hospital rather than Pleasants' Asylum was best entitled to the possession of the Tenter House land and premises; however, he further directed that Fr Spratt's claim to occupy the premises should be considered, as *'the giving of shelter to destitute females, without distinction to creed, was a work of charity in accordance with the benevolent intentions of Mr Pleasants on behalf of the poor'*. The members of the Pleasants' Trust and the authorities of Cork Street Fever Hospital were willing to entertain Spratt's offer and the judge ordered a valuation of the Night Refuge premises to see if Spratt's offer was a reasonable one. The valuer, Geale, endorsed the figure of £1,100 as being the correct value. Spratt no longer being alive, his case was represented by Canon Farrell, parish priest of St Catherine's, Meath Street, who took over as guardian of the Refuge. Canon Farrell promised to deliver the £1,100 asking price and requested the Court to convey the property to himself, to John's brother, Fr James, and to Cardinal Cullen, as the three trustees. Mrs Barrett who represented the deceased executors of Thomas Pleasants' will, agreed to all of this and the governors of the Cork Street Fever Hospital willingly went along with the proposal,

---

51.  The Pleasants' Asylum, Camden Street, Dublin, was founded in 1818. One of its three governors in these years was Rev John J. MacSorley of St Peter's Parish who worked closely with Spratt on various local issues.

since they were about to become the beneficiaries of the price. Canon
Farrell indicated that the money could be paid with no delay.[52] On 11th
July 1871 £1,100 was handed over to the Governors of the Cork Street
Fever Hospital and the ownership of Spratt's Night Refuge came to the
diocesan trustees, Cardinal Cullen, Canon Farrell and Fr James Spratt.[53]

*The Night Refuge under Mercy*

It had been John Spratt's intention one day to have the Sisters of Mercy
take over the Refuge.[54] His unexpected demise hastened that day. Canon
Farrell immediately secured the agreement of these Sisters to take over
the running of the Refuge – no easy matter. It no doubt helped that less
than one month later, the Refuge received the bequest of £100 from the
Amiens Street builder, Patrick Murphy, which he had made on 7th March
1871.[55] When Canon Farrell paid an inspection visit that August he found
the many hundreds of beds all clean and tidy with their coarse linen
sheets, blankets and rug quilts; however, the relentless traffic of destitute
women and children, some 267,000 of them as overnight guests since
its foundation, left its mark.[56] The nuns very quickly had to commence
repairs, including new windows, all at a cost of some £400.[57] By the time
all the furnishing was completed, as a result of the total refurbishment,

the Refuge was some £500
in debt by December 1872.[58]
Undaunted, Canon Farrell
and the Sisters of Mercy had
ambitious plans for the Refuge
and its neighbourhood. He
had already begun and was near
to completing new schools for
the girls in the locality, near
Weavers' Square. A site in

**Fig 131.** *The Mercy Convent, Brickfield Lane.*

52. *SNL*, 25th June 1871; *FJ*, 29th June 1871.
53. *DEM*, 12th July 1871, report on the transaction at the Rolls Court, on Tuesday,
    11th July 1871.
54. *FJ*, 30th July 1872.
55. *FJ*, 1st Aug 1871.
56. *FJ*, 30th Aug 1871. It was reported that he had accommodated a remarkable
    267,371 persons up to 24th Aug 1871.
57. *FJ*, 30th July 1872.
58. *FJ*, 4th Dec 1872.

Ormond Street, where six dilapidated houses had long gone, had been acquired on which to build a new convent and chapel and to make thereby a new main entrance to the Night Refuge and these schools.[59] A bequest of £50 from Dr Flanagan of Celbridge, that December, was a timely help.[60] Within two years the new schools had taken in some 1,000 children from the neighbourhood of the Refuge and in July 1874 the foundation stone for the connected convent and chapel at Brickfield Lane had been set in place by Fr H McManus, Canon Farrell's successor as parish priest of St Catherine's.[61] The initial refurbishment of the Refuge in 1872 must have been inadequate: twelve years later the rooms were described as ill-ventilated yet draughty, some of them too dark and dank to be used and the toilet arrangements 'defective'. As of 1st May 1884 the nuns closed the Refuge down entirely for at least six months, to gut it, reconstruct and modernise it.[62] At the point of closure it was accommodating 700 to 800 souls, so what happened to them is not quite clear. It was reported that the sisters found alternative accommodation for them.[63] Its four floors, *'one of which had always been useless'* were reduced to three, with higher ceilings. Hot and cold running water was installed. At one end of the building a semi-commercial laundry was constructed to provide work for those who wanted to stay on during the daytime hours. At the other end there was erected *'a sewing room where the better class of refugees...may earn their board and lodging for a time'*, and a new registry office or reception was installed. The capacity was thereby extended so that the Refuge could now provide bed accommodation for up to 1,400 a week against the 900 formerly. At times in the past, the 900 was exceeded and presumably the unfortunates doubled up or slept on the floors.[64] The entire operation cost in the region of £3,000 and the Sisters were anxiously seeking support.[65] A not insignificant contribution came their way in September 1884 when the will of Viscount Netterville provided £1,000.[66] The Refuge re-opened its doors on 1st November

---

59.  *FJ*, 4th Dec 1872.
60.  *FJ*, 13th Dec 1872.
61.  *FJ*, 15th July 1874.
62.  *FJ*, 23rd Dec 1884.
63.  *FJ*, 23rd April 1884.
64.  *FJ*, 23rd Dec 1884.
65.  Ibid.
66.  *FJ*, 14th April 1884.

1884, with some 88 destitutes, including children, coming for shelter in that first new week.[67] Within a month its numbers had risen back up to close on 400.[68] These numbers of destitute using the Refuge rose steadily over the following year so that by the last week of December 1885 some 901, including 163 children, had received shelter.[69] The poverty in the city remained relentless as the published weekly returns for the Refuge recorded: in 1890, in the week ending 22nd February, some 1,022 destitutes were accommodated and at the end of March the figure reached 1,054, including 145 children.[70] Spratt's name was still remembered in these returns where the advertisements for St Joseph's Night Refuge continued to record *Founded by the late Very Rev Dr Spratt, A.D. 1861*'.[71] He so continued to be remembered by name in the Night Refuge's own public notices down to late September 1900.[72] Thereafter, such notices dropped the mention of his name, although, as late as December 1906, a report on the Refuge mentioned John Spratt as the founder.[73] The same appeals for charity continued to appear in the press down to 4th December 1920.[74] If Spratt's name no longer appeared in public notices, the Refuge itself certainly did: as late as March 1944 it could record that, over the previous year, it had sheltered 10,352 souls and had fed some 20,704 while in the month of February 1944 alone it had accommodated 1,398 and fed some 3,396.[75] It was still going strong a century after it was founded by Fr Spratt and in its centenary year it still commanded the affectionate support of some Dublin citizens, as when, in May 1961, it reportedly received £500 from the will of widow Frances O'Farrell of Ballsbridge.[76] It still received no state aid, and despite being entirely reliant on charity, it continued to shelter close on 20,000 persons a year, or over 380 a week, and provided some 35,000 meals. It was, without doubt, John Spratt's most enduring charitable legacy.

---

67.  *FJ*, 10th Nov 1884.
68.  *FJ*, 15th Dec 1884, week ending 13th Dec 1884.
69.  *FJ*, 28th Dec 1885.
70.  *FJ*, 24th Feb, 8th April 1890.
71.  *FJ*, 29th Dec 1890.
72.  *FJ*, 25th Sept 1900.
73.  *Irish Times*, 14th Dec 1906.
74.  *WFJ*, 4th Dec 1910.
75.  *Irish Independent*, 9th March 1944.
76.  *Irish Independent*, 16th May 1961.

# CHAPTER TWENTY

## *A Downright and Prostrating Destitution, 1860-1867*

Some months before Fr John took the steps to establish his Night Refuge for destitute women and children, he became preoccupied with a different destitution, first in the West of Ireland and, soon after, in his native city. Severe drought in the late spring and summer of 1859, followed by the wettest three consecutive years of the century, 1860-62, produced a severe agricultural depression over 1859-64.[1] Patrick Malone, parish priest of Belmullet, Co Mayo, in June 1860 reported on the reappearance of hunger, fever and dysentery and claimed that some 900 to 1,000 families in his area were in a starving state. He rejected statements made in Parliament at this time that the landlords and the poor law commissioners had done their duty in the face of this distress. He contended that of twenty-five landed proprietors in his region of Erris, only four had done anything to assist their tenants, while *'the Commissioners have offered the workhouse and no more'*. Fr Malone, having seen some 2,000 perish in a single workhouse in 1847, was not confident that sending people into such a setting was any solution. As to the reality and extent of this new distress, the coastguards at Belmullet corroborated his account. Desperate for financial aid, Fr Malone felt that if *'our poor people'* could just hold out for two or three weeks more, they would be self-supporting again, and *'will have escaped a total annihilation which the workhouse application would ensure'*.[2]

John Spratt responded positively and energetically to Fr Malone's

---

1. J. S. Donnelly, Jr, 'The Irish Agricultural Depression of 1859-64', in *Irish Economic and Social History*, 3, 1976, p. 34.
2. *DEP*, 21st June 1860.

pleas for help. Just how long before the middle of June 1860 it was before Fr John began organising aid for Erris is not certain, but, in the course of that month alone, he sent sums of £39, £8 and £14 to the Belmullet parish priest, that last sum being a gift from Spratt's great benefactor of an earlier distress, Andreas George Moller.[3] In the course of the next month, the friar sent additional sums of £20 and £10, the latter even as his old friend, Martin A Brennan, now editing his own newspaper, *The Connaught Patriot*, was sending a like sum from Tuam. Apart from the *Connaught Telegraph*, Brennan's *Patriot* was the first newspaper to highlight the dreadful situation unfolding in Erris.[4] It may well be that Brennan had kept Spratt informed of the disaster unfolding in the far west. Whatever the case, at the beginning of July Fr Malone expressed his *'profound gratitude'* to the Carmelite because, although a few deaths had occurred, *'through your agency the lives of hundreds will have been rescued'*. Malone conceded that *'even the poor law authorities, dreading the consequences of their past neglect, have given temporary [outdoor] relief in a few instances'*, but, this was *'in so scanty a measure as to make one disgusted with their administration'*.[5] The Carmelite, of course, was far from being the only benefactor to Fr Malone and the Erris Distress Fund: sums came from different parts of Ireland and England at this time. However, Spratt's contribution was acknowledged as outstanding. As most of the Erris destitute had survived the crisis by the end of that July, Fr Malone thanked all who had been *'so wonderfully instrumental in saving the lives of "thousands",'* but he thanked in particular, Fr Spratt, who had been the biggest channel of aid.[6] Of 590 separate acknowledged donations, the Carmelite friar had forwarded some 77 of them.[7]

*Ravages Returning*

Sadly, within a year the problem returned: appalling weather once again ruined the harvest of both food and fuel. The Dublin alderman, Peter Paul M'Swiney, was so exercised by the recurrent words of woe from

3. *DEP*, 14th, 21st June 1860; *DWN*, 30th June 1860.
4. *Connaught Patriot*, 14th April, 5th, 12th May, 16th, 30th June, 14th, 21st July 1860; *EF*, 4th, 27th July 1860.
5. *EF*, 4th July 1860.
6. *DWN*, 4th Aug 1860.
7. *Report of the Mansion House Committee for Relief of Distress in Ireland*, Dublin 1862, pp. 17-30.

the West that he urged a special meeting of Dublin City Council. He called on his fellow councillors to consider the gathering crisis and to condemn the Chief Secretary, Sir Robert Peel, for dismissing it.[8] As reports of the looming disaster multiplied, Peel had paid a visit to the west of Ireland in October 1861, famously or infamously covering three hundred miles in three days, and declaring, when he had reached Sligo, that *'the West is prosperous'*. This was the exact opposite to what M'Swiney's commercial contacts were telling him as he was informed that the cereal crop was down from 56 to 75% in some areas, that two thirds of the potato crop had failed and that the turf was too sodden to be saved.

The special meeting of the City Council was held on 26th November 1861 and it called upon the Lord Mayor, Richard Atkinson, to set up a Mansion House Relief Committee and also to prepare a memorial to the Lord Lieutenant calling on government to address the deepening crisis. Not the least remarkable aspect of this unfolding situation was the disbelief and division of opinion it generated. Some sections of the public and some organs of the press denied there was any crisis looming and implied that the whole business was a sectarian scare,

**Fig 132.** *The Mansion House, Dublin.*

8.  *DDE*, 27th Nov 1861.

manufactured by Catholics and nationalists from ulterior motives. Thus the *Dublin Daily Express*, in reporting that the Lord Lieutenant had agreed to receive a deputation of city councillors on the matter, for 30th December, commented that it did not see the point of this, in respect of *'the alleged famine in the West of Ireland'*. It denounced councillors such as M'Swiney, Thomas Reynolds and Sir John Gray as *'famine-mongers'*.[9] Apart from visiting the Lord Lieutenant, however, Dublin City Council gave unintended support to distress sceptics by seeming to do nothing to establish a relief committee. As Lord Mayor Atkinson's term of office was expiring at the end of the calendar year, no Mansion House Committee had been set up before the end of 1861: it would be late February 1862 before the new Lord Mayor, Denis Moylan, eventually convened a meeting.[10]

### Re-enter Reverend Spratt

By this stage, Fr John, now immersed in his infant Night Refuge, was at risk of becoming further enmeshed in the crisis of the West. At the end of January 1862 he received a donation of £50 for relief of distress in Connaught from his old supporter, Richard Devereux of Wexford.[11] They had met in Dublin the previous December and doubtless had discussed the unfolding situation. Devereux was concerned that nothing had been done to initiate formal relief efforts and he urged that a committee of the charitable in Dublin would establish such a relief organisation as Spratt had done in 1849. The Wexford merchant prince appreciated how widely engaged and deeply committed Spratt then was, in a range of other charitable commitments, but added that *'your love for the poor will, I am sure, if possible, cause you to undertake this charitable work'*.[12]

Three days later, Spratt contacted Gray of the *Freeman's Journal*, reminding the newspaper man of the great work Gray himself had done for famine relief, back in 1849, and modestly claiming that *'although I was so much before the public, I was only the representative of you and others who were really the workers'*. Saying that he himself would willingly take up such public work again in the future, he pleaded that, just then, he was too

---

9.   *DDE*, 20th Dec 1861.

10.  *FJ*, 21st Feb 1862.

11.  *EF*, 3rd Feb 1862.

12.  *EF*, 6th Feb 1862, Devereux to Spratt, 31st January 1862.

heavily committed to the Night Refuge, to sustain which he had to raise £9 every week. He felt, therefore, that he could not risk *'the shelter and subsistence of 500 to 700 poor homeless females and children'* by taking on this new responsibility. Offering to co-operate, he hoped that some other person – presumably Gray himself – would launch an initiative for the West.[13] For all that, he found it impossible to ignore the charitable trust that others reposed in him. Thus, the very next day, he had to acknowledge and dispatch £10 from Charles Putland of Bray Head, for the destitute of the west of Ireland.[14]

The matter of an organised response was finally addressed when M'Swiney's proposed meeting to establish a Mansion House Relief Committee was at last convened by the new Lord Mayor, on 17th February, probably after pressure from Gray. The latter was one of a small group which included Alderman Reynolds and Captain Knox of the *Irish Times* who had met with Lord Mayor Moylan a few days before, to prepare for this public meeting.[15] Leading councillors and aldermen such as M'Swiney and A M Sullivan, together with prominent Catholic clergymen such as Drs Cullen, Woodlock and O'Connell, were present: and so too, inevitably, was Dr Spratt.[16] It was Fr John who seconded Gray in thanking the Lord Mayor for having called this meeting which established the Mansion House Relief Committee. Equally inevitably, he now found himself a member, attending its first business meeting on 20th February.[17] Having been slow to get established, the Mansion House Relief Committee was quick in raising and dispatching funds: £150 was recorded in donations that very foundation day, and a further £90 one week later. As for Fr John, despite trying to cope with overseeing the care of 1,000 destitutes in his own Night Refuge at this very time, he proved the most regular attender of all at the weekly business meetings of the new body, from its inception to its dissolution some years later. Indeed, frequently enough he chaired its

---

13. *EF*, 6th Feb 1862, Spratt to Gray, 2nd February 1862.
14. *SNL*, 7th Feb 1862. Charles Putland (1813-1876), an improving landlord, generous to his tenants in Cork and Wicklow, he made significant contributions to the development of Bray town. See B. Hourican, 'Charles Putland', in *DIB*, vol. 8, p. 332.
15. *EF*, 17th Feb 1862.
16. Ibid.
17. *FJ*, 21st Feb 1862.

meetings, more often than any other individual, apart, perhaps, from the Lord Mayor.[18] Consequently, despite his protestation to Devereux, he quickly found himself at the centre of what proved a major relief project, national and international.

*Private versus public aid*

The Committee believed that the Government and some newspapers were completely mistaken in thinking that the existing regime of the poor law would be adequate to meet the emergency. In the Committee's view, given the past record of the poor law and the attitude of its guardians whose doling out of assistance was niggardly in the extreme, the system was totally inadequate to the nature and the scale of the challenge. Certainly, the most recent study of official poor relief in the west of Ireland supports the idea of the inadequacy of the system there to cope with extensive distress.[19] Spratt and his charity colleagues felt there was no alternative now than to target independent financial support.[20] Indeed, it could not but deplore the attitude of the Government, notably in the person of Chief Secretary Peel, and the attitude of a section of the Protestant evangelical press that *'the cry of distress was in great measure artificial and chiefly sectarian'*.[21] The men of the Mansion House found that in over 100 poor law unions, the giving of outdoor relief to the sick *'has been a dead letter'*. In consequence of these attitudes, they argued that contributions to their Committee had been partly stifled and confined, with a few exceptions – notably the Society of Friends – to one section of the community.[22] In the course of its proceedings it made highly successful appeals for funds, even as the crisis deepened. During the first four weeks from its launch, the Mansion House Relief Committee had received over £850 and had disbursed aid at the rate of £120 a week. Over the months from 17th February to 10th August 1862 the organisation raised some £5,179

---

18. He chaired meetings, for example, on 14th April, 19th May, 9th, 30th June, 17th July 1862, for which see *IT*, 15th April, *CT*, 24th May, *IT*, 10th June, 1st, 17th July 1862 respectively.

19. D. S. Lucey, 'Poor relief in the West of Ireland, 1861-1911', in V. Crossman & P. Gray, eds., *Poverty and Welfare in Ireland, 1838-1948*, Dublin 2011, pp. 37-52.

20. *Report of the Mansion House Committee for Relief of Distress in Ireland*, Dublin 1862, p. 4.

21. Ibid, p. 5; see also O'Neill, 'The charities and famine in mid-nineteenth century Ireland', p. 152.

22. Ibid, p. 7.

and distributed it to Protestant and Catholic clergymen and to local relief committees.[23] In the United States of America, despite civil war and its attendant hardships, the Irish were not slow to offer support: as early as March 1862 Spratt was to be found thanking a citizen of New York for offering to raise money among the Irish there.[24] As it transpired, of that total of £5,179, raised over February to August 1862, some £3,300 came from overseas and £1,037 of that from America. The Irish in England were no less forthcoming: at a meeting of the Committee which Spratt chaired that April, Archbishop Cullen handed in a generous £250 from a relief committee of Liverpool, this at a time when Lancashire itself was experiencing hardship from its own *'cotton famine'*, caused by the American Civil War.[25] Indeed, some £1,000 of that £5,179 came from England, and mainly from Liverpool.[26] Further afield in France, that June, a single sermon preached in the Basilica of Sainte-Clotilde, Paris, and attended by the Empress, raised some £418.[27] Spratt remained active on the Committee, as member and sometime chairman, even as the numbers in his own Refuge reached a record 1,200 in the second week of May.[28] By the end of that month, the Mansion House Committee was dispensing some £400 a week in aid.[29] Some individuals within Ireland itself proved hugely generous: by early June, Charles Putland had contributed his fourth gift of £20, while the Dame Street watchmaker and jeweller, John Donegan, by the end of that month had already contributed his twelfth subscription of the like amount.[30] By the time the subscription lists closed, Donegan had made

---

23. Ibid, pp. 6, 13.
24. *IT*, 1st April 1862.
25. *IT*, 15th April 1862. For the Lancashire Cotton Famine see, inter al., G. R. Boyer, 'Poor Relief, Informal Assistance and Short Time during the Lancashire Cotton Famine', *Explorations in Economic History*, 34, 1997, pp. 56-76.
26. *Report of the Central Committee for Relief of Distress in Ireland, 1862-3*, Dublin 1864, p. 4. The "Mansion House Committee" came in time to be also called "The Central Committee" and sometimes also simply "The Irish Committee".
27. *FJ*, 17th June 1862.
28. Those seeking shelter in the Night Refuge weekly, rose from 1,119 in the week ending 3rd May to 1,201 by the end of the following week: see *FJ*, 3rd, 12th May 1862.
29. *FJ*, 4th June 1862.
30. *IT*, 10th, 27th June 1862. For Donegan, see *Thom's Directory for the year 1862*, p. 1217.

nineteen donations totalling £310, and Putland nine totalling £160.[31] Through June and July, disbursements continued weekly, mainly to counties Mayo, Roscommon, Galway and Kerry.

By the end of July 1862 the most pressing wave of distress was receding and the Committee felt it could now hold its final gathering on 20th August.[32] Spratt, of course, was present when Dr Cullen chaired what they thought would be their last meeting, as good weather had finally brought hopes for a better harvest. That last event, vocal in its expressions of gratitude to its donors in Ireland and abroad, was equally forthright in its attacks upon the British Government for its *'indifference'*. They could neither forgive nor forget Chief Secretary Peel's comment in the House of Commons on 15th February 1862 that

> the case of Ireland was greatly exaggerated. He protested indignantly against the imaginary sufferings of Ireland being paraded before Europe as most distasteful to the feelings of the Irish people.[33]

Spratt seconded the resolution of Peter Paul M'Swiney adopting the report of the Committee and censuring the government for its inaction.

*Resurrecting the Relief Committee*
This, however, was not the end of the story. Having disbanded after this meeting, the Mansion House Relief Committee, including Spratt, had to be reconvened momentarily, in early November 1862, to acknowledge a remarkable donation of £500 from an Irish relief committee in Melbourne.[34] Unfortunately, it soon had to resurrect itself again, less temporarily, as yet another appallingly wet autumn and early winter brought a renewal of misery. Three days before Christmas 1862, apprised of *'an immense number of applications'* for help, the old guard of Spratt, M'Swiney and company had to reconvene at the Mansion House to consider the situation. This time the distress was not confined to the western counties but was manifest in towns and cities even in the east, Dublin included. The Committee hazarded

---

31. *Report of the Mansion House Committee for Relief of Distress in Ireland*, pp. 21, 26.
32. *FJ*, 14th Aug 1862.
33. *EF*, 21st Aug 1862.
34. *CT*, 8th Nov 1862.

that '*the ensuing year would be one of unsurpassed distress among small farmers and the labouring class in every county of Ireland*'. That very meeting raised and distributed £345 to places as varied as Skibbereen, Castletownsend, Clifden, Galway and Roscommon, but also to several conferences of St Vincent de Paul in Dublin, and even £10 to Spratt's Night Refuge.[35] Given their dismal predictions for the year ahead, they could not have been surprised that their renewed activities would take them far into the following year. This time, even the *Dublin Daily Express* must have been experiencing a pang of conscience as it republished the names of the members '*who formed the celebrated Mansion House Committee*', in case the public had forgotten who they were.[36]

This resurrected committee which would now also come to be alternatively called the "Central Relief Committee" and the "Irish Relief Committee" – the latter, presumably, to distinguish it from the various Lancashire relief committees – held a general meeting at the Mansion House on 5th January 1863, to prepare for the worst. As one member, Dr Phelan, noted, '*they had now been visited with three successive bad harvests*'. Phelan feared that the Committee in its previous recent existence had been characterised as denominationally and socially too narrow in its membership and direction. He suggested that they should now dissolve and then come together in a more representative way, in order to include '*the landed proprietary of all denominations*'. He believed that the original Mansion House Committee had been regarded in some quarters, notably by the *Dublin Evening Mail*, as being sectarian, as almost exclusively a Roman Catholic body. His attempt to be helpful was taken as singularly unhelpful. Professor Kavanagh of the Catholic University was among a number of committee members who had to point out that prominent Protestants such as Captain Knox of the *Irish Times* and Dr Gray of the *Freeman's Journal* had been and still were leading members. Consequently, the committee members rejected Dr Phelan's suggestion, insisting that it was not for them to dissolve but for others to join them.[37] Their search for charitable funds quickly gained support, with the Protestant Lord Mayor, John Vereker, handing in donations of £100, £10 of it from himself and £35 from Guinness' Brewery.[38]

---

35. *EF*, 23rd Dec 1862.
36. *DDE*, 6th Jan 1863.
37. *IT*, 6th Jan 1863.
38. *IT*, 23rd Jan 1863.

*'A downright and prostrating destitution'*

The distress was now as noticeable in Dublin as in the West, as the capital city experienced its own *'cotton famine'*: its female cotton stocking weavers were experiencing extensive unemployment as much as those in Lancashire. So great was the drain on charity funds in Dublin that the Roomkeepers Society had exhausted their own reserves and were in debt, to the extent of £160, for the first time in their seventy-three year history. They were immediately granted £30 by the Mansion House Committee even as other grants went to the poor of the West.[39]   At this point, in January 1863, the South Dublin Union Workhouse had not a single empty bed, in some cases people were *'doubling up'* as some 3,069 unfortunates crowded its wards. Towards the end of that month the local distress in Dublin led to a public meeting in the vestry room of St Bride's parish church. Here its incumbent, William Carroll, was joined by John Spratt and other prominent citizens, including Captain Knox, Jonathan Pim and the Lord Mayor, as they sought support for their own poor, Protestant and Catholic alike. Carroll spoke movingly of *'a downright and prostrating destitution'*. He explained that in his own parochial school the attendances had dropped due to lack of clothing and footwear for the children. Spratt endorsed all that Carroll reported

**Fig 133.**  *St Bride's Church and National School stood near the corner of Bride Street and Bride Road. They were demolished in 1900.*

39.  Ibid.

on the occasion and a denominationally mixed committee was set up to collect local funds to relieve local and national poverty, with Carroll and Spratt being designated as the authorised collectors.[40] As the *Irish Times* noted:

> The Rev Dr Spratt was found in the vestry of a Protestant church, side by side with the Rector, to co-operate in the work. Charity knows no distinction of creed.[41]

A few days later, Carroll and Spratt, at a meeting of the Central Relief Committee, as the Mansion House Relief Committee was being increasingly called, handed in £50 they had collected locally and Rev Carroll's presence was greeted with some delight since he was the first Protestant clergyman to join the Committee. He pointed out that his presence there was with the full endorsement of his Protestant parishioners.[42] Meanwhile, in their own locality, the two clergymen had dispensed some £20 in supplying bread and coal to 174 families, 86 Catholic and 88 Protestant, while a further 200 local supplicant households had still to be assisted.[43] By the end of February, with the help of diverse donations which included £100 from Dublin pawnbrokers, the Roomkeepers had to be further bailed out with a grant of a similar amount. Indeed, by late March of that year, the Roomkeepers had been granted some £880 by the Mansion House Committee to

**Fig 134.** *Jonathan Pim, MP.*

40.  *FJ*, 27th Jan 1863.
41.  *IT*, 27th Jan 1863.
42.  *DDE*, 30th Jan 1863.
43.  *DDE*, 6th Feb 1863.

aid in the relief of Dublin distress.[44] Though never remarked upon at the time, it was hardly unhelpful that Spratt was a prominent member and office-holder in both bodies. Indeed, his own Night Refuge secured a total of £60 from the same source.[45] However, as if to underline the Relief Committee's unsectarian nature, other recipients of its support at this time included the Association of Distressed Protestants and the Society of St Vincent de Paul: the former was granted a total of £100 and the latter a total of £600.[46] At the same time, it is the case that most of the disbursements went much further afield, to the poor and hungry from Letterkenny to Dungarvan, Loughrea to Skibbereen. By the end of April 1863 the Relief Committee had raised almost £8,500 and had dispensed as much.[47]

### Aid from Overseas

The response from abroad was impressive; that from America, remarkable. By the end of May 1863 relief efforts in New York City alone had raised £5,500.[48] Over the whole life of the resurrected Relief Committee, from late 1862 to August of 1863, of a total of £29,217 raised, some £18,808, or two thirds, came from the United States of America, as against £2,084 from Ireland and £873 from England and Scotland. Such sums were those which came to the Central Relief Committee and did not include remittances sent directly to others. The Committee reckoned that a total of £300,000 had been donated from America. Individual prelates, doubtless, would have been significant recipients of separate donations. In Archbishop Cullen's case, the £9,000 which he received directly, he gave into the funds of the Committee. With far fewer Irish immigrants, Australia and Tasmania remitted a remarkable £5,356 to the Mansion House Relief Committee.[49]

By early August 1863 the worst was over and the funds of the Committee were exhausted. The Lord Mayor now convened a public

---

44. *FJ*, 20th March 1863. However, the *Report of the Central Committee for Relief of Distress in Ireland, 1862-3*, p. 102, gives the total sum as £680.
45. *Report of the Central Committee for Relief of Distress in Ireland, 1862-3*, p. 105.
46. *DDE*, 6th Feb 1863; *IT*, 27th Feb 1863; *Report of the Central Committee for Relief of Distress in Ireland, 1862-3*, pp. 95, 103.
47. *IT*, 1st May 1863.
48. *DWN*, 30th May 1863.
49. *Report of the Central Committee for Relief of Distress in Ireland, 1862-3*, pp. 4-6.

meeting so that the Committee could give an account of itself and present its formal *Report*, as it had now *'ceased its labours'* and could respond no longer to any further relief applications. Rev Carroll spoke at this meeting, recalling how he and Spratt had been criticised in some of the press for having collected £50 from the parishioners of St Bride's and given it to the Central Relief Committee who in turn made a grant of £25 to the poor of the parish as part of their City of Dublin allocations. That hostile press had insinuated that these parishioners had been swindled out of the balance of £25 that had been allocated elsewhere. Such hostile reports caused him and Spratt grief as, in the end, they had raised and donated from the parish some £60 for the Central Relief Committee but the parish had in fact received a total of £175 in allocations from the Committee. This sum had enabled them to help some 6,000 to 7,000 parishioners in their days of need.[50]

In opening the meeting, Lord Mayor Vereker struck a note highly critical of the government. He pointed out that Ireland, distressed as it was, had contributed £20,000 to the relief of distress in Lancashire whose people had had the support of that government and the press. Similar support had not been the case in Ireland where *'by one portion of the press they were demonised as famine-mongers, banded together to falsify and misrepresent facts. They were told that the Irish famine was a humbug and a myth'*, yet, when they had collected and disbursed close on £30,000, those who had denounced them were then *'obliged to hold their tongues...the Chancellor of the Exchequer [was] obliged to admit the Irish famine ...'.*

The Committee Secretary's *Report* continued in this vein of reproach, noting that in the Queen's Speech at the prorogation of Parliament, her ministers had come forward and deplored the severe distress; this was a bit late since the previous denial of that distress by

**Fig 135.** *An 1862 image depicting the Lancashire 'Cotton Famine'.*

---

50. *DDE,* 7th Aug 1863.

the Chief Secretary and the Irish Government had the effect of deterring people from supporting the relief efforts. It noted sourly *'His Excellency the Lord Lieutenant never contributed to our funds'* but *'as if in condemnation of our body, he subscribed a trifling sum to the Committee of the Society of Friends who very humanely acted as a Relief Committee...he thus ignored the two main churches of Ireland'.* Captain Knox of the *Irish Times* fully endorsed the *Report* and noted how *'efforts had been made to undermine the Committee*

**Fig 136.** *Captain Knox.*

*"by introducing elements of religious disunion"': 'he came to the Committee as a Protestant and a Conservative and he [now] left it on its dissolution as good a Protestant and a Conservative as he ever was'.*[51]

As the *Report* itself observed:

> The Protestant Lord Mayor, the Catholic Archbishop, the Protestant and Catholic clergy, the Catholic and Protestant laity of the city united together, as one man, in the holy name of common charity.[52]

This had been intended as the final meeting of the Central Relief Committee but it proved otherwise. A year and half later, in February 1865, it had to reconvene in special assembly to finally bring its work to a close. Spratt, like Captain Knox and ex-Lord Mayor Vereker, were all there to decide what to do about funds which had been donated since their closing meeting of 6th August 1863. A sum of £132 was still to their credit and the question of its final disposal had to be addressed. Vereker suggested £20 each to Galway and Limerick City

51. *DDE*, 7th Aug 1863; *SNL*, 7th Aug 1863.
52. *Report of the Central Committee for Relief of Distress in Ireland, 1862-3*, p. 9.

charities, £20 for the Coombe Hospital, £20 for the Rotunda, £20 for the Roomkeepers, £10 for the Night Refuge and the remainder to their Reverends, Carroll and Spratt, to help the poor in their districts.[53] Thus, at last, the Central Relief Committee, in the 1860s, came to its end.

*From Distress to Disease*

For Carroll and Spratt, however, it would not be too long before their commitment to public charity would bring them to common cause once more. In October 1866, they found themselves attending another public meeting in the Mansion House – summoned there by the threat of cholera. This latest threat, since the earlier epidemics in 1832 and 1849, first manifested in Ireland that July: on the 27th, a fifteen year old Dublin girl, Jane Magee, of No. 2 City Quay, became the first victim of cholera in Ireland. She had just returned from Liverpool. Four days later, her friend, Mary Anne Meyler, who had tended her in her last illness also died, followed by Mary Anne's father, Andrew Meyler, that same evening.[54] Within a fortnight there were at least four other such fatalities in Dublin, two of adult men who had returned separately from Liverpool, and two destitutes from the Bow Street Night Asylum.[55] Soon deaths were reported from Drogheda, Mallow and Westport.[56] By that stage, arrangements were being made by the Poor Law guardians of Dublin to have any suspected cases sent to the Meath Street, Hardwicke and Sir Patrick Dun's hospitals. Furthermore, preparing for the worst, some 200 cholera sheds were now being erected in Kilmainham.[57] Over the next month, the incidence of deaths from the disease rose gradually but steadily. Over the last three weeks of September and the first week of October the cholera deaths in Dublin rose from 52 to 55, to 65 and to 96.[58]

It was in this situation that a North City dispensary doctor, Albert Speedy, on 29th September urged the immediate institution of a cholera relief fund.[59] His call resulted in a meeting of prominent citizens in

53.  *FJ*, 24th Feb 1865.
54.  *FJ*, 31st July 1866; *EF*, 1st Aug 1866.
55.  *DWN*, 18th Aug 1861, citing *DDE*, 13th Aug.
56.  *DWN*, 25th Aug, 1st Sept 1866.
57.  *DWN*, 18th Aug 1866.
58.  *DWN*, 6th Oct 1866.
59.  *SNL*, 20th Oct 1866.

the Mansion House on 9th October, to consider how best to help fellows rendered destitute by the *'ravages of cholera'* in the city. Those present included Lord Naas, the Chief Secretary, the Lord Mayor, James Mackey, Dr Trench, Archbishop of Dublin, and other worthies. Carroll and Spratt also attended.[60] Support and apologies came from Archbishop Cullen. The last-named, in his letter of apology, stressed the need for an effective committee, one

**Fig 137.** *James Mackey, Lord Mayor.*

composed of people who really had first-hand, direct experience of the poor and their needs. He instanced the earlier distress relief committee of the 1860s and specifically mentioned Spratt and M'Swiney, Richard Devitt and Dean O'Connell as having been the *'most active in the management of that Committee'*, and hoped they might be engaged again.[61] This was duly noted and the resulting Cholera Relief Committee included all four, together with the physician son of an old associate of Spratt, Dr Thomas Hayden.[62] Another medical man present, Dr Burke, noted that, to-date, cholera deaths numbered 300 to 400, although he now thought it was diminishing in Dublin, but extending in the suburbs, especially in Kingstown and Donnybrook. The distress was serious enough as not only did families lose their breadwinners but, often enough, their goods had to be destroyed by the local health officials as an antidote to the spread of the disease. Dean O'Connell moved and Fr Spratt seconded the appointment of treasurers to the fund. The meeting ended with generous donations coming from those present, including £25 each from Naas, Trench and Sir James Power.

---

60.  *DEP*, 9th Oct 1866.

61.  *DEP*, 10th Oct 1866, Cullen to Lord Mayor, 8th October 1866.

62.  *FJ*, 10th Oct 1866. Dr Thomas Hayden was a member of Spratt's CYMS and his father, Dr George, had died in 1857: see *Cork Examiner*, 29th July 1857 for Dr George Hayden's death notice.

**Fig 138.** *Lord Naas.*

Within days over £1,000 had been raised and the Cholera Relief Committee was soon meeting several times a week. Among one of its early actions was to agree to offer financial support to those exclusively charity hospitals who took in cholera sufferers. Another was to urge rectors and parish priests to furnish lists of orphaned children.[63] By mid-October the Cholera Relief Committee had raised £2,400 and both in its general committee and the subcommittee for allocations to parishes, Spratt was assiduous in his attendance: as in previous such organisations he proved to be the most faithful presence in the work. His subcommittee, by mid-October, was meeting daily in the face of the crisis, and, indeed, by that stage he had become the honorary secretary,[64] along with Archdeacon Lee and Dr E D Mapother, the Medical Officer for Dublin.[65] By late October, as they gained a command of the situation, they were meeting thrice weekly. By the end of that month they had raised £2,932, had disbursed £616 and had evolved their grants into four categories: first was an *'anticipatory'* grant to the Protestant and Catholic parish clergy to enable them to give immediate aid in face of a desperate need; second was a grant to each affected family, limited to five shillings per family member; third was a special grant to a remaining spouse where husband or wife had died of the disease; and finally, they agreed a special final grant for children who had been left as orphans. Some of these children had been sent to foster parents in the country and others placed in different occupations as apprentices. It was left to the local clergy to determine the manner in which these grants were provided. At their meeting on

63. *DEP*, 13th Oct 1866; *IT*, 15th Oct 1866; *SNL*, 18th Oct 1866; *FJ*, 19th Oct 1866.
64. *FJ*, 19th, 22nd Oct 1866.
65. *FJ*, 19th March 1867 lists them.

25th October another problem for the affected poor was discussed: this was the distressing challenge of actually conveying their dead ones to the cemeteries. The poor law authorities were empowered to provide coffins and shrouds but not conveyance, as there were insufficient cholera carts.

This situation soon brought the Carmelite friar once again into conflict with the South Dublin Union poor law guardians. On 26th October he and three others, including the Protestant Archbishop, went as a deputation to Lord Naas at Dublin Castle to complain at the tardiness of the South Dublin Union in supplying carts for the conveyance of the dead and of its delaying in granting them an interview. They also complained that the cholera sheds at Kilmainham were too far afield for many of the poor to reach them and that what was needed were local cholera reception houses in different parts of the south city, such as had been provided in the epidemics of 1832 and 1849. The South Dublin Union's first action thereafter was to insist that their cholera conveyance supply was *adequate at present* and would be increased if found necessary.[66]

By early November the Committee, its Protestant and Catholic clergy and laity working in complete harmony, had raised £3,533 and had dispensed £790 in grants.[67] The rate of applications for grants was reported to be declining and this was taken as a sign that the disease itself was waning. So Archdeacon Lee reported on 8th November and Spratt confirmed this as his experience of the situation. Consequently their suggestion to meet twice weekly instead of three days a week was adopted.[68] They were still meeting in early December 1866 at which point they had raised £3,901 and dispensed £1,131 in grants.[69] At that point the cholera was on a downward trend. In four weeks of November, Dublin experienced 234 cholera deaths, with 68, 63, 48 and 55 in each successive week.[70] By the end of that year, the cholera had ceased but it had left a trail of orphans in its wake. By the first week in January 1867 Archbishop Trench informed his committee colleagues

66. *DEM*, 30th Oct 1866.
67. *FJ*, 9th Nov 1866.
68. Ibid.
69. *IT*, 7th Dec 1866.
70. *DDE*, 8th Dec 1866, report of the Dublin Medical Officer of Health, E D Mapother.

that they were now dealing with 197 cholera orphan applications.

The final meeting of the Cholera Relief Committee was held on 18th March 1867 with the Lord Mayor as Chairman. The sixteen present – equally balanced between Protestant and Catholic clergy, included Carroll and Spratt among them. While the clergy on the Committee worked harmoniously together, when it came to the disbursement of local grants each clergyman dispensed only to the destitute of his own denomination. Of the anticipatory grants to these clergy, some £400 had been allocated, almost £40 of which was returned, unused. As to family grants and household goods replacement, over £1060 had been assigned. In regard to orphans, some 265 applications had been examined and some 43 of these were struck out. In effect, the cases of some 222 orphans, 12 years of age and under, received assistance. Each orphanage admission was supported by a grant of £7 and some £1505 was thereby granted to 108 children placed in orphanages. The total income of the Committee, including deposit interest, amounted to £4095 and a sum of £210 was left as a start-up contingency for a future return of the disease. As the proceedings moved towards a close, Carroll and Spratt moved a vote of thanks to the Lord Mayor. Thereupon Dean O'Connell moved an extraordinarily warm resolution of praise and thanks to the Established Church's Archdeacon Lee: although simultaneously Chaplain to Archbishop Trench, Rector of a large Dublin parish, and Professor of Divinity in Trinity College, he gave great time and devotion to the Cholera Relief Committee. It may have been this kind of tribute from Fr O'Connell, that led one of the listeners, Spratt's friend Rev Carroll, to surmise just four years later that the *'system of mutual anathema is passing away'*.[71] Archdeacon Lee expressed himself overwhelmed by *'his friend'* Dean O'Connell's remarks and then turned to the meeting to pass a vote of thanks to Spratt as honorary secretary, but Spratt would have none of it, insisting *'the work was done by the Archdeacon'*.[72]

71. *FJ*, 19th March 1867 for O'Connell's tribute; *EF*, 30th May 1871 for Rev Carroll's comment.
72. *FJ*, 19th March 1867.

# CHAPTER TWENTY-ONE

## *The Politics of Community and Nation, 1860-1871*

From the start of the 1860s, and throughout that decade, Friar John found himself engaged on multiple fronts simultaneously. There was his ongoing commitment to the teetotal movement, to his schools, orphanage, Roomkeepers Society, and the relief of distress in the west, apart altogether from his conventual and community commitments. To these were added new engagements, local and national. Among the local ones were his support for the provision of clean water supply to Dublin City, for the opening of St Stephen's Green as a public park, and for the Sunday opening of the Botanic Gardens. Concurrent with these came a major commitment to the creation of the O'Connell Monument: this latter was a campaign of interminable meetings of which he chaired many, sometimes in the midst of bitter acrimony and uproar and one which had not concluded before he died. It was at the level of ward politics that Fr John's engagement began in his quest to commemorate O'Connell, starting in October 1862 but that quest soon moved from the local to the national arena.

However, the politics of contemporary concerns, as much as the politics of historic commemoration, engaged him just as directly in both local and national strivings from the start of that same decade. It was, above all else, the decade of the Fenians and of their fraught relationship with the Catholic Church. The friction was evident from the beginning of the 1860s, with the affair of the funeral of Terence Bellew McManus who had died in San Francisco in January 1861. Two months after his death, a meeting in Dublin established the National Brotherhood of Saint Patrick and it was this body which determined to bring the remains of McManus home and to stage in the process a great nationalist gesture. The question as to where he was to *'lie in state'* immediately divided opinion. It led to a rupture between Archbishop Cullen and the Catholic Church in Dublin on the one hand and the Fenians on the other.[1] Cullen forbade any lying in state in his cathedral in Marlborough Street and declined even to receive a deputation on the subject. It appears that the organisers then approached

**Fig 139.** *Terrence Bellew McManus.*

Fr John for permission to have the remains lie for honouring, before burial, in his Carmelite church. However, as the *Evening Packet* described it, Fr Spratt *'seemed to have had his instructions and also refused the use of his cathedral in Whitefriar Street'.*[2] Spratt's response did not endear him to the Fenians, as later events would testify. In the meantime, however, the friar's immediate political interest at this time was more mundane – to secure his and his confreres' right to vote in the municipal elections.

### The Friar as Ward Boss

On 28th October 1861, even as the ructions over the remains of McManus were intensifying, Spratt appeared before the Municipal Revision Court to stake his claim to the franchise and to assert the claims of ten of his Whitefriar Street confreres to exercise the vote in their local Royal Exchange Ward. The Conservative agent, Hyndman, a leading figure of the Dublin Freemasons, objected to the eleven Carmelites

---

1. O. P. Rafferty, *The Catholic Church and the Protestant State: nineteenth century realities*, Ch. 7, 'Cardinal Cullen, early Fenianism and the McManus funeral affair', pp. 142-58.
2. *DEPC*, 21st Oct 1861.

**Fig 140.** *Richard Atkinson, Lord Mayor.*

being entered on the voters' register as they had no *'prima facie case'*.[3] Spratt explained that he had lived in Whitefriar Street since 1827[4] and that he and two other Carmelites, Thomas Bennett and John Carr, were co-lessees of the friary and that the others who resided there had equal rights in that property: they all paid the rents and rates for the premises between them. The Conservative opposition argued that the friars were not householders but lodgers, since they admitted that, in theory, they could be removed at the command of their superior, the Prior.[5] Against this, the Carmelites' defence counsel argued that the friars were joint householders since they paid municipal rates or taxes and, so long as they paid their rent and rates, they were entitled to the vote. It emerged that the ten Carmelites had previously held the municipal vote up to 1860 in which year they were removed from the register due to an oversight or error in the matter of payment of local taxes.[6]

3. Hyndman's memorial on the wall of the mortuary chapel of Mount Jerome Cemetery states this affiliation.

4. From this it would appear that he did not move from the friary in French Street until that year. As regards some of the others, in 1861 Fr Carr had been living in Whitefriar Street Friary from 1851 and Frs Bennett and McGee since 1855: see *FJ*, 29th Oct 1861.

5. The Conservatives cited precedents for this position: one such, the so-called Gorman case, in which a distiller occupying a distillery house was denied the vote on the grounds that he could be dismissed from employment and consequently be evicted from his dwelling; another was the case, *Heath versus Hynes*, where members of an incorporated hospital and occupying apartments in it were deemed not to be entitled to the vote.

6. *SNL*, 29th Oct 1861. The ten Carmelite names given were: Thomas Bennett, John Carr, Cornelius Crotty, Eugene Cullen, Michael Gilligan, Henry McGee, John Mulvihille, John Spratt, Peter Ward and John Berkeley (sic). The final surname should perhaps have been that of John Elias Bartley (1832-1895): see GMA, *Catalogus Fratrum*, p. 4 where there is no name of Berkeley but where that of Bartley is recorded.

No decision was come to on that day as the Lord Mayor, Atkinson, reserved judgement while his revision court considered whether or not the friars were householders *'within the meaning of the Act'*. It was an important case since it suggested that the clergy of all religious orders in the city would be affected by it. In the event, on the very next day, 29th October, Spratt and his confreres were victorious, the court deciding unanimously that the *'various claims of the applicants had been substantiated'*.[7] It was, it may be added, very much Spratt's victory as, over the decades, he appears to have been the only Calced Carmelite to take such political initiatives.

He continued to be politically engaged for the rest of the decade. He became actively involved in the Central Franchise Association, a body operating from at least July 1862 to promote and defend the registration of Liberal voters or Liberal claimants to the vote. He was involved in the discussions of this body in December 1862 when they met to consider how best to unite the entire Liberal Party *'into an effective organisation to prepare for the forthcoming poor law revision'*.[8] Such political engagement by him, far from being frowned on, can only have been encouraged, since his friend, the diocesan curate, P J Gilligan, had led the way and since Dr Cullen himself had, like Gilligan and Yore, contributed to the funds of the Central Franchise Association.[9] What was principally at stake in this immediate concern was a struggle for control of the workhouses in Dublin. The Catholic Church authorities were concerned with the situation, for example, in the South Dublin Union. This, in late September 1862 had over 2,650 poor inmates, only 700 of whom were Protestants: yet there were only four Catholic ward masters and three Catholic ward mistresses to cater for the large Catholic majority of the workhouse inmates.[10] The result of the efforts in Spratt's own Royal Exchange Ward were mixed, with a Conservative, Dockrell, and a Liberal, Carroll, being returned.[11]

---

7. *DEM*, 30th Oct 1861.
8. *FJ*, 31st Dec 1862.
9. For Fr Gilligan's initiative, see *DEP*, 23rd Sept 1862. He chaired the first ward meeting, that of Usher's Quay, to get Liberal supporters to bestir themselves and hoped other wards would follow this example. For this, Cullen's and Yore's financial contributions, see *FJ*, 13th Oct 1862.
10. *DEP*, 23rd Sept 1862; according to P. J. Gilligan.
11. *IT*, 1st April 1863.

Such disappointment does not seem to have deterred the friar from continued political activity. Within months, in August 1863, he was actually the President of the Royal Exchange Liberal Club and was actively involved in the preparations for the next round of municipal elections, due that November.[12]   One of his confreres, Michael Gilligan, then President of Terenure College, soon got involved in these elections when he claimed the right to be included in the municipal voting register. The clerk of the church in Whitefriar Street, William Devereux, testified that friar Michael Gilligan had been resident in that friary for the previous three years and, indeed, had secured the municipal vote the previous year. Now Fr Gilligan was being challenged on the ground that he was only a lodger in the friary. It was left to the Lord Mayor to decide Gilligan's eligibility but what that decision may have been is not reported.[13]   It is likely that John Spratt was present at this hearing but it is not recorded. However, he was certainly present at the revision court the following year when the two friars, John Hall, who was then a chaplain in the South Dublin Union Workhouse, and Thomas Doyle, who was then teaching in their Dominic Street Academy, sought the vote on the grounds of residence in the friary.[14]   In support of his confreres, Friar John testified that Fr Doyle had been living in Whitefriar Street for ten years and Fr Hall for the previous seven. The Carmelites' Conservative opponents argued that only actual lessees were entitled to the vote and that those friars whose names were not on the leases had no voting entitlement. As in previous years, the court postponed a decision and it is unfortunate that the outcome is not evident.[15]   In the course of the following year the Conservatives made strenuous efforts to have Spratt himself, and his close friend, the Discalced Carmelite Bishop, Dr Whelan, disfranchised. This was in relation to the poor law elections of 1865.[16]   Again, it is not certain if these efforts were successful. However, that summer Fr John was active in the Royal Exchange Ward in calling for support for the National Association of Ireland.

---

12.  *DEP*, 23rd Sept 1862; according to P. J. Gilligan.
13.  *DDE*, 29th, 30th Oct 1863; *IT*, *SNL*, *FJ*, 30th, 31st Oct 1863 respectively: these last three newspaper sources have little or no reporting on this municipal revision case.
14.  *EF*, 29th Oct 1864.
15.  *SNL*, 29th Oct 1864.
16.  *FJ*, 18th March 1865.

*The National Association*

A body established by Catholic laymen and supported by Dr Cullen, to press for Church of Ireland disestablishment, Catholic education and agrarian reform, the National Association of Ireland had been founded on 29th December 1864, with Peter Paul McSwiney, now Lord Mayor, presiding.[17] The meeting had been convened on foot of a requisition signed by many hundreds of Catholics, headed by Archbishop Cullen and twenty-three other bishops; Spratt was among the many hundreds of clerical signatories as were ten other of his Whitefriar Street confreres.[18] When some 2,000 assembled at the Rotunda on 29th December, Spratt found himself sitting among the bishops on the platform. Rightly so, he may have thought, as he was among the original twenty-seven foundation members: Spratt was the sole Carmelite among the founding fathers. For Cullen, this new organisation represented his first foray into national politics since the 1850s. The new body, as a pressure group, refused to support any parliamentary candidate who failed to stand up for tenant rights, in the form of compensation for improvements they made to the land, and for disestablishment and disendowment of the Established Church in Ireland. As with every other organisation or institution which Spratt joined, he proved a faithful attender at its regular business meetings through the spring of 1865 when it counted over 300 full and 700 associate enrolments.[19] In June of that year Fr John brought the politics of the Association into his own locality when he headed the list of signatories calling on the ratepayers of the Royal Exchange Ward to meet to consider how best they could assist the NAI in its endeavours.[20]

At this point, the NAI would need all the help it could get. Three months before, in April, the organisation came close to splitting over the question of pledging parliamentary independence and the issue of accepting or refusing to accept offers of government places. Cullen

---

17.  E. R. Norman, *The Catholic Church and Ireland in the Age of Rebellion, 1859-1873*, London 1965, p. 139; P. J. Corish, 'Cardinal Cullen and the National Association of Ireland', *Reportorium Novum*, iii, No. 1, 1962. The laymen included Peter Paul McSwiney, Professor Kavanagh, Richard Devitt, Sir John Gray and John Blake Dillon.

18.  *DWN*, 17th Dec 1864; Norman, p. 140.

19.  *EF*, 20th, 22nd Feb 1865; *CT*, 25th Feb 1865.

20.  *EF*, 6th June 1865.

**Fig 141.** *William Gladstone.*

was against a ban on accepting office and he opposed any change to the NAI constitution which sought to introduce a pledge of independent opposition. Significantly, in the general election that July, the NAI's influence was only *'marginal'*, as O'Carroll relates,[21] and although the leader, Dillon, secured election in Tipperary, its general lack of success merely reflected its weakened condition after the divisions of April to June 1865.[22] For all that, however, it did provide evidence of some activity. At a committee meeting which Fr John attended, in October 1865, it claimed to have been responsible for organising a total of 1,204 petitions, bearing 436,000 signatures seeking parliamentary support for land reform, church disestablishment and education. As Norman concluded, it paved the way for allying the Irish Catholic body with the British Liberal Party and thereby helped to prepare the path for the Irish measures of William Gladstone's first administration of 1868 to 1874.[23] At the same time, it may be fair to suggest that the physical force activities of the Fenians, over 1865-1867, had not a little to do in moving Gladstone to take a more practical reforming interest in Ireland. It was, therefore, in this context, a timely question when Dr Leahy of Cashel reminded his NAI audience that there were only two ways of pursuing redress – the peaceful way of O'Connell or the way of physical force.

By that point, the way of physical force appeared to be gaining momentum as the Fenian movement, to the dismay of Cullen and the NAI, appeared to be growing in popularity among the ordinary

21. O'Carroll, p. 194.
22. Norman, p. 171.
23. Ibid, pp. 172-3.

people. The sudden death of Dillon that September left the NAI somewhat leaderless and, over the course of the following year, it was effectively moribund, giving up its own offices in October 1867.[24] It remained formally in existence long enough to see the enactment of the disestablishment of the Church of Ireland; at a meeting in March 1869, as this Bill was making its way through parliament, Spratt moved a resolution urging that some of the surplus revenues of that Church might be devoted to land reclamation and to enable some tenant farmers to become proprietors.[25] Whether or not he remained an active committee member thereafter is not certain: he was not listed among those attending its important meeting on 1st February 1870 when it issued an *Address to the People of Ireland* summarising its history, celebrating its victory in the struggle for disestablishment, and directing attention to the question of the land.[26] Indeed, his attention over the life of the NAI had been more strongly engaged by other political causes, most notably with the Fenians and the amnesty movement, with the electoral battles in Dublin City and with the politics of his own Carmelite Order in Ireland.

*The Friar and the Fenians*

If the NAI had hoped to frustrate or forestall the Fenians, it signally failed to do so. The latter movement gathered pace from 1865 and achieved international attention by a series of military episodes. These included the rescuing of their leader, James Stephens, from jail in Dublin that November; Fenian incursions into Canada in April and May 1866, the arms raid on Chester Castle on 11th February 1867 and the abortive forays into Iveragh, Co. Kerry, and near Kells, Co. Meath, the very next day. Following this, the British government suspended *Habeas Corpus* and, on 5th and 6th March, the principal attempt at insurrection took place in Dublin and Munster. This outbreak resulted in the mass arrests of hundreds of suspected Fenians: by May 1867 some 169 of these had been sent for trial, 8 convicted of high treason, 6 sentenced to death and 25 sentenced to long terms of penal servitude.[27] Those facing death

---

24. O'Carroll, p. 202.
25. *FJ*, 11th March 1869.
26. *DEP, FJ*, 2nd Feb 1870.
27. O. P. Rafferty, *The Church, the State and the Fenian Threat, 1861-1875*, London 1999, p. 97; L. Ó'Broin, *Fenian Fever: an Anglo-American Dilemma*, New York 1971, p. 174.

sentences included Captain John McCafferty, Colonel Thomas Bourke and Patrick Doran. McCafferty had been arrested in Queenstown in April 1865, had been deported to America but had returned to lead the Rising in 1867. Bourke, his fellow Irish American officer, had been wounded and captured in the outbreak in Tipperary. Doran had been involved in the attempted rising in Co. Dublin. The latter was afforded clemency but Bourke was scheduled for execution on 29th May.[28]

At no stage that is recorded, did Spratt express any opinion in print, condemnatory or otherwise, on the Fenian movement up to this point. However, with the convictions for high treason, of Doran, McCafferty and Bourke, he lost no time in taking an initiative to press for clemency. Together with his CYMS colleague, Canon Pope, he thereby laid the foundations of the amnesty movement which resulted in the establishment of the Amnesty Committee and later, of the Amnesty Association.[29] They organised a requisition calling on the Lord Mayor to convene a public meeting that might petition the Queen to extend mercy *'to the unfortunate Fenians'*. By 11th May 1867 they had secured some four hundred signatures and three days later the Lord Mayor convened that meeting at the Mansion House. It was attended by those noted opponents of the death penalty, James Haughton and Alfred Webb, together with other familiar Spratt associates. Motioning the Lord Mayor to assume the chair, Spratt then read a letter from Cullen, an arch-enemy of the Fenians. Deploring the way in which the *'people'* ignored his advice to stay away from revolutionary movements, the Cardinal Archbishop commented:

> I have learned with much pleasure that you intend to take part in the meeting to be held today to invoke Her Majesty's clemency... This is not the first time that you have proved by your activity that the Catholic priest is in his fitting place wherever a work of mercy is to be performed...your exertions command my warmest sympathy,

28. Rafferty, p. 97; P. O'Conchubhair, *The Fenians were dreadful men': the 1867 Rising*, Cork 2011, pp. 31-32, 139; B. Jenkins, *The Fenian Problem: Insurgency and Terrorism in a Liberal State, 1858-1874*, Liverpool 2008, p. 93; (Jenkins errs in naming Patrick Doran as Patrick Dolan).
29. Norman, p. 127.

and he hoped that an act of royal clemency *'will restore good feeling among the people'.*[30] Despite such activities, it appeared that preparations were in train for Bourke's execution and it was not until 27th May that Bourke and six others had their death sentences commuted to penal servitude.[31] Cullen who had intervened with Dublin Castle on the matter, thought that his intercession was decisive but Rafferty has shown that the cabinet decision to commute rather than to execute had been taken before news of Cullen's intervention had reached them: the decision, therefore, had more to do with domestic political calculation than with Irish feelings and Irish pressure groups. It was reported from Dublin that some Fenians were actually disappointed that Bourke had been spared as this deprived them of a martyr whose death would have supplied oxygen for the revival of the movement.[32] In this, the Fenians would not for long be disappointed.

That August 1867, while preparing Fenians in England for a renewed attempt at rebellion, two Irish American Fenian soldiers, Colonel Thomas Kelly and Captain Timothy Deasy, had been arrested. On 18th September, while being taken to court for trial, a successful attempt to rescue them resulted in the death of the Manchester police escort, Sergeant Brett, and in the arrest of several alleged Fenian participants. Three of these, William Allen, Michael Larkin and Michael O'Brien, were sentenced to death, to be executed on 23rd November 1867. Once again, petitions for clemency were organised in Ireland, signed widely by Catholic and Protestant clergy alike. On 19th November John Spratt convened the Grand Carmelite Confraternity whose members agreed to sign the petition, and Spratt himself went about the city to solicit additional support.[33]

This time the petitions were in vain and the Fenian movement secured its martyrs, with the executions of Allen, Larkin and O'Brien on 23rd November. There was a sequel. Whereas Allen and O'Brien were

---

30.  *FJ*, 9th, 11th May 1867; *DEM*, 14th May 1867; Cullen to Spratt, 14th May 1867. V. Comerford, *The Fenians in Context: Irish politics and society, 1848-82*, Dublin 1998, p. 144, misdates this meeting to 13th May 1866 and errs in naming McSwiney, instead of William Joynt, as Lord Mayor; McSwiney had been Lord Mayor in 1864.

31.  Comerford, p. 145; Jenkins, pp. 95-96; J. O'Neill, *The Manchester Martyrs*, Cork 2012, pp. 55-56.

32.  Rafferty, pp. 97-98.

33.  *EF*, 20th, 21st Nov 1867.

**Fig 142.** *The trial of the 'Manchester Martyrs'.*

unmarried, the diminutive, thirty-two year old tailor, Michael Larkin, left behind a widow, four children and his recently widowed mother. Patrick Larkin, his only son, was given refuge by Spratt in his St Peter's Orphanage in York Street.[34] The hope was expressed that those who attended the Manchester Martyr's first anniversary commemoration in Glasnevin Cemetery would see their way to give practical point to their patriotism by contributing to St Peter's and St Joseph's Orphanages.

In the provision of refuge in St Peter's Orphanage, Patrick Larkin was not the only orphaned son of a Fenian. In October 1868 there occurred the sudden death of a suspected Fenian, William Sheedy. He had been arrested and taken from his home in North King Street, and, neither tried nor convicted, was incarcerated in Mountjoy Jail for two years, before release in August 1868. Two months later he dropped dead in Strand Street, his death brought on, so it was asserted, by the rigours of his jailing. In October a committee was put together to aid

34.  *The Irishman*, 18th July 1868, 2nd Jan 1869. As for the other children, the eldest daughter, Margaret, was initially sheltered in a convent in London; the second eldest, Mary Anne, was placed with the Sisters of Mercy in their St Joseph's Convent in Dublin's Mountjoy Street where she was later joined by Margaret, and the youngest child remained with Larkin's widow in Manchester.

his dependants and that month they approached Fr John who agreed to take two of the Sheedy boys into St Peter's. The elder of the two had to be discharged from the Orphanage for reasons unstated, but he was replaced by his youngest brother.[35]

As for the remaining Fenian prisoners, meetings to press for their release began with Cork City Council on 3rd August 1868, followed by a meeting in Dublin's Mechanics Institute at which Isaac Butt presided, on 12th November and which Spratt attended.[36] These were followed on 26th January 1869 by a great gathering in Dublin to press for their release. Spratt did not attend this but penned an apology the day before and expressed his warm support for the movement then beginning.[37] This meeting began the organising of signatures to an amnesty petition and on 9th February Spratt attended a large follow-up assembly where he seconded a resolution that a national petition of 100,000 signatures be presented at the earliest opportunity.[38] A modest success was recorded when some 49 *'non-military'*, out of a remaining total of 81 Fenian prisoners, were released under amnesty a month after this meeting.[39]

### Fenian friction

For all that, John Spratt's standing with the Fenian press and with some sections of the amnesty movement at this time was problematic. For one thing, when the Bill to disestablish the Church of Ireland passed its final hurdle, in the Lords, in late July 1869, Spratt, like the rest of his Roman Catholic fellow-clergy, was gratified and he soon called on the Irish people to be *'jubilant, joyous and gracious'* at the good which this enactment would bring in its train. He urged his fellow-citizens, in gratitude, to turn out in numbers at Kingstown, to welcome the return of the Lord Lieutenant, Spencer, on 6th August 1869. He himself hurried there along with Rev Carroll, and they were on the welcoming platform when the Lord Mayor, on his Excellency's disembarking,

---

35. *The Irishman*, 10th Oct 1868, 13th Feb 1869.
36. *DEP, FJ*, 13th Nov 1868.
37. *The Irishman*, 30th Jan 1869.
38. *FJ, IT*, 10th Feb 1869.
39. Rafferty, p. 120; Jenkins, p. 270; Comerford, pp. 165-166; E. Larkin, *The Consolidation of the Catholic Church in Ireland, 1860-1870*, Dublin 1987, p. 641.

introduced the Carmelite to the Viceroy.[40]  The ultra-nationalist *The Flag of Ireland* was not impressed:

> A fulsome gush of loyalty has burst forth from the lips of…John Spratt, D.D.  No more zealous or pious clergyman, we are sure, exists than Dr Spratt, but from having too much heart in this instance he has lost his head.[41]

Such criticism did not deflect him from becoming involved in the emerging amnesty movement.  On 5th November 1868 his long-time friend and associate in his Cuffe Lane Irish Total Abstinence Society, the bricklayer-poet, John McCorry, convened the meeting which established the Irish Liberation Society, better known as the Amnesty Committee.[42]  McCorry was no Fenian and his Amnesty Committee was a moderate body which organised a great church door collection to raise funds to press for further release of Fenian prisoners even after the first wave of releases in March 1869.  By late April it had collected over £2,000, but a dispute developed over how this was to be allocated and, by May 1869, the Amnesty Committee had split in two, with the more radical and strident part emerging eventually, over May and June 1869, as the Amnesty Association.[43]  The key organiser of the latter was the Fenian, John Nolan, secretary of the original Amnesty Committee who, ironically, was an employee of the moderate nationalist Peter Paul McSwiney's Sackville Street drapery business.[44]  With Nolan, was Isaac Butt as President, who had come to a new prominence as the defence counsel for Fenian prisoners.  This new body preferred

---

40.  *DEM*, 6th Aug 1869.
41.  *The Flag of Ireland*, 7th Aug 1869.
42.  *DDE*, 6th Nov 1868.  The original name may have been ironic, intended as a jibe at the contemporary UK Liberation Society which was set up to seek disestablishment of the Church of England, whereas McCorry and his supporters were seeking the liberation of Irishmen from jail.  Known as 'the toiling minstrel', McCorry died after a fall from scaffolding while working on a building at Clondalkin.  A self-educated and gifted individual, his poetry won high praise from Lady Wilde who spoke of his *wonderful excellence, considering the little time he could bestow on self-culture*: for his life, see *DWN*, 23rd Sept 1871.  As to the foundation meeting, Larkin, *The Consolidation*, misdates it to 12th November when the second such meeting was presided over by Isaac Butt.
43.  Larkin, p. 644.
44.  Comerford, p. 170.

a more aggressive approach for release of the remaining prisoners and conducted a vigorous campaign over the ill-treatment of jailed Fenians, notably in the case of Jeremiah O'Donovan Rossa in Chatham Jail.

In the course of 1869 Spratt became caught up in the excitements of the amnesty cause and soon found his relations with the Amnesty Association to be complex. It was noted earlier how actively the Carmelite had become engaged in the Liberal politics

**Fig 143.** *Isaac Butt, MP.*

of the Royal Exchange Ward. In late August 1869 some twenty-eight members of the Ward's Liberal Club, joining forces with colleagues in the Mansion House and Fitzwilliam Wards, called on Spratt to preside over a meeting of their voting citizens to aid the Amnesty Association in its campaign. This he duly did, at a time when the campaign had become energetic and vocal.[45] Typical of this energy was a great demonstration at Drogheda, on 22nd August, when thousands travelled from Dublin, Meath and Louth to lend their support to the cause. Meticulously organised by Nolan who had arranged for excursion trains, the occasion commenced with Mass, followed by a procession and then a meeting where strident speeches were the order of the day. Some 20,000 to 30,000 paraded to the People's Park for the event and it is noteworthy that the procession was led by Spratt's ITAA Temperance Band. Interestingly, he himself was neither present nor sent a note of apology, as others did.[46] However, when his own Royal Exchange Ward meeting was held three days later, the large attendance included the Amnesty Association's Nolan. W J Battersby, who had not been publicly linked with Spratt for many years, was present and proposed

---

45. *FJ*, 23rd Aug 1869.
46. *EF*, 23rd Aug 1869.

the friar as chairman.  In opening the meeting Spratt delivered one of the most significant speeches of his public life.  He adopted a tone of humble deference to the authorities, urging that an appeal to *the brightest and most gracious prerogative of the Crown – that of mercy and forgiveness'* – was *'a noble one'*, and then went on to censure the more strident speeches that had become the tenor of recent amnesty gatherings:

> I must avow that, at many meetings held ostensibly for the same object, language has, in my humble opinion, been made use of, better calculated to defeat than to forward the end proposed.

He continued, at unusual length, to berate the unwisdom of defiant language aimed at *'winning the empty cheers of the giddy and unreflective'*: it was language that, for the poor prisoners, only served *'to turn the key rather than open the door'*.  He went on:

> we are not to forget or lay aside the dignity of men or in any way to depart from what is due to our country.  In our upright, manly, yet respectful attitude, let us point to the suffering prisoners and say – *'our brothers have erred with the ardour and inexperience of youth'*.

These remarks, reportedly, were received with *'loud and prolonged applause'*.[47]  It would transpire, however, that this classic position of O'Connellite liberalism was anathema to the nationalism of the Irish Republican Brotherhood.  In the meantime, Spratt continued his amnesty activity.  In late September 1869 he actually used the usual Sunday evening meeting of his Cuffe Street ITAA to further the cause in a quite specific way.  On 19th September, with the hall *'filled to capacity'*, he led the meeting, along with James Haughton, in proposing a memorial to the Queen, to be addressed by way of Prime Minister Gladstone, calling for amnesty.  Drawn up and dated 19th September, it bore the signatures of Spratt and Haughton.[48]  Their memorial duly dispatched, within a matter of days a reply from Gladstone was addressed to Spratt, promising to lay the Irish Total Abstinence Society's memorial before the Queen and praising its *'loyal and becoming terms...and the soundness of*

47.  *FJ*, 26th Aug 1869.
48.  *FJ*, 23rd Sept 1869.

*judgement which they exhibit in attaching its true character to the offences unhappily committed by the persons now in confinement'.*[49] The Fenian press was aghast. *The Irishman* thundered:

> In reply to Dr Spratt and the other authors of the humiliating petition from the temperance people, Mr Gladstone hints that he may liberate the prisoners if we in Ireland only acknowledged that they committed *'a crime which admits of no justification'* – which, it is needless to say, we in Ireland won't admit...Mr. Gladstone and his friends would do well to consider the effect of refusing the constitutional demand of a whole people. It might lead to an unpleasantly *'unconstitutional'* demand.[50]

The *Flag of Ireland* was even more enraged:

> Mr Gladstone's letter to the teetotal flunkeys bears only one interpretation...to the Irish people that, unless they go down on their knees...there is no hope for the release of the prisoners.[51]

A week later, a monster amnesty demonstration was held where, according to police reports, some 200,000 gathered in a great field near Phibsborough in Dublin. Described as the culmination of the campaign, and addressed by George H Moore in a brilliant speech, there was no sign of John Spratt's presence, although, yet again, as at Drogheda, his own temperance band played a prominent part in marshalling the multitude of contingents to their allotted places.[52] However, the friar was not silenced. A fortnight later he addressed a public letter to both the Amnesty Association and to the original Amnesty Committee. He did not pull his punches and told them that it was in their power to bring the prisoners' sufferings to an end or to *'prolong them for years to come'*. He reiterated that defiant language could only damage the cause, and commented:

---

49. *IT*, 28th Sept 1869.
50. *The Irishman*, 2nd Oct 1869.
51. *The Flag of Ireland*, 2nd Oct 1869.
52. *IT*, 11th Oct 1869.

> While you are breathing the fresh air and enjoying the blessed
> light of liberty, turning what ought to be an occasion of mourning
> and humiliation into holiday displays, the unfortunate victims of
> political excitement are expiating their offences against the law,
> by terrible sufferings.

Observing that Gladstone had rejected their demands for additional
amnesty, Spratt pointed out that the Prime Minister had not shut the
door. The friar thereupon called on the amnesty movement organisers
to allow excitement to calm down and to *'abandon at once an agitation
which has proved useless, nay, mischievous'*.[53] The more moderate Amnesty
Committee responded to his plea by stating their total concurrence
with his view of the matter and expressing the wish that the rival
Amnesty Association might follow suit.[54] However, the two organs
of the Association were not impressed. From *The Irishman* came the
comment:

> We need hardly say much about Sir Oracle Spratt – a very
> respectable person in every respect, save as a politician.

Its editor added, acidly, that the Carmelite friar was stuck in the politics
of fifty years before: while he was preaching loyalty to the Crown, he
was caught in a contradiction since, as a friar, he was daily in breach of
the law by contravening the provisions of the Catholic Relief Act of
1829 which outlawed regular clergy.[55]

On the same date, the *Flag of Ireland* devoted a hostile editorial to the
Carmelite, stating that *'the cobbler should stick to his last'*: while conceding
that *'everyone'* admired Spratt as a teetotal advocate, *'the duty of the Irish
people in the Amnesty Movement he does not understand'*. It denounced
Spratt's *'very silly and humiliating letter'* calling for an end to the agitation,
and added: *'of course, no one but the veriest flunkey in Ireland would be silly
enough to accept the suggestion'*.[56] The attacks did not end there: they were

---

53. *DEP*, 27th Oct 1869.
54. *SNL*, 29th Oct 1869, James Carroll, Secretary, Central Amnesty Committee, to
    Spratt.
55. *The Irishman*, 30th Oct 1869.
56. *The Flag of Ireland*, 30th Oct 1869.

renewed in December 1869, but John Spratt no longer responded,[57] although one correspondent to the press did come to his defence: writing in January 1870 'An Observer' denounced *The Irishman* for its attacks on Spratt, especially as coming from its owner who once had stood as a Tory candidate for Limerick city.[58] Yet there was a sense in which the Carmelite's position was endorsed by no less a person than the Amnesty Association president, Isaac Butt. Butt recognised the situation as spelled out by Gladstone, that amnesty could come, but not by the coercive pressure of mass meetings. Butt therefore, from mid-October 1869, had been trying to curtail the demonstrations and to calm down the excitement, just as Spratt had advised, but the Association's secretary, Nolan, took a different view. Nevertheless, Spratt's (and Butt's) position was somehow vindicated when, on 11th November 1870, the Gladstone cabinet agreed to a Fenian amnesty – significantly after a long period of quiescence and inactivity on the part of the Amnesty Association. By mid-January 1871 some 30 Fenian prisoners had been released, though not those involved in the Manchester rescue of Kelly and Deasy, nor those who had tried to subvert soldiers.[59] Spratt had made a not insignificant contribution to the amnesty issue but it was only one strand of his many-sided political engagements at this time.

*Electoral Reform and Registration*

The Carmelite friar continued his role in the Central Franchise Association and, as the prospect of a general election loomed, two developments in 1868 lent a new urgency to the activities of this body. One was the passing of the Representation of the People (Ireland) Act which came into law on 13th July and which reduced the qualification for the rated-occupier franchise from £8 to £4 and, more significantly, introduced the lodger franchise for parliamentary elections in Ireland. The other was the looming prospect of a general election, which came to pass in November of that year. In making preparations to ensure that the Conservative and Orange parliamentary stranglehold on Dublin City could be successfully challenged, the Central Franchise

---

57. *The Irishman*, 24th Dec 1869.
58. *DEP*, 4th Jan 1870, 'The Anti-Priest Movement', by 'An Observer'.
59. Comerford, pp. 174, 184; Jenkins pp. 306-313.

Association, at the end of June 1868, set up a Registration Committee and the Carmelite friar secured a place on this.[60] He supported a motion that they issue circulars seeking funding to cover registration and related organisational expenses: furthermore, at Alderman McSwiney's urging, it was agreed that ward meetings be energised into local registration efforts, as sole reliance on the central body could not guarantee success. A few days after this, on 7th July, Fr John, as President of the Royal Exchange Liberal Club, chaired a meeting to consider *'the best means of organising the Liberal interests of the Ward in carrying out the new parliamentary franchise'*. As he himself put it, *'they had met to give hearty support to the Central Franchise Association to free the city from misrepresentation'*, as *'for too long they had the infliction of Vance and Grogan'*. Indeed, not since 1837 to 1841 did Liberals and Repealers occupy the two city seats. From 1841 to 1867 the Conservatives dominated, and while the Repealer, John Reynolds, shared one of the two Dublin City seats with the Conservative Grogan from 1847 until 1852. However from 1852 until 1865 the two seats were held by the Tories, Grogan and Vance, and from 1865 till 1868 the Conservative Benjamin Lee Guinness shared with the Liberal Jonathan Pim. So Spratt was on the mark when he attacked the Conservative predominance. His close involvement in local liberal politics was further evident when, a week later, he attended a meeting for an identical purpose, of the Mansion House Ward which was actually held in the premises of St Peter's Orphanage in York Street: it may be reasonably assumed that he had organised the venue.[61] Although the Central Franchise Association was focussed on getting every eligible voter registered to the exclusion or deferral of discussion on specific candidates, nevertheless the emergence of the prominent Quaker, Jonathan Pim, as a Liberal candidate was welcomed. Spratt continued to busy himself in the Liberal cause when he attended yet another such gathering in early August, this time of the South City Ward: here he seconded a Central Franchise Association motion urging the various city ward committees not to put forward lodger claimants to the vote who paid less than 4 shillings weekly.[62]

Friar John showed a very active involvement in the municipal

---

60.  *FJ*, 1st July 1868.

61.  *FJ*, 8th July 1868.

62.  *DEP*, 16th July 1868. It is also interesting to note that the orphanage schoolmaster, Michael O'Connolly, was among those who attended.

politics of the Royal Exchange Ward, of whose Liberal Club, Friar John
was President, in the later 1860s; nevertheless, it was the increasingly
compelling attraction of parliamentary elections that most deeply
engaged the public Spratt as the decade saw hopes for a Gladstonian
Liberal triumph, with its concomitant promise of redress for Ireland.
In this climate of expectation possession of the vote became now more
urgent than ever for the friar. Consequently, when in September 1868,
the revision of Dublin's parliamentary register commenced, he and
eighteen other Carmelites of Whitefriar Street put forward their claims
as joint rated occupiers of *'four houses in Aungier Place'*. Objections were
raised by their opponents because the address of the premises as given in
the rate-books was Aungier Lane, not Aungier Place. It is not clear how
these objections were overcome, but John enjoyed a signal victory as he
and his eighteen brother Carmelites exercised the vote in the election
on 18th November that year.[63]  At the time, Aungier Street had only 15
lodger, and only 32 rated occupier voters, so the Carmelites constituted
more than 50% of the ratepayer voters. Unsurprisingly, to a man they
plumped for the Catholic, Dominic Corrigan, and the Quaker, Jonathan
Pim.[64]  Securing the vote was ever a struggle, especially for the religious.
John's brother, James, and five other Augustinians of John Street, were
denied the vote on the basis that there were more claimants out of their
premises than the rated amount would admit of. An identical rejection
was the fate of six Franciscans of Merchant's Quay: and among the
Discalced Carmelites of Clarendon Street, only Fr Daniel Fogarty, out
of eleven of the friars there, voted.[65]

As the general election loomed, John was among the prominent
public figures to call for a mass meeting of Dublin's Liberal voters

---

63. The nineteen were listed as James Behan, John Brennan, John Carr, Cornelius
    Crotty, Eugene Cullen, Thomas Cullen, Thomas Doyle, Joseph Flood, Michael
    Gilligan, John Hall, John Laybourne, Matthew McDonnell, Henry McGee, Patrick
    O'Farrell, Patrick O'Toole, Nicholas Staples, John Spratt, Peter Ward and Joseph
    Bultor [sic], presumably the latter is a misspelling for Joseph Butler (1844-1918),
    for whom see GMA, *Catalogus Fratrum*.
64. Anon, *City of Dublin Election, 18th November 1868, List of Electors*, Dublin 1868.
    This source, in the National Library of Ireland, appears to have been the poll-
    book compiled by the agents for Corrigan and Pim.
65. *FJ*, 29th Sept 1868; *DDE*, 1st Oct 1868. *The City of Dublin Election, 18th November
    1868, List of Electors*, as cited in note 117, lists no votes cast by any members of
    either community.

**Fig 144.** *Sir Dominic Corrigan, MP.*

to promote the return of Corrigan and Pim.[66] The ensuing meeting in the Rotunda, on 2nd November, proved tense as the emotive issue of the Fenian amnesty threatened to derail the Liberal train. Pim, one of Dublin's two city MPs since 1865, was challenged on his support in parliament for the suspension of *Habeas Corpus*; his defence was to assert that he had been one of only eighteen Irish MPs to move an amendment to have that suspension reviewed every three months.

Spratt was to the fore in this meeting, conveying a letter of apology he had received that very day from Cardinal Cullen, and moving the first resolution calling for religious equality and disestablishment of the Church of Ireland. He also intervened effectively to secure a hearing for the MP Cogan who was barracked and heckled by Fenian supporters over his vote on the *Habeas Corpus* issue.[67] Two days later, he attended a crowded meeting of Liberal supporters of Usher's, Merchant's and Wood Quays where Corrigan delivered a blistering attack on the Conservative candidate, Arthur Guinness, and on the Established Church.[68] Two days later again, in his Cuffe Lane Temperance Hall, Spratt chaired a crowded meeting of the combined Royal Exchange, Mansion House and Fitzwilliam Ward electors, with Corrigan and Pim both present. Corrigan again launched a fierce attack on Arthur Guinness who had not, he asserted, followed his father, Benjamin Lee Guinness, in supporting religious equality. Speaking at the end of the meeting, the Carmelite declared his total support for Corrigan and Pim, but also conveyed his apprehension that his fellow friars were very

---

66. *DDE*, 30th Oct 1868.
67. *DEM*, 2nd Nov 1868; *DEP*, 2nd, 3rd Nov 1868; *The Irishman*, 7th Nov 1868.
68. *FJ*, 5th Nov 1868.

anxious about the Liberal candidates' chances of success: he concluded:

> Forty years ago he stood by O'Connell in the first great struggle
> for liberty and he thanked God he was as well that day and was as
> able to engage in the mighty effort now being made to complete
> the work of emancipation.[69]

Spratt and his fellow-Liberals, however, were destined to disappointment
when it came to the Catholic candidate. While Pim was returned, in
second place, Corrigan came last of the four candidates and, doubtless
to his and Spratt's chagrin, the arch-opponent, Guinness, topped the
poll. It may have been some consolation that it had been a very close-
run battle, with only 208 votes separating the first from the fourth
candidate, and only a single vote separating Guinness from Pim. The
results were:

| | |
|---|---|
| Guinness | 5,587 |
| Pim | 5,586 |
| Plunkett | 5,459 |
| Corrigan | 5,379[70] |

It transpired that Guinness had secured victory by purchasing votes of
the freemen electors for cash. Spratt thereupon became involved in the
successful Liberal campaign to have Guinness unseated and became
active in the resulting by-election, with Corrigan once again in the lists
to fill the vacancy.[71] Critical to the hoped-for success in this battle
was the effective registration of the new lodger voters: it was reckoned
that, for the impending by-election, there could be as many as 1,200
additional Liberal voters as against an additional 300 Conservatives.
Consequently, it now became imperative for the city Liberal agents to
register as many of these 1,200 as possible. In May 1869, at a meeting
of the city's Liberals, where Corrigan explained that they would need

---

69. *DEP*, 7th Nov 1868.
70. *Warder and Dublin Weekly Mail*, 21st Nov 1868. *The Dictionary of Irish Biography* (1st
    edition) entry on Arthur Guinness by Diarmaid Ferriter states that having
    'inherited' his father's Dublin City seat, he failed to retain it in the 1868 general
    election.
71. *FJ*, 11th Feb 1869.

a fighting fund of £1,000 to meet the costs of effective registration, Spratt now found himself as one of three treasurers appointed to raise and account for this funding. They started well, as on the night of this meeting, they raised £356.[72] However, the road to the £1,000 proved a long one and by October 1869 they had managed to reach only £500.[73] While the revision court registration process ended on 25th October, it was not until 18th August 1870 that the by-election was held, with Corrigan, at last, topping the poll.[74]

## A Cardinal crossed

The struggle for that victory was not without controversy and casualties, the most significant of the latter being John Spratt himself. The Carmelite had been working assiduously in Corrigan's support right up to the beginning of July 1870. On 8th July he was prominent at a campaign meeting in the Rotunda, where his brother James was also present, and Fr John spoke up strongly for Corrigan.[75] However, in a matter of days, difficulties arose. At the Rotunda meeting, Corrigan had expressed support for 'mixed' or non-sectarian education. Unfortunately, the senior diocesan clergy, in Cullen's absence at the Vatican Council in Rome, took exception to these views. Cullen's vicar-general, Edward McCabe, lost no time in complaining to the Cardinal:

> Sir Dominic Corrigan is in the field for Dublin again. I fear he will do mischief on the education question if he is returned. I contributed a small stone to erect a barrier to his great progress by writing a short letter to Alderman McSwiney. I wish we had your Eminence here, for, if Dublin return him with the very meagre address which is expected from him, his return will injure the cause...I wrote to Dr Spratt and took the opportunity of telling him that as he became sponsor for Sir Dominic, he made himself responsible for his election address.[76]

72.  EF, 20th May 1869.
73.  DEP, 5th Oct 1869.
74.  FJ, 20th Aug 1870.
75.  FJ, 9th July 1870.
76.  DDA, Cullen Papers, 321/7/III/45, McCabe to Cullen, 10th July 1870.

John Spratt, as Corrigan's most prominent clerical supporter, was told in no uncertain terms, to convey to Corrigan that if the latter wished to represent Dublin City in Parliament, he would have to conform to their views on the education question. It came as a bolt from the blue to Corrigan and Spratt alike. The friar was now in the unenviable situation of having to write and question the education views of one whom he had been supporting politically for two years. On the very next day of McCabe's complaint to Cullen, the Carmelite was compelled to

**Fig 145.** *Cardinal Edward McCabe, succeeded Paul Cullen as Archbishop of Dublin.*

write to Sir Dominic and he copied it to the Cardinal's office. Referring to Corrigan's Rotunda speech of the week before, Spratt was present to hear that speech but now had to confess to Corrigan that

> since then I have become aware that, with reference to the education question, the views you are supposed to maintain cause very great uneasiness and dissatisfaction in high quarters among the clergy.

He went on:

> to yourself individually there is and can be amongst us but one feeling, that of friendly admiration, but the education question being the only one now left unsettled, upon which as Catholics we have a natural interest, the Clergy and Catholics generally have a right to make quite sure that their future representative in Parliament shall fully, fairly and unconditionally represent that most important question.

He ended:

> I would not trouble you but that I have had the best reason
> for arriving at the conviction that this is a matter of the last
> importance as regards success in the approaching election.[77]

Corrigan replied to Spratt the same day, thanking the friar for giving
him the opportunity *'of stating what my views are on Education – what I
understand by 'Freedom of Education'.* These views which, he remarked,
had for long been in the public domain, were, as regards university
education, that Ireland should have a single, national university, engaged
not in teaching but exclusively in examining and in the awarding of
degrees; that all degrees, emoluments and honours should be open
equally to all candidates without distinction: *'that the whole business of the
University should be to ascertain what a man knows and not where he learned it'.*
As to primary education, there should be the same freedom; that the
State should give equally and impartially to all denominations, *'to those
who desire denominational education and to those who do not'.* He continued:

> We are both anxious for the success of the Liberal Party. I
> would therefore earnestly ask you and your friends to attend the
> meeting summoned for tomorrow. There is no time to be lost.
> The election will soon be upon us, and it is above all important
> that there should be no disunion among us…

and concluded, *'if my views do not obtain general approval I will at once
withdraw'.*[78] This letter, too, ended up in the Cardinal's office, but also saw
publication in the daily press, presumably courtesy of the Carmelite.[79]
However, Spratt was still not clear of trouble. Vicar General McCabe,
who had been on diocesan spiritual retreat that week, emerged from it
to complain yet again to Cullen in Rome, asserting that

---

77. RCPI, *Sir Dominic Corrigan Letters*, DC/4/2/1, Spratt to Corrigan, 12th July 1870;
    DDA, *Cullen Papers*, 321/1/III/8/1, Spratt to Corrigan 11th July 1870.
78. RCPI, *Corrigan Letters*, Corrigan to Spratt, 12th July 1870.
79. DDA, *Cullen Papers*, 321/1/III/8/2, Corrigan to Spratt, 12th July 1870; *FJ*, 15th
    July 1870. As to the meeting, there is no report that it was held or that Spratt
    attended it.

amongst his many good deeds, I fear Dr Spratt has done some mischief by taking up Sir Dominic Corrigan. The latter has been giving out that the letter which he published last week was considered quite satisfactory. I suspect Dr Spratt gave him some such assurance. I sent a note to Dr Spratt last night telling him that, in my opinion, the letter was the reverse of satisfactory.[80]

By this stage the airing of this disagreement was in full public view and while the Conservatives had not chosen a candidate to replace the unseated Arthur Guinness, the Liberal electors were now divided due to the Spratt-Corrigan contretemps. As the on-looking *Saunders' Newsletter* observed,

> there would seem to be only a single way of settling the difference and that is one which Sir Dominic Corrigan would not seem likely to follow, or at least, has not thought proper to adopt.[81]

Cullen now entered the lists directly, with a long open letter to Corrigan on 6th August, commenting that Corrigan's support for *'mixed education'* was founded *'upon infidel principles'*. As for primary education, *'the demands of Catholics comprise Catholic schools, Catholic teachers, Catholic training schools, Catholic books and Catholic Inspectors. Less than this will not satisfy the Catholics of Ireland'*. Cullen concluded in no uncertain terms:

> I think a sentence in your letter to Dr Spratt will be turned against you by your opponents. You say that *'on University Education my views have been for some years before the public. I entertain the same views now'*. Many Catholics will say that they cannot support you because, some years ago, you wrote very strongly in support of mixed education and the Queen's Colleges and you now profess your adherence to what you wrote then. The only way I see for getting out of this difficulty is by publishing a distinct condemnation of those colleges and of the principle on which they are founded.[82]

---

80. DDA, *Cullen Papers*, 321/7/III/48, McCabe to Cullen, 18th July 1870.
81. *SNL*, 22nd July 1870.
82. DDA, *Cullen Papers*, 321/7/I/9, Cullen to Corrigan, 6th August 1870; RCPI, *Corrigan Letters*, Cullen to Corrigan, 7th August 1870.

Corrigan responded to this pressure by insisting he was going to stand for parliament with or without the support of the church. Cullen, in turn, kept up the pressure by ordering a deputation of Bartholomew Woodlock, who was Rector of the Catholic University and, as it happened, was Corrigan's brother-in-law, along with Canon Farrell, and the doubtlessly embarrassed Carmelite friar. They were to call on Corrigan with a view to persuading him to toe the line. The emissaries pressed to know if he would support continued endowment of Trinity College and of the Protestant Royal and Charter Schools or instead promote redistribution of such funding so as to ensure equal education rights for all.[83] He replied that as to private endowment of Protestant education institutions, parliament could not interfere: as to public endowment, he supported equal financial treatment for all and was opposed to the public financing of any proselytising education bodies.

Cullen, as Corrigan's biographer noted, considered this a capitulation by Corrigan and allegedly went on to vote for him.[84] The resultant poll on 18th August 1870 saw Corrigan triumph by 4,468 to 3,444 for the Home Rule candidate, Captain Edward Robert King Harman, and with a single vote for the third candidate, David Robert Plunkett.[85] The victorious Corrigan however, in the course of his own parliamentary career, continued to advocate his views on mixed education against the more militant denominationalism of Cardinal Cullen, and, ironically, only a year after his return to parliament, went on to be elected Vice-Chancellor of the Queen's University.[86]

The baronet doctor and the Cardinal Archbishop may well have thought that each had achieved the victory, and perhaps they had: as the *Warder* sarcastically put it, '*Sir Dominic Corrigan was returned on Thursday, by a majority of 756, to represent Cardinal Cullen in the Parliament at Westminster*'.[87] The only one who privately must have felt compromised and defeated was the Carmelite friar. Having campaigned for Corrigan

83. E. O'Brien, *Conscience and Conflict: a biography of Sir Dominic Corrigan, 1802-1880*, Dublin 1983, p. 311.
84. Ibid, p. 312. O'Brien, quotes Cullen correspondence in which Cullen is reported to have also voted for the Quaker Pim. This, presumably, is to mistake the 1870 by-election for the 1868 general election as Pim, already an MP, was not a candidate in 1870. O'Brien's source is MacSuibhne, *Cullen*, vol. 4, p. 243.
85. *DDE*, 20th Aug 1870; *DWN*, 27th Aug 1870.
86. O'Brien, p. 285.
87. *The Warder and Dublin Weekly Mail*, 20th Aug 1870.

from 1868 until the Rotunda meeting of 8th July 1870, there is no sign that he took part in any celebrations of Corrigan's electoral triumph: their only contact thereafter may well have been a long conversation they had on the subject of temperance on the day before Spratt died.[88] There is a sense that John Spratt's political engagements through and beyond the 1860s came at a considerable cost to himself and, indeed, to his confreres.

*Carmelite Politics 1860-1871*

By the middle of the 1850s Friar John, as earlier noted, was the best-known Irish Carmelite, even in Rome. Then, in June 1863, he finally secured formal recognition and the most senior responsibility when Prior General Savini appointed him as Vicar Provincial. This followed the end of Thomas Bennett's terms as Provincial and the appointment was made pending the intended holding of a Provincial Chapter in 1863. However, for reasons not clear, that Chapter was never held and Savini, having appointed Spratt as Provincial that October, confirmed that appointment the following month. He would remain as Provincial from then until the end of his days, in 1871, a considerable burden on top of already crowded hours. The position brought new and onerous responsibilities at a time when the number of Carmelite friars in Whitefriar Street and in Ireland as a whole was growing significantly: the number of friars in Whitefriar Street during Spratt's tenure as Provincial went from 12 in 1863 to 14 in 1869 and reached 21 in 1871.[89] It was also at a time when his charitable and political commitments were multiplying. His concerns now embraced the manifold cares

**Fig 146.** *Angelo Savini, O.Carm.*

---

88.  There are no extant Spratt-Corrigan letters following their exchange of correspondence on 12th July 1870. For their final conversation see Chapter Twenty-Four.

89.  W. J. Battersby, *Catholic Directory*; 1863, p. 165, 1869, p. 144, 1871, p. 148.

of any Provincial, from schools to colleges, from finances to friaries, from the reception and oversight of novices, the ordinations and funerals of friars to the minutiae of discipline and observance, apart altogether from the demands of the liturgical year. Nevertheless, in April 1864 he felt able to report to Savini that *'all were happy and seemed to enjoy a peace which they had not experienced for years'.*[90] Hardly a compliment to his diligent predecessor, Bennett, the peace proved one of a calm before a storm. Although Savini pressed Spratt to do something about establishing a Carmelite presence in England for the first time since the Reformation, he demurred and claimed that he needed all the priests he could get for his various Irish foundations.

Spratt's first term concluded in April 1866, but he was re-appointed, a sure-enough sign of the Prior General's approval.[91] Indeed, Savini wrote to Cullen at the end of May urging him to ignore any murmurings from discontented friars, *'respectable in many respects, but not for their humility'*: he asked that *'you freely support my Provincial, John, and with him the true interests of my Irish Province'.*[92] It is interesting to note that no Irish provincial chapter was held then and that Spratt requested that no defined term of office be laid down for him.[93] He now instituted a rigorous regime of observance that would have done Fr Bennett proud. He issued a series of decrees: friars were forbidden to go from friary to friary without

**Fig 147.** *Andrew Farrington, O. Carm.*

90.  O'Dwyer, *Irish Carmelites*, p. 235, citing AO Rome II, Hib, 14th April 1864.
91.  Ibid, p. 237.
92.  DDA, *Cullen Papers*, 327/6/1866, Savini to Cullen, 31st May 1866.
93.  GMA, *Scrapbook A*, p. 59: letter of appointment; also O'Dwyer, op.cit., pp. 237, 252, n. 332.

the Provincial's permission; they were to be within the walls before bedtime; weekly statements of account had to be read out in each community; priests were to say Mass daily unless excused by illness; all were to attend meditation at 7 am in winter and at 6 am in summer, and suitable spiritual works were to be read aloud during dinner. By the summer of 1867 rumblings of discontent were audible. Some twenty-five friars wrote jointly to Rome to complain of Spratt's regime and they requested a formal visitation of the Province. His refusal to allow the Prior of Knocktopher, Fr Martin Bruton, to go on the American mission had to be overridden by Savini. Furthermore, when the young friar, Andrew Farrington, then only three years a priest,[94] asked permission to go on the missions to Wales or America, he was given short shrift:

Rev and Dear Sir,

I received a letter, by this day's post, from the Most Revd Father General of our Order telling me to cancel the *'obedience for Merthyr'* and to inform you that you are to remain in the Convent of Knocktopher where your services are required. You are, thus, for the present, deprived of an opportunity of wandering through the woods of Maryland or the mountains of Wales. Do take my advice, give up self-will and renounce the spirit of disobedience, and if you do not, believe me, you will get on the high road to ruin. You are young – not in age – but in Religion, therefore I give you this advice because I know you want experience.

As I am writing, I deem it my duty to inform a Canonist like yourself of the fact that His Holiness Pope Pius IX has given extraordinary jurisdiction to the Cardinal Archbishop of Dublin as Delegate Apostolic, over the Friars of Ireland.

Yours sincerely,

John Spratt, V. Provincial.[95]

---

94. GMA, *Catalogus Fratrum*, p. 6. Born in 1840, Farrington entered the Order in December 1860, ordained in 1865 and died in May 1921. As Spratt's first biographer, he did not mention this matter in the biography; see A. E. Farrington, *Rev Dr Spratt, O.C.C.: His Life and Times*, Dublin 1893.
95. GMA, *IRE 040/0001*, John Spratt to Andrew Farrington, 24th January 1868.

The tone of this letter does little credit to Fr John whose public charm and agreeability were a byword. It can be explained in part, perhaps, by his annoyance that Farrington had sought the support of his own Prior, William Withers, and the support of Savini himself, no less. Savini initially had supported Farrington's wish until Spratt pleaded with the Prior General, successfully, to cancel that permission, or 'obedience' as it was then called.

This was by no means the only letter of such tenor at this time: Withers himself had received a stiff enough missive from Spratt over the Farrington business. It may all suggest that Spratt was becoming rattled as a potential mutiny of the friars was taking shape. Twenty-seven of them soon signed a petition to the Prior General in Rome requesting that an Irish Provincial Chapter be held at Easter 1868. All six friaries in Ireland subscribed to this petition, including Whitefriar Street itself. Savini had to tell Spratt about the petition which, on 28th February 1868, Spratt discounted as being inspired by malcontent younger friars and that the older men stood by him. He added that if the General wished to find a successor to Spratt, he would have to clear it with Cardinal Cullen, to whom he would now submit Savini's letter and his own reply to it.[96]

In the midst of this turmoil, one week later Spratt issued a new printed decree to outlaw the taking of drink except during or immediately after dinner, and this he duly copied to the Cardinal.[97] It appears too, that Spratt now sent two senior confreres, Henry McGee and Cornelius Crotty, to Rome to present his case against the dissidents: so the unhappier members of the Whitefriar Street community argued when eighteen of them, on 2nd March 1868, again petitioned the Prior General to intervene. Withers too, now weighed in with a letter to Savini, and signed by his confreres, Farrington and Eugene Cullen, arguing that McGee and Crotty did not represent the views of the Irish Province; they requested the General to undertake a visitation, and complained that Spratt was devoting too much time and attention to matters outside of the Order. There was by now an extensive feeling among the friars that a Chapter was urgently needed.

96.  DDA, *Cullen Papers*, 341/1/6, Spratt to Savini, 28th February 1868.
97.  Ibid, 341.1/6, printed decree of 6th March 1868.

Well-disposed to Fr John as Cardinal Cullen was at this time, he could no longer ignore the murmurings below deck. On 22nd March 1868 he wrote to the Cardinal Prefect of Propaganda Fide, Alessandro Barnabo.[98] He spoke of Spratt as an *'excellent religious and highly esteemed here in Dublin'*:

> He does much for the cause of Temperance, maintains an orphanage and schools for the poor. He has founded a night refuge for all who cannot pay the rent. But, despite all these good qualities, he has not been able to maintain the religious system introduced by Fr Bennett.

Then, in a classic of understatement, Cullen added:

> It may be that he is too occupied with external matters and that he does not attend sufficiently to the affairs of the monastery.

In fairness to the Cardinal, he did not rush to judgement. Consulting some of the older Carmelites, he commented:

> From what I can gather, there is no great reason for complaints on either side,

and sagely added:

> But, both Fr Spratt and the younger members are both heated and will probably say things against each other, founded more on imagination than on real truth.

Cullen himself either could not or would not suggest a solution but left it up to the Prefect of Propaganda to do so.[99] The Prefect now contacted Savini who appears to have suggested to Spratt that the friar might consider his position. Such appears to be the case from Fr John's response, as cited by O'Dwyer:

---

98. Alessandro Barnabo (1801-1874) was Prefect of Propaganda from 1856 to 1874.
99. O'Dwyer, *Irish Carmelites*, p. 240.

> Having accepted the office of Provincial of Ireland – of which
> I was not ambitious – with the approbation of the Archbishop,
> Apostolic Delegate and now Cardinal, I could not renounce it
> without his approval.[100]

The Cardinal Archbishop of Dublin concluded that only two men of the Order in Ireland were fit to replace Spratt: John Carr, Prior of Whitefriar Street, and Thomas Bennett. Carr declined the position and Bennett was then too ill to take it up again. As a consequence, John Spratt survived the mutiny and went on to preach a splendid sermon on the occasion of the dedication of the new Carmelite church in Moate, Co Westmeath. The storm of discontent eventually subsided. Between then and May of 1871, as seen already in part, he remained as busy as ever in public affairs and political struggles. Indeed, during these years, as during the many before, he remained committed to his original and most enduring public cause, the campaign for temperance and teetotalism.

---

100. Ibid, p. 240.

**Fig 148.** *The Irish Province of Carmelites' Provincial Chapter 1871.*

**Back row, left to right:** *Baptist Michael Daly (1850-1919), Joseph John Brennan (1846-1912), Peter John Wheatley (1836-1919), Dominic Terence Sheridan (1836-1892), Elias James Davis (1836-1902), Bartholomew Patrick Duggan (1843-1911).*

**Second row, left to right:** *Spirdion Joseph (1823-1894), Stanislaus Thomas Bartley (1844-1915), Patrick Edward Southwell (1841-1922), Aloysius Michael Moore (1837-1895), Albert William Blanchfield (1844-1900), Patrick Thomas Davis (1842-1904), Ignatius James Behan (1842-1922).*

**Third row, left to right:** *Angelus Martin Bruton (d.1875), Elias John Bartley (1832-1895), Laurence Patrick O'Toole (1836-1894), Joseph Michael Gilligan (1832-1888), Albert Patrick O'Farrell (1836-1892), Mary Peter Ward (1831-1916), Vincent Joseph Butler (1844-1918), Elias Andrew Farrington (1840-1922), Paul Philip Mc Donnell (1835-1902), John of the Cross Thomas Doyle (1839-1912), Albert Nicholas Staples (1835-1921), Brocard John Leybourne (1838-1911).*

**Fourth row, left to right:** *Eugene Cullen (d. 1879), Clemens Patrick Parr (d. 1881), Simon Henry Mc Gee (d. 1879), Simon John Carr (1816-1893), Angelo Savini (Prior General), Aloysius Mary Galli (Socius), Joseph Cornelius Crotty (d.1883), Joseph John Hall (1831-1897), Charles William Withers (d.1877).*

# CHAPTER TWENTY-TWO

## *The Last Campaign, 1861-1871*

Friar John was committed to public health and welfare, not least by promoting recreational alternatives to the tavern. From the start of the 1860s he supported the campaign for the opening of Stephen's Green to the public[1] and it was also borne out in another campaign, for the opening of the Botanic Gardens, Glasnevin, on Sundays. His comrade, Haughton, was one of the pioneers of this movement. As a member of the Royal Dublin Society which had the management of

**Fig 149.** *The Botanic Gardens, c. 1900.*

1. D. McCabe, *St Stephen's Green, Dublin, 1660-1875*, Dublin 2011, p. 2.

the Botanic Gardens, Haughton had three times in the course of the 1850s brought a motion to have the Gardens open on Sundays, the only day when working people could hope to visit. Three times this motion was rejected, with excuses which ranged from fear of working class vandalism to fear of violation of the Sabbath.[2] In exasperation, Haughton then commenced a public campaign in the early 1860s, holding committee meetings in his own Eccles Street home from February 1861.[3]

From the outset, the Carmelite friar became involved and joined Haughton in organising a petition to parliament. They pointed out that the Botanic Gardens were funded from the public purse but their management was entirely in the control of the Royal Dublin Society: it was the latter which determined the days, the hours and the terms of admission of visitors. The petitioners remarked that these times and terms

> operate to the virtual exclusion of the professional, mercantile, operative and all the industrial classes of the community...who so largely contribute to the public taxes out of which these Gardens were maintained.[4]

The petitioners contrasted the situation, where RDS members were allowed access on Sundays from 2 pm while ordinary Dubliners were excluded on that day, with that which prevailed in Great Britain where the public at large were admitted. Under pressure, the RDS relented and at a special meeting on 13th July 1861 they agreed to Sunday opening of the Gardens to the public.[5] Fears of vandalism by the great unwashed proved unfounded, as its Director, David Moore, hastened to assure all concerned.[6] This, however, was not the end of the matter. The RDS had decided that they would admit the public to the grounds from 2.30 pm, but as the village public houses in Glasnevin opened at 2 pm on

2. *SNL*, 10th May 1858; *Farmers' Gazette and Journal of Practical Horticulture*, 19th June 1858, 18 June 1859; *SNL*, 1st Nov 1859; *IT*, 3rd Nov 1859; *FJ*, 4th Nov 1859.
3. *IT*, 31st Jan 1861.
4. *EF*, 21st Feb, 1861; *DWN*, 23rd Feb 1861.
5. *FJ*, 20th July 1861; C. Nelson & E McCracken, *The Brightest Jewel: A History of the National Botanic Gardens, Glasnevin, Dublin*, Kilkenny 1987, pp. 129-131.
6. Nelson & McCracken, p. 131.

Sundays, as everywhere else, this was not acceptable to the temperance crusader. Fr John considered access to public amenities as a preventive measure, as offering an outlet other than the public house. Reviewing the situation as it had developed by 1865, he observed that young men arriving at 2 pm in the expectation that the Botanic Gardens, like the Zoological Gardens, would be then open, soon entered the public houses instead. He claimed that *'the vigilance of the police is asleep in so quiet and innocent-looking a place as Glasnevin'*, with the result that the publicans there opened even earlier than the law allowed. He concluded by urging the RDS to open at 2 pm instead of 2.30 pm, but with what outcome is not clear. The campaign was but one further chapter in John Spratt's unrelenting crusade for the temperance cause.

*From rallies to remonstrances*

By the end of the 1850s, Spratt's great open-air temperance assemblies of the summer months, as in the Phoenix Park, Donnybrook or Harold's Cross, were no longer a recurrent or regular feature of his teetotal evangelism. There were occasional open-air gatherings, as at Brickfield Lane, across the road from his Night Refuge, in May 1861, where he administered the pledge to *'several hundred'* people, but these events were by now few and far between.[7] His direct appeal to the people was largely confined to the Sunday evening gatherings of his Irish Total Abstinence Association in Cuffe Lane which continued year by year up to 1871. Furthermore, annually at New Year resolution time, he attracted sizeable numbers to his Cuffe Lane Temperance Hall, on each 31st December or 1st January, where they came to take the pledge at his hands while the ITAA band played festive airs. As late as 1st January 1871 some 1,600 persons are reported to have turned up for this, determined to amend their ways for the year or years ahead.[8] At these weekly or annual Cuffe Lane gatherings he continued to be supported by a cohort of unfailing stalwarts: most notable among them, his tireless friend, Haughton. There too were that *'fluent, ready and able speaker'*, John Mooney of Kilmainham, the bricklayer-poet John McCorry and the eloquent George Barber. While the friar administered

7.  *DEP*, 21st May 1861.
8.  *EF*, 3rd Jan 1871. For other such annual occasions, see *FJ*, 4th Jan 1860; *SNL*, 31st Dec 1861; *FJ*, 3rd Jan 1865; *EF*, 1st Jan 1866; *FJ*, 5th Jan 1869; *EF*, 3rd Jan 1870.

the pledge they delivered their stirring exhortations. Others came to speak at these weekly assemblies, from across the city and across the denominations. They included James Alexander Mowatt, an insurance agent of North Strand, always a formidable speaker, and the Scot, Thomas Wallace Russell, who was the southern Irish agent of the Presbyterian-dominated Irish Temperance League, together with others who represented different teetotal bodies.

**Fig 150.** *Thomas Wallace Russell.*

However, there was a sense, hinted at by Fr John himself, that he and his closest comrades now constituted an *'old guard'* and, at the end of the 1860s, he expressed anxiety for the future. Addressing his Cuffe Lane audience, on 7th February 1869, he observed that while their weekly meetings had been going on well for the previous thirty years, he hoped that younger men would come forward. He could have added, but did not, that it might be a good thing too if some fellow priests might present themselves for the cause. As will be seen shortly, with only a single exception in these years, they did not. Furthermore, the great body of Dublin Catholic temperance and teetotal societies that featured in the pages of Battersby's *Directory* in the later 1840s and early 1850s had long gone by 1860: they withered on the vine, one by one, until Spratt's Cuffe Lane society was the sole Catholic body still meeting throughout the 1860s and a little beyond.

*A short-lived resurgence*

Towards the end of the 1860s, from about the autumn of 1868, a revival appeared to begin. That sole Catholic clerical exception to Spratt's solitary eminence was a diocesan curate, Fr C P Meehan, who emerged as a local champion for the cause. At Alderman Crotty's 'Great Rooms', in Christchurch Place, he organised the Hibernian

Total Abstinence Association from at least September 1868. As with Spratt's Cuffe Lane body, it was interdenominational. On Sunday 20th September, for example, Fr Meehan engaged the support of Russell and Mowatt and also of Daniel P Foxwell, the Catholic agent of the United Kingdom Alliance in Ireland. They were greeted by an audience of some 2,000 and also by the brass band of the local Skinners' Society or trade union.[9] While the Hibernian continued to attract large numbers to its Christchurch Place meetings – some 2,500 on one Sunday in October 1868, for example – another new society began meeting under the direction of Spratt's supporter, John Mooney. He had established a group at his Teetotal Hall in Henrietta Street by the end of October, with the brass band of the local Stonecutters' Society providing the entertainment.[10] Then in December, at a meeting in Spratt's Temperance Hall, it was announced that yet another teetotal society was about to open, in Poolbeg Street. The speaker, W H Squires, exulted that *'thus they were spreading a network of meetings over the city'*. The teetotal mission of this latest arrival was especially directed at the coal porters and dockers of the city's quays.[11] Before the year ended, Spratt and Haughton were rejoicing at *'a grand revival of teetotalism in Dublin'*, with their Cuffe Lane Hall now more crowded than ever. The Unitarian teetotaller, always generous in his praise of the Carmelite, referred to the *'2,000 to 3,000 persons all gathered together under the banner of teetotalism which you have so faithfully held aloft for over a quarter of a century'*. He then went on to praise Fr Meehan's *'wonderful success'* up in Christchurch Place.[12]

This revival, however, appears to have been short-lived. By January 1871 the Poolbeg Street body was no longer earning a mention and a similar silence had descended upon Fr Meehan's Christchurch Place society and upon John Mooney's Henrietta Street group by December of that year. In effect, the temperance campaign as a direct moral appeal to the person had ceased to revive as a mass movement in Spratt's own

9.  *FJ*, 22nd Sept 1868. For Russell and Mowatt, see Malcolm, *Ireland Sober, Ireland Free*, pp. 152, 171, 173. It is not clear from the contemporary sources if Fr Meehan's Hibernian Total Abstinence Association was another name for, or a different body to, the St John Baptist Total Abstinence Society which he conducted in the same place and for which see *FJ*, 22nd Sept 1868, and *DWN*, 21st Jan 1869.
10. *Flag of Ireland*, 31st Oct 1868; *EF*, 3rd Jan 1870.
11. *FJ*, 7th, 14th Dec 1868.
12. *FJ*, 15th Dec 1868, Haughton to Spratt, 14th December 1868.

lifetime after 1860. He himself, in terms of such direct evangelical appeal to the individual, confined his unceasing efforts to the Cuffe Street Temperance Hall and to his Carmelite Whitefriar Street Church. It was against this background that the friar's campaign against drink, after 1860, took a new direction as he joined with others to seek reform and sobriety by legislative means alongside his old direct appeal to the person.

### New directions

The temperance movement in Ireland from the mid-1850s to the late 1870s generally manifested as remarkably denominational. In terms of members and organisations it was now, as originally, dominated by Protestants, generally Dissenters, and particularly by Presbyterians and Quakers. In terms of geography, it was strongest in Ulster. To a degree also, it was seen as identified with Sabbath observance or sabbatarianism, and to that extent was increasingly off-putting to many Irish Catholic religious leaders who were, in any case, already amply suspicious of the proselytising potential inherent even in the temperance movement. The movement in these decades after 1850 was in sharp contrast to its outlook and activity in the two decades from 1830 in that it now became markedly political. Its dominant Protestant wing increasingly looked for legislation to secure sobriety. By contrast, as Elizabeth Malcolm has indicated, the Catholic component sought to integrate the movement into the framework of devotional organisations and practice then developing apace.[13] One example, from John Spratt's old stomping ground of Harold's Cross, bears this out: in the late 1840s and early 1850s the temperance movement in that neighbourhood expressed itself in Spratt's great outdoor rallies on Harold's Cross Green; however, by the end of the 1870s Catholic temperance and practice there was expressed by and embedded in the Harold's Cross Temperance Sodality, firmly located within the physical and moral confines of the local Catholic church.[14]

Overall, the movement in Ireland over 1850 to 1880 was not only partitioned denominationally and geographically, it was also deeply divided over political and legislative strategy. This took three distinct

---

13. Malcolm, p. 151.
14. *FJ*, 15th Dec 1879.

**Fig 151.** *A Dublin Total Abstinence Society Coffee Stall.*

forms. Firstly, there were those who sought to abolish the Sunday trade in drink and who sought some kind of 'Sunday Closing' act. Secondly, there were the abolitionist or prohibitionist teetotallers who wanted the compulsory suppression of the trade seven days a week and nationwide. Thirdly, there were the proponents of the so-called 'Permissive Bill' which sought to empower the ratepayers of a given area to determine if their district would permit or forbid the sale of liquor within that area. In terms of inspiration to action, all three had in common that they took motivation from across the Atlantic Ocean or from across the Irish Sea. One of the earliest sources of inspiration came from the United States of America, where, in the state of Maine, in the year 1851, a law was passed prohibiting the sale of liquor anywhere in the state. The so-called Maine Law became a mantra for the Irish and the British prohibitionists. Two years later there was established by the Irish-born Quaker, Nathaniel Card, in Manchester, the United Kingdom Alliance for the Suppression of the Traffic in Intoxicating Liquors.[15] In 1854 the Forbes Mackenzie Act brought Sunday closing to Scotland.[16] In the following year a branch of the prohibitionist UKA was established

---

15. B. Harrison, *Drink and the Victorians: The Temperance Question in England, 1815-1872*, London 1971, p. 197; N. Longmate, *The Water-Drinkers: A history of temperance*, London 1968, pp. 136-7.

16. B. Harrison, p. 238. The act was called after its promoter, the Liverpool Conservative MP, William Forbes Mackenzie (1807-1862).

in Belfast, and in 1858 a branch was set up in Dublin, of which Spratt became a member.[17] That same year witnessed the foundation in Belfast of the Irish Temperance League which, dominated by Presbyterians, became the principal prohibitionist body in Ireland. Its Dublin branch was founded in 1865. One year later again, Dublin was birth-place to the Irish Sunday Closing Association. Little love was lost between those of the UKA and ITL, on the one hand, who sought total prohibition and those of the ISCA, on the other, who aimed for the more limited closing of public houses on Sundays. However, they did work together, with the prohibitionists at times believing that Sunday closing could be regarded as a first step towards complete closing. Such a position was held notably by Spratt's friend, Haughton.

With the singular exception of John Spratt who managed well to work with Protestants of all confessions, the Catholic Church tended to stand aloof from the legislative campaign, at least as far as it involved prohibition. Insofar as any Catholic bishops were supporters of temperance or teetotalism, their approach was voluntarist rather than legislative or coercive. Thus it was that, in 1857, Bishop Thomas Furlong of Ferns secured voluntary closing of public houses on Sundays in his diocese. Four years later his example was followed by Archbishop Patrick Leahy of Cashel. It would be fourteen years later again that three other prelates followed, John MacEvilly of Galway, Patrick Moran of Ossory, and Francis McCormack of Achonry.[18] For the most part, however, senior Catholic clergy, when not directly opposed to teetotalism and its movements, were wary, none more so than Paul Cullen in Dublin. Personally, he preferred moderation to teetotalism; politically, he was deeply suspicious of the Protestant-dominated, sabbatarian-coloured Irish temperance movement. He must have been perplexed by the quite central role that Fr John Spratt came to play in it.

### The Quest for Sunday Closing

Given such suspicions, the ease with which the Carmelite friar participated in and took leadership positions over the legislative

---

17. So James Haughton indicated in a speech in Dublin in 1864: see *EF*, 3rd Feb 1864.
18. *IT*, 20th Oct 1875. This history of Catholic bishops securing Sunday closing in their dioceses was provided by the Quaker, Henry Wigham, at a conference in Dublin in October 1875.

campaigns for temperance in the 1860s is notable. Among the clergy
of his own friary he was alone: among the Catholic clergy of the
Dublin diocese he was unique in his public commitment to a political
dimension for the temperance cause. Thus, from the beginning of the
1860s, Fr John threw himself into the quest for Sunday closing. In May
of 1860 he and Haughton were involved in securing the signatures of
some 12,000 Dublin citizens to a parliamentary petition calling for the
Sunday closing of public houses, signatures that included the names of
clergy of several denominations. They were keen to stress that

> there is, in this instance, a most gratifying absence of party and
> sectarian feeling and a happy unanimity in favour of an object in
> which men of all parties take an interest.[19]

It turned out to be just the first step on a very long road whose
destination would never be reached by either man.

In August 1861 both men became caught up when the British
Association for the Advancement of Science held its congress in
Dublin. The keynote speaker was the aged Whig-Liberal reformer,
Henry Brougham, and joining him there was the UKA propagandist, Dr
Frederick Richard Lees, the York Street Congregationalist, Dr William
Urwick, and the Anglican firebrand millenarian, Dr Tresham Gregg. On
this occasion Brougham and Lees were seeking support for a permissive
bill, one allowing for local determination to ban the sale of liquor, and
this on the basis that to secure local option for prohibition in one place
could lead to its adoption in others. The Carmelite friar was present
at the opening meeting and it appears that he was scheduled to deliver
a paper on temperance, but for reasons not clear, he did not do so. A
disappointed Haughton publicly expressed regret at Spratt's failure to
deliver as promised and ended up delivering one himself. However,
he was unstinting in his praise of Spratt's devotion to the cause and
paid a fulsome tribute to the friar's work.[20] A year later, he and Spratt
were to have attended the International Temperance and Prohibition
Convention in London and both of them, listed as vice-presidents,
were to have read papers at this gathering in Hanover Square. It is

19. *CT*, 12th May 1860.
20. *IT*, 22nd Aug 1861.

**Fig 152.** *James Haughton.*

not clear that Spratt ever travelled to this event, although Haughton and Urwick did.[21] Two years later, in April 1863, an English Sunday Closing Bill was brought forward in the House of Commons by the Hull City MP, John Somes. Spratt now wrote to those Catholic bishops who had been promoting voluntary Sunday closing in their dioceses to seek support, and also contacted the Primate, Joseph Dixon of Armagh, who had been similarly engaged.[22] Dixon responded positively and added that if Sunday closing had been observed more widely, then little more would have been heard of *'those abominable secret societies which have worked so much mischief to our country'*.[23] In a similar response, Furlong also gave his support. He candidly confessed that it needed *'all the vigilance and energy of the clergy to ensure its general observance'* and that he and his clergy could not control non-Catholic publicans: so, he concluded that only the coercion *'of the civil law can make such observance universal and thoroughly effective'*.[24] Likewise, Bishop David Moriarty of Kerry supported Spratt's endeavour, while remarking that the high duty of whiskey and the poverty of the people combined to promote temperance in his own diocese. He regretted that the existing law which closed public houses on Sundays up to 2 pm was not more strictly enforced and agreed that a legislated Sunday closing *'would have a very beneficial effect'*.[25] Such episcopal endorsements, while encouraging, did nothing to advance the destiny of Somes' bill which soon went down to defeat by a large majority. The friar and his supportive bishops

---

21. *IT*, 3rd Sept 1862; *London Evening Standard*, 4th Sept 1862 reports on the presence of Haughton and Urwick, but there is no mention of Spratt in this or in other London newspapers of the time.
22. *The Irishman*, 25th April 1863, Spratt to Dixon, 3rd April 1863.
23. *IT*, 25th April 1863.
24. *FJ*, 25th April 1863, Furlong to Spratt, 6th April 1863.
25. *FJ*, 25th April 1863, Moriarty to Spratt, 21st April 1863.

cannot have been reassured when it emerged that, in this defeat, out of 105 Irish MPs only 38 had troubled to vote and only 20 of them in favour of whom only 6 were Irish Catholic members.[26]

Worse was to follow. In order to increase revenues and to encourage the consumption of beer over spirits, the government had passed two acts that caused dismay to Spratt and his temperance colleagues: the Revenue Act of 1863 and the Beerhouses Act of 1864.[27] The former allowed wholesale beer sellers to acquire retail licences to sell beer off the premises in any quantity less than 4.5 gallons, without the need for a magistrate's certificate. The latter unwittingly allowed retail beer sellers to obtain a licence without a magistrate's certificate, merely by first purchasing a wholesale licence from the excise authorities. The result was an explosion in the numbers of beerhouses, from over 300 in Ireland in 1864 to over 1,220 by 1873.[28] Already in May 1863, Spratt wrote to Cullen alerting him to the problem of the now 600 plus uncontrolled beerhouses or *'dens of iniquity'* in the capital.[29] The legislation amounted to the encouragement of drinking dens, with a concentration of them in Dublin City.

There was consternation in Dublin temperance circles. In response, Spratt organised a great meeting in the Rotunda, in February 1864. He featured as the key speaker and, to loud cheers, he attacked *'those dens of immorality under the name of beer houses which had now assumed so fearful and so formidable an aspect'*. He deplored the granting of licences to *'questionable characters'* and that these *'wretched dens were haunted from midnight to six o'clock in the morning by the most depraved members of society'*. Since the proliferation of beer houses, the streets had become *'scenes of savage and ferocious assaults'* and, within these dens, *'music and dancing [were] kept up until daylight'*, and *'scenes of riot, disorder, bloodshed and of the most immoral character were enacted within these places licenced and protected by law...'*. Alderman Reynolds argued that it would be pointless to try to suppress the entire drink trade by legislation such as the Maine Law, yet it was imperative to mitigate the evil of the 700 beer houses in Dublin, where the owners could obtain a licence for twelve shillings and six pence, no questions asked. He called for legislation to curtail the evil

26.  Malcolm, pp. 192,194.
27.  26 & 27 Vict. c. 33 and 27 & 28 Vict. c. 35 respectively.
28.  Malcolm, pp. 211-212.
29.  DDA, *Cullen Papers*, 340/8/III/24, Spratt to Cullen, 11th May 1863.

and Spratt's Anglican friend and neighbour, Rev William Carroll, went on to praise the Carmelite for having taken this initiative. Fr John had already prepared the text of a memorial calling for legislative redress; the meeting adopted this and agreed to seek a meeting with the Chief Secretary, Peel, and a delegation to London was appointed for this purpose.[30] That delegation, comprising Sir John Gray and his son of the same name, Aldermen Tom Reynolds and William Lane Joynt, met with Peel in London and to their gratification he indicated that a bill *favourable to the wishes of the citizens*' would be introduced '*immediately*'. That 'immediately', despite Peel's writing to assure Spratt in April 1864, took from ten to thirteen years before legislation in 1874 and 1877 addressed the beer house problem.[31] However, more immediately, what transpired was that the MP Somes reintroduced his English Sunday Closing Bill in April 1864 and it was now proposed to extend its hoped-for provisions to Ireland. Spratt was quick off the mark to get back to those bishops, Dixon, Leahy and Furlong, who had supported him in 1863 and to seek the renewal of that support. This he duly secured and now with the additions of Bishop Laurence Gillooly of Elphin and of Hamilton Verschoyle, Church of Ireland Bishop of Kilmore.[32] The enthusiastic Leahy remarked that '*in fact, we have a Somes' bill in full operation in this diocese*', by voluntary influence and with the happy result of '*full churches, empty jails*'.[33] Even Archbishop Cullen, who later on may have been ambivalent about Spratt's campaign for Sunday closing, now seemed to come on board without reservation. In a letter to the friar on 14th April he declared his full support for the inclusion of Ireland in Somes' latest bill, and equally, his backing for the abolition of the beer

---

30. *EF*, 3rd Feb 1864. That it was Spratt's initiative is clear from the remarks of Carroll, James Haughton and Samuel McComas on the occasion.
31. DDA, *Cullen Papers*, 320/5/13, Peel to Spratt, 29th April 1864. The 1874 Licensing Act obliged wholesale beer sellers to now obtain a magistrate's certificate. The 1877 Beer Licences Regulation (Ireland) Act laid down that beer house premises must have a rateable valuation of at least £15 before a licence could be granted. The numbers of beer houses thereupon fell from 1,223 in 1873 to 635 in 1878-9, while the numbers of retail beer sellers fell from 939 to 466; see Malcolm, p. 212.
32. *FJ*, 14th April 1864, Dixon to Spratt, 13th April 1864; *FJ*, 16th April 1864, Furlong to Spratt, 10 April 1864; *CT*, 23rd April 1864, Leahy to Spratt, 12th April 1864; *FJ*, 20th April 1864, Gillooly to Spratt, 18th April 1864; *DDE*, 18th April 1864, C. M. Verschoyle to Spratt, 12th April 1864.
33. *CT*, 23rd Apr 1864.

**Fig 153.** *Sir Wilfrid Lawson, MP.*

houses: he wished Spratt *'every success in your zealous efforts'.*[34]   Once again, however, Somes's bill failed.

It now fell to the radical MP and prohibitionist, Sir Wilfrid Lawson, to attempt legislation for a permissive bill.  In Ireland, the Irish Temperance League, which had just opened a Dublin office in January 1865, rallied to the Lawson initiative.  Although the League was resolutely prohibitionist and determinedly Protestant, the Carmelite friar had no qualms about throwing his influence behind it.

At its first major public meeting in Dublin in April 1865, Fr John was prominent and, alone among Catholic clergymen, joined with Dr Urwick of York Street and other Dissenter clergymen in support of Lawson's endeavour.[35]  The ITL's leading figure and agent outside of Ulster was the energetic temperance evangelist, the Scot, Thomas Wallace Russell, who managed the ITL's Dublin office.  Russell worked closely enough with John Spratt and was known to speak at the friar's Cuffe Lane Temperance Hall meetings on Sundays.[36]  Furthermore, he was instrumental in securing a 50,000 copy reprinting of Spratt's 1849 tract, *An Appeal to the People on the Horrid Crime of Drunkenness.*

Lawson's 1865 parliamentary initiative having shared a similar fate to Somes', the Dublin campaigners now redirected their efforts to local pressure.  In the autumn of 1866 Spratt joined his ITL comrades, Russell, Mowatt, Urwick and Haughton, on a deputation to the Dublin City Recorder, Frederick Shaw.  Their object was to persuade him to curtail the renewal of licences willy-nilly.  The friar had already obtained the signatures of several hundred citizens and these signatories claimed that in 1865 some 16,192 cases of drunkenness had come before the

---

34.  Ibid, 23rd Apr 1864, Cullen to Spratt, 14th April 1864.
35.  *DDE*, 22nd April 1865. For the ITL's activities in Dublin at this time, see *DDE*, 24th March 1865; *IT*, 26th April, 1st May 1865; *SNL*, 2nd, 9th April 1865; *DDE*, 24th Aug 1865.
36.  For this, see *DDE*, 11th Sept 1865; *EF*, 4th Sept 1866.

Dublin police magistrates, an increase of 3,000 over the figures for 1864. Spratt read out the memorial calling for a remedy. The deputation received an unsympathetic hearing from Shaw who asserted that over his experience of 29 years as Recorder, the number of public houses had declined from 1,600 to 800. These figures were hardly credible but it appears that they were not contested by the delegation.

Nothing achieved, nothing daunted, Spratt in that autumn of 1866 bent his efforts to persuading the publicans themselves to support the campaign for Sunday closing. At first he appears to have been well-received: James Carey, leading figure in the Licenced Grocers' and Vintners' Association, a parishioner of Spratt's and a supporter of the friar's various charities, told him, on Saturday 6th October 1866, that his Association was willing to support the Sunday closing cause. Like other virtuous causes of the age, such as the campaign for the abolition of night baking, or the struggle for the achievement of a Saturday half-holiday, or the eight-hour working day, it was grand in theory, but not in practice, since it could only work if universally adopted in the trade. Spratt was innocent enough to take Carey at his word. Russell of the ITL, however, did not lay much store in Carey's assurances: he argued that if the LGVA were sincere, why then did they not simply follow the example of the publicans in Dr Leahy's Cashel diocese? Although Russell and his ITL wanted total prohibition, they were willing to support Sunday closing as a stepping-stone, but the Scot reminded the Carmelite that the LGVA had rejoiced when Somes' bill had been defeated.[37] Spratt's reaction to Russell's observations is not evident but, one month later, the friar was a prime mover in the foundation of a new body.

### The Irish Sunday Closing Association

On 29th November 1866 an array of temperance crusaders from Belfast, Dublin and England gathered in the Rotunda, Dublin, to form an association to secure the Sunday closing of public houses in Ireland, by means of parliamentary legislation. Those attending included the most prominent and active Quakers such as the Wighams, Pims and Allens, together with other Nonconformists such as Samuel McComas, William Urwick, George Leatham of Belfast and James

---

37. *SNL*, 9th Oct 1866.

Haughton. Once again, Spratt was the sole Dublin-based Catholic clergyman participating and it was he who moved and Urwick seconded the founding resolution.[38] Spratt became joint secretary, along with Henry Wigham, with the latter's co-religionist, Thomas Pim junior, as chairman. The new body followed upon a similar one founded in Belfast in 1864 but which had folded following the defeat of Somes' legislative efforts. The new body was destined to a longer life but also to a protracted struggle. Haughton supported it, but without great hopes or enthusiasm, but the Dublin Quakers were zealous in their endorsement and generous in their funding of it.[39]

After foundation, the first public outing for the ISCA came when it persuaded the Lord Mayor to chair a meeting in the Mansion House to promote the cause and to press the city's MPs to back an Irish Sunday closing bill.[40] In one regard, the occasion represented something of a coup for the infant ICSA since they managed to secure, at the head of the list of 700 signatories requesting this meeting, the names of the two archbishops of Dublin, Drs Cullen and Trench. It may not be wide of the mark to suggest that this owed a great deal to Spratt himself: as seen in an earlier chapter, at this very time he had close and cordial relations with Archbishop Trench, as much as he now had, for the time being, with Cullen.[41] These worthies apart, leading citizens attended: these included the High Sheriff, Fitzgibbon, and the police magistrate, Frank Thorpe Porter, together with long-standing associates of Spratt in earlier campaigns and battles, such as the Rev Thomas Shore, formerly of the Roomkeepers and now chaplain to Mountjoy Jail, and Andrew Bagot of manufacture-revival days. Nonetheless, not everything went along the lines of securing total agreement on the nature and the pursuit of Sunday closing. For one thing, the High Sheriff wanted to see early closing on Saturday evenings as well as Sunday closing, a position that Cullen seems also to have favoured. Fitzgibbon's motion on this matter

---

38. *FJ*, 30th Nov 1866. The full title of the organisation was The Irish Association for the Closing of Public Houses on Sunday, but it soon came to be known simply as The Irish Sunday Closing Association. It is hereafter abbreviated to ISCA.

39. Malcolm, p. 195. Henry Bewley donated £50, the Pims £35, Richard Allen £10 and the Wighams £15. Haughton gave £1. It is not clear how much, if anything, Spratt contributed in cash.

40. *DEM*, 19th Dec 1866.

41. See Chapter Fourteen for his relations with Trench, and Chapter Eighteen for his relations with Cullen at this time.

was actually carried on the occasion. However, strong opposition to any form of closing was expressed by the publican and town councillor, Cornelius Dennehy, one of Spratt's foremost opponents on the issue. Dennehy condemned proposals for closing on any day as a piece of class-inspired propaganda designed to deprive the working man of his simple pleasures. He noted that the ISCA was not proposing to ban the Sunday selling of drink in restaurants, cafés and hotels, frequented exclusively by the better off. He insisted, not unreasonably, that '*it was no business of one class of the community to make rules or regulations to bind another class*' and he moved an amendment to this effect. Spratt's ally, James Alexander Mowatt, '*a working man and son of a working man*', countered Dennehy whose proposed amendment came from those who made their own gains by persuading working men to spend their wages on drink. Dennehy's amendment was lost.

Spratt made an impressive speech on the occasion, remarking that the sellers of goods other than liquor were prohibited from trading on Sundays. He spoke up also in the cause of young men who worked their Sundays in public houses, several thousand of them who were deprived of this day of rest.[42] The ISCA did well in getting this publicity for its cause and it went on soon after, in January 1867, to form a Ladies Committee to garner practical help in the preparation and collection of petitions.[43] Spratt and Wigham pressed on through 1867 in securing signatures for Sunday closing memorials. By May of that year they had generated some 500 petitions with 38,000 names, some 16,000 of them in Dublin, including those of over 200 publicans.[44] Furthermore, they had secured the signatures of Cardinal Cullen and ten other bishops to a declaration calling on Irish MPs in favour of Sunday closing legislation.[45] At the same time the friar kept up his direct appeals to the ordinary folk and on 4th July 1867 he issued *An Address to the Working People*, calling on them to forswear drink.[46] This tract caused outrage in the ranks of the publicans, as shall emerge.

It proved challenging to persuade any Irish MP to support the cause, let alone to sponsor a bill, but eventually, in the spring of 1867 Major

---

42. *FJ*, *IT*, 20th Dec 1866.
43. *DDE*, 16th Jan 1867.
44. *DDE*, 6th May 1867.
45. Malcolm, p. 182.
46. *DEP*, 4th July 1867.

Myles O'Reilly, MP for Longford, took up the crusade. That July he secured a second reading for his bill to prohibit drinking in public houses on Sunday but allowing for off-premises sales between 1 and 2.30 pm and between 8 and 9 pm on that day. In Dublin the LGVA grew alarmed and rallied to oppose it. In the process, their spokesman, Carey, launched a blistering attack on John Spratt over the latter's *Address to the Working People*. The Carmelite had had copies printed and posted on placards throughout the city.[47] Carey commented:

> Dr Spratt might tell them that it was a scandalous thing to have houses open on Sundays but he believed it was a greater scandal for himself to be giving the pledge to men whom he must have known would break it again.[48]

Carey's anger at Spratt was hardly surprising since the Carmelite in that address had not moderated his own language. Spratt had written of *'liquors which brutalise men'*, and of *'the house of drunkenness which is the bane of Ireland'*. He went further:

> Can it be possible that drunkard-makers are not aware of the progressive debasement and shame which their establishments are working...they see it written in the squalid and haggard countenances of their wretched customers: death, hell and the drunkard-maker – beyond this partnership, none are profited.[49]

It was a sore point, and an old one at that, as some senior ecclesiastics even in Fr Mathew's day had worried about the wholesale administering of a pledge to weak and vulnerable people. As for Carey, the friar had accepted his assurances that the LGVA favoured Sunday closing. T W Russell's assessment of this had proven shrewder since Carey now made his way to London to lobby the Chief Secretary, Lord Naas, against O'Reilly's bill. The result was that Naas succeeded in having the bill killed off by referring it to a select committee of the House, and this so late in the session as to ensure its abortion. Others, however,

---

47. *EF*, 11th July 1867.
48. Ibid.
49. *DEP*, 4th July 1867: J. Spratt, *An Address to the Working People*.

entered the public prints in Spratt's defence against the vitriol of the vintners: such champions wanted a public meeting convened to endorse and sustain the friar against the fury of the publicans. It was notable that it was laymen and mainly Protestants, not fellow-Carmelites or even diocesan confreres, who rose to his defence.[50] One of these defenders, Joseph Rogers, wanted to see 100,000 copies of Spratt's *Address* printed and distributed throughout Ireland as a counter-attack on the publicans.[51] A supportive meeting was held, in the

**Fig 154.** *Major Myles O'Reilly, MP.*

Cuffe Lane Temperance Hall, with some 600 to 800 reported present to hear his praetorian guard of Haughton, Barber and Mowatt rise to his defence and to ask, *'who ever thought that there would be a citizen of Dublin found who would pour forth abuse on one of the most charitable, inoffensive inhabitants of our city?'* [52] Carey might well have wondered if they were reading the same text of Spratt's *Address* as he. In reference to Carey's attack on Spratt for administering the pledge to men whom he knew would break it, Mowatt remarked that it was the vintners who caused such men to break their pledge; and, as for pledge-breaking, what then of town councillor Carey's promise to Spratt that the LGVA would support Sunday closing? A resolution of support for the friar was thereupon passed with acclamation.

The battle for a bill continued the following year, 1868, when Major O'Reilly introduced a revised version. Cardinal Cullen wrote to Spratt on 27th February to encourage him in his ongoing Sunday closing campaign and to hope that the re-introduced measure might this time be successful.[53] So too did Nicholas Conaty, Bishop of Kilmore since 1865. In a very warm letter to the Carmelite, and describing the success

50. See, for example, *EF*, 13th July 1867, Thomas O'Hanlon to editor, 11th July 1867; *DEP*, 13th July 1867, George Barker to editor, 12th July.
51. *FJ*, 15th July 1867, Joseph Rogers to editor, 14th July 1867.
52. *DEP*, 15th July 1867.
53. *FJ*, 16th March 1868, Cullen to Spratt, 27th February 1868.

of voluntary Sunday closing in his own diocese, Conaty nevertheless wished the friar that *'your exertions in supporting Major O'Reilly's Bill will be crowned with success'.*[54] They were all, again, to be disappointed: O'Reilly's bill was sent to another select committee where it was so drastically mangled that he discarded it.[55] Undeterred, in the following session of 1869, he resurrected an amended version which the new Chief Secretary, Chichester Fortescue, professed to support; however, that June the latter announced there were government plans for a total review of the licensing system and the Longford MP was induced to withdraw his proposed measure.

*From Sunday Closing to Local Option*

With the campaign for Sunday closing becoming stalled by repeated parliamentary reverses, the temperance movement as a whole in 1869 began to refocus its hopes and efforts on its preferred alternative: it now concentrated its lobbying on a campaign for a permissive bill such as had been championed in parliament by Sir Wilfrid Lawson since 1864.[56] Lawson came to Dublin in March 1868 to promote the permissive bill cause. Most of the usual Dublin temperance crusaders met him for breakfast at the Shelbourne Hotel. Spratt was not there, but sent apologies. It was probably because of Lawson's visit that the ITL now added to its title so that it became The Irish Temperance League and Permissive Bill Association.[57] Although Spratt did not or could not attend, his comrades Haughton and Mowatt were present, delivering strong speeches, as did Dr Stewart of the famous Lucan Mental Hospital who claimed that most mental illness was caused by abuse of stimulants *'which commenced in moderate drinking and terminated in madness'.*[58] As for Spratt himself, the social highlight of his temperance days at this time came a month later when the Prince of Wales visited the Catholic University. Cardinal Cullen, as host, introduced the

---

54.  *DEP*, 20th March 1868, Conaty to Spratt, 18th March 1868.
55.  Malcolm, pp. 199-200.
56.  Harrison, p. 254.
57.  See *EF*, 28th March 1868, where it is still called simply The Irish Temperance League, and then *SNL*, 30th March 1868, where it now becomes The Irish Temperance League and Permissive Bill Association. Malcolm dates the simply-styled Irish Permissive Bill Association to January 1869: Malcolm, p. 177.
58.  *SNL*, 30th March 1868.

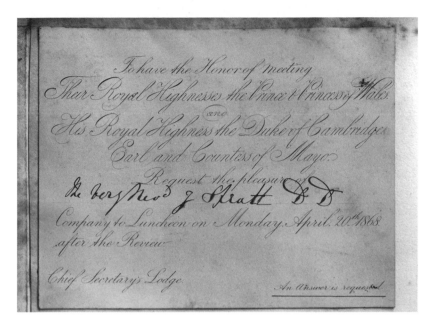

**Fig 155.** *Invitation to Luncheon with the Prince and Princess of Wales in GMA, Scrapbook A.*

Carmelite to the Prince as *'the apostle of temperance'*, and, according to one account, the Prince *'bowed in a very marked manner to the Rev Dr Spratt'*.[59] Indeed, the Prince had just at this time invited Spratt to dinner at the Vice-Regal Lodge.[60]  Back to the reality of the daily struggle for the cause, although Spratt could not attend the welcome to Lawson, he maintained at this time a close, comradely relationship with the leaders of the ITL.  On 13th September 1868, for example, Russell of the League and Daniel Foxwell, the Catholic agent of the UKA in Ireland, both spoke at Spratt's Cuffe Lane Hall during his usual Sunday pledge-giving assembly.[61]  A week later he hosted a very large meeting of some 1,000 to 1,500 people at the Hall to consider *'The Great Question'* of the liquor traffic in Ireland.  Foxwell spoke at length, as did Haughton, Mowatt and A M Sullivan, in support of a UKA draft permissive bill, while the friar paid tribute to the memory of his friend and neighbour,

---

59.  *FJ*, *IT*, 22nd April 1868.
60.  GMA, Box 78, *Scrapbook G*, Prince of Wales to Spratt, 20th April 1868.  Spratt was more than once invited to high society dinners and lunches in these years: Lady Naas invited him in December 1869 for which, ibid.
61.  *FJ*, 14th Sept 1868.

Dr Urwick, who had died that July after 39 years as pastor at York Street, and after a long life spent in the temperance cause.[62]

After the disappointments of the recurrent failures of Sunday closing bills, the period from the autumn of 1868 to the summer of 1869 was, at last, a heartening time for Spratt and his temperance comrades: the UKA was pressing the cause of permissive legislation with renewed urgency, and in Dublin temperance fortunes seemed to be reviving as three new halls opened in the city.[63] It was in this period too, with Cullen's approbation, that Spratt emulated the example of Dr Leahy of Cashel by establishing an 'Association of Prayer' for the conversion of addicted drunkards. The hope was that the Association might be warmly taken up by Dublin clergy and laity alike, and even be introduced into the schools.[64] It may not have been a momentous event but it was one sign of that development, noted by Malcolm, whereby temperance in Catholic circles came to be incorporated within the faith's devotional structure.

In parliament, meanwhile, a new Sunday closing bill had secured a second reading in March 1869 and a permissive bill was about to be introduced, both to the extreme concern of the LGVA.[65] However, as so often in the past, Lawson's Permissive Bill was rejected, this time by 200 to 94 and, as before, only one third of Irish MPs bothered to vote: yet, for the first time, a small majority of those Irish members supported the measure, 20 for with 15 against; but it was hardly evidence that the tide had begun to turn, as far as the attitude of Irish MPs went. Nevertheless, Spratt and Russell, as secretaries of the ISCA, rallied for a new push at the start of 1870. That January

**Fig 156.** *Chief Secretary Chichester Fortescue.*

62. *FJ*, 22nd Sept 1868.
63. See pp. 483-484.
64. *EF*, 4th March 1869.
65. *FJ*, 11th March 1869.

they organised a large interdenominational deputation to the Chief Secretary. This included the usual Dublin Quakers, the leading Dublin Presbyterian, Dr Kirkpatrick, the founding president of the Belfast ITL, William Scott, as well as Russell and Spratt. The Carmelite introduced the delegation and asked Fortescue if the government would include a Sunday closing clause in any bill to reform the licensing system.[66] The friar told Fortescue that he had visited every drink trader in Dublin – a not inconsiderable feat since there were over 1,000 of them – and claimed that *'a very large majority were in favour of Sunday Closing'*. Fortescue professed to be taken aback at the radicalism of their aim to achieve total closing on Sundays at the expense of *'considerable inconvenience to the public'*. He may have recalled the riots that broke out in England in 1855 when a Sunday closing measure was proposed.[67] When Kirkpatrick insisted that his Presbyterian General Assembly fully supported total Sunday closing, as did Rev William Carroll in respect of the Church of Ireland Convocation, Fortescue remained unimpressed and sceptical, even as he indicated the government's commitment to some kind of licensing reform. Spratt was deeply disappointed at Fortescue's response, not least because of his concern for the several thousand young men working in public houses who were deprived of Sunday rest and were working in *'a demoralizing slavery'*.[68] The Carmelite and the ISCA did not accept the outcome of their meeting with Fortescue and instead now began to urge Dublin City Council in turn to press the Chief Secretary. Spratt and Wigham now sent in a memorial to the Corporation on this matter.

*A Corporation at odds*
A battle now commenced in City Hall between councillors supportive of Spratt and his cause on the one hand and councillors who themselves were publicans or friends of publicans on the other. Among the latter group was Spratt's old foe, James Carey. When Spratt's memorial was supported and seconded by resolution, Carey moved a clever amendment by shifting the focus to the disreputable beer houses: his motion called on government to address the beer house scandal

66. *SNL*, 17th Jan 1870.
67. Harrison, pp. 201, 215, 238–9.
68. *DEP*, 7th Feb 1870, John Spratt to the Committee of the Grocers' Assistants Association, 3rd February 1870.

by removing the right of the Excise authorities to grant beer house licences. Carey's amendment was lost, with only 9 for and 22 against.[69] Spratt and his comrades then opened up a new line of attack when they petitioned the Corporation itself to adopt a permissive or local option approach. Within the Council it was promoted by A M Sullivan who proposed a consultative vote of the ratepayers before a licence could be granted. On 30th June 1870, in what was described as the most crowded meeting in thirty years, the Council debated the issue for over four hours. Before them was a motion drafted by Spratt that *'the Dublin Corporation, elected by the people, would vote to trust the people with a voice upon the licensing system'*. Despite a vigorous opposition from the publican lobby, this motion was carried by 24 to 18. As Sullivan's *Nation* commented:

> Thus, the first blow has been given in Dublin to that system of licensing for the drink traffic which crowds our cities and towns with public houses and which is a powerful agency for the demoralisation and ruin of the people.[70]

It proved to be a short-lived victory. At a resumed meeting of the Corporation, with the whip out for the drink lobby councillors, and with the temperance supporters taken unawares, Cornelius Dennehy moved against the ratepayer control resolution. He argued that it was unwise to remove licence control away from the *'judicial and magisterial authorities'* to *'the haphazard votes of a section of the community'* and when pushed to a ballot, Dennehy's position was carried by 18 to 12.[71]

Frustrated in this recourse, Spratt at the end of 1870 took part in yet another deputation to Fortescue at Dublin Castle. This time it was a more imposing delegation that presented itself, with the two Dublin City MPs, Corrigan and Pim, and a long list of local authority representatives from Belfast, Carlow, Clonmel, Dungannon, Limerick, Omagh and Dublin itself, together with the leading members of the ISCA. Spratt read out a letter of support from Cardinal Cullen which urged that the law which forbade Sunday trading in other goods be extended to liquor. Acknowledging the extensive and representative

---

69.  *FJ*, 8th March 1870.
70.  *DWN*, 18th June 1870.
71.  *EF*, 21st June 1870.

nature of this delegation, Fortescue, nevertheless, still maintained a position of scepticism. He concluded by stressing once again that the issue of public inconvenience, in such total closing as they proposed, simply could not be ignored.[72] Apparently undaunted by this, Spratt and the ISCA organised yet another descent upon Dublin Castle, in February 1871, this time to meet with the new Chief Secretary, the Marquis of Hartington, who had just taken up office on 13th January. This time they had organised an even weightier delegation, now with five MPs in tow, together with Canon McCabe, Spratt and several Church of Ireland clergymen, as well as the usual contingent from the temperance ranks. Hartington argued that to close the licensed public houses on Sunday would only drive the drinkers into beer houses and illegal outlets. To this McCabe replied that the beer houses and illegal outlets should be closed down in any case. Effectively, however, the new Chief Secretary left the delegation with good wishes and no promises, beyond a vague valediction of *'waiting for a more comprehensive measure to be introduced'.*[73]

When at last the Liberal government introduced that comprehensive measure, in 1871, it fell in the face of fierce opposition. A year later, Sir Dominic Corrigan, an ardent Sunday Closing advocate but an opponent of prohibition, tried to introduce his own Sunday Closing bill, to replicate the Scottish example, but it too failed.[74] Six more years passed before a modest version of Sunday closing was achieved when the O'Conor Don, MP for Roscommon, successfully promoted a measure that had been pioneered in the House originally by the Presbyterian clergyman and MP for Londonderry, Richard Smyth; but when it finally passed the House on 10th August and received the royal assent on 15th August 1878,[75] it fatally excluded cities and towns with a population exceeding ten thousand. It would have proved too little and too late for John Spratt.

*Back to the Beginning*
In the years of great expectations and of dashed hopes for a legislative remedy, the Carmelite friar and his closest temperance colleagues kept

72. *DEP*, 22nd Dec 1870.
73. *EF*, 3rd Feb 1871.
74. Malcolm, pp. 219-220.
75. Ibid, p. 249.

up their weekly meetings in the Cuffe Lane Temperance Hall and, in the summer months from the late 1860s, Fr John led his teetotal followers on rail excursions and outings to Wicklow and Wexford, accompanied by his beloved ITAA brass band. He continued his pledge-giving in that Hall and in his nearby Whitefriar Street Church until the very day he died. As Fr John came towards the end of his days he became anxious about securing successors to take up the cause. They were not forthcoming. In August 1871, as his Cuffe Lane society set out on their first summer excursion after his death, passing Whitefriar Street Church on their outward journey, they hoped *'some clergyman will be found to grasp the standard of temperance so ably carried by this good priest for thirty-three years'*.[76] That December, his old comrade John Mooney, speaking at the Sunday evening assembly in the Hall, hoped that before long

> another good priest would be found ready to take his place, but until then, those who came to the Hall to take the pledge, should be contented with making a manly determination within themselves to renounce forever strong drink which was the curse and ruin of thousands.[77]

This did not happen. Soon other stalwarts followed Fr John to the great beyond: John McCorry passed away on 10th September 1871, James Haughton on 20th February 1873, John Mooney on 23rd December 1878 and George Barber in August 1885.[78]

It was another teetotal pioneer of a later age, the clergyman, historian and future Bishop of Sydney, Michael Kelly, who provided the first historical assessment of John Spratt's temperance crusade. His conclusion was not totally favourable: he considered that Fr John, like Fr Mathew before him, had failed. They left memories but no successors nor successor organisations to carry on that struggle.[79] Although Kelly praised the work and dedication of Mathew and Spratt, it was a harsh judgement if a partly true one as far as temperance in Catholicism went.

---

76. *FJ*, 22nd Aug 1871.
77. *FJ*, 11th Dec 1871.
78. *DWN*, 23rd Sept 1871; *FJ*, 21st Feb 1872; *FJ*, 26th Dec 1878; *Flag of Ireland*, 15th Aug 1885, respectively.
79. M. Kelly, 'The suppression of intemperance – Part II', *Irish Ecclesiastical Record*, 3rd series, vol. x, 1889, pp. 623-643; Malcolm, p. 190.

Whereas in the 1840s, Fr John had clerical supporters in Frs O'Connell and Yore, by the 1860s he was, in Dublin, virtually alone as a priest temperance crusader. For all that, within the wider movement, he had a unique gift among Catholic clergymen for his ability to co-operate across denominational lines. This, in its way, ensured that the cause endured beyond his death, not within the confines of the Catholic confession but in those transcending organisations that continued the work for years after his own passing.

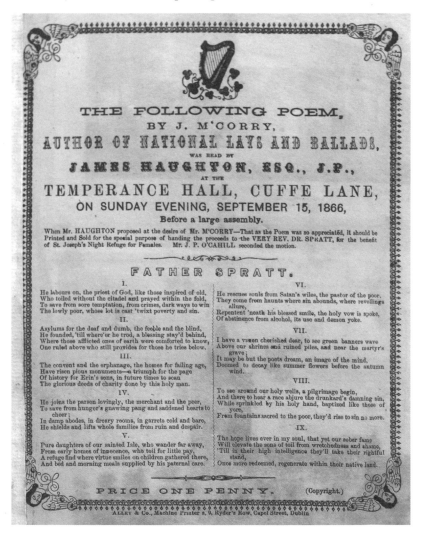

**Fig 157.** *A poem written by J. M'Corry in* Scrapbook A.

# CHAPTER TWENTY-THREE

## *Death and Thereafter*

On Sunday 21st May 1871 Fr John administered the pledge at his usual weekly gathering in the Cuffe Lane Temperance Hall. It was the last time he would do so there, after weekly meetings for over 30 years. Six days later, on Saturday 26th, he took breakfast as usual at 10 o'clock in the friary, and proceeded to the chapel house where he gave the pledge to two women. He then made his way to the vestry to write up their certificates and here, awaiting him, was a man who came to conclude the legal business of securing the future of the Night Refuge. A sudden weakness overcoming him, he sank into the arms of this visitor and expired before medical aid arrived.[1] It was not unfitting that he died between the public cause that was his oldest and most enduring, temperance, and the major cause that was his most recent and perhaps the dearest to his heart, the Night Refuge. His death certificate gave his age, wrongly, as 73, as did the brass plate on his coffin, the former stating that he died of disease of the heart, of unknown duration.[2]

Apart from a fall in December 1868 in which he sustained a shoulder injury, Father John enjoyed robust health until towards the end of his life. Around January he had been feeling unwell enough to consult two eminent physicians in respect of gangrene in the toe, arising from poor circulation and they, apparently, had prescribed alcohol, which he declined to take.[3] If he was now beginning to feel unwell, it was

---

1. *EF*, 29th May 1871.
2. Registry of Births, Marriages and Deaths, Dublin, *Death Certificate of John Spratt*, 7th June 1871.
3. *Dublin Shipping and Mercantile Gazette*, 30th May 1871.

**Fig 158.** *John Spratt.*

hardly surprising. The immediately-preceding years had been ones of growing pressure and increasing stress. For one, there was the virtual mutiny he faced, as Provincial, by his younger Carmelite confreres with their remonstrances to Rome against his administration. For another, and more recently than that, there had been the Corrigan education controversy and the humiliation he had been subjected to by Canon McCabe and Cardinal Cullen.[4] Then again, he had been pilloried by republican nationalists in the amnesty agitation and had been attacked by the publicans for his Sunday closing agitation.[5] To these sudden stresses had been added his ongoing worry for the upkeep of the Night Refuge and of St Peter's Orphanage which were peculiarly personal responsibilities, on top of the shared responsibility for his schools, the Roomkeepers Society, and the Asylum for the Female Blind in Portobello. Apart from his ongoing charity work, he had also taken up the cause of raising money for the French who had been suffering as a result of the Franco-Prussian War: in particular, the villagers between Metz and Sedan were reported as suffering severe privation.[6]

---

4. For both see Chapter Twenty-One.
5. See Chapters Twenty-One and Twenty-Two.
6. DDA, *Cullen Papers*, 321/1/III/20, List of subscriptions sent by Spratt to Cullen, 20th December 1870; also see *EF*, 25th Oct 1870; *FJ*, 2nd Dec 1870; *EF*, 8th Dec 1870, 26th, 28th, 31st Jan 1871.

Furthermore it seems he had recently completed a translation, from Italian, of *The Life of St Angelo, Martyr,* which James Duffy published for him, posthumously, that October.[7] In the week before his passing, he had been distinctly ailing,[8] yet he managed to remain active. On the day before his death, for example, he and Sir Dominic Corrigan, presumably now reconciled, had spoken together at length on the temperance cause.[9] His sudden demise, therefore, came as a profound shock to his confreres, comrades, and the wider public. His confrere, Henry McGee, as Vicar Prior in Whitefriar Street, informed Prior General Savini, two days later. He told him that Fr John *'had shown some signs of a heart malady but nobody expected the end'.* McGee explained how Spratt *'was carrying out a great act of charity by buying a house which he had had an eye on for a while, to offer a night refuge to poor women and children. He died just after signing the contract'.*[10]

Typical of the many reactions was that of the *Evening Freeman* which described the news *'as the message of a national calamity'.*[11] A litany of tributes soon poured forth: *'a truly good and amiable man...pure of all party feeling and utterly unsullied by bigotry'*, wrote one unnamed admirer.[12] Haughton spoke of *'the irreparable loss which the [temperance] movement had sustained'.*[13] Archdeacon Redmond of Arklow wrote:

> I have had the honour and happiness of his friendship for forty years and I never knew a more simple, humble or a more unaffectedly dignified man. He was emphatically unselfish and animated with good will to all men...He delighted in joining his separated brethren in works of benevolence...the Vincent de Paul of Dublin...His Night Refuge alone would be enough to immortalise him.[14]

In like spirit, the distinguished lawyer, academic and MP for Tipperary, Denis Caulfield Heron, also saw the friar's ecumenism as an outstanding

7. *FJ,* 11th Oct 1871.
8. *SNL,* 29th May 1871.
9. *EF,* 26th June 1871, speech by Corrigan at a meeting in Whitefriar Street Church on Sunday 25th June 1871.
10. CISA Archives, *AO Rome, Hib 3,* McGee to Savini, 29th May 1871.
11. *EF,* 29th May 1871.
12. *Dublin Shipping and Mercantile Gazette,* 30th May 1871.
13. *FJ,* 5th June 1871.
14. *EF,* 30th May 1871, Archdeacon Redmond to editor, 30th May 1871.

feature of his character and career: *'he forgot the dogmas which divided them in the immortal hopes which united them'.*[15] In reviewing the legion of tributes, perhaps the most memorable and original was that of his Church of Ireland friend and fellow-worker for the poor, William Carroll, Rector of St Bride's. John had died on the eve of Pentecost and on the very next day, William Carroll, dwelling on the mystery of that feast day, then turned to the loss of his friend. He spoke in depth of the history of the Order of which the friar had been so distinguished a member and referred to the long history of the Carmelites, Dominicans and Franciscans whose *'abbeys and possessions in Ireland were robbed by Henry the Eighth'.* Carroll stressed *'the immense service which these Orders rendered to humanity'* and went on to consider John Spratt:

> I always had the feeling that he was a genuine and genial representative of the benevolence and charity and traditions of his Carmelite fraternity. For many years, as you all know, it was my privilege to have been associated with Dr Spratt in many works of charity, morality and Christian sympathy…In the wretched religious distractions which divide and harass our country it is unusual thus to allude to a brother of a different sect; but there are signs and tendencies abroad which seem to indicate that this practical system of mutual anathema is passing away… On almost all speculative points I differed from Dr Spratt, but as surely as I believe in a God, I believe that his religion is as saving a religion as mine…this Carmelite friar…so long a shining light amongst us.[16]

Finally, one of the most unusual yet significant tributes came from the pen of a pseudonymous woman, 'Ierne' who wrote *'it was the women of Dublin who would most feel the death of Dr Spratt'*, as he was the one, uniquely, who provided shelter for the homeless among women.[17]

*Obsequies*
The funeral Mass in the church that John built was presided over by Cardinal Cullen, attended by one of the friar's closest clerical friends,

---

15. *EF*, 26th June 1871.
16. *FJ*, 30th May 1871.
17. *DWN*, 1st July 1871, 'Ierne' to editor.

the Discalced Carmelite friar, William Joseph Whelan, quondam Bishop of Bombay.[18] The church was crowded for hours before the Office of the Dead commenced at eleven o'clock and the congregation witnessed an imposing turn-out of senior diocesan clergy and heads of all the leading religious orders. With the Cardinal and the Bishop in the sanctuary, the Mass was celebrated by his Carmelite confrere, Henry McGee. Following the two-hour long ceremony in the church, the ensuing funeral procession proved to be *'one of the most imposing that has ever passed through the streets of Dublin'.*[19] The vast cortege, gathering more mourners as it wended its way, *'was probably the largest seen in the city or in Ireland since that of O'Connell'.* Estimated at 30,000, it comprised people of all classes and creeds as it proceeded towards Glasnevin.[20] The great file was led by his own and other temperance societies and lobbies, including the Irish Permissive Bill Association and the Wesleyan Band of Hope, Sandymount; next, the Coal Porters' Society and the religious confraternities, the children of his schools, his fellow-members of the Roomkeepers Society, and the trades of Dublin. There followed the hearse, drawn by six black horses, accompanied by outriders and running footmen, followed by the boys of St Peter's Orphanage and then his beloved ITAA brass band. Among the immense number of carriages were those of William Carroll and of the Methodist minister, James Tobias, together with all the worthies of the state, the bench, town and gown. Yet, it was well-remarked that

> Long and imposing funeral processions have followed to the tomb men for whom a dozen persons did not feel sincere regret; but every one of the thousands who looked on yesterday's procession was a sincere and earnest mourner…her citizens watched with sincerest sorrow, with many a prayer and tear.[21]

On arrival at Glasnevin Cemetery, where Dr Whelan received the remains, John was laid to rest in the Carmelite plot and there had his

18. John Francis (William Joseph) Whelan (1798-1876) was Vicar Apostolic of Bombay from 1848 to 1850: thereafter he spent the rest of his life in the Clarendon Street friary.
19. *FJ*, 31st May 1871.
20. *DDE*, 31st May 1871.
21. *FJ*, 31st May 1871.

name inscribed in due course, on the monument to the Carmelites who had gone before him.

In Rome, too, where the news had reached them from Fr Carr, as Prior of Whitefriar Street, the Carmelites held a Solemn Mass on 6th June in the church of their community at Santa Maria in Traspontina, which was draped in black for the occasion. It was here that the Prior General, Angelo Savini, lived and he, together with the Procurator General, Fr Elias Maggi, and the Prior, Fr Caruso, presided at the service.[22] Back in Dublin, on 26th June, Fr John's month's mind was observed in a packed Whitefriar Street Church. The Solemn Office of the Dead was sung, led once again by Bishop Whelan, with the Psalms being chanted by the full choir of the Carmelite priests.[23]

The Carmelite plot in Glasnevin proved not to be John's final resting place. Having interred him there and having entered his age incorrectly as 73, as per the brass plate on his coffin, the cemetery authorities corrected that record on 27th June 1873, on receipt of his baptismal certificate, and now entered his age as 75.[24] They then made the gift of a private vault in the O'Connell Circle, beneath the tower, close by the grave of his hero, the Liberator, and next to his old friend, Fr William Yore. Over this vault, at his own expense, Fr James, the Augustinian, erected a splendid memorial of a Celtic cross on a four-sided base, all standing eighteen feet high. Three of its sides featured panels depicting scenes of

**Fig 159.** *The vault of John and James Spratt, in the O'Connell Circle, Glasnevin Cemetery.*

22. *FJ*, 21st June 1871.
23. *EF*, 27th June 1871.
24. Glasnevin Cemetery Archives, Dublin Cemeteries Committee, *Register of Interments*, vol. 9, p. 61. Errors about John Spratt's age abounded: see *Appendix 1*.

John's life and achievements. The northern panel showed the friar administering the pledge; the eastern one presented the frontage of his Night Refuge; that on the south displayed an image of the exterior of his Whitefriar Street Church, while that on the west bore the following inscription:

Blessed are the dead who die in the Lord; they rest
From their labours and their works follow them.
Sacred to the Memory of the

Very Rev John Spratt, D.D.

Who departed this life on the eve of Pentecost, 1871,
In the 75th year of his age and the 51st of his Sacred Ministry.
He was for many years the Provincial of the Carmelite Order in Ireland.
It was by his exertions and under his superintendence that the Church of that Order was erected in Whitefriar Street, A.D. 1826 & 1827.
He was the vigilant guardian of St Peter's Orphanage from its foundation, and for upwards of 40 years he was Honorary Secretary of the Roomkeepers Society.
He was one of the first to join Fr Mathew in the temperance crusade, and, with Monsignor Yore, he continued to be the untiring champion of it to his latest moment.
He was the zealous founder of St Joseph's Night Refuge, Cork-street, for the Homeless Poor. The Asylum for the Female Catholic Blind, formerly at Portobello, and now at Merrion, was one of his happiest inspirations.
To him also, the Schools of Whitefriar Street, male and female, owe their origin and efficiency.
A place of refreshment, light and joy to his soul, and to all the souls who have departed with the sign of faith, and that rest in the sleep of peace.

Fr James, the last survivor of the three brothers, died on Friday 6th June 1879[25] in his 76th year. Close to John in life and death, he was laid

---

25. Glasnevin Cemetery Archives, Dublin Cemeteries Committee, *Register of Interments*, vol. 12, 9th June 1879.

to rest in the same vault within the O'Connell Circle, on 9th June 1879. Fr John's death suddenly left vacant the position of Provincial. In due course and with due decorum, the Prior of Whitefriar Street, John Carr was appointed temporarily as Vicar Provincial by the Prior General until a proper Chapter of the Order could be organised. That Chapter, the first full one since 1849, was presided over by Prior General Savini himself, at the end of August 1871. At this, Fr Carr was overwhelmingly elected Provincial with John Hall as Prior in Whitefriar Street.[26]

**Fig 160.** *Fr John Carr, O.Carm.*

### The Estate, the Order, the Family and Rome

John Spratt died intestate. This was despite having been twice asked to make a will and twice declining. As late as March 1871, eight weeks before his death, his Prior at Whitefriar Street, requested him to do so, but to no avail.[27] On 24th June James Spratt was appointed administrator of John's estate.[28] He lost no time and entered upon his task with zeal. Fr Carr, in two letters to Savini, within a fortnight of the grant of administration, described how James Spratt brusquely entered the friary and his brother's room, took all the clothes, money and moveable goods and threatened legal action if impeded. Carr added that it took the intervention of the Cardinal Archbishop of Dublin to prevent the situation becoming a public scandal.[29] What Fr James discovered was a matter of some astonishment to the Whitefriar Street brethren: a sum of the equivalent of 96,150 French francs for charity and a personal sum of 7,250 French francs equivalent, together described by Fr Carr to his Prior General as *'an enormous sum of money'*: Carr was embarrassed

26. O'Dwyer, *Irish Carmelites*, pp. 260-262. Hall had been appointed as Prior initially when Carr became Vicar Provincial.
27. CISA Archives, *Hib 1*, Carr to Savini, 30th June 1871.
28. NAI, *Wills and Administrations*, year 1871, p. 558.
29. CISA, *Hib 1*, Carr to Savini, 30th June, 4th July 1871.

and apologetic to Savini, adding, *'how could it [be] that our Vicar Provincial had his own money, as it were: it is enough to say that he was the only one among our fathers...'.*[30] It turned out that the money destined for charity had been made up into parcels and labelled with the name of the intended charity. The money described by Carr as 'personal' was reckoned by the Church authorities to amount to £500 sterling in the money of that time: this would be consistent with the grant of administration which fell within the category of under £600.

At this point the surviving children of Spratt's brother, Michael and of his sister, Mary Anne, came forward to claim the inheritance of Spratt's £500. Those concerned were firstly, Michael Thomas and Eleanor, the son and daughter of Michael; and secondly, the surviving four sons and surviving one daughter of Mary Anne Vickers, née Spratt: these were James, Richard, Joseph, Nicholas and Elizabeth. To prevent any scandal that might arise from any legal contest between these people and the Carmelites, Cardinal Cullen was consulted and, on 11th July 1871, he sought the advice of the Pope. The Pontiff and his closest advisors agreed that as the family were *'poor'*, the money should be given to them.[31]

As for John's other effects, it would appear that they remained with Fr James for the time being. The Carmelite friar, in the course of his life, had been given various gifts, some valuable such as Alderman Tom Reynolds's gold ring, some sentimental, such as the beautiful onyx ring with cameo of the Virgin, the gift of Pope Gregory XVI, or the relics of St Valentine. Other valuable artefacts came his way as personal 'finds' or discoveries made by workmen and which they gave to him, such as the precious gilded bishop's crozier found, apparently, in Christchurch during building excavations. Then again, he was himself the purchaser

30. Ibid, Carr to Savini, 30th June 1871. Unfortunately, the end of the letter is missing and there is no extant copy in the Gort Muire Archives. It is difficult to offer an equivalent in today's euro currency, but one advisor has suggested that the 96,150 French francs would be the equivalent of circa 300,000 euro today. On that basis, Spratt's own 7,250 French francs would equate to 23,000 euro today.
31. Propaganda Fide Archives, *Scritture Riferite nei Congressi, Irlanda,* vol. 36, 1868-75, pp. 891, 942; DDA, *Cullen Papers,* 326/5/1/29, Cullen to Pope Pius IX, 11th July 1871. It is to be noted that these documents referred to John Spratt's nephew, Michael, as Michael John whereas, in fact, he was Michael Thomas, the one who had erected the memorial stone to his father, Michael senior, and which memorial gives the name Michael Thomas as son.

of rare books and artefacts, not least the historic Virgin of Dublin which to this day is to be found in the Whitefriar Street Church. Apart from seeing to the granting of the £500 to the surviving relatives, James had also to ensure that any outstanding creditors were paid. To this end he placed a notice in the national press at the end of June 1871 giving potential creditors until 21st August to lodge their claims. Since nothing further was heard on this score, it would appear that any or all outstanding debts had been settled.

As for John's belongings, whether auctioned or retained by James until his own death, some of them made an appearance in odd circumstances. In January 1876, an ebony walking cane, silver-topped and with Fr John's name engraved, appeared as a prize at a bazaar being held at the Passionists' Mount Argus church, as did his alarm clock, at a church bazaar in Rathmines exactly four years later.[32] More significantly, a large scrapbook into which the friar had pasted newspaper cuttings and pictures, together with a large, contemporary water-colour of Lord Edward Fitzgerald under which Spratt had written a description of the nobleman, came into the hands of a dealer, Fetherston of Coppinger Row.[33] Furthermore, an autograph letter of Daniel O'Connell to John Spratt, of the year 1838, was privately put up for sale in 1882.[34] Finally, a silver snuff box, engraved with John's name, was put on sale a year later, while a similar item, presented to him by his Irish Total Abstinence Association in 1842, was offered for sale in June 1886.[35]

*Remembering John Spratt*

The rapid disposal of Fr John's worldly goods did not mirror the dispersal of the memories of the man. Immediately after his funeral, moves were made to remember him by memorial, apart from that erected by his brother, Fr James. It speaks well to the affection or the respect in which he was held that, the very day after his funeral,

32. *DWN*, 15th Jan 1876, 15th Jan 1880.
33. *FJ*, 21st Sept 1880. What happened to the scrapbook thereafter is, as yet, uncertain. The Carmelite Archives in Gort Muire contain a number of Spratt scrapbooks and this one may be among them, gifted to or purchased back by them, as one of the GMA scrapbooks contains a watercolour portrait of Lord Edward Fitzgerald.
34. *FJ*, 10th Aug 1882. Its whereabouts today are not known to this writer.
35. *FJ*, 26th June 1886. This last item did the rounds. It was offered for sale again in February and in July 1887, at a bazaar prize-draw for the Dominican Orphanage, Eccles Street, Dublin: see *FJ*, 11th Feb, 26th July 1887.

an editorial in the *Freeman's Journal* urged that *'his memory should not be allowed to die away from amongst us'* and suggested a *'People's Penny Collection'* to source the funds to create one.[36]   Six days later, the Carmelite Confraternity in Whitefriar Street convened to establish a committee and to inaugurate a subscription fund, with the Carmelite, Fr Sheridan, in the chair and Michael O'Connolly, the St Peter's Orphanage master, as one of its honorary secretaries.[37]  Sheridan gave the project a definite steer when he commented that he felt Fr John's greatest interest was in St Peter's Orphanage and that the best memorial would be to raise funds to endow it.  He noted that since its foundation some 500 orphans had found shelter in it.  The Confraternity therefore agreed to hold a public meeting in Whitefriar Street Church to promote this suggestion.[38]

When that meeting was duly held, on Sunday 25th June, the church was crowded.  The gathering included Sir William Wilde, Sir Dominic Corrigan, A M Sullivan and leading members of the Dublin labour movement.[39]  Interestingly, the Lord Mayor, who presided, mentioned the Night Refuge in his opening remarks, suggesting that this was

John Spratt's pre-eminent achievement.  In a sense he was right, for, although the friar had a long history as spiritual guardian of St Peter's, he had not been its founder – contrary to what is stated on his Glasnevin monument – whereas the Refuge had been his sole initiative and creation.[40]  However, not wishing to introduce a discordant note, the Lord Mayor professed to

**Fig 161.**  *Sir William Wilde.*

---

36.  *FJ*, 31st May 1871, 'A Monument to Dr Spratt'.
37.  *EF*, 8th, 16th June 1871.  The thirty-five year old Fr Terence Sheridan became Prior of Kildare in 1875.  He was one of the Carmelite pioneers in Australia in the 1880s: see O'Dwyer, *Irish Carmelites*, p. 303.
38.  *The Irishman*, 17th June 1871.
39.  *DDE*, 26th June 1871.
40.  The Orphanage was founded by a workman named Halligan, in 1817, and Spratt did not become involved until 1823: see *SNL*, 10th June 1871.

agree with Fr Sheridan that if Spratt could be asked, he would have chosen the Orphanage. In the light of what was later to unfold, it was a singularly unfortunate decision. While others, such as the positivist and biographer of Auguste Comte, Henry Dix Hutton, spoke up for the Night Refuge, the consensus was that since the Refuge '*had been provided for*', then the Orphanage was the better choice as a memorial. Corrigan, who reminded his audience that the very church where they now met was also a result of the friar's initiative and energies. He went on to suggest also that the dining room of the Orphanage should be adorned with a full length portrait of the friar.

John Keegan, the secretary of the United Trades Association, recalled Spratt's great efforts for the revival of Irish manufactures twenty years before and drew attention to the Carmelite's great love of art. Keegan suggested that they should be ambitious and build a new orphanage and install on its forecourt a statue of the friar.[41] No new orphanage was ever built and no statue made.

It was actually on the premises of the Orphanage at 44 York Street that the members of the Spratt Memorial Committee held their meetings. They decided on a general circular to the public at large and a particular circular to be sent to the trades unions, tontine and benefit societies and the confraternities.[42] Soon enough donations began to come in, modest in the main, but including ten guineas each from the distillers Sir James Power and his son, John Talbot Power, MP, and £20 from the Wexford MP, Matthew D'Arcy. By mid-July the fund had reached £260 and the committee decided the time had come to issue a fund-raising circular to the Irish of America and Australia.[43] That September also, the committee chaired by Wilde, resolved to explore the possible purchase of the Cahill bust of Spratt: Fr Sheridan and John Keegan went to inspect and found that this '*admirable likeness and beautiful work of art*' could be had for £60.[44] Fr Sheridan wanted the decision to purchase postponed,

---

41. *EF*, 26th June 1871.
42. *FJ*, 6th July 1871.
43. His death and the memorial fund were noticed in the American, Australian and New Zealand press: see for examples, *The Morning Star and Catholic Register* (New Orleans), 23rd July 1871; *The Ballarat Star*, 31st July 1871; *The Argus* (Melbourne), 31st July 1871; *West Coast Times* (New Zealand), 12th Aug 1871; *Taranaki Herald*, (New Zealand), 12th Aug 1871; Launceston Examiner (Tasmania), 3rd Aug 1871.
44. *SNL*, 2nd, 9th Sept 1871.

**Fig 162.** *Bust of John Spratt, by James Cahill.*

presumably because the funds were not accumulating as greatly as the initial burst of enthusiasm might have indicated. Keegan, for one, bore this out when he apologised on behalf of the trade unions for their tardiness in subscribing. This he attributed to *'a crisis among the trades'.* However, Fr Sheridan was outvoted and the decision to purchase the bust was taken, with Keegan offering to make a suitable pedestal for it at his personal expense. The bust was duly purchased and stands still today in the Carmelite Community Centre, Whitefriar Street.[45]

*Faltering funds*

As the inflow of funds decelerated, it was decided to hold ward meetings throughout the city in order to regenerate momentum. However, while the Spratt Memorial Committee professed itself satisfied with the progress made, the editor of the *Freeman's Journal* chose to disagree, and complained that *'the result is far away short of the merits of the man…the people of Dublin have scarcely subscribed £500'.* The editor remarked that there were names absent from the lists, names which ought to have been prominent. It added that Dublin artisans and labourers owed much to Spratt's memory and deserved to be denounced as thankless *'if they fail in a magnanimous fulfilment of their obligations to their benefactor'.*[46] However, money from the ward meetings began to come in: over £120 from the prosperous Mansion House Ward, much more modest sums from others.[47] Still, the *Freeman's* editor berated the tardiness or niggardliness of certain sectors and now singled out the temperance or teetotal lobby in particular. He remarked that they had not raised or donated a penny for the fund although they had no difficulty in raising over £100,000 for

---

45. *FJ*, 16th Sept, 27th Oct 1871.
46. *FJ*, 18th Oct 1871.
47. *FJ*, 16th Nov 1871. The others included £25 from the less affluent North City Ward.

teetotal propaganda.[48]

The rebuke brought a frank and stinging retort from T W Russell. He held it was to the credit of the teetotal community that they had not come forward to contribute since *'the Memorial Committee is very much composed of publicans'*, and rhetorically inquired *'is it not a fact that the paid secretary of the Memorial Committee is also the paid secretary of the Licensed Grocers' and Vintners' Society? Just fancy the teetotallers of Dublin co-operating with such men'*.[49] In a time and a society so Bible-conscious, it must have struck many that the teetotal protest smacked of the Pharisee. Dr McSwiney who chaired the next meeting of the Memorial Committee responded that the memorial was to commemorate the friar *'as priest, patriot and universal philanthropist'*, and that, of the original committee of 49, only 2 had been publicans: the committee, augmented by ward representatives, now numbered 75, of whom 13 were publicans and the presence of the latter merely reflected the universal esteem in which Fr Spratt was held. Furthermore, the then secretary had only been brought on board recently and was not there during the first five months of the committee's existence, yet Russell and his comrades had failed to engage or support even during that period.[50] The maligned secretary of the Memorial Committee, Michael Dwyer, also challenged Russell, pointing out that the two publican members of the original committee happened to be the aldermen of the Mansion House and Royal Exchange Wards and that no one from the Licensed Grocers was involved in the early stages. He explained that once the first fervour of the campaign had subsided, in order to guarantee even a modest success, the Committee had had to ask the licensed trade for assistance and asked Dwyer himself if he would come on board. Dwyer concluded his response by pointing out that these publican members showed *'genuine charity'* in casting aside personal feelings when their assistance was requested. Given Spratt's attacks on the trade, it was a generous response.[51] The row rumbled on, with publican John Doyle of Wexford Street also attacking Russell and the teetotal lobby, noting that the latter put in no appearance to help the Orphanage when Fr Spratt died. He added that the Carmelite friar had never any problem working in the Roomkeepers Society for over forty

48. *FJ*, 9th Jan 1872.
49. *FJ*, 16th Jan 1872, T. W. Russell to editor, 9th January 1872.
50. *FJ*, 19th Jan 1872.
51. Ibid.

years where the majority of active members were licensed grocers and vintners. He suggested that teetotallers such as Russell needed to learn charity towards their neighbours.[52]

By April 1872, money from the city's trade unions began to come, in sums ranging from the fifteen shillings of the Spratt-family trade of tanners to the £5 from the coachmakers.[53] However, by the time of the first anniversary of the friar's death, the flow had diminished to a trickle. On Tuesday 29th April Wilde chaired one of the last reported meetings of the Spratt Memorial Committee and the list closed. Given the modest dimensions of the final total sum, of £415, it could be argued that it was as well that the Committee had not sought to erect a physical monument but had instead settled on a bursary.[54] As against this, the Orphanage did not survive beyond the year 1879, having been brought to ruin in a legal dispute between its lay management committee on the one hand and the Carmelite friars and the Dublin diocesan authorities on the other. At the end of the proceedings not a shilling was left to support any orphan: so much for that particular memorial to Fr Spratt.[55]

### Twilight of the ITAA

Other institutions that might have kept John Spratt's memory alive also fell by the wayside or metamorphosed into something other than that which he had founded and fostered. This became notably the case with his Cuffe Lane Irish Total Abstinence Association, with its Temperance Hall and its associated ITAA brass band. That hall, originally their church when he first entered the Carmelites, and still their church when he returned from Spain in 1822, became a hallowed place in his life for over thirty years.

On the second Sunday evening after John's death, his Irish Total

---

52. *FJ*, 20th Jan 1872, John Doyle to editor, 16th January 1872.
53. *FJ*, 5th, 12th, 22nd April, 3rd May 1872.
54. *FJ*, 3rd May 1872. Only one further meeting was reported in mid-June which acknowledged a donation of £5 from the journeymen bakers, for which see *FJ*, 15th June 1872. No final list of subscriptions appears to have been published anywhere.
55. See F. A. D'Arcy, 'The rise and decline of St Peter's Orphanage, York Street, Dublin, 1817-1879', *forthcoming*; also, DDA, *Cullen Papers*, 329/6/4, *High Court of Justice in Ireland, Chancery Division, Master of the Rolls: the Attorney General versus McGee and Others, Statement of Claim, 22 February 1878.*

Abstinence Association met to hear James Haughton speak of *'the irreparable loss which the movement had sustained'*, and he hoped the ITAA committee members would keep up the Sunday gatherings.[56] Recalling the friar *'so greatly loved by all who knew him'*, and commenting that *'a better man than Fr Spratt has not lived amongst us'*, the Unitarian philanthropist urged the committee to hold an urgent meeting to consider the future.[57] It is not evident that this meeting took place or, if it did, whether or not it had any positive outcome. On balance, it probably did convene, but certain it is that once John Spratt was gone, it seemed as though the publicity value of the weekly gatherings at Cuffe Lane Temperance Hall had gone with him. There is no doubt that Spratt had an entrée to the press, and especially to the *Freeman's Journal*, from his long friendship and collaboration with its editors, the Gray family. To some extent also, so did James Haughton, but he too was by now failing and would himself soon be no more. Those left behind in Cuffe Lane did not possess the national reputations nor could they command the national attention as these two had done for half a century. The movement in general in Dublin continued on without Spratt and Haughton, but was hardly the stronger for it.[58]

No Carmelite came forward to replace John Spratt at the Hall and no priest to assume its leadership. James Haughton tried, after his friend's death, to get other clergymen to take up the challenge, to no avail. He recalled visiting the Hall one Sunday evening where the people asked if he himself would administer the pledge.[59] The ITAA continued, under a nine-man committee led by one M Burke as secretary. It was as much a social club and a benefit society as a teetotal body and for some years continued its annual summer excursions and continued prudently to provide for life's emergencies.[60] James Haughton died on 20th February 1873 and the ITAA and its benefit arm assembled in 'Dr Spratt's Hall' to honour Haughton's memory and to arrange with Spratt's beloved brass

56. *FJ*, 5th June 1871.
57. *FJ*, 7th June 1871, Haughton to editor, 1st June 1871.
58. For the temperance movement from the last quarter of the nineteenth century, see D. Ferriter, *A Nation of Extremes: The Pioneers in Twentieth-century Ireland*, Dublin 1999; and Malcolm, *Ireland sober, Ireland free*.
59. S. Haughton, *Memoir of James Haughton*, Dublin 1877, pp. 270-272.
60. *FJ*, 22nd Aug 1871, 7th July 1873, 15th Aug 1876 for the excursions; 5th Jan 1874, 5th Jan 1875 for its benefit meetings.

band, under Mr Tighe, to take part in Haughton's funeral procession.[61]
Samuel Haughton, James' son, in thanking the ITAA for its expressions
of sympathy, remarked, *'I fear that Rev Fr Spratt's place has never been filled'.*[62]
The ITAA survived into the later 1870s and in October 1877 it joined
in a great social occasion to mark the birthday of Fr Mathew, this time
in the Dublin Total Abstinence League and Working Men's Club, 41
York Street: some 70 sat down to tea and to dance the evening hours
away. Thereafter, however, the ITAA as teetotal body or as tontine
society ceased to garner a mention in the press and how long beyond
the late 1870s it may have survived is not yet known.

*A Hall of memories*
As for Fr John's Temperance Hall itself, it was not long before it was
gradually taken over by a branch of the Ancient Order of Foresters.
They too had a brass band which soon began meeting in the Hall, at
least by March 1872.[63] By that August the building was being referred to

**Fig 163.** *Sackville Street (O'Connell Street), in the late 19th century.*

61. *FJ*, 24th Feb 1873.
62. *FJ*, 24th Feb, 3rd March 1873. Samuel, who wrote a life of his father, repeated
    that note of regret; see S. Haughton, *Memoir*, pp. 270-272. This Samuel is not to
    be confused with the contemporary Rev Dr Samuel Haughton of TCD, an error
    which appears in the *Dictionary of National Biography*. For this see Quaker Historical
    Archives, Dublin, J. Kelly Haughton to O. Goodbody, 23rd October 1971.
63. *FJ*, 9th March 1872.

as 'The Foresters' Home, late Dr Spratt's Hall, for the Ancient Order of Foresters, Dublin District'.[64] When Spratt's ITAA held its annual soiree in October 1872, in the Hall, a distinct note of nostalgia prevailed: they remembered *'the late Dr Spratt's Hall where thousands took the pledge…but all that is now a thing of the past and Dr Spratt has only left his society to perpetuate his memory…'*. Unfortunately, the ITAA being unable to pay the rent, became tenants of the Foresters who now took it over and refurbished it.[65] On 28th August 1875 the property at 12 Upper Mercer Street and the buildings behind it on Cuffe Lane, *'formerly used as Dr Spratt's Hall'*, and still used by the Foresters and the ITAA, were put up for auction in a sheriff's sale. Despite the sale, the Foresters and ITAA continued to meet there, and when the property was re-advertised for sale in 1876, the Hall had now officially become The Foresters' Hall.[66]

*The Brass Band's last days*

Just as John Spratt's name gradually disappeared from his Temperance Hall, so too it did, at length, from that of his ITAA Brass Band. The band appears to have been fortunate in the support of its conductor, John Tighe, who continued to lead it for many years. In 1875 it still numbered some 32 members, including two of his sons. Most notably, and aptly, it participated in the great parade of 1875 that marked the unveiling of the O'Connell Monument that John Spratt had done so much to promote. Here, on this remarkable occasion, the Dublin Coal Porters, all one thousand of them, were accompanied by *'Dr Spratt's Band, attired in regimental suits'*.[67] Then, with that event over, the Band changed its name. At its own inaugural soiree in 'The Foresters' Hall, Cuffe Lane', the band was unveiled as 'The City of Dublin Brass Band'.[68] So it continued thereafter, dissociated from Spratt's name, but not perhaps entirely from his ideals. It continued to support the Dublin teetotal movement into the 1880s, as, for example, entertaining meetings of St Joseph's Total Abstinence League, Grenville Street, and St Nicholas of Myra's Total Abstinence League, Francis Street, and the

---

64. *FJ*, 12th Aug 1872.

65. FJ, 10th Oct 1872.

66. *FJ*, 27th Aug, 19th Oct 1875, 19th June 1876. The Foresters had a 31-year lease on the Hall from 1st April 1872 at £25 per year, which they regularly paid.

67. *IT*, 7th Aug 1875.

68. *FJ*, 10th Oct 1875.

Dublin Total Abstinence Union at the Rotunda, in October 1883.[69] By 1894 it featured as the first band to play in the Phoenix Park's summer season,[70] but by then its engagements were purely social and not distinguishable from those of any other of the city's bands at the time.

*Forgetting and Remembering*
Fr John's name also disappeared in time from its association with his beloved Night Refuge. Although the Sisters of Mercy had stepped into the void created by his death and had taken over the responsibility soon after, his name continued to appear in public advertisements for the charity, but not after the year 1900. Nevertheless, his portrait featured prominently on the Refuge's premises which now take the form of the Sophia Housing Association charity. Likewise, his image still presides in the premises of the Sick and Indigent Roomkeepers Society, even after their move from their historic location in No. 2 Palace Street to No 34 and then to No 74 Upper Leeson Street.[71] As Friar John Spratt's name gradually disappeared from public awareness over the decades after 1871, all that remains is to consider his historic legacy.

**Fig 164.** *Sophia Housing Project, Cork Street.*

---

69.  *FJ*, 30th Oct 1883.
70.  *FJ*, 2nd May 1894.
71.  *IT*, 19th Jan 2011.

# CHAPTER TWENTY-FOUR

## *The Legacy*

Much of Friar John's achievement lived after him, in works that he founded or causes that he served: his St Peter's Schools in Whitefriar Street flourished: likewise, to this day, his Whitefriar Street Church with its St Valentine's Shrine and its Virgin of Dublin: and, of course, the Carmelite Order that he served so long. Yet, for all that, he is hardly remembered today beyond the confines of the Carmelites: John Spratt deserved better of his city and his country. His concern for his fellow-citizens has not been reciprocated: certainly, the city fathers have done nothing to honour his memory despite his many different commitments towards a better life for all. He was a man of peace and compassion, courageous in campaigns whether for clemency, or civil rights, religious equality, social reform or political liberty. Without question, he was the most persistent political priest in the Dublin of his age, and one of the most so in the Ireland of his times. The temper of those times changed profoundly between the 1820s and 1830s, on the one hand, and the 1860s and early 1870s on the other, and, in so doing, they left him in some ways as an apparent anachronism. The politics of O'Connellite liberalism, which he maintained to the end of his days, would be swept away by the new belligerence of Fenian and Home Rule nationalism from the 1860s. Thenceforward, the echoes of louder voices and extremer champions would come to be recalled in the public statuary, the folk memory and the historical writing of this city and country alike. Nor can it be said that he ever fully reconciled his political liberalism with his Catholic fidelity: the attacks, military and intellectual, of Italian liberals, republicans and nationalists on the

Papacy and the Papal States constituted an unresolved challenge. John Spratt was a practical man, not a theorist. For all that, his political contribution during that period of markedly fluid politics in the mid-nineteenth century was a very considerable one in raising political awareness and contributing to political action. Even as his political and religious liberalism brought him into campaigning comradeship with leading Unitarian and Quaker Dissenters, he did not share their *laissez-faire* or economic liberalism: as we have seen, where situations required it, he believed in state intervention. His economics, what he called *'the economy of mercy'*, came from an older, traditional Catholic moral economy that still had relevance beyond his age. At the same time, for all his being steeped in traditional Catholic theology, he was remarkably a moderniser among Irishmen. Friar that he was, he never looked back to a supposed golden age of saints and scholars: rather, he wanted that his fellow Irishmen be sober, industrious, dignified and free. Education and industry, with habits of self-discipline leading to self-worth were his goals for his fellow-citizens and fellow-countrymen: these goals underlay his campaigns for temperance, for schools and for the revival of Irish industry.

He was, however, first and foremost a conventual religious, ministering to his people through the word and the deed. Given this confessional contribution as friar and pastor, it remains remarkable just how interconfessional or ecumenical he was: without question, uniquely so for his age. To the extent that this left him out of step with his Cardinal Archbishop and with a Church that was now coming into its own dominance, speaks eloquently and carries convincingly beyond his time: this, more than anything else, perhaps, justifies his remembrance and reconsideration.

# APPENDICES

# APPENDIX 1

## *The Spratt Family: problems of dates and names*

Biographers and historians of John Spratt and the Spratt family have differed widely on such a fundamental matter as John's date of birth, have been largely silent on the nature and extent of his family and have overlooked problems in the Christian names of his mother and youngest sister. First came the account by his close acquaintance, the Catholic publisher, W J Battersby, in 1871. Then followed the biography by his younger Carmelite confrere, Andrew Elias Farrington, in 1893. Next there were the three accounts by the Irish Carmelite historian, Peter O'Dwyer, in 1968, 1971 and 1988. Finally, and most recently, there is an entry in the *Dictionary of Irish Biography* by David Murphy in 2009.[1] None have anything to say about John's father, most have little to say of his mother and siblings, and differ in assigning the date of his birth and, in consequence, of his age at death.

Battersby, who credibly claimed to have known John well for over half a century, presented him as the eldest son, born in 1794. Another contemporary and close associate of John in the 1840s and

---

1.  W. J. Battersby, *Authentic life and acts of the Very Rev Dr Spratt, S.T.M., Provincial, O.C.C.*, Dublin 1871; A. E. Farrington, *Rev Dr Spratt, O.C.C.: his life and times*, Dublin 1893; P. O'Dwyer, *John Francis Spratt, O.Carm., 1796-1871: a Dissertation submitted to the Faculty of Church History of the Pontifical Gregorian University*, Rome 1968; *Father John Spratt: beloved of Dublin's Poor: a centenary souvenir, 1871-1971*, Dublin 1971; *The Irish Carmelites (of the Ancient Observance)*, Dublin 1988; D. Murphy, 'John Francis Spratt, 1796-1871' in J. McGuire & J. Quinn, eds., *Dictionary of Irish Biography, from the earliest times to the year 2009*, 8 vols., Cambridge 2009, vol. iii, p. 1099. There are other biographical accounts in A. Webb, *A Compendium of Irish Biography*, Dublin 1878, p. 487; J. S. Crone, *A Concise Dictionary of Irish Biography*, Dublin 1928, pp. 236-37.

528

1850s, in the Irish temperance and home manufacture movements, Martin A. O'Brennan, writing in 1858, gave John's year of birth as 1798.[2] Farrington states unequivocally that he was born in 1795 while O'Dwyer and Murphy give the year as 1796. The Catholic registers for the relevant parish, St Catherine of Alexandria in Meath Street, unfortunately have no entries for the years 1794 to 1799. One of its Baptismal Registers from 1781 stops at 1794 and that for 1794 to 1824 actually starts only as of November 1799. These original registers are now in the Dublin Diocesan Archives. The confusion is compounded by a letter of reference for John Spratt by Irish Carmelite Provincial, Patrick O'Farrell, dated 20th August 1816, in which he gives John's birth date as 5th January 1798.[3] O'Dwyer mentions this fact in his *Dissertation*, p. 28; but he erroneously attributes the same error to Farrington; and while Farrington does, in fact, commit an error, he does so by dating John's birth as 31st January 1795, perhaps intending to have written 31st December 1795.[4]

*The Clan*

There is no published family history of the Spratt clan in Ireland. Such Spratts as there were in John's own lifetime were concentrated in a few locations. Most notably, they were in the north of the island, especially in and around Belfast, Lisburn and Irvinestown. There was a scattering of them elsewhere in the North, with a few families in Derry and Donegal.[5] In the south of the country there was a cluster in Cork, especially around Youghal, and in Waterford around Lismore and Cappoquin. Finally, there were Spratts in County Dublin around the Naul and in Dublin City from the eighteenth century if not earlier. The earliest record for Dublin that this writer has found is that of William Sprat [sic], locksmith, who was admitted to the freedom of the city

2. Battersby, p. 5; M. A. O'Brennan, *O'Brennan's Antiquities*, 2 vols., Dublin 1858-1860, 2nd ed., vol. 1, pp. 389-390. John was actually a subscriber in aid of publication of this work.
3. For O'Farrell's letter of 20th August 1816, see GMA, *Scrapbook A*, p. 4.
4. O'Dwyer, *Dissertation*, p. 28, citing Farrington, p. 196.
5. A number of Spratt men are listed by O'Herlihy as R.I.C. members in Donegal in the later nineteenth century: see J. O'Herlihy, *The Royal Irish Constabulary: a complete alphabetical list of Officers and Men, 1816-1922*, Dublin 1999, p. 438.

in 1709.[6]  A very English name, it is not yet certain when its earliest bearers were to be found in Ireland.  It is likely that they were of the Old English in Ireland, as, in the year 1343, one Richard Spratt or Sprot was Constable of Roscommon Castle.[7]

*The immediate family*

As for John's immediate family, we now know approximately when his father, James, was born.  This was in or about the year 1758.  The writer of his death notice remarked that James had lived at his Cork Street home and business for 70 years when he died on 4th December 1828.[8] As for his mother, there are differing versions as to her Christian name: most published accounts have her as Elizabeth Bollard: so Farrington, O'Dwyer and Murphy state.  However, it would appear that their sole source for this Christian name is a letter of Bishop Petrus Antonius de Trevilla of Cordoba, dated 17th April 1818, whereby Spratt was certified as having received the tonsure.  In this document it is stated that he was the legitimate son of James Spratt and Elizabeth Bollard.[9] However, the critically relevant extant records, apart from this, have her as Esther Mary Bollard.  Such is how her name appears in the Catholic parish registers for St Catherine's in September 1790 when she and her husband, entered as Esther and James, were named as the parents of a son, James, and similarly in September 1792 for the baptism of a second son, Michael.[10]  Prior to this, in November 1786, Esther Bollard was a godparent in a separate non-family baptism.  So again she appears, with husband James in 1800, on the occasion of the baptism of another of their own children, Catherine, and identically in 1806 on the baptism of a further child of theirs, also called Esther.[11]  As grandparents and sponsors of their grandchild, Nicholas Vickers, she was known as Esther.  However, a year before that, on the baptism of another grandchild, Richard Vickers, at St Catherine's, she was entered

---

6.  *Ancient Freemen of the City of Dublin*, in www.databases.dublincity.ie, accessed 19/06/2017.

7.  J. d'Alton, *The History of Ireland: from the earliest period to the year 1245*, 2 vols., Dublin 1845, vol. 2, p. 121.

8.  *Freeman's Journal*, Sat 6th Dec 1828.

9.  GMA, *Scrapbook A*, p. 5.

10. DDA, St Catherine's RC Parish Register, *Baptisms from April 1781 to February 1794*, under dates 20th September 1790 and 16th September 1792 respectively.

11. Ibid, 11th September 1800, 8th April 1806 respectively.

as Elizabeth, as she was also in September 1817, when she and husband James were sponsors at the baptism of the child of friends, Thomas and Bridget Moore.[12] Finally, when their daughter, Catherine, entered the Carmelite convent at Firhouse, Tallaght, Co Dublin, in June 1856, the official record clearly stated that her parents were James Spratt and Esther Bollard.[13] Her second name was Mary: perhaps she had a third forename as Elizabeth or was known familiarly by that Christian name.

The parish records have no record of the year of Esther's birth but if her death notice is to be relied upon, she was 75 years old when she died in December 1836.[14] Presumably she was born in 1761 and would have been, therefore, three years younger than her husband James. These facts apart, almost nothing is known of her own parents or siblings, although one piece of evidence suggests that she probably had a brother, Richard.[15] As to her marriage to James, no record has yet been found to prove the date of this. O'Dwyer cites the marriage register of St Catherine's to state that they were married on 16th September 1792. However, the original of this register has no record of any such marriage on that date but instead, it records for that date the baptism of their second, and eldest surviving son, Michael.[16]

As for Michael, following marriage to his wife, Anna, they had at least five children: Michael junior was baptised on 22nd December 1825, James on 27th December 1827, Andrew on 9th May 1828; then two others followed, Eleanor and John, but their birth or baptismal dates are not yet known. As head of the family after James senior died in 1828, Michael lived at No. 105 Cork Street, next door to his mother and there ran the family tannery business. Over the years 1828 to 1830 he may have moved house, temporarily, for in those years he was listed as living at Rehoboth Place, at Dolphin's Barn, off the South Circular

---

12. Ibid, 6th February 1823, 18th September 1824 respectively.
13. Carmelite Monastery, Firhouse, *Archives*, reception of Catherine Spratt on 8th June 1856.
14. *DEP*, 3rd Dec 1836.
15. Richard Bollard is listed as godfather to Michael Spratt on his baptism on 16th September 1792 : DDA, St Catherine's Parish Registers, *Baptisms from April 1781 to February 1794*.
16. O'Dwyer, *Irish Carmelites*, p. 244, note 23. The extant Catholic and Church of Ireland Parish registers for the period 1770-1820 have no record of the marriage of James Spratt and Esther Bollard.

Road. Indeed, in 1830, his mother Esther is listed as living with him and his family at this address. However, by 1832 at least, Esther was back at No. 104 and Michael back next door.[17] Following Esther's death in 1836 Michael remained at No. 105 until 1838. The further details of Michael senior's life feature significantly in the main text of this work, so suffice it to say here that he and John were followed in the list of family births by their first sister Mary Ann, who was born probably circa 1798. When in 1818 she married Joseph Vickers, this was done by licence. Whether or not this was because there may have been a significant property settlement involved or because the marriage was one of mixed denominations is not evident from the extant records, but all of the children of this marriage were baptised in the Catholic Church.[18] Out of this Spratt-Vickers marriage came six children: James in 1821, Richard in 1823, Nicholas in 1824, Catherine in 1826 and also Joseph and Elizabeth whose dates are not evident. The Vickers (or Vicars) had been tallow chandlers of Francis Street for close on a century up to 1848 when apparently they ceased to trade, at least under that name. One ancestor, William Vickers, had been a tallow chandler in Francis Street from at least 1767 to 1791 and had previously been a tanner from the early 1760s at least. He was succeeded in 1791 by Robert Vickers, presumably his son, who plied his trade in his own name down to 1843. Thereafter, the business appeared as Vickers & Co. Chandlers until 1848, after which year it disappeared from the trade directories. The marriage link between the two families was very much one between related trades.

Following Mary Ann, the next-born was Catherine, in 1800. Nothing is known of her life until she entered the Carmelite Convent at Firhouse in County Dublin in 1856. Then came James, born in 1803. In 1827 he was received into the Augustinian Order, for the Dublin friary and then entered the novitiate in Rome, taking his simple vows in

---

17.  J. S. Folds, *The Post Office Annual Directory for 1832*, p. 208; for 1833, p. 232; and *Pettigrew & Oulton, 1834*, p. 39. Interestingly, there was by 1836 a Carmelite Convent and School catering for 300 pupils in Rehoboth: *SNL*, 26th Oct 1839 records a bequest of £30 'for the use of the convent at Rehoboth' from one James Barrett, late of Baggot Street'.

18.  Registry of Deeds, Year 1818, *Licence no. 518*. Unfortunately, the Registry has no record of any property settlement involving Mary Ann Spratt and/or Joseph Vickers.

1828.[19] In or around 1829 he was ordained and began his philosophy studies in the town of Fermo, in the Marché on the Italian east coast. In 1830 he was appointed to the Augustinian Priory of Santa Maria in Posterula, Rome, and was elected prior there in 1834 at the age of 28 – not quite emulating John who had been 27 when elected Carmelite Prior in Dublin in 1823. James was actually on a rare visit home to Dublin in 1834 when he was summoned back to Rome to become Prior of Posterula.[20] He therefore missed the deaths and funerals of his father and mother. He returned to Dublin in the early 1840s. From 1843 to 1851 Battersby's and Thom's Directories feature his name as a member of the John's Lane Augustinian community. It is likely that he returned to Italy in the latter year but he reappeared in the national press from 1857 and in the directories from 1858.[21] He then remained on in the Dublin friary until his death on 6th June 1879.

In regard to their youngest sister, she was baptised simply as Esther Spratt, in April 1806.[22] Yet, when she died at the early age of thirty-four in late 1840, she was described as *'Eliza, daughter of the late James Spratt, Esq., of Cork Street'.*[23] Her two Christian names, appearing in different contexts, therefore replicated those of her mother. At some point, in the 1820s or earlier 1830s perhaps, she moved to Monkstown. Unmarried, it is possible she worked there in some capacity for one of the two families in the Church Street brewing partnership of Andrew and Michael Thunder. Describing themselves betimes as *'Brewers to His Excellency the Lord Lieutenant of Ireland'* they had established themselves in two fine mansions, by the mid-1830s. Michael lived at 'Windsor' and Andrew at 'Ashton Park'.[24] Andrew was undoubtedly a family friend: in 1827 he acted as godfather and sponsor to Fr. John's nephew, James, son of John's older brother, Michael. The co-sponsor with Andrew was Eliza Spratt.[25] When Eliza passed away at the age of 34 in 1840 her

19. DDA, *Cullen Papers*, 332/7/29 & 30, James Spratt, OSA, by Archbishop Cullen, 11th Aug 1855.
20. Ibid.
21. *FJ*, 2nd Sept 1857 reports his role in the Triduum ceremonies for the Feast of St Augustine, 28th August.
22. DDA, St Catherine's RC Parish Register, *Baptisms from April 1781 to February 1794*, under date 8th April 1806.
23. *DMR*, 2nd Nov 1840.
24. S. Lewis, *A Topographical Dictionary of Ireland*, 2 vols., 1837, i. 390.
25. www.Irishgenealogy.ie, RC Parish of St James, July 1827

death notice stated that she died in Monkstown.[26]

So much for the birth or baptismal dates of John, his parents and siblings, it remains to note that because of conflicting versions of the date of his own birth, it is hardly surprising that his age at death is also a subject of divergent accounts. His death certificate gave his age, wrongly, as 73, stating that he died of disease of the heart, of unknown duration.[27] Having interred him in Glasnevin, the cemetery officials entered his age incorrectly as 73, as per the brass plate on his coffin; they corrected that record on 27th June 1873, on receipt of his baptismal certificate, and now entered his age as 75.[28] Indeed, errors about John Spratt's age abounded. Reporting on his death, *Saunders' Newsletter* thought he was *'about eighty years of age'*.[29] Sir Dominic Corrigan was categoric in insisting that Spratt was 81.[30] The *Dublin Shipping and Mercantile Gazette* repeated the oft-stated misconception that he was born in 1798, making him 73, as stated on his official death certificate which had been testified to by confrere, Fr McGee.[31] His friend Battersby, who claimed to have known him well, stated that John was 77.[32] Presumably it was John's brother, Fr James, who produced the baptismal certificate for the cemetery authorities, though why he himself did not correct the mistake at the time of John's funeral is a mystery.

26. *DMR*, 2nd Nov 1840: "Deaths ...at Monkstown, Eliza, daughter of the late James Spratt, Esq., of Cork Street".

27. Registry of Births, Marriages and Deaths, Dublin, *Death Certificate of John Spratt*, 7th June 1871.

28. Glasnevin Cemetery Archives, Dublin Cemeteries Committee, *Register of Interments*, vol. 9, p. 61.

29. *Saunders' Newsletter*, 29th May 1871.

30. *EF*, 26th June 1871.

31. *Dublin Shipping and Mercantile Gazette*, 30th May 1871.

32. W. J. Battersby, *Authentic Life and Acts of the Very Rev Dr Spratt*, Dublin 1871, p. 14.

# APPENDIX 2

---

## *The Catholic Church in Dublin in an age of repression and reconstruction, c. 1740-1840*

The Catholic Church in Dublin diocese and Dublin city had been well served in cautious progress by its two long-serving archbishops, John Carpenter (1769-1786) and John Thomas Troy (1786-1823).[1] Under them, great strides were made in the improvement of clerical discipline and in introducing the rigours of Roman observance. However, apart from the problems of a still hostile political and religious environment, they faced a great challenge in the rapid growth of population and in finding an adequate supply of priests and churches. This situation was hardly unique for the Catholic Church in Ireland or in Dublin city. Throughout the western world the population explosion of the eighteenth and nineteenth centuries posed a daunting challenge for all Christian denominations. As to Ireland, in 1770 some 1,600 priests served a population of 2.65 million – a ratio of 1 to 1656: by the year 1800 this had deteriorated to a situation whereby 1,860 priests served a population of 4.2 million – a ratio of 1 to 2,260. Despite strenuous efforts, the situation continued to worsen, at least until the Great Famine. By 1840 the Catholic Church had 2,400 priests serving a population of 6.6 million – a ratio of 1 to 2,750. Put in another way, over the forty years from 1800 the number of priests rose by 35%

---

1. H. Fenning, 'The Archbishops of Dublin, 1693-1786' in J. Kelly & D. Keogh, pp. 175-214 and D. Keogh, 'The pattern of the flock: John Thomas Troy, 1786-1823' in ibid., pp. 215-236.

whereas the population rose by over 50%.[2] As Larkin put it, in respect of Ireland as a whole:

> a ratio of one priest to 1,660 people in 1770 already represented a heavy pastoral load, and the increase of that load by 66 per cent to 2,750 in 1840, simply turned a very difficult situation into a virtually impossible one.[3]

In Dublin the demographic change dramatically altered the relative strength of Catholic and Protestant persuasions. By the early 1730s Dublin had become a predominantly Protestant city, with three Protestants for every two Catholics. By 1750 the situation was reversing and by the mid-1760s, when the entire city's population was around 145,000, there were three Catholics for every two Protestants. That disparity intensified over the next century.[4] As for the diocese of Dublin where there were 169 priests for 255,000 people in 1800 – a ratio of 1 to 1,509, by 1840 there were 195 priests for 401,000 people – a ratio of 1 to 2,056.[5] However, the latter was a more than favourable ratio compared with the national average of 1 per 2,676 circa 1800. Yet remarkably, with the church emerging from the penal era, Dublin ratios, as Sean Connolly has indicated, had deteriorated from the situation prevailing at the height of the penal regime: in 1731 the national average was 1 priest to 1,587 Catholics.[6] On the eve of the Great Famine the ratio had deteriorated further at 1 to 2,996. While the opening of Carlow College in 1793 and Maynooth College as a seminary in 1795 helped a stressful situation from being even worse, this was for a time offset

2.  E. Larkin, *The Pastoral Role of the Roman Catholic Church in Pre-Famine Ireland, 1750-1850*, Dublin 2006, p. 9., D. J. Keenan, *The Catholic Church in Nineteenth-Century Ireland: a Sociological Study*, Dublin 1983, p. 59; S. Connolly, *Religion and Society in Nineteenth-Century Ireland*, reprint ed., Dublin 1994, pp. 56-57; T. Inglis, *Moral Monopoly: the Catholic Church in Modern Irish Society*, Dublin 1987, p. 117.
3.  E. Larkin, 'Before the devotional revolution', in J. H. Murphy, ed., *Evangelicals and Catholics in Nineteenth-Century Ireland*, Dublin 2005, p. 17.
4.  P. Fagan, 'The population of Dublin in the eighteenth century with particular reference to the proportions of Catholics and Protestants', *Eighteenth Century Ireland*, vol. 6, 1991, pp. 140-143, 156. See also H. Fenning, 'The Archbishops of Dublin', p. 203.
5.  Larkin, p. 271.
6.  S. J. Connolly, *Priests and People in Pre-Famine Ireland, 1780-1845*, Dublin 1982, pp. 32-33.

by the revolutionary upheavals on the continent which closed the Irish seminaries there. The deteriorating ratio of priests to parishioners was, perhaps, counterbalanced by the growing discipline, zeal and efficiency of the clergy in the century from 1770. As Larkin summarised it:

> the response of the Irish Church was both impressive and imaginative. Impressive because the Church did increase the total number of clergy by more than 1000 between 1770 and 1845, provided nearly 2,000 chapels between 1790 and 1845, reformed the conduct and behaviour of the clergy over the same period, and created virtually a new seminary system that by 1845 supplied the Church with some 100 priests annually.[7]

Within the urban and rural diocese of Dublin a very great deal was accomplished in terms of clerical discipline and pastoral care by Archbishops Carpenter and Troy. When Troy took up his episcopal challenge in 1786, his diocese had 45 parishes, 9 of them in the city of Dublin. He had some 100 priests in the city and 54 in the rural parts of his diocese. Under Troy and his successors, Murray and Cullen, the diocese experienced an unprecedented expansion of activity: by 1864 the number of parishes had risen to 50, the number of churches built between 1800 and 1864 was 119, together with 41 convents, 15 hospitals and 10 colleges and seminaries.[8]

---

7. E. Larkin, pp. 5, 150-151. See also B. Grimes, 'Funding a Roman Catholic Church in Nineteenth-Century Ireland', *Architectural History*, vol. 52, 2009, pp. 147-168.
8. M. O'Reilly, *Progress of Catholicity in Ireland in the Nineteenth Century*, Dublin 1865, p. 33. See also B. Grimes, *Commodious Temples: Roman Catholic Church building in nineteenth century Dublin*, Dublin 2010, p. 9.

## APPENDIX 3

---

## *The Carmelites of New Row and Ash Street, Dublin, in the 18th century*

As they began their gradual return from the continent the first settlement of the Calced Carmelites may have been in New Row. The southern end of this street linked Blackpitts to the Coombe. Below and beside New Row there flowed the Blackpitts River, a tributary of the Poddle. It was a street in an area of tanners and weavers, brewers and distillers, dwelling in some cases in tall, gable-ended 'Dutch Billy' houses, at one stage homes to prosperous manufacturing families.[1] It was here in New Row in the year 1677 that the Dublin Quakers first set up their Meeting House. However, the noise and unpleasant surroundings led them to abandon it as a place of worship and, instead, they leased it out as a warehouse, from November 1686.[2]

It was over forty years later, in 1728, that one Francis Lehy, *'a friar of the Mitigated Carmelite Order'*, took up a lease on this warehouse as the first Post-Reformation home for his Dublin Carmelites: so it was asserted in a report of an investigation into Roman Catholic Chapels

---

1. J. W. deCourcy, *The Liffey in Dublin*, Dublin 1996, pp. 306, 405; D. Dickson, *Dublin: the making of a capital city*, Dublin 2014, p. 91; C. Lennon, *Irish Historic Towns Atlas: No.19, Dublin, Part II, 1610-1756*, Dublin 2008, p. 6; P. Pearson, *The Heart of Dublin: resurgence of a historic city*, Dublin 2000, pp. 219, 223, 272; J. Prunty, *Dublin Slums 1800-1925: a study in Urban Geography*, Dublin 1998, p. 52.

2. R. L. Greaves, *Dublin's Merchant Quaker: Anthony Sharp and the Community of Friends, 1643-1707*, Stanford, 1998, p. 151; T. Wight & J. Rutty, *A History of the Rise and Progress of People called Quakers in Ireland from the year 1653 to 1700*, Dublin 1751, pp. 344-346; D. M. Butler, *The Quaker Meeting Houses of Ireland*, Dublin 2004, pp. 45-46.

in Dublin in the year 1749.[3] The locating of Catholic friaries, chapels
and churches in former warehouses and stables was not uncommon in
earlier eighteenth-century Dublin.[4] How long the Carmelites stayed in
New Row is uncertain. The 1749 *Report* conveys the impression that
it was vacated almost immediately after Fr Lehy had taken possession
of it; and in an appendix to his own edition of this *Report*, Nicholas
Donnelly implies that they left in the same year, 1728, as they had
come.[5] The explanation given by the 1749 *Report*'s author was that *'being
reproved for his indiscretion in taking the Meeting House, which might have given
offence to his superiors, he quitted it'*.[6] Following Nuala Burke's view on this,
David Butler, in his *Quaker Meeting Houses in Ireland*, commented that

> a continental visitor suggested to the Friars that the past Quaker
> connection could give offence to the religious superiors of the
> Order, upon which they left the building.[7]

Certainly, there was no love lost between Quakers and Catholics in early
eighteenth-century Dublin, to judge from the fact that the Quakers'
new Meeting House in Meath Street was attacked and sacked by an irate
Catholic crowd in 1720.[8]

However, in a report of the year 1731 on 'the State of Popery in
Ireland', the Vicar of St Catherine's, the Rev Henry Echlin, mentioned
that *'one [other] mass house is at the bottom of New Row near where Wormwood
Gate stood and belongs to Fryars Carmelite'*. His report noted that these
premises catered for seven priests, *'six of whom are resident in the parish'*,
and he added that *'the said Mass house has been lately rebuilt and enlarged'*.

---

3. N. Donnelly, ed., *Roman Catholics: State and Condition of Roman Catholic Chapels in Dublin both Secular and Regular A.D. 1749*, Dublin 1904, p. 17. This account erroneously states that the New Row premises were vacated by the Quakers upon their moving to Eustace Street at that time – but, as noted earlier, the Friends had abandoned it as a Meeting House forty-two years earlier. O'Dwyer, p. 129 follows Donnelly in this misconception.
4. N. Burke, 'A hidden church'? The structure of Catholic Dublin in the mid-eighteenth century', *Archivium Hibernicum*, vol. 31, 1974, pp. 86-87.
5. Donnelly, p. 37, Note N.
6. Ibid, p. 17; Burke, p. 90.
7. Butler, op.cit., p. 46, citing *The Journal of the Friends Historical Society*, 1975, p. 380.
8. P. Fagan, 'The Dublin Catholic Mob, 1700-1750', *Eighteenth Century Ireland*, vol. 4, 1989, p. 134.

It is possible, however, that he was actually referring to a friary of the Discalced Carmelites who by the early eighteenth century were said to have been located in or near the place called Wormwood Gate.[9] What threatens confusion here is the fact that in eighteenth century Dublin, according to Rocque's map of 1756 and Taylor's map of 1816 there were two New Rows, or, a single New Row, separated by the length of Francis Street: the southern section housing the Quaker Meeting House and Calced Carmelite community, and the northern one housing the Discalced Carmelites at Wormwoodgate.[10]

This might well explain how, in that same source of the year 1731, the curates and churchwardens of the Church of Ireland Parish of St Nicholas Without reported in November, that

> there is another large Mass-house or Friary erected in Ash-Street in the said Parish, since his present Majesties [sic] accession to the throne to which seven priests or Friars belong, and that several others, as we are informed, officiate in it.[11]

It is clear enough that however long or short their location in New Row may have been, by the early 1730s the Calced Carmelites were certainly established in Ash Street, a short walk away across to the other side of the Coombe. At one stage in their time there, in the early 1740s, they found themselves coming to the aid of the local parish priest of St Nicholas, Fr Richard Lincoln. Over the period 1742-1748, a dispute between himself and the local Franciscans over control of the Church of St Nicholas of Myra, forced him to say Mass for six months *'at the Carmelite Chapel which is in this parish'*. With the support of his archbishop, Fr Lincoln eventually triumphed. What his triumph accomplished for relations between the Ash Street Franciscans and Carmelites is not evident.[12]

---

9.  J. P. Rushe, *Carmel in Ireland: a narrative of the Irish Province of Teresian or Discalced Carmelites, A.D. 1625-1896*, Dublin 1903, p. 142.
10. Lennon, Map 16.
11. 'Report on the State of Popery in Ireland, 1731, *Archivium Hibernicum*, vol. 4, 1915, p. 146.
12. C. Giblin, 'Ten documents relating to diocesan affairs, 1740-1784, from Franciscan Library, Killiney', *Collectanea Hibernica*, No. 20, 1978, pp. 61-68.

*Priors and Friars*

Little enough is currently known as to who precisely were the members of this Ash Street Friary. There is no succession list of the Priors of Ash Street: the names of some have come down but few enough of them perhaps. James of St Bernard appears to have been Prior of the Discalced at Wormwood Gate at the time of John Garzia's *Report* of 1722, and O'Dwyer records that Francis Leahy [otherwise Lahy or Lehy] took possession of the Calced New Row Friary in 1728.[13] In 1741, following upon the first Irish Provincial Chapter since the Reformation, Matthew Lyons was elected Prior, in succession to Eugene Swiney whose own career was somewhat unusual: in 1750 he became a clergyman of the Church of Ireland, *'persecuted the Order for ten years'*, came back to the fold and was sent out to Spain.[14] Lyons had been Commissary General of the Irish Province circa 1729, with a brief to secure recruits and to recover Irish friaries which had been lost to the Order. Six years later, in 1737, when the Irish Province was fully restored, he became Provincial. In the following year he attended the General Chapter of the Order under Prior General Benzoni. It is not clear at this point how long Matthew Lyons held the office of Prior. Almost certainly he was Prior when in May 1739 he signed a thirty-one year lease for Ash Street which he secured from the Meath Street merchant and property owner, Samuel Onge.[15] The next holder of the position as is currently evident was the colourful Francis Mannin, subsequently Provincial. Indeed there now began an era when he and his confrere, Peter Bermingham, would alternate in offices between Provincial of Ireland and Prior of Dublin, well into the mid-1770s. They may well have been close friends for both had been trained in Spain, receiving Minor Orders together and being ordained together in Barcelona in 1741. Following his ordination, Mannin had asked to be allowed to proceed to France or Germany to study dogmatic theology in order to strengthen his preparation for the Irish Mission. The authorities in Catalonia and Rome were not

---

13. K. MacGrath, 'John Garzia, a noted priest-catcher and his activities, 1717-1723', *Irish Ecclesiastical Record*, vol. 72, Dec 1949, p. 512.
14. O'Dwyer, pp. 130, 135. No other details of Eugene Swiney have yet come to hand and his name appears under various spellings in the different sources.
15. Registry of Deeds, *Book 94*, p. 341, No. 66611, Memorial of lease dated 16th May 1739, between Samuel Onge and Matthew Lyons & Owen Swiney. One of the witnesses to this was Robert Lyons.

persuaded, and, unfairly or not, felt that he and his Irish confrere were more interested in travel and in independent living than in returning to Ireland. Return they did, however, and Mannin went on to become a distinguished Provincial of the Order until his death, aged about 65, in October 1775.[16] During the 1760s he worked hard to try to secure a novitiate house on the continent to ensure the survival of the Order in Ireland. His alternating successor, Bermingham, survived him by at least a decade. Bermingham had been disappointed in the expectation of becoming a bishop, a role for which Mannin had recommended him: but, with Archbishop Carpenter's failure to support this, he would live with the consolation of being Provincial for an extensive period, from 1768 until 1778, following a previous term over the years 1756-1762. Bermingham was Prior of Ash Street, probably over the period 1762-1768, again in the mid-1770s and finally in the mid-1780s. By that stage another two young, Spanish-educated Carmelites had returned to Ireland and were destined to hold office as Dublin Priors and Irish Provincials, Thomas O'Mahony and James [O'] Farrell. They were both assigned to Ash Street on their return. O'Mahony was elected Provincial for the years 1788 to 1792, during which time O'Farrrell was Prior of Ash Street. He later then became Provincial from 1792 to 1805. In the later 1780s Fr John Neilan was Prior, certainly so from at least 1787 until 1791.

One of the key concerns of the Order was that of questing or fundraising and Fr Neilan, like most of his community, was active in the seeking of alms over the wider Dublin region. Community member William Barry, from 1798 to 1805, was one of the most energetic of the Ash Street friars in this regard, as was Fr Thomas Finny from 1797. Fr Neilan's successor as Prior was Fr Michael Molloy who held the office from 1791 until 1805. In the latter year he was elected Provincial and remained in the post until 1813, and died in January 1815.[17] The last Prior of Ash Street was Richard Cosgrave who was in office from 1805 until 1808 at least. It was, therefore, on his watch that the historic move from Ash Street to French Street was made. Described by the press as

16. O'Dwyer, pp. 135, 146-150, 154, 159, 161. Mannin was one of those who took the Oath of Allegiance which would have been in or about 1774 where it was stated that he was then 65 years of age. See R. Walsh, 'A list of Ecclesiastics who took the Oath of Allegiance', *Archivium Hibernicum*, vol. 1, 1912, pp. 62, 46-76.

17. GMA, *Ash Street Account Book*, p. 83; O'Dwyer, p. 163-4.

*'innocent and harmless during life, sincere in his attachments and hospitable from principle'*, he was only fifty two when he died in French Street on 12th March 1816.[18]

---

18. *FJ.*, 13th March 1816, cited in O'Dwyer, p. 243, n. 16.

# APPENDIX 4

---

## *The Burials Dispute in the 1820s and after*

*An unfortunate episode*

On Sunday 7th September 1823 a well-known young Dublin man, Arthur D'Arcy, of the family who owned the Anchor Brewery, died following a fall from his horse on the previous Thursday. Although a Catholic, his funeral and burial were to take place in the Church of Ireland parish graveyard of St Kevin's, in Camden Row. Burial of Catholics in Church of Ireland graveyards had for long been the custom in the city - and elsewhere in the country - since the Catholics had no cemetery of their own. Under the penal laws, they were forbidden to have the Catholic funeral service and prayers conducted aloud by their priests in vestments, in Church of Ireland graveyards. In consequence, and by custom, their priests, without formal attire or ceremony, simply uttered a few quiet prayers and the relatives of the deceased paid the appropriate fees to the Church of Ireland parish authorities.

Arthur D'Arcy was taken for burial to St Kevin's on Tuesday 9th September. As the funeral party gathered, Dr Michael Blake, Catholic Priest of St Michael's & St John's in Exchange Street, removing his hat, was about to say a few words when Sexton Dunn of St Kevin's, intervened to tell him to desist. According to Blake, and to Arthur D'Arcy's close friends, he was told '*I must not offer any prayer over that grave'*. On asking by whose authority Dunn commanded this, he was told that it was by order of Dr Magee, the Church of Ireland Archbishop of Dublin. Blake then whispered to those standing nearby, including

544

Arthur D'Arcy's friends, John and Denis Redmond of Rathmines,[1] that he had been prohibited from saying any prayers and advised the immediate mourners to say their own silent prayers for the deceased. They then dispersed quietly, the vast majority of the funeral entourage being unaware, at first, of what had just transpired.

However, it did not take long before the incident blew up into a major storm of mutual recrimination between Catholic and Church of Ireland spokesmen. The unfortunate Archbishop Magee, only recently installed Protestant Archbishop, was completely unaware of what had transpired, he at that time visiting a sick relative in England. Further, his Archdeacon, the Minister of St Kevin's, John Torrens, confirmed that he had never received any instructions on the matter from Archbishop Magee and that he himself had not assigned any specific instructions to Sexton Dunn in respect of Arthur D'Arcy's funeral. He clarified that the Sexton was acting according *'to former longstanding regulations which prohibited any clergyman from officiating in a church-yard, without the express permission of the Incumbent, and that this permission could only be granted to clergy of the Established Church'.*[2] However, Magee very soon became caught up in the vortex of recrimination caused by the zeal of his St Kevin's sexton. The fiasco of the funeral of Arthur D'Arcy lit a fuse that led to an explosion over the rights and wrongs of what became known as the Burials Question. The incident went all the way up to the House of Lords and resulted in attempts at burials legislation that sought to prevent similar disputes in future.[3] Such disputes continued however – a similar unfortunate episode occurred in Youghal in April 1824,[4] while a year later, the well-known Catholic Priest, Dr William Yore, was prohibited from reciting prayers at the burial in St Mark's Churchyard of a Mr Bergin of Essex Street.[5] In October 1829 a Mrs O'Brien, a

---

1. *FJ*, 24th Sept, citing Michael Blake to Editor, *The Evening Herald*, on 18th Sept 1823. See also *FJ*, 9th Sept, 8th, 13th, 17th Oct 1823.

2. FJ, 20th Apr 1824, John Torrens, Archdeacon of Dublin, to the editor of *The Courier*, 13th April 1824.

3. There is no detailed recent treatment of this issue but W. J. Fitzpatrick, *History of the Dublin Catholic Cemeteries*, Dublin 1900, pp. 2-16 and M. Ronan, *Apostle of Catholic Dublin: Father Henry Young*, Dublin 1944, pp. 114-116, provide the most detailed accounts. See also F. O'Ferrall, *Catholic Emancipation*, p. 49; T. McGrath, *Public Ministry of Bishop James Doyle*, pp. 119-121.

4. *FJ*, 1st May 1824.

5. *FJ*, 5th March 1825.

Catholic of Marlborough Street, died and her funeral took place to St Thomas's Churchyard. When the mourning party were informed that no funeral service would be permitted within the precincts, they stopped the procession, conducted the Catholic funeral service in the street and then processed into the graveyard for the interment.[6]

The eruption of the Burials Question was significant on several counts. It increased interdenominational tensions at the very time when the evangelical revival was sweeping into Ireland. It gave the Catholic Association the gift of a grievance that aided it in its efforts to mobilise Catholics, lay and clerical alike. There followed, not long after, the adoption of the penny-a month 'Catholic Rent' as a way of recruiting the mass of the Catholic lay and clerical populations in the quest for Catholic Emancipation. By contributing to what Bartlett has called *'the grievance apparatus of the Catholic Association'*,[7] it intensified the thrust for parliamentary representation. Most immediately, it caused a flurry of activity at Westminster that led to hurried and, in the end, ineffectual remedial legislation – the unfortunately misnamed Easement of Burials Bill.

---

6. *FJ*, 10th Oct 1825. As late as 1838 another conflict over Catholic funeral rites in a Church of Ireland graveyard occurred in relation to Derry Cathedral. See *FJ*, 6th Apr 1838.
7. T. Bartlett, *The Fall and Rise of the Irish Nation: The Catholic Question, 1690-1830*, Dublin 1992, pp. 332-333.

# Appendix 5

## The Penal Clauses of the Catholic Relief Act, 1829 [1]

Clause XXVIII:

And whereas Jesuits, and members of other religious orders, communities, or societies of the Church of Rome, bound by monastic or religious vows, are resident within the United Kingdom; and it is expedient to make provision for the gradual suppression and the final prohibition of the same therein: Be it therefore enacted, that every Jesuit and every member of any other religious order, community, or society of the Church of Rome, bound by monastic or religious vows, who at the time of the commencement of this Act shall be within the United Kingdom, shall within six calendar months of the commencement of this Act deliver to the clerk of the peace of the county or place where such person shall reside, or to his deputy, a notice or statement in the form and containing the particulars required to be set forth in the schedule to this Act annexed...and in case any person shall offend... he shall forfeit and pay to His Majesty, for every calendar month during which he shall remain in the United Kingdom without having delivered such notice or statement as is herein-before required, the sum of fifty pounds.

Clause XXIX:

if any Jesuit, or member of any such religious order, community,

---

1. *Public General Statutes: 10 George IV. c.7: An Act for the Relief of His Majesty's Roman Catholic Subjects.*

or society as aforesaid, shall, after the commencement of this Act, come in to this realm, he shall be deemed and taken to be guilty of a misdemeanour, and, being thereof lawfully convicted, shall be sentenced and ordered to be banished from the United Kingdom for the term of his natural life.

Clause XXXIII:

And be it further enacted, that in case any Jesuit, or member of any such religious order, community, or society as aforesaid, shall, after the commencement of this Act, within any part of the United Kingdom, admit any person to become a regular ecclesiastic, or brother or member of any such religious order, community, or society, or be aiding or consenting thereto, or shall administer or cause to be administered, or be aiding or assisting in the administering or taking, any oath, vow or engagement purporting or intended to bind the person taking the same to the rules, ordinances, or ceremonies of such religious order, community, or society, every person offending in the premises in England and Ireland shall be deemed guilty of a misdemeanour, and in Scotland shall be punished by fine and imprisonment.

Clause XXXIV:

…..in case any person shall, after the commencement of this Act, within any part of the United Kingdom, be admitted or become a Jesuit, or brother or member of any other such religious order, community, or society as aforesaid, such person shall be deemed and taken to be guilty of a misdemeanour, and being thereof lawfully convicted shall be sentenced and ordered to be banished from the United Kingdom for the term of his natural life.

# APPENDIX 6

---

## *The Carmelite and other Schools of the Whitefriar Street neighbourhood in the 1820s: some problems of evidence*

An examination of the extant evidence in regard to schools in St Peter's Parish in the period 1800 to 1830 unearths a surprisingly complex, even confusing situation especially in the 1820s. The Church of Ireland had no day school in St Peter's and only one such school for boys in the neighbouring parish of St Brigid's, to judge by the evidence of parliamentary commissions and returns in the 1820s. In 1821 St Peter's only had one school for Protestant children, a boarding establishment of some thirty to forty girls: the annual income of this, some £560, was provided by private subscription and charity sermons. However the local Church of Ireland authorities, in a parliamentary return of 26th February 1823, declared that they intended to establish a parochial school and a Sunday school *'with as little delay as possible'.*[1]

As for Catholic educational provision in St Peter's Parish and neighbourhood, the situation appears complex, even confusing: leaving aside the Carmelite Cuffe Lane School founded circa 1806-1808, whose later history is not known, from 1820 there were two and possibly four, schools. Firstly, there was St Patrick's General Free School in Cuffe Lane, founded by the Carmelites in 1820, and taught by laymen James Crowe and Michael Dallagher: between them they earned £55 per annum for their labours. They catered for some 200-300 pupils, some paying a few pence, the others free, in a schoolhouse whose condition in 1826, was described as *'very bad'*. Next, close by, in a room in a lodging house there was St Peter's French Street Chapel School catering for between 87 and

---

1. Parliamentary Papers, H. C. 1823 (229), *Accounts relating to diocesan and parish schools in Ireland in 1821*, pp. 52-23.

549

110 children, taught by one Anne Ellis for as little as 7 shillings and 7 pence a week.[2] Like its neighbouring St Patrick's, it was partly free and partly funded from the pennies of the poor scholars.[3] Separately from these, or so it would seem, was St Peter's Orphan Institution of Cuffe Lane where, in 1826, a house was rented by the Carmelites but not yet converted by them into a schoolhouse: pending completion of which the children were fostered out to the country. This orphan institution was created by or cared for by the French Street Carmelite Confraternity of the Blessed Virgin Mary. In the middle of the 1820s it cared for some 44 orphans at an annual cost of £250, obtained by subscription and charity sermon. It was described as being located in St Andrew's Parish – and presumably this referred to the Catholic Parish of St Andrew's of which French Street, or Upper Mercer Street, was a part. Finally there was a fourth, Carmelite-sponsored school, St Patrick's Free School of Redmond's Hill. It consisted of *'a spacious room'* in a house on Redmond's Hill, rented at a cost of 3s 4d per week: a large room, presumably, it was described as catering for 100 pupils and, reportedly, was taught by one Anne Elliott for £22 per year, her salary provided by the *'subscriptions of a few pious individuals'*, with some of the scholars contributing one penny a week.[4] It is conceivable that this entity was one and the same as the 'French Street Chapel School' taught by Anne Ellis: perhaps the two 'Annes' were one and the same person, these apparent separate identities simply being an error of transcription or misprint in the parliamentary return: each occupied a large room in a house and the 7s 7d a week paid to one was close to the £22 per year paid to the other. The only problem with this suggestion is their apparently distinct addresses, the one at Redmond's Hill, the other at French Street Chapel – unless the latter was just an eponymous or generalised address.

Farrington states that John had established his (first) school in the year 1822, in Great Longford Street, but that its number of pupils grew

2. The average wage for a Dublin city labourer at that time would have been 10 to 12 shillings a week, and for a tradesman such as a carpenter, some 50 shillings a week. See F. A. D'Arcy, 'Wages of labourers in the Dublin Building Industry, 1667-1918', *Saothar*, 14, 1989, pp. 17-34, and 'Wages of Skilled Workers in the Dublin Building Industry, 1667-1918', *Saothar*, 15, 1990, pp. 21-38.
3. Parliamentary Papers, H. C. 1826-7 (12), *Second Report of the Commissions of Irish Education Inquiry*, p. 102.
4. Ibid, p. 100.

so rapidly that, in 1824, he moved it to Whitefriar Street. O'Dwyer is sceptical about this, speculating that John, just back from Spain, was hardly in a position to have established a school as quickly as the year 1822. It can now be added that nowhere in the manuscript volume, *Accounts of Whitefriar Street Church and Schools*, is there any mention of the location 'Longford Street', nor is there any mention of this location for the school in any of the newspapers nor in any of the Dublin trade and street directories for the 1820s and 1830s.[5] The school in Longford Street is not mentioned either in any of the parliamentary papers of the period: what is mentioned, in both a parliamentary return of 1831-32 and in the *First Report of the Commissioners for inquiring into the condition of the poorer classes in Ireland*, in 1836, in a table of Roman Catholic Female Daily Schools within the City of Dublin, is a Mount Carmel School for Girls, *'founded 1824'*, and which, in 1836, had 176 girls on the rolls and 125 in daily attendance, with 80 of them paying one penny a week. This may well have been the school for girls that the Carmelites had publicly expressed their hopes for at the charity dinner of October 1823. The name St Andrew's was retained until the year 1846 when Fr John got the approval of the Commissioners to change its name to St Peter's Female National School.[6] Perplexingly, in a corresponding table of 'Male Daily Schools within the City of Dublin' there is no mention of any Carmelite school for boys.[7]

If Farrington were correct in stating that John had established his (first) school in the year 1822, in Great Longford Street, it is conceivable that his school or 'schools' were housed originally in some of the several lodging houses of Great or Little Longford Street but even the evidence of contemporary maps is of no help in this matter. The only extant Carmelite evidence is the manuscript financial account for John Spratt's school, the earliest entries for which are for the year 1824, but interestingly, this source never mentions the name 'Longford Street'.[8]

---

5. Farrington, p. 116; O'Dwyer, *Dissertation*, p. 54; GMA, *Accounts of Whitefriar Street Church and Schools*, p. 91.

6. See p. 11 below.

7. Parl. Papers, H. C. 1831-32 (445), *A Return of the number of applications to the Board of Education for new schools under their system, or for assistance in behalf of schools already established*, p. 10; *Appendix to the First Report of the Commissioners for inquiring into the condition of the Poorer Classes in Ireland*, p. 12aa, Table No. 9, and p. 11aa, Table 7, respectively.

8. GMA, *Accounts of Whitefriar Street Church and Schools*.

# APPENDIX 7

## Michael Thomas Spratt
## (1825-1885)

Born in 1825, eldest son of Michael and Anna, and Fr John's nephew, Michael Thomas Spratt, had as eventful a career as his father. As an eighteen-year-old, in 1843, he was collecting Daniel O'Connell's 'Repeal Rent' in Sandymount and was still doing so a year later.[1] At that stage, as a clerk in the Repeal Association, he became involved in an incident involving a forged £50 note. It transpires that a confidence trickster, John Coffey, had presented the note at the Association's offices, on the pretext of joining the Association and then securing the balance of £49 after deducting the membership fee. Young Michael Thomas took the man to a bank to have the transaction carried through. Here the forgery was discovered and both were detained by the police. Michael Thomas was originally charged but then released and the culprit was committed for trial.[2] Almost a decade later, now living in Wharton Terrace, Michael Thomas attended a demonstration of the Catholics of Ireland that had been organised by his uncle, Fr John, among others, to protest against a bill for the inquisitorial inspection of convents.[3] As for his occupation, he appears to have been a 'law clerk' or 'commission agent'. He was presented in such a capacity as acting in a land deal before the Encumbered Estates Court in 1853.[4] However, two years later, like his father, he appeared before the Insolvent Debtors Court

---

1. *DWN*, 2nd Sept 1843; *DWR*, 20nd July 1844.
2. *Statesman and Dublin Christian Record*, 18th June 1844; *DEM*, 21st June 1844. Interestingly, the only reports were carried by the anti-O'Connell, Conservative press.
3. *FJ*, 10th June 1853.
4. *Allnutt's Irish Land Schedule*, 15th Aug 1853.

where his various addresses coincided with those of the late Michael Spratt senior.[5] He had been, it appears, obtaining goods without paying for them and had been arrested. At a hearing in early May 1855 he offered to pay some of the debt in cash, up front, if the proceedings might be stayed. The case was adjourned for a fortnight but what transpired thereafter is not evident. Another misfortune followed. In December 1860, his wife Susan died in childbirth, aged only 30 years.[6] They already had at least one child at the time, two-year old Kathleen Mary Anne.[7] Michael Thomas emigrated to New Zealand, perhaps immediately after this. It was probably from here that he organised the tombstone in memory of his father, at Glasnevin. In 1870 he married an English widow, Maria Louisa Bell of Cockermouth, Cumbria, in St Joseph's Catholic Cathedral, Dunedin.[8] Within three years they had separated, with Michael Thomas declining responsibility for debts she was incurring. He went to live north of Dunedin, at Oamaru, was involved in a series of property dealings and legal disputes in the course of the 1870s, and died at his home there on 28th December 1885 at sixty years of age.[9] It is evident that he kept up some kind of contact with his homeland, as the death of his mother in 1870 was noticed in the Otago press.

---

5. *FJ*, 18th Apr 1855; *DEP*, 19th Apr 1855; *General Advertiser*, 21st Apr 1855.
6. The headstone gives her date of death as 29th December 1861, but the cemetery archives record her burial as on 31st December 1860.
7. Register of the Parish of St Andrew's, *Book 18*, p. 131, date of baptism, 5th August 1859.
8. *Otago Daily Times*, 19th Apr 1870.
9. For the marital trouble, see *Otago Daily Times*, 30th Jan 1873, case of Webb versus Spratt for recovery of debt. For his death notice, see *Otago Daily Times*, 29th Dec 1885. His age at death was given as 55, but he was, in fact, 60 years old, being baptised on 22nd December 1825: for this, see the Parish Register of St James' Catholic Church, Dublin, 22nd Dec 1825.

# APPENDIX 8

---

## *The Night Refuge: Weekly returns of the numbers of women and children accommodated*

**Table No 1:**  Weekly returns of the numbers of women and children, 5th Apr 1861 to 27 March 1862:

| Week Ending | Servants | Children | Overall total |
|---|---|---|---|
| 5th Apr | 346 | 290 | 963 |
| 12th Apr | 376 | 204 | 896 |
| 19th Apr | 387 | 148 | 850 |
| 26th Apr | 371 | 184 | 872 |
| 3rd May | 308 | 181 | 794 |
| 10th May | 373 | 162 | 726 |
| 17th May | 348 | 110 | 616 |
| 24th May | 366 | 146 | 688 |
| 30th May | 336 | 125 | 601 |
| 6th June | 368 | 140 | 658 |
| 13th June | 382 | 126 | 659 |
| 20th June | 341 | 123 | 595 |
| 27th June | 365 | 84 | 524 |
| 5th July | 236 | 42 | 384 |
| 12th July | 146 | 44 | 248 |
| 18th July | 186 | 49 | 263 |
| 25th July | 204 | 38 | 273 |
| 1 Aug | 163 | 41 | 250 |
| 8th Aug | 208 | 43 | 286 |

| Week Ending | Servants | Children | Overall total |
| --- | --- | --- | --- |
| 15th Aug | 180 | 24 | 240 |
| 22nd Aug | N/A | N/A | N/A |
| 29th Aug | 133 | 28 | 216 |
| 5th Sept | 132 | 34 | 206 |
| 12th Sept | 101 | 47 | 202 |
| 19th Sept | 116 | 32 | 209 |
| 26th Sept | 119 | 32 | 201 |
| 3rd Oct | 104 | 33 | 201 |
| 10th Oct | 136 | 26 | 219 |
| 17th Oct | 117 | 19 | 180 |
| 24th Oct | 140 | 38 | 254 |
| 31st Oct | 156 | 36 | 251 |
| 7th Nov | 161 | 30 | 236 |
| 14th Nov | 198 | 36 | 285 |
| 21st Nov | 187 | 40 | 278 |
| 28th Nov | 138 | 43 | 252 |
| 5th Dec | 197 | 65 | 365 |
| 12th Dec | 219 | 61 | 394 |
| 19th Dec | 253 | 71 | 477 |
| 26th Dec | 299 | 105 | 585 |
| 2nd Jan | 370 | 101 | 630 |
| 9th Jan | 405 | 96 | 664 |
| 16th Jan | 390 | 109 | 689 |
| 23rd Jan | 367 | 112 | 676 |
| 30th Jan | 390 | 132 | 796 |
| 6th Feb | 392 | 133 | 860 |
| 13th Feb | 361 | 148 | 836 |
| 20th Feb | 326 | 176 | 903 |
| 27th Feb | 406 | 160 | 1,002 |
| 6th March | 390 | 190 | 1,085 |
| 13th March | 434 | 189 | 1,041 |
| 20th March | 409 | 199 | 1,114 |
| 27th March | 490 | 208 | 1,142 |

**Table No 2:**   Weekly returns of the numbers of women and children, 6th May 1870 to 15th May 1871:

| | | | | |
|---|---|---|---|---|
| 6 May | 751 | | 20 Oct | 568 |
| 11 May | 720 | | 27 Oct | 532 |
| 19 May | 745 | | 3 Nov | 575 |
| 26 May | 750 | | 10 Nov | 607 |
| 2 June | 708 | | 17 Nov | 582 |
| 9 June | 714 | | 24 Nov | 564 |
| 16 June | 690 | | 2 Dec | 592 |
| 23 June | 609 | | 8 Dec | 620 |
| 30 June | 643 | | 15 Dec | 624 |
| 7 July | 502 | | 24 Dec | 602 |
| 15 July | 572 | | 31 Dec | 590 |
| 21 July | 576 | | 6 Jan | 608 |
| 4 Aug | n/a | | 13 Jan | 620 |
| 11 Aug | 470 | | 19 Jan | 599 |
| 18 Aug | 490 | | 26 Jan | n/a |
| 25 Aug | n/a | | 2 Feb | 596 |
| 1 Sept | 563 | | 9 Feb | 565 |
| 8 Sept | n/a | | 10 March | 567 |
| 15 Sept | 578 | | 6 Apr | 648 |
| 22 Sept | 557 | | 20 Apr | 617 |
| 29 Sept | 590 | | 27 Apr | 671 |
| 6 Oct | 585 | | 15 May | 678 |
| 13 Oct | n/a | | | |

# BIBLIOGRAPHY

1. Publications by John Spratt

2. Publications about or addressed to John Spratt

3. Manuscript Sources

4. Newspapers and Periodicals

5. Directories

6. Official Publications

7. Printed Sources to 1900

8. Historical Works since 1901

9. Dissertations and Theses

10. Biographical Dictionaries and Modern Reference Works

11. Internet Websites

## 1.  Publications by John Spratt:

*(other than letters to the press: where only sole copies are thought to be extant, these are in the Carmelite Library and Archive, Gort Muire, Dublin, unless a different location is stated)*

*A novena, or nine days' devotion to the ever glorious and blessed Virgin Mary of Mount Carmel, compiled from [sic] the use of those pious individuals who wear the holy scapular*, 30 pp., Dublin, Richard Coyne, Capel Street, 1824.  There is a subsequent 35 pp edition of this, undated, in the Royal Irish Academy, Haliday Pamphlet No. 1427, catalogued under the year 1828; it is slightly different by inclusion of meditations interspersed with the prayers.

*The Sincere Christian's Manual of Devotion or Selection of Prayers Arranged Principally for the Use of the Members of the Sodality of the Holy Scapular*, 1st ed [?], Dublin 1828.  It is not certain if this edition appeared in print: Spratt's 35 page edition of his *A novena, or nine days' devotion* carries a publisher's notice that *The Sincere Christian's Manual* is 'In the Press'.  The earliest extant edition is that published by John Coyne, Dublin 1837.

*A Sermon on the Love of God*, 18 pp., T & S Courtney, 1st ed Dublin 1830, later ed., Dublin 1837.  It was announced for publication in 1828 but the earliest extant copy is dated 1830, in Royal Irish Academy Haliday Tracts.

*The Parents' Guide*, Dublin 1830, or 1831 ?  Publisher and printer unknown, apparently there is no extant copy in any of the major libraries in the English-speaking world, or in Rome.  Spratt sent a copy to Bishop Doyle of Kildare & Leighlin who acknowledged having received and read it, in March 1831.

*The Novena, or Nine Days' Devotion to the Seraphic Mother, Saint Teresa of Jesus*, 22pp., J. Coyne, Dublin, n.d., c. 1835.

*An Eulogium on the Ever Blessed Virgin Mary of Mount Carmel, chiefly from the Spanish*, 72 pp., J. O'Sullivan, Dublin 1835.

*The Sincere Christian's Manual of Devotion, or selection of prayers arranged principally for the use of members of the Sodality of the Holy Scapular*, 395 pp., John Coyne, Dublin 1837.

*Manual of Prayers* [?], Catholic Book Society, Dublin 1838.  No extant copy of this has been found to-date: it is mentioned under this title by W. J. Battersby in his *Catholic Directory* for the year 1838, p. 9, as No. 251 in a list of 'cheap books' published by the Catholic Book Society.  It may have been a cheap reprint or edition of *The Sincere Christian's Manual of Devotion*, listed in the previous entry above.

*Address of the Christian Doctrine Societies of the City of Dublin…to Daniel O'Connell… John Spratt, D.D., 5th September 1844*, 2 pp.; undated but clearly 1844.

*Sermon on the Passion and Death of Our Lord and Saviour Jesus Christ, by the Very Rev J. Spratt, preached in the Carmelite Church, Whitefriar Street, Dublin, on Good Friday, April. 9th, 1841.* This was published in *The Catholic Luminary*, No. 22, Sat 10th April 1841, pp. 507-12.

*The Carmelite Manual: containing a selection of beautiful prayers, and various practices of piety*, Dublin 1846. There is a copy of this in the British Library while there is a later, 5th edition, published by James Duffy, 526 pp., Dublin 1861.

*Distress of the People*, 2pp., Dublin 1846: printed circular of 3rd Nov 1846, no publisher given.

*Address from the Members of the Cuffe Street Temperance Society to their Brethren in America*, [co-authored with James Haughton], in *The Irish Patriot – Daniel O'Connell's Legacy to Irish Americans*, 32 pp., from *Selected Americana from Sabin's Dictionary of books relating to America*, Philadelphia 1847; copy in National Library of Scotland.

*Whitefriar Street Schools: to the Friends of the Education of the Poor*, 1 p., 25th Oct 1848.

*General Relief Committee, Royal Exchange….J. Spratt, D.D.,12 July 1849*, 1 p., Dublin 1849.

*An Appeal to the People on the Horrid Crime of Drunkenness.*, 64 pp., Battersby, Dublin 1849. Marsh's Library, Dublin, possesses a 32 page edition which is catalogued as being published 'circa 1848' and printed by Thomas Edmondson, 9 Dame Street, for the Irish Temperance League, Southern Branch: however, the Irish Temperance League was not founded until 1858 and its Southern Branch, in Dublin, not until 1864. The Royal Irish Academy's copy is of the 1849 edition with 64 pp.; an edition was printed in London as late as 1870, held by the University of London Library.

*The Triumph of Mary, the Mother of God: being a discussion in the reign of Edward VI between a rom. Cath. Priest and a puritanical preacher, transcribed and revised*, iv, 192 pp., C. M. Warren, Dublin 1849; copy in Library, Trinity College Dublin.

*The Real Presence of the Body and Blood of Our Lord Jesus Christ in the Holy Eucharist Demonstrated. From the Diary of an Irish Farmer*, viii, 96 pp., John Fowler, Dublin 1850.

*To the Most Rev. and Right Rev, the Catholic Archbishops and Bishops of Ireland...John Spratt, D.D., 30th Jan 1850*, 2 pp., Dublin 1850.

*The Catholic University of Ireland....the Address of the Central Committee in Dublin appointed to collect donations...John Spratt, 9th Feb 1850*, 2 pp., Dublin 1850, no publisher given.

*Great Schools of Education & Industry, Whitefriar Street...to the Charitable and Humane...John Spratt, D.D., 7th Oct 1850*, 1 p., Dublin 1850.

*The Holy Bible Alone is not the Rule of Faith*, 85 pp., James Duffy, Dublin 1852; copy in Lambeth Palace Library.

'An Appeal to the People on Drunkenness', in *Duffy's Fireside Magazine*, No xxxviii, Dec 1853.

'Ancient sculptured stone from the vicinity of St Audeon's Church, Dublin', *Journal of the Kilkenny and South East of Ireland Antiquarian Society*, series 1, vol. iii, part 2, 1855, pp. 277-79.

'Stone articles found near the old church of Carrigacurra, county of Wicklow', *Journal of the Kilkenny and South East of Ireland Antiquarian Society*, new series, vol.1, 1856-7, part ii, 1857, *Proceedings and Papers*, p. 358.

'Wilson's Dublin Tradesman's token, found in an ancient well in Aungier Street, Dublin', *Journal of the Kilkenny and South East Ireland Antiquarian Society*, new series, vol. 2, part 1, 1858, p. 62.

'A leaden 'Bulla' of Pope Gregory IX', *Journal of the Kilkenny and South East of Ireland Antiquarian Society*, new series, vol. 2, 1858, part 1, p. 201.

*An Appeal on behalf of the Catholic Blind Asylum*, (unsigned), 1 p., Dublin 1858.

'The original brass matrix of the seal of the Rev James Verschoyle, afterwards Bishop of Killala', *Journal of the Kilkenny and South East Ireland Antiquarian Society*, series 2, vol. iii, part 1, 1860, p. 82.

*Copy of a letter to the President of the Catholic Young Men's Society...John Spratt, D.D., 19 Feb 1861*, 1 p., Dublin 1861.

*Circular letter to Dublin Catholics regarding the election of overseers of deserted children*, 2 pp., Dublin 1863, no publisher given; copy in National Library of Ireland.

*The Address of the Orphan Boys...to the Rev William H Anderdon*, 1 p.: no date, but probably 1865, as in October 1865 Anderdon left Dublin for London, permanently.

*Short Instructions for the Sacrament of Confirmation for the use of the Whitefriar Street Schools*, 16 pp., Henry E. Byrne, Dublin 1865.

*Fr Spratt's Address to the Working People...reprinted from the Dublin Evening Freeman, 4 July 1867*, 2 pp., Dublin 1861, no publisher stated.

*A Sermon on the Passion and Death of Our Lord and Saviour Jesus Christ, preached on Good Friday, 1869, in the Carmelite Church of Dublin*, 24 pp., McKernan, Dublin 1869; copy in Royal Irish Academy.

*A Sermon on the Parable of the Prodigal Son*, 20 pp., McKernan, Dublin 1870; copy in National Library of Ireland.

*The History of John Connolly or, Cruelty to Animals Punished. Printed and published for the use of the children in the Very Rev Dr Spratt's Free Schools, Whitefriar Street*, 32 pp., Dublin 1871; neither the name of the author nor the publisher are stated but the work is almost certainly by John Spratt.

**Undated publications:**

*Cruelty to Animals*, 1 p., Byrne, Longford Street, Dublin: unsigned but the phrasing is identical to that in one of Spratt's handwritten sermons as entered in GMA. Box 73.

*To Her Majesty's Commissioners of National Education in Ireland, the Memorial of the undersigned Rev John Spratt, Manager of the National Schools in Whitefriar Street*, 1 p., Dublin.

**Unsigned publication:**

Anon, possibly by Spratt: *Devotions in honour of St Valentinus, Martyr, whose sacred body is deposited in the Carmelite Church, Whitefriar Street*, 8 pp., printed by J. O'Sullivan, Dublin, 1838; copy in Royal Irish Academy.

**Posthumous publications:**

Petrie, G., 'Description of an antique statue of the Madonna in Dublin, forwarded by the Very Rev Dr Spratt for publication', *Irish Ecclesiastical Record*, vol. vii, July 1871, pp. 474-475.

*Life of St Angelo, Martyr, of the Order of the B.V.M. of Mount Carmel, translated by the Very Rev John Spratt, D.D.*, ? pp., James Duffy, Dublin 1890; there may have been earlier editions after Spratt's death in 1871.

## 2. Publications about or addressed to John Spratt:
*(in chronological order)*

*Most Important Letters of the Right Rev Dr Fleming, Catholic Bishop of Newfoundland to the Very Rev John Spratt of Aungier-Street on the state of religion in that country*, 16 pp., W. Powell, Thomas Street, Dublin 1835; copy in Royal Irish Academy.

O'Brennan, M. A., *O'Brennan's Antiquities*, 2 vols, Dublin, 1858-60, vol 2, *A School History of Ireland*, Dublin 1860.

Davenport Hill, M., *Our Exemplars, poor and rich: or, biographical sketches of men and women who have, by an extraordinary use of the opportunities, benefitted their fellow-creatures*, pp. xviii, 342, Petter & Galvin, 1861: copy in Library of Congress.

Haughton, J., 'Memoir of the Very Rev Dr. Spratt of Dublin', *Catholic Telegraph*, 28th Nov 1863.

Battersby, W. J., *Authentic Life and Acts of the Very Rev Dr Spratt, S.T.M., Provincial, O.C.C.*, 24 pp., Dublin 1871.

Sadleir, J., *An elicy [sic] on the much lamented death of the Very Rev'd Dr Spratt*, Dublin 1871; copy in National Library of Ireland.

Anon, 'Biogram No 49 – The Very Rev John Spratt', *Irish Monthly*, Dec 1877, pp. 706-7.

Webb, A., 'John Spratt, D.D.', in A. Webb, *Compendium of Irish Biography*, Dublin 1878, p. 487.

Farrington, A. E., *Rev Dr Spratt, O.C.C.: His Life and Times*, Dublin 1893.

Anon., 'St Joseph's Night Refuge', No VIII in a series 'Our Dublin Charities', *The Irish Rosary*, vol. 1, No. 8, November 1897, pp.392-99.

Crone, J. S., *A Concise Dictionary of Irish Biography*, Dublin 1928, pp. 236-37.

O'Dwyer, P., *Father John Spratt: beloved of Dublin's poor, Centenary Souvenir, 1871-1971*, pp. 62, Dublin 1971.

O'Dwyer, P., *The Irish Carmelites*, Dublin 1988.

Murphy, D., 'John Francis Spratt (1796-1871)', *Dictionary of Irish Biography*, vol. 8, Cambridge 2009, p. 1099.

## 3. Manuscript Sources:

### Capuchin Friars, Church Street, Dublin:
Theobald Mathew Papers.

### Carmelites of the Ancient Observance, Gort Muire, Dublin:
Carmelite Papers, including extensive nineteenth-century correspondence of individual Carmelite friars, priors and provincials with each other, with the Prior General in Rome and with  Vatican officials; Spratt's manuscript and printed correspondence, notes and scrapbooks; the Catalogus Fratrum.

### Carmelites of the Ancient Observance, Collegio Internazionale S Alberto, Rome:
Carmelite Papers relating to the Irish Province: over two hundred letters between Carmelites in Ireland and Rome: records of Irish Provincial and General Chapters and Acts; many of these have been microfilmed by Peter O'Dwyer and the microfilms deposited in the Gort Muire Archives.

### Dromore Diocesan Archives:
Correspondence of Michael Blake, Bishop of Dromore (1833-60).

### Dublin Diocesan Archives:
Original registers of baptisms and marriages of various Dublin parishes; the papers of Archbishop Murray, Cardinal Cullen, Archdeacon Hamilton, Bartholomew Woodlock; papers of the Catholic Association; papers relating to the Catholic University and to various religious orders of priests, nuns and brothers.

### Glasnevin Cemetery Archives:
Proceedings of Catholic Cemetery Committee, 1846-1855.
Dublin Cemeteries Committee, Minute Books of Proceedings of General Meetings, (1850-1886).
Register of Interments, 1871-1880.

### National Archives of Ireland:
Chief Secretary's Office Registered Papers.
Commissioners of National Education ED/1 – ED/4/: Applications, Registers, Salaries.

North Dublin Union Minute Books.
Official Papers.
Records of the Sick & Indigent Roomkeepers Society.
Society of Friends Central Relief Committee.
Wills & Administrations.

**National Library of Ireland:**
Graham Papers (microfilm), n. 2924-2967, p. 2545-88.
Leahy Papers (microfilm) n. 5705-8, p. 6005-8.
Ms Special List 173: M. Tierney, ed., *Calendar of Dr Slattery Papers*, Cashel Diocesan Archives.
Ms 35452, *A Fortnight's Visit to Ireland with a glance at the City of Dublin*, August 1839.

**Propaganda Fide Archives, Rome:**
Udienze, Indice, vols. 7 to 20, 1829-72.
Scritture Originali Riferite nella Congresi, Irlanda, vol. 35, 1865-67, vol. 36, 1868-75.

**Registry of Births, Marriages and Deaths, Dublin:**
Death certificates for various members of the Spratt and Vickers families.

**Registry of Deeds, Dublin:**
Marriage Licences, 1800-1899.
Transcript Books, 1825-1886.

**Royal College of Physicians of Ireland, Dublin:**
Sir Dominic Corrigan Papers: Non-Denominational Education, DC/4/2/1-DC/4/2/14.

**Society of Friends, Dublin: Quaker Historical Library:**
Material relating to James Haughton and John Spratt, including a pledge certificate of August 1845 signed by John Spratt.
Miscellaneous correspondence, tracts and images relating to famine relief and the temperance movement in nineteenth-century Ireland.

## 4. Newspapers and Periodicals:

*Advocate, or Irish Industrial Journal*
*Allnutt's Irish Land Schedule*
*The Ballarat Star*
*The Banner of the Truth*
*The Catholic Luminary and Ecclesiastical Repertory*
*The Catholic Magazine and Review*

*The Catholic Penny Magazine*
*Catholic Telegraph*
*Connaught Patriot*
*Cork Examiner*
*Dublin Builder*
*Dublin Daily Express*
*Dublin Evening Mail*
*Dublin Evening Packet and Correspondent*
*Dublin Evening Post*
*Dublin Gazette*
*Dublin Mercantile Advertiser*
*Dublin Monitor*
*Dublin Morning Register*
*Dublin Observer*
*Dublin Penny Journal*
*Dublin Shipping and Mercantile Gazette*
*Dublin Temperance Gazette*
*Dublin Weekly Herald*
*Dublin Weekly Nation*
*Dublin Weekly Register*
*Duffy's Fireside Magazine*
*Duffy's Catholic Magazine*
*Evening Freeman*
*Evening Telegraph*
*Farmers' Gazette and Journal of Practical Horticulture*
*Flag of Ireland*
*Freeman's Journal*
*General Advertiser*
*Hibernian Journal or Chronicle of Liberty*
*Hibernian Temperance Journal*
*The Irishman*
*Irish Builder*
*Irish Catholic Magazine*
*Irish Monthly*
*Irish Rosary*
*Irish Temperance and Literary Gazette*
*Irish Times*
*Irish Trades' Advocate*
*Irish World*
*Journal of the Kilkenny and South East of Ireland Antiquarian Society*
*Kilkenny Journal*
*Kennedy's British and Irish Catholic Magazine*
*Launceston Examiner (Tasmania)*

*Leinster Express*
*Limerick and Clare Examiner*
*Limerick Reporter*
*Liverpool Mercury*
*Lloyd's Weekly Newspaper*
*London Evening Standard*
*Morning Star and Catholic Register (New Orleans)*
*Newry Examiner*
*Northern Whig*
*Otago Daily Times*
*Penny Despatch*
*The Pilot*
*Public Ledger and Daily Advertiser*
*Roscommon Journal*
*Saunders' Newsletter*
*Statesman and Dublin Christian Record*
*Taranaki Herald, (New Zealand)*
*The Tablet*
*The Times*
*Tipperary Free Press*
*Tipperary Vindicator*
*Vindicator (Belfast)*
*Warder and Dublin Weekly Mail*
*Waterford Mail*
*Weekly Freeman's Journal*
*Weekly Telegraph*
*Wexford Independent*

## 5. Directories:

Battersby, W. J., *The Catholic Directory*, 1836-1874.
Folds, J. S., *The Post Office Annual Directory*, 1832-1833.
Pettigrew & Oulton, *The Dublin Almanac and General Register of Ireland*, 1834-45.
*Thom's Irish Almanac and Official Directory*, 1844-1871.
*Watson's*, or *The Gentleman's & Citizen's Almanac*, 1835.
*Wilson's Dublin Directory*, 1800-39.
Young, H, *The Catholic Directory*, 1821.

## 6. Official Publications:

*Census of Ireland for the year 1851, Part V, Table of Deaths, vol. i,* Dublin 1856.
*Census of Ireland for the Year 1861,* Dublin 1863.
*Hansard, Parliamentary Debates,* 3rd series.

**Parliamentary Papers:**

H.C. 1823(229), *Accounts relating to diocesan and parish schools in Ireland in 1821*.
HC 1824 (51), *Fifth Report from the Select Committee on Artizans and Machinery*.
H.C. 1826-7 (12), *Second Report of the Commissioners of Irish Education Inquiry*.
H.C. 1831-32 (445), *A Return of the number of applications to the Board of Education for new schools under their system, or for assistance in behalf of schools already established*.
H.C. 1835 (300), *Second Report of the Commissioners of National Education in Ireland for the year ending 31st March 1835*.
H.C. 1835 (390), *Return of books, schools and of Roman Catholic, Protestant and children of other denominations, under the superintendence of the Commissioners of National Education*.
H.C. 1836, (43), *Third Report of the Commissioners for inquiring into the Condition of the Poorer Classes in Ireland*. xxx, Appendix C, Part II.
H.C. 1837 (483), *Report of the Select Committee on the Plan of Education for Ireland*.
H.C. 1839 (429) *Education (Ireland)*.
H.C. 1840 (246), *Sixth Report of the Commissioners*.
H.C. 1842 (353), *Seventh Report of the Commissioners...for the year 1840*.
H.C. 1844 (569), *Tenth Report of the Commissioners*.
H.C. 1845 (650), *Appendix to the Eleventh Report of the Commissioners*.
H.C. 1847 (32), *Thirteenth Report of the Commissioners*.
H.C. 1847-8 (693), *Report from the Select Committee on Savings Banks (Ireland)*.
H.C. 1849 (21), *Savings Banks (Ireland): Minutes of Evidence taken before the Select Committee on Savings Banks (Ireland)*.
H.C. 1849 (437), *First Report from the Select Committee on Savings Banks*.
H.C. 1849 (1066), *The Fifteenth Report...for the year 1848*.
H.C. 1849 (21) *Savings Banks Ireland: Minutes of Evidence taken before the Select Committee on Savings Banks (Ireland)*.
H.C. 1850 (649), *Report from the Select Committee on Savings Banks*.
H.C. 1851 (295), *Return showing how the sum of £30,000 voted by the House of Commons for the relief of depositors in the late Savings Bank, Cuffe Street, Dublin, has been disposed of*.
H.C. 1857-58 (411), *Report from the Select Committee on Savings Banks*.
H.C.1860, LVIII, (901), *Minutes of Evidence before Guardians of the South Dublin Union and Assistant Poor Law Commissioner*.

**Public General Statutes:**

40 Geo. III, c. 75, *An Act for the better Discovery of 'charitable donations and bequests'*, 1800.

10 Geo. IV, c. 7, *An Act for the Relief of His Majesty's Roman Catholic Subjects*, 1829.

7 & 8 Vict. c. 97, *An Act for the more effectual Application of Charitable Donations and Bequests in Ireland*, 1844.

10 Vict. c. 7, *An Act for the temporary Relief of destitute Persons in Ireland*, 1847.

10 Vict. c. 31, *An Act to make further Provision for the Relief of the Destitute Poor in Ireland*, 1847.

10 & 11 Vict. c. 90, *An Act to provide for the Execution of the Laws for relief of the Poor in Ireland*, 1847.

25 Vict. c. 22, *An Act to continue certain Duties of Customs and Inland Revenue*, 1862.

26 & 27 Vict. c. 33, *An Act for granting to Her Majesty certain Duties of Inland Revenue, and to amend the Laws relating to the Inland Revenue*, 1863.

27 & 28 Vict. c. 35, *An Act for more effectually regulating the Sale of Beer in Ireland*, 1864.

37 & 38 Vict. c. 69, *An Act to Amend the Laws relating to the sale and consumption of Intoxicating Liquors in Ireland*, 1874.

40 & 41 Vict. c. 4, *An Act to amend the Law relating to the granting of Licences for the sale of Beer, Ale and Porter in Ireland*, 1877.

## 7. Printed Sources to 1900: (in alphabetical order)

*Annual Report of the Charitable Society for the relief of the Sick and Indigent Roomkeepers in the City of Dublin*, 1833.

Anon., *A Letter to a Member of the Dublin Temperance Society on the supposed value of ardent spirits in relation to National Wealth*, Dublin 1830.

Anon., *A Statement of the Charitable Society for the relief of Sick and Indigent Roomkeepers of all religious persuasions in the City of Dublin for the Year 1823*, Dublin 1824.

Anon., *A Statement of the Charitable Society for the relief of Sick and Indigent Roomkeepers of all religious persuasions in the City of Dublin for the year 1833*, Dublin 1834.

Anon., *A Statement of the Efforts Made by the Committee Desirous for Reforms in the Molyneux Asylum for Blind Females*, Dublin 1857.

Anon., *Address of the Dublin Temperance Society to their fellow citizens*, Dublin 1830.

Anon., *An Accurate report of the Proceedings of the Very Rev. Theobald Mathew in Dublin in the Cause of Temperance, when eighty thousand took the pledge*, 76 pp., Dublin 1840.

Anon., *Appeal from the Hibernian Temperance Society to all persons interested in the real welfare of Ireland*, Dublin 1830.

Anon., *Auxiliary Societies: Observations, Anecdotes respecting Temperance*, Dublin 1830.

Anon., *City of Dublin Election, May 1859, List of Electors in the year 1859*, Dublin 1859.

Anon., *City of Dublin Election, 18 Nov 1868, List of Electors.*

Anon., *Devotions in honour of St. Valentinus, Martyr, whose sacred body is deposited in the Carmelite Church, Whitefriar Street.* 8 pp., Dublin 1838.

Anon., *First Annual Report of the Dublin Auxiliary to the United Kingdom Alliance*, Dublin 1855.

Anon., *First Annual Report of the Dublin Juvenile Temperance Society on Total Abstinence Principles*, Dublin 1838.

Anon., *First Report of the Irish Permissive Bill Association*, Dublin 1869.

Anon., *Four Dialogues between the Apostle, St Peter and His Holiness of the Pope of Rome on the most important controverted doctrines and the Order of the Scapular or Carmelites, by a Friend to St Peter*, Dublin 1811.

Anon., *Hibernian Temperance Society. Proceedings of the First Annual Meeting held at the Rotunda on the 7th of April 1830*, Dublin 1830.

Anon., *Irish Permissive Bill Association, General Council Meeting, 25 May 1869*, Dublin 1869.

Anon., *Public Announcement of the Hibernian Temperance Society at its First General Meeting*, Dublin 1830.

Anon., *Report of the Central Committee for Relief of Distress in Ireland, 1862-3*, Dublin 1864.

Anon, *Report of the Mansion House Committee for Relief of Distress in Ireland*, Dublin 1862.

Anon., *Report of the Speech of P.C. Crampton, Surgeon-General, President of the Hibernian Temperance Society*, Dublin 1830.

Anon, *Rules To Be Observed by the Subscribing Members of the Venerable Confraternity of Our Blessed Lady of Mount Carmel*, Dublin 1835.

Anon., *Sketch of the Rise and Progress of Temperance Societies: Hibernian Temperance Society, Paper A*, Dublin 1830.

Anon., 'St Joseph's Night Refuge', No VIII in a series 'Our Charities', *The Irish Rosary*, vol. 1, 1897, pp. 392-99.

Anon, *The Irish Franchise and Registration Question*, London 1841.

Anon., *Third annual Report of the Dublin Auxiliary to the United Kingdom Alliance*, Dublin 1857.

Archdall, M., *Monasticon Hibernicum*, Dublin 1786.

Balch, W. S., *Ireland As I Saw It: The Character, Condition, and Prospects of the People*, New York 1850.

Bermingham, J., *A Memoir of the Very Rev Theobald Mathew with an account of the rise and progress of Temperance in Ireland*, Dublin 1840.

Bradburne, S., *Tudor, City of Dublin Election, July 15th 1865, List of Electors for the year 1865*, Dublin 1865.

Calahorra, F., *Breve Compendio del Origen y Antiquedad de la Santa Religion del Carmen*, Madrid 1766.

Coleman, T. A., *A Brief Account of the Indulgences, Privileges and Favours conferred on the Order, Confraternities and Churches of the Most Glorious Mother of God, The Virgin Mary of Mount Carmel*, Dublin 1826.

[Colgan], *The Very Rev R. J. C., DD., The Rules and Statutes together with the Ceremonial of the Brothers and Sisters of the Third Order of the Blessed Virgin Mary of Mount Carmel*, Dublin 1844.

de Capell Brooke, A., *Sketches in Spain and Morocco*, 2 vols., London 1831.

Doyle, J., *Letter of the late Right Reverend Dr Doyle on temperance societies, with the answer of James Henry, M.D., Fellow of the Royal College of Physicians, Dublin*, Dublin 1830.

Dubbin, J. P., *Observations in Europe, Principally in France and Great Britain, 2 vols.,* New York 1844.

Finny, T., *Ordo Divini Officii Pro Anno MDCCCXX…*, Dublin 1820.

Fitzpatrick, W. J., *The life, times and contemporaries of Lord Cloncurry,* Dublin 1855.

Fitzpatrick, W. J., *History of the Dublin Catholic Cemeteries*, Dublin 1900.

Forbes, J., *Memorandums Made in Ireland in the Autumn of 1852*, 2 vols., London 1853.

Hall, S. C. & A. M., *Ireland, its scenery and character*, 3 vols., London 1841.

Haughton, S., *Memoir of James Haughton*, Dublin 1877.

Hole, J. R., *A Little Tour in Ireland by an Oxonian*, London 1892.

Kennedy, T., & Sullivan, W. K., *On the industrial training institutions of Belgium and on the possibility of organising an analogous system in connection with the national schools of Ireland*, Dublin 1855.

King Harman, L. H., & Allnutt, H., *The Veil Partly Withdrawn, or further revelations in connection with the Molyneux Asylum for Blind Females, Peter Street, Dublin*, Dublin 1857.

Lewis, S., *A Topographical Dictionary of Ireland*, 2 vols., London 1837.

McGregor, J. J., *The New Picture of Dublin*, Dublin 1828.

Mackey, J., *Speech of John Mackey at the Hibernian Temperance Society*, Dublin 1837.

Magee, W., *A charge delivered at his primary visitation in St Patrick's Cathedral, Dublin, on Thursday 27th of October, 1822*, Dublin 1822.

Maguire, J. F., *The Industrial Movement in Ireland as illustrated by the National Exhibition of 1852*, Cork 1853.

Meagher, W., *Notices of the life and character of His Grace Most Rev Dr Daniel Murray, late Archbishop of Dublin*, Dublin 1853.

Miley, J., D.D., *Will Teetotalism Last? An Exhortation to the People on the Heinous Guilt and Disastrous Consequences of the Violation of the Pledge*, 22 pp., Dublin 1840.

Molyneux, E., *A practical Treatise of the law of elections in Ireland as altered by the Reform Act*, Dublin 1835.

Mooney, T. A., *History of Ireland, from its first settlement to the present time*, 1st ed. 1845, 2nd ed. Boston 1846.

Mooney, T. A., *Nine years in America, in a series of letters to his cousin, Patrick Mooney, a farmer in Ireland*, Dublin 1850.

Mooney, T. A., *The People's History of Ireland*, 2 vols., Dublin 1869-70.

Moran, P. F., *Pastoral letters and other writings of Cardinal Cullen*, 3 vols., Dublin, 1882.

O'Brennan, M. A., *O'Brennan's Antiquities*, 2 vols., Dublin 1858-1860.

O'Connell, D., *Seven Letters on the Reform Bill and the law of elections in Ireland*, Dublin 1835.

O'Reilly, M., *Progress of Catholicity in Ireland in the Nineteenth Century*, Dublin 1865.

Perraud, A., *Études sur l'Irlande Contemporaine*, Paris 1862.

Perraud, A., *Ireland in 1862*, Dublin 1863.

Ray, T. M., *A List of the Constituency of Dublin as registered prior to the City of Dublin Election in January 1835*, pp. 160, Dublin 1835.

Rodenberg, J., *The Island of the Saints*, London 1858.

Rodenberg, J., *A Pilgrimage Through Ireland*, London 1860.

Roussel, N., *Trois Mois en Irlande*, Paris 1853.

Scally, M., *The Teetotaler's Catechism*, Dublin 1846.

Sheil, J. B., *History of the Temperance Movement in Ireland*, Dublin 1843.

Shore, T., *Case of the Rev Thomas R Shore and the Protestant Orphan Society, with a statement of the circumstances under which he was removed from the Society...*, Dublin 1851.

Starrat, M., *History of Ancient and Modern Dublin; or, Visitors' Guide to the Metropolis of Ireland*, Dublin 1832.

Urwick, W., ed., *The life and letters of William Urwick, D.D., of Dublin,* London 1870.

Walmesley, C., *The general history of the Christian church: from her birth to her final triumphant state in Heaven, chiefly deduced from the Apocalypse of St John the Apostle. By Signor Pastorini,* Dublin 1771.

White, F., *Report and Observations on the State of the Poor of Dublin,* Dublin 1833.

Wight, T. & Rutty, J., *A History of the Rise and Progress of People called Quakers in Ireland from the year 1653 to 1700,* Dublin 1751.

## 8. Historical Works since 1901:

Alexander, A., *Infinitesimal: how a Dangerous Mathematical Theory shaped the Modern World,* London 2015.

Andrews, H., *The Lion of the West: a biography of John McHale,* Dublin 2001.

Andrews, H., 'Thomas Crosthwaite, (c.1782-1870)', *Dictionary of Irish Biography,* vol. 2, pp. 1042-3.

Anon, 'Report on the State of Popery in Ireland, 1731', *Archivium Hibernicum,* vol. 4, 1915, pp. 124-59.

Anon, *Catholic Young Men's Society of Ireland: Centenary Record, 1849-1949,* Dublin 1949.

Bartlett, T., *The Fall and Rise of the Irish Nation: The Catholic Question, 1690-1830,* Dublin 1992.

Bartlett, T., 'The penal laws against Irish Catholics: were they too good for them?', in O. P. Rafferty, ed., *Irish Catholic Identities,* Manchester 2013, pp. 154-170.

Begadon, C., 'Catholic Devotional Literature in Dublin, 1800-1830', and 'Catholic Religious Publishing, 1800-1891' in J. H. Murphy, ed., *The Irish Book in English, 1800-1891,* Oxford 2011, pp. 331-341 and 371-378.

Begadon, C. 'The Renewal of Catholic Religious culture in eighteenth-century Dublin' in J. Bergin, E. Magennis, L. Ní Mhunghaile & P. Walsh, eds., *New Perspectives on the Penal Laws,* Dublin 2011.

Bergström-Allen, J. & Copsey, R., *Thomas Netter of Walden: Carmelite, Diplomat and Theologian,* Faversham 2009.

Bourke, A., ed., *The Field Day Anthology of Irish writing*, vol. 5, *Irish Women's Writing and Traditions*, Cork 2002.

Bowen, D., *Paul Cardinal Cullen and the Shaping of Modern Irish Catholicism*, Dublin 1983.

Bowen, D., *The Protestant Crusade in Ireland, 1800-70*, Dublin 1978.

Boylan, A., 'Women in groups: an analysis of women's benevolent organisations in New York and Boston, 1797-1840', in *Journal of American History*, 71, 1984, pp. 497-523.

Briggs, A., 'Cholera and society', *Past & Present*, 19, 1961, pp. 76-96.

Broderick, J. H., *The Holy See and the Irish Movement for the Repeal of the Union with England, 1829-1847*, Rome 1951.

Brown, S. J., 'The New Reformation Movement in the Church of Ireland, 1801-1829', in S. J. Brown, & D. W. Miller, eds., *Piety and Power in Ireland, 1760-1960: essays in honour of Emmett Larkin*, Indiana 2000.

Burke, H., *The People and the Poor Law in Nineteenth Century Ireland*, Dublin 1987.

Burke, N., 'A hidden church'? The structure of Catholic Dublin in the mid-eighteenth century', *Archivium Hibernicum*, vol. 31, 1974, pp. 86-87.

Burke, W. P. , *The Irish Priests in the Penal Times, 1660-1760*, 1968 reprint of 1st ed, Waterford 1914.

Butler, D. M., *The Quaker Meeting Houses of Ireland*, Dublin 2004.

Carr, R., *Spain 1808-1975*, Oxford 1983.

Carretero, I. M., *Exclaustracion y Restauracion Del Carmen en España, 1771-1910*, Roma 1996.

Casey, C., *Dublin, The City within the Grand and the Royal Canals*, New Haven and London 2005.

Cathcart, K. J., *The Letters of Peter lePage Renouf, 1822-1897*, 4 vols., Dublin 2002-4.

Clark, A., 'Orphans and the Poor Law: Rage against the machine', in V. Crossman, & P. Gray, eds., *Poverty and Welfare in Ireland, 1838-1948*, Dublin 2011, pp. 97-114.

Collins, J., *Life in Old Dublin*, Dublin 1913.

Comerford, V., 'Ireland, 1850-1870: post-famine and mid-Victorian', in W. E. Vaughan, ed., *A new history of Ireland*, vol. 5, *Ireland under the Union,1801-1870*, Oxford 1989, pp. 372-95.

Comerford, V., *The Fenians in Context: Irish Politics and Society, 1848-82*, Dublin 1998.

Conlan, P., *Franciscan Ireland*, Mullingar 1988.

Conlan, P., 'Reforming and seeking an identity', in E. Bhreathnach, J. MacMahon & J. McCafferty, eds., *The Irish Franciscans, 1534-1990*, Dublin 2009, pp. 102-131.

Connolly, C., 'Prince Hohenloe's Miracles: Supernaturalism and the Irish Public Sphere' in D. Duff & C. Jones, eds., *Scotland, Ireland and the Romantic Aesthetic*, Lewisburg 2007, pp. 236-257.

Connolly, S. J., *Priests and People in Pre-Famine Ireland, 1780-1845*, Dublin 1982.

Connolly, S. J., *Religion and Society in Nineteenth-Century Ireland*, reprint.ed., Dublin 1994.

Corbett, A., Pochin Mould, D. & Dixon, C., *Whitefriars Street Church*, Dublin 1964.

Corish, P. J., *The Catholic Community in the Seventeenth and Eighteenth Centuries*, Dublin 1981.

Crawford, J., " 'An overriding providence' : the life and ministry of Tresham Dames Gregg (1800-1881)" in T. C. Barnard & W. G. Neely, eds., *The Clergy of the Church of Ireland, 1000-2000*, Dublin 2006, pp. 157-168.

Crawford, J., *The Church of Ireland in Victorian Dublin*, Dublin 2005.

Crossman, V., 'The humanization of the Irish poor laws: reassessing developments in social welfare in post-Famine Ireland', in A. Gestrich, S. King & L. Raphael, eds., *Being Poor in Modern Europe: historical perspectives, 1800-1940*, Oxford 2006, pp. 229-49.

Crossman, V., *Politics, pauperism and power in late nineteenth-century Ireland*, Manchester 2006.

Crossman, V., 'Middle class attitudes to poverty and welfare in post-Famine Ireland', in F. Lane, ed., *Politics, Society and the Middle Class in Ireland*, Basingstoke 2010.

Crossman, V., *Poverty and the Poor Law in Ireland, 1850-1914*, Liverpool 2013.

Crossman, V. & Gray, P., eds., *Poverty and Welfare in Ireland, 1838-1948*, Dublin 2011.

Cunningham, P. 'The Catholic Directory for 1821', *Reportorium Novum*, vol. 2, No. 2, 1960, pp. 324-363.

Curran, M. J., 'Archbishop Carpenter's Epistolae (1770-1780)', *Reportorium Novum*, vol. 1, No. 2, 1956, pp. 381-405.

Curtis, M., *Portobello*, Dublin 2012.

D'Arcy, F. A., 'Religion, radicalism and rebellion in nineteenth-century Ireland: the case of Thaddeus O'Malley', in J. Devlin & R. Fanning, eds., *Religion and Rebellion*, Dublin 1997, pp. 97-105.

D'Arcy, F. A., 'Federalist, social radical and anti-sectarian: Thaddeus O'Malley (1797-1877)', in G. Moran, ed., *Radical Irish Priests, 1660-1970*, Dublin 1998, pp. 91-110.

D'Arcy, F. A., 'The decline and fall of Donnybrook Fair: moral reform and social control in nineteenth century Dublin', *Saothar*, 13, 1988, pp. 7-21.

D'Arcy, F. A., 'Wages of labourers in the Dublin Building Industry, 1667-1918', *Saothar*, 14, 1989, pp. 17-34.

D'Arcy, F. A., 'Wages of Skilled Workers in the Dublin Building Industry, 1667-1918', *Saothar*, 15, 1990, pp. 21-38.

D'Arcy, F. A., *Terenure College, 1860-2010: A History*, Dublin 2009.

Darcy, J. B., *Fire upon the Earth : the life and times of Bishop Michael Anthony Fleming, O.S.F.*, St. John's Newfoundland 2003.

Davis, R., *The Young Ireland Movement*, Dublin 1987.

de Courcy, J. W., *The Liffey in Dublin*, Dublin 1996.

Devlin, J. & Fanning, R., eds., *Religion and Rebellion*, Dublin 1997.

Dickson, D., ed., *The Gorgeous Mask: Dublin, 1700-1850*, Dublin 1987.

Di Martino, V. & R., *Irish Rome: Roma Irlandese*, Rome 2015.

Dickson, D., *Dublin: the making of a capital city*, Dublin 2014.

Donnelly, Jr, J. S., 'The Irish Agricultural Depression of 1859-64', *Irish Economic and Social History*, 3, 1976, pp. 33-54.

Donnelly, N., ed., *Roman Catholics. State and Condition of Roman Catholic Chapels in Dublin both Secular and Regular A.D. 1749*, Dublin 1904.

Doyle, C., 'Thomas Pleasants (1728-1818)', *Dictionary of Irish Biography*, vol. 8, pp. 151-2.

Edwards R. D., & Williams, T. D., eds., *The Great Famine: Studies in Irish History, 1845-52*, Dublin 1957 (1997 ed).

Egan, M. J., *Life of Dan O'Brien, Founder of the Catholic Young Men's Society*, Dublin 1949.

Elmes, R. M., *Catalogue of Engraved Irish Portraits*, Dublin 1975.

Esdaile, C. J., *Spain in the Liberal Age: From Constitution to Civil War, 1808-1939*, London 2000.

Fagan, P., *Catholics in a Protestant Country: the papist constituency in Eighteenth-Century Dublin*, Dublin 1988.

Fagan, P., *Dublin's Turbulent Priest: Cornelius Nary, 1658-1738*, Dublin 1991.

Fagan, P. 'The Dublin Catholic Mob, 1700-1750', *Eighteenth Century Ireland*, vol. 4, 1989, pp. 133-142.

Fagan, P. 'The population of Dublin in the Eighteenth Century with particular reference to the proportions of Catholics and Protestants', *Eighteenth Century Ireland*, vol. 6, 1991, pp. 140-143.

Fenning, H., 'The Archbishops of Dublin, 1693-1786' in J. Kelly & D. Keogh, eds., *History of the Catholic Diocese of Dublin*, Dublin 2000, pp. 175-214.

Fenning, H., *The Undoing of the Friars in Ireland*, Louvain 1972.

Fenning, H., 'Dublin imprints of Catholic interest: 1701-1739', *Collectanea Hibernica*, 39-40, 1997-1998, pp. 106-154.

Fenning, H., 'Dublin imprints of Catholic interest: 1740-1759', *Collectanea Hibernica*, 41, 1999, pp. 65-116.

Fenning, H., 'Dublin imprints of Catholic interest: 1760-69', *Collectanea Hibernica*, 42, 2000, pp. 85-119.

Fenning, H., 'Dublin imprints of Catholic interest: 1770-1782', *Collectanea Hibernica*, 43, 2001, pp. 161-208.

Fenning, H., 'Dublin imprints of Catholic interest:1783-1789', *Collectanea Hibernica*, 44-45, 2002-2003, pp. 79-126.

Fenning, H., 'Dublin imprints of Catholic interest: 1790-1795', *Collectanea Hibernica*, 46-47, 2004-2005, pp. 72-141.

Fenning, H., 'Dublin imprints of Catholic interest: 1796-1799', *Collectanea Hibernica*, 48, 2006, pp. 72-141.

Fenning, H., 'Dublin imprints of Catholic interest: 1800-09', *Archivium Hibernicum*, 61, 2008, pp. 246-324.

Ferriter, D., *A Nation of Extremes: The Pioneers in Twentieth-century Ireland*, Dublin 1999.

Ferriter, D., 'Arthur Edward Guinness (1840-1915)', in *The Dictionary of Irish Biography* (1st edition), Cambridge 2009, pp. 316-17.

Fleetwood, J., *The Irish Body Snatchers: a history of body snatching in Ireland*, Dublin 1988.

Fleming, N. C., & O'Day, A., eds., *The Longman Handbook of Modern Irish History since 1800*, London 2005.

Fr Augustine, *Footprints of Fr Mathew, OFM, Cap: apostle of temperance*, Dublin 1947.

Geary, L. M., 'Prince Hohenloe, Signor Pastorini and Miraculous Healing in Early Nineteenth-Century Ireland', in G. Jones & E. Malcolm, eds., *Medicine, Disease and the State in Ireland, 1650-1940*, Cork 1999.

Geary, L. M., ed., *Rebellion and remembrance in modern Ireland*, Dublin 2001.

Geary, L. & Walsh, O., *Philanthropy in nineteenth-century Ireland*, Dublin 2015.

Geoghegan, P. M., *King Dan, The Rise of Daniel O'Connell, 1775-1829*, Dublin 2008.

Geoghegan, P. M., *Liberator: The Life and Death of Daniel O'Connell, 1830-1847*, Dublin 2010.

Gestritch, A., King, S., & Raphael, L., eds., *Being Poor in Modern Europe: historical perspectives, 1800-1940*, Oxford 2006.

Giblin, C., 'Papers of Richard Joachim Hayes, O.F.M., 1810-1824', *Collectanea Hibernica*, 21-22, 1979-80, pp. 120-134.

Giblin, C., 'Ten documents relating to diocesan affairs, 1740-1784, from Franciscan Library, Killiney', *Collectanea Hibernica*, 20, 1978, pp. 61-68.

Gil, A., 'Documenta', *Zelo*, vol. 10, No. 2, Summer 1958, pp. 90-97.

Grace, P. A., 'In time of cholera', *Irish Journal of Medical Science*, vol. 183, No. 1, March 2014, pp. 133-37.

Greaves, R. L., *Dublin's Merchant Quaker: Anthony Sharp and the Community of Friends, 1643-1707*, Stanford 1998.

Grehan, A., *Aungier Street: revitalising an historic neighbourhood (Dublin City Council)*, Dublin 2013.

Gribben, A., ed., *The Great Famine and the Irish Diaspora in America*, Amherst 1999.

Gribben, C. & Holmes, A. R., eds., *Protestant Millennialism, Evangelicalism, and Irish Society, 1790-2005*, Basingstoke 2006.

Grimes, B. *'Commodius Temples': Roman Catholic Church building in nineteenth century Dublin*, Dublin 2010.

Grimes, B., 'Funding a Roman Catholic Church in Nineteenth-Century Ireland', *Architectural History*, vol. 52, 2009, pp. 147-168.

Harrison, B., *Drink and the Victorians: The Temperance Question in England, 1815-1872*, London 1971.

Harrison, R., *Richard Davis Webb, Dublin Quaker Printer 1805-1872*, Cork 1993.

Henry, B., *Dublin Hanged: crime, law enforcement and punishment in late eighteenth-century Dublin*, Dublin 1994.

Hill, J., & Lennon, C., eds., *Luxury and Austerity*, Dublin 1999, pp. 137-161.

Holmes, J., 'Irish evangelicals and the British evangelical community, 1820's-1870's', in J. H. Murphy, ed., *Evangelicals and Catholics in nineteenth century Ireland*, Dublin 2005, pp. 209-222.

Hoppen, K. T., *Elections, Politics and Society in Ireland, 1832-1885*, Oxford 1984.

Hoppen, K. T., *Ireland since 1800: Conflict and Conformity*, 1st ed., London 1989.

Hourican, B., 'Charles Putland', *Dictionary of Irish Biography*, vol. 8, p. 332.

Inglis, T., *Moral Monopoly: the Catholic Church in Modern Irish Society*, Dublin 1987.

Jackson, A., *Ireland, 1798-1998*, Oxford 1999.

Jenkins, B., *The Fenian Problem: Insurgency and Terrorism in a Liberal State, 1858-1874*, Liverpool 2008.

Kearney, H. F., 'Father Mathew: Apostle of Modernisation' in A. Cosgrove & D. McCartney, eds., *Studies in Irish History*, Dublin 1979, pp. 164-175.

Keenan, D. J., *The Catholic Church in Nineteenth-Century Ireland: a Sociological Study*, Dublin 1983.

Kelly, J. J., 'The impact of the penal laws', in J. J. Kelly & D. Keogh, eds., *History of the Catholic Diocese of Dublin*, Dublin 2000, pp. 144-145.

Kelly, M., 'The suppression of intemperance – Part II', *Irish Ecclesiastical Record*, 3rd series, vol. x, No. 7, July 1889, pp. 237-45.

Kent, W. H., 'Catholic Theology in England', *The Dublin Review*, vol. 109, July-Oct 1891, pp. 92-106.

Keogh, D., 'The pattern of the flock: John Thomas Troy, 1786-1823' in J. J. Kelly & D. Keogh, eds., *History of the Catholic Diocese of Dublin*, Dublin 2000, pp. 215-236.

Keogh, D., & McDonnell, A., eds., *Cardinal Paul Cullen and his World*, Dublin 2011.

Keogh, D., 'Evangelising the Faithful: Edmund Rice and the reformation of nineteenth-century Irish Catholicism', in C. Lennon, ed., *Confraternities and Sodalities in Ireland: charity, devotion and sociability*, Dublin 2012, pp. 57-75.

Kerr, D. A., *The Catholic Church and the Famine*, Dublin 1996.

Kerr, D. A., *Peel, Priests and Politics: Sir Robert Peel's Administration and the Roman Catholic Church in Ireland, 1841-1846*, Oxford 1982.

Kerrigan, C., *Fr Mathew and the Irish Temperance Movement, 1838-1849*, Cork 1992.

Kinealy, C., *Repeal and Revolution: 1848 in Ireland*, Manchester 2009.

Lahey, R. J., 'Fleming, Michael Anthony, 1792-1850', *Dictionary of Canadian Biography*, vol. 2, 1836-1850, Toronto 2003-2005.

Lane, F., ed., *Politics, Society and the Middle Class in Ireland*, Basingstoke 2010.

Larkin, E., *The Consolidation of the Catholic Church in Ireland, 1860-1870*, Dublin 1987.

Larkin, E., 'Before the devotional revolution', in J. H. Murphy, ed., *Evangelicals and Catholics in Nineteenth-Century Ireland*, Dublin 2005, pp. 15-37.

Larkin, E., *The Pastoral Role of the Roman Catholic Church in Pre-Famine Ireland, 1750-1850*, Dublin 2006.

Leichty, J., 'The popular reformation comes to Ireland: the case of John Walker and the foundation of the Church of God, 1804', in R. V. Comerford, M. Cullen, J. R. Hill & C. Lennon, eds., *Religion, Conflict and Co-existence in Ireland*, Dublin, 1990.

Lennon, C., ed., *Confraternities and sodalities in Ireland: charity, devotion and sociability*, Dublin 2012.

Lennon, C., *Irish Historic Towns Atlas: No.19, Dublin, Part II, 1610-1756*, Dublin 2008.

Lindemann, A. S., *A History of European Socialism*, New Haven 1983.

Lindsay, D., *Dublin's Oldest Charity: the Sick and Indigent Roomkeepers Society, 1790-1990*, Dublin 1990.

Lindsay, D., 'The Sick and Indigent Roomkeepers' Society', in D. Dickson, ed., *The Gorgeous Mask: Dublin, 1700-1850*, Dublin 1987.

Loeber, R., Campbell, H., Hurley, L., Montague, J. & Rowley, E., eds., *Architecture, 1600-2000*, being vol. IV of A. Carpenter et al., eds, *Art and Architecture of Ireland*, 5 vols., Dublin 2014.

Longmate, N., *King Cholera: the biography of a disease*, London 1966.

Longmate, N., *The Water-Drinkers: A history of temperance*, London 1968.

Lucey, D. S., 'Poor relief in the West of Ireland, 1861-1911', in V. Crossman & P. Gray, eds., *Poverty and Welfare in Ireland, 1838-1948*, Dublin 2011, pp. 37-52.

Luddy, M., *Women and Philanthropy in nineteenth-century Ireland*, Cambridge 1995.

Luddy, M., 'Philanthropy in Nineteenth-Century Ireland', in A Bourke, ed., *The Field Day Anthology of Irish writing*, vol. 5, *Irish Women's Writing and Traditions*, Cork 2002, pp. 691-92.

McCabe, D., *St. Stephen's Green, Dublin, 1660-1875*, Dublin 2011.

McCartney, D., *UCD: A National Idea*, Dublin 1999.

MacDonagh, O., *The Emancipist, Daniel O'Connell, 1830-47*, London 1989.

McEvansoneya, P., 'Cultural philanthropy in mid-nineteenth-century Ireland' in L. Geary & O. Walsh, *Philanthropy in nineteenth-century Ireland*, Dublin 2015, pp. 210-224.

MacGrath, K., 'John Garzia, a noted priest-catcher and his activities, 1717-1723', *Irish Ecclesiastical Record*, vol. 72, Dec. 1949, pp. 494-514.

McGrath, T., *Politics, interdenominational relations and education in the public ministry of Bishop James Doyle of Kildare and Leighlin, 1786-1834*, Dublin 1999.

McGrath, T., *Religious Renewal and Reform in the Pastoral Ministry of Bishop James Doyle of Kildare and Leighlin, 1786-1834*, Dublin 1999.

MacSuibhne, P., *Paul Cullen and his contemporaries*, 5 vols., Naas 1961-77.

Macauley, A., '"Strong views in very strong forms": Paul Cullen, Archbishop of Armagh (1849-52)', in D. Keogh & A. McDonnell, eds., *Cardinal Paul Cullen and his World*, Dublin 2011.

Magnier, L., 'Recent find in the Archives', *Carmelite Contact*, Issue 32, Summer 2015, p. 10.

Malcolm, E., *'Ireland sober, Ireland free': drink and temperance in nineteenth-century Ireland*, Dublin 1986.

Meagher, J., 'Glimpses of eighteenth-century priests', *Reportorium Novum*, vol. 2, No.1, 1958, pp. 129-147.

Mearns, A., *The Bitter Cry of Outcast London*, London 1883.

Mitchell, D., *A 'Peculiar' Place: the Adelaide Hospital Dublin: its times, places and personalities, 1839 to 1989*, Dublin 1989.

Mitchell, R., 'Thomas Weld, (1773-1837), Cardinal', *Oxford Dictionary of National Biography*, Oxford, 2004-15.

Moffitt, M., *The Society for Irish Church Missions to the Roman Catholics, 1849-1950*, Manchester 2010.

Moore, M. J., 'Irish Cresset-Stones', *Journal of the Royal Society of Antiquaries of Ireland*, vol. 114, 1984, pp. 98-116.

Mulligan, F., *William Dargan: An Honourable Life, 1799-1867*, Dublin 2013.

Murphy, D., 'John Francis Spratt, 1796-1871' in J. McGuire & J. Quinn, eds., *Dictionary of Irish Biography, from the earliest times to the year 2009*, 8 vols., Cambridge 2009, vol. iii, p. 1099.

Murphy, J. H., ed., *Evangelicals and Catholics in nineteenth century Ireland*, Dublin 2005.

Murphy, J. H., ed., *The Irish Book in English, 1800-1891*, Oxford 2011.

Murphy, P., ed., *Sculpture, 1600-2000*, being vol. III, of A. Carpenter et al. eds., *Art and Architecture of Ireland*, Dublin 2014.

Nelson, C., & McCracken, E., *The Brightest Jewel: A History of the National Botanic Gardens, Glasnevin, Dublin*, Kilkenny 1987.

Norman, E. R., *The Catholic Church and Ireland in the Age of Rebellion*, London 1965.

Norman, E. R., *Anti-Catholicism in Victorian England*, London 1968.

Norman, E. R., *The English Catholic Church in the Nineteenth Century*, Oxford 1984.

Nowlan, K. B., *The Politics of Repeal*, London 1965.

O'Brien, E., *Conscience and Conflict: a biography of Sir Dominic Corrigan, 1802-1880*, Dublin 1983.

Ó Broin, L., *Fenian Fever: an Anglo-American Dilemma*, New York 1971.

O'Carroll, C., *Paul Cardinal Cullen, portrait of a Practical Nationalist*, Dublin 2008.

Ó'Conchubhair, P., *'The Fenians were dreadful men': the 1867 Rising*, Cork 2011.

O'Dwyer, P., *Father John Spratt: beloved of Dublin's Poor: a centenary souvenir, 1871-1971*, Dublin 1971.

O'Dwyer, P., *The Irish Carmelites (of the Ancient Observance)*, Dublin 1988.

O'Ferrall, F., *Catholic Emancipation: Daniel O'Connell and the birth of Irish Democracy, 1820-1830*, Dublin 1985.

Ó Gráda, C., *Ireland Before and After the Famine: Explorations in Economic History, 1800-1925*, Manchester 1988.

Ó Gráda, C., *Black '47 and Beyond, Princeton*, New Jersey 1991.

Ó Gráda, C., & Guinnane, T. W., 'Mortality in the North Dublin Union during the Great Famine', in C. Ó Gráda, ed., *Ireland's Great Famine*, Dublin 2006.

Ó Gráda, C., ed., *Ireland's Great Famine*, Dublin 2006.

Ó Gráda, C., *The early history of Irish savings banks, UCD School of Economics Working Paper*, WP 08/04, Feb 2008, unpaginated.

Ó Gráda, C., 'Savings banks, famine and financial contagion: Ireland in the 1840s and 1850s', *Irish Economic and Social History*, vol. 36, No. 1, 2009, pp. 21-36.

O'Herlihy, J., *The Royal Irish Constabulary: a complete alphabetical list of Officers and Men, 1816-1922*, Dublin 1999.

O'Neill, J., *The Manchester Martyrs*, Cork 2012.

O'Neill, T., 'A Bad Year for the Liberties', in E. Gillespie, ed., *The Liberties of Dublin*, Dublin 1972.

O'Neill, T. 'The organisation and administration of relief, 1845-52' in R. D. Edwards, & T. D. Williams, eds., *The Great Famine: Studies in Irish History, 1845-52*, 1997 ed., pp. 243-244.

O'Neill, T., 'The charities and famine in mid-nineteenth century Ireland', in J. Hill & C. Lennon, eds., *Luxury and Austerity*, Dublin 1999, pp. 137-161.

O'Reilly, B., *The life of the Most Rev Dr McHale, Archbishop of Tuam*, 2 vols., New York 1890.

Ossory Fitzpatrick, S. A., *Dublin: A Historical and Topographical Account of the City*, Cork 1977.

O'Toole, D., 'The employment crisis of 1826', in D. Dickson, ed., *The Gorgeous Mask: Dublin 1700-1850*, Dublin 1987, pp. 157-171.

Owens, G., 'Popular mobilisation and the rising of 1848: the clubs of the Irish Confederation', in L. M. Geary, ed., *Rebellion and remembrance in modern Ireland*, Dublin 2001.

Padbury, J., 'Mary Hayden, 1862-1942, Feminist', in *Studies*, vol. 98, 2009, pp. 145-158.

Pearson, P., *The Heart of Dublin: resurgence of a historic city*, Dublin 2000.

Pollard, R., *The Avenue: a history of the Claremont Institution*, Dublin 2006.

Potterton, H., *The O'Connell Monument*, 11pp., Dublin 1973.

Prunty, J., *Dublin Slums 1800-1925; a study in Urban Geography*, Dublin 1998.

Prunty, J., 'Battle plans and battlegrounds: Protestant mission activity in the Dublin slums, 1840's – 1880's', in C. Gribben & A. R. Holmes, eds., *Protestant Millennialism, Evangelicalism, and Irish Society, 1790-2005*, Basingstoke 2006, pp. 119-143.

Quinn, J., 'John Mitchel' in *Dictionary of Irish Biography*, vol. 6, pp. 523-27.

Quinn, J. F., *Fr Mathew's Crusade: temperance in nineteenth-century Ireland and America*, Boston 2002.

Rafferty, O. P., *The Church, the State and the Fenian Threat, 1861-1875*, London 1999.

Rafferty, O. P., *The Catholic Church and the Protestant State: nineteenth century realities*, Dublin 2008.

Reeve, H., *The Greville Memoirs*, 8 vols., London 1898.

Reynolds, J. A., *The Catholic Emancipation Crisis in Ireland, 1823-1829*, New Haven 1954.

Robins, J., *The Lost Children: A Study of Charity Children in Ireland, 1700-1900*, Dublin 1980.

Robins, J., *The Miasma: Epidemic and Panic in nineteenth-century Ireland*, Dublin 1995.

Ronan, M., *Apostle of Catholic Dublin: Father Henry Young*, Dublin 1944.

Ronan, M., *The Parish of St Michan*, Dublin 1948.

Rowlands, J., 'James Haughton and Young Ireland', *Carloviana*, Christmas 1971, pp. 9-12.

Rushe, J. P., *Carmel in Ireland: a narrative of the Irish Province of Teresian or Discalced Carmelites, A.D. 1625-1896*, Dublin 1903.

Smet, J., *The Mirror of Carmel: a brief history of the Carmelite Order*, Darien, Illinois 2011.

Stalley, R., *The Cistercian Monasteries of Ireland*, London & New Haven, 1987.

Stead, W. T., 'The Maiden Tribute of Modern Babylon', *Pall Mall Gazette*, 6th, 7th, 8th, 10th July 1885.

Strange, J., & Toomre, J., 'Alexis Soyer and the Irish Famine', in A. Gribben, ed., *The Great Famine and the Irish Diaspora in America*, Amherst 1999, pp. 66-84.

Sullivan, M. C., *Catherine McAuley and the Tradition of Mercy*, Dublin 1995.

Sullivan, M. C., *The Path of Mercy: the life of Catherine McAuley*, Dublin, 2012.

Swift, R., & Kinealy, C., eds., *Politics and Power in Victorian Ireland*, Dublin 2006.

Townend, P. A., *Father Mathew, temperance and Irish identity*, Dublin 2002.

Turner, F. J., 'Thomas Weld (1750-1810), landowner and benefactor', *Oxford Dictionary of National Biography*, Oxford 2004-15.

Tutty, M. J.,' Dublin's Oldest Charity', *Dublin Historical Record*, XVI, 3, March 1961, pp. 73-74.

Vaughan, W. E., ed., *A New History of Ireland*, vol. 5, *Ireland under the Union, 1801-1870*, Oxford 1989.

Wall, T., 'Catholic Periodicals of the Past: 1: The Catholic Penny Magazine, 1834-35', *Irish Ecclesiastical Record*, vol. 101, Jan-June 19643, pp. 234-244.

Wall, T., 'Catholic periodicals of the past: 2: the Catholic Book Society and the Irish Catholic Magazine', *Irish Ecclesiastical Record*, vol. 102, Jan-June 1964, pp. 289-303.

Walsh, R. 'A list of Ecclesiastics who took the Oath of Allegiance', *Archivium Hibernicum*, vol. 1, 1912, pp. 46-76.

Walsh, R. 'A List of the Regulars Registered in Ireland, pursuant to the Catholic Relief Act of 1829', *Archivium Hibernicum*, vol. 3,1914, pp. 34-48.

Walsh, W. J., *O'Connell, Archbishop Murray and the Board of Charitable Bequests*, Dublin 1916.

Watchorn, F., *Crumlin and the way it was*, Dublin 1985.

Whelan, I. 'The Bible Gentry: Evangelical Religion, Aristocracy and the New Moral Order in the early nineteenth century', in C. Gribben & A. R. Holmes, eds., *Protestant Millennialism, Evangelicalism and Irish Society, 1790-2005*, London 2006.

Whelan, I., *The Bible War in Ireland: the 'Second Reformation' and the Polarization of Protestant-Catholic Relations, 1800-1840*, Dublin 2005.

Woodham-Smith, C., *The Great Hunger*, London 1962.

Woods, A., *Dublin Outsiders: a history of the Mendicity Institution, 1818-1998*, Dublin 1998.

Woods, C. J., 'Sir John Gray, (1816-1875)', *Dictionary of Irish Biography*, vol. 4, pp. 223-225.

## 9. Dissertations and Theses:

Bretherton, G., *The Irish Temperance Movement, 1829-1847*, Ph.D. Columbia University 1978.

Callaghan, O., *The impact of the Great Famine on a city: a study of Dublin, 1845-1850*, BA thesis, UCD, NUI, 1971.

D'Arcy, F. A., *Dublin Artisan Opinion, Activity and Organisation, 1820-1850*, MA thesis, UCD, NUI, 1968.

Lyne, G., *The General Association of Ireland, 1836-1837*, MA thesis, UCD, NUI, 1968.

O'Dwyer, P., *John Francis Spratt, O.Carm.,1796-1871: a Dissertation submitted to the Faculty of Church History of the Pontifical Gregorian University*, Rome 1968.

O'Neill, T. P., *The State, Poverty and Distress in Ireland, 1815-1845*, PhD Dissertation, UCD, NUI, 1971.

## 10. Biographical Dictionaries and Modern Reference Works:

Boase, F., *Modern English Biography since…1850*, 3 vols, Truro 1892-1901.

Cannadine, D., ed., *Oxford Dictionary of National Biography*, Oxford 2004-15.

Crone, J. S., *A Concise Dictionary of Irish Biography*, Dublin 1928.

*Dictionary of Canadian Biography*, Toronto, 2003-17.

McGuire, J. & Quinn, J., eds., *Dictionary of Irish Biography, from the earliest times to the year 2009*, 8 vols., Cambridge 2009.

Moody, T. W., Martin, F. X., & Byrne, F. J., *A new History of Ireland*, vol. viii, *A Chronology of Irish History to 1976*, Oxford 2011.

Webb, A., *A Compendium of Irish Biography*, Dublin 1878.

## 11. Internet Websites:

http://www.britishnewspaperarchive.co.uk/
www.databases.dublincity.ie,
www.findmypast.ie/
http://www.Irishgenealogy.ie,

# ILLUSTRATIONS

*All images courtesy of the Gort Muire Library and Archives, unless otherwise indicated.*

**Cover Design:** The cover is a composite of three images: An exterior view of the original church at Whitefriar Street, engraving by George Petrie, printed by Fisher Son & Co., 1829. Source: Public Domain; Lithograph of Fr John Spratt, as President of the Irish Total Abstinence Society, by Forster & Co., Courtesy of the National Library of Ireland,[1] Call no. EP SPRA-JO (2) IV; Sackville Street, Dublin City, Co. Dublin, Courtesy of the NLI, Call no. L_CAB_02921.

**Fig 1.** Sketch of a young John Spratt, in Gort Muire Archives, *Scrapbook A*. The artist is unknown.

**Fig 2.** The Carmelite Church in Cordoba, photographed in the 19th century. Image courtesy of Paco Muñoz.

**Fig 3.** Drawing of the Portlester Chapel of St Audoen's Church, Dublin, in ruins, with no roof. Originally published in the *Dublin Penny Journal*, vol. 1, No. 26, December 22nd 1832. Source: Public Domain.

**Fig 4.** Map of Dublin 1798. Original Cartographer: William M Wilson. Source: Public Domain. Additions and modifications by illustrator.

**Fig 5.** The former Carmelite Church and Temperance Hall at French Street.

**Fig 6.** Photograph of a young Fr John Spratt.

**Fig 7.** Bust of William Magee, Church of Ireland Archbishop of Dublin, which can be found in Trinity College Library. Photograph by illustrator.

---

1. Hereafter NLI.

**Fig 8.** Monument of Dr Daniel Murray, Catholic Archbishop of Dublin, in St Mary's Pro-Cathedral, Dublin. Photograph by illustrator.

**Fig 9.** Fr John Spratt's Catholic Association membership card.

**Fig 10.** Exterior view of the original church at Whitefriar Street. Engraving by George Petrie. Printed by Fisher Son & Co., 1829. Source: Public Domain. Photographed and edited by illustrator.

**Fig 11.** Interior view of the original church at Whitefriar Street. Engraving by George Petrie. Printed by Fisher Son & Co., 1829. Source: Public Domain. Photographed and edited by illustrator.

**Fig 12.** Spratt's annotation in Archdall's *Monasticon* states the statue was 'Removed in 1822/3 by Dr Spratt. This statue is preserved in the Carmelite Church of Dublin. See page 213.'

**Fig 13.** The statue of Our Lady of Dublin in Whitefriar Street Church.

**Fig 14.** Aloysius Scalabrini, O.Carm. Courtesy of CISA, Rome.

**Fig 15.** A 19th century image depicting Resurrection Men. Original publication unknown. Source: Public Domain.

**Fig 16.** The Cork Street Fever Hospital and House of Recovery. Opened in 1804, the hospital was inundated over the next three decades with the Fever Epidemic of 1817/1819, the Typhus Epidemic of 1826 and the Cholera Epidemic of 1832. Reproduced by kind permission of the Royal College of Physicians of Ireland. Reference: RCPI Archival Collections: CSFH/7/1/6

**Fig 17.** Samuel Rosborough (1757-1832). Reproduced by kind permission of the Sick and Indigent Roomkeepers Society.

**Fig 18.** The former headquarters of the Sick and Indigent Roomkeepers Society, on Palace Street. Reproduced by kind permission of the Sick and Indigent Roomkeepers Society.

**Fig 19.** 'Honest Tom' Steele (1788-1848). Attributed to Joseph Patrick Haverty, (1794-1864), after an oil painting. Printed by Engelmann Craf, Condet & Co. Image used courtesy of the NLI. Call no. PD 2120 TX (1) 3. Cropped and edited by illustrator.

**Fig 20.** An invitation to Dinner.

**Fig 21.** The Old Methodist Meeting House in Whitefriar Street.

**Fig 22.** The facade and pulpit of Chiesa dei Santi Nomi di Gesù e Maria, Rome. Reproduced by kind permission of Alessio Damato and Marie-Lan Nguyen respectively.

**Fig 23.** The relics of St Valentine at Whitefriar Street Church. Image courtesy of Michael Conway.

**Fig 24.** Bishop Michael A. Fleming. Courtesy of the Archives of the Roman Catholic Archdiocese of St. John's.

**Fig 25.** The Basilica Cathedral of St John the Baptist. Courtesy of St. Johns Newfoundland and Labrador, Basilica Heritage Foundation.

**Fig 26.** Spratt's *Manual of Devotion*, with inscription from Daniel O'Connell.

**Fig 27.** Daniel O'Connell. Original photograph by the World History Archive Source: Public Domain.

**Fig 28.** Aloysius Calamata, O.Carm. Photo courtesy of CISA, Rome.

**Fig 29.** Pope Gregory XVI. Source: Public Domain.

**Fig 30.** Portrait of Fr Theobald Mathew by James Butler Brennan, in Crawford Art Gallery, Cork. Cat. No. 2732-P.

**Fig 31.** James Haughton. Source: Public Domain. Editing and cropping by illustrator.

**Fig 32.** A scene at Donnybrook Fair, by Samuel Watson, c.1842. Sourced at TRIARC - Modern and Contemporary Irish Art Collection (Digital Image Collection).

**Fig 33.** Temperance Association Card of Thomas Kent signed by Fr. Theobald Mathew, OFM Cap., 12th April 1838. Courtesy of Capuchin Archives.

**Fig 34.** Daniel O'Connell speaks at the monster meeting in Trim. © Lebrecht Music and Arts Photo Library.

**Fig 35.** Temperance medal of John Spratt. The front (face) shows the Good Shepherd. The outer-rim inscription reads 'I have found the sheep that was lost Luke Chap. 15 v. 6'. The obverse: Cruciform text of pledge reads: 'I have voluntarily promised in the presence of the Revd. Dr. Spratt to abstain from all spiritous liquors and intoxicating drinks except used medicinally and then by order of a medical man and the discountenance of all the vices and practices of intemperance and also to attend to my religious duties'. The outer-rim inscription reads 'The Dublin Total Abstinence Pledge The Very Revd. Dr. Spratt Patron 1840'. The maker of the medal was J. Taylor. Courtesy of the Capuchin Archives.

**Fig 36.** John Spratt's book *An Appeal to the People on the Horrid Crime of Drunkenness*.

**Fig 37.** Cardinal Giacomo Fransoni. Source: Public Domain.

**Fig 38.** The Rotunda, Dublin. Original photograph from The Lawrence Photograph Collection. Courtesy of the NLI. Call no. L_ROY_00302

**Fig 39.** John Spratt's Volunteers of 1782 Revived membership card, dated 10th November 1844, in GMA Archives, Scrapbook A.

**Fig 40.** Fr Thomas Bennett, O.Carm. Portrait in Whitefriar Street Carmelite community.

**Fig 41.** The crypt of Daniel O'Connell, Glasnevin cemetery.

**Fig 42.** Portrait of Sir Robert Peel, 2nd Baronet by Henry William Pickersgill. Image: Public Domain.

**Fig 43.** Marble Statue of Archbishop John McHale in the grounds of the Cathedral of the Assumption. Sculpted by Sir Thomas Farrell. Image courtesy of Andreas F. Borchert.

**Fig 44.** Portrait of Lord Lieutenant Heytesbury. Artist unknown. Source: Public Domain.

**Fig 45.** A clipping from the *Freeman's Journal*, 6th Dec 1844, in GMA, *Scrapbook A*, showing Archbishop Murray's letter of 3rd December.

**Fig 46.** Scene at the gate of the workhouse, c. 1846. Originally published in J. C. Ridpath, *Ridpath's history of the world : being an account of the principal events in the career of the human race from the beginnings of civilization to the present time, comprising the development of social institutions and the story of all nations*, Cincinnati 1907. Source: Public Domain.

**Fig 47.** Portrait of Archdeacon John Torrens. Attributed to George Sanders (b. 1810), after an original painting by James Godsell Middleton. Courtesy of the NLI. Call no. P TORR-JO (1) IV

**Fig 48.** Drawing of Alexis Soyer. Artist unknown. Source: Public Domain.

**Fig 49.** Alexis Soyer's soup kitchen on the esplanade of the Royal Barracks. Originally published in *The Illustrated London News*, 17 April 1847.

**Fig 50.** Statue of Sir John Gray on O'Connell Street, Dublin.

**Fig 51.** John Bright, MP. Source: Public Domain

**Fig 52.** Young Irelanders (clockwise from top left): Michael Doheny, William Smith O'Brien, John Blake Dillon, Thomas Devin O'Reilly, Thomas Francis Meagher and Charles Gavan Duffy. A composite image by the illustrator.

**Fig 53.** Lithograph of John Mitchel. By Charles Baugniet, published by and after Professor Gluckman. Source: Public Domain.

**Fig 54.** John Reynolds, MP. By J. H. Lynch. Printed by Professor Glukman. Source: Public Domain.

**Fig 55.** George Villiers, 4th Earl of Clarendon. Source: Public Domain.

**Fig 56.** Pope Pius IX. Source: Public Domain.

**Fig 57.** The headquarters of the Bricklayers' and Stonecutters' Guild, originally built as St Peter's Parish Savings Bank. Source: Public Domain.

**Fig 58.** St Peter's, Church of Ireland, Aungier Street, as it was rebuilt in 1867. The church closed in 1950, and was demolished in 1983.

**Fig 59.** Valentine Brown Lawless, 2nd Baron Cloncurry. Artist unknown.

**Fig 60.** Drawing of Thomas Mooney, originally printed in *The Irish World*, 26th May 1888. Courtesy of the National Library of Ireland.

**Fig 61.** A view from Capel Street overlooking Essex Bridge, by James Malton. Originally published in 1797. Source: Public Domain.

**Fig 62.** The Royal Exchange, Dublin in 1810 (Modern day City Hall). Originally drawn by Samuel Frederick Brocas, and engraved by Henry Brocas.

**Fig 63.** Benjamin Lee Guinness. Source: Public Domain.

**Fig 64.** Dr R R Madden. Originally published in *The United Irishmen: their lives and times, with several additional memoirs, and authentic documents, heretofore unpublished, the whole matter newly arranged and revised*, Dublin 1858. Source: Public Domain.

**Fig 65.** The Great National Industrial Exhibition, RDS, Dublin 1853. Image courtesy of JDP Econ.

**Fig 66.** William Dargan. Source: Public Domain.

**Fig 67.** Former Methodist Centenary Church, Stephen's Green, now the Department of Justice.

**Fig 68.** The Mortuary Chapel in Goldenbridge Cemetery, erected in 1829.

**Fig 69.** A 19th century illustration of a funeral taking place in Glasnevin Cemetery. Originally published in *The Graphic*, 20th May 1882.

**Fig 70.** A letter written by Fr Spratt on behalf of the new industrial school.

**Fig 71.** An untitled newspaper clipping from GMA, *Scrapbook A*, discussing the delivery of some lace work to Lady Clarendon, subsequent at her visit to the school.

**Fig 72.** Dr. Daniel Cahill. On stone by Harriet Osborne O' Hagen, Printed by Maclure, Macdonald & Macgregor. Courtesy of the NLI. Call no. EP CAHI-DA (1) IV

**Fig 73.** Richard Baptist O'Brien. Originally published in Kevin Condon, c.m. *The Missionary College of All Hallows 1842-1891*, All Hallows College, Dublin 1986.

**Fig 74.** Dr Franc Sadlier. Portrait in Provost's House, Trinity College.

**Fig 75.** Richard MacDonnell (1787-1867), Provost of Trinity College, Dublin By Stephen Catterson Smith, the Elder, oil on canvas. Source: Public Domain.

**Fig 76.** Dr Richard Chenevix Trench. Originally published in *Richard Chenevix Trench, Archbishop: Letters and Memorials*, London 1888. Source: Public Domain.

**Fig 77.** A sketch of the Adelaide Hospital. Source: Public Domain.

**Fig 78.** St Vincent's Hospital at Stephen's Green. Image courtesy of the Sisters of Charity.

**Fig 79.** Fr Joseph Crotty, O.Carm.

**Fig 80.** A liturgical celebration in Whitefriar Street Church, c.1920s.

**Fig 81.** Lord Cloncurry's estate at Lyons, Co. Kildare. Source: Public Domain.

**Fig 82.** Michael Spratt's Headstone. Courtesy of Connor Dodd, of the Glasnevin Trust.

**Fig 83.** Headstone of Sister Mary John Spratt at Firhouse Carmelite Convent. Image courtesy of Michael Troy, O.Carm.

**Fig 84.** Portrait of Fr Matthew Flanagan in St Nicholas of Myra Church.

**Fig 85.** The Blessed Stone, currently located in St Audeon's.

**Fig 86.** An image of the pedestal for the Blessed Stone, designed by Spratt, in GMA, *Scrapbook A*.

**Fig 87.** An example of a 'bulla' or leaden seal of Pope Gregory IX, one of which was donated to the National Museum of Ireland by Spratt. Courtesy of Surrey County Council. Find ID 407324.

**Fig 88.** George William Frederick Howard, 7th Earl of Carlisle, by Thomas Cranfield, published by Mason & Co (Robert Hindry Mason), early-mid 1860s. Courtesy of the National Portrait Gallery, London.

**Fig 89.** Painting of Fr John Spratt currently at Whitefriar Street Church.

**Fig 90.** Portrait of John Spratt at the current headquarters of the Sick and Indigent Roomkeepers Society. Courtesy of the Society.

**Fig 91.** Painting of John Spratt, previously housed in the St Joseph's Night Refuge. Courtesy of the Sisters of Mercy Archives.

**Fig 92.** Bust of John Spratt by the eminent sculptor, James Cahill, currently situated in the Whitefriar Street Community Centre.

**Fig 93.** Two images of John Spratt from the Gort Muire Archives. The source is unknown.

**Fig 94.** Lithograph of Fr John Spratt, by Forster & Co., Crow Street, Dublin. Courtesy of the NLI. Call no. EP SPRA-JO (1) IV.

**Fig 95.** Lithograph of Fr John Spratt, as President of the Irish Total Abstinence Society, also by Forster & Co. Courtesy of the NLI. Call no. EP SPRA-JO (2) IV.

**Fig 96.** Lithograph of Dr John Spratt, as President of the Irish Total Abstinence Society. Courtesy of the NLI. Call no. EP SPRA-JO (3) I.

**Fig 97.** An Irish Total Abstinence Association Pledge signed by Spratt. Image courtesy of the Irish Quaker Historical Library, Dublin.

**Fig 98.** Wooden plaque on frame of portrait of John Spratt in the Roomkeepers Society dates the portrait to 1872. Courtesy of the Roomkeepers Society.

**Fig 99.** A leather tag identifying the statue of Our Lady of Dublin.

**Fig 100.** *Scrapbook A* at the Gort Muire Archives.

**Fig 101.** The Shrine of Our Lady of Dublin in Whitefriar Street Church.

**Fig 102.** One of Spratt's prayer books with his name inscribed on brass clasp.

**Fig 103.** The breviaries of John Spratt in the Gort Muire Library.

**Fig 104 - 108** Photographs showing various aspects of Spratt's monument in the O'Connell circle, Glasnevin.

**Fig 109.** The oldest of the Carmelite Plots in Glasnevin Cemetery, dating from 1853.

**Fig 110.** Dr William Urwick. Engraved by J. Cochran after a photograph by Maull & Polyblank. Courtesy of the NLI. Call no. EP URWI-WI (1) II.

**Fig 111.** Rev Dean Andrew O'Connell. Courtesy of the NLI. Call no. EP OCON-AN (1A) III.

**Fig 112.** Donnybrook Fair 1859, by Erskine Nichol. Source: Public Domain.

**Fig 113.** A poster printed by Joseph Dillon advertising the Fair. Reproduced by kind permission of the Royal College of Physicians of Ireland.

**Fig 114.** Church of the Sacred Heart, Donnybrook.

**Fig 115.** Cardinal Paul Cullen. Image courtesy of Pictorial Press Ltd.

**Fig 116.** Cardinal Nicholas Wiseman. The National Portrait Gallery, London. Reference: NPG Ax18313. Source: Public Domain.

**Fig 117.** John Sadleir, MP. From a daguerreotype by William Edward Kilburn. Source: Public Domain.

**Fig 118.** Frederick Lucas. Source: Public Domain.

**Fig 119.** Portrait of Cardinal John Henry Newman by Sir John Everett Millais. Reference no. NPG 5295. Source: Public Domain.

**Fig 120.** Newman House, Stephen's Green, formerly the Catholic University of Ireland.

**Fig 121.** The Christian Union Buildings in Lower Abbey Street were erected on the site of the Metropolitan Hall, formerly the Music Hall. Courtesy of the NLI. Call no. L_ROY_08561.

**Fig 122.** Portrait of Sir Peter Le Page Renouf, by Alberto de Rohden. Courtesy of Guernsey Museums and Galleries. Accession no. GUEMG: GMAG 1976.133

**Fig 123.** *Patrick O'Brien, MP*. Originally published in *The Black & White Parliamentary Album 1895*, The Black and White Publishing Co. Ltd, 63 Fleet Street, London. Source: Public Domain.

**Fig 124.** Monsignor William Yore. Portrait in the Deaf Heritage Centre.

**Fig 125.** Portobello College, formerly the Portobello Hotel.

**Fig 126.** A M Sullivan. Engraving by Charles Malcolm Grey. Courtesy of the NLI. Call no. EP SULL-AM (1) II.

**Fig 127.** Cardinal Adolphe Perraud. Source: Public Domain.

**Fig 128.** South view of the Stove Tenter House in 1818. Engraving by B. Brunton. Courtesy of the NLI. Call no. ET A327 .

**Fig 129.** St Joseph's Night Refuge for the Homeless Poor.

**Fig 130.** Benjamin Lee Guinness. Drawn by W. A. Wragg; engraved by Day & Son. Courtesy of the NLI. Call no. EP GUIN-BE (1) III.

**Fig 131.** The Mercy Convent, Brickfield Lane. Originally published in *The Irish Rosary*, vol. 1, No. 8, November 1894, p. 396. Image courtesy of the Central Catholic Library, Dublin.

**Fig 132.** The Mansion House, Dublin.

**Fig 133.** St Bride's Church and National School stood near the corner of Bride Street and Bride Road. They were demolished in 1900. Image courtesy of the Iveagh Trust.

**Fig 134.** Jonathan Pim, MP. By Thomas Cranfield, albumen carte-de-visite, 1860s. Courtesy of the National Portrait Gallery. Ref no. NPG Ax8649

**Fig 135.** An 1862 image depicting the Lancashire 'Cotton Famine'. Originally published in Life Photo Archive. Source: Public Domain.

**Fig 136.** Captain Knox. Source: Public Domain.

**Fig 137.** James Mackey, Lord Mayor of Dublin. Source: Public Domain.

**Fig 138.** Richard Bourke, 6th Earl of Mayo, styled Lord Naas. Source: Public Domain.

**Fig 139.** Terence Bellew McManus as he stood in the Dock in Clonmel Courthouse, 10th October, 1848. Originally published in the *Supplement to the Irish Fireside,* 16th September 1885. Courtesy of the NLI. Call no. Irish Fireside 1885 September 16 (A).

**Fig 140.** Portrait of the Right Hon. Richard Atkinson, Lord Mayor of Dublin. Originally published in *The Illustrated London News*, 16th January 1961. Source: Public Domain.

**Fig 141.** Portrait of William Gladstone. Originally published in Goldwyn Smith, *My memory of Gladstone*, London 1904. Source: Public Domain.

**Fig 142.** The trial of the 'Manchester Martyrs'. Originally published in *The Illustrated London News*, 9th November 1867. Source: Public Domain.

**Fig 143.** Portrait of Issac Butt, MP, by John Butler Yeats. Courtesy of the National Portrait Gallery, London. Ref. NPG 3831.

**Fig 144.** Sir Dominic Corrigan, MP. Image Courtesy of Wellcome Library, London.

**Fig 145.** Cardinal Edward McCabe, succeeded Paul Cullen as Archbishop of Dublin. Source: Public Domain.

**Fig 146.** Angelo Savini, O.Carm. Courtesy of CISA, Rome.

**Fig 147.** Andrew Farrington.

**Fig 148.** The Irish Province of Carmelites' Provincial Chapter 1871. For list of Carmelites, see p. 479.

**Fig 149.** The Botanic Gardens. Courtesy of the NLI. Call no. EAS_1750.

**Fig 150.** Thomas Wallace Russell. Courtesy of the NLI. Call no. EP RUSS-TH (1) II.

**Fig 151.** A Dublin Total Abstinence Society Coffee Stall. Image courtesy of the Irish Quaker Historical Library, Dublin.

**Fig 152.** James Haughton. Image courtesy of the Irish Quaker Historical Library, Dublin.

**Fig 153.** Sir Wilfrid Lawson, MP, 2nd Baronet of Brayton circa 1900. Source: Public Domain.

**Fig 154.** Major Myles O'Reilly. Source: Public Domain.

**Fig 155.** Invitation to Luncheon with the Prince and Princess of Wales in GMA, *Scrapbook A*.

**Fig 156.** Chief Secretary Chichester Fortescue. Originally published in Lady Strachey, ed., *The Later Letters of Edward Lear*, London 1911. Source: Public Domain.

**Fig 157.** A poem by J M'Corry, read by James Haughton, at a temperance gathering on 15th September 1866. GMA, *Scrapbook A*.

**Fig 158.** John Spratt.

**Fig 159.** The vault of John and James Spratt in the O'Connell Circle, Glasnevin Cemetery.

**Fig 160.** Fr John Carr, O.Carm..

**Fig 161.** Sir William Wilde. Source: Public Domain.

**Fig 162.** Bust of John Spratt, by James Cahill.

**Fig 163.** Sackville Street (O'Connell Street), in the late 19th century. Courtesy of the NLI. Call no. L CAB 02921.

**Fig 164.** Sophia Housing Project, Cork Street.

# INDEX

# M

# O

# P